ZWILLIN
J.A. HENCK

Complete B

Knife Skills

The Essential Guide to Use, Techniques & Care

Jeffrey Elliot & James P. DeWan

Robert
ROSE

ZWILLING J.A. HENCKELS Complete Book of Knife Skills
Text copyright © 2010 Jeffrey Elliot and James P. DeWan
Photographs and illustrations copyright © 2010 Robert Rose Inc.
Cover and text design copyright © 2010 Robert Rose Inc.

ZWILLING®, TWIN®, MIYABI®, and are registered trademarks of ZWILLING J.A. HENCKELS AG, Solingen, Germany, used with permission by the trademark owner.

No part of this publication may be reproduced, stored in a retrieval system or transmitted, in any form or by any means, without the prior written consent of the publisher or a licence from the Canadian Copyright Licensing Agency (Access Copyright). For an Access Copyright licence, visit www.accesscopyright.ca or call toll-free: 1-800-893-5777.

For complete cataloguing information, see page 394.

Disclaimer
Knives are created for particular jobs. It is important that the knife you use is for the purpose intended. Knives can be dangerous if used improperly or for the wrong purpose. Please be careful in the use of a knife for any of the purposes and projects included in this publication. Knives, of course, should be kept away from children and from those persons who, for whatever reason, are incapable of or incompetent in using a knife.

The publisher does not take any responsibility for the use of any knife for any portion or portions of the project included herein. If there is any concern about the use of a knife, please do not proceed without proper assistance.

The publisher has made all reasonable efforts to provide up-to-date and accurate information in respect to the projects included in this publication, but the material is "as is," without any warranty by the publisher, and the publisher shall have no liability to you or to any third party in any way relating to the utilization of any knife in respect to this publication.

If you choose to use the information in this publication, it shall be at your own risk and the publisher is no way responsible for the use of such information by you, and such information is provided as a "guide only."

Editor: Sue Sumeraj
Proofreaders: Sheila Wawanash and Gillian Watts
Indexer: Gillian Watts
Design and Production: Joseph Gisini / PageWave Graphics Inc., www.pagewavegraphics.com
Photography: Al MacDonald, www.foodphotostudio.com
Hand Model: Mark Steuer
Title Page and Chapter Openers:
Photography: Colin Erricson, www.erricsonphoto.com
Associate Photographer: Matt Johannsson
Food Styling: Kathryn Robertson and Kate Bush
Prop Styling: Charlene Erricson
Illustrations: Crowle Art Group
Photography of Knife Edge (page 42): Courtesy of Brent Beach
Chef coats: Courtesy of Chefwear, www.chefwear.com

We acknowledge the financial support of the Government of Canada through the Book Publishing Industry Development Program (BPIDP) for our publishing activities.

Published by Robert Rose Inc.
120 Eglinton Avenue East, Suite 800, Toronto, Ontario, Canada M4P 1E2
Tel: (416) 322-6552 Fax: (416) 322-6936
www.robertrose.ca

Printed and bound in China

3 4 5 6 7 8 9 PPLS 18 17 16 15 14 13

Contents

Introduction

We once saw the great Chinese chef Martin Yan give a cooking demonstration. At one point, he took a beautiful, fat yellow bell pepper and, after removing both ends, cut away the entire seed pod in one quick motion, which left him with a single long, rectangular piece of pepper. (We'll show you how to do this on page 145). Next, he laid the pepper skin side down on his cutting board and began to work on the flesh. He took his cleaver (which is what most Chinese chefs use for the majority of their work) and, slicing horizontally across the surface of the pepper, removed a paper-thin slice and set it aside. Then he cut another paper-thin slice, and another, and another. In all, he cut seven perfect slices from that pepper, the last of which he placed over the label on a bottle of fish sauce. We could read the label through the slice of pepper.

Chef Yan's expertise comes from years of practice. We're not suggesting that, to be a great cook, you need to be able to pull off fancy moves like his. But to be able to cook effectively, you must be able to handle a knife safely, and with precision and speed. Martin Yan started cooking as a child, so by the time he was an adult, he'd had a decade of experience with using a knife. Most of us aren't so fortunate; in fact, home cooks may never learn to use a knife correctly at all. And that's why we've written this book: because whether you're a culinary professional or simply an interested home cook, learning to use a knife properly is a fundamental skill that no one should be without.

Why Knife Skills Are Important

Anyone who wants to cook — whether professionally or at home — needs to know how to use a knife. And that doesn't just mean knowing how to cut various vegetables into various shapes, though that's certainly part of it. It also means knowing how to hold a knife and, equally importantly, how to hold the item you're cutting in a way that prevents you from cutting yourself. Learning how to hold and use a knife correctly will not only help you work more safely, but will also enable you to work faster, making you much more efficient in the kitchen.

If safety and speed weren't enough incentive, good knife skills also allow you to cut your food uniformly. Uniformity is important for two reasons. First, pieces of an individual food that are the same size and shape cook at the same rate. Imagine, for example, that you have a craving for home fries: diced potatoes sautéed in hot fat with a little onion and garlic. If you cut your potatoes into a ragtag collection of shapes and sizes, the small pieces will cook much more quickly than the large ones, so when the small pieces are done, the large pieces will be just this side of raw. Worse, by the time the larger pieces are done, the small ones will be beyond overcooked. But if you cut your potatoes into beautiful, nearly perfect ½-inch (12 mm) dice, not only will they cook together perfectly, but they'll look fantastic, too.

And that's the second reason to cut everything into uniform sizes and shapes: presentation. There's a definite elegance to perfectly cut, perfectly sized vegetables that simply cannot be attained with rough cuts. Restaurant patrons may not understand the principles of even cooking that lie behind uniform cuts, but their subconscious registers that if you aim for perfection with something as seemingly insignificant as your vegetable cuts, then you must take the same care with every aspect of preparation. When you're cooking at home, presentation may matter less, but making food look beautiful will certainly wow your guests and make your family feel loved and special.

The Science of Cooking

Before we discuss this book's approach to teaching knife skills, let's talk a little about cooking in general, because once we have a shared interpretation of what cooking is, we'll be able to place the acquisition of knife skills into this broader context.

Cooking is the manipulation of food for the purpose of rendering it suitable for consumption. Like everything else in the universe, cooking is subject to the laws of nature, so when we cook, we can control the outcome if we understand the applicable natural laws. In other words, once we know the science of cooking, we know what will happen before we start. There is no more guesswork, no more wondering how a dish will turn out.

Cooking cannot simply be about following recipes, because recipes are little more than maps. If you don't know how to read a road map, you won't reach your destination. Further, a road map leaves out a lot of important information, such as what the weather is like on the day you're driving, how much traffic there is and what condition the road is in. Likewise, a recipe cannot possibly account for all of the factors that affect successful cooking, such as the amount of water in one tomato versus another, the temperature of your burner when it's on "medium" heat or the ability of your pans to conduct heat. The best way to navigate in a kitchen is to learn as much as you can about the natural laws behind cooking before you ever pick up a recipe.

To be a good cook, it helps to be conversant in many different fields, both hard sciences and social sciences. Here are just a few examples:

- **Chemistry:** Understanding the chemical makeup of ingredients enables us to predict how they will react to heat or cold, or to other ingredients. It tells us why sugar melts, then turns yellow, light brown, dark brown and black, why we use baking powder and why meat browns in the skillet.
- **Anatomy:** Knowing how an animal is put together tells us how to take it apart. Knowledge of the skeletal structure of a chicken, for example, allows us to break it down in minutes.
- **Mathematics:** Without an understanding of numbers and ratios, you'd never be able to recreate a dish. Imagine trying to cook using multiple ingredients with no concept of what "how much" means.
- **Biology:** This life science tells us why veal bones make better stocks than beef bones, and what happens to chlorophyll (the pigment that makes plants green) when it comes into contact with acid.
- **Physics:** It's the laws of physics that allow us to toss food in a pan. When we move the pan forward, the food also moves forward, because it is riding on the surface of the pan. When we stop the pan, momentum continues to carry the food forward. This momentum, combined with a subtle upward flick of the wrist, propels the food up the sides of the pan and into the air, where it sails in a perfect parabola back into the pan.
- **Geography:** The geographical origin of a given dish or cuisine can tell us a lot about what to expect from it, as the cuisine of any region is heavily influenced by ingredients that are locally available in that region. Dishes from hot-weather climates, for example, typically contain a lot of spices.
- **History:** The story of a dish is an echo of the story of the people who created it. To understand the popularity of chile peppers in Asian cuisine, for example, follow the paths of the New World explorers.

- **Sociology:** Knowledge of different cultures tells us what foods people include in or exclude from their cuisine, and what meanings they ascribe to particular ingredients. For example, you'll have a better chance of finding a recipe for pork loin from countries that are predominantly Christian, as Judaism and Islam place religious restrictions on the consumption of pork.

This is one of the things we've always loved about cooking: the range of knowledge you acquire when you're learning how to do it well. Simply put, the better informed you are in all things, the better cook you will be, with or without recipes.

The key to cooking, then, is understanding your ingredients: what they're made of (protein, starch, fiber, etc.), how they're put together (where are the seeds? what's the skeletal structure like?), how they interact with each other and how they react over time when exposed to various types of heat. Knowing that the seed of a mango is shaped roughly like a spearhead dictates how you cut the flesh into pieces. Knowing that acid affects protein the same way heat does will help you prepare the South American dish ceviche, in which raw fish is "cooked" in an acid such as lime juice. Knowing in advance what's going to happen to an egg if you crack it into a pot of water that's boiling at 212°F (100°C), rather than the much lower poaching temperature of 160°F to 180°F (71°C to 82°C), will help you avoid a stringy, soggy, disgusting mess.

In addition to learning as much as you can about ingredients, to become a skilled cook you must have a good understanding of method and technique. Method is the order in which you put ingredients together; technique is what you do to food to get it ready to cook: cutting up vegetables, scaling a fish, pounding meat to tenderize it and so on. This book is almost entirely about technique — specifically, knife technique. As such, it is an important tool in your quest to become a great cook.

If you know your ingredients *and* you know your methods and techniques, you'll be able to cook virtually anything. And that's a great place to be.

How to Use This Book

There are many different styles of learning — everyone has different needs and different ways of assimilating information. Thus, we have done our best to incorporate as many useful tools as possible into this book:

Concise and detailed written instructions

We've analyzed exactly what has to happen in any given technique, then we've described it in detail, giving you as many specifics as possible, whether it's telling you the correct angle at which to hold your knife or explaining the relative amount of force you need to apply.

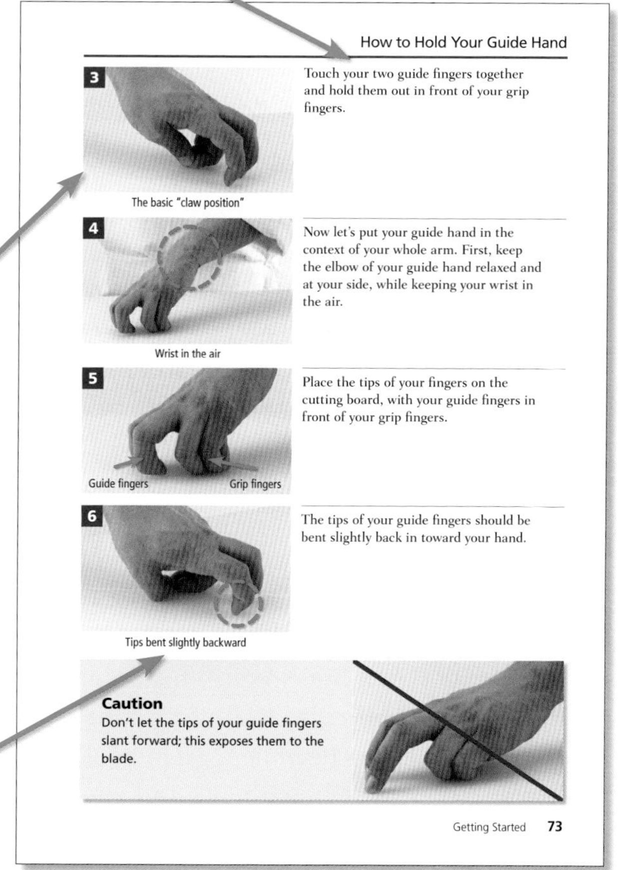

How to Hold Your Guide Hand

3 Touch your two guide fingers together and hold them out in front of your grip fingers.

The basic "claw position"

4 Now let's put your guide hand in the context of your whole arm. First, keep the elbow of your guide hand relaxed and at your side, while keeping your wrist in the air.

Wrist in the air

5 Place the tips of your fingers on the cutting board, with your guide fingers in front of your grip fingers.

Guide fingers

Grip fingers

6 The tips of your guide fingers should be bent slightly back in toward your hand.

Tips bent slightly backward

Caution

Don't let the tips of your guide fingers slant forward; this exposes them to the blade.

Getting Started 73

Pictures

Reading instructions without accompanying visual aids requires an almost photographic imagination that most of us do not possess. So we've supplied the pictures. Each technique is accompanied by a series of photographs that illustrate exactly what we're trying to convey in the instructions.

Directed Focus

In any photo, the number of details can overwhelm your eye to the point that you don't know what you're supposed to be seeing. Show the same photo to five people and you're likely to get five different answers to the question "What did you see?" That's why we've included helpful graphics, such as arrows and labels, with many of the photos, to point out exactly where you're supposed to be looking and indicate what you're supposed to be getting out of it.

After years of teaching, we've concluded that everyone is his or her own best teacher; the job of the professional teacher, then, is to teach us how to teach ourselves. You'll notice a pattern as you read through this book: we have broken every action down into its smallest parts. Holding a knife, for example, is not simply a matter of grabbing the handle with your dominant hand. Every finger has a role to play. Our instructions, pictures and graphics will help you become aware of what each of your fingers should be doing at any given time: what it should be touching, what angle it should be at, how it should be working with your other fingers and so on.

This awareness of details, once achieved, will carry over into other learning venues: for example, you'll have a better sense of what to look for the next time you take a cooking class, or go to a professional chef demo, or even watch a cooking show on television. It's easy to get lured into watching the action. When the chef cuts a zucchini into half-moons, we watch the thin slices fall neatly away from the knife. When she's honing the blade, we watch the edge of her knife as it scrapes along the length of the steel. But you'll learn much more about the technique being demonstrated if you look for the small details behind the action. Instead of watching the pieces of zucchini, watch the chef's guide hand (the one not holding the knife). Where are her fingers in relation to the blade of the knife? At what angle is she holding her wrist? At what angle is she facing the board? Likewise, instead of watching the blade travel down the steel, observe the chef's posture. Is she standing erect or is she bent slightly at the waist? Where are her elbows in relation to her body? Is she holding the steel parallel to the ground or perpendicular or at an angle? Does her movement come from her elbow, her wrist or both?

Train yourself to look for those details and you'll open yourself up to a wealth of information that most chefs won't think to mention because, for them, it's instinctual. And ultimately, that's what you want: to get to a place where your knife technique is instinctual, a muscle memory. This book will show you just how to get there.

Throughout this book, we'll be using the terms "knife hand" and "guide hand." Your knife hand, naturally, holds the knife, while your guide hand holds the food you're cutting. Your dominant hand should be your knife hand.

About the Knife Recommendations in this Book

When deciding what knife to use for a specific technique, there are several factors to take into consideration: the size of the item you're cutting, whether you'll be using a slicing motion or a chopping motion and your own preference. For each of the techniques in this book, we will recommend the knife or knives we feel are most appropriate for the job; however, that doesn't mean they are the only suitable choices.

For the most part, we suggest using a chef's knife or a Santoku — two interchangeable multi-purpose knives — but you could also use a Gyutoh, which is the Japanese version of the chef's knife.

If you are cutting vegetables and the recommended knife is a Santoku, you could use a Nakiri, Kamagata, Chinese cleaver or Usuba — all knives of similar shape and function as the Santoku.

A paring knife can be replaced by its big brothers the utility knife, the Shotoh or the Chutoh, or by a Kudamono.

When it comes to carving, we most often recommend the Western carving knife, but you can substitute its Eastern cousin the Sujihiki or, for boneless meat, the Yanagiba or the Takobiki (or any of the variations on those knives).

Practice Makes Perfect

When we're born, we know how to breathe, how to suckle, how to sleep, how to cry and how to fill a diaper. Everything else is a learned skill. The reason we're so good at walking, shaking hands, opening a door — the reason we can do these things without thinking — is that we've done them over and over and over again, hundreds or thousands of times. And because we've done them so many times, our muscles have learned how to do them for us. They've memorized these tasks. Hence, the term "muscle memory."

Muscle memory is the result of repeated movement over a period of time. With repetition, the brain remembers the movement, making it progressively easier to do, to the point where the movement can be performed without the brain needing to think about it. When we walk, for example, we don't have to think, "Use the muscles of the left leg to pick up the left foot and, balancing on the right foot alone, move the left foot forward from the hip until it is well in front of the right foot, but not so far as to be uncomfortable. Set the left foot down on the ground heel first and immediately pick up the right foot, moving it forward ...” No, we just walk.

It’s the reason that great sports stars are great: they practice making the same motion thousands, if not millions of times, whether it’s a golf swing, a tennis backhand or a pitched baseball. The more you do something, the easier it becomes and the more likely it is that your muscles will remember it so you don’t have to. Chef Tim Bucci, a culinary instructor and silver medalist in the Culinary Olympics, sums it up succinctly: “Practice makes permanent.”

Thus, we recommend that you practice the techniques in this book as much as possible. Go to your local market and buy a 10-pound (5 kg) bag of potatoes or a jumbo sack of onions, then practice your cuts. If you feel, as many people do, that it’s simply not right to waste food, save your practice cuts and turn them into soup. Practice at every opportunity. Even when a recipe calls for “rough cuts,” take the time to make them perfect. The more you practice, the better and faster you’ll get, and the sooner you’ll reach the point where you realize that your knife skills are pretty good. And once that happens, you’ll be well on your way to becoming a great cook.

PROFESSIONAL "S"
ICE HARDENED
NO STAIN

Chapter 1

Everything You Need to Know About Knives

In this chapter, we'll give you a little background on the history of cutting tools, as well as a brief description of the modern knife-making process. We'll teach you the parts of the knife, explain the different blade styles and describe the most common knives — both Western and Japanese — on the market today. Finally, we'll show you how to take care of your knives, from storing to honing to sharpening, so they'll last as long as possible.

The History of Cutlery

The earliest tools used by humans were cutting tools, and the earliest of these date back nearly three million years. These tools were primitive, single-edge stone tools made by flaking rock against rock. Flint was at first the rock of choice but was later replaced by harder obsidian, which can hold an edge better. By 50,000 BC, these early stone knives had evolved to double-edge tools.

The rest of the history of cutlery is closely related to the history of metal, for as metallurgy advanced, so did cutlery. First came copper, which was soon abandoned because it was too soft a metal to hold an edge. By 1500 BC, the skills required to make bronze (an alloy of copper and tin) had spread to Europe. Knives were cast, then hammered to create harder edges. Bronze knives were much sharper and thinner than their stone predecessors.

The next great advance in cutlery was the discovery of iron, which gave weight and strength to blades and increased their cutting ability. Iron was also far more abundant and less expensive than copper.

The modern age of cutlery was ushered in by metalsmiths in India, who invented steel by heating and cooling iron and charcoal together repeatedly, during which process the iron acquired some of the charcoal's carbon. By the 10th century, steel manufacture had reached Europe. Carbon steel has its disadvantages, though: it easily corrodes, rusts and pits, and will not hold an edge well.

The term "Damascus steel" is commonly associated with Japanese knives today, but as the name implies, it was originally made in the Middle East, using steel from India called wootz. The method for making true Damascus steel was lost in the 18th century. Today, Damascus patterns are created by pattern welding, in which different steels that polish differently are forged together to create decorative patterns on the edge of the blade.

MIYABI 7000D Santoku

In the early part of the 20th century came the discovery that steel gained corrosion resistance when chromium was added to it. High-carbon stainless steel — made by adding additional metals, such as molybdenum, vanadium or cobalt — was the next step, in the 1920s.

Today, many knives, particularly premium knives from Japan, are made using high-carbon "super steels," which are extremely hard and tough. They are usually sandwiched between layers of softer steel. VG-10 steel can be hardened to HRC 61 on the Rockwell scale (see page 43). SG-2, a powdered steel, can be hardened to HRC 63, as powdering creates an equal distribution of uniformly sized carbon atoms, giving the steel a superior metallic structure. ZDP-189, the hardest steel currently on the market, can reach HRC 67 thanks to its high carbon and vanadium content. Many of these super steels are exclusive to one or two knife companies.

There are some titanium knives on the market, though production is limited because titanium is so expensive. Titanium is lightweight and very resistant to corrosion, but it doesn't hold an edge well and dulls quickly.

Some companies also make knives from very hard ceramics, such as zirconium oxide (also known as zirconia). Because it is so hard, ceramic holds an edge very well; however, its initial sharpness doesn't compare to that of steel, and when ceramic knives get dull they must be professionally sharpened.

One of the most interesting super steels is Cronidur 30, in which some of the carbon is replaced by nitrogen. It was initially developed to make the ball bearings used in the Space Shuttle. Before Cronidur 30, the shuttle would burn through a set of bearings every launch. Now that the bearings are made from this super steel, they last through 30 to 40 launches.

When used to manufacture cutlery, this steel provides amazing edge retention and corrosion resistance. The only Cronidur 30 knives on the market at the time of publication are found in the TWIN 1731 and TWIN Cronidur lines by ZWILLING J.A. HENCKELS.

TWIN 1731 chef's knife

How Knives Are Made

Knives today are either forged or stamped. Both methods start with a coil of steel that is as thick and wide as it needs to be for the length of the knives that will be made from it. A coil that will be turned into chef's knives, for example, is wider than a coil that will be used to make paring knives.

The coil is put on a coiling machine, which unrolls it and feeds it into a 400-ton press. The press uses a die to cut the coil into blanks the width of the knives they are to become.

At this point, the stamping and forging processes diverge. In the stamping process, the blanks are passed on to another die, which cuts out the knives. In the forging process, the first step for the cut blank is upset forging, in which the section of the blank that will become the bolster (the thick piece of steel between the blade and the handle) is super-heated, then the two ends of the blank are pushed toward each other, causing the heated section to bulge.

The blank is now ready to be forged again to form the bolster. It is moved from the upset forging machine while still hot and placed on another 400-ton press fitted with a forging die, which slams down on it, creating the beginnings of a bolster. The resulting blank looks like this:

Some knives undergo a type of forging called hot drop forging, in which the hot blank is hammered into a die, rather than having a die slam down onto the metal. An example of this type of forging is the TWIN Cuisine line by ZWILLING J.A. HENCKELS. In this line of knives, the tang runs horizontally, not vertically like the blade.

TWIN Cuisine paring knife

Next, the blank is transferred to another press, where a trimming die cuts out the knife, giving it three clearly defined parts: the blade, the bolster and the tang (the part that will be inserted into the handle).

The leftover trim goes on to be recycled.

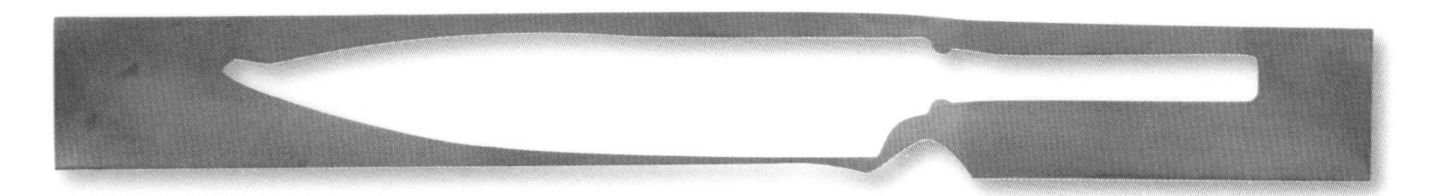

The blade is far from finished. First, the bolster is milled on a tooling machine to prepare it for the application of the handle. Then the bolster and the back of the blade are ground to create their finished shape.

The next stage, in which the steel is hardened by heating and rapid cooling, ensures that the molecular structure of the steel is the best it can be. The correct hardening temperature and the duration of the treatment are subject to narrow limits and must be precisely maintained. The cutting abilities and corrosion resistance of the blade depend entirely on the right heat treatment. While the better stamped knives will also go through this step, most inexpensive stamped knives will not.

Once it is hardened, the knife is ready for grinding and polishing. Both forged and stamped knives go through these steps. Most knives are taper-ground, meaning they taper in a V shape from the spine to the edge. The more finely the surface of the blade is ground and polished, the more resistant to rust it will be. At this point, the knife is still not sharp.

Next, the handle is attached to the blade. For a riveted handle, two handle pieces (called scales) are affixed to the tang by metal pins (called rivets). In this type of handle, the edges of the tang are still visible on the finished knife (see the knife on page 19).

If the handle will fully enclose the tang, the tang is heated (as is the bolster on a forged knife). Then the handle is filled with adhesive and the tang is inserted into it. An adjusting robot smoothes the connection between the handle and the bolster in five stages (fewer in the case of a stamped knife), each of which uses a successively finer belt sander. In some cases, highly trained technicians are required to make adjustments by hand.

Next, highly skilled craftspeople sharpen the knife in a multi-step process involving grinding wheels and belts of varying coarseness. Finally, the blade is embossed with company logos and information about the knife, branding stickers are added, and the knife goes through a final inspection before it is packaged.

Some knives are made in pieces, which are then welded together. This process might be used on inexpensive knives, as a cost-saving measure, or on high-end knives, as a way to use the best steel for each individual piece. Japanese knife manufacturers, for example, often make the bolster, blade and tang separately to ensure that each incorporates the type of steel best suited for its use. In the case of hollow-handled knives, which have no tang, the blade is welded to the handle.

Parts of the Knife

The parts of a knife are pretty much the same for all knives, with a few exceptions based on whether the knife is stamped or forged, serrated or fine-edge, symmetric or asymmetric, riveted or non-riveted. To illustrate the parts, we will use a classic forged chef's knife.

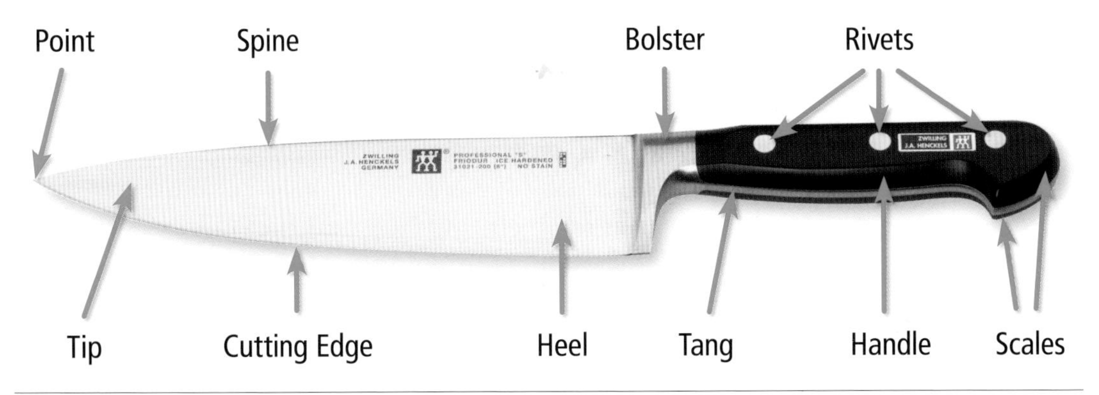

TWIN Professional "S" chef's knife

The **point** is where the spine and the cutting edge come together. It is used for delicate work and to pierce foods.

> When you are trussing a chicken without using string, you use the point of a chef's knife or boning knife to pierce the flaps, which hang down from the cavity, and insert the ends of the legs through the holes.

The **tip** is the first third of the blade. Because most blades taper in thickness from heel to point, the tip is the thinnest, lightest part of a knife, and is therefore well suited to delicate work such as chiffonading basil or cutting soft fruits and vegetables.

The **spine** is the top of the blade. On forged knives, it is usually thicker than the rest of the blade, and can be squared or rounded. In the basic grip (explained on page 70), the thumb and index finger pinch the blade below the spine. Professional chefs who use their knives frequently develop a distinctive callus on their index finger from the spine.

> Because of its thickness and weight, the spine of a chef's knife can be used to crush garlic quickly. Place a clove of garlic parallel to and near the edge of your cutting board. Turn the knife upside down and smash down on the garlic with the spine. Move your knife slightly down the clove after each downward stroke until the whole clove is crushed.

Forged knives have a **bolster**, located where the blade and the handle meet. The bolster protects fingers from the edge while lending weight and balance to the knife. Bolsters can be closed (also called full), as in the labeled knife pictured on page 19, or open (half), as in the picture below. A closed bolster extends from the spine to the edge of the blade at the heel, so that part of the edge is dull. An open bolster stops short of the edge, so it gives you more cutting edge and is easier to hone and sharpen, as the bolster doesn't get in the way. The open bolster pictured below is also ergonomic, meaning that it was designed to be comfortable when you are gripping the knife by the blade, as in the basic grip (see page 70).

TWIN 1731 chef's knife showing open bolster

The **handle** is what you hold the knife by. Handles come in many shapes, sizes and materials, and can be solid or hollow. Common materials for handles are wood, plastic and composite resin. Common shapes include classic handles (as in the labeled knife pictured on page 19), ergonomic handles and D-shaped handles (often seen in classical Japanese knives). The handle should feel good in your hand so that, over time, you begin to feel as if the knife is an extension of your hand.

TWIN Five Star serrated utility knife showing ergonomic handle

MIYABI 7000D Gyutoh showing D-shaped handle

End cap detail

The **tang** is the steel that extends from the blade or the bolster into the handle. The tang gives a knife strength, durability, balance and weight. It can be full or partial (or, in hollow-handled knives, non-existent). Knives with full tangs are considered stronger and more reliable for heavy work.

TWIN Professional "S" chef's knife showing full tang

Partial tang of a TWIN Four Star before insertion into handle

The **scales** are pieces of wood, plastic or composite resin that enclose the tang to form the handle on a riveted knife. There is one on each side of the tang, and they are held together by metal pins called **rivets**.

The **heel** of the knife is the back third of the cutting edge, up to the bolster. It is thicker and heavier at the spine than the rest of the blade and is therefore well suited to heavier work, such as cutting through thick skin and chicken bones.

Although a chef's knife is thick enough and heavy enough to cut through most bones, it's not a good idea to use it on any bones thicker than chicken bones, as doing so can damage the edge. That job is best left to a meat cleaver, which has a sturdy edge specifically designed for this task.

The **cutting edge** is the part of the knife that does the work. There are many different types of cutting edges, each suited to specific tasks.

Blade Styles

Cutting edges can be taper-ground, convex-ground or hollow-ground; fine, serrated, scalloped or Granton; and symmetric or asymmetric.

Edge Shapes

Taper-ground edges are the most common. The knives are made from a single sheet of metal that is ground so that the blade tapers from the spine to the edge, resulting in a distinctive V-shaped blade. This edge is stable and sturdy, capable of cutting through a wide variety of foods. It is typically found on all-purpose knives, such as chef's knives, utility knives and paring knives. These knives usually taper from the heel of the knife to the tip as well (called distal tapering).

In **convex-ground edges**, the sides of the blade arc near the edge, creating a wider area directly behind the edge than in a taper-ground edge. These edges are extremely sturdy, though not as sharp as other edge styles. They are suitable for heavy tasks such as chopping through bone, which is why you will most likely encounter this edge on cleavers.

Hollow-ground edges are made by beginning the grinding process lower down on the blade (typically a quarter to halfway down), creating a concave slope at the edge. The resulting edge can be very sharp. This edge can sometimes be found on slicing knives and on knives sold at an entry-level price.

Types of Edge

Fine edges are straight and uninterrupted from heel to point. They are relatively easy to sharpen, give the user greater accuracy and control, and make cleaner cuts than serrated edges.

Fine edge

Serrated and **micro-serrated edges** have saw-like teeth running along them. The actual cutting surface lies between and is protected by these protrusions, so the edge needs sharpening less often because the cutting surface never comes in contact with the board. When the need for sharpening does arise, it is nearly impossible to sharpen these knives at home, as special tools are needed, so it is best to send them to a professional. You could also simply replace the knife when it gets dull; a typical serrated knife lasts 10 to 15 years, depending on the level of usage. Serrated edges are used to cut items with harder outsides than insides, which is why you often find them on bread and tomato knives. Entry-level knives also often feature serrated or micro-serrated edges, because they are low maintenance.

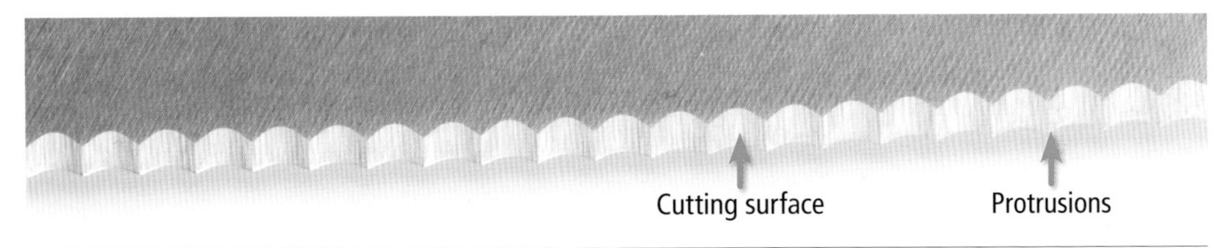

Serrated edge

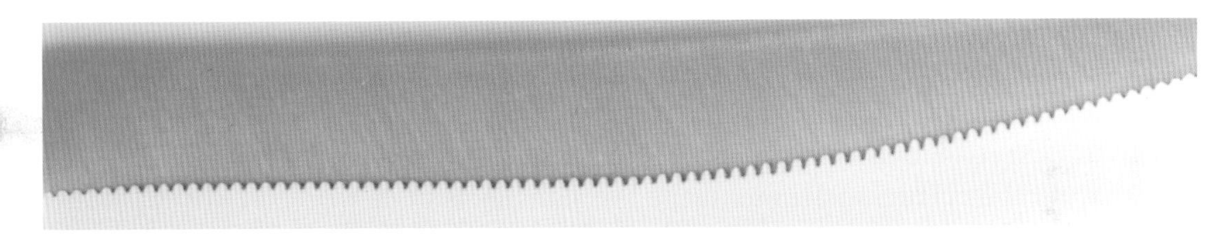

Micro-serrated edge

Scalloped edges are the reverse of serrated edges: instead of the cutting edge arching inward between teeth, a series of arches bend outward from the blade. The properties of and uses for a scalloped blade are similar to those of serrated blades, but the edges are less resilient to wear. Scalloped edges can be found on bread knives and slicing knives.

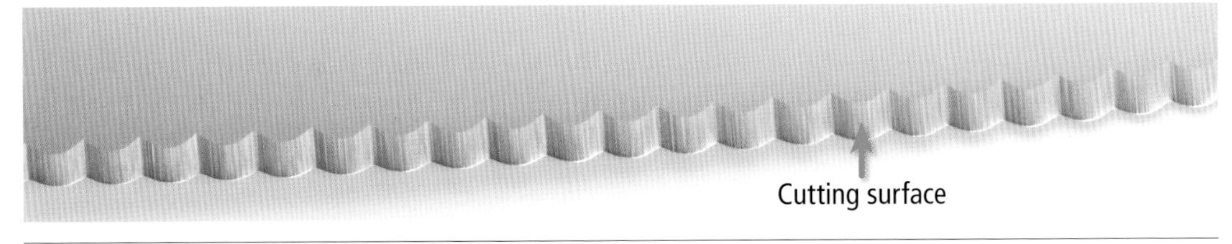

Scalloped edge

Granton edges have hollows, called grantons or kullens, ground into the side of the blade. The grantons create pockets of air between the side of the blade and the food, reducing friction and helping to keep food from sticking to the sides of the blade. These edges are most effective on thin knives, such as knives used to slice meat and fish, as the grantons cover a large portion of the surface area of the side of the blade. In recent years, grantons have been added to chef's knives and Santokus; they may add some benefit to these knives, but they are less effective than when used on slicers.

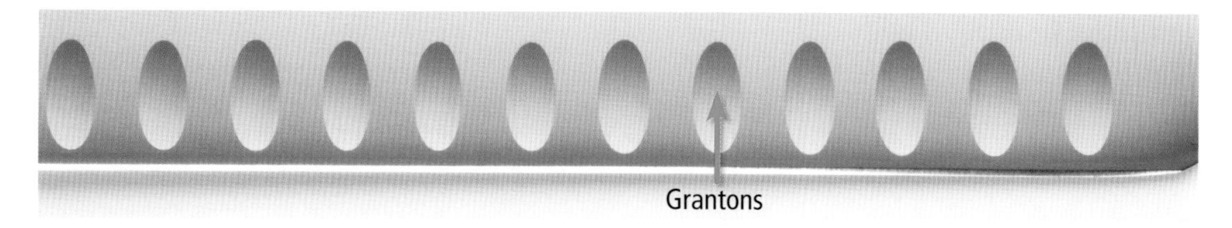

Granton edge

Symmetric vs. Asymmetric Edges

An understanding of the geometry of symmetric and asymmetric edges requires a discussion of the differences between Western and Japanese approaches to the culinary arts. In Japan, food is often consumed raw, or with minimal preparation, so its structural integrity must remain as close to its original state as possible. The sharper the cutting instrument, the less damage is done to the cells that hold the ingredient together and the slower the cell degradation that begins when the food is cut. Therefore, Japan has some of the sharpest knives around.

The way to get sharper edges on a knife is to decrease the angle of the edge. Western knives and Western-style Japanese knives are symmetrically double-beveled, meaning the angle of slope is the same on both sides of the knife. But whereas in Western knives this angle is usually between 20 and 30 degrees on each side, for a total angle of 40 to 60 degrees, in Western-style Japanese knives, the angle is reduced to 10 to 20 degrees per side, for a total angle of 20 to 40 degrees.

Japan's traditional knives are asymmetrically single-beveled, meaning one side is either flat or slightly concave, while the other has a beveled edge of between 10 and 20 degrees (so the total angle is 10 to 20 degrees) that slopes down from the side of the blade. These are extremely sharp and cause the least amount of cellular structural damage when slicing, which is why you find them on knives used for sashimi and other raw fish preparations. Japan also makes asymmetrically double-beveled knives, which have different-size bevels on either side of the blade. The common ratios used are 70:30 and 90:10.

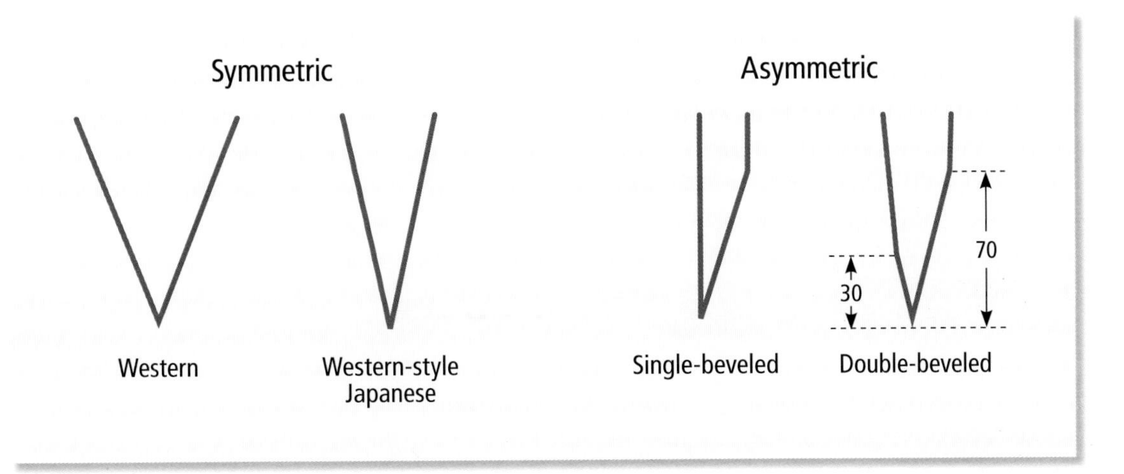

Single-beveled knives come in both right-handed and left-handed models, but left-handed models usually need to be custom-ordered and are more expensive, as the demand for them is far less (about 10% of the population is left-handed). So left-handed apprentice chefs often learn to use their right hand until they can afford left-handed knives.

Types of Knives

There are countless varieties of knives, from general-purpose knives, such as the chef's knife, to the ultra-specialized knives of Japan, such as the Fugubiki, which is designed to slice the highly poisonous puffer fish, fugu, with precision, to avoid releasing toxins into the flesh. An entire book could be devoted to listing and classifying cutlery, but we'll limit our discussion to the most common knives (though we will mention a few exotic ones). We'll also talk about other cutting tools used in the kitchen.

Improper preparation of fugu can be fatal. About six deaths a year in Japan are attributed to fugu poisoning.

Multi-Purpose Knives

The **chef's knife** (sometimes called a cook's knife or a French knife) is arguably the most important tool in the kitchen. Almost any cutting you need to do, from slicing a watermelon to dicing a shallot, can be accomplished with a chef's knife (or one of its close relatives, the Gyutoh or the Santoku). Chef's knives range in length from 6 inches (15 cm) to over 12 inches (30 cm). Ten inches (25 cm) is the standard for professionals, while 8 inches (20 cm) is the most common length for chef's knives used in the home (it's the size typically included in prepackaged knife block sets). As with all knives, you should choose the largest knife that's comfortable in your hand — the larger it is, the more things you can do with it.

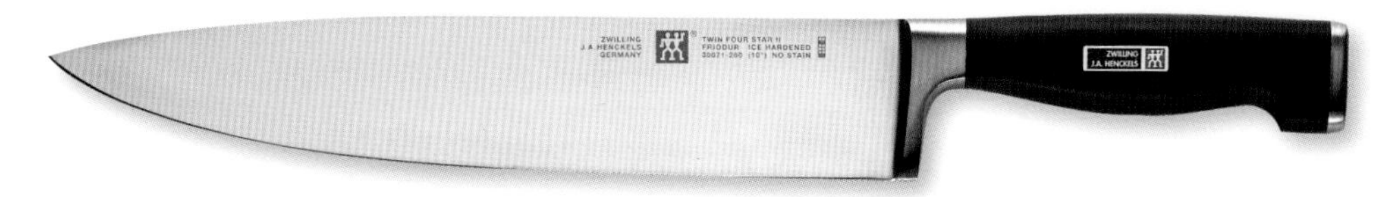

TWIN Four Star II chef's knife

The **Gyutoh** is considered a Western-style knife in Japan. It can have a traditional D-shaped handle, as seen on page 27, or a Western-style riveted handle. *Gyu* means "cow," and *oh* means "sword," which indicates that the Gyutoh was originally considered a meat knife, but it has come to be used more like a chef's knife. In recent years, the Gyutoh has risen in popularity in Western kitchens due to its extreme sharpness. However, because it is more fragile than a chef's knife, with a harder, thinner blade, there are some things you would do with a chef's knife that you should not do with a Gyutoh, such as cutting through small bones or smashing garlic. Gyutohs are sold in lengths ranging from 210 to 300 millimeters (about 8 to 12 inches).

MIYABI 7000MC Gyutoh

The **Santoku** is closely related to the chef's knife and the Gyutoh. The word loosely translates as "three virtues," indicating that it can be used to cut meat, fish or vegetables. It was adapted by the Japanese from the Western chef's knife, but has a straighter edge that is suited to the Japanese cutting style of chopping rather than rocking, as you would with the curved edge of a chef's knife. Santokus are growing in popularity in the West and are usually fairly short, sold in lengths of either 150 or 180 millimeters (about 6 or 7 inches). In Japan they are almost solely used in the home and are rarely seen in professional kitchens.

MIYABI 7000D Santoku

The **Chinese cleaver** (also known as a vegetable cleaver) is an Eastern alternative to the chef's knife. It is used for chopping, for slicing fish and vegetables and for cutting boneless meats. Chinese cleavers typically range in length from 7 to 9 inches (18 to 23 cm) and are thinner and lighter than meat cleavers (see page 34). The broad side of the blade is great for scooping cut items off the cutting board.

TWIN Signature Chinese cleaver

Usuba, **Kamagata** and **Nakiri** knives are Japanese adaptations of the Chinese cleaver and are used to cut vegetables. The Usuba and Kamagata are single-beveled knives; the Nakiri is double-beveled. The Kamagata's blade has a curved front, like that of a Santoku, while the other two have squared tips. The thin blades on these knives make them ideal for specialized tasks such as cutting ribbons out of daikon and cucumber. Their blades are also less broad than that of the Chinese cleaver.

MIYABI 5000S Usuba

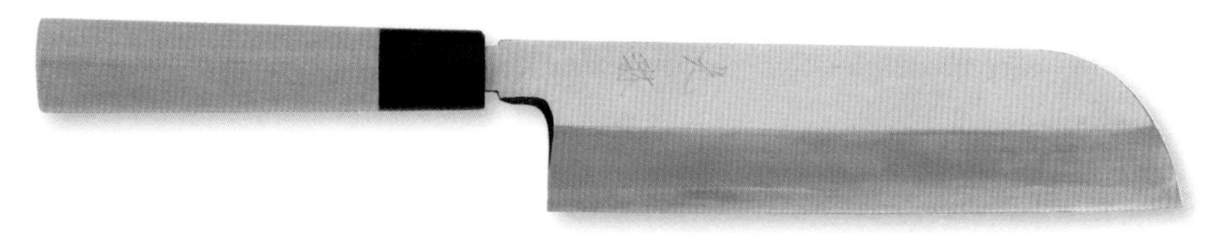

Kamagata

Nakiri

Paring knives, which can be viewed as small chef's knives, are used when a chef's knife would be cumbersome. Tasks such as hulling strawberries or dicing shallots are easier with a smaller knife. Paring knives range in length from 2 to 4 inches (5 to 10 cm); the larger the knife, the more uses you'll find for it.

TWIN Profection paring knife

The **Kudamono** (also known as a fruit knife or a sheep's foot parer), is a miniature version of a Santoku and is used much like a parer.

MIYABI 5000S Kudamono

The most unusual member of the paring knife family is variously called a **tourné knife**, a peeler and a bird's beak. The first name can be attributed to the fact that the arc of the blade is perfectly suited to the French cut called tourné (see page 109). That arc also helps you follow the curve of fruits and vegetables while peeling, thus the name "peeler." As for "bird's beak," the origin of that name should be fairly obvious from the photo.

TWIN Professional "S" peeler

Utility knives (also known as petty knives or sandwich knives) are longer than paring knives but shorter than chef's knives, and are therefore suited to cutting items of medium size. They are quite portable and can often be found on picnics and fishing trips. The Japanese use Shotohs and Chutohs in place of paring knives; these two knives have the same shape, but the Chutoh is slightly longer.

TWIN Profection utility knife

MIYABI 5000S Shotoh

MIYABI 7000D Chutoh

Slicing Knives

Slicing knives (also called **carving knives**) are long and thin, enabling you to make clean slices with one stroke of the blade. They range in length from 8 to 12 inches (20 to 30 cm), and come in different shapes and with different edges, depending on their intended use. The most utilitarian is the generic slicing knife, or what the Japanese call a **Sujihiki**.

TWIN Professional "S" carving knife

The companion to the carving knife is the meat fork, which can be used to hold the meat while you're slicing. Meat forks are also used to lift cuts of meat while cooking and, in restaurants, to swirl and plate pastas.

TWIN Four Star II carving fork

At buffet carving stations, you'll often see servers using long hollow-edge slicers with rounded tips. In the past, these were typically used to carve large steamship rounds of beef, hence they came to be called **roast beef carvers** (though they are also commonly known simply as hollow-edge slicers). Because these knives were so frequently used on buffet lines, the round tip evolved as a safety measure.

TWIN Professional "S" hollow-edge slicer

The thinnest and most flexible slicing knife is called either a **salmon slicer** or a **ham slicer**, depending on what country you're in. It's used to make the thinnest slices of smoked salmon and prosciutto.

TWIN Four Star II salmon slicer

The **Yanagiba** is a specialized single-beveled slicer for cutting sashimi. *Yanagi* means "willow" and *ba* means "blade," indicating the shape of the blade. The Yanagiba is the most important knife for a sushi chef. These slicers are typically between 10 and 12 inches (25 and 30 cm) in length but can be much longer.

MIYABI 7000 Pro Yanagiba

In Japan, there are numerous specialized slicers, all variations of the Yanagiba. The Fugubiki, a thinner version of the Yanagiba, is used to cut slices of fugu (blowfish) so thin that you can see the decoration of the plate through them. The Takobiki looks like a square-tipped Yanagiba and is used to slice octopus. The Sakimaru Takobiki has a tip that is angled forward like a slash on a keyboard; it was developed to satisfy a regional preference.

Steak knives are designed for use at the dining table, and are therefore small, so they'll fit in with other flatware. They are used to cut cooked meats and other items that are hard to cut with a butter knife, such as hard root vegetables. Steak knives can be either serrated or fine-edge. Fine-edge steak knives are more easily sharpened and make cleaner (less ragged-looking) cuts.

TWIN Professional "S" steak knife

Bread knives are serrated knives that are particular good for cutting through the hard crusts of bread or anything with a soft interior and a hard exterior. They are typically 8 to 10 inches (20 to 30 cm) in length, though longer knives are available for commercial use. Some bread knives have an L-shaped (offset) blade to keep the cutter's knuckles from hitting the board.

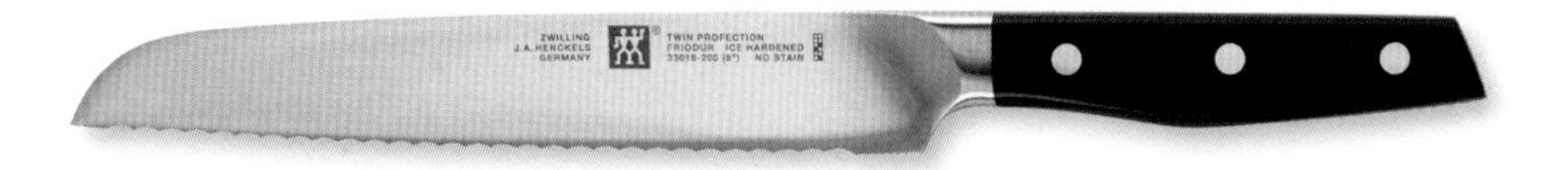

TWIN Profection bread knife

Scalloped slicers fall in between bread knives and slicing knives. They make excellent slicers, as the scalloping gives you more edge surface than a fine-edge knife of the same length would have, but they lack the pointed teeth of a serrated edge.

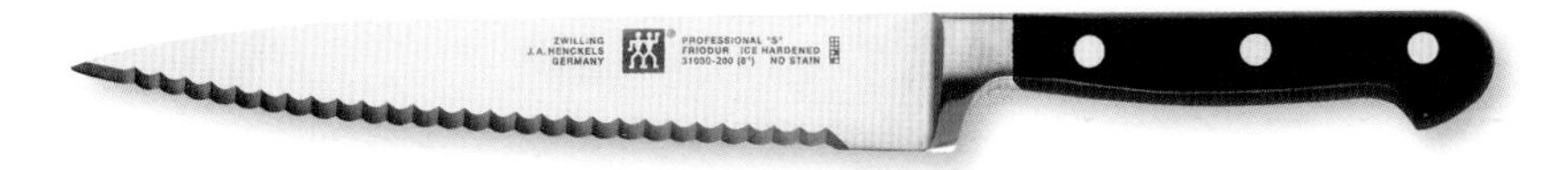

TWIN Professional "S" scalloped slicer

Tomato knives are small serrated knives for, as the name suggests, slicing tomatoes. They are usually around 5 inches (13 cm) long.

TWIN Five Star serrated utility knife

Some people prefer to use a serrated knife to cut tomatoes because of the tomato's combination of tough skin and soft interior. However, as long as you keep your knives sharp, a fine-edge knife is actually better for the task, as the resulting slices look cleaner.

Butchering Knives

Western and Japanese knife manufacturers take very different approaches when it comes to designing knives for butchering meat, poultry and fish. In general, Western butchering knives are narrower, thinner and more flexible than Japanese butchering knives.

Boning knives are long and somewhat flexible, perfect for working around bones and getting between joints. They are typically between 5 and 6 inches (13 and 15 cm) long. The thin, narrow blade allows for greater control of the tip as it works its way under silverskin and between muscle groups.

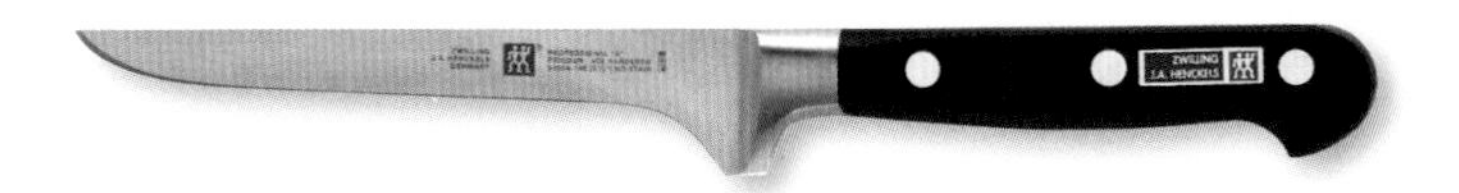

TWIN Professional "S" boning knife

Boning knives work well for both meat and poultry, but when working with fish, Western chefs want their knives even longer and more flexible, and a **fillet knife** gets them as close to the bone as possible.

TWIN Professional "S" fillet knife

The **scimitar** is a large knife for cutting large pieces of raw meat. Its name and shape are derived from the curved scimitar sword, which originated in the Middle East. Scimitars are typically 12 inches (30 cm) or longer.

Scimitar

The **meat cleaver** is a large, heavy, rectangular knife with a convex edge that's good for chopping through bones and tendons. You can also use the side of a cleaver to smash things like garlic.

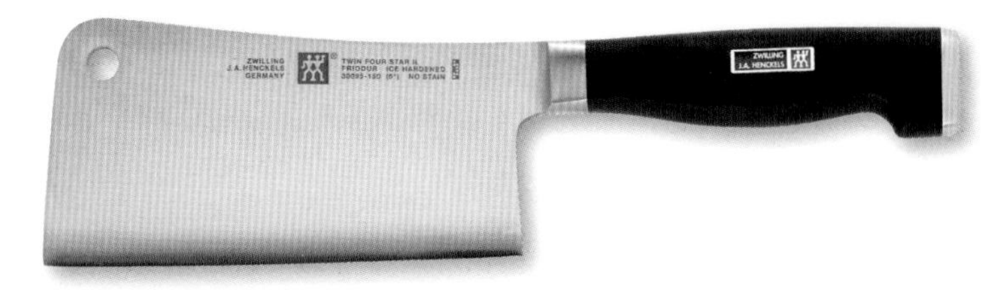

TWIN Four Star II cleaver

The **Deba** is a thick, stiff, single-beveled knife of extreme sharpness, used by Japanese cooks to butcher boneless meat and to fillet fish. In the latter use, the beveled blade enables them to get very close to the bone, and the blade's width allows them to remove the fillet in fewer strokes and therefore more cleanly.

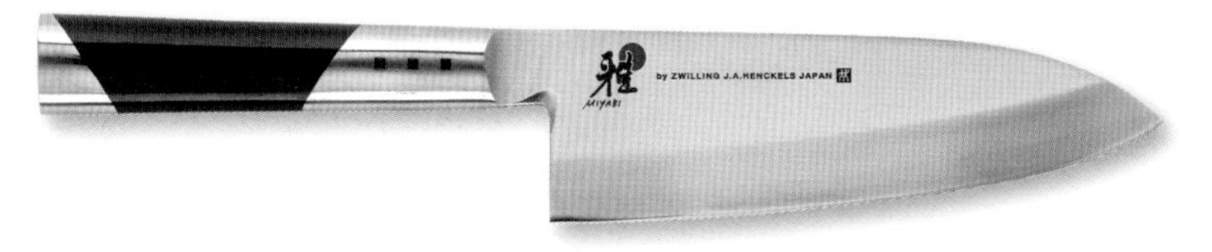

MIYABI 7000 Pro Deba

For smaller fish, a **Kodeba** is used. (Ko means "small," so "small Deba.)

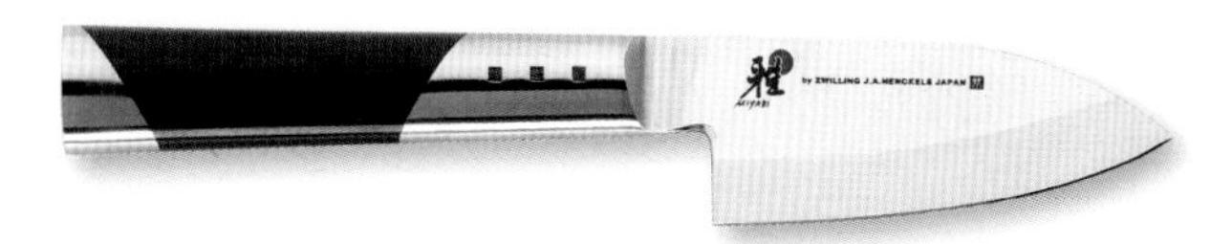

MIYABI 7000 Pro Kodeba

When working with bone-in meat, the Japanese use a short, stiff, narrow knife called a **Hankotsu**.

Hankotsu

For poultry, they use a wider knife called a **Garasuki** (which has no Western counterpart) to separate the meat and cut through bone.

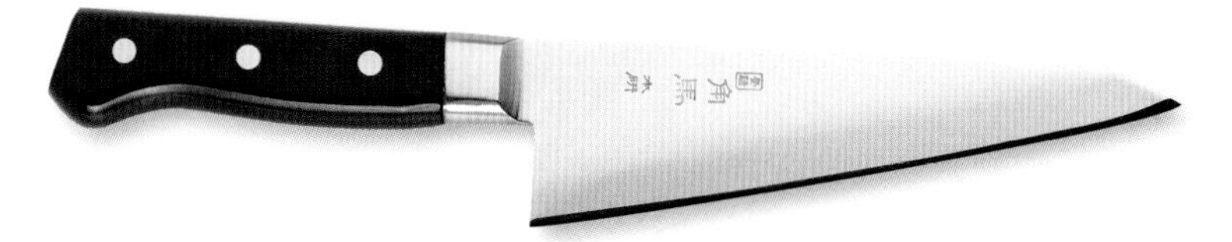

Garasuki

The Garasuki was developed in Japanese restaurants that specialize in preparing chicken.

The **Honesuki** falls between a Hankotsu and a Garasuki in width, and is more of an all-purpose knife for boning meat and poultry.

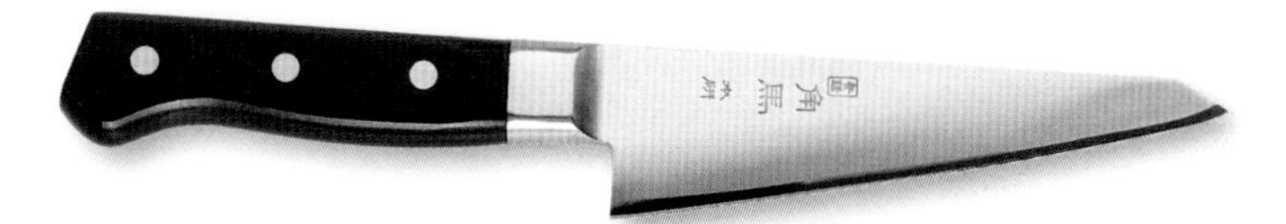

Honesuki

The largest and most impressive-looking butchering knife is the **Maguro** of Japan. These knives look more like swords than kitchen cutlery. They are most often seen at Tsukiji Fish Market in Tokyo, where fishmongers use them to cut up large tuna (the purpose for which they were designed).

The Mezzaluna

The **mezzaluna**'s curved half-moon blade makes it the ideal knife for mincing and for chopping herbs. It comes in single- and double-bladed designs. Some models have knobs on each end of the blade for handles; others have an arcing handle that attaches to each end of the blade.

TWIN Select double mezzaluna

Other Cutting Tools

Many cutting tools used in the kitchen are not technically knives, as they don't have a true cutting edge. Most have names that are descriptive of their main use.

Kitchen shears and **poultry shears** are well suited to a number of tasks, such as cutting the fins off fish or cutting through the small bones of poultry. Poultry shears often have longer blades than all-purpose kitchen shears, sometimes with a slight curl.

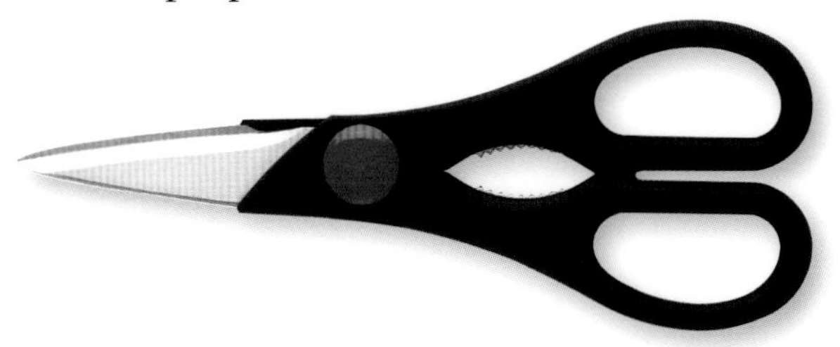

TWIN kitchen shears

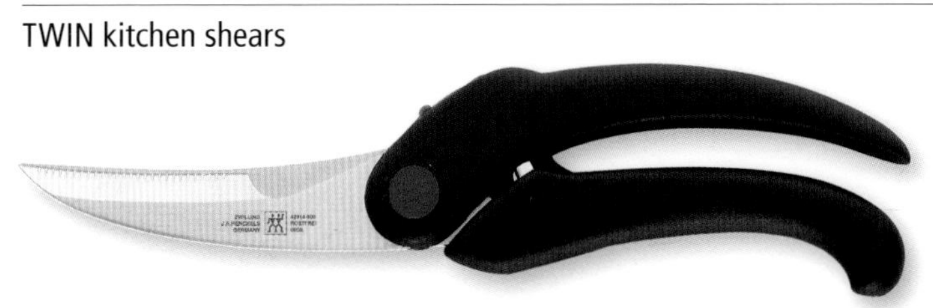

TWIN poultry shears

The **oyster knife** is designed for shucking oysters. These rigid knives are typically 3 inches (7.5 cm) long, with dull edges on both sides and either a straight or a slightly curled blunt tip. Similar in shape and use are **clam knives** and **scallop knives**, which have a sharpened edge on one side. Clam knives are narrower and longer than oyster and scallop knives. The stiffness of these knives allows them to break the hinges of bivalves.

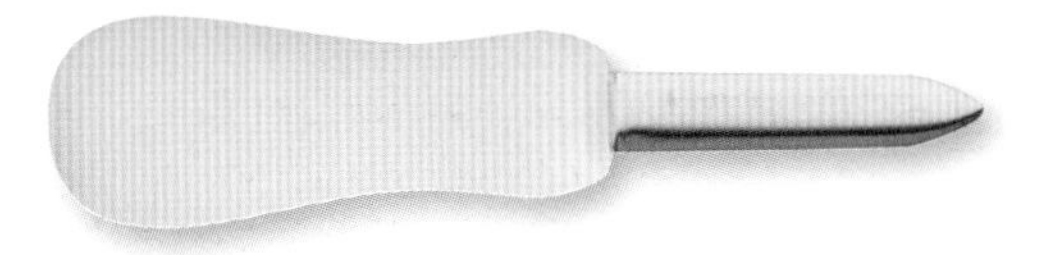

Oyster knife

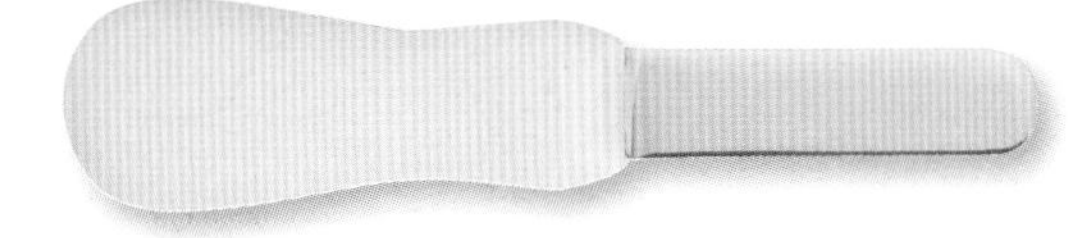

Clam knife

Scallop knife

The **shrimp deveining knife** has a curved blade that follows the curve of a shrimp's back to remove the intestine. While this arguably makes the job a little bit easier, it can be accomplished just as well with a paring knife or tourné knife.

Shrimp deveining knife

Channel knives (also called canal knives) and **zesters** are used for similar purposes and can often be found combined into one tool. Channel knives have one circular blade; zesters have four or five. Channel knives are typically used to make citrus twists for cocktails; zesters are typically used to zest citrus fruit. Both can also be used to cut channels in fruits and vegetables before slicing, to make decorative slices.

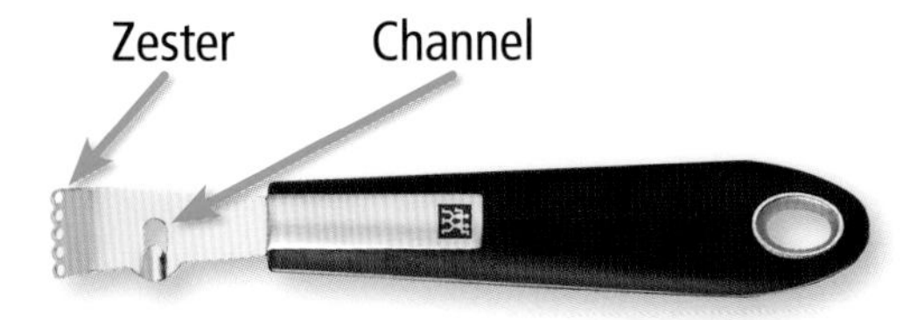

TWIN Cuisine zester/channel knife

Peelers are used for just that: peeling fruits, vegetables and tubers. Like channel knives and zesters, they can also be used to make decorative slices. They are composed of two facing blades, which can be either stationary or swiveling. Stationary peelers work best with straight produce, such as carrots, whereas swivel peelers are better for rounded fruits and vegetables.

TWIN Cuisine stationary peeler

TWIN Pure swivel peeler

Corers are designed to remove the stem and core from fruits and vegetables such as apples and tomatoes. They consist of a long shaft crowned by a circular cutting tool. Some corers are designed to segment as well as core.

TWIN Pure apple corer

The **pizza cutter** is a round blade attached to a hub on a handle. Its spinning action allows it to easily slice pizza.

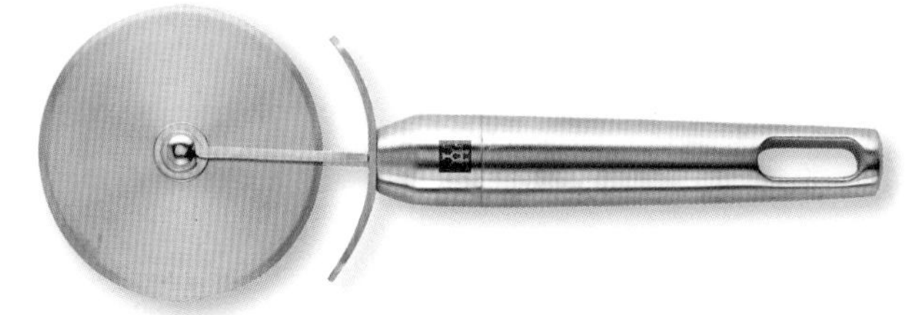

TWIN Pure pizza cutter

Graters come in all shapes and sizes and can be used for any number of tasks, from grating nutmeg and zesting lemons to shredding potatoes or cheeses.

TWIN Pure grater

Many **cheese knives** are designed to work with specific sizes and styles of cheese. For large wheels of hard cheese, there are long blades with handles on each end. For soft cheeses, there are knives with thin blades. For Parmesan cheese, there are small, stiff, heart-shaped knives designed to pry off wedges. There are also all-purpose cheese knives, many with a forked tip for spearing cut pieces of cheese.

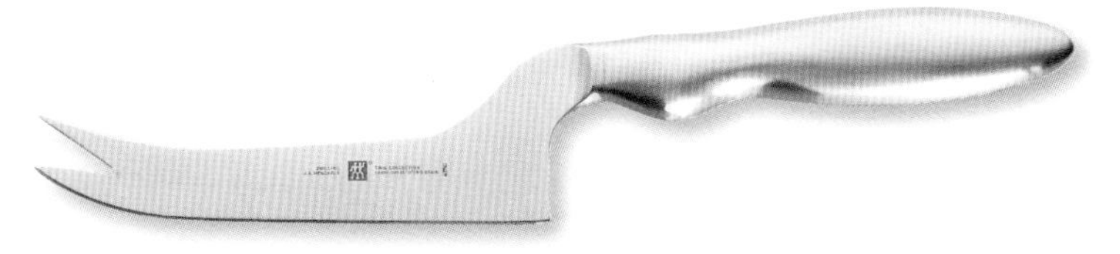

TWIN Collection fork-tip cheese knife

The **mandoline** is an excellent tool for slicing large quantities of produce evenly and quickly. The blade is stationary and the food being cut is moved against it. It can be raised or lowered to change the thickness of the slice. Many mandolines come with additional blades for making juliennes, batons and gaufrettes. Some mandolines have stands; others are hand-held.

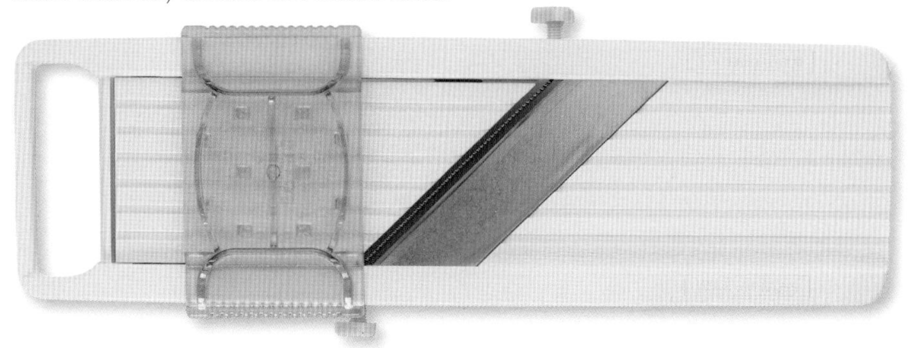

Japanese mandoline

A **truffle slicer** is related to the mandolin in that the blade is stationary and the truffle moves against it. However, the blade cannot be adjusted as widely for thickness, as the truffle slicer is intended to shave very thin pieces of truffle. It can also be used to shave chocolate.

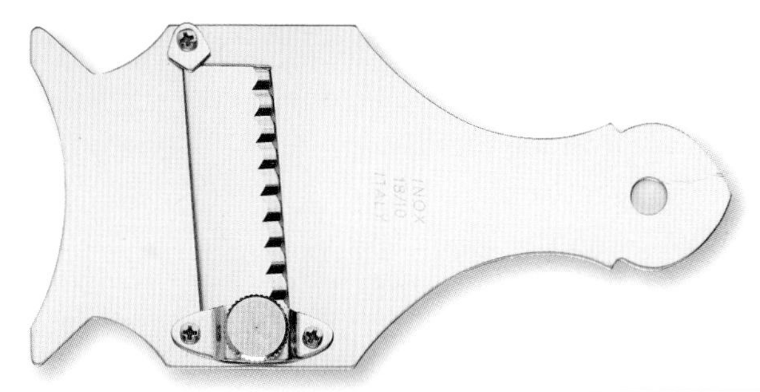

Truffle slicer

Melon ballers come in various sizes and shapes, and are used to cut balls out of fruits such as melons and vegetables like potatoes.

TWIN Pure melon scoop

In French cooking, the term "Parisienne" is used to describe food that has been cut into balls.

A **grapefruit knife** is a small serrated knife used to halve and segment citrus fruit. The blade curls at the tip, allowing you to follow the curve of the fruit while cutting between the rind and the flesh.

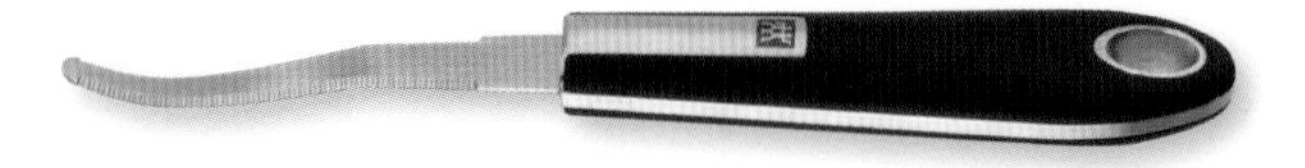

TWIN Cuisine grapefruit knife

A **butter curler**, which has a blade shaped like a question mark, makes delicate curls of butter or chocolate for garnish.

Butter curler

Electric Cutting Machines

A **meat slicer** (also called a deli slicer) is used to slice deli meats and charcuterie. It has a rotating circular blade that can be adjusted for thickness. The item being sliced sits in a movable cradle, which slides back and forth against the spinning blade. In restaurants, deli slicers are often used to cut large amounts of produce rapidly.

Food processors, by means of interchangeable blades, can slice, chop and grate at high speed. For chopping, the blade spins at the bottom of a bowl filled with food. For slicing and grating, the blade spins at the top of the bowl while the food being cut is pushed against it from above. Food processors typically have two speed settings, as well as a pulse option.

Blenders can be used to chop and purée by means of a multi-speed rotating blade at the bottom of a pitcher.

Hand blenders (also called immersion blenders or stick blenders) have rotating blades at the end of a stick or wand. You can use them in any container, including cooking pots, to purée solids or whip or emulsify liquids.

Buffalo choppers combine vertical rotating blades with a spinning donut-shaped bowl to uniformly chop food to the desired size. They are most often used in professional kitchens.

Knife Care

A good knife is an investment. With proper care, it will last a lifetime, so keep the following maintenance tips in mind:

- No steel is completely "stainless"; with improper care, it will stain, pit or rust. Always rinse off acidic foods (citrus juice, tomatoes, mustard, ketchup, etc.) from a blade after use, as acid can cause slight tarnishing. Should the blade show signs of staining, use a non-abrasive metal polish to clean it.
- Do not put knives in the dishwasher, even if they are said to be dishwasher-safe. Banging against other cutlery, the dishwasher racks or pots and pans will nick the blades. Dishwashers also cause wood handles to discolor and crack.
- To clean a knife, wipe it with a wet cloth and dishwashing detergent. Dry it immediately. Dry from the spine of the knife to the cutting edge, and from the heel to the point, to avoid poking or cutting yourself.
- For wood-handled knives, in addition to immediately drying the handle after washing it, you should occasionally apply mineral oil to the handle to help maintain the finish. This will also help protect the handle from moisture damage.
- Try not to put a good knife in a drawer unless you have an in-drawer knife tray, a knife sheath or edge guard, or a box for the knife. Jumbling knives in a drawer along with other cutlery may cause irreparable blade damage. This type of storage also results in a higher incidence of injury, as you may not see the knife when you're reaching into the drawer.

Proper Knife Storage

Knives must be stored in a safe place to protect the cutting edge and guard against injuries. Many professional chefs carry their kitchen tools in an attaché case, toolbox or knife roll. At home, knives can be stored in a knife block, in an in-drawer knife tray, in protective sleeves or edge guards, or on a magnetic wall mount.

- The ubiquitous countertop **wooden knife block** offers easy access to your knives and fits underneath kitchen cabinets. The size of these blocks varies depending on how many knives they are designed to store. Look for blocks with horizontal slats so that the knives don't rest on their edges.

- **Wooden in-drawer knife trays** are convenient if you like the features of a knife block but want to store knives in a drawer, leaving your countertop clear.
- A **protective sleeve** slides over the blade of a knife like a glove slides over your hand. Once inside protective sleeves, knives can be stored in a drawer, knife roll or case.
- An **edge guard** slides onto a knife edge as if you were slicing into it. Better ones are lined to keep them from scratching the sides of the blade. Once protected by edge guards, knives can be stored in a drawer, knife roll or case.
- **Magnetic wall mounts** allow easy access to your knives when you don't have a lot of counter space. Make sure the magnets are strong enough to hold knives securely in place. And never try to hang a knife that isn't clean: grease interferes with the magnet's ability to hold the knife.

> Higher-end knives often come packaged in boxes and can continue to be stored in these boxes if space allows.

Honing a Knife

If you were to examine a knife under a microscope, you'd see that the edge is made up of thousands of small cutting teeth, called burrs. Through use, these fine teeth eventually get bent, dulling the knife. Honing the knife with a honing steel realigns the burrs.

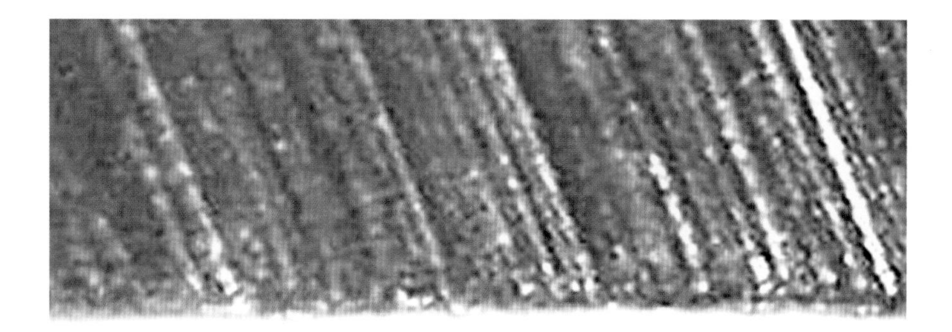

Honing vs. Sharpening

Honing is maintaining the edge; sharpening is repairing the edge. Sharpening should be performed when honing no longer returns the edge to sharpness. Just as with an automobile, the more care you take to maintain a knife, the less often you have to repair it. And as with a car, repairing a knife is more costly than maintenance, because when sharpening you are removing metal from your knife by grinding it away.

Honing steels are sold in varying degrees of coarseness. They typically range from 9 to 12 inches (23 to 30 cm) in length; your steel should be about 2 inches (5 cm) longer than the knife you are trying to hone. Honing steels are slightly magnetic, so they'll pick up any particles of metal removed from the knife during honing.

TWIN Professional steel

Understanding the Rockwell Scale

Before you ever purchase a honing steel, it's important to know how hard the steel in your knives is. The hardness rating is expressed as a number on the Rockwell scale. To determine a steel's Hardness Rockwell C (HRC) rating, a diamond-tipped pin is pressed into the metal, then the depth of penetration for a given amount of force is measured. Knives are made of some of the hardest metal you'll encounter. As a point of comparison, the metal used to make buildings is about HRC 15. The metal in a typical Western kitchen knife is HRC 57, while the metal in Japanese knives can range from HRC 60 to HRC 67.

Your honing steel must have an HRC higher than that of your knives; otherwise, you'll damage both. Most steels come in an HRC between 60 and 65. For this reason, many Japanese knives must be honed on a fine-grit whetstone rather than on a steel.

Important Things to Remember When Using a Honing Steel

- Use a honing steel that is longer than your knife.
- Make sure your knife and honing steel are both clean and dry.
- Hold your knife against the honing steel at roughly the same angle as the factory-applied angle on the edge of the knife. For Western knives, this is usually between 20 and 30 degrees; for Japanese knives, this is between 10 and 20 degrees.

An easy honing angle for a Western knife is 22.5 degrees. To find this angle, hold your knife at 90 degrees, then halve that to find 45 degrees, then halve it again to find 22.5 degrees. You could also use the angle of the bolster as your guide, as the angle of most Western bolsters is between 20 and 25 degrees.

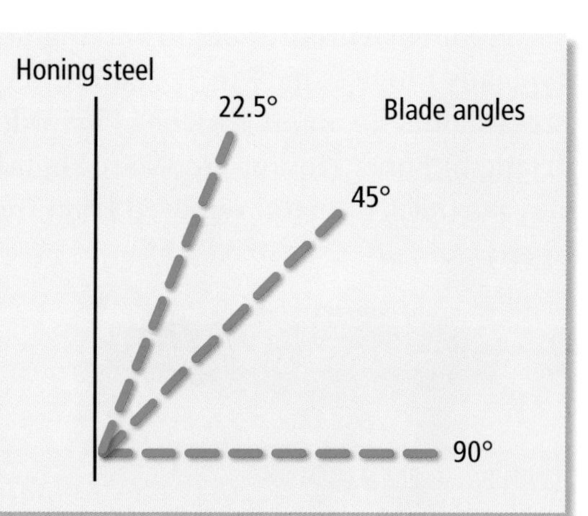

- Maintain the same angle every time you hone.
- Do not press the knife against the honing steel or apply force. The weight of the knife is enough to do the job.
- Use the whole length of both the knife and the honing steel, to avoid creating a bow in the knife.
- When you're done honing, clean and dry both knife and honing steel to remove any metal particles that may have come off during honing.
- Honing steels have a lifespan of between 10 to 15 years, depending on usage. They should be replaced when they lose their effectiveness.

When you are learning to use a honing steel, use a junk knife and honing steel to practice. These can often be found at garage sales and thrift shops. Go slowly at first. As you practice, you'll gradually be able to hone faster.

How to Use a Honing Steel

There are several ways to use a honing steel; we've provided instructions for two methods we consider safe. Method 1 is the safest, as the edge of the knife is never pointed toward yourself or anyone else. Method 2 requires extra vigilance, as you are moving the knife in the air, with the edge facing out.

Throughout this book, we'll be using the terms "knife hand" and "guide hand." Your knife hand, naturally, holds the knife, while your guide hand holds the food you're cutting — or, in this case, the honing steel. Your dominant hand should be your knife hand.

Method 1

Holding the honing steel in your guide hand, place it perpendicular to the counter, with the tip resting on the counter or on a cutting board.

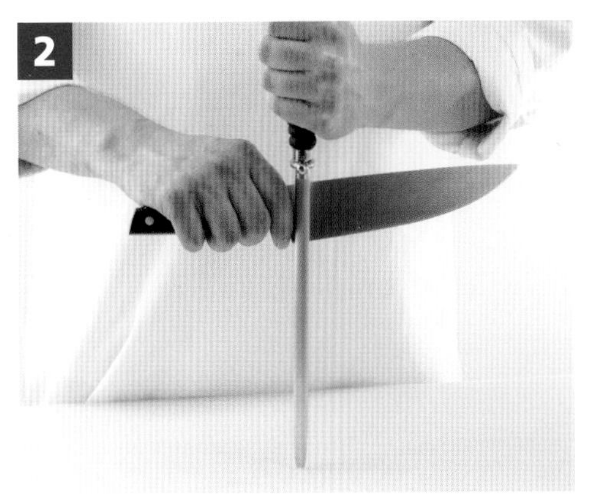

Holding the knife in your knife hand, line up the spine with the handle of the steel, with the cutting edge of the heel resting against the steel at the desired angle. (It doesn't matter which side of the steel you rest the edge on, as you'll be repeating the steps on both sides.)

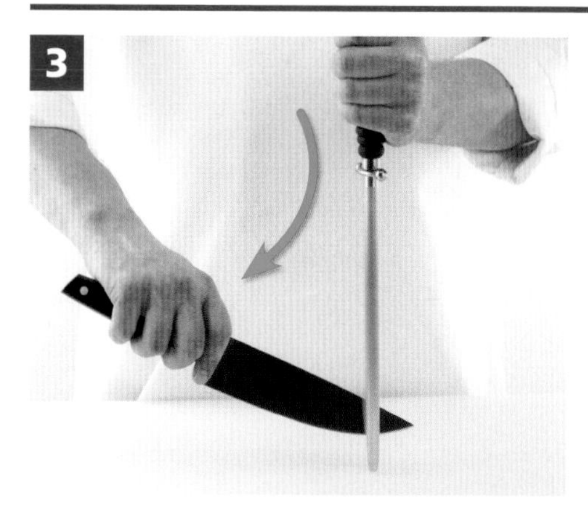

Simultaneously pulling the elbow of your knife hand back and moving your forearm down, pull the knife across and down the steel, moving from heel to point.

Move the blade to the other side of the honing steel. Line up the spine with the handle of the steel, with the cutting edge of the heel resting against the steel at the desired angle.

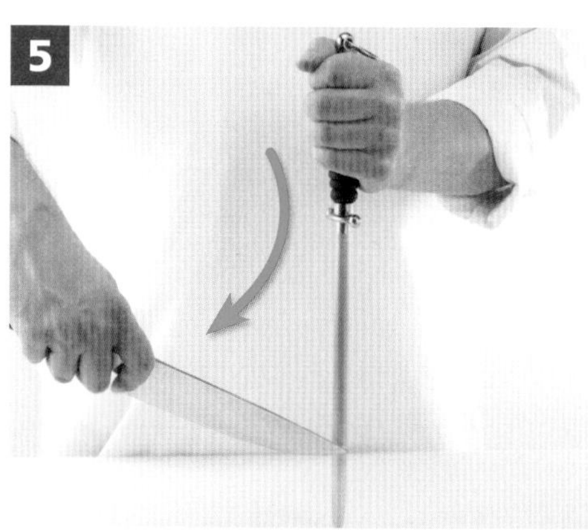

Simultaneously pulling the elbow of your knife hand back and moving your forearm down, pull the knife across and down the steel, moving from heel to point.

Repeat steps 2 to 5 until your edge is restored, anywhere from three to five times on each side of the blade.

> Most people don't hone or sharpen their knives nearly enough, if at all. That's why it's important to buy a good-quality knife with strong edge retention. The better the edge retention, the less often the edge will need to be maintained or repaired.

Method 2

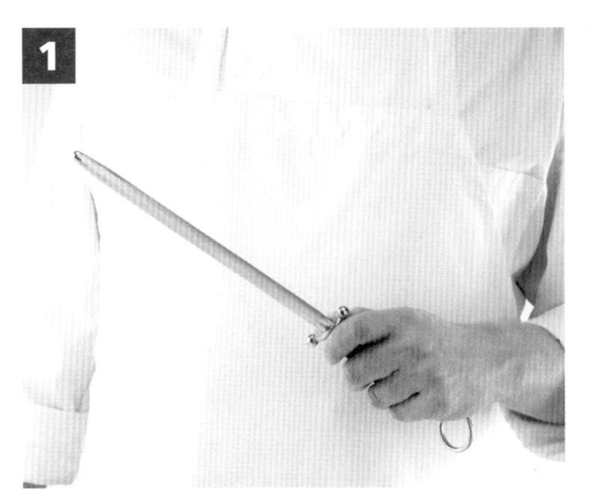

Hold the honing steel in the air, tip up, then point the tip away from you at a 45-degree angle and toward your knife hand at a 45-degree angle.

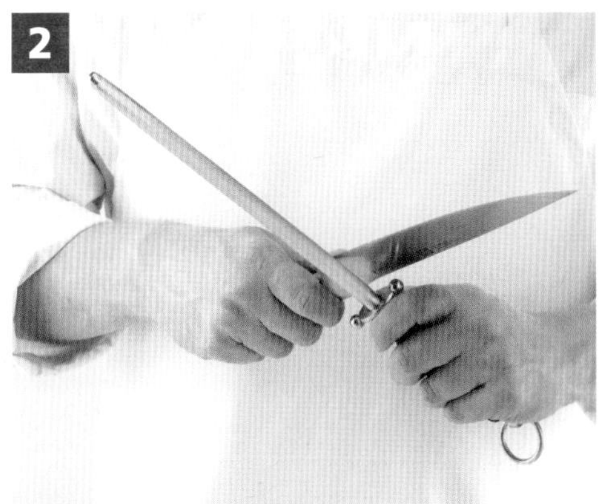

Line up the spine of the knife with the handle of the steel, with the cutting edge of the heel of the knife resting against the steel at the desired angle. (It doesn't matter which side of the steel you rest the edge on, as you'll be repeating the steps on both sides.)

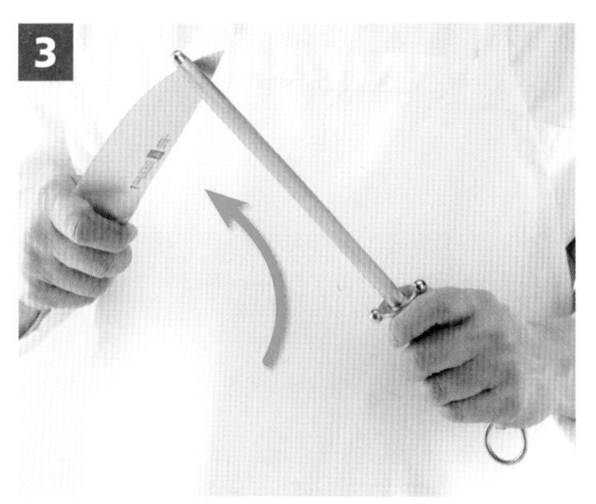

Simultaneously moving your elbow away from your body and moving your forearm up, pull the knife across and up the steel, moving from heel to point.

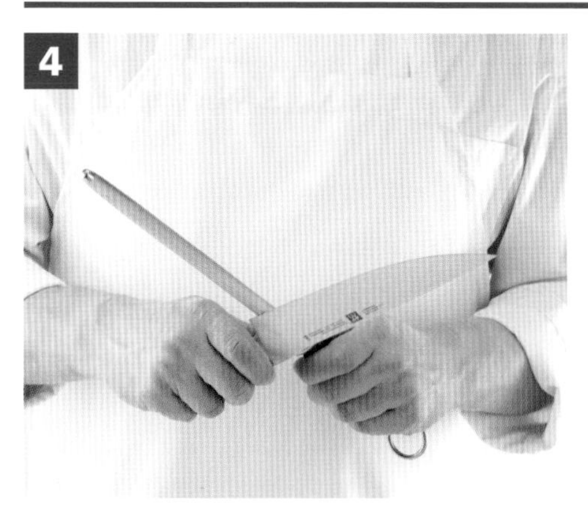

Move the blade over the top of the honing steel to the other side. Line up the spine of the knife with the handle of the steel, with the cutting edge of the heel of the knife resting against the steel at the desired angle.

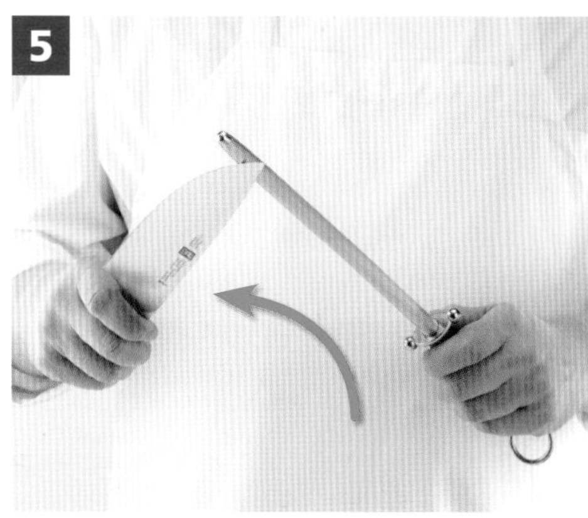

Simultaneously moving your elbow away from your body and moving your forearm up, pull the knife across and up the steel, moving from heel to point.

Repeat steps 2 to 5 until your edge is restored, anywhere from three to five times on each side of the blade.

> You'll often see chefs do the mirror action of this airborne honing method: they start at the tip of the steel, with the edge of the knife facing them, then pull the knife down the steel and toward themselves. We don't recommend this method, as the chance of injury is increased.

Sharpening a Knife

When a honing steel no longer returns a knife's edge to sharpness, you can try a sharpening steel, such as a ceramic steel or a diamond-coated steel, which removes some metal from the blade, thereby sharpening it.

TWIN diamond steel

But your best bet is to move on to a true sharpening agent: a pull-through sharpener (good), an electric sharpener (better) or a whetstone (best).

True Grit

When you want to smooth wood, you need something abrasive — sandpaper — to do so. Similarly, when you want to sharpen a knife, you need something abrasive to remove the metal from the cutting edge. As with sandpaper, all sharpening devices have a particular grade of grit. And as with smoothing wood, when sharpening a knife you start with a coarser grit and work your way to a finer one. Sharpening devices range from 250 grit to 10,000 grit; the lower the number, the coarser the grit. The duller the knife, the coarser the sharpening device you start with.

Pull-Through Sharpeners

There are two types of pull-through sharpeners: those with grinding wheels and those with rods. Wheel sharpeners have one or two pairs of overlapping wheels. When a sharpener has one pair of wheels, they are typically either coarse or fine. Of the sharpeners that have two pairs of wheels, some have one pair of coarse wheels and one pair of fine wheels; others have a coarse and a fine wheel in each pair.

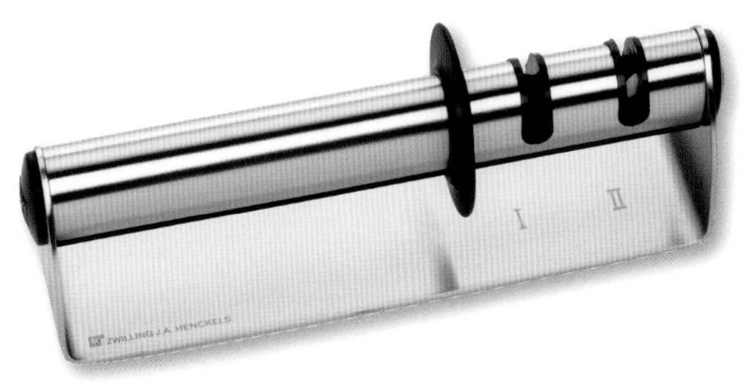

TWIN Sharp Select stainless steel pull-through sharpener

Rod sharpeners have one or more pairs of rods crossed to make a V, as when your fingers are laced together. Each of the two rods in a pair has the same grit. If the sharpener has more than one pair, they typically progress from coarse grit at the back to fine grit at the front.

Rod sharpener

In either case, to sharpen a knife, you pull it through the V-shaped opening between the wheels or rods:

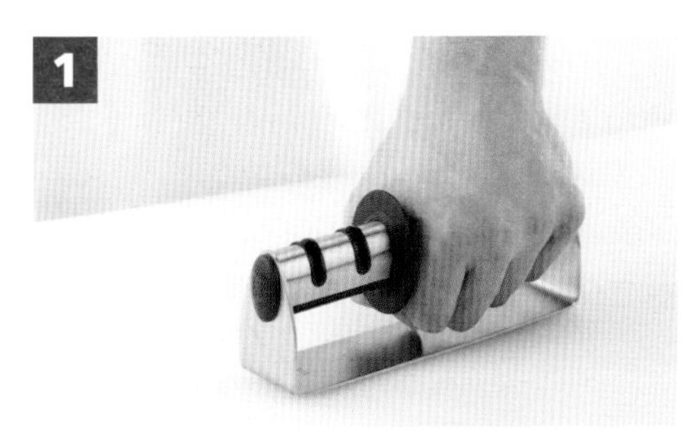

1. Stabilize the sharpener with your guide hand.

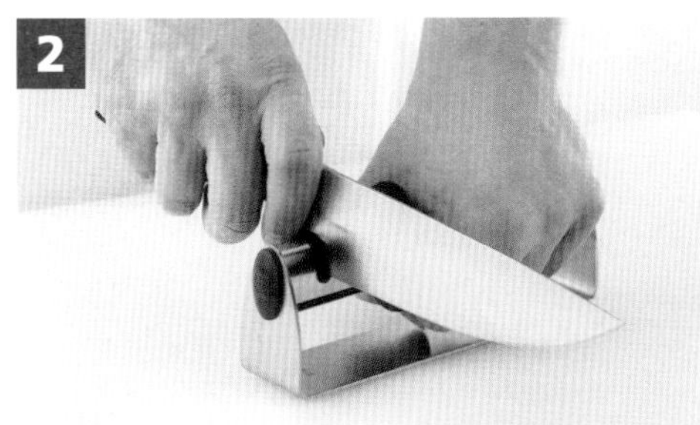

2. Place the knife in the sharpener, with the edge of the heel resting on the wheels or rods. The knife should be perpendicular to the counter.

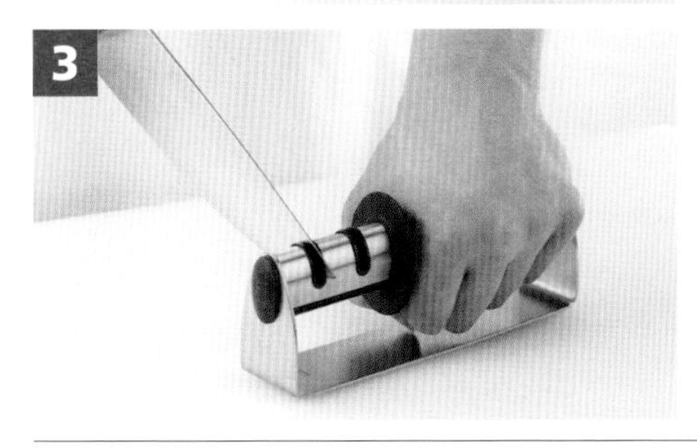

3. Without applying pressure, pull the knife through to the tip, letting the weight of the knife do the work.

Repeat steps 2 and 3 until the desired sharpness is achieved.

Electric Sharpeners

There are many types of electric sharpeners on the market. Look for a model that allows you to adjust the angle or that offers a choice of angles. Some models allow you to do one side of the blade at a time; most do both at the same time. Operation is similar to that of a pull-through sharpener (see above). If used improperly, the combination of coarse grinding wheels and high speed can damage knives beyond repair.

Whetstones

A whetstone is the best way to sharpen a knife because of the control it allows — you can choose your own angle and grit. Whetstones fall into four basic types: oil stones, water stones, diamond stones and our recommended choice, ceramic stones.

Lubricants aid the whetstone in its grinding action and also help to suspend and carry away the fine metal filings, called swarf, so that they are not ground into the stone's surface.

Oil stones require oil as a lubricant; mineral oil is a good choice. They can be composed of natural stone or synthetic materials, and usually come in one grit. Restaurants, though, often have a tri-stone, which has three grits — coarse, medium and fine — that can be rotated.

Oil stone

Water stones need to be soaked in water for at least 10 minutes before use. They are typically made of a compressed material, such as silicon carbide (Carborundum) or aluminum oxide (corundum). These materials wear down fairly quickly because they are quite soft. But on the plus side, water stones usually have a fine grit and sharpen knives quickly.

Water stone

Diamond stones are made of metal embedded with bits of diamond. By varying the amount and size of the diamonds, manufacturers can control the grit of the stone. These stones last a long time but are, unsurprisingly, fairly expensive.

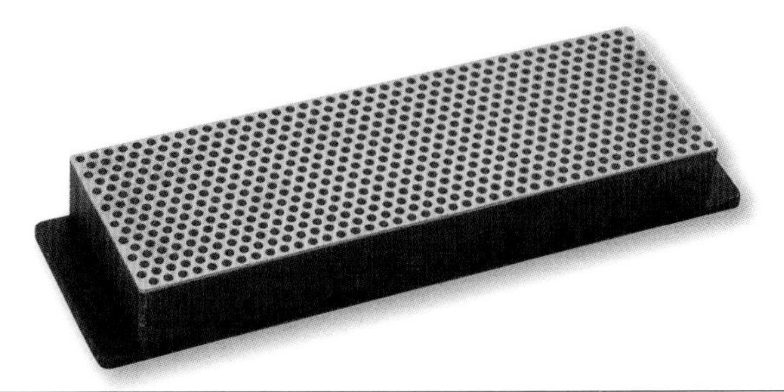

Diamond stone

Ceramic stones require water for lubrication but, unlike water stones, need only a light film of water before they are ready to go. Because of their hardness they last a very long time, which compensates for their high price. They typically come in one or two grits, which can be quite fine.

TWIN Finishing Stone Pro ceramic stone

Japanese knives are typically both honed and sharpened on whetstones. Professional chefs in Japanese restaurants often sharpen their knives daily, or even several times a day. For that reason, they mainly use fine-grit stones, rarely dipping below 3,000 grit when maintaining the edge and using up to 10,000 grit when polishing the edge.

For Western knives, you'd use a lower-grit whetstone. If your knife is very dull, it needs intensive repair, and you can use a stone with a grit as low as 250; for maintenance, start with a grit of 1,000 and work your way up to the highest grit you have.

Important Things to Remember When Using a Whetstone

- Use the middle three fingers of your guide hand to stabilize the blade against the stone.
- Do not press down on the knife; let its weight do the work.
- If your stone doesn't have a case with feet to stabilize it, place a wet towel underneath it, as you would with a cutting board.
- Align the stone so the long edge is perpendicular to the edge of the counter.
- Hold the blade against the stone at the correct angle (see page 44). Because a knife tapers from heel to point as well as from spine to edge, you may need to make the angle slightly wider as you move from heel to point.
- Maintain the same angle every time you sharpen.
- Make sure to sharpen the entire knife, from heel to point; otherwise, you will create a bow in it.

How to Use a Whetstone

There are a number of ways to use a whetstone; no one way is the best. We've provided instructions for two methods, one Eastern and one Western. In the Western method, you move the knife diagonally across the stone, sharpening from point to heel in one motion. In the Eastern method, you sharpen the edge in three segments: the tip, the middle and the heel.

You can use any type of stone, but we'll demonstrate using a ceramic stone. Start by drizzling water over the surface of the stone and keep a small bowl of water nearby, as you'll need to periodically lubricate the stone as you use it.

> When you're using the Western method, knives with an open bolster or no bolster are easier to sharpen than knives with a closed bolster, as you can move the knife completely across the stone without impediment.

Western Method

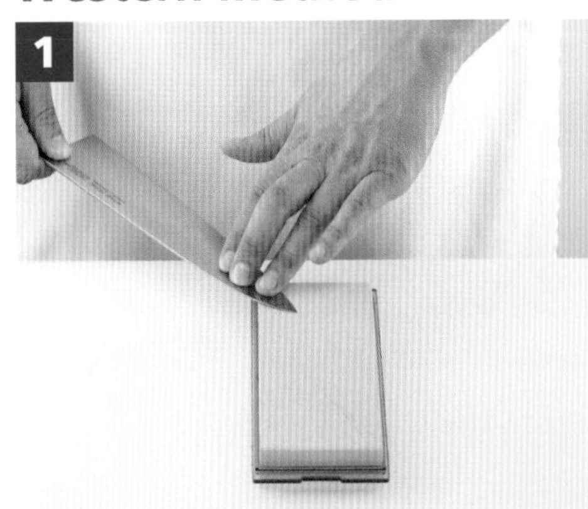

Place the point of the knife at the lower knife-hand corner of the stone, with the edge of the blade facing toward your guide hand and resting on the stone at the desired angle.

Slowly slide the knife diagonally across the stone, moving it simultaneously away from you and from point to heel.

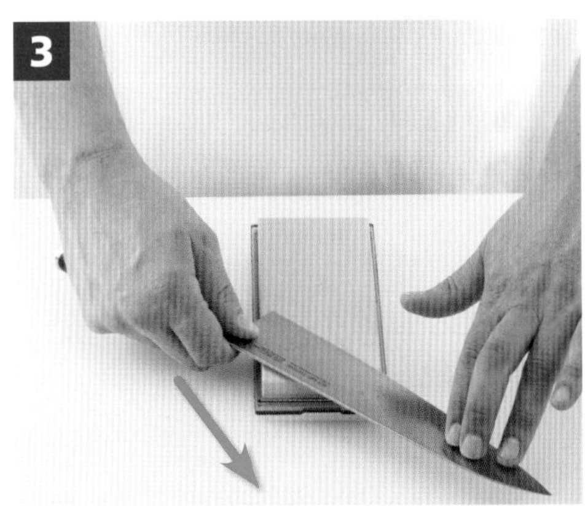

Continue moving the knife across the stone until the heel comes off the upper guide-hand corner. Repeat steps 1 to 3 four more times.

If your knife has a closed bolster, move the heel of the knife until it hits the lower knife-hand corner of the stone in step 3.

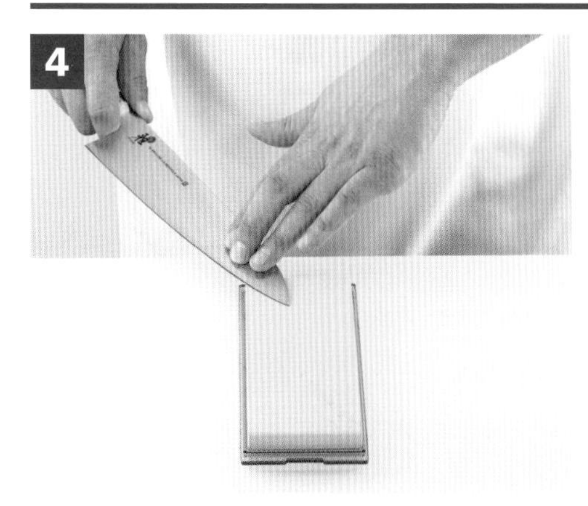

4

Flip the knife over and place the point at the lower knife-hand corner of the stone, with the edge of the blade facing away from your guide hand and resting on the stone at the desired angle.

5

Repeat steps 2 and 3.

Check your knife for sharpness (see box, below). If it's still dull, repeat steps 1 to 5. If it's sharp, repeat steps 1 through 5 on a finer-grit stone.

To test the sharpness of your knife, try to cut a piece of paper. With a dull knife, you'll make a jagged cut, almost tearing through the paper. A sharp knife will sail right through, leaving a clean cut.

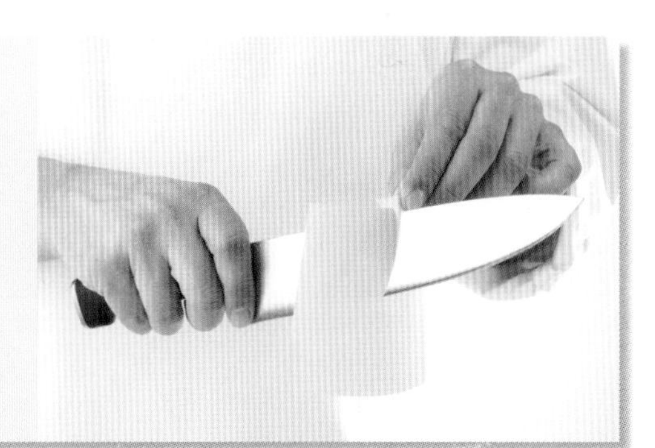

Eastern Method

First, hold the blade with the edge facing toward you and resting on the stone at the desired angle.

Tip

1. Align the tip segment of the knife with the lower edge of the stone.

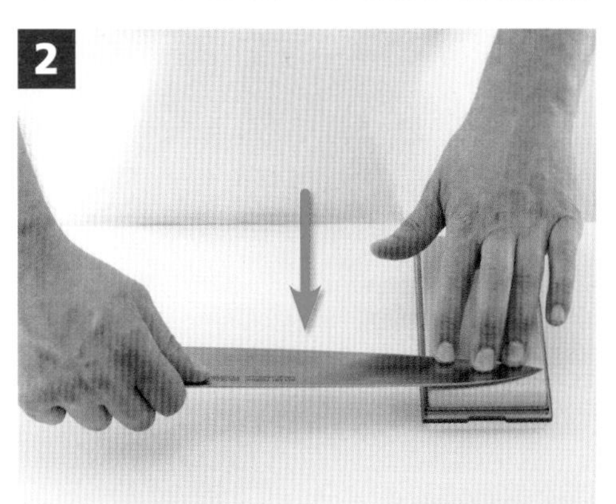

2. Slide the knife straight to the upper edge of the stone.

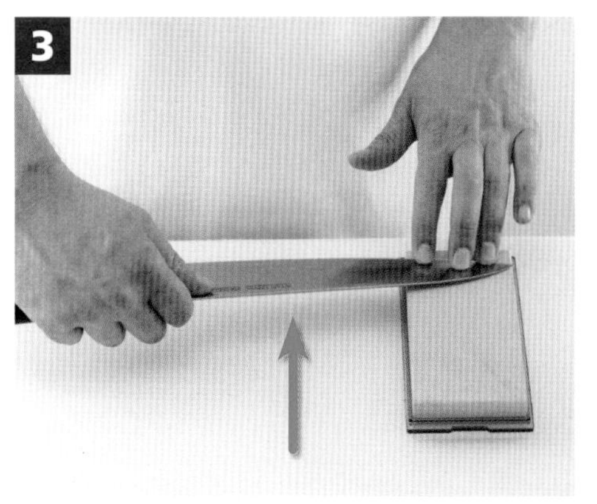

3. Slide the knife straight back to the lower edge of the stone. Repeat steps 1 to 3 three to four more times.

Middle

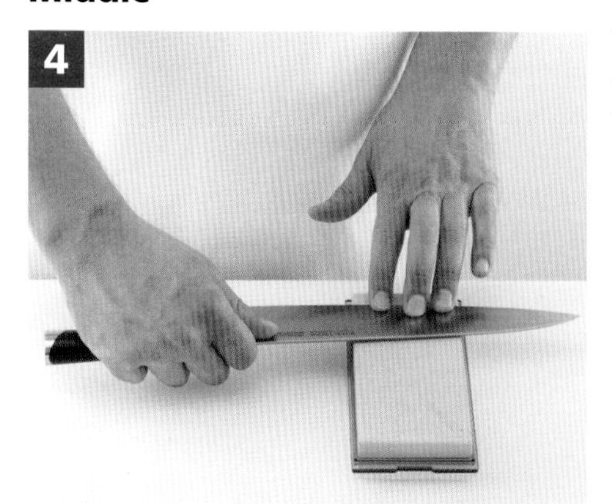

Align the middle segment of the knife with the lower edge of the stone.

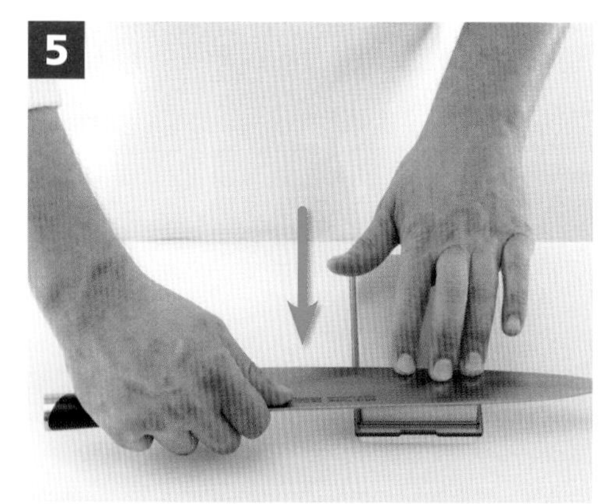

Slide the knife straight to the upper edge of the stone.

Slide the knife straight back to the lower edge of the stone. Repeat steps 4 to 6 three to four more times.

Heel

Align the heel segment of the knife with the lower edge of the stone.

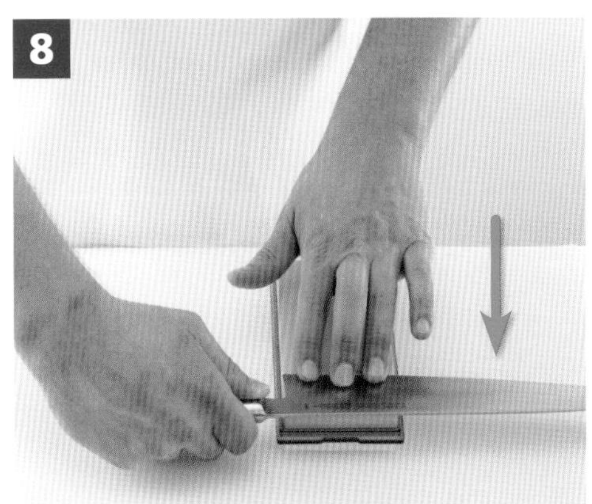

Slide the knife straight to the upper edge of the stone.

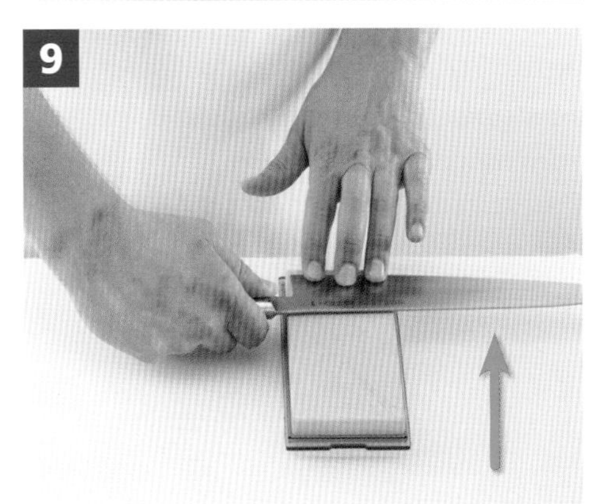

Slide the knife straight back to the lower edge of the stone. Repeat steps 7 to 9 three to four more times.

To sharpen the other side of the blade, turn it over so that the edge is facing away from you at the desired angle.

Heel

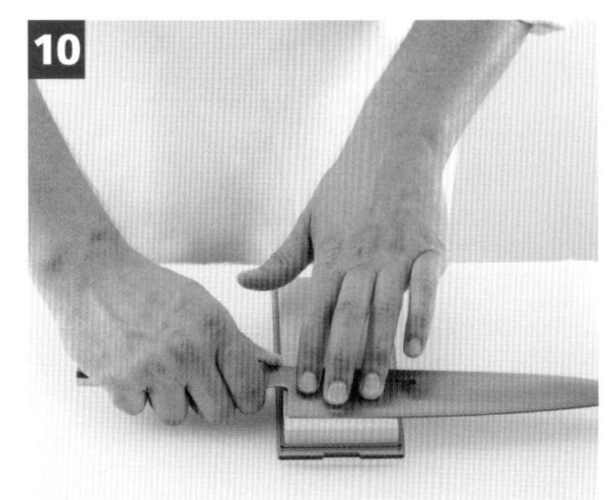

Align the heel segment of the knife with the upper edge of the stone.

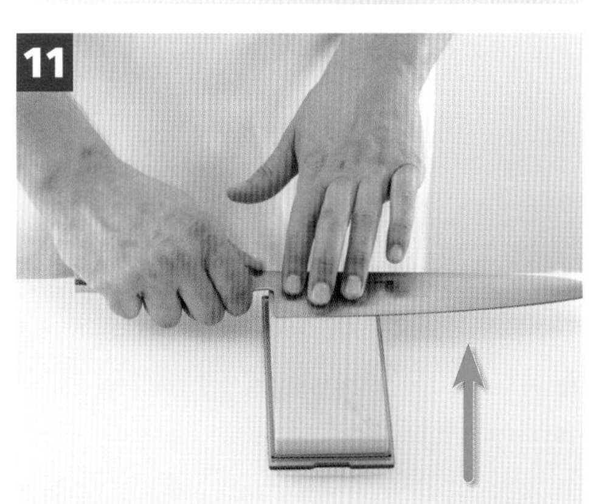

Slide the knife straight to the lower edge of the stone.

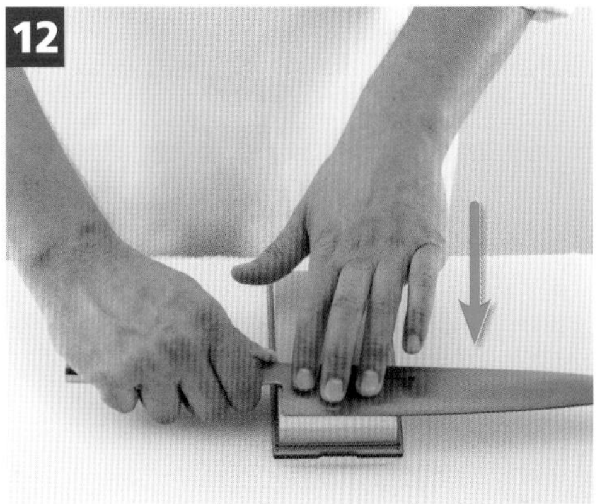

Slide the knife straight back to the upper edge of the stone. Repeat steps 10 to 12 three to four more times.

Middle

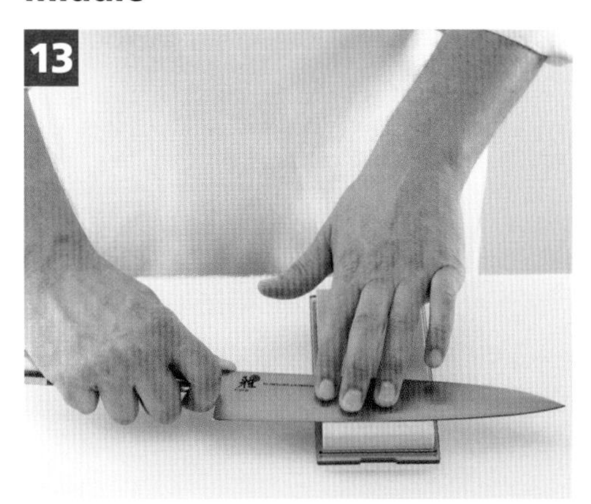

Align the middle segment of the knife with the upper edge of the stone.

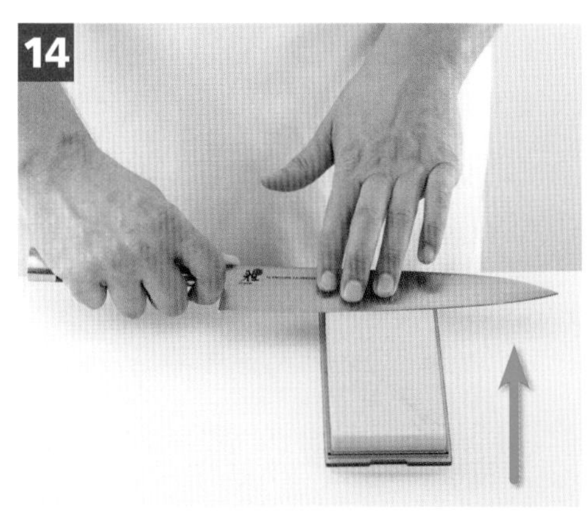

Slide the knife straight to the lower edge of the stone.

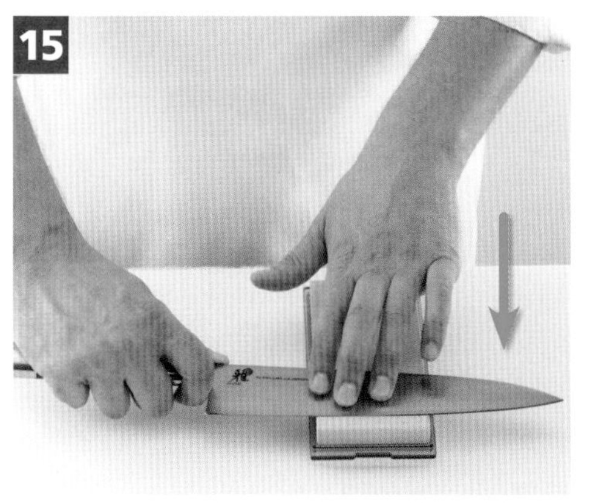

Slide the knife straight back to the upper edge of the stone. Repeat steps 13 to 15 three to four more times.

Tip

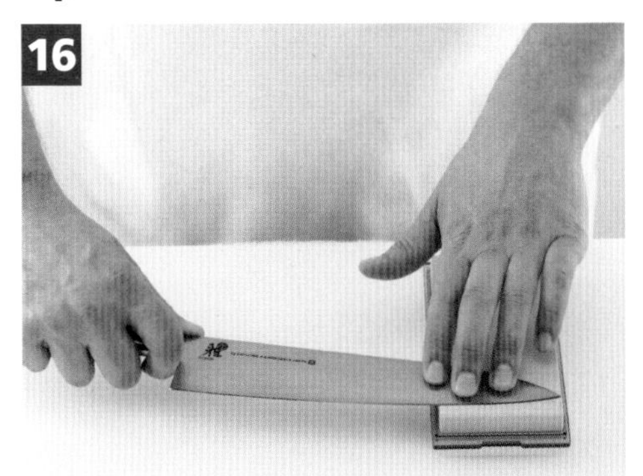

Align the tip segment of the knife with the upper edge of the stone.

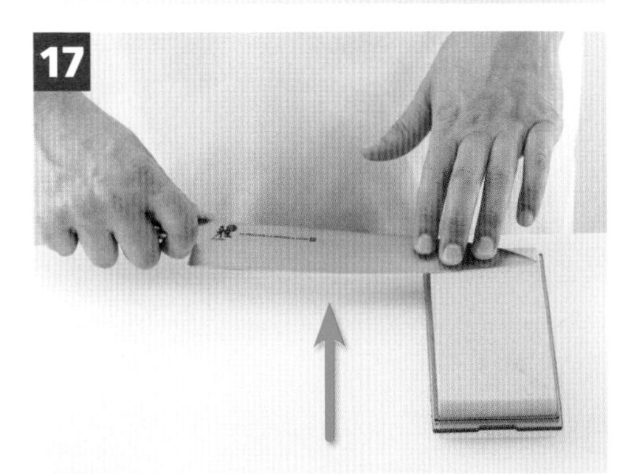

Slide the knife straight to the lower edge of the stone.

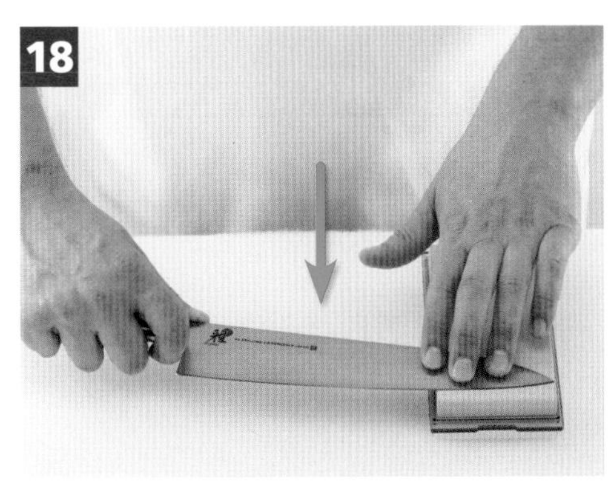

Slide the knife straight back to the upper edge of the stone. Repeat steps 16 to 18 three to four more times.

Check your knife for sharpness (see box, page 55). If it's still dull, repeat steps 1 to 18. If it's sharp, repeat steps 1 to 18 on a finer-grit stone.

In many cities, you can find professional knife-sharpening companies that will sharpen knives, scissors, lawnmower blades — basically anything with an edge. If no one offers such a service where you live, there are several mail-away sharpening companies to choose from. Make sure to use the same company every time you get your knife sharpened, as they will always sharpen at the same angle.

PROFESSIONAL "S"
FRIODUR ICE HARDENED
31021-200 (8")
NO STAIN

Chapter 2

Getting Started

Professional cooks differ from home cooks in many ways, mainly because the demands of the professional kitchen are different from those of the home kitchen. Making the same dish 10 or 20 times a day, day in and day out, leads to a speed and confidence that most home cooks, who may go weeks or months before repeating a dish, have difficulty achieving. Nonetheless, there are many practices common among professionals that can greatly improve the home cook's command of the kitchen. The concepts and techniques explained in this chapter are essential to success in any kitchen, whether home or professional.

The Benefits of Mise en Place

The French term *mise en place* translates (more or less) as "putting in place." The easiest way to describe mise en place is to conjure up images of TV chefs. When they say, "Add the onions to the pan and sauté," they don't then go to a cutting board and cut up onions. They simply dump a bowl of previously chopped onions into the pan. Before they begin cooking, they have all the ingredients needed for the dish chopped, sliced, poured and measured into individual bowls or containers, so that everything is ready to be added at the appropriate time. This keeps them from a frantic race to get the garlic minced before the onion burns, or to get all the carrots chopped before the simmering water evaporates.

Mise en place means that you've read the recipe, understood its every component and done all of your ingredient prep work before you set a pan on the flame. (One exception: because an oven takes a while to heat up, you can turn it on while you prep.) Moreover, you've assembled all the equipment you'll need while cooking: the pots and pans, whisks and spoons, aprons and towels, utensils and paraphernalia. Food can burn just as easily while you're looking for a clean spatula.

Some chefs even talk about "mental mise en place," which simply means that when you're in the kitchen, you're focused on the task at hand. You're not thinking about your taxes or your weekend or your kids' homework. You're thinking about the food and what you'll be doing with it. Staying focused allows you to work quickly, safely and efficiently, three hallmarks of the professional cook. If you can't work quickly, you'll never last in a professional kitchen. If you can't work safely, you can't work quickly, because speed is a direct result of the confidence that comes from frequent repetition of a task without injury (not to mention that injury slows us down). And if you can't work efficiently, you will waste both time and product.

The organized cook is the speedy cook. When all of your ingredients are prepped and ready, when all of your pots and utensils are at hand, you'll be able to prepare your meal quickly and efficiently, without infuriating setbacks or wasted food. At the same time, the organized cook is the safer cook: when everything is in its place, you're far less likely to cut your hand on an errant knife.

Setting Up Your Work Station

The centerpiece of a cook's work station is the cutting board. Other elements include assorted bowls for various purposes, dry and damp towels, pots and pans and, of course, knives and utensils.

Cutting Boards

There are many types of cutting boards on the market, made from a number of different materials. We prefer boards made from wood and plastic, as ceramic, glass or metal cutting boards will dull your blades.

End-grain wooden boards are more durable than edge-grain boards and are gentler on the edge of your knife.

End-grain board

Edge-grain board

If storage space allows, it's a good idea to have multiple cutting boards, to avoid cross-contamination. Plastic cutting boards make this easy, as you can color-code them: red for raw meats, yellow for poultry, blue for fish and seafood, green for produce, white for dairy. It's also a good idea to have a separate board for garlic and onions, to prevent the transfer of these strong flavors.

To avoid harmful bacteria growth, it's important to thoroughly clean cutting boards immediately after use. Plastic boards can be put in the dishwasher, but the heat will cause wooden boards to warp and split. Instead, use hot running water and dish soap to clean wooden boards, scrub vigorously, then let air-dry. For extra sanitation, spray your boards down with a 3:1 mixture of water to vinegar and let air-dry.

To ensure that your prep goes smoothly, quickly and safely, anchor your board to the counter with a dampened thin dish towel. Fold the towel in half and lay it on the counter. Place your board on top, orienting it so that one long side is flush with the edge of the counter. Make sure the corners of the damp towel aren't peeking out from beneath the edges of the board. (It looks sloppy, but more importantly it makes it harder to keep a clean and sanitary work station, because it will catch bits of food and soak up any liquids, such as juice or blood, that drip from your board.) Place your fingertips on the board and try moving it, to make sure it won't slip.

You could use a damp paper towel to anchor your board, but cloth towels generally work better. Or try the type of plastic non-slip webbing that's meant to go under a rug — it works well!

Bowls

When getting your work station ready, you'll need to assemble several bowls of various sizes, for different purposes. First off, you'll want to keep a large metal bowl at your station for garbage and scraps. As it fills up, empty it into the garbage can or put it aside to take out to the compost heap.

Gather all of your raw produce into another large bowl. Keeping raw food off the counter aids in organization and sanitation.

When you're going to be prepping proteins, such as meat, fish or chicken, have a bowl of ice on hand to keep them cold (or simply leave them in the refrigerator until you're ready to work with them). Rather than setting food directly on the ice, place it in another bowl on top of the ice, or place a layer of plastic wrap or foil over the ice and lay the food on top.

You'll also want to have a selection of bowls into which you can measure ingredients as you finish preparing them. Items that are added to the pan at the same time (onions and peppers, for example, or mixes of dried spices) can go into the same bowl.

Towels

Professional cooks use dry towels in place of oven mitts. (Oven mitts are bulky and have only one use, whereas dry towels take up less space and have numerous uses in the kitchen.) Fold a dry towel into quarters to increase its ability to insulate your hands, and you can remove anything from the oven. Just make absolutely sure your towel is dry, because water conducts heat very, very well. If you pick up a hot pan with a wet towel, you will burn yourself.

You'll also need a dry towel next to your cutting board to keep your knives on, so you know where they are and they won't move if bumped.

In addition, you'll want to have a couple of damp towels handy, one to wipe down your station and another to hold your cutting board in place (see page 66).

Pots and Pans

Your inclination may be to leave your pots and pans where they are, stored and out of the way until you need them. But we recommend that, as part of your prep work, you get out the pots and pans you'll be using, placing them either next to your station or next to the stove, so all you have to do is grab each one as you need it. It's always best to have everything at its handiest, and this will prevent you from the sudden last-minute realization that the very pot you need is in the dishwasher.

Knives and Utensils

Read through (or think through) your recipe with an eye to what steps you'll need to follow and how best to accomplish them. What are the most appropriate knives for your various tasks? How will you remove food from the skillet — with tongs? a spatula? a wooden spoon? If you make these decisions before you start cooking and lay out the knives and utensils you'll need as you go along, the entire process will go more smoothly.

Basic Knife Safety Measures

Understanding how to use knives safely is the first step to achieving good knife skills. Here are some important points to keep in mind:

- Keep your knives sharp (see page 49). A sharp knife is safer than a dull one because it requires less pressure when you're cutting. The knife will not slip or twist in your hand as easily, and you'll have better control of the blade. When you do cut yourself (and we all cut ourselves occasionally), the wound will be even and clean, not ragged, and more likely to heal quickly.
- Use the correct size and type of knife for the job. You'll have better control and will work faster and more efficiently. (Imagine how slow it would be to dice a butternut squash with a paring knife instead of a chef's knife.)
- Use knives only for their intended purpose. A knife is not a screwdriver, a box cutter or a can opener.
- Hold the knife firmly in your hand and cut away from your body.
- When your knives are not in use, make sure they are kept in plain sight, not covered by a towel, a napkin or anything else. A hidden knife is a dangerous knife. After handling a knife, lay it down in a cleared area, with the blade pointed away from the edge of the table or cutting area, so that it is visible to everyone and can't be knocked off the counter.
- When handing a knife to someone, hold it by the bolster or top of the handle, with the cutting edge facing away from your palm, and extend it toward the other person handle first; better yet, place the knife on the counter, with the handle facing the other person.

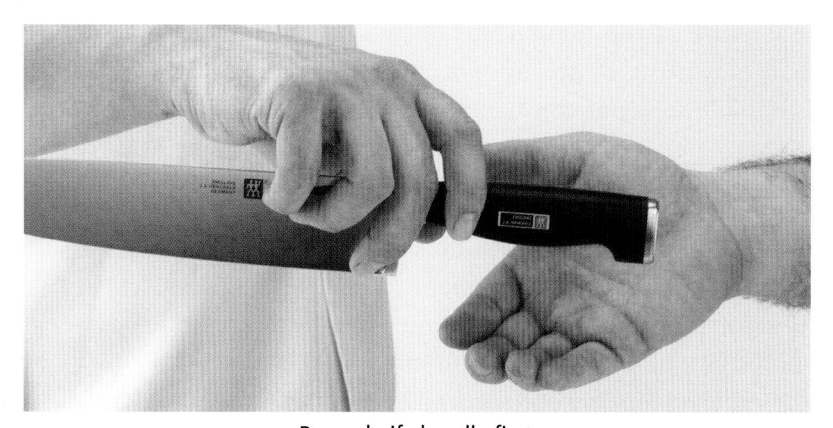

Pass a knife handle first

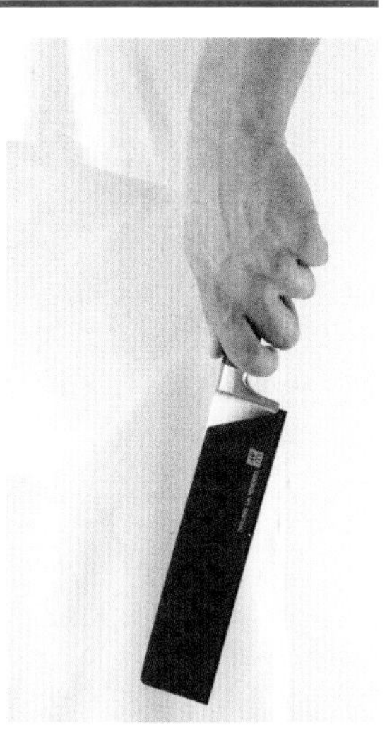
The correct way to carry a knife

- Do not reach blindly for a knife. Reach deliberately for the handle.
- Never try to catch a falling knife. It may be difficult to rein in your natural reflexes, which compel you to try to catch something that is falling, but *resist* or you will cut yourself. Back away and let the knife fall.
- Wear closed-toed shoes when you're in the kitchen, to protect your feet in case a knife should fall.
- Try not to walk around carrying a knife. If you must, carry it in your less dominant hand. If you should trip, you'll throw out your dominant hand to brace yourself, and if there is anyone in front of you, you might stab them. Keep the knife close to your side, with the tip facing down and the edge facing backwards. If your knife has a sheath or an edge guard, use it.
- Store knives properly, as discussed on page 41.
- Keep knives well out of the reach of children.
- Never test the sharpness of a knife by running your finger along the edge. Instead, try slicing a sheet of paper (see page 55).
- Wash sharp knives separately. Do not wash them with other utensils and do not leave them sitting in the sink, where they can get covered with dishes or soapy water and may not be visible. In addition to the safety risk, a knife left in the sink is more susceptible to rust.
- Dry each knife separately, with the cutting edge pointed away from your hand. Dry the blade from the spine to the edge and from the heel to the point, to avoid poking or cutting yourself.

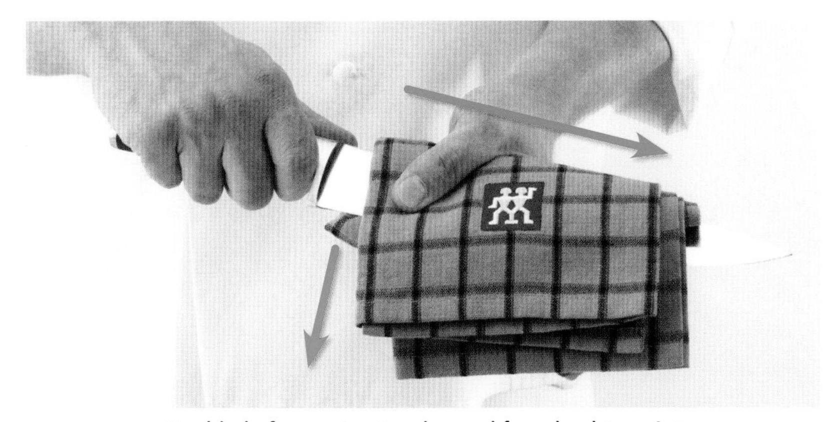
Dry blade from spine to edge and from heel to point

How to Hold a Chef's Knife

While there are many different types and styles of knives, most professional chefs in the West do the majority of their work with a chef's knife. (Japanese chefs routinely use a variety of knives, while Chinese chefs may use a cleaver for even the smallest tasks, such as slicing jalapeños.) The basic grip demonstrated below is the classic Western way of holding a chef's knife. It provides stability, so you are always in control of the blade. It will probably feel awkward at first, but be patient and practice; soon the knife will feel as natural in your hand as a toothbrush.

Throughout this book, we'll be using the terms "knife hand" and "guide hand." Your knife hand, naturally, holds the knife. Your guide hand holds the food you're cutting, while simultaneously guiding the blade. It is most common for people to use their dominant hand as their knife hand. So if you're left-handed, your left hand will be your knife hand and your right hand will be your guide hand.

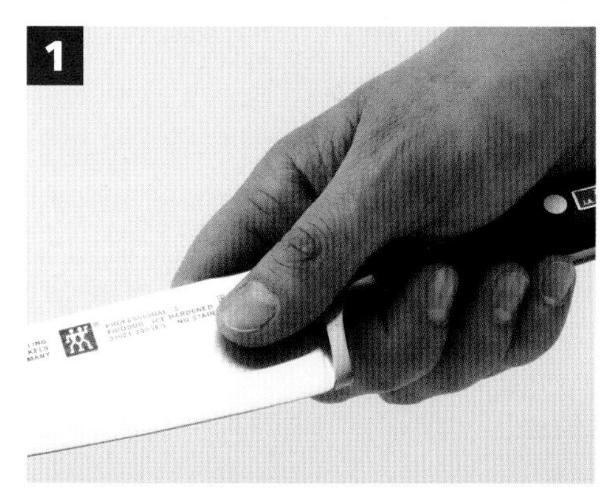

Pinch the blade of the knife between the thumb and index finger of your knife hand, just in front of the handle.

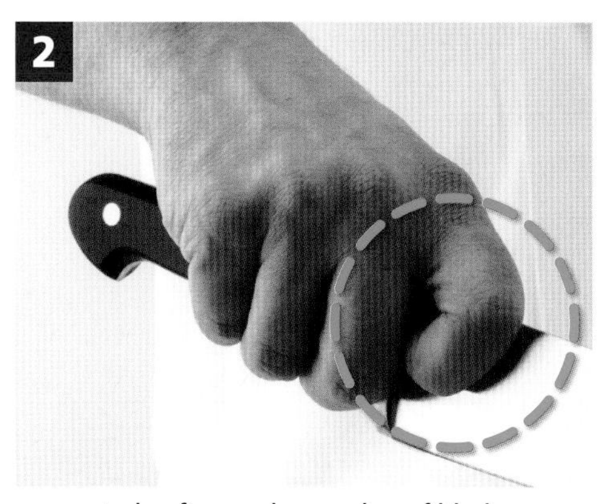

Index finger above edge of blade

Keep your index finger curled above the edge of the blade and therefore out of harm's way.

3

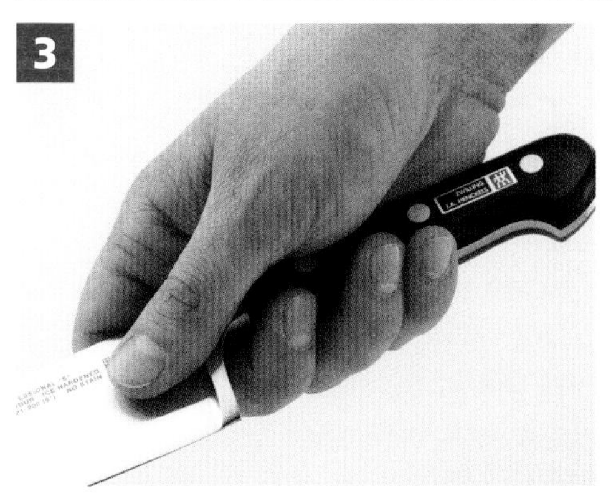

Curl your remaining three fingers around the handle, holding it snugly but comfortably against your palm. The side of your middle finger closest to your thumb should be against the bolster of the knife (or, if the knife does not have a bolster, around the heel of the knife). This is your basic knife grip. Below are two more angles.

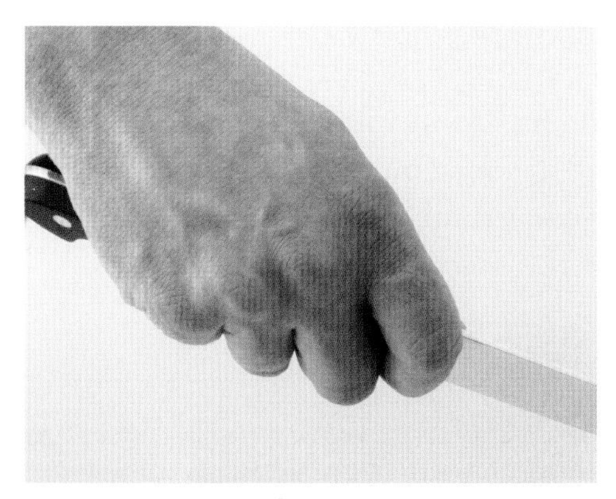

View from above

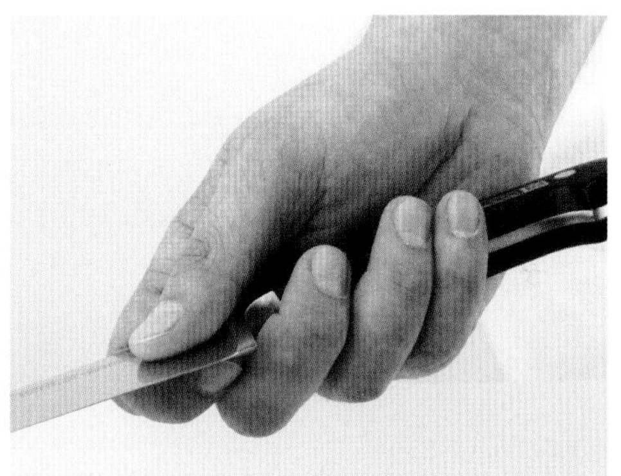

View from below

Japanese chefs sometimes extend their index finger along the spine of their knives, but we don't recommend this practice. In Japan, meats are generally boneless by the time they reach the kitchen, and the vegetables used tend to be on the soft side, so there is less risk that the chef will lose control of the knife. In the West, we use a lot of hard root vegetables and often cut meats off the bone. Cutting these items requires much more control to prevent your blade from slipping while you're cutting. Therefore, we recommend pinching the blade between thumb and index finger as described in step 1.

How to Hold Your Guide Hand

Before we show you how to cut up food, we want to give you a general idea of what your guide hand will be doing while you're cutting. The best way to hold your guide hand is in what we call the "claw position" (for reasons that will become apparent when you look at the pictures). In many ways, this position is the hardest thing you'll have to learn, because, as you'll discover, it's a little awkward and more than a little intimidating, as the blade of the knife will be directly against one or two of your fingers. But in terms of safety, this position can't be beat: done correctly, it greatly reduces the risk that you will cut yourself.

When talking about your guide hand, we'll refer to your index finger and/or middle finger as the "guide fingers," because more often than not they will act in tandem. We'll refer to your thumb, ring finger and pinky as the "grip fingers," as they are the ones that will hold the food while you cut it.

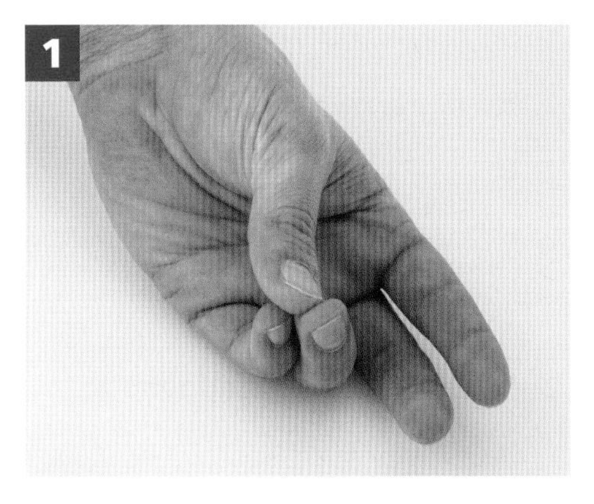

Touch the tip of your thumb to the tips of your ring finger and pinky.

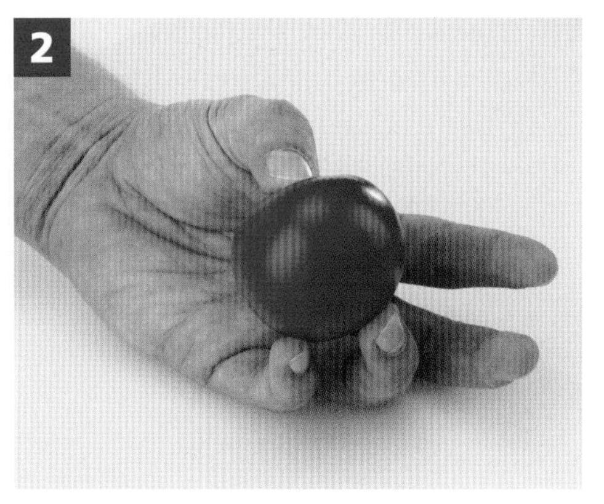

Though we're not there yet, ultimately these are the fingers you'll use to hold your food.

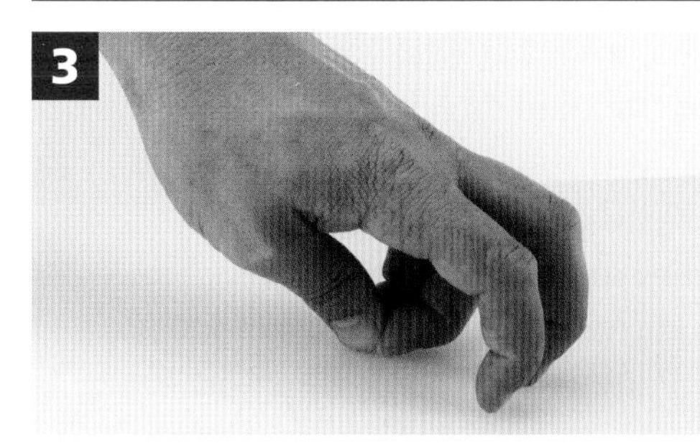

The basic "claw position"

Touch your two guide fingers together and hold them out in front of your grip fingers.

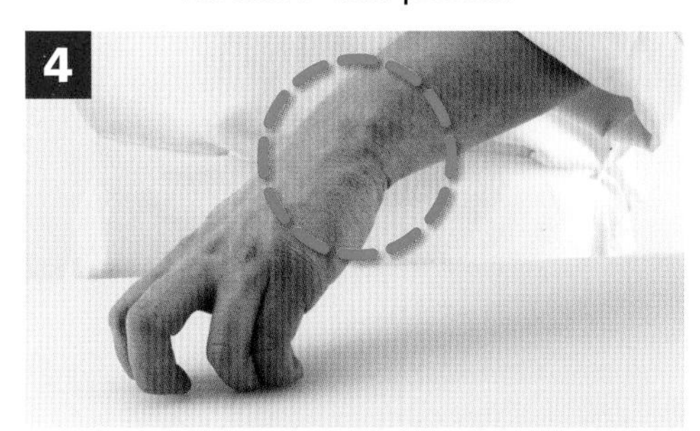

Wrist in the air

Now let's put your guide hand in the context of your whole arm. First, keep the elbow of your guide hand relaxed and at your side, while keeping your wrist in the air.

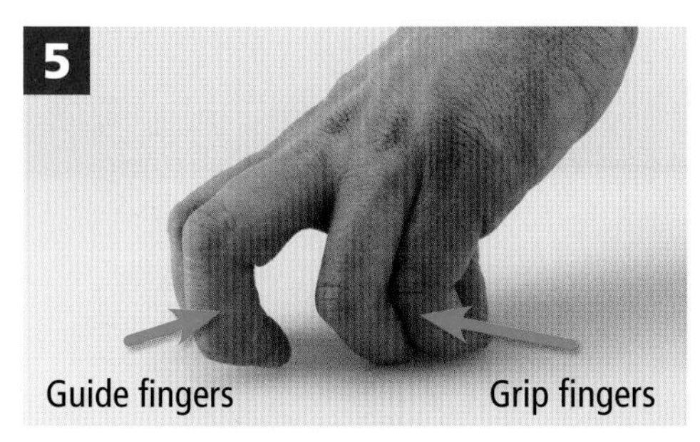

Place the tips of your fingers on the cutting board, with your guide fingers in front of your grip fingers.

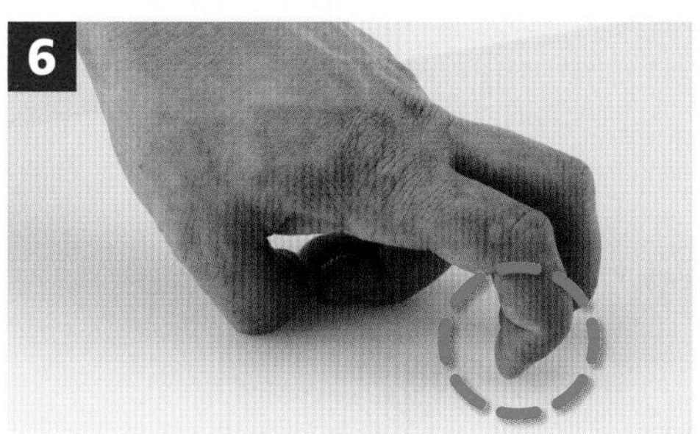

Tips bent slightly backward

The tips of your guide fingers should be bent slightly back in toward your hand.

Caution

Don't let the tips of your guide fingers slant forward; this exposes them to the blade.

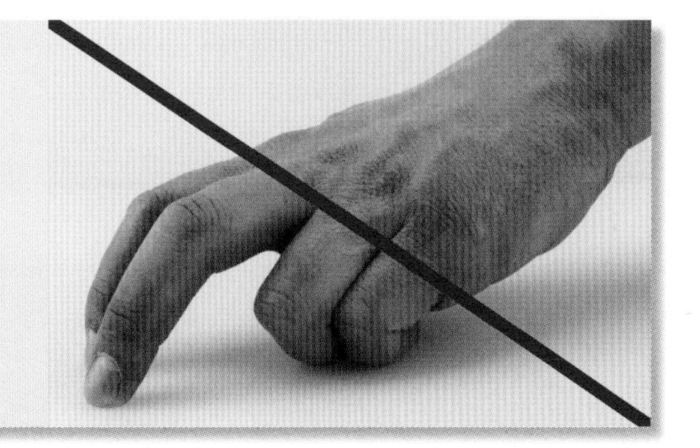

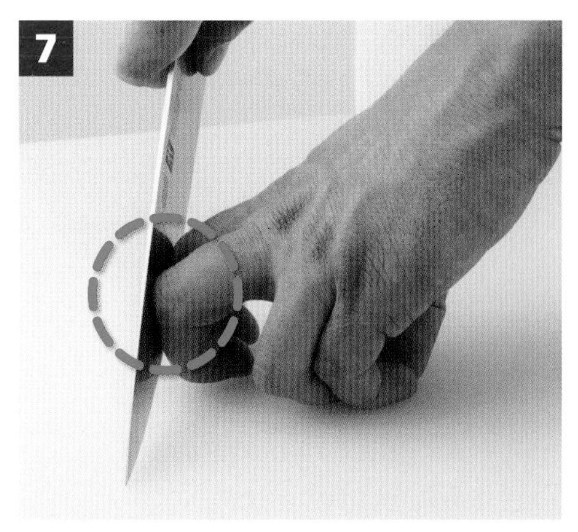
Blade against middle segment of guide fingers

Okay, here comes the scary part: Rest the side of the blade against the middle segment of your guide fingers. We know, it's weird; instinct tells us to keep the blade as far from our fingers as possible. Still, this is the safest way to use a knife. With the blade going straight up and down against your guide fingers, and the tips of your fingers bent back and away from the blade, there's no way for you to cut yourself.

Other Options

Everyone's hands are different, and finger lengths vary dramatically from person to person. Thus, there are various ways to hold the guide hand safely. You can choose to rest the blade against the middle segment of both guide fingers, as in photo 7 above, against the middle segment of one guide finger or against the knuckle of one or both guide fingers. The important thing is to keep the blade flush against your finger(s) at all times as you use the knife. Feeling the pressure of the blade helps you keep track of where it is and allows you to determine more easily and exactly the size of the cuts you're making. No matter what, make sure to keep the nail segment of your fingers bent back and away from the blade, as this removes any chance that the knife will come down on your fingers.

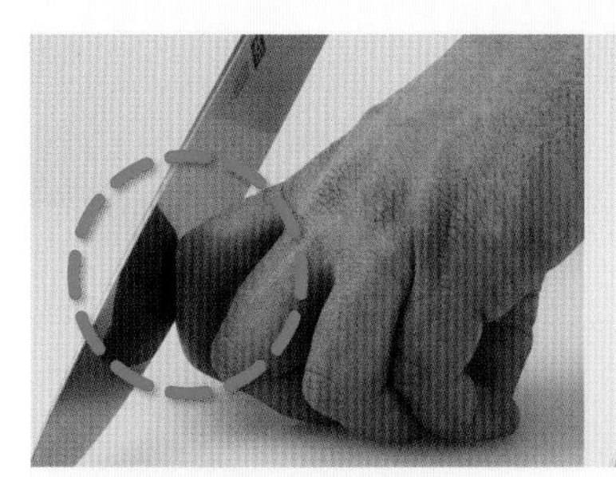
Blade against middle segment of index finger

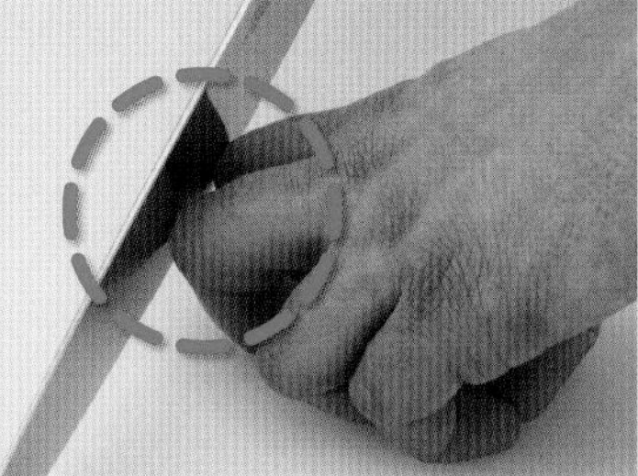
Blade against knuckles of guide fingers

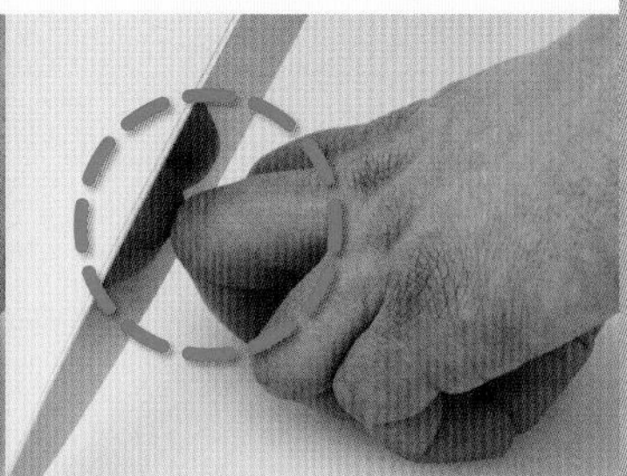
Blade against knuckle of middle finger

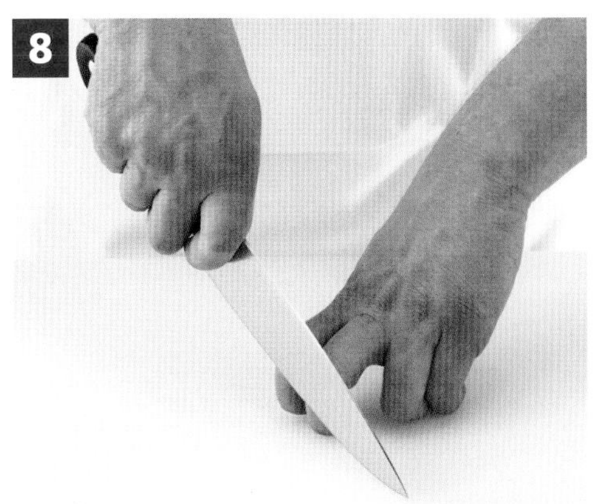

Watch as we move the blade of the knife up and down, as if we were cutting something.

Observe how the blade stays flush against the guide fingers.

Grip fingers well back

At the same time, notice how the grip fingers are kept well back from the knife and the guide fingers. It's important to keep those fingers anchored.

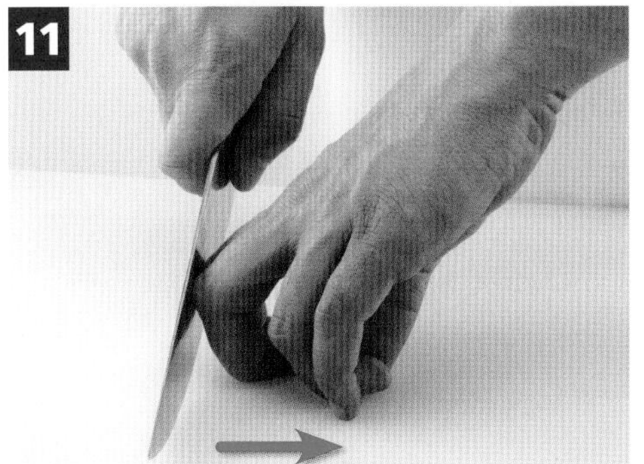

As you cut, draw your guide fingers back toward your grip fingers, always keeping the blade of the knife pressed firmly against your guide fingers.

Caution

Here are a couple of things to avoid when you're cutting:

Never allow your fingers to become splayed out in front of the food. You're simply asking to cut yourself when you do that.

At the same time, never let your grip fingers creep up past your guide fingers. That's the surest way to lose a thin slice of thumb or pinky.

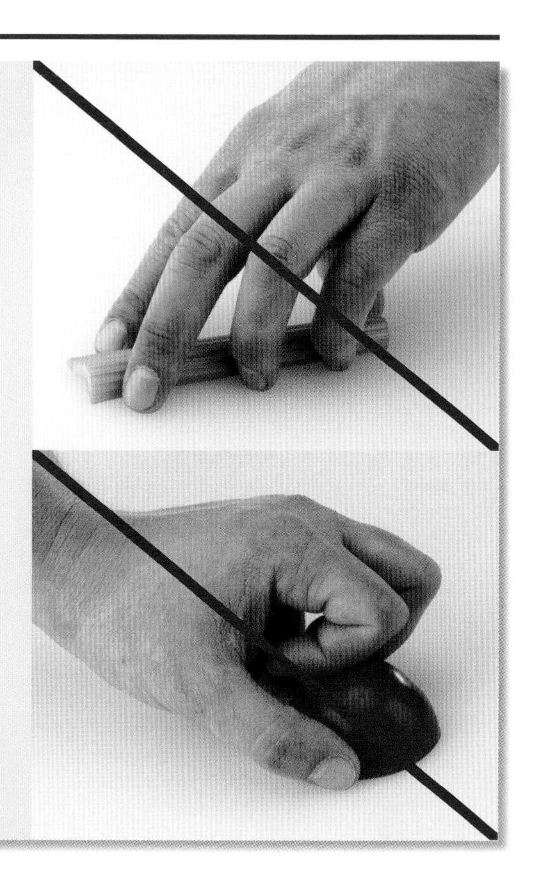

Using a Chef's Knife

The most common techniques performed with a chef's knife — slicing and chopping — can be applied to many items and types of cuts. Take time to practice the motions involved, developing muscle memory, before trying to cut anything. Once you have the hang of slicing and chopping without food, practice some more with stalks of celery, which we've used in the photos to illustrate the techniques. Go slowly at first, then gradually pick up speed.

A third technique, mincing, is used to cut vegetables and herbs into very small pieces very quickly. Because mincing involves fairly simple, straight-forward motions, you can practice using a clove of garlic, as we've done in our instructions.

When using a knife, always stand facing the cutting board, with both feet firmly planted on the ground, shoulders' width apart.

Slicing

Slicing involves moving your wrist in a circular motion. You'll use this technique for thin items, such as celery and zucchini, and for classic cuts such as batonnets and dice.

First, focus on your knife hand.

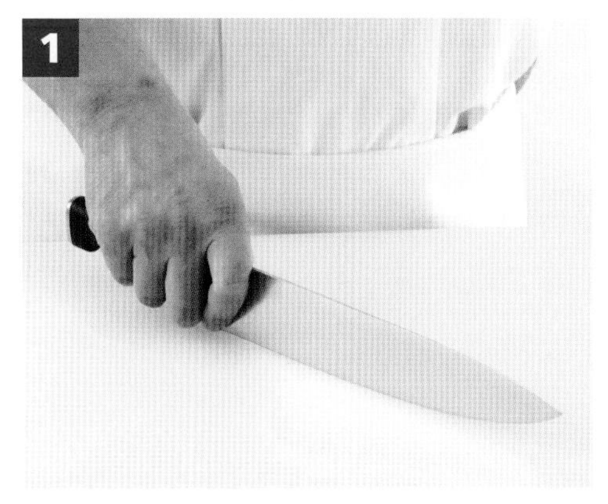

Hold the knife with the cutting edge flat against the cutting board, as if you've just cut something.

Pull up on the handle as you simultaneously pull back the blade, drawing the point of the blade back across the board.

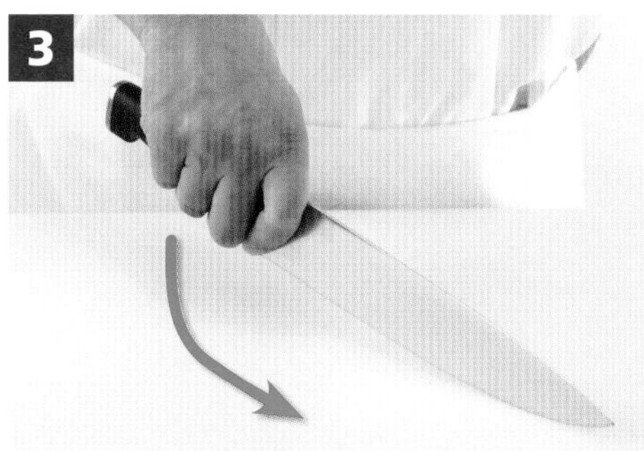

To slice, press down on the handle as you simultaneously move the point of the blade forward. Make sure the knife stays in contact with the board at all times.

Be sure to do the "up" and "back" motions simultaneously in step 2, and the "down" and "forward" motions simultaneously in step 3. It's "up and back," not "up, then back." It's "down and forward," not "down, then forward." If you separate the movements, your wrist will be tracing a square instead of a circle.

Now let's bring in the guide hand.

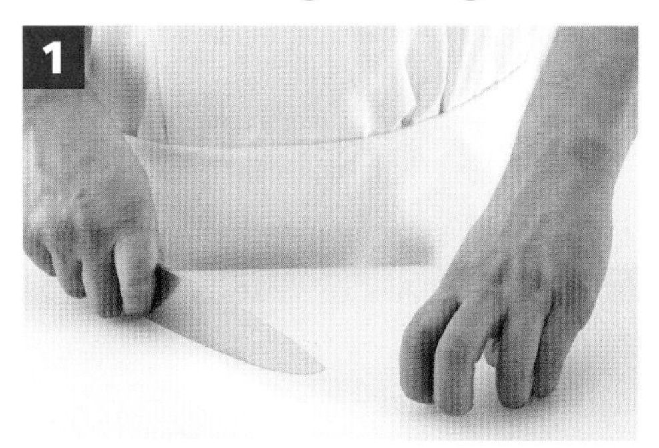

Place your guide hand on the cutting board, in the claw position.

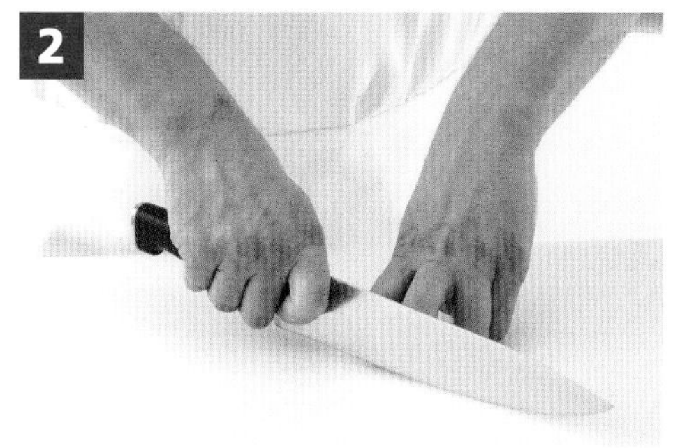

Place the edge of the blade flat against the board, pressing the side of the blade against your guide fingers.

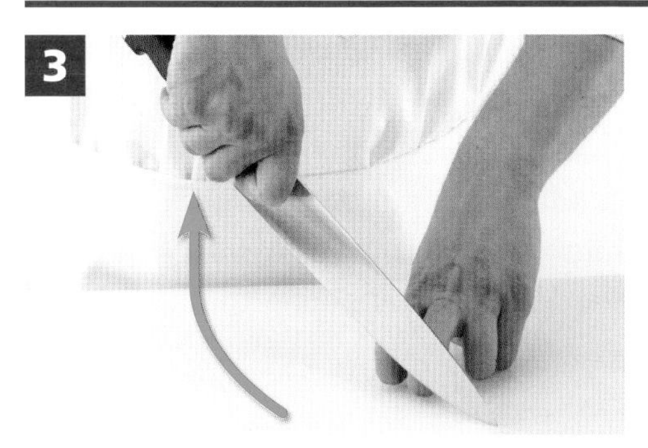

Keeping the blade against your guide fingers, pull up on the handle as you simultaneously pull back the blade, drawing the point of the blade back across the board.

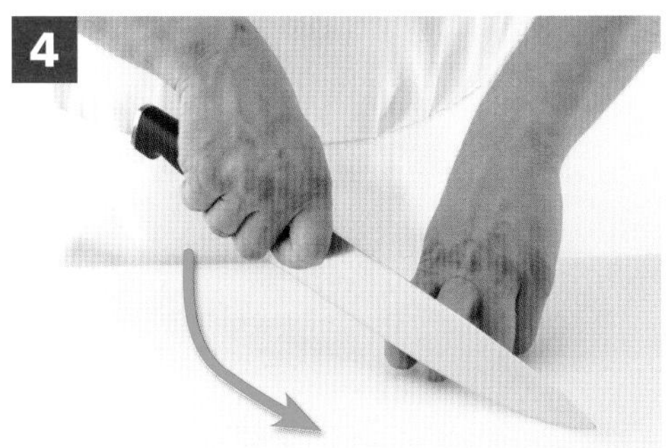

Still keeping the blade against your guide fingers, press down on the handle as you simultaneously move the point of the blade forward. Make sure the knife stays in contact with the board.

There's one last component of this technique, and that's moving your guide fingers back while your grip fingers stay anchored to the board.

Moving your guide fingers back.

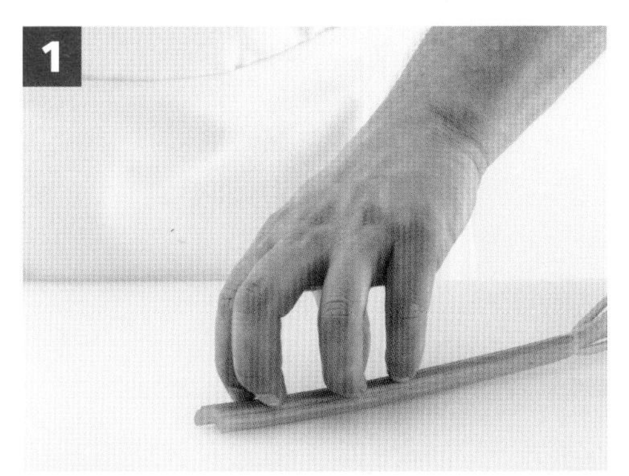

Place your guide hand on the cutting board, in the claw position.

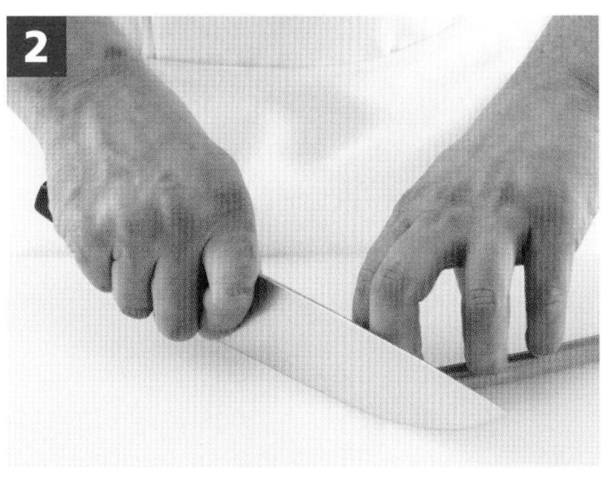

Place the edge of the blade flat against the board, pressing the side of the blade against your guide fingers.

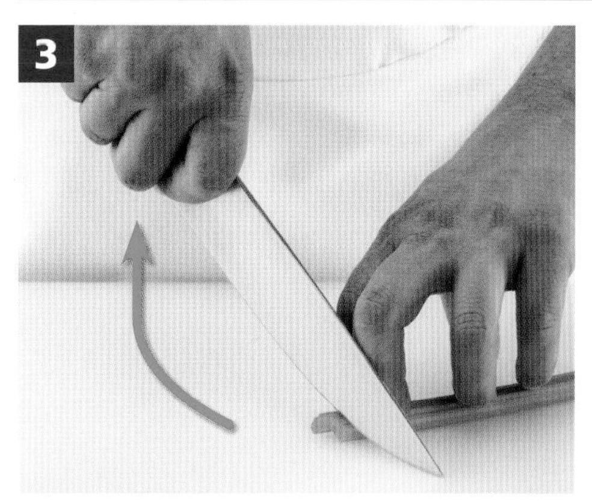

Pull up on the handle and simultaneously pull back the blade, drawing the point of the blade back across the board. As you draw the blade back, move your guide fingers about $1/4$ inch (6 mm) toward your grip fingers. Make sure to keep the blade pressed against your guide fingers as you pull them back.

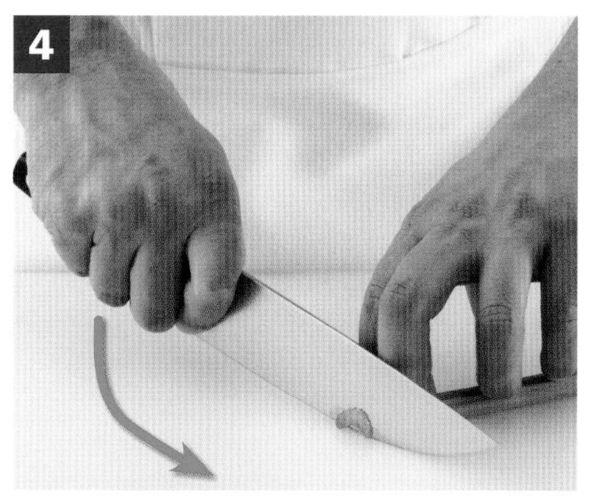

Stop your guide fingers and press down on the handle as you simultaneously move the point of the blade forward.

Repeat steps 3 and 4 until your guide fingers are almost, but not quite, all the way back to your grip fingers.

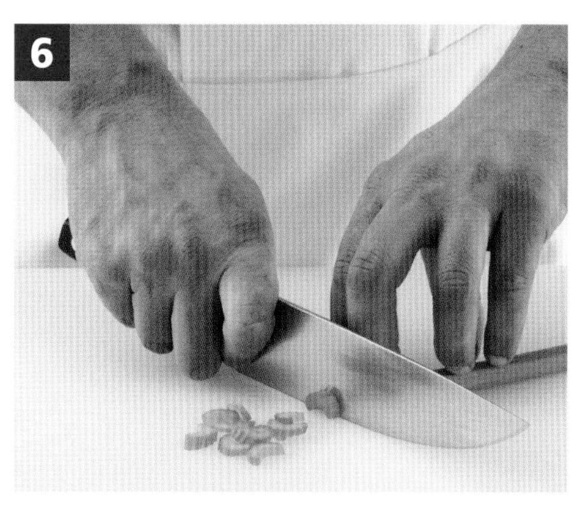

If there's more of the item left to cut when your guide fingers have nearly reached your grip fingers (as with long items, such as celery or zucchini), simply move your grip fingers farther back, set up your guide hand in the claw position and begin the process again.

Chopping

Chopping is a straight up-and-down motion that's used for items that come apart easily, such as mushrooms or onions. Unlike with slicing, the knife comes completely off the board, so it needs the guide hand to steady it.

Practicing the chopping motion.

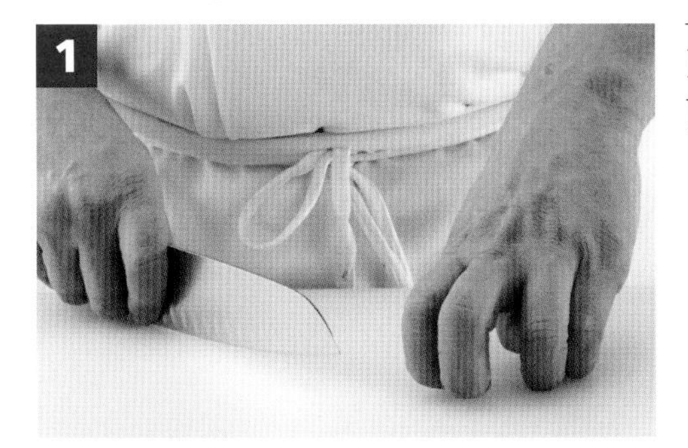

Place your guide hand on the cutting board, in the claw position.

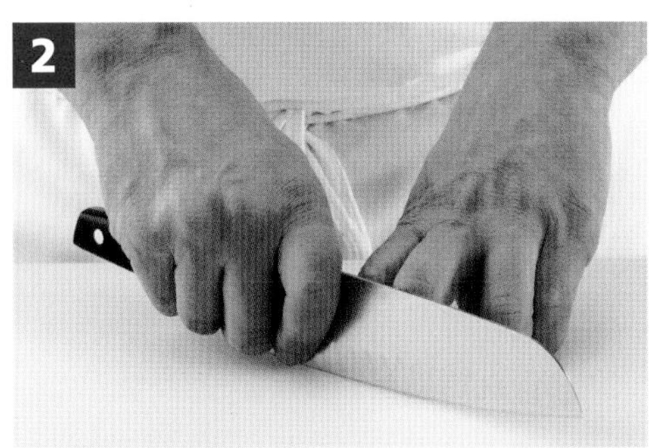

Place the edge of the blade flat against the board, pressing the side of the blade against your guide fingers.

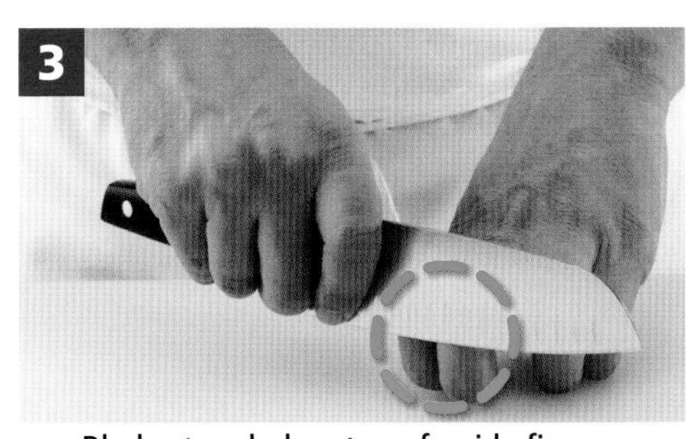

Blade stays below top of guide fingers

Moving from the wrist, raise your knife hand so that the edge of the blade comes almost to the top of your guide fingers, keeping it in constant contact with your fingers. Do not allow the blade to rise above your fingers.

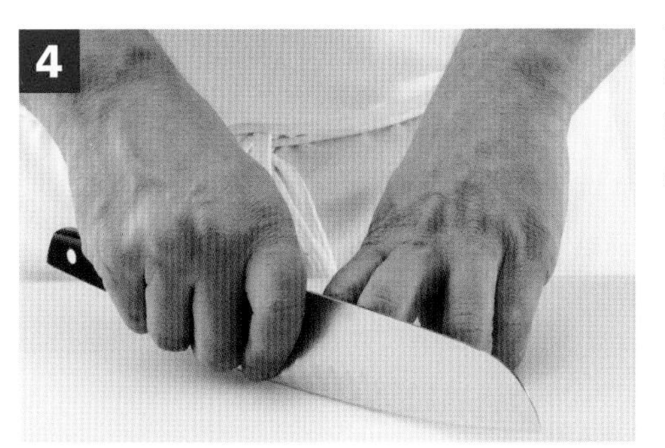

Still working from the wrist, slowly bring the blade back down until it comes to rest again on the board.

Caution

If the blade rises above your guide fingers, there's a risk it will come back down on top of your fingers rather than alongside them.

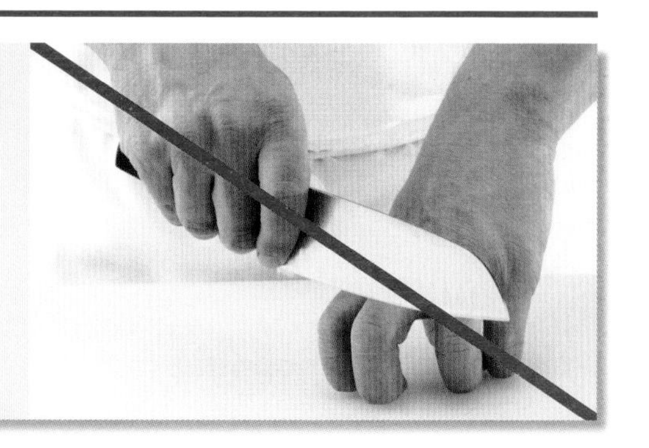

Now move your guide fingers back toward your grip fingers as you repeat the chopping motion.

Moving your guide fingers back.

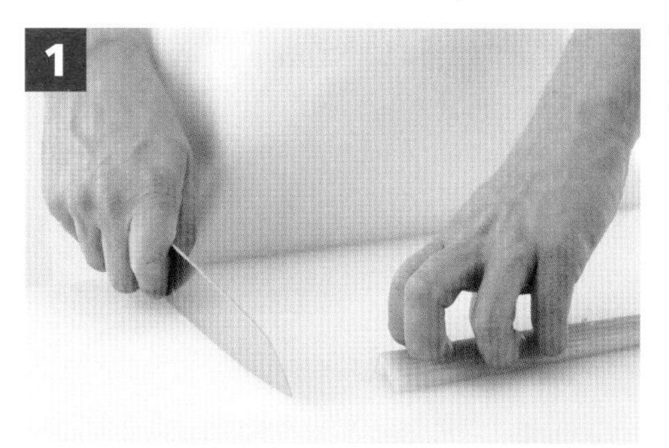

Place your guide hand on the cutting board, in the claw position.

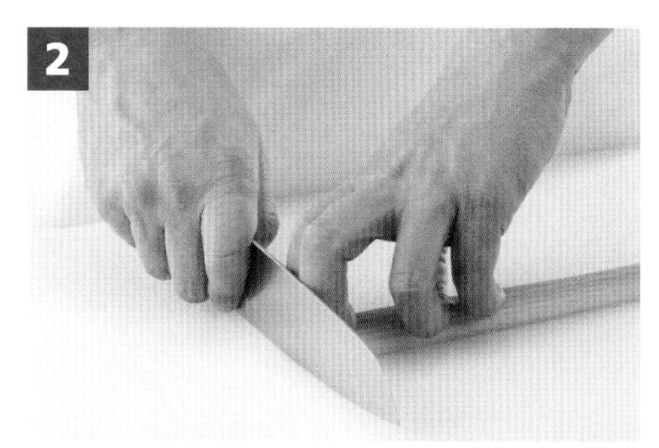

Place the edge of the blade flat against the board, pressing the side of the blade against your guide fingers.

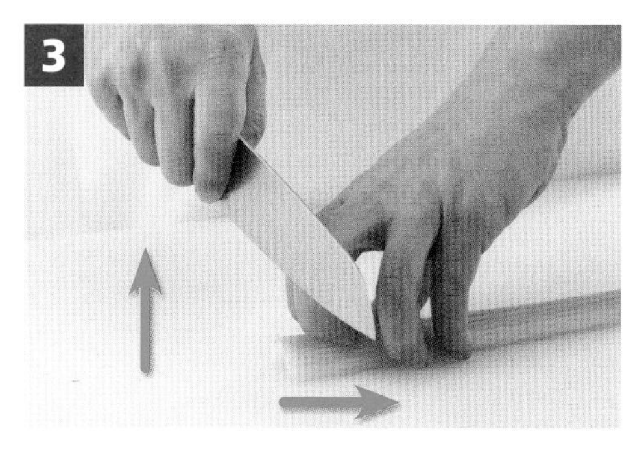

Moving from the wrist, raise your knife hand so that the edge of the blade comes almost to the top of your guide fingers. As you bring the blade up, move your guide fingers $\frac{1}{4}$ inch (6 mm) toward your grip fingers. Make sure to keep the blade pressed against your guide fingers as you pull them back.

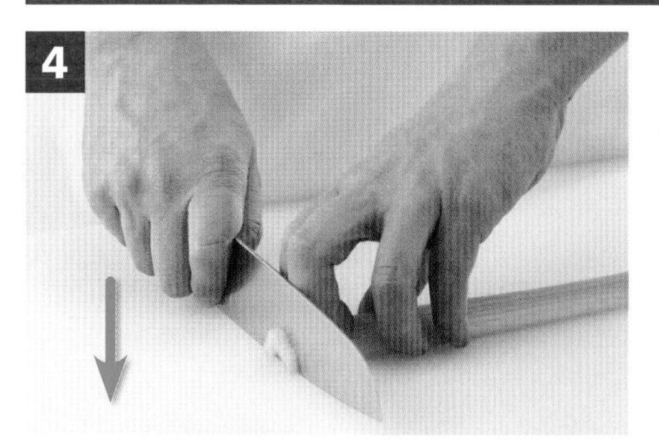

4

Stop your guide fingers. Still working from the wrist, slowly bring the blade back down until it comes to rest again on the board.

5

Repeat steps 3 and 4 until your guide fingers are almost, but not quite, all the way back to your grip fingers.

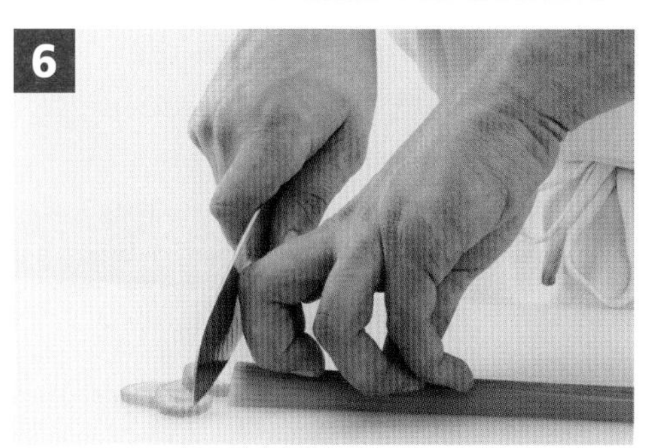

6

If there's more of the item left to cut when your guide fingers have nearly reached your grip fingers (as with long items, such as celery or zucchini), simply move your grip fingers farther back, set up your hand in the claw position and begin the process again.

Mincing

This technique can be used on garlic, nuts, parsley or anything else you want cut into very small pieces very quickly. The tiny pieces cook quickly and distribute their flavor evenly throughout a dish. In mincing, your hands work together differently than in most other techniques: the palm of the guide hand anchors the tip of the knife, while the knife hand works the blade straight up and down like a paper cutter.

Garlic is probably the most commonly minced vegetable, so we'll use a garlic clove to demonstrate the technique. We'll give instructions for mincing just a single clove, but you can do several at once if you wish. The more time you spend mincing, the smaller the pieces will be.

Mincing Garlic

First, peel a garlic clove (see page 168) and set it on the cutting board. It doesn't matter if the clove is in one piece or was broken up when you were peeling it.

Place the flat side of your knife directly on top of the clove. Form your guide hand into a fist and bring it down on the side of the knife with as much force as needed to smash the clove. If the garlic has been smashed into several pieces, gather them into a pile.

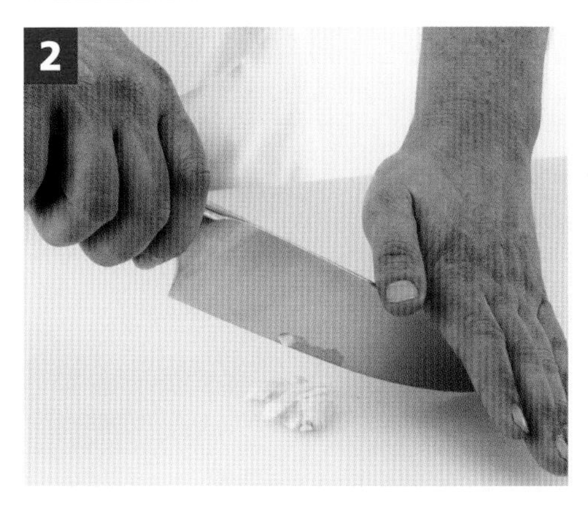

Hold the knife at a 45-degree angle directly over the pile of garlic, with the point on the board. Anchor the tip of the blade with the palm of your guide hand, keeping your fingers arched up and away from the blade.

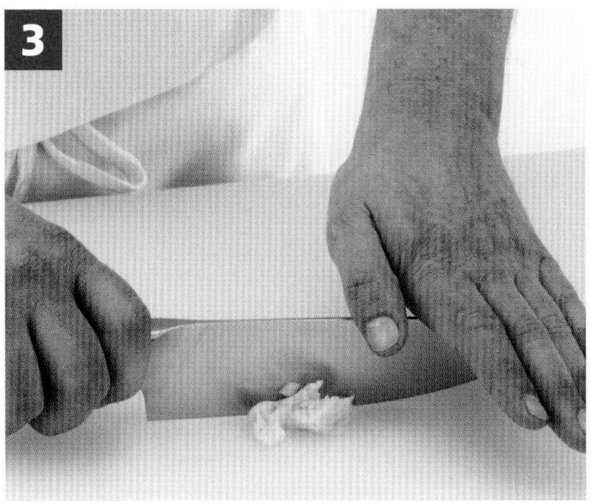

Continuing to anchor the tip, bring the blade straight up and down repeatedly — like working a paper cutter — while simultaneously moving the blade horizontally, back and forth across the garlic. Continue mincing until the garlic pieces are as small as desired.

When you're mincing herbs, nuts, mushrooms — anything other than garlic — start with coarsely chopped pieces, gather them into a pile, then continue with step 2.

Other Knife Grips

The vast majority of knife work is done with the basic grip described on page 70. A number of tasks, however, require specialized grips.

The Paring/Tourné Grip

This grip is used with a paring knife or a tourné knife when you're peeling produce or creating tourné vegetables (see page 109).

Hold your knife hand with the palm up and the fingers outstretched. Lay the knife across the top of your palm, where it meets the fingers, with the blade edge facing your thumb

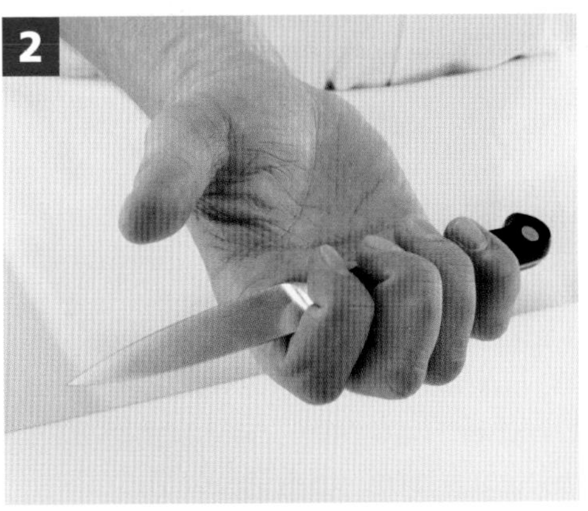

Curl your fingers around the knife handle. Your index finger will be curled over the spine of the blade rather than over the handle.

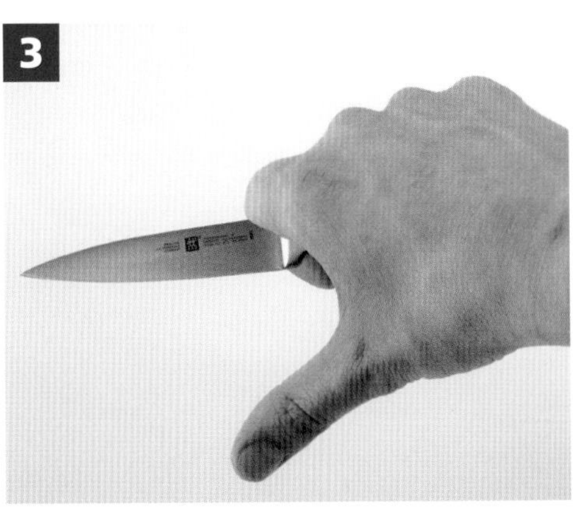

Flip your hand over, keeping your thumb extended. (Your thumb will ultimately be placed on the bottom of the fruit or vegetable you're paring.)

The Stabbing and Reverse Stabbing Grips

The stabbing grip and the reverse stabbing grip are used for a handful of techniques, including boning out a leg of lamb and splitting a lobster. The only difference between the two grips is that the direction of the blade is reversed.

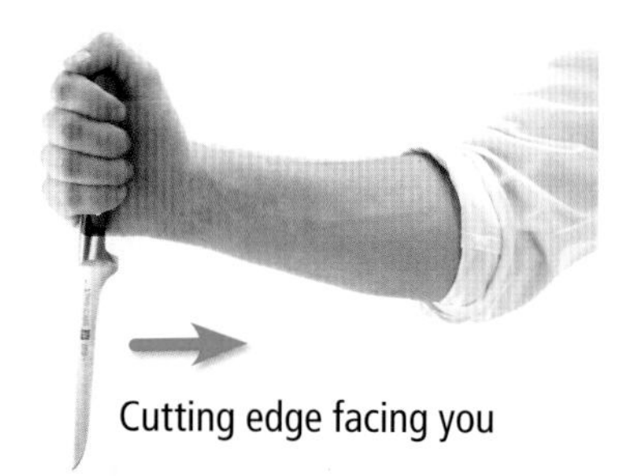

For the **stabbing grip**, wrap all four fingers around the handle and encircle it with your thumb. Point the blade down, with the edge facing back toward you.

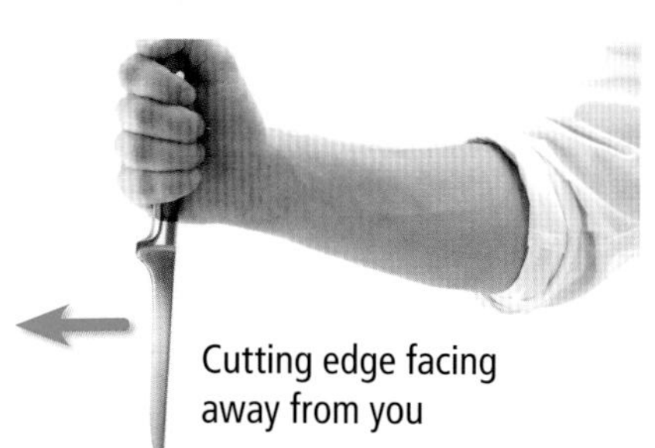

For the **reverse stabbing grip**, turn the knife so that the edge is facing away from you.

The Shucking Grip

The shucking grip is used most notably for opening clams and oysters, but it's also used with a paring knife for such tasks as removing the eyes from pineapples or potatoes and stemming tomatoes or strawberries.

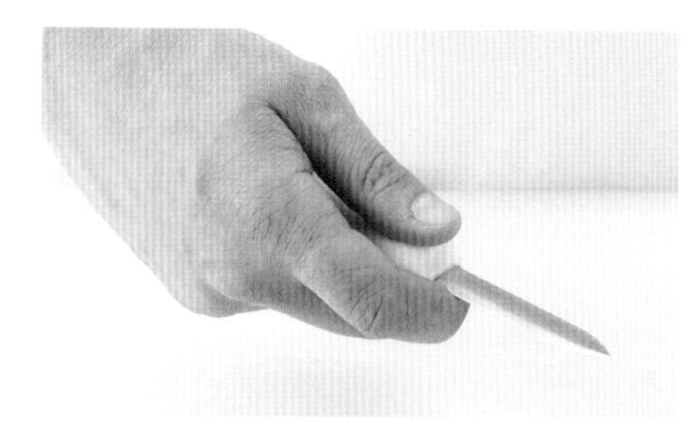

Hold the knife in the basic grip described on page 70, but with the blade parallel to the board, rather than perpendicular to it. If you're using a paring knife, your thumb and index finger will still pinch the blade, but with a shorter clam or oyster knife, your thumb can rest on the handle instead.

While the clam knife has one sharpened edge, the oyster knife is dull on both sides, so you won't have to worry about which direction the edge is facing.

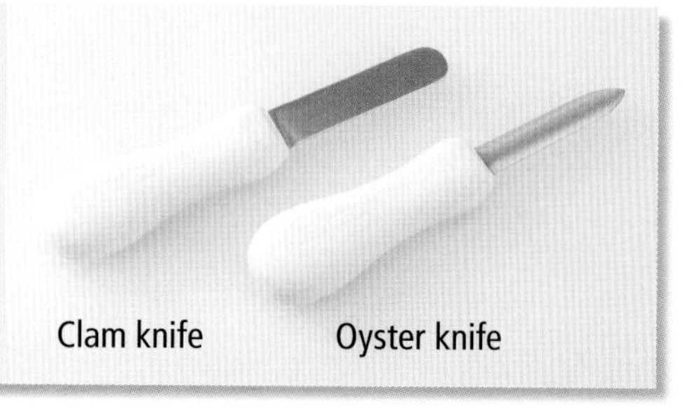

The Fluting Grip

This grip is used when you're carving decorative patterns into a vegetable or fruit. It is most commonly done with a paring knife or tourné knife.

1 With the edge of the knife facing away from your hand, rest the tip and middle segment of your knife-hand index finger against the middle of the blade. Place the tip of your middle finger just below the tip of your index finger.

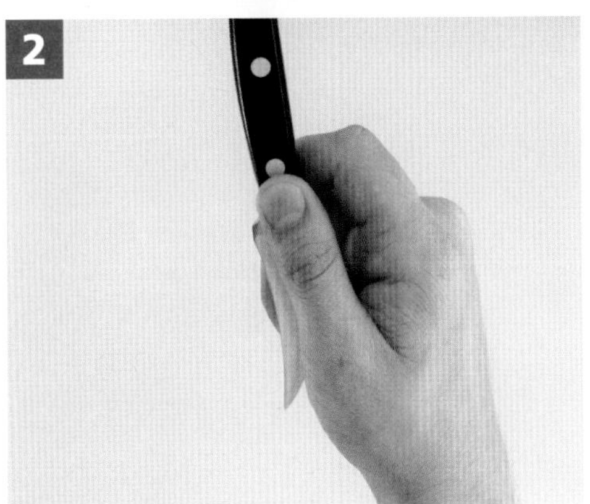

2 Press your knife-hand thumb against the blade, holding it against your index and middle fingers.

The fluting grip is similar to holding a pen, but with one major difference: a pen is held at an angle, with the middle resting against the soft, fleshy spot between your thumb and index finger, while a knife in the fluting grip is held so that the blade is vertical.

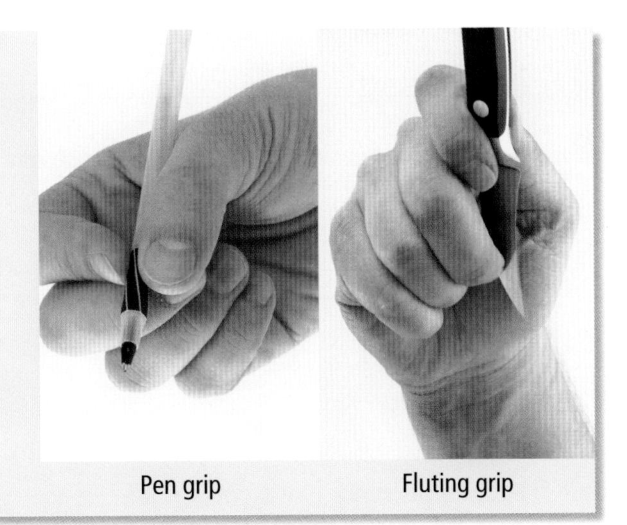

Pen grip　　Fluting grip

Chapter 3

Basic Vegetable Cuts

Vegetable pieces that are attractive and cook evenly are essential to the preparation of quality food. While there are only a few basic shapes and sizes to learn, their importance cannot be overestimated. The ability to produce perfect basic cuts is a hallmark of excellent knife skills.

Sticks

RECOMMENDED KNIFE

Chef's knife or Santoku

One of the most common shapes for vegetables is the stick, a long rectangular shape with perfectly square ends. There are five stick sizes, each with its own name: pont-neuf sticks, batons, batonnets, juliennes and fine juliennes. Unfortunately, there is no universal agreement on the proper measurements for each size. Listed below are the dimensions we cut our sticks to, but different sources will tell you alternative lengths and widths, and each chef seems to have his own preference. However, it hardly matters, as the technique for cutting sticks is the same regardless of the size; once you learn the technique, it's easy to adjust the size of your sticks to satisfy your chef's demands or to suit the dish you're preparing.

We'll use a potato for our demonstration, but the technique can be used on any large vegetable and some fruits. It can even be used on cheese, cooked meats and breads.

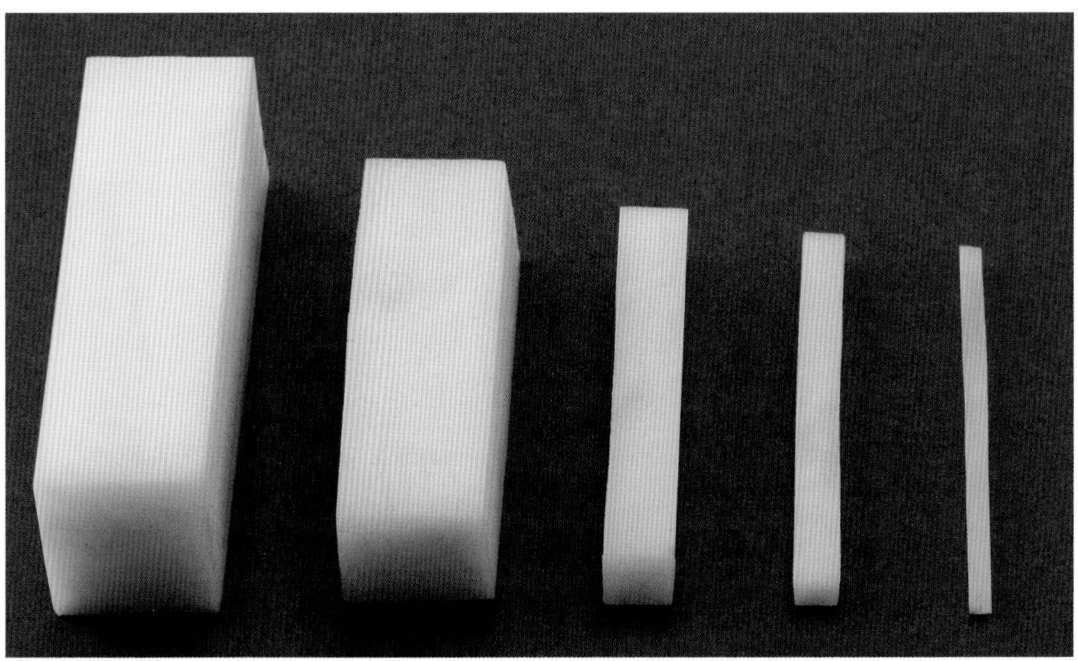

Pont-neuf	Baton	Batonnet	Julienne	Fine julienne
3" x $\frac{3}{4}$" x $\frac{3}{4}$"	$2\frac{1}{2}$" x $\frac{1}{2}$" x $\frac{1}{2}$"	$2\frac{1}{2}$" x $\frac{1}{4}$" x $\frac{1}{4}$"	2" x $\frac{1}{8}$" x $\frac{1}{8}$"	2" x $\frac{1}{16}$" x $\frac{1}{16}$"
(7.5 x 2 x 2 cm)	(6 cm x 12 mm x 12 mm)	(6 cm x 6 mm x 6 mm)	(5 cm x 3 mm x 3 mm)	(5 cm x 2 mm x 2 mm)

The first thing we're going to do after peeling is cut the potato into a box shape. In the interest of showing you the best possible results, we'll demonstrate the way they'd do it in a restaurant, where everything has to look perfect. For the home cook, your standards can be as high or as low as you make them. Remember, though, that the more even your cuts, the more evenly the food will cook and the better-looking your finished dish will be.

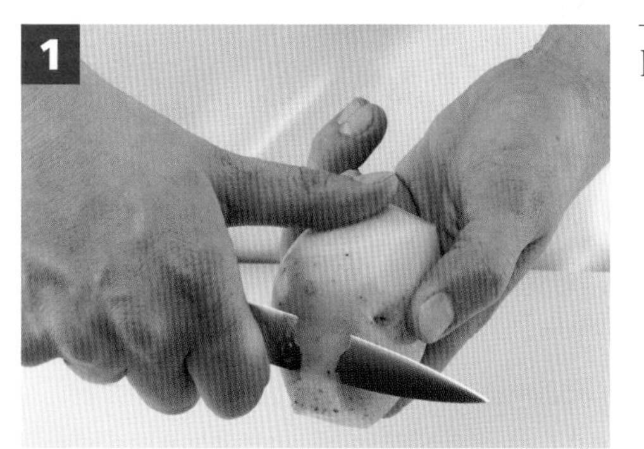

Peel the potato (see page 206 or page 207).

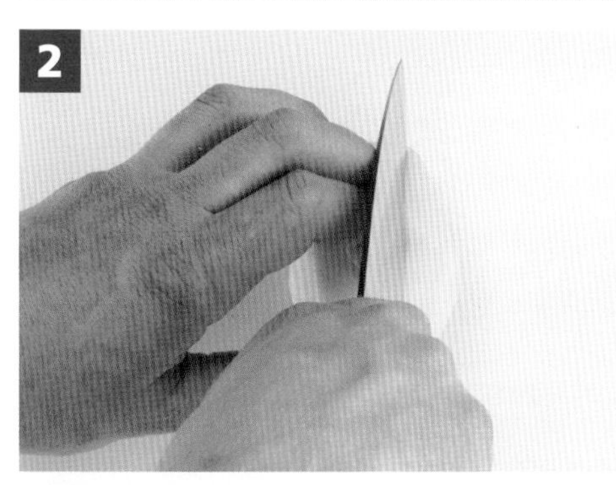

Keeping the knife blade perpendicular to the cutting board, cut a thin slice from one long side of the potato to create a flat surface. Be sure to keep your guide hand in the claw position.

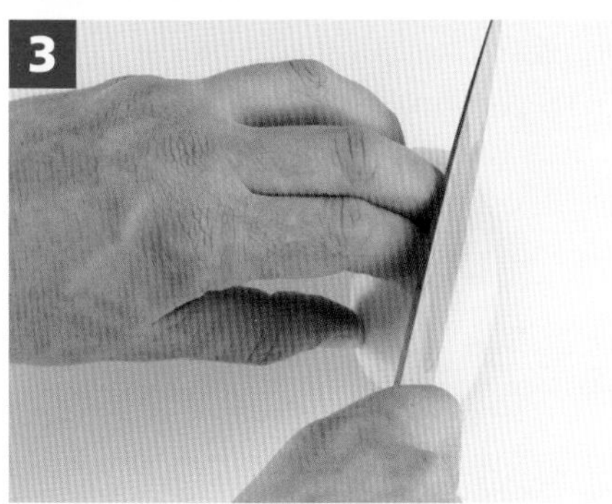

Rest the potato on that flat surface and cut another thin slice from the side closest to your knife hand.

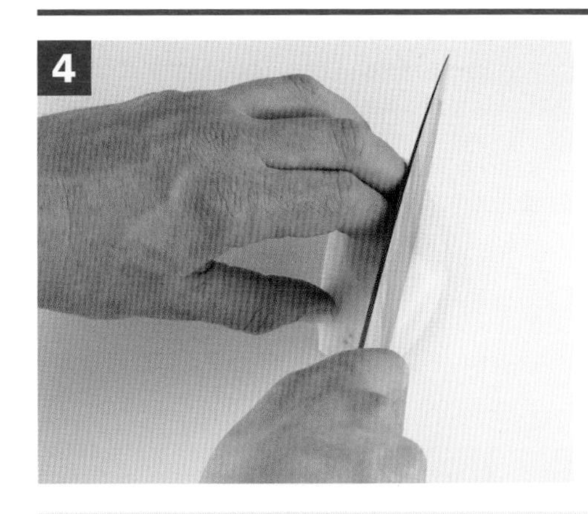

Roll the potato over onto this new surface and cut a third slice from the side closest to your knife hand.

Cutting a potato into a box is not as easy as it sounds. To do it properly, your knife must be perfectly perpendicular to the cutting board. If it tilts even a little bit in either direction, you'll end up with an oddly shaped box. As with everything else in the world, the more you practice, the better you'll get.

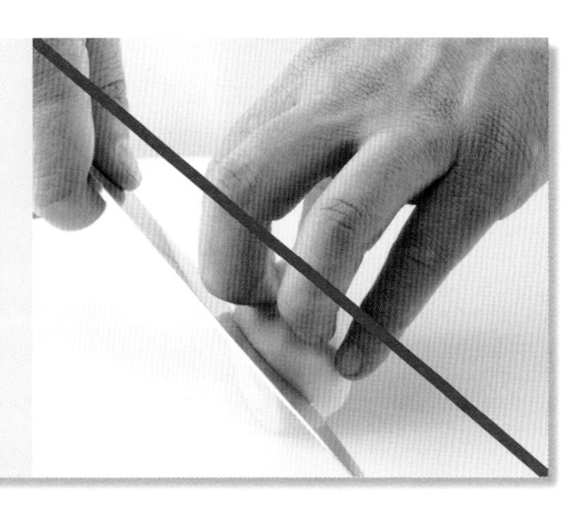

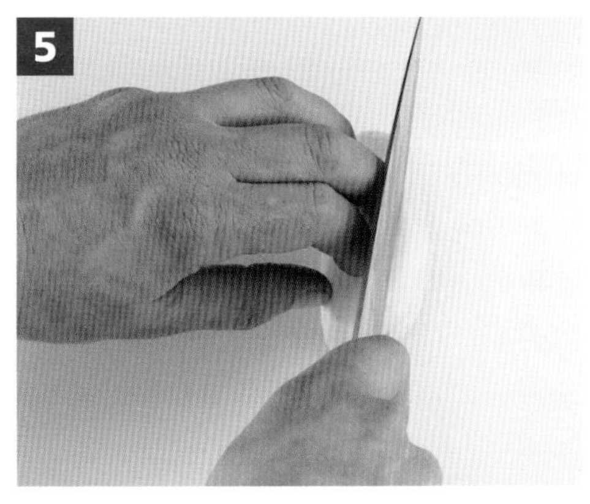

Roll the potato over onto the third surface and cut off the remaining round edge.

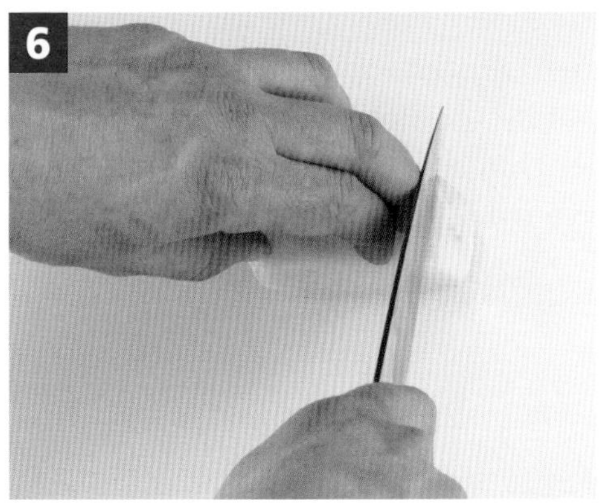

Rotate the potato 90 degrees and cut off one short end, again keeping the blade perpendicular to the board.

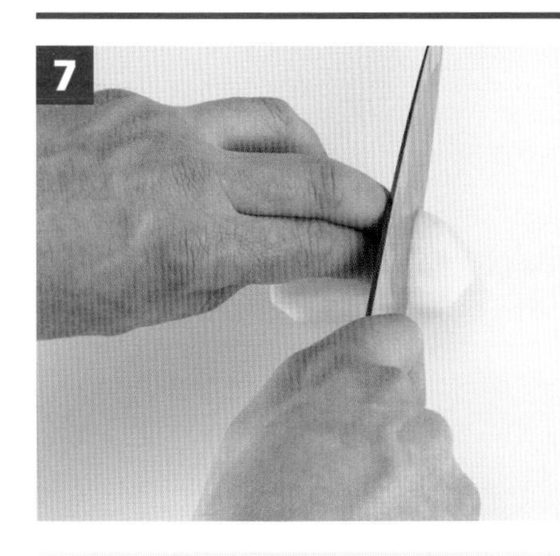

Rotate the potato 180 degrees and cut off the other end. In a restaurant, you'd make the box exactly 3 inches (7.5 cm) long for pont-neuf sticks, 2½ inches (6 cm) long for batons or batonnets, or 2 inches (5 cm) long for juliennes or fine juliennes. At home, all that's really important is that the pieces are short enough that they are easy to eat.

Next we're going to cut the box into individual planks. The width of the plank will determine the name of the cut. For this demonstration, we'll make batonnets, which means we'll cut the planks to ¼-inch (6 mm) thickness. Once you get good at this, you can simply eyeball the cuts. For now, though, we recommend using a small ruler to measure your cuts.

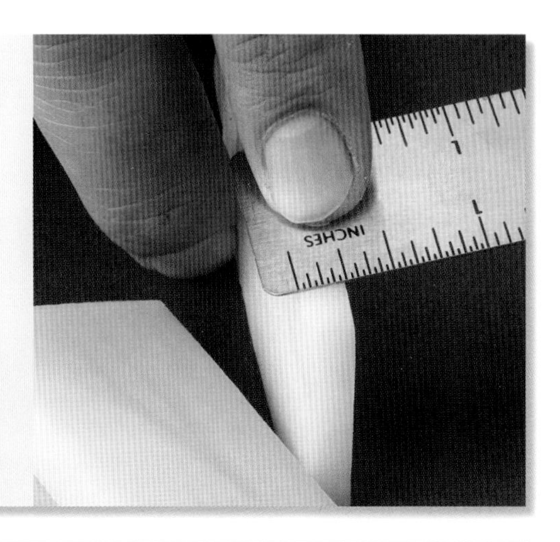

Clear off all the scrap from your cutting board and place the box on it, with the long side parallel to your knife blade. Steady the box with your guide hand in the claw position and cut off a ¼-inch (6 mm) slice from a long side. Repeat this step until you have cut the potato completely into ¼-inch (5 mm) planks.

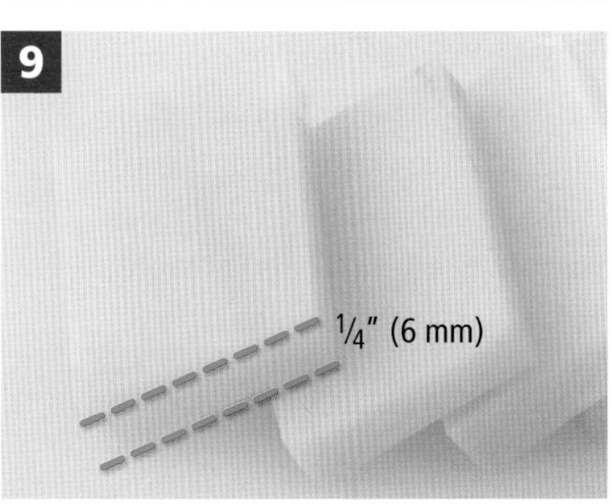

To ensure an even slice, make sure your knife edge is perfectly parallel to the side of the box and perfectly perpendicular to the cutting board. You want the edge of this plank to be exactly ¼ inch (6 mm) thick all the way around.

The final step is to cut the planks into ¼-inch (6 mm) strips. You'll end up with 2½-inch (6 cm) long pieces with ends that are perfect ¼-inch (6 mm) squares. When you get good at this, you can stack several planks and cut them all at once. To start with, though, we'll cut one plank at a time.

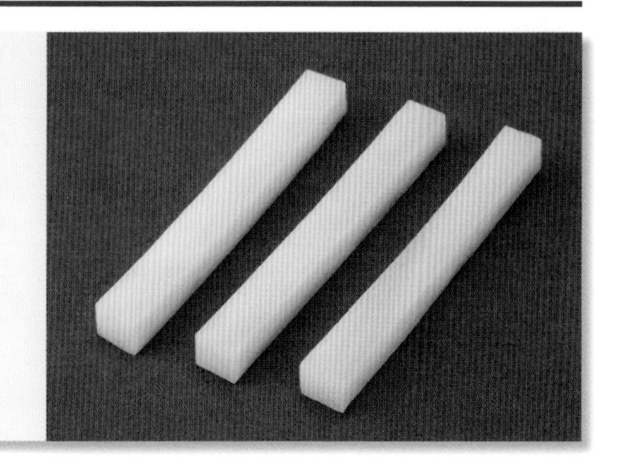

Lay one plank lengthwise on your cutting board. Hold it with your guide hand in the claw position and cut off one ¼-inch (6 mm) slice. Repeat this step until you have cut the plank completely into ¼-inch (6 mm) strips.

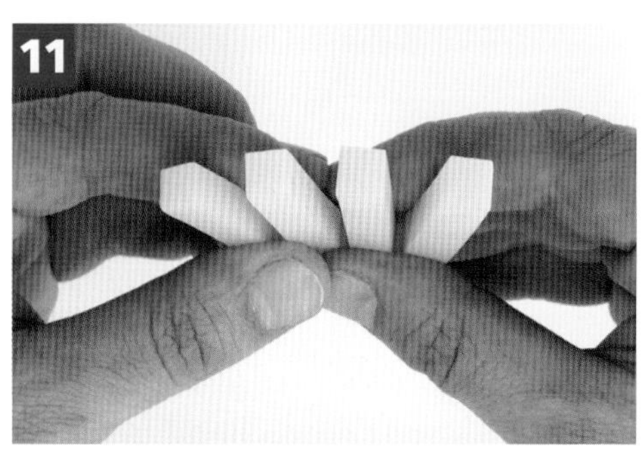

Examine both ends of your strips to make sure they are perfect squares. Repeat steps 10 and 11 until all the planks are cut into batonnets.

Slicing vs. Chopping

Several factors come into play when you are deciding whether to cut using a slicing motion (see page 77) or a chopping motion (see page 81). First and foremost is the nature of the item you are cutting. Some foods, such as butternut squash, are simply too big to slice. Other items, such as mushrooms, have a soft texture that lends itself to chopping. The second factor is your choice of knife. The curve of a chef's knife makes slicing easy, while the straighter edge of a Santoku makes it a great chopper. The final consideration is your own preference: some people are more comfortable chopping, while others prefer slicing. In this book, we'll use the verb "cut" where either technique can be used, and "slice" or "chop" when a specific motion is preferred.

Dice

Dice, like sticks, come in several sizes, each with its own name. In fact, dice are simply sticks cut into perfect cubes. So for every size of stick, there are corresponding dice.

RECOMMENDED KNIFE

Chef's knife or Santoku

Large dice
(from pont-neuf sticks)
¾" x ¾" x ¾" (2 x 2 x 2 cm)

Medium dice
(from batons)
½" x ½" x ½" (12 x 12 x 12 mm)

Small dice
(from batonnets)
¼" x ¼" x ¼" (6 x 6 x 6 mm)

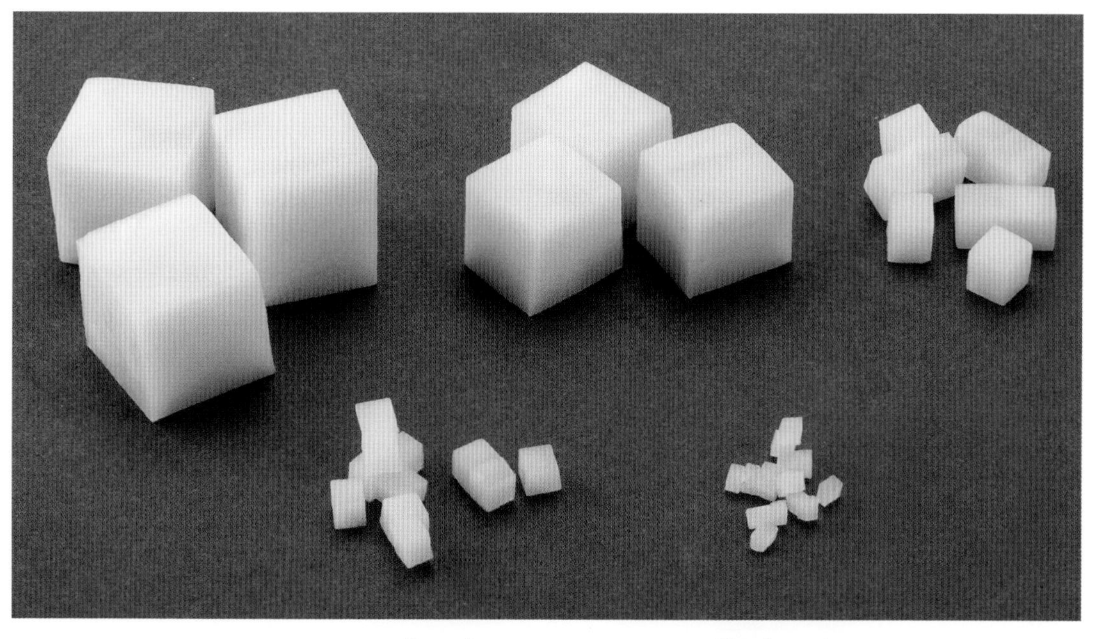

Brunoise
(from juliennes)
⅛" x ⅛" x ⅛"
(3 x 3 x 3 mm)

Fine brunoise
(from fine juliennes)
1/16" x 1/16" x 1/16"
(2 x 2 x 2 mm)

To begin cutting dice, first cut sticks (see page 90). As with stick cuts, the technique for dice is identical for every size. We'll give instructions for medium dice, which means we'll start with batons. For other dice, simply start with the corresponding sticks.

Dice

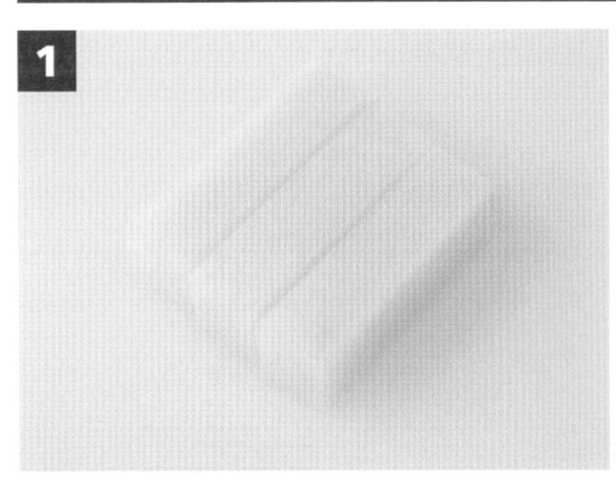

1 Line up several batons side by side on your cutting board.

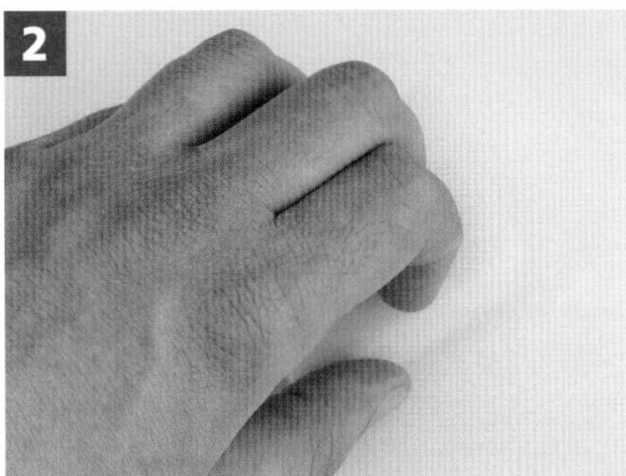

2 Hold them down with your guide hand in the claw position.

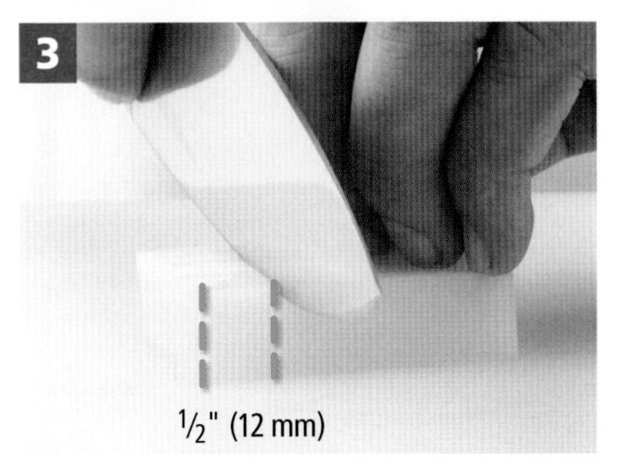

3 Position your guide fingers so that, when the knife blade is flush against them, it is exactly ½ inch (12 mm) in from the end, then cut straight down.

4 Repeat step 3 until the batons are completely cut into medium dice.

We recommend using a ruler to measure your cuts at first. The more you do this, the better you'll get at eyeballing the sizes.

Practical Uses for Your Scraps

In the course of cutting perfect sticks and dice, you're going to create a lot of scrap pieces as you trim away the rounded edges that define the exterior of the vegetable. One of the guiding principles of the restaurant business is cost control. The lower you can get your costs, the more profit you can make. Thus, very little goes to waste in a professional kitchen. Meat scraps are turned into sausage and pâté. Stale bread becomes croutons. And vegetable peelings are used for stocks, sauces, soups and purées. If the menu features deep-fried julienned potatoes, there will be another item on the menu that uses the scraps, such as mashed potatoes or vichyssoise. Kitchen scraps may also be used for "family meal," the food served to the staff, which does not need to be of the same high quality as the food served to customers.

Home cooks do not generally have the same opportunity to use up scraps, simply because they don't work with the same volume of food. One option for the waste-wary home cook is simply to cut the scraps into shapes that are close to your intended cuts; at home, it doesn't really matter if they're not perfect. You could also put the scraps in an airtight container or freezer bag as you create them, and freeze them until you have enough collected to make a batch of stock. Or, if you have a garden and the ability to compost, you can throw your scraps onto the compost heap — at least they'll be helping to enrich the next generation of vegetables!

Chiffonade

This technique is used to create long, thin strands of certain herbs, such as basil, sage or mint, or leafy vegetables, such as spinach and lettuce. The root, *chiffon*, is the French word for "rag," and a pile of chiffonaded vegetables does indeed resemble a pile of green rags.

RECOMMENDED KNIFE
Chef's knife or Santoku

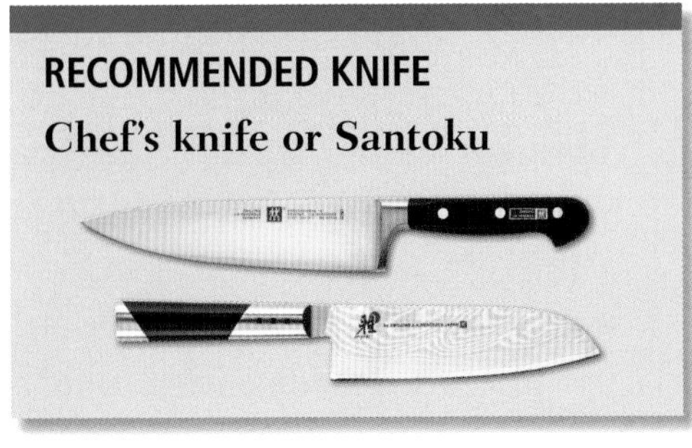

There's no right or wrong when it comes to the size of chiffonade. Your decision about how thick to make it will depend on how you plan to use it. Very fine chiffonade, for example, looks elegant sprinkled on top of a cold plate, but would wither and shrivel if added to a hot dish. The more you cook, the better you'll understand how various sizes of chiffonade are used.

Here, we'll teach you two ways to cut chiffonade. While these techniques produce similar results, close examination will reveal that the individual pieces created using the classic technique are much more precise and beautiful than the pieces created with the "quick and dirty" technique. Which technique you choose will depend on how much time you have and how important the look of the final product is.

When chiffonading, use the thinner, lighter tip of your knife, rather than the heel, to make your cuts. The leaves will end up less bruised and will stay greener through preparation and service.

To practice, we suggest using baby spinach. It's much cheaper than fresh herbs and has a smooth texture that makes it easier to work with than regular spinach.

Chiffonade cut using the classic technique

Chiffonade cut using the "quick and dirty" technique

The Classic Technique

Lay 8 to 10 baby spinach leaves, top side down, on your cutting board, one on top of another. Don't bother to pull off the stems; just make sure they're all pointing the same way, away from where your knife will be.

The tops of most leaves have a waxy coating that helps water roll off while the leaves are on the plant. But that coating also makes your knife more likely to slip when you're cutting. The underside of a leaf is rougher and grips the knife better, making for cleaner cuts. So always cut leafy vegetables and herbs with the top side down.

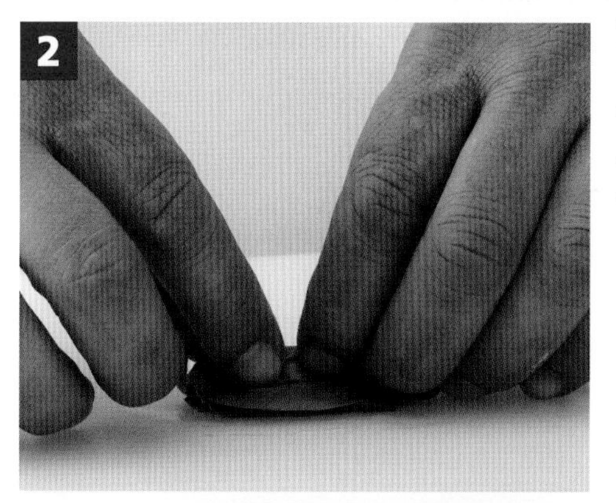

Flip the stack over so that the underside of the outer leaf ends up on the outside and roll up the leaves lengthwise, fairly tightly, like rolling a tiny carpet.

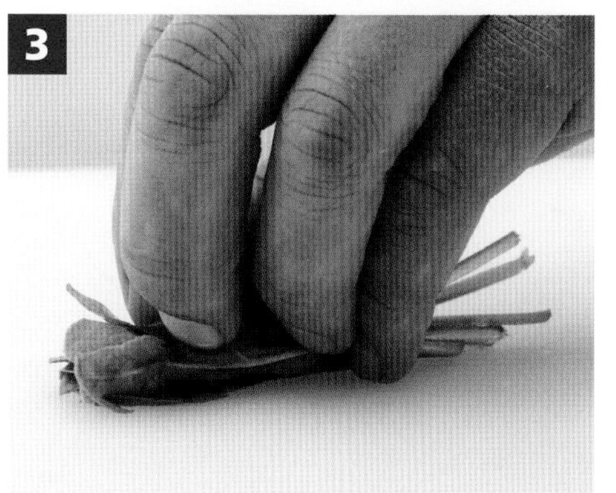

Steady the roll with your guide hand in the claw position, close to the end of the roll.

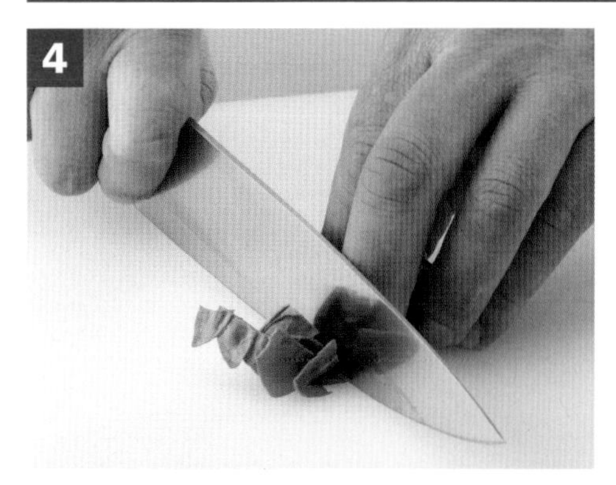

With the knife blade flush against your guide fingers, cut off a piece of the roll to even up the end. Discard this first piece.

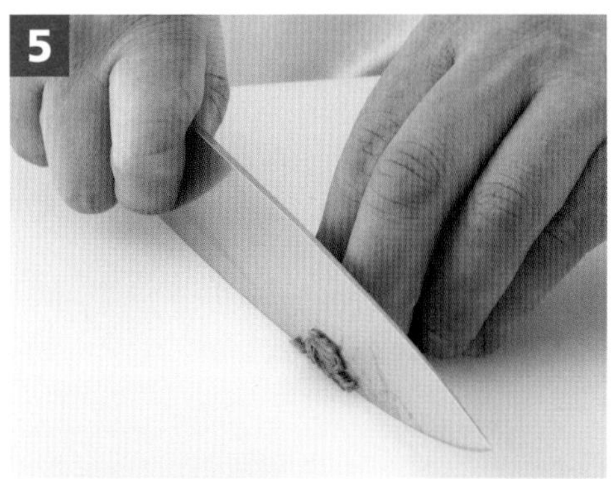

Move your guide fingers back toward your grip fingers and cut off a very thin slice. (The less you move your fingers back, the thinner the slices will be.)

Repeat step 5 until you have cut the entire roll (excluding the stems) into a neat pile. Discard the stems.

The "Quick and Dirty" Technique

Grab some baby spinach leaves with your guide hand and crush them into a tight wad. (Pull the stems off first, if you prefer.) Place the wad on the cutting board, anchoring the back with your grip fingers while holding down the front with your guide fingers in the claw position.

With the knife blade flush against your guide fingers, cut off a piece of the wad to even up the end. Discard this first piece.

Move your guide fingers back toward your grip fingers and cut off a very thin slice.

Because the leaves will expand and the wad will come apart as you loosen your grip (and sometimes even if you don't), you will have to constantly readjust your grip on the wad to keep it compact. As your guide fingers are moving back, use your grip fingers to mash down the leaves and force them under your guide fingers. (Imagine that you're forcing the wad under a tiny door and, as each bit squeezes through, you cut it off.)

Repeat step 3 until you have cut the entire wad into a messy pile.

This "quick and dirty" technique will result in bruised greens that will brown quickly as time goes by. But if you're using the chiffonade immediately or cooking it, you'll likely never notice the difference.

Rondelles

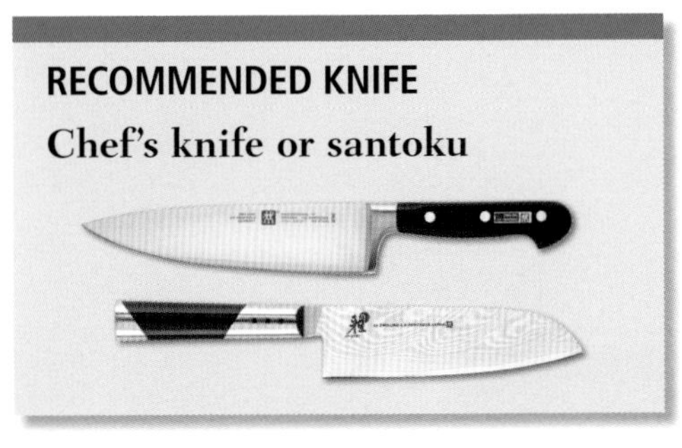
RECOMMENDED KNIFE

Chef's knife or santoku

Rondelles are simple rounds or ovals cut from conical or cylindrical vegetables, such as carrots, parsnips, cucumbers or burdock. Because the width of these vegetables varies along their length, the pieces cut from them will be of variable diameters; for this reason, there can be no precise dimensions for rondelles.

Rondelles are typically anywhere from ⅛ to ½ inch (3 to 12 mm) thick. When deciding how thick or thin to make your pieces, consider the cooking method you intend to use, bearing in mind that thicker pieces take longer to cook than thin pieces. Rondelles intended for a dish that will be cooked over high heat for a short time, such as a sauté or stir-fry, will benefit from a thinner cut. For a dish that will be cooked more slowly over lower heat (such as glazed carrots), a thicker cut would be better.

To demonstrate the technique, we'll use a carrot.

⅛" (3 mm) rondelles | ¼" (6 mm) rondelles | ½" (12 mm) rondelles

1

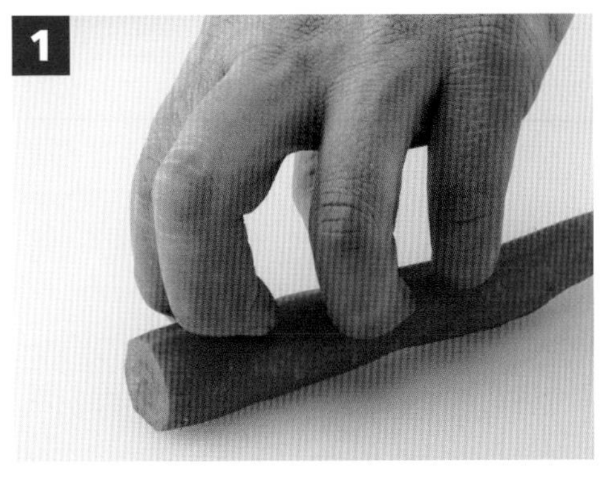

Peel the carrot, if desired, and trim off the ends. Steady the carrot with your guide hand in the claw position.

2 With the knife blade flush against your guide fingers, cut a round of the desired thickness.

3 Repeat step 2, taking care to make each successive piece the same thickness, until the entire carrot is cut into rondelles.

To make ovals, or bias cuts, hold the knife at an angle to the carrot (or vice versa), rather than perpendicular. The sharper the angle, the longer the ovals will be. You'll end up with slightly more waste from the end pieces, but only slightly more.

For more decorative rondelles, scrape the vegetable in several places along its length, using a fork, zester, peeler or channel knife, before cutting it into rounds or ovals.

The Oblique Cut

The oblique cut (also called the roll cut) is a quick, easy cut designed for conical vegetables such as carrots and parsnips. It allows you to adjust for the tapering of the vegetable so that each piece comes out roughly the same size. This is one of the few cuts for which the knife is not pressed against the guide fingers; instead, your guide hand will be performing a rolling motion. For the demo, we'll use a carrot.

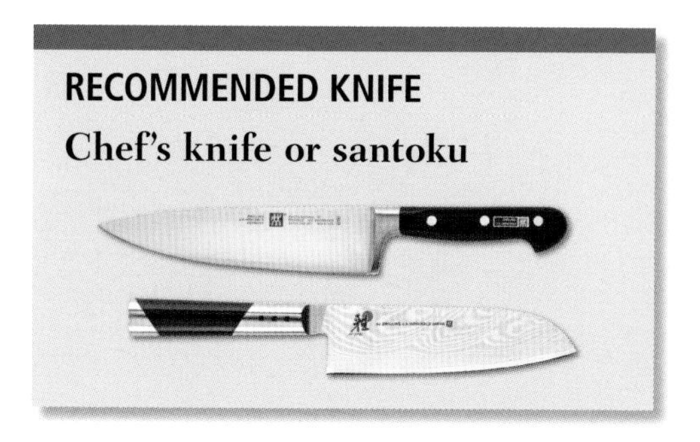

RECOMMENDED KNIFE

Chef's knife or santoku

Oblique-cut carrots

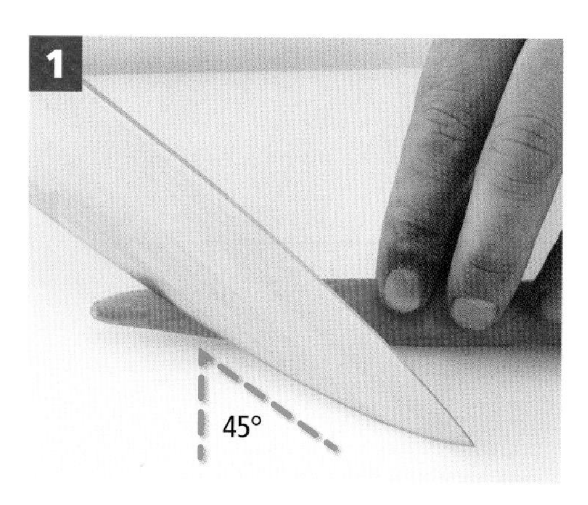

If desired, peel the carrot. Lay the carrot on the cutting board with the root end facing your knife hand. Holding the knife at a 45-degree angle to the carrot, cut off and discard the root end.

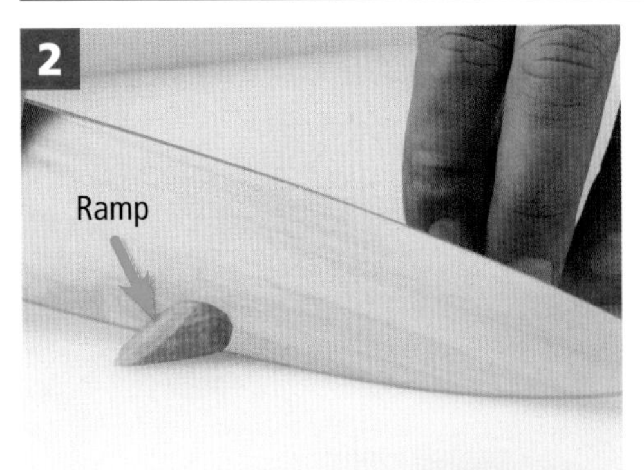

Cut surface looks like a ramp

Rotate the carrot 90 degrees (a quarter-turn) toward you, so that the slanting cut surface looks like a little ramp leading up to the top of the carrot. Keep your knife at a 45-degree angle to the carrot and cut off another piece.

Rotate the carrot another 90 degrees and cut off another piece. As the carrot gets thicker, decrease the angle of your cut so that your pieces remain roughly the same size, though a slightly different shape.

Continue rotating and cutting at an angle until the entire carrot is cut.

The oblique cut is a great choice if you plan to make glazed carrots, because it creates a large amount of surface area on each piece, which means the carrots will cook quickly. In the time it takes for the cooking liquid to evaporate, the carrots will be perfectly cooked.

The Paysanne Cut

The paysanne cut (also called the tile cut) is similar to cutting medium dice, except that, rather than cubes, it produces flatter squares with the dimensions $\frac{1}{2}$ by $\frac{1}{2}$ by $\frac{1}{8}$ inch (12 by 12 by 3 mm). To practice, start with a potato baton (see page 90). Once you get the hang of the technique, you can line up several batons side by side.

RECOMMENDED KNIFE

Chef's knife or Santoku

Potato paysannes

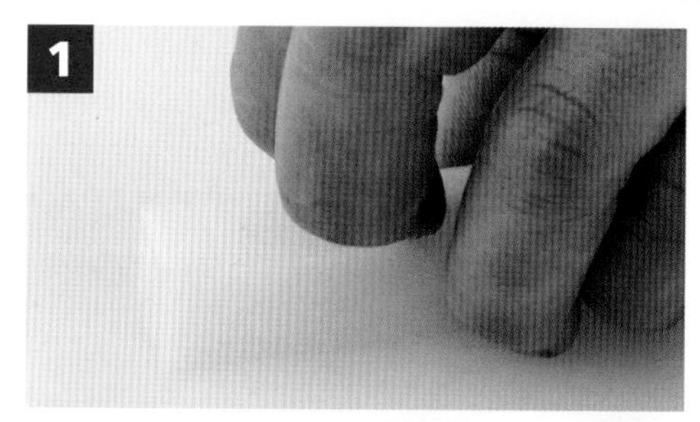

Steady the baton with your guide hand in the claw position.

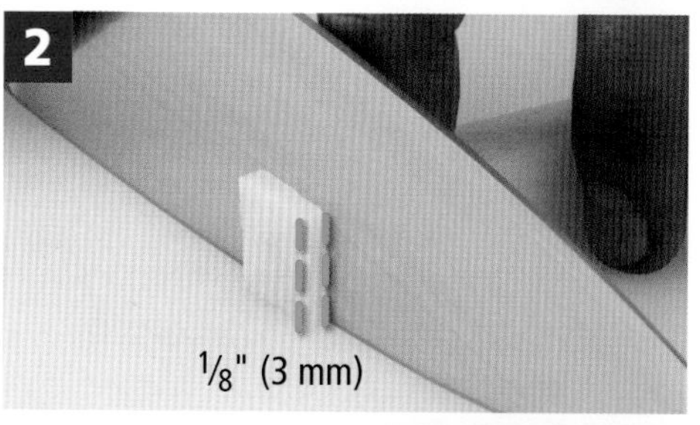

Position your guide fingers so that when the knife blade is flush against them, it is exactly $\frac{1}{8}$ inch (3 mm) in from the end. Cut straight down.

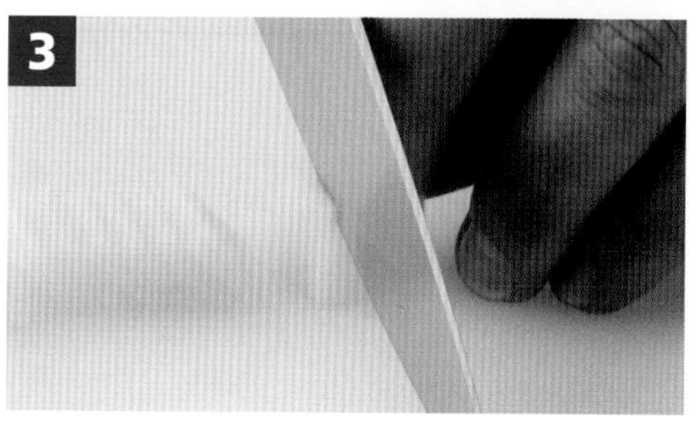

Repeat step 2 until the entire baton is cut into paysannes.

The Lozenge Cut

The lozenge cut is a diamond shape whose measurements are roughly $\frac{1}{2}$ by $\frac{1}{2}$ by $\frac{1}{8}$ inch (12 by 12 by 3 mm). It's similar to the paysanne cut (see page 106), but because of its angles it is produced slightly differently. Once again we'll use a potato for practice, though this cut can be used on any number of vegetables.

RECOMMENDED KNIFE

Chef's knife or Santoku

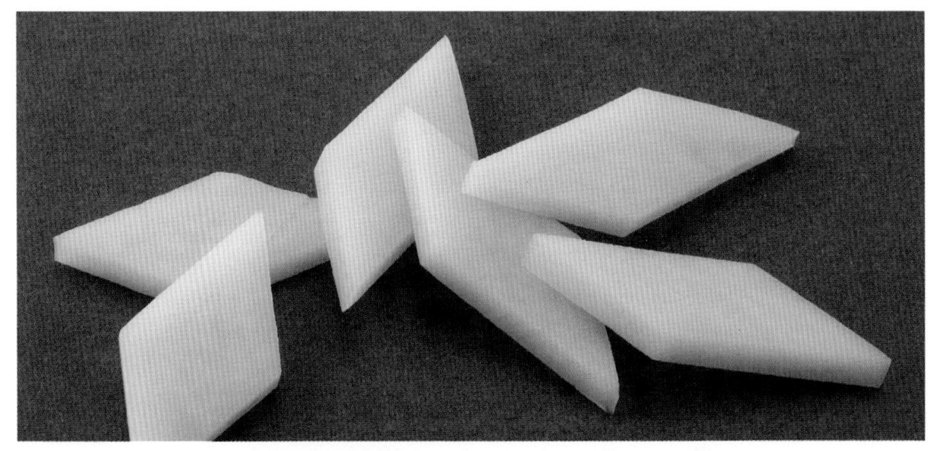

Potato lozenges

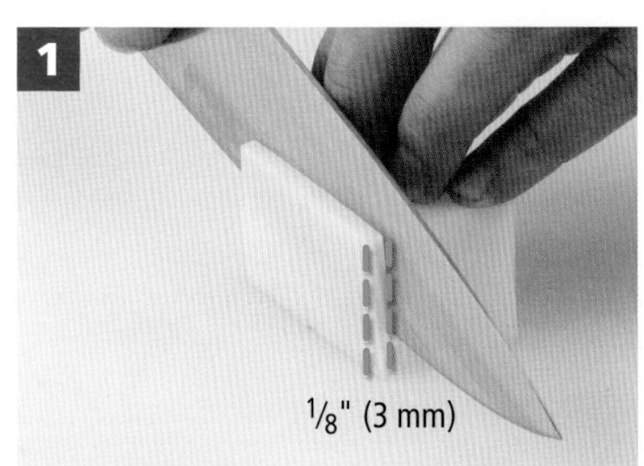

Start by squaring off the potato and cutting it into $\frac{1}{8}$-inch (3 mm) planks. (See pages 91–93, steps 1 to 9, but cut $\frac{1}{8}$-inch (3 mm) planks rather than $\frac{1}{4}$-inch (6 mm) planks.)

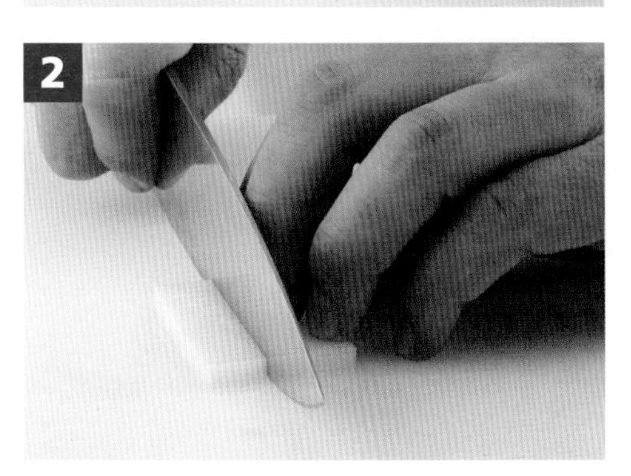

Lay one plank lengthwise on the cutting board and cut it into $\frac{1}{2}$-inch (12 mm) strips. (As you get better at this, you can stack several planks to make the work go more quickly.)

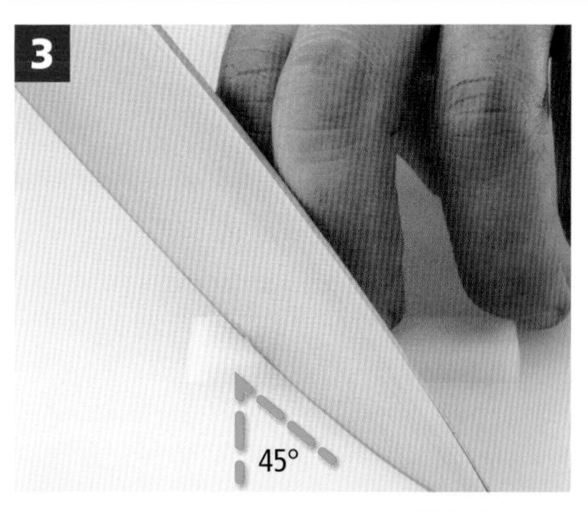

Starting with one ½-inch (12 mm) strip, place your guide fingers on top, close to one end, at a 45-degree angle. Your thumb, ring finger and pinky, rather than gripping the potato strip, will be off to the side, as necessitated by the angle of your guide fingers.

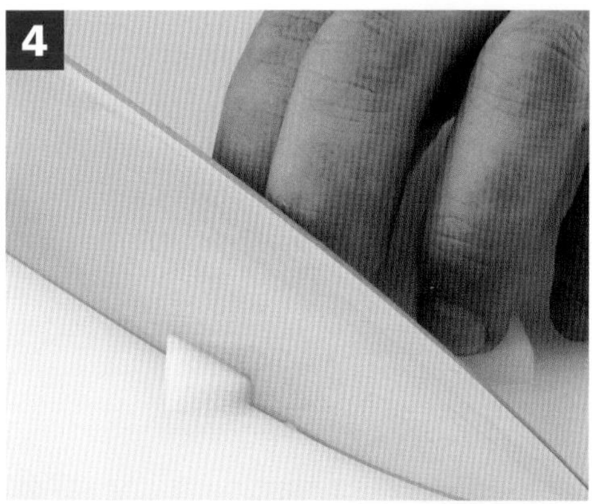

Cut a perfect triangle off the end of the strip. (This piece may be discarded or saved for scraps.)

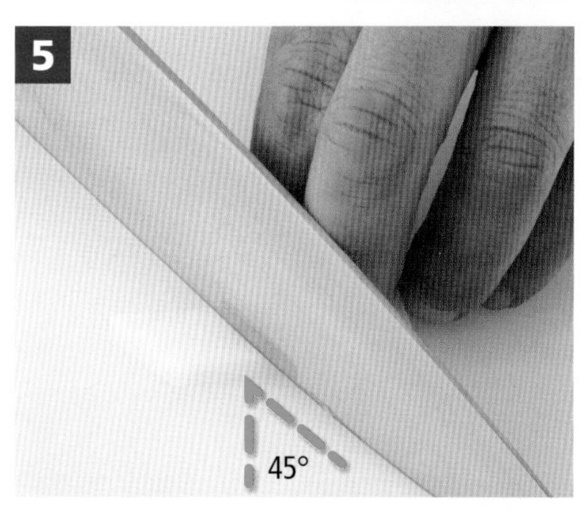

Keeping the knife blade flush against your guide fingers, move the knife back ½ inch (12 mm) and make another 45-degree cut.

Repeat step 4 until the entire strip has been cut into lozenges.

The Tourné Cut

This cut, a seven-sided barrel shape similar in appearance to an American football, is arguably the most challenging to create, and especially to do well. *Tourné* is French for "turned," and in this technique the vegetable is turned after each cut. Though you can do this cut with a paring knife, the curved shape of the tourné knife will make it easier to follow the arcs you are trying to cut.

RECOMMENDED KNIFE

Tourné knife or paring knife

The technique, which is similar to peeling a potato the "old school" way (page 206), can be used on any hard vegetable. Potatoes are the most common choice, but it will also work on carrots, beets, turnips and so on. We'll write the instructions using potatoes. For instructions on the knife grip, see page 85.

Because this cut is so challenging, you can expect the learning curve to be a bit steeper than for most of the other cuts. Try not to get frustrated; as you keep practicing, you'll get the hang of it.

Potato tourné

Practicing the Motion

Before you try the technique with a potato (or any other vegetable), we recommend practicing the motion with an egg.

1. Hold your guide hand with the palm up and the fingers relaxed and slightly curled. Rest the egg on the middle, ring and pinky fingers and support it with your thumb and index finger.

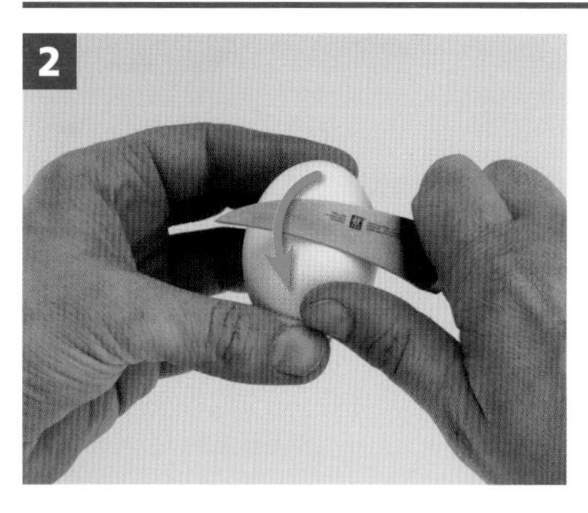

Place the thumb of your knife hand at the bottom of the egg, roughly perpendicular to the thumb of your guide hand, and place the knife blade near the top of the egg. Drag the knife down to your thumb, following the curve of the egg. Rotate the egg, raise the knife back to the top and repeat the motion.

Keep rotating and dragging the knife down until the motion begins to feel comfortable. This may take some time, so be patient.

Cutting a Tourné

With this technique, there's no need to peel the potato (or other vegetable) first; the peel will be cut away in the course of cutting the tourné.

Cut the potato into chunks roughly 2 inches (5 cm) long and 1 to 2 inches (2.5 to 5 cm) wide and thick. (If you're using a conical vegetable, such as a carrot, cut it into 2-inch/5 cm lengths.)

Rest a potato chunk on the index, middle and ring fingers of your guide hand and support it with your thumb.

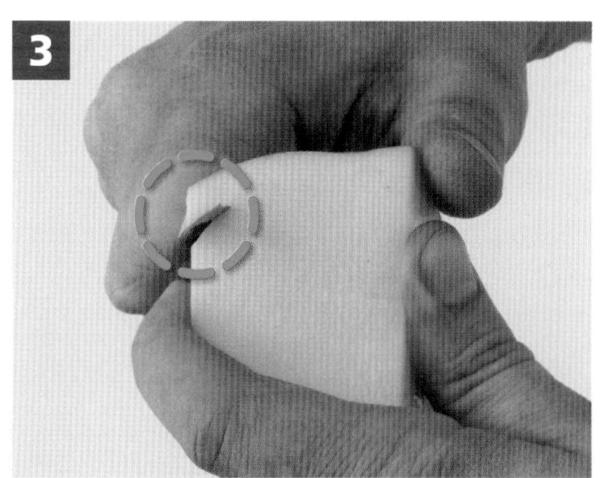

Knife just in front of center

Place the thumb of your knife hand at the bottom of the chunk, perpendicular to the thumb of your guide hand, and place the knife blade on the top of the chunk, cutting into the flesh just in front of the center of the chunk.

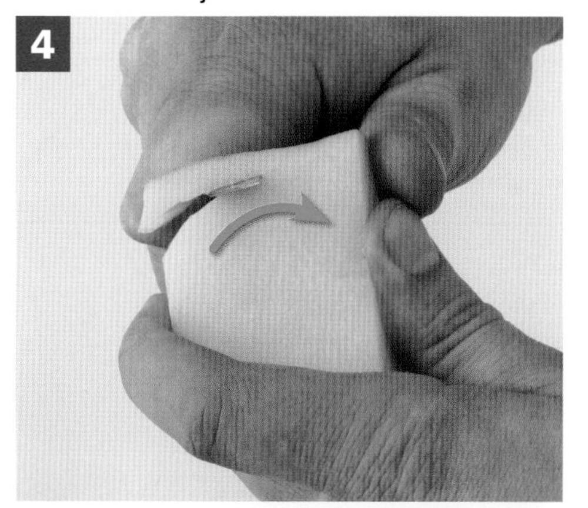

Notice that the blade is not perpendicular to the side of the potato chunk. Rather, the spine is tilted slightly back. This is because you're not going to be cutting straight down the potato. You'll be cutting in an arc, like you're following the shape of an egg. Think of the shape you're going for — a barrel with seven sides — and let that image inform your hand how to move.

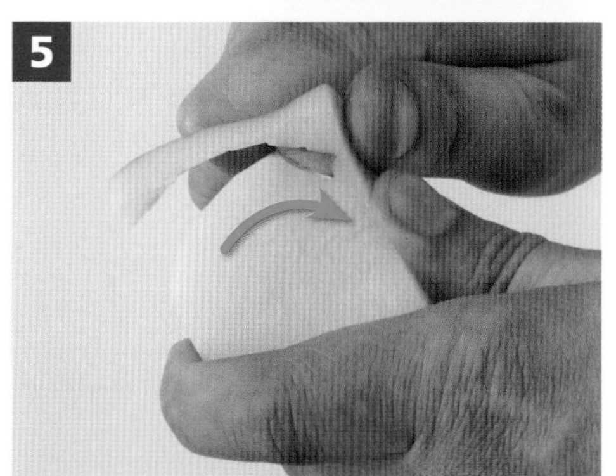

Tilt the edge of the blade out as you move it in an outward arc to the midpoint of the chunk, then tilt it in as you move it in an inward arc down to the bottom. By the time you reach the bottom, the knife should again be just in front of the center of the chunk.

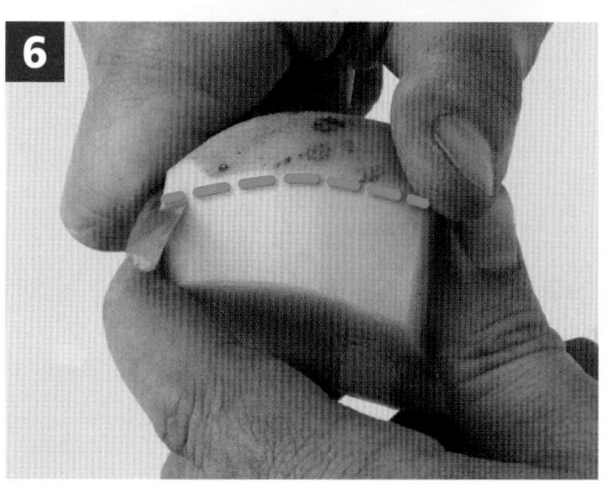

Use edge of previous cut as guide

Using the thumb and index finger of your guide hand, rotate the potato chunk so that the edge of the first cut is facing you. You'll use that edge as a guide for the next cut.

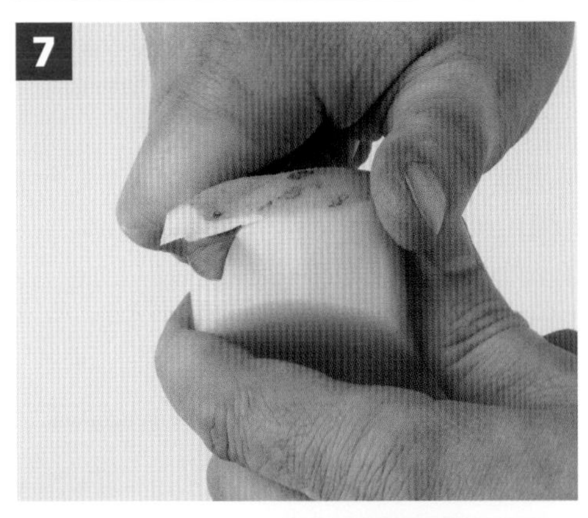

Place the blade back on top of the potato chunk, just in front of the center of the chunk.

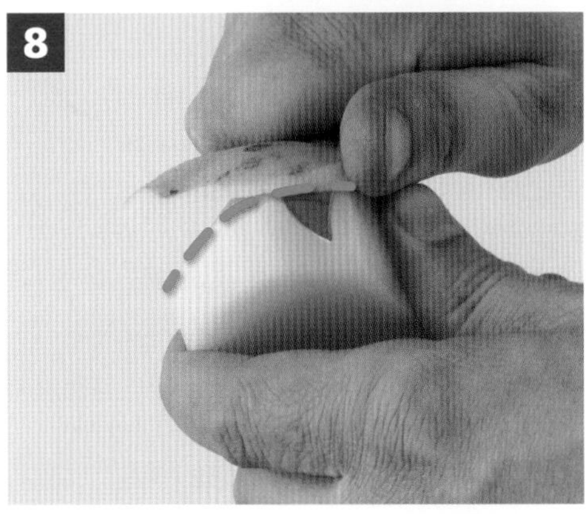

Use edge of previous cut as guide

Cut another arc as you did in step 5, using the edge of your previous cut as your guide for the edge of this new cut.

Repeat this process five more times, so that you end up with a seven-sided barrel shape.

Remember, the keys to this technique are practice and patience. Save the scraps and imperfect shapes you create, simmer them in water until they're tender and turn them into delicious mashed potatoes.

Things That Can Go Wrong

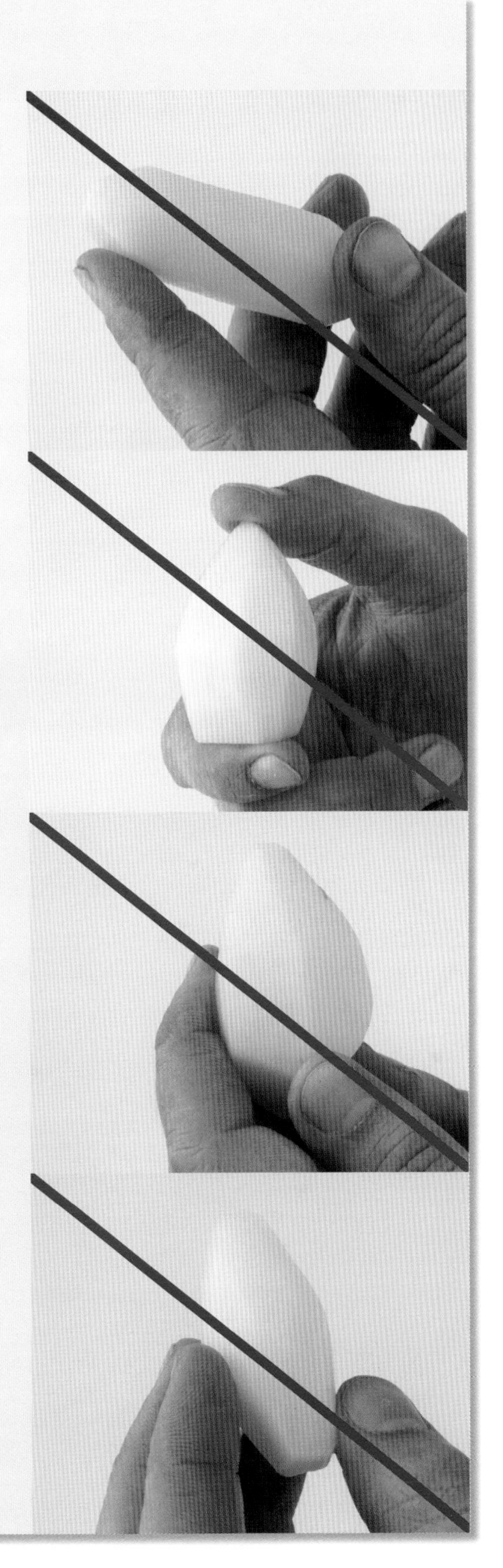

If you start too close to the front of the potato chunk at the top and end too close to the front of the chunk on the bottom, you'll wind up with ends that are too wide, and your tourné will look too cylindrical.

Even if you start just in front of the center at the top, you may at first have difficulty bringing the knife back to the center at the bottom. This will give your tourné a pear-shaped look, which is close, but no cigar.

If your cuts are too wide, you'll end up with too few sides.

If your cuts are too narrow, you'll end up with too many sides.

Chapter 4

Cutting Fruits and Vegetables

Some fruits and vegetables are not as easily turned into perfect sticks or dice because of their shape and structure. These items must be cut up using techniques designed just for them. In this chapter, we'll demonstrate the most common of these techniques. By the time you master them, you'll have an understanding of the relationship between vegetable structure and knife technique, and will be able to handle any unusual item with confidence.

Apples

The techniques for cutting apples into slices, sticks and dice are fairly straightforward, but of course, with apples, you have the added complication of the core, which must be removed before you start cutting. In addition, many recipes specify peeling the apple, so we've given you instructions for that, too.

Peeling an Apple

Because the peel of an apple is edible, it is not always necessary to remove it before coring and chopping. However, if you choose to do so, it should be done first. Use a large knife to cut off the ends, after which you can use either a paring knife or a peeler to remove the peel. In our instructions, we'll use a paring knife, but a peeler can be used in the same way.

RECOMMENDED TOOLS

Chef's knife or Santoku; paring knife, tourné knife or peeler

1 Set the apple on its side, with the top facing your knife hand. Using the chef's knife or Santoku, cut off a thin piece from the top.

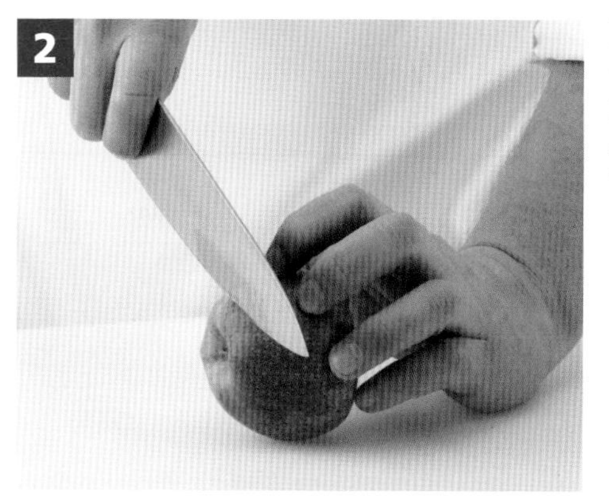

2 Rotate the apple so that the bottom is facing your knife hand. Cut off a thin piece from the bottom.

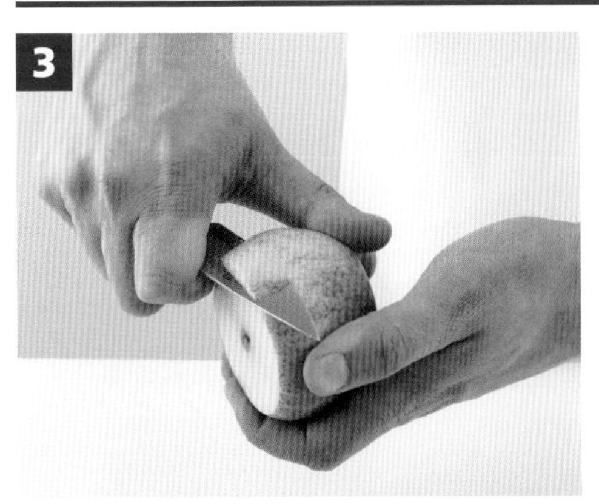

Hold the paring knife in the paring grip (see page 85). Hold the apple in your guide hand. Rest the thumb of your knife hand at the bottom of the apple and place the blade at the top. Draw the knife toward your thumb, just underneath the apple peel, to remove a thin slice of peel.

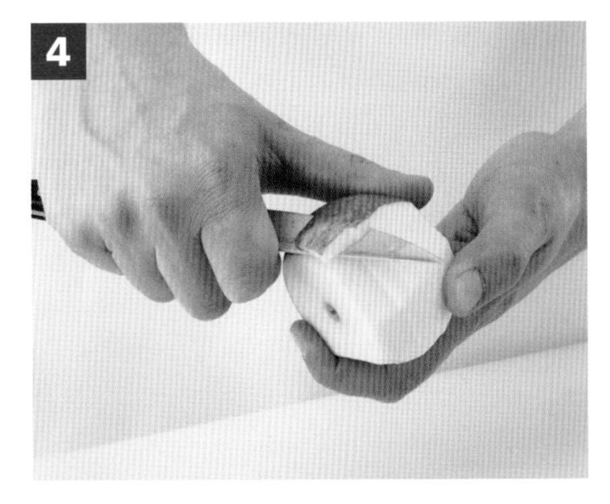

Rotate the apple and repeat step 3 until the apple is completely peeled.

You can also use a paring knife to peel the skin off an apple in one piece by working the knife under the skin in a spiral starting from the top of the apple down to the bottom.

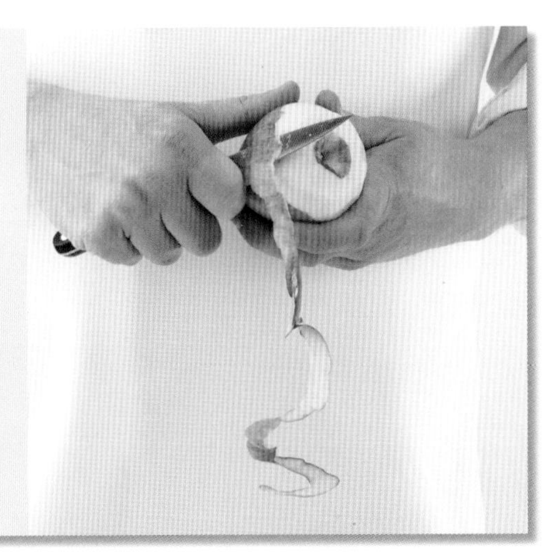

Removing the Core (Fast Method)

Choose this method over the tidy method (page 119) if time is of the essence and you don't mind ending up with pieces of different sizes.

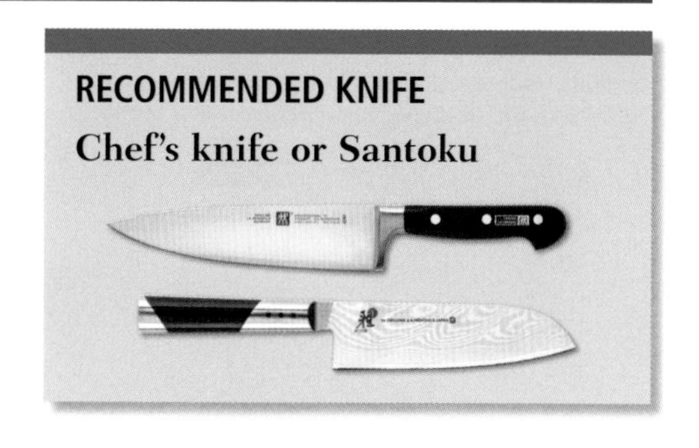

RECOMMENDED KNIFE

Chef's knife or Santoku

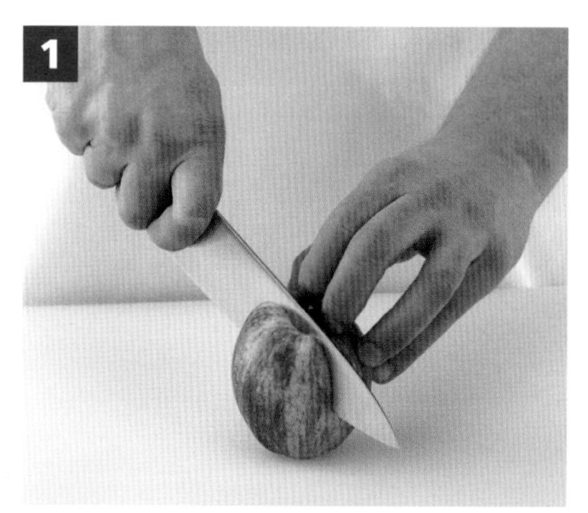

1 Place the apple right side up on the cutting board and hold it with your guide hand in the claw position. Place the knife blade about 1/2 inch (12 mm) from the center — the approximate radius of the core — and flush against your guide fingers. Cut straight down.

2 Rotate the apple 180 degrees and make a second cut, parallel to the first, on the other side.

3 Lay the apple on one of the cut sides, place the blade about 1/2 inch (12 mm) from the center on your knife-hand side and cut off the third side.

Rotate the apple 180 degrees and repeat step 3 to cut off the fourth side.

You now have two large pieces and two smaller pieces, along with a box that holds the core. Because the core itself is not rectangular, you will be wasting a bit of the apple, but the amount of waste is minimal and the speed at which these cuts can be made more than makes up for the loss. Anyway, as a reward you can eat the flesh off the core while you cook.

Removing the Core (Tidy Method)

Choose this method over the fast method (page 118) if you want to end up with four pieces of the same size.

RECOMMENDED KNIVES

Chef's knife or Santoku; paring knife or tourné knife

Set the apple right side up on the cutting board and hold it with your guide hand in the claw position, just to the side of center. Place the blade of the chef's knife right in the center, pressed firmly against your guide fingers.

Cut straight down through the apple to divide it in half.

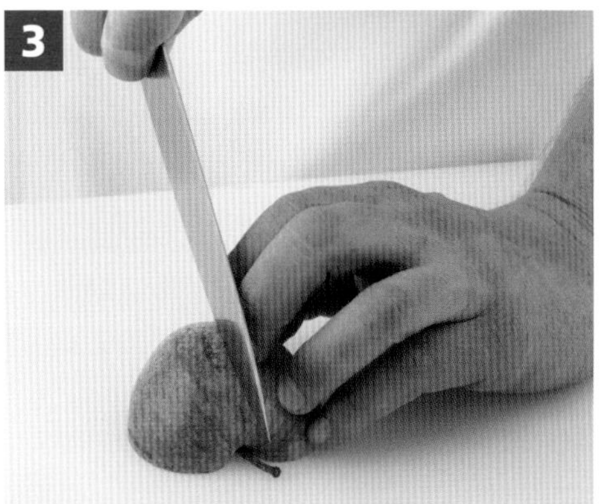

Lay one half cut side down, with the top or bottom pointing toward you. Steady it with your guide hand in the claw position, just to the side of center. Place the blade right in the center, pressed firmly against your guide fingers.

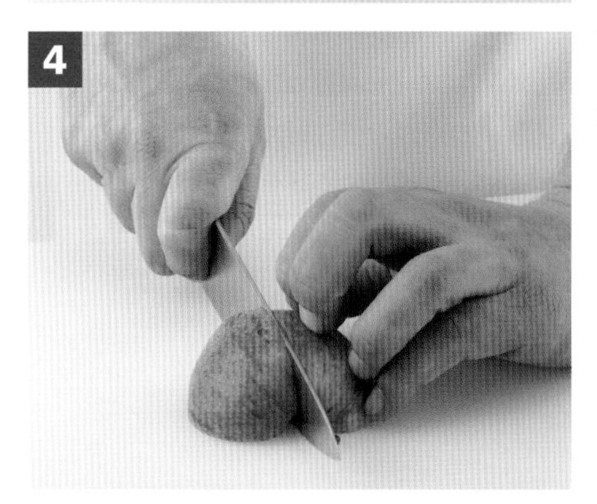

Cut straight down to divide the apple half into two equal pieces.

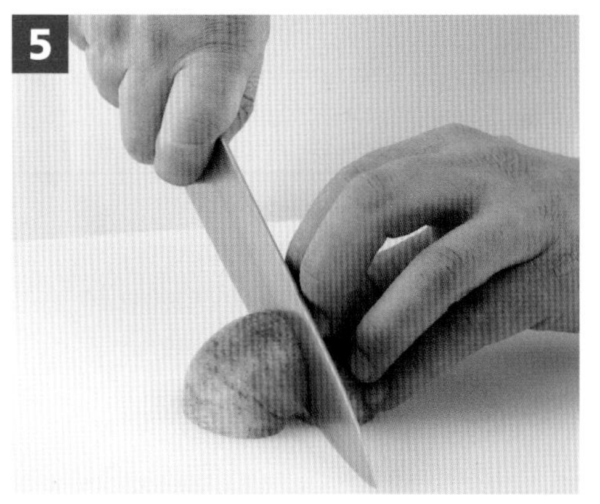

Repeat steps 3 and 4 with the other apple half. You now have four quarters of the same size, with cut sides that form a perfect 90-degree angle.

Hold one apple quarter in your guide hand, with the corner facing you. Place your thumb on one side and your guide fingers on the other.

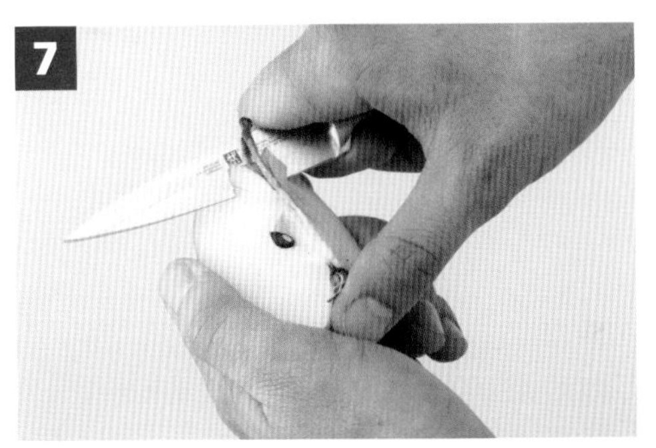

Hold your paring knife in the paring grip (see page 85). Place the blade on the top of the corner and your knife-hand thumb on the bottom of the corner.

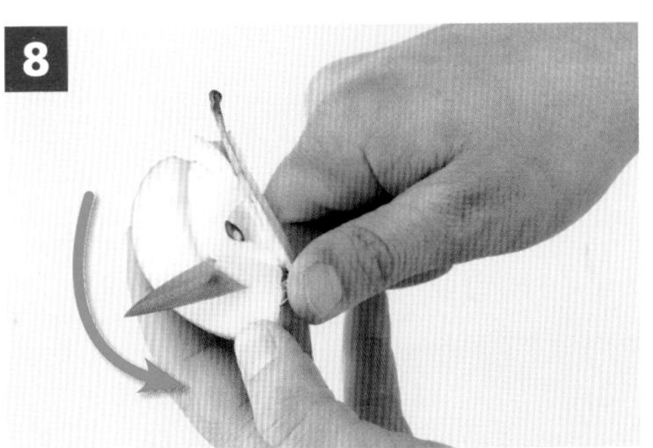

To cut away the core, draw the blade down to your knife-hand thumb, cutting in toward the center of the apple and back out in an even arc.

Repeat steps 6 to 8 with the other three apple quarters.

To prevent your apple pieces from turning brown when they're exposed to the air, place them in a bowl of acidulated water as you cut them. Use a mixture of 1 part lemon juice to 4 parts water.

Cutting Slices

The apple's structure — crisp, with plenty of juice to lubricate the knife so it doesn't stick — makes it the perfect candidate for the chopping technique (see page 81). So even though you're cutting slices, you're actually chopping!

The instructions below assume that you have already cored the apple using the fast method (see page 118) and will be using one of the large pieces created in that process. You can, of course, cut the other three pieces the same way.

RECOMMENDED KNIFE

Chef's knife or Santoku

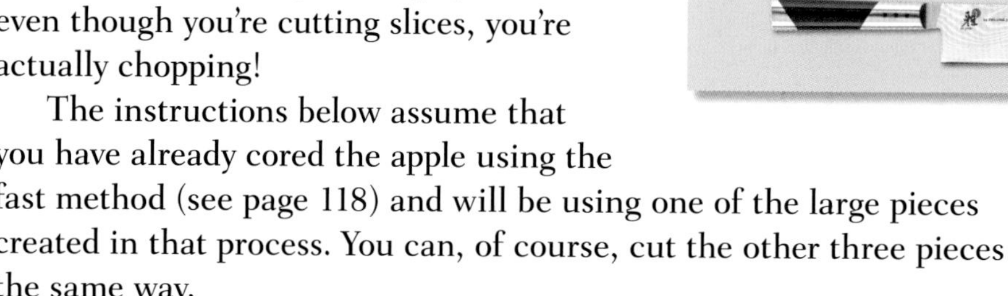

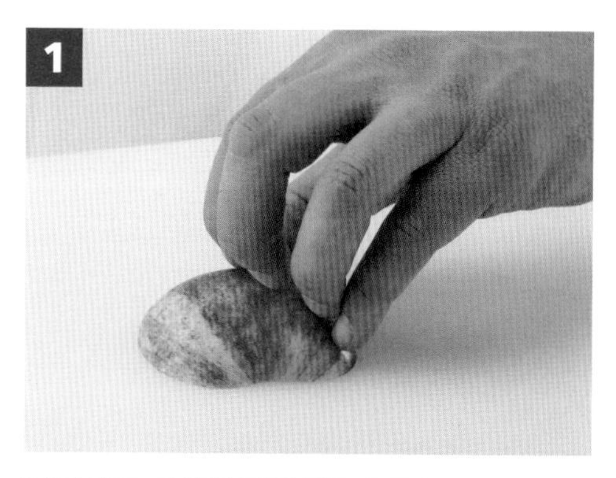

1. Place one of the two large apple pieces on the board, cut side down. Steady it with your guide hand in the claw position.

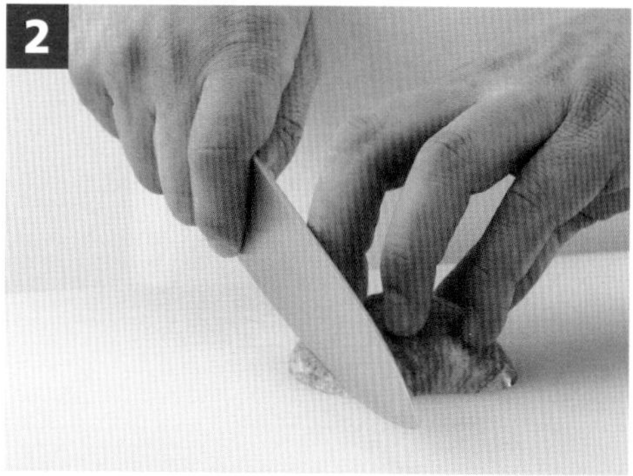

2. Place the knife blade flush against your guide fingers and cut straight down to create your first slice.

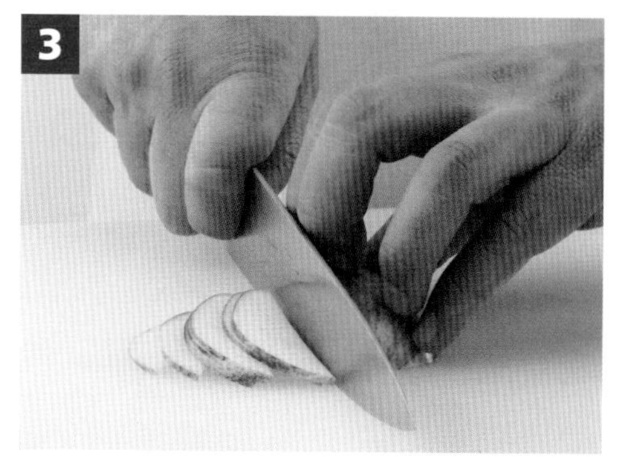

3. Keeping the blade against your guide fingers, move them back slightly and cut off another slice.

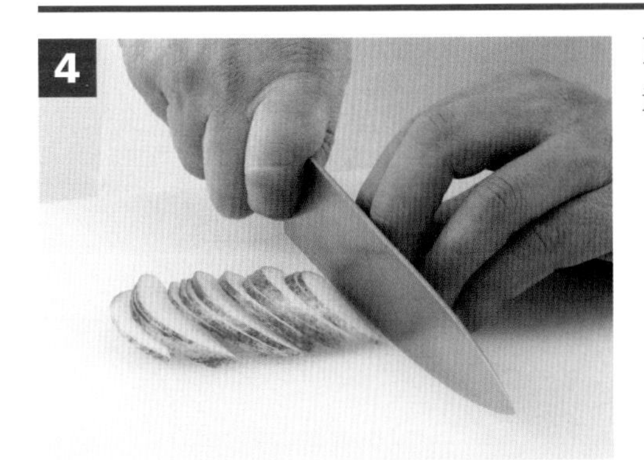

4 Repeat step 3 until the entire apple piece is cut into slices.

You can also cut an apple into slices using the fan method described for an avocado on page 137.

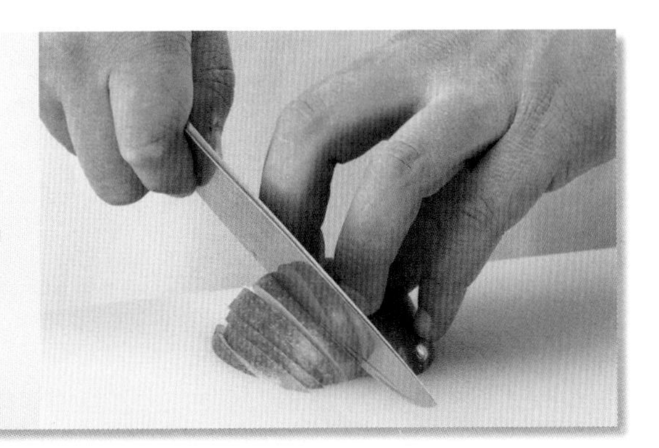

Cutting Sticks and Dice

RECOMMENDED KNIFE

Chef's knife or Santoku

Because an apple slice has a rounded edge, it's not feasible to cut it into a box shape, as we do with potatoes and other vegetables (see page 91). Thus, the sticks we cut from our apple slices will end up being different lengths. Don't worry about it; even the top chefs accept this constraint.

Work with one apple slice at a time until you feel comfortable with the technique. At that point, you can start stacking some of the slices to increase your efficiency.

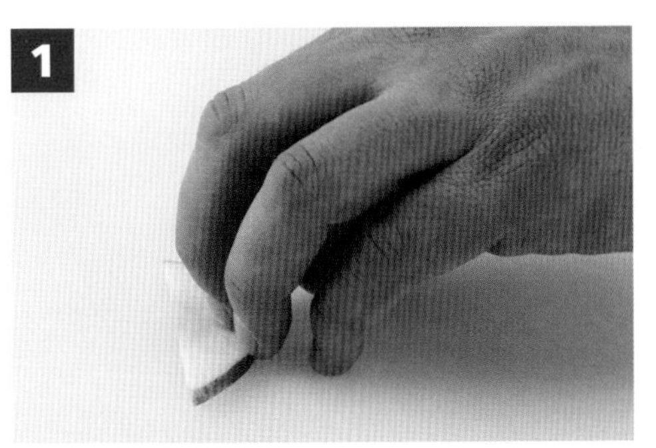

1 To cut sticks, lay an apple slice on the board, with the straight edge facing your knife hand. Steady it with your guide hand in the claw position.

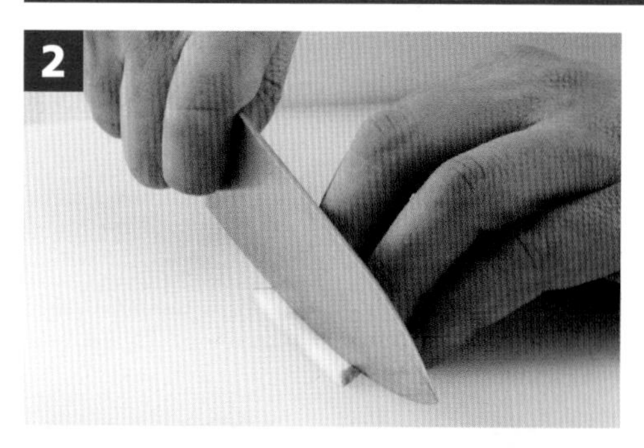

Place the knife blade flush against your guide fingers. Make sure the distance from the edge of the slice to your knife is the same as the thickness of the slice. Cut straight down to create your first stick.

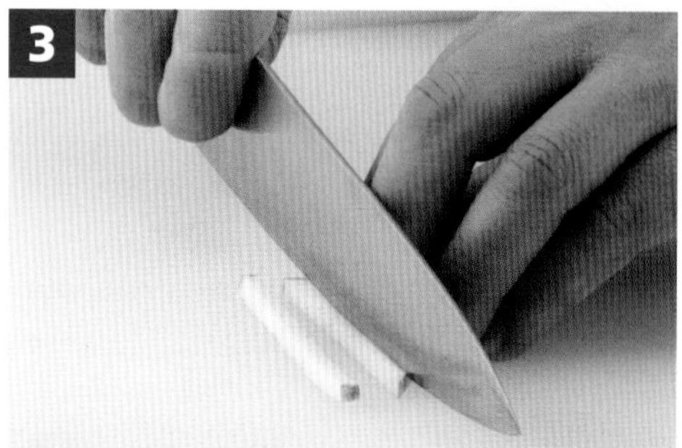

Keeping the blade against your guide fingers, move them back the appropriate amount and cut off another stick.

Repeat step 3 until the entire apple slice is cut into sticks.

If your apple slices are ½ inch (12 mm) thick, cut ½-inch (12 mm) strips; that way, each stick will have a perfect square at each end.

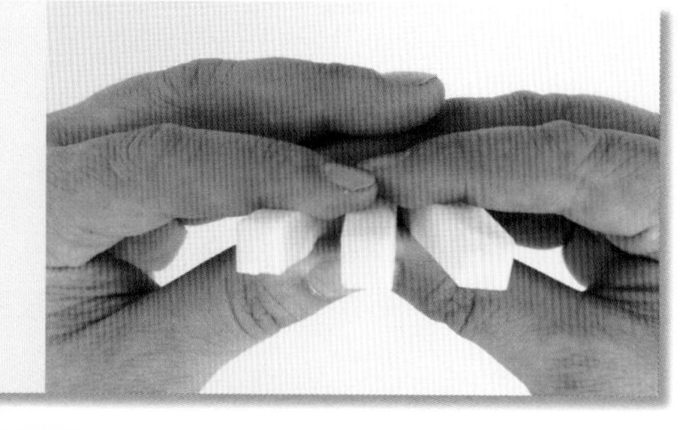

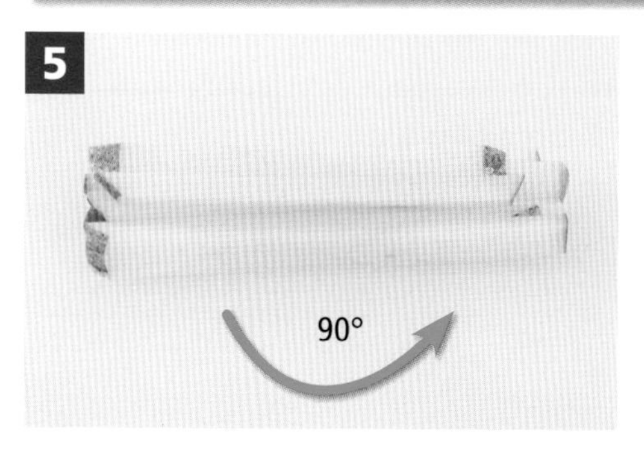

To cut dice, gather the sticks into a neat pile, then rotate them 90 degrees.

Steady the sticks with your guide hand in the claw position. Place the knife blade flush against your guide fingers. Make sure the distance from the edge of the sticks to your knife is the same as the width of a stick. Cut straight down to create your first set of dice.

Keeping the blade against your guide fingers, move them back the appropriate amount and cut off another set of dice.

Repeat step 7 until the sticks are completely cut into dice.

Do the Ripe Thing

Throughout this book, we will be teaching you to cut fruits and vegetables into uniform shapes that both look attractive and, more importantly, cook evenly. One way to make this task easier is to purchase fruits and vegetables that are uniform in shape and size. Also, try to buy produce when it is in season and ripe (or hold on to it until it's ripe). This will make cutting easier, as the item will have its optimal texture.

Artichokes

Artichokes are a challenge because of the sharp points on the ends of the leaves. Once you trim those away, however, the base of the leaves and the artichoke heart make for wonderful eating.

The first step is to hold the artichoke in your guide hand and carefully pull off the outer layer of leaves with your knife hand. Next, you must decide whether or not you want to cut off the stem. For some dishes — especially when you're using baby artichokes or cutting the artichoke in half lengthwise, as for grilling — you may want to leave the stem on. If you do, trim off the end, then peel the stem with a paring knife or peeler (see page 128, steps 2 and 3).

If you want to remove the stem, allowing the artichoke to sit upright on the plate, simply lay the artichoke on the cutting board, with the stem facing your knife hand. Steady the artichoke with your guide hand and use a chef's knife to cut away the stem at the base of the artichoke.

Preparing an Artichoke with Leaves On

Artichoke leaves make a delicious and fun appetizer. Steam the artichokes and serve with a dipping sauce. To eat, pull off the leaves and scrape the flesh from the heart with your teeth.

RECOMMENDED TOOLS

Chef's knife or Santoku; kitchen shears

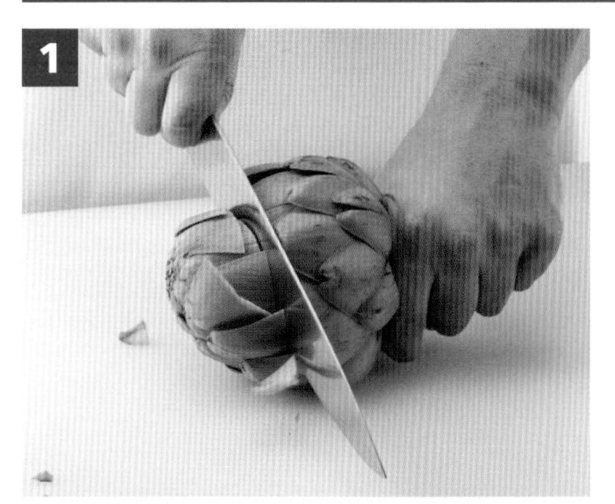

Lay the artichoke on the cutting board, with the top facing your knife hand. Steady it with your guide hand and use the chef's knife to cut away the top 2 inches (5 cm).

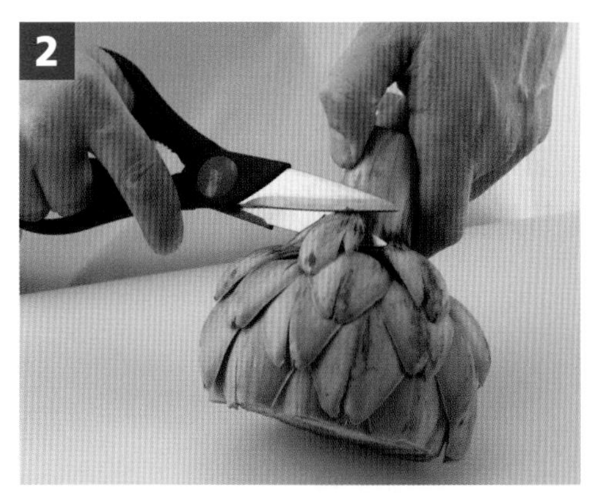

If any points remain, hold the artichoke in your guide hand and use the kitchen shears to snip away the sharp tips of the remaining leaves. The artichoke is now ready to cook.

Preparing an Artichoke Heart

Artichoke hearts can be shaved on a mandoline and tossed raw with a vinaigrette, or cut into dice and added to soups and sauces.

RECOMMENDED TOOLS

Chef's knife or Santoku; paring knife; spoon

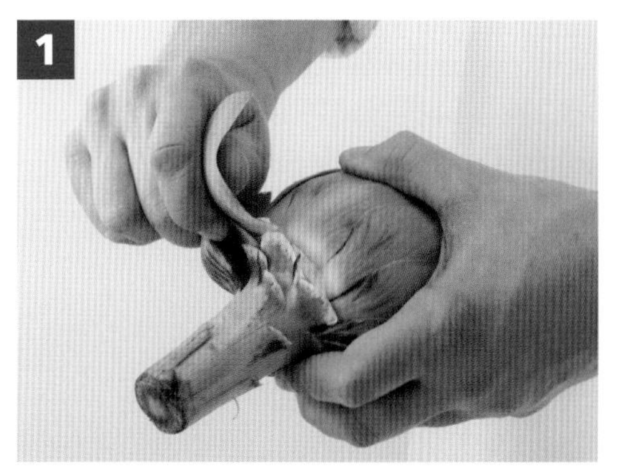

With your guide hand, hold the artichoke by the top. Use your knife hand to peel away the leaves around the bottom.

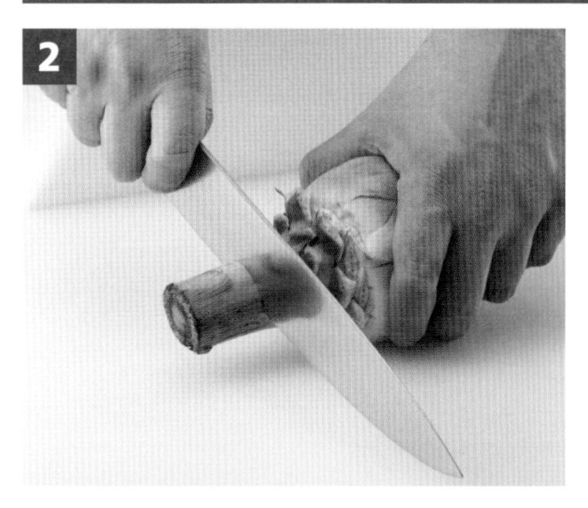

Lay the artichoke on the cutting board, with the stem facing your knife hand. Steady it with your guide hand and use the chef's knife to cut straight down to remove the bottom of the stem.

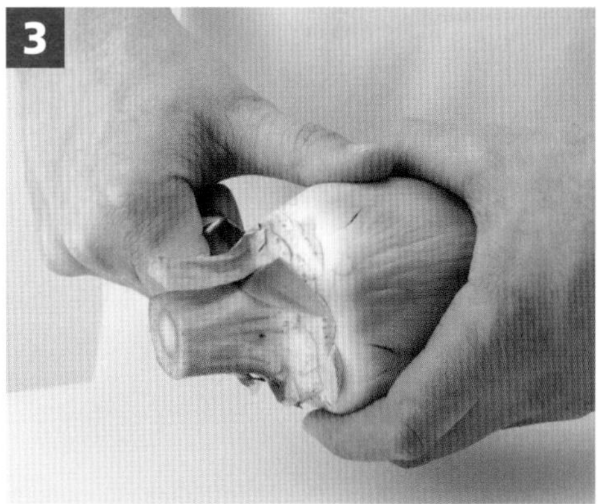

With your guide hand, hold the artichoke by the top. Hold the paring knife in the paring grip (see page 85). Peel the outside of the stem, keeping your knife-hand thumb anchored on the leaves.

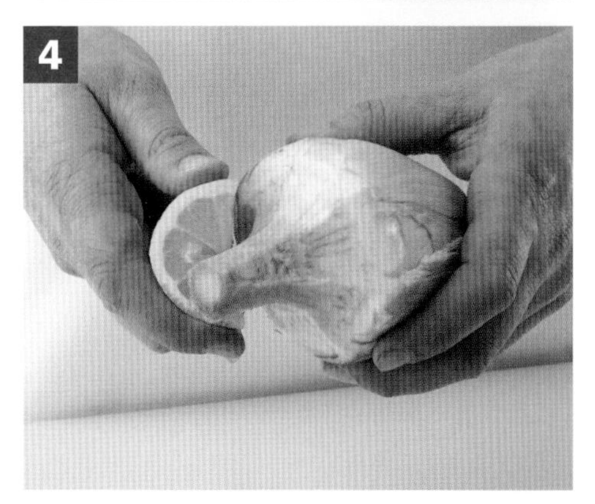

Rub the entire cut surface of the artichoke with a piece of lemon or put it in a bowl of acidulated water to keep it from oxidizing and turning brown.

Lay the artichoke on the board, with the top end facing your knife hand. Place the blade of the chef's knife on top of the artichoke, about 1 inch (2.5 cm) above the stem, and cut straight down to remove the remaining leaves.

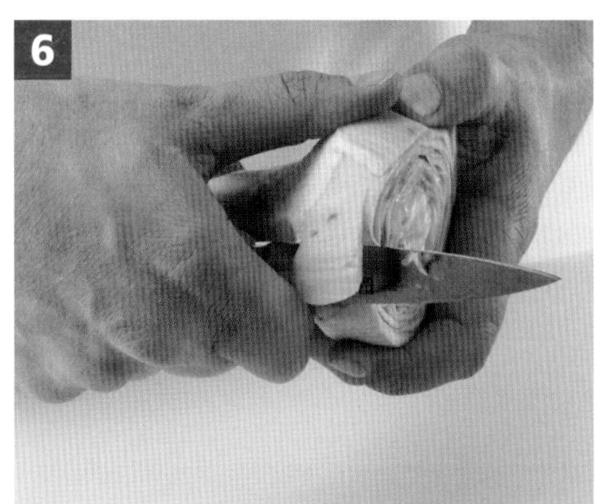

Hold the artichoke bottom in your guide hand, with the side facing you. Hold the paring knife in the paring grip (see page 85). Place the blade along the side and anchor your knife hand by placing your thumb as far around the top edge as you can reach.

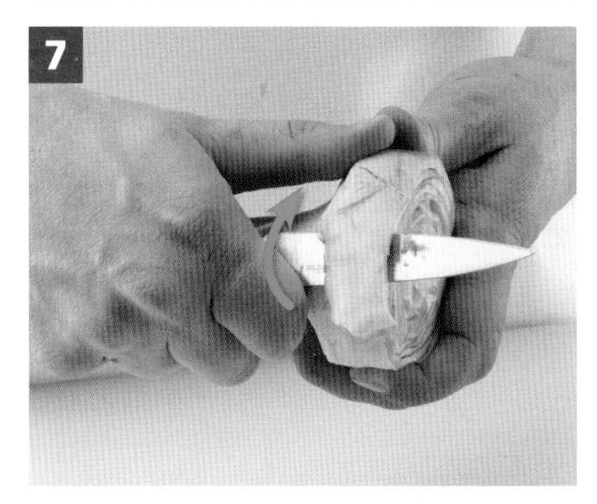

Draw the knife toward your thumb while simultaneously using your guide hand to rotate the artichoke into the blade, trimming off the skin around the entire edge.

Use the spoon to remove the purplish, feathery choke from the center. Discard the choke.

The artichoke heart is typically cut into halves or quarters for use.

Avocados

While there are many types of avocados, the most widely available variety is the Hass avocado, which has a dark green, pebbly peel that becomes almost black when the fruit is ripe. Unlike many other fruits, avocados are peeled after they're cut in half and the seed removed.

Pitting an Avocado

To remove the seed, we take advantage of its relative hardness and its location in the center of the avocado.

RECOMMENDED KNIFE

Chef's knife or Santoku

1. Hold the avocado in your guide hand with the tapered end between your thumb and index finger and the wider end resting in your palm.

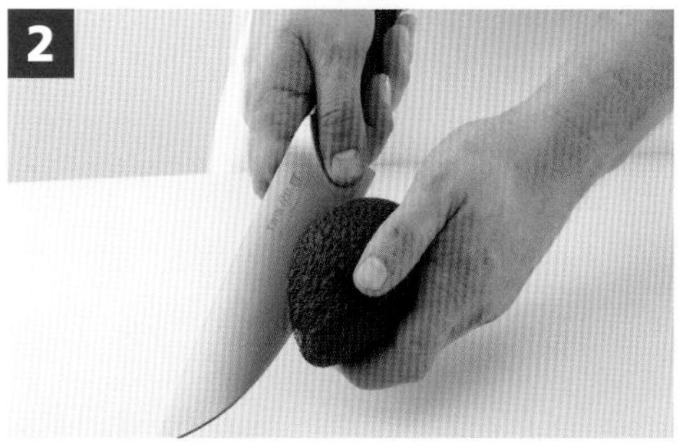

2. Place the knife blade along the vertical center of the avocado. Cut through the skin and into the flesh until the blade hits the seed.

3. Maintaining constant contact between the blade and the seed, use your guide hand to rotate the top of the avocado into the blade, cutting through the skin and flesh.

4

Continue rotating the avocado into the knife until you have turned it 360 degrees and cut all the way around the seed.

5

Set your knife down and grab one side of the avocado in each hand. Twist the halves in opposite directions to loosen one of them from the seed.

6

Pull the two halves apart. One half will have the seed still attached; the other will have a crater where the seed was resting.

7

To remove the seed, hold that half in your guide hand, skin side down, with the tapered end between your thumb and index finger and the wider end in your palm.

8

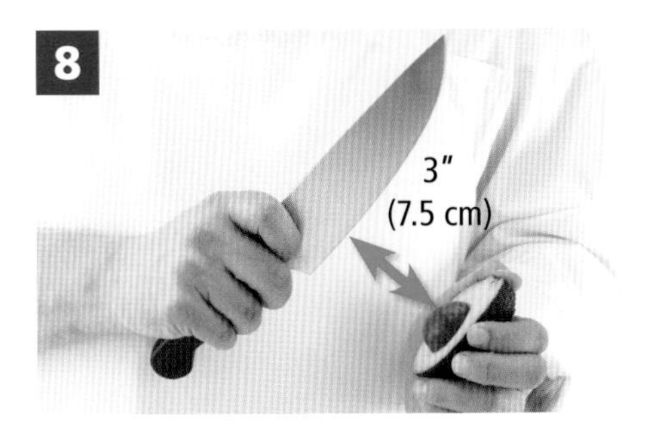

Hold the knife about 3 inches (7.5 cm) above the seed, positioning the blade so that the heel is directly over the center of the seed.

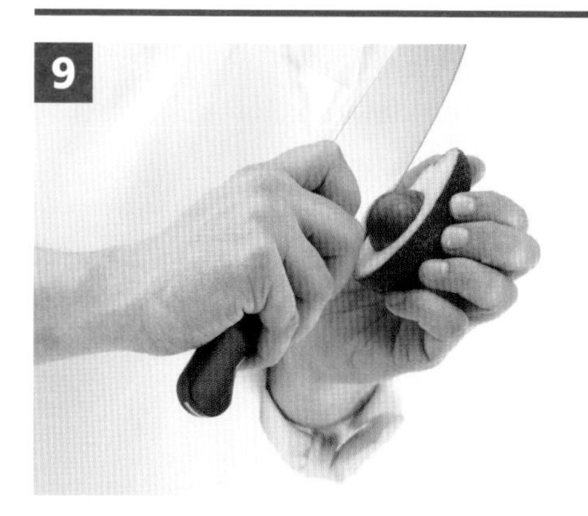

Moving from the wrist, make a light chopping motion down onto the seed, burying the blade $\frac{1}{4}$ to $\frac{1}{2}$ inch (6 to 12 mm) into the seed.

When we say a "light" chopping motion, we mean a *light* chopping motion. You don't want to cut through the seed, just embed the blade in it. If you hit the seed too hard, the knife might pass all the way through to the flesh of the avocado, through the flesh to the skin, through the skin to your fingers and, in the worst-case scenario, through your fingers. To figure out the appropriate amount of force, start by bringing the knife down so lightly that it bounces off the seed, then gradually increase your force until the knife is embedded in the seed.

Twist the knife and the avocado in opposite directions to loosen the seed.

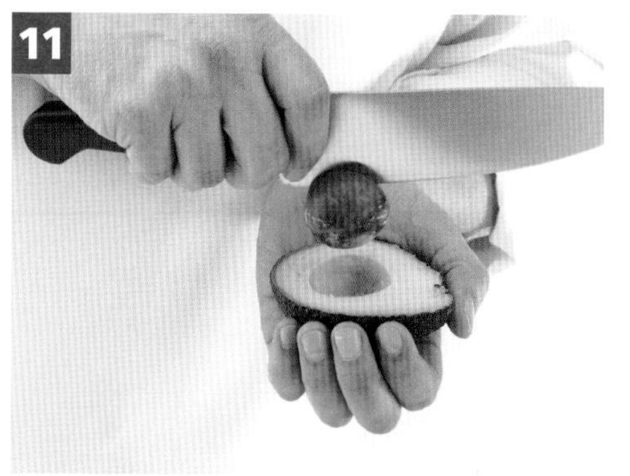

Pull the seed out, still attached to the knife. Wrap your guide hand with a dish towel and carefully pull the slippery seed off the blade.

Peeling an Avocado

The skin of an avocado is not edible, so it must be removed. There are a number of ways to do this (you can even use a spoon!), all of them equally effective. We'll show you our favorite.

RECOMMENDED KNIFE

Paring knife

1

Hold an avocado half in your guide hand and cut a small nick in one edge of the skin. Place the knife blade beneath the flap of skin you've just cut and lift it slightly.

2

Grab the skin flap between the blade and the thumb of your knife hand and lift it, pulling your knife hand back gradually to peel the skin away from the flesh.

3

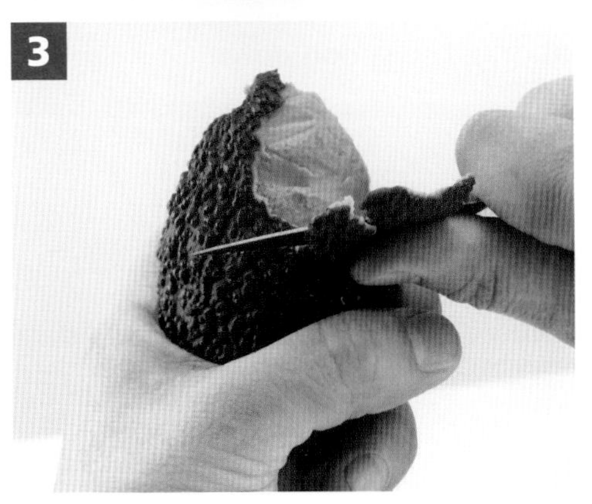

As you peel, the skin will tear and you'll have to start over again, so repeat steps 1 and 2 as many times as you need to until the avocado is peeled.

Using a Spoon to Peel an Avocado

1

Hold an avocado half in your guide hand with the tapered end between your thumb and index finger and the wider end resting in your palm. Slip the tip of the spoon under the skin at the top of the avocado and push it down between the skin and the flesh.

2

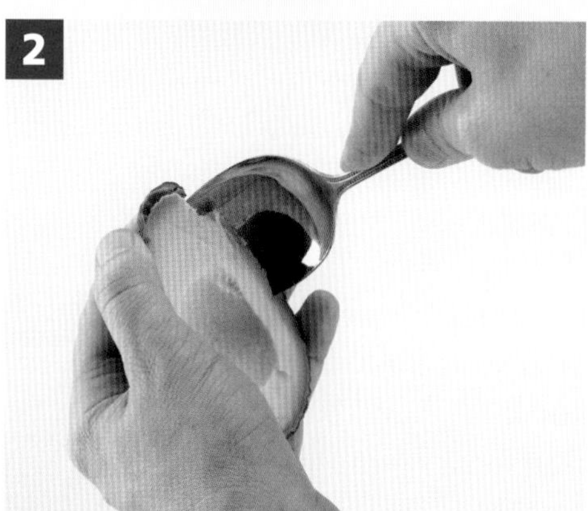

Rotate the spoon handle down so that it's at a 90-degree angle to the avocado.

3

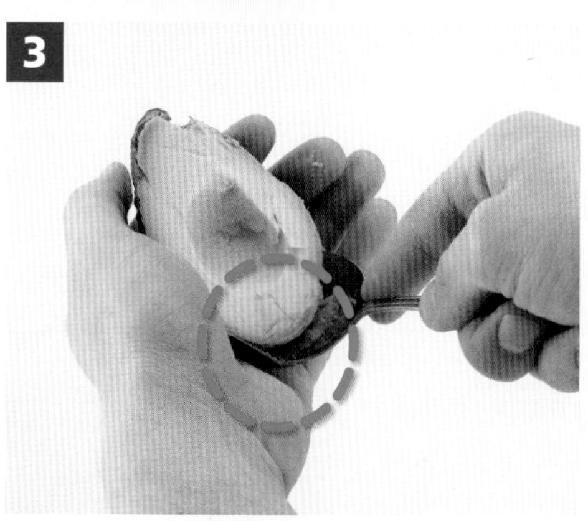

Spoon edge scrapes along skin

Drag the spoon toward you along the side of the avocado that's supported by your middle, ring and pinky fingers. Hold the spoon at an angle so that the edge scrapes against the inside of the skin as you drag the spoon down.

4

When you reach the bottom of the avocado, rotate it 180 degrees, so that the bottom ends up between your thumb and index finger. Keep the spoon between the skin and the flesh as you turn the avocado.

5

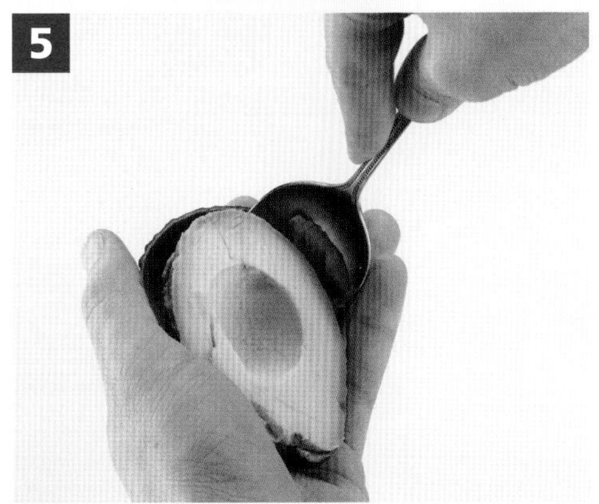

Drag the edge of the spoon around the wide end of the avocado and back toward you, freeing the remaining flesh.

6

With a little practice, the avocado flesh will come out in one piece, with nothing stuck to the skin. If there is much left on the skin, use your spoon to scrape it out.

Cutting Slices (Fast Method)

Avocado slices are great on sandwiches and salads. Whether you cut the slices the long way, the short way or on a diagonal is entirely up to you. Ask yourself, "What would be the most attractive and functional presentation of these slices?" and you can't go wrong.

RECOMMENDED KNIFE

Chef's knife or Santoku

Choose this method over the fan method (page 137) if time is of the essence and perfectly even slices are not required.

1 Place a peeled avocado half on the cutting board, cut side down. Steady the avocado with your guide hand in the claw position.

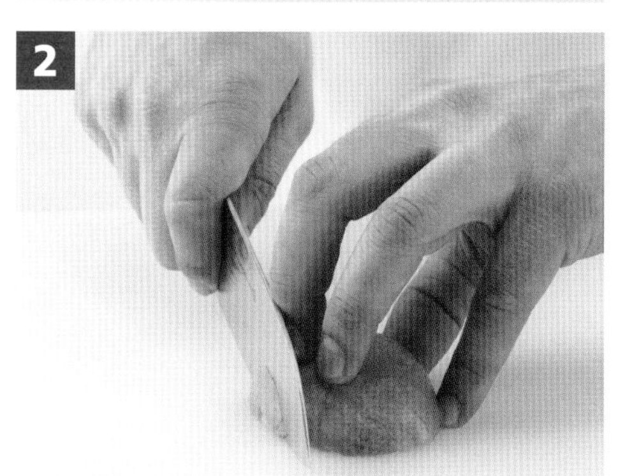

2 Place the knife blade flush against your guide fingers and cut straight down to create your first slice.

3 Keeping the blade against your guide fingers, move them back slightly and cut off another slice.

4

Repeat step 3 until the entire avocado half is cut into slices.

Cutting Slices (Fan Method)

If you want to cut perfectly even $1/4$-inch (6 mm) slices, choose this method over the fast method (page 136).

RECOMMENDED KNIFE

Chef's knife or Santoku

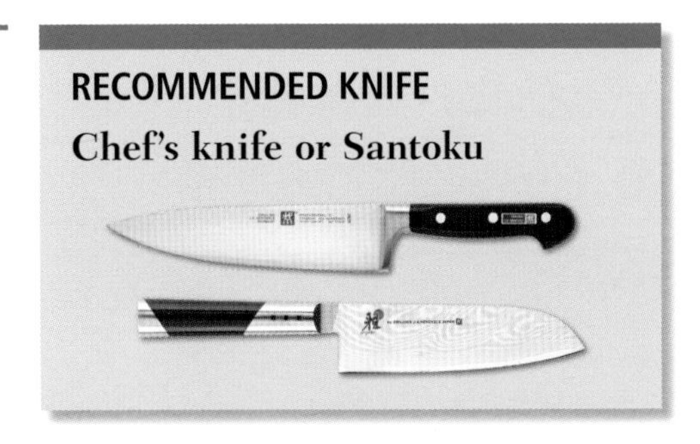

1

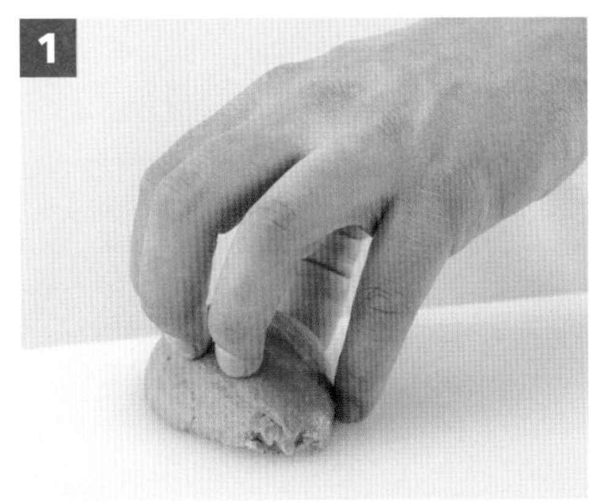

Place a peeled avocado half on the cutting board, cut side down, with the wide end facing you. The avocado should be fairly close to the edge of the cutting board nearest you. Steady the avocado with your guide hand.

The avocado should be close enough to the edge of the board that the knife handle is beyond the edge of the board, not directly above it. If you hold the handle directly above the board, you'll have a tendency to tilt the knife toward the tip, which will result in uneven slices.

Place the knife blade ¼ inch (6 mm) in from the knife-hand side and angle it so that the spine is just slightly higher than parallel to the board. Cut through the avocado to the point where the centerline of the avocado touches the board.

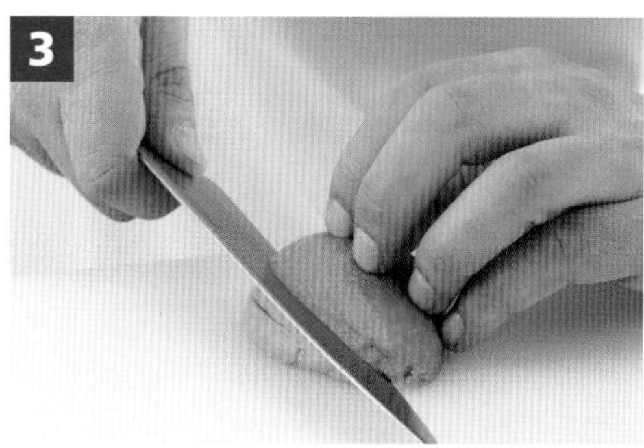

Move the knife up ¼ inch (6 mm) and increase the angle of the blade slightly. Cut through to the junction of the centerline and the board.

When deciding how much to increase the angle of your knife between cuts, keep in mind that the knife should be vertical by the time you get to the center of the avocado. Figure out how many ¼-inch (6 mm) slices you'll be making to that point and adjust your angle accordingly.

Repeat step 3, increasing the angle of the blade slightly after every cut, until you reach the center point of the avocado. The knife should be perpendicular to the board at this point. Cut straight down through the avocado.

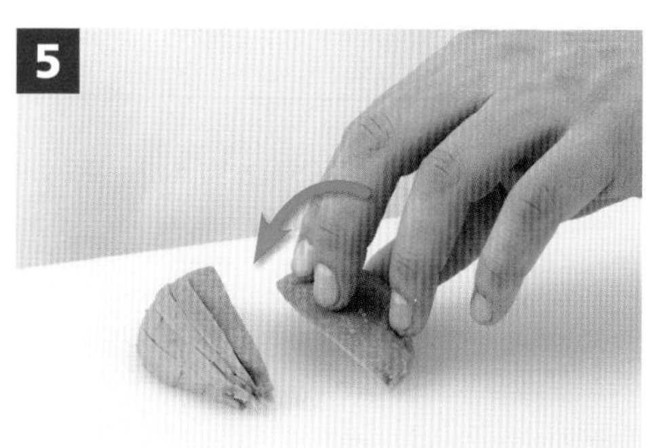

Move the slices you've already cut out of the way and push the remaining half over onto the new cut side.

Repeat steps 2 to 4 until the second half is cut into $\frac{1}{4}$-inch (6 mm) slices.

This technique for cutting even slices will work on most round fruits and vegetables.

Dicing a Peeled Avocado

Dicing a peeled avocado half is a more delicate operation than dicing an unpeeled one (see page 143), but it gives much more even results. If appearances are important to you, go with this technique.

Place a peeled avocado half on the board, cut side down, with the top facing your knife. The avocado should be fairly close to the edge of the cutting board nearest you. Steady the avocado with your guide hand.

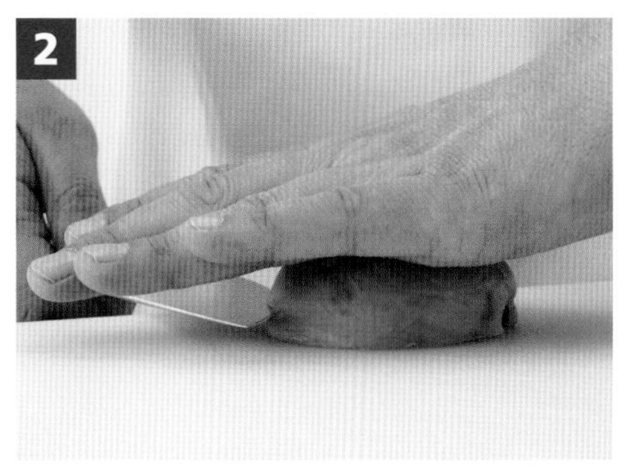

Hold the knife just above the board, with the blade parallel to the board.

The avocado should be close enough to the edge of the board that the knife handle is beyond the edge of the board, not directly above it. If you hold the handle directly above the board, you'll have a tendency to tilt the knife toward the tip, which will result in uneven slices. (Note: In the picture, the guide hand has been removed for clarity.)

3 Cut straight through the avocado horizontally at the desired height. Narrower cuts will produce smaller dice and wider cuts will produce larger dice. Leave the avocado slices stacked as you cut them.

4 Raise your knife and make a second horizontal cut the same width as the first. (Depending on the size of the avocado and the preferred size of your dice, you may not need to make this second cut, or you may make up to four horizontal cuts.)

5 When you have completed your horizontal cuts, place your guide hand on top of the stack in the claw position.

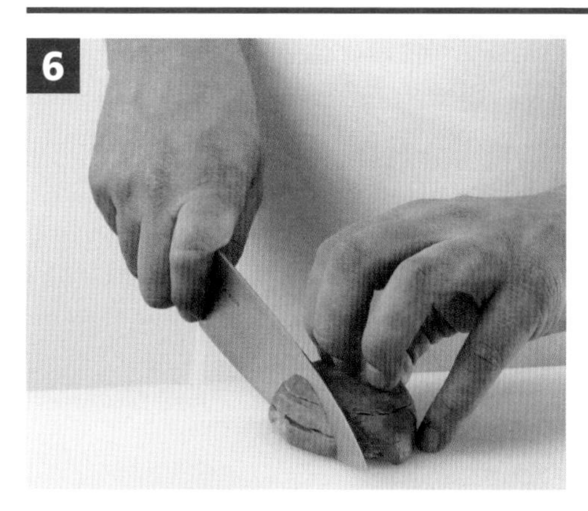

Place the knife blade against your guide fingers. Make sure the distance from the edge of the stack to your knife is the same as the width of your horizontal cuts. Cut straight down to create your first set of sticks.

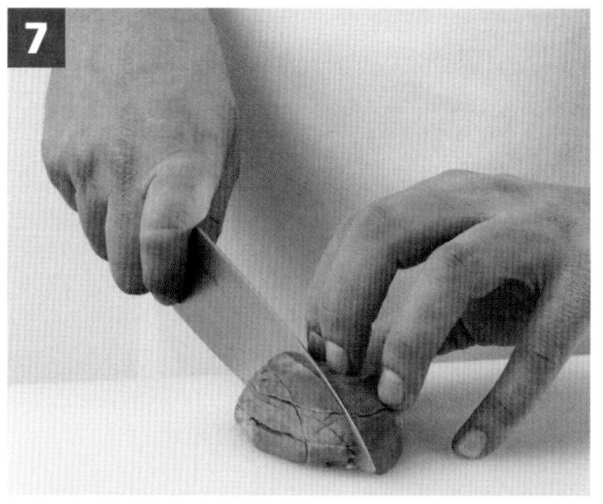

Keeping the blade against your guide fingers, move them back the appropriate amount and cut off another set of sticks.

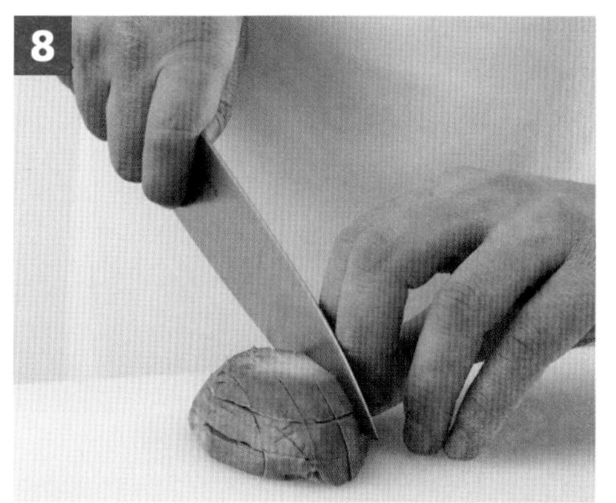

Repeat step 7 until the entire stack is cut into sticks.

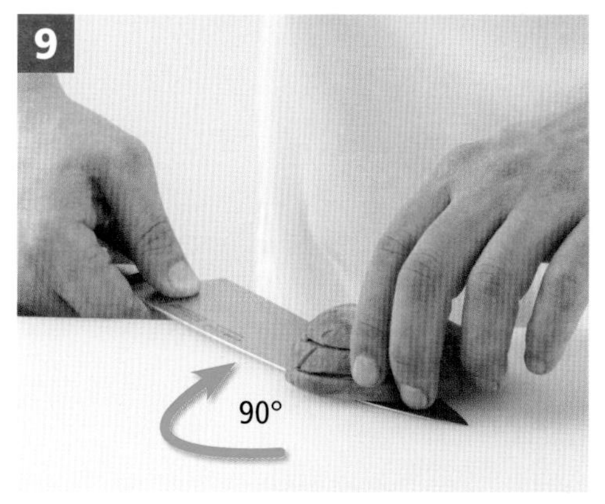

Slide your knife under the stack and use it to carefully rotate the sticks 90 degrees.

Steady the sticks with your hand in the claw position. Place the knife blade flush against your guide fingers. Make sure the distance from the edge of the sticks to your knife is the same as the width of a stick. Cut straight down to create your first set of dice.

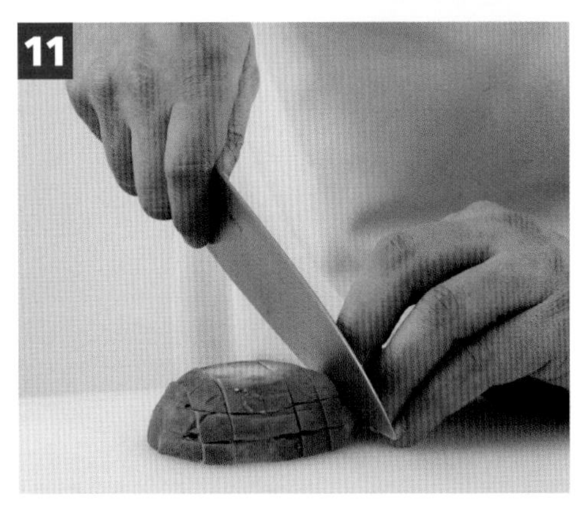

Keeping the blade against your guide fingers, move them back the appropriate amount and cut off another set of dice.

Repeat step 11 until the sticks are completely cut into dice.

Dicing an Unpeeled Avocado

Dicing an unpeeled avocado half is much quicker and easier than dicing a peeled one (see page 139), but the resulting dice are not as even. If that doesn't bother you, go with this technique.

1. Hold an unpeeled avocado half, skin side down, in your guide hand, with the tapered end between your thumb and index finger and the wider end resting in your palm. Make sure you have a clear view of the entire surface of the flesh.

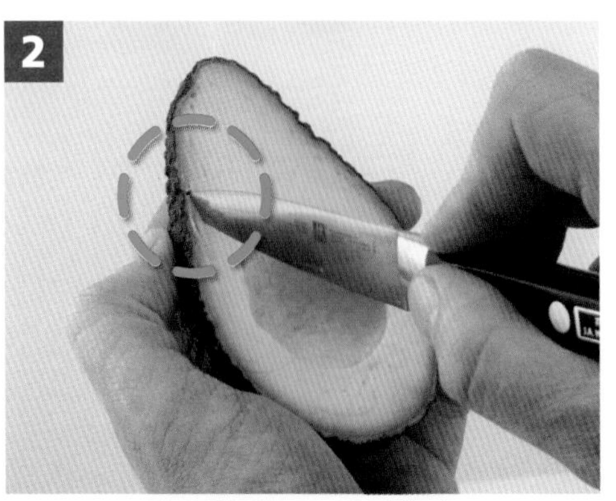

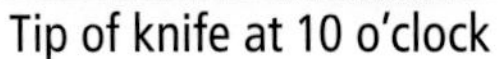
Tip of knife at 10 o'clock

2. Insert the tip of your knife into the flesh of the avocado at the 10 o'clock position (if the top of the avocado is 12 o'clock).

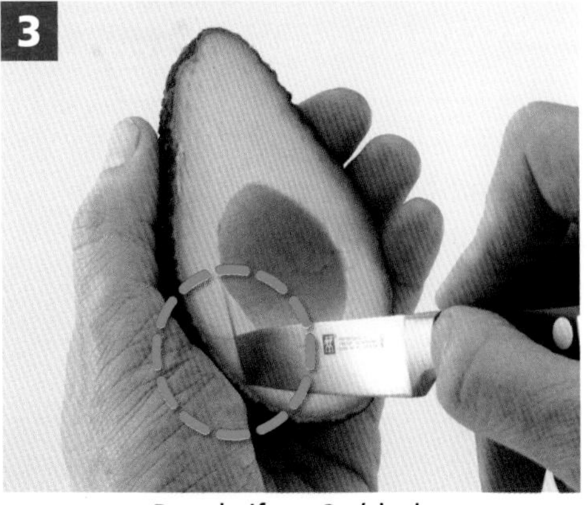
Drag knife to 8 o'clock

3. Drag the knife gently through the flesh on a straight line to 8 o'clock, allowing the point to just scratch along the inside of the skin at the bottom of the flesh.

4

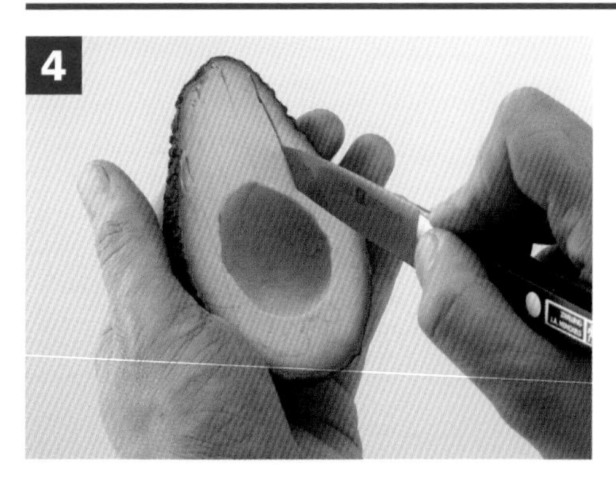

Use the same technique to make a series of evenly spaced parallel cuts through the avocado.

Remember, when you're cutting through the flesh, with every knife stroke you want to cut all the way down to, *but not through,* the avocado skin.

5

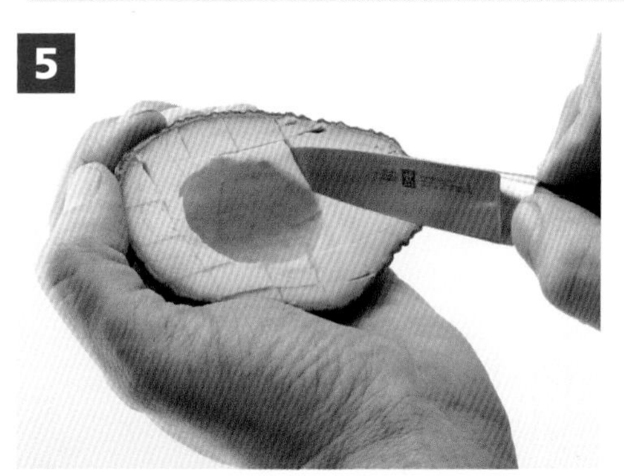

Rotate the avocado 90 degrees in your palm and cut another series of evenly spaced parallel lines.

6

The avocado should now be crisscrossed with a series of squares, and the squares should, in theory, all be the same size.

7

Holding the avocado in your guide hand, use a large spoon to scrape the dice out of the skin. (If you need more guidance, follow the directions for Using a Spoon to Peel an Avocado, page 134.)

Bell and Chile Peppers

Bell peppers (also called sweet peppers) and all chile peppers (jalapeño, serrano, habanero, etc.) are species in the capsicum genus, and they all have a similar internal structure, with a cluster of seeds attached to the stem and the ribs. Before you can cut a pepper into sticks or dice, you'll need to remove the core and the ribs.

Coring a Pepper

There are numerous ways to cut up peppers, but we love this one because it's so quick. In a nutshell, we simply cut off both ends, then place the knife inside the pepper and roll the pepper forward, cutting away the core and seeds in one easy motion. We'll demonstrate the technique with a green bell pepper, but it can be used on any large capsicum.

RECOMMENDED KNIFE

Chef's knife or Santoku

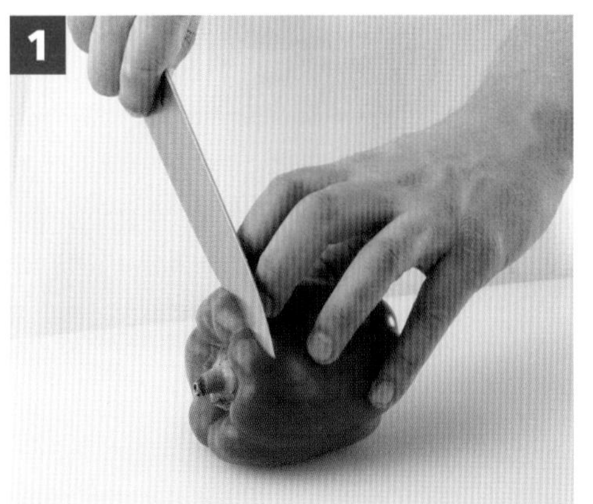

Place the pepper on the cutting board with one end facing your knife hand. (We'll be cutting off both ends, so it doesn't matter where you start.) Steady the pepper with your guide hand.

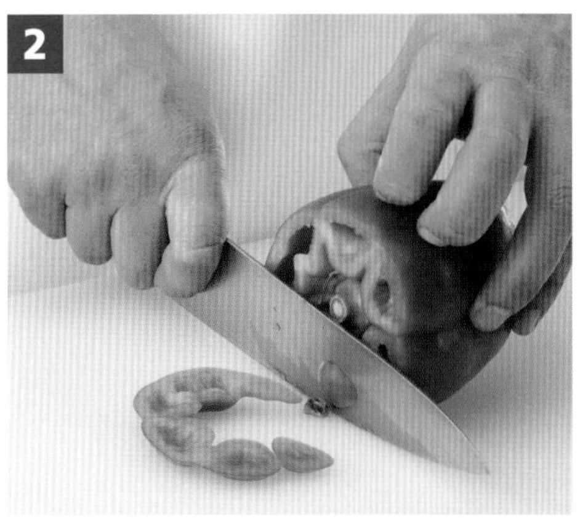

Cut off just enough of the end to allow you to see inside the pepper.

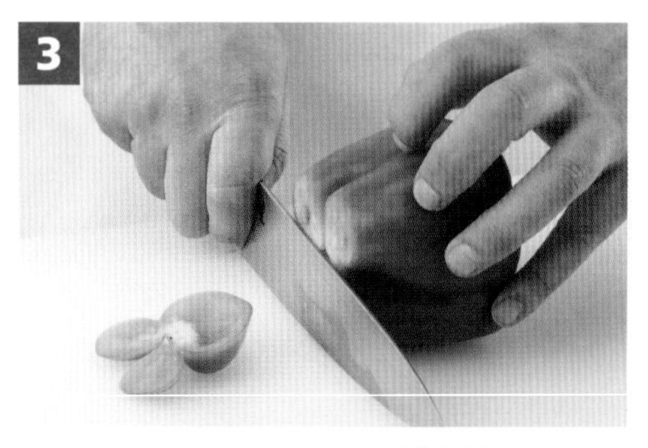

Rotate the pepper and cut off the other end.

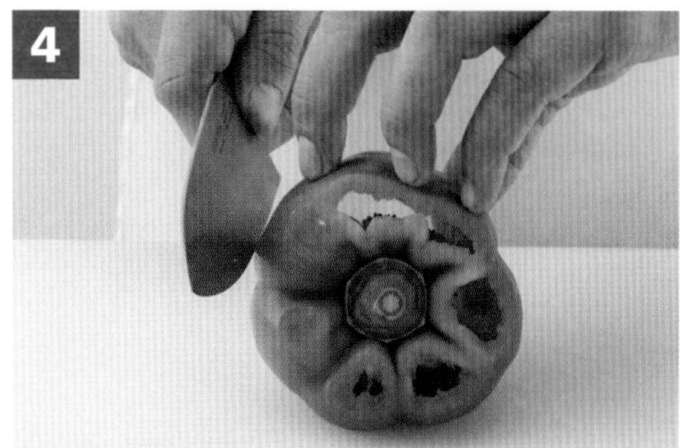

Turn the pepper until one of the cut ends is facing you. Steady the pepper with your guide hand.

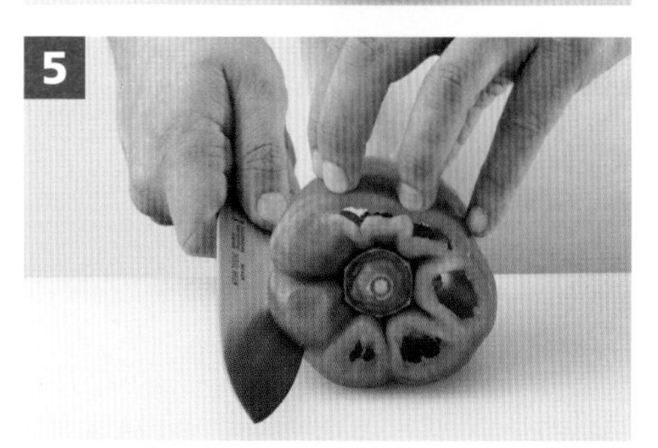

Hold the knife about 1 inch (2.5 cm) above the board and place the edge of the blade against the pepper. Cut into the pepper, angling the blade slightly downward.

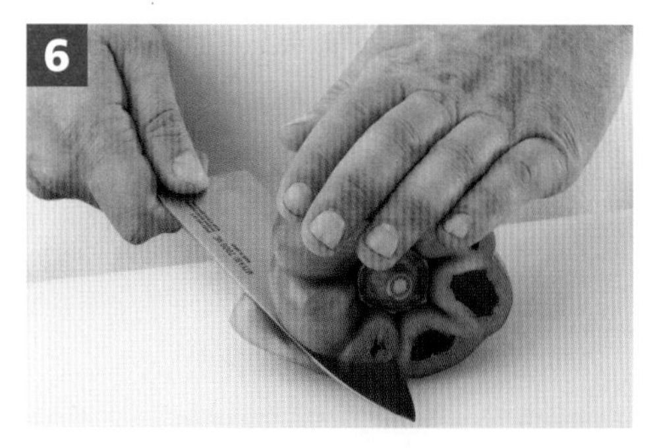

Bring the blade down parallel to the board and trap the flesh of the pepper between it and the board.

Slide your knife horizontally across the surface of the flesh, cutting through the ribs as you reach them.

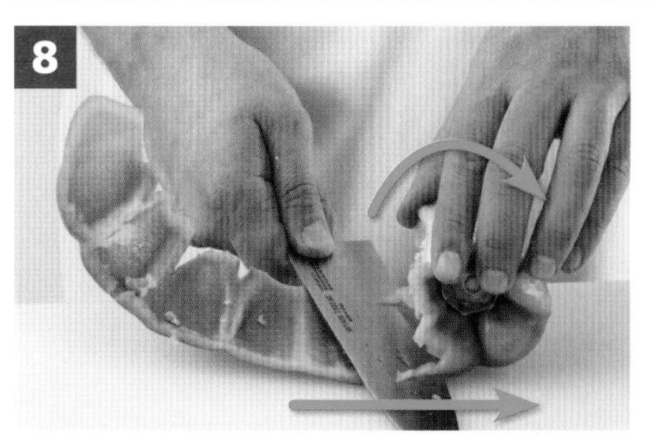

As you cut, use your guide hand to roll the pepper in the same direction the knife is moving. Imagine that the flesh of the pepper is like the tread of a tank, rolling out in front of the knife.

When the knife reaches the end of the pepper, the entire core should come out in one piece, and all of the white ribs should be removed. You'll be left with one long rectangle of pepper flesh.

If you haven't gotten all of the ribs, carefully go back over the pepper again, keeping your knife parallel to the board.

At this point, the pepper can be cut into sticks, dice, paysannes or lozenges (see chapter 3) or into threads (see page 374). We suggest cutting the pepper flesh in half first to make it easier to handle. We also advise keeping peppers skin side down on your cutting board. With the waxy skin side up, it's a little easier for your knife to slip.

Don't forget about the two end pieces. While they're harder to work with because of their shape, they can still be cut into rough sticks or dice.

Broccoli

Broccoli is one of the few vegetables whose different parts require different treatments, both in their prep and in their cooking. The tender florets are removed easily with a chef's knife or Santoku, while the woody, fibrous stalk needs to be peeled before it is cut.

Removing the Florets

Depending on what you're using them for, you can remove the florets in big pieces or smaller pieces. Examine the broccoli stalk and you'll see that, because many small florets go into making up larger florets, which then join together to make the entire head, the closer to the top of the head you cut, the smaller the florets you'll get.

Regardless of what size florets you choose to cut, you need to start by stripping off the leaves clustered near the florets. For this, you can use a paring knife or just pull them off by hand.

RECOMMENDED KNIFE

Chef's knife, paring knife or Santoku

1

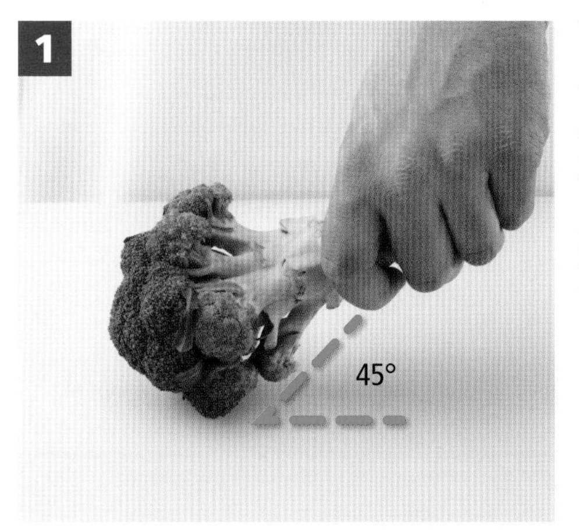

Lay the broccoli sideways on the cutting board, with the florets facing your knife hand. Wrap your guide hand around the bottom of the stalk and tilt it up until it makes a 45-degree angle with the board, leaving the florets resting on the board.

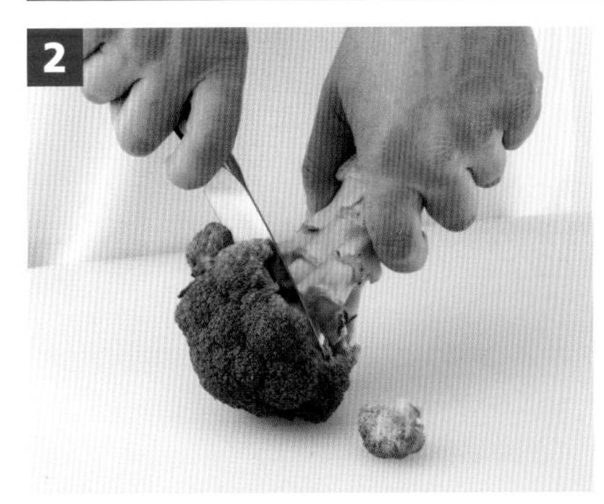

Decide how big you want your florets to be, then place your knife on the appropriate place on the stem of a floret and cut it off.

Turn the broccoli stalk with your guide hand and make another cut next to the first one. Continue turning and cutting florets until they have all been cut off.

Peeling and Cutting the Stalk

The broccoli stalk doesn't have much going for it, it would seem. It's tough, woody and a pallid green so inferior to the florets' lovely deep shade. On the other hand, it contains fiber and flavor and is easy to work with, once you peel it. Depending on the size of the stalk, you can peel it at a 45-degree angle (see page 207) or in your hand (see page 206).

Once it's peeled, you can cut it into rondelles (page 102), sticks (page 90), tournés (page 109) or dice (page 95), or you can simply give it a rough chop and use it to make cream of broccoli soup.

Rondelles Dice Tourné

Cauliflower

Cauliflower is similar in structure to broccoli, but the stem is shorter and the florets are more tightly packed.

Removing the Stem

The only odd thing about cauliflower is its large, thick stem, which should be removed before you break up the florets. After the stem is removed, you can either use your hands or a paring knife to break the cauliflower head into large or small florets, or use your knife to give it a rough chop.

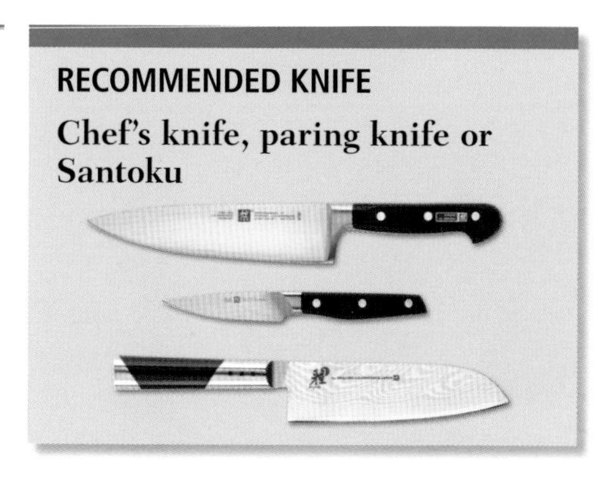

RECOMMENDED KNIFE

Chef's knife, paring knife or Santoku

1 Place the cauliflower upside down on the cutting board and steady it with your guide hand. Holding the knife at a 45-degree angle to the board, place the point against the stem where it meets the florets.

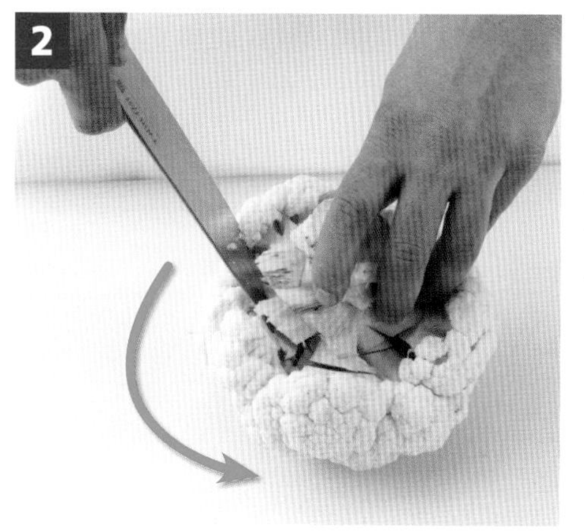

2 Use your guide hand to turn the cauliflower into the knife as you cut through the stem, keeping the blade at a 45-degree angle. Cut all the way around the stem until it can be lifted away from the head.

Celery

A common ingredient in French cuisine is a mix of aromatic vegetables called mirepoix. Classically, it's a 2-1-1 mix of diced onion, carrot and celery. Depending on the dish, the mirepoix may be part of the final product, in which case it is cut into perfect dice, or it may be strained out (as it is with stock), in which case a very rough chop is acceptable.

Celery is also a common ingredient in soups, stir-fries, braises and salads, so we'll give you a couple of suggestions for attractive cuts.

> Some recipes call for the removal of the long fibrous "strings" on the outside of a celery stalk. This is easily done: just scrape the celery with the spine of your knife.

Cutting Batonnets

Celery can be a challenge because its two ends are very different. The root end is flat and wide, while the top end branches off into several smaller, thinner pieces. When you're cutting batonnets, you'll need to deal with each of these ends in turn. In addition, the stalk is arch-shaped, rather than round. This is fairly easy to resolve, though: you simply need to cut each length of stalk into three sticks.

RECOMMENDED KNIFE

Chef's knife or Santoku

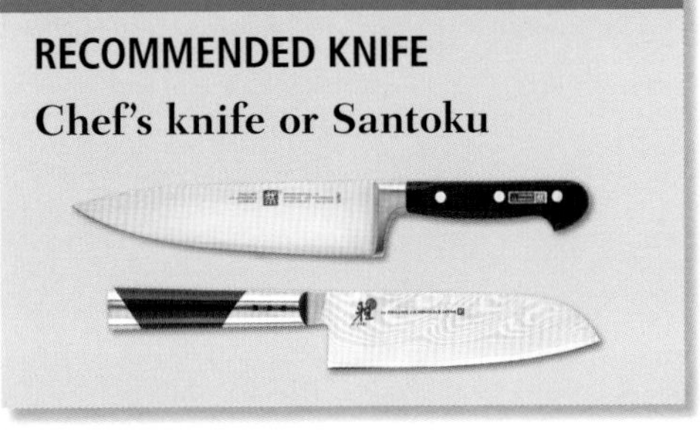

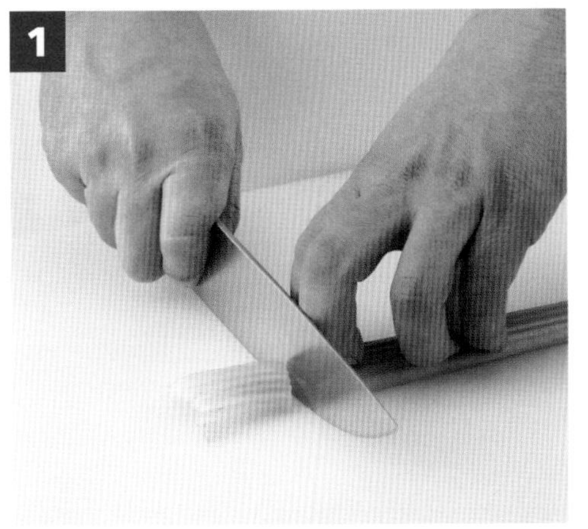

1. Lay a celery stalk on the cutting board, hollow side down, with the root end facing your knife hand, and steady it with your guide hand in the claw position. Trim off the bottom end of the stalk, up to the point where the pale green section starts, and reserve it for stock.

2

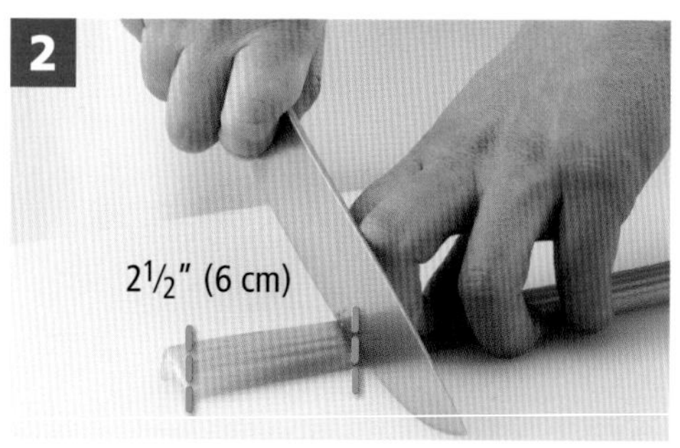

Move your guide fingers back far enough to allow you to cut off a piece of stalk that's about 2½ inches (6 cm) long.

3

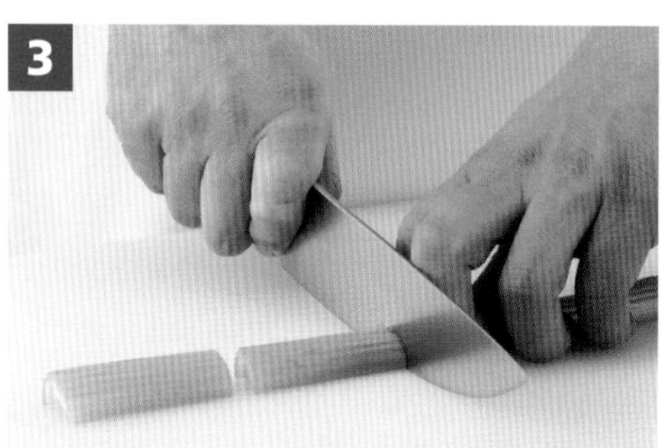

Continue moving your guide hand back and cutting the stalk into 2½-inch (6 cm) lengths, stopping at the juncture where the stalk splits into several branches. Set the top section aside.

4

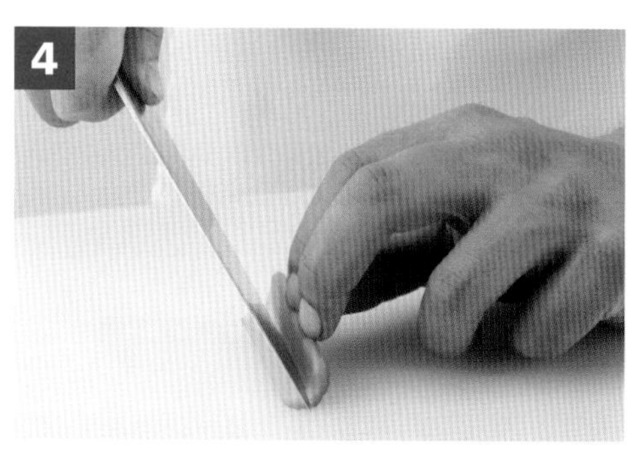

Place one length of stalk parallel to your knife and hold the piece so that one long edge is lying flat on the board (rather than the center point of the arch resting on the board). Cut lengthwise to remove about one-third of the piece.

5

Lay the remaining piece flat on the board and anchor it on one long edge with your guide fingers in the claw position. Cut this piece in half lengthwise.

You now have three pieces of roughly the same size. Even though they are not squared off on the ends, they will function more or less like batonnets.

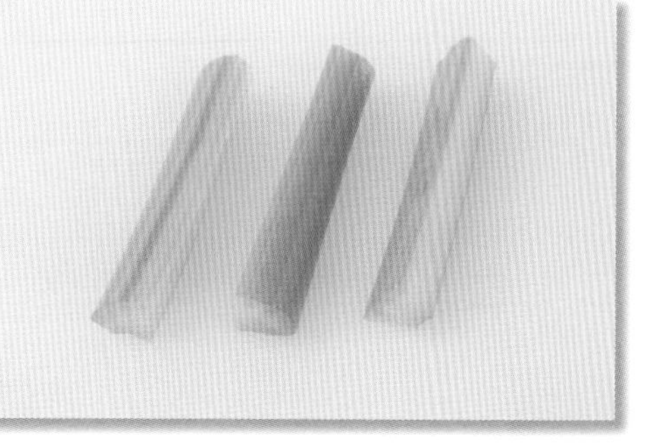

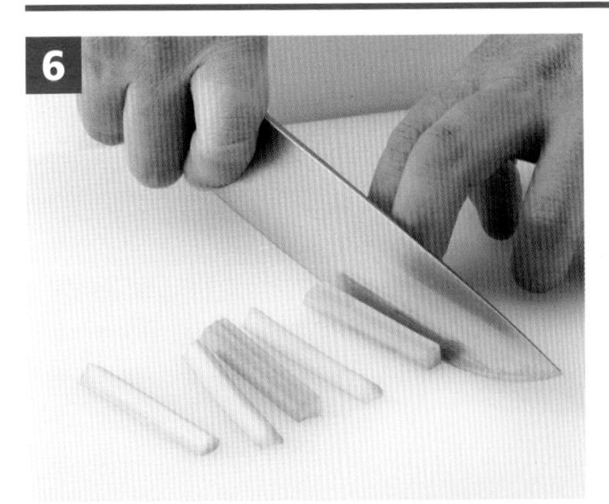

Cut each of the remaining $2\frac{1}{2}$-inch (6 cm) lengths into three pieces.

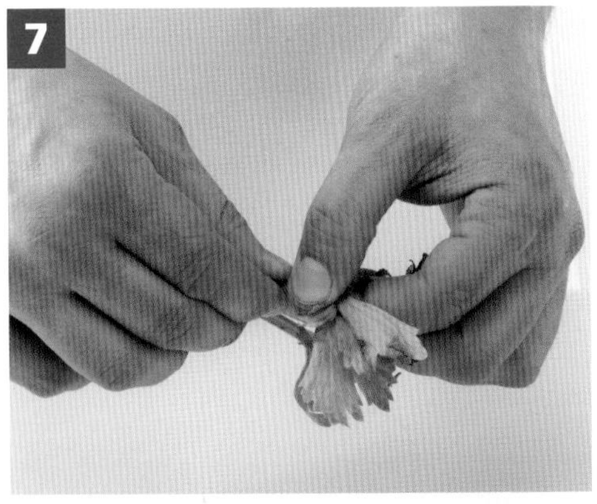

Pull or cut off any leaves from the top section of the celery stalk.

Stand the top section on end and, steadying it with your guide hand, separate the smaller branches from the main piece. Reserve the branches for stock.

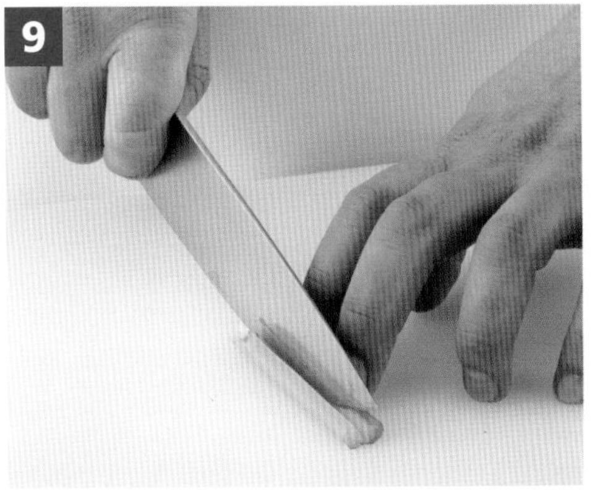

Cut the main piece in half.

Cutting Small Dice

Once you've cut batonnets (see page 151), you're most of the way to small dice. When you're first practicing your cuts, you may want to work with one batonnet at a time until you get the hang of cutting dice. Once you're comfortable with the technique, you can cut several batonnets at one time, as we do in the instructions below.

RECOMMENDED KNIFE

Chef's knife or Santoku

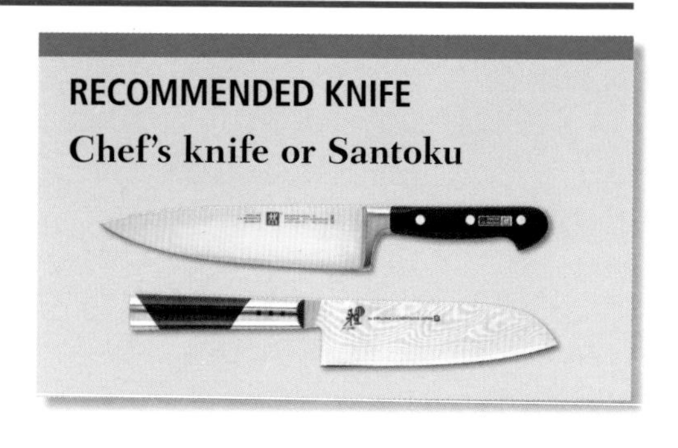

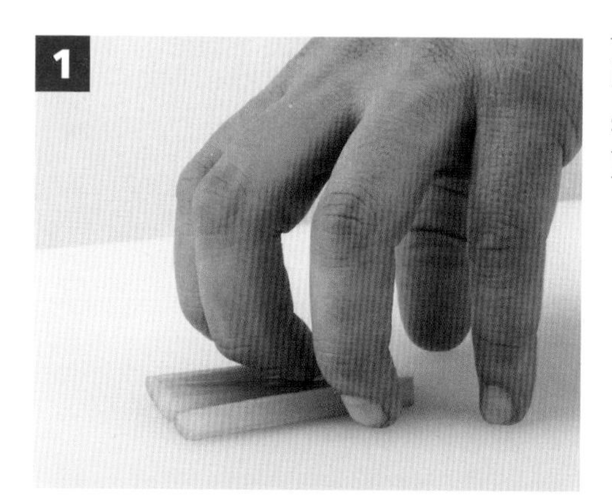

1. Line up several celery batonnets side by side and steady them with your guide hand in the claw position.

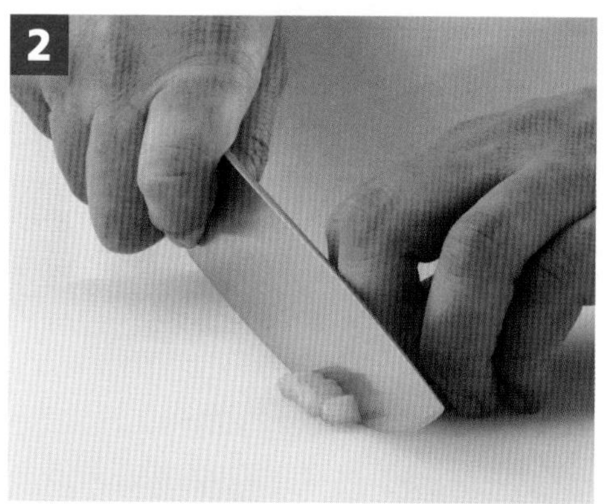

2. Place the knife blade flush against your guide fingers. Make sure the distance from the edge of the batonnets to your knife is the same as the width of a batonnet. Cut straight down to create your first set of dice.

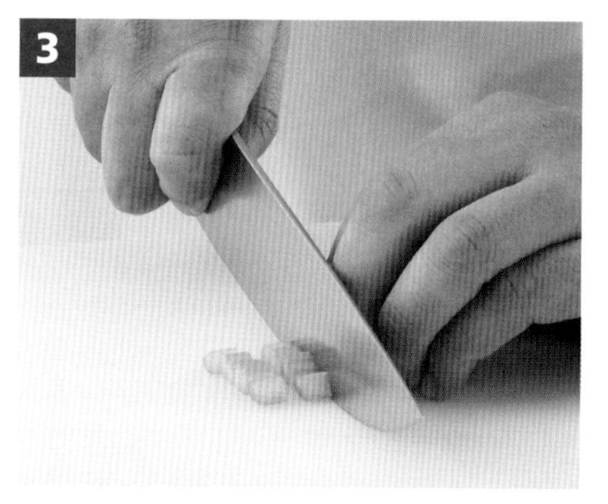

3. Keeping the blade against your guide fingers, move them back the appropriate amount and cut off another set of dice.

Repeat step 3 until the batonnets are completely cut into dice.

Cutting Flakes

This is an attractive, wing-shaped cut that looks great in stir-fries and other dishes. We'll show you two ways to do it; you can choose the one you like best. Because this technique is used to produce attractive pieces, it's best to start with a stalk that has already been trimmed on top and bottom.

Changing the angle of your knife will change the look of the flake. There's no right or wrong about how the flakes should look; you can decide what shape you like best. In our demos, we'll use a 45-degree angle.

RECOMMENDED KNIFE

Chef's knife or Santoku

Flakes cut at a 30° angle

Flakes cut at a 45° angle

Flakes cut at a 60° angle

Technique 1

1

Lay the stalk on the cutting board, hollow side down. Steady it with your guide hand in the claw position.

2

Place the blade on the stalk, about $\frac{3}{4}$ inch (2 cm) in from the knife-hand side, and tilt the spine of the blade until it's at about a 45-degree angle to the stalk, with the spine pressed against your guide fingers. Cut down through the stalk at that angle. This first piece is scrap.

3

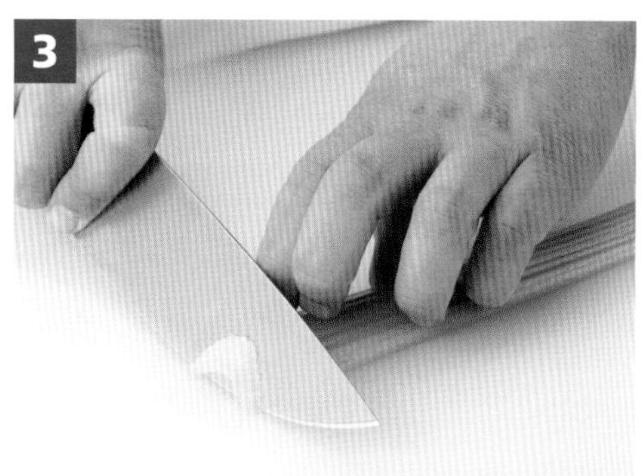

Keeping the spine of the blade against your guide fingers, move them back about $\frac{1}{8}$ inch (3 mm) and cut off another piece at the same angle. This is your first useable piece.

4

Continue moving the knife back and cutting at a 45-degree angle until the entire stalk is cut into flakes. Discard the uneven scrap piece from the end.

Technique 2

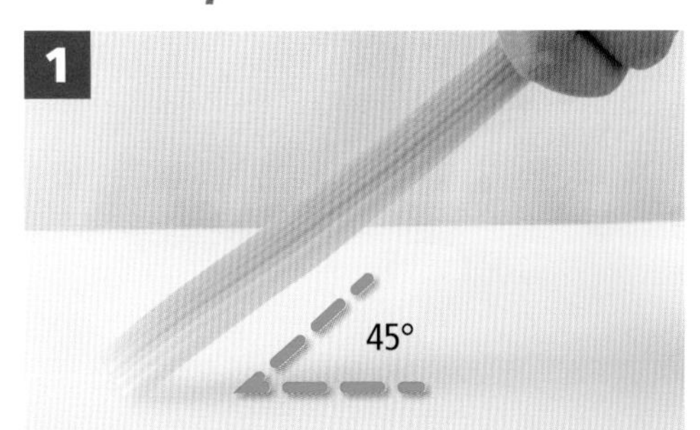

Lay the stalk on the cutting board, hollow side down. Using your guide hand, lift one end so that the stalk is at a 45-degree angle to the cutting board.

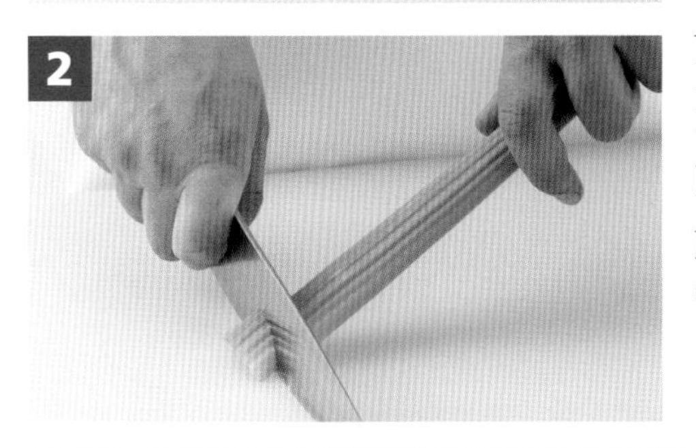

Place the blade on the stalk, about 3⁄4 inch (2 cm) in from the knife-hand side. Make sure your blade is perpendicular to the board and cut straight down. This first piece is scrap.

This technique is somewhat unusual in that the weight of the stalk is resting on the two pillars of the arch at the bottom end. When you cut down, you increase the pressure on those pillars. However, once you cut all the way through, the first piece falls away and the stalk drops straight down onto two new pillars. Thus, unlike most techniques, where you move the knife across the food toward the guide hand, in this case your guide hand feeds the food to the knife, while your knife hand remains in the same place.

Place the blade on the stalk, about 1⁄8 inch (3 mm) in from the knife-hand side, and make another cut straight down. This is your first useable piece.

Each time you cut a piece and the stalk drops to the board, make sure your blade is positioned about 1⁄8 inch (3 mm) in from the knife-hand side and continue cutting straight down until the entire stalk is cut into flakes. Discard the uneven scrap piece from the end.

Cutting Paysannes

This is probably the most common cut for celery. Start with a stalk that has been trimmed on top and bottom. You can cut the pieces to any size you like, depending on how you plan to use them.

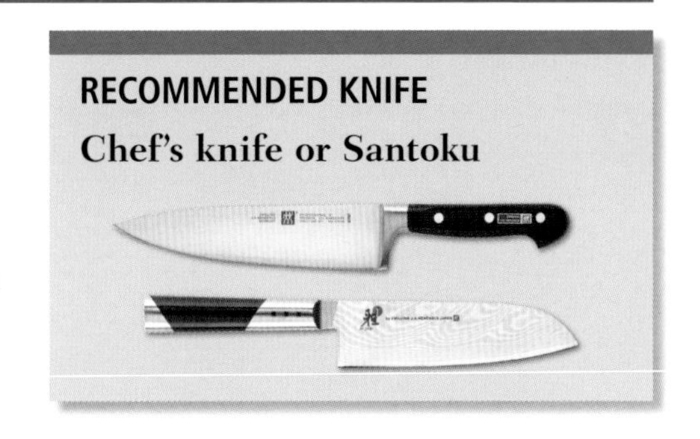

RECOMMENDED KNIFE

Chef's knife or Santoku

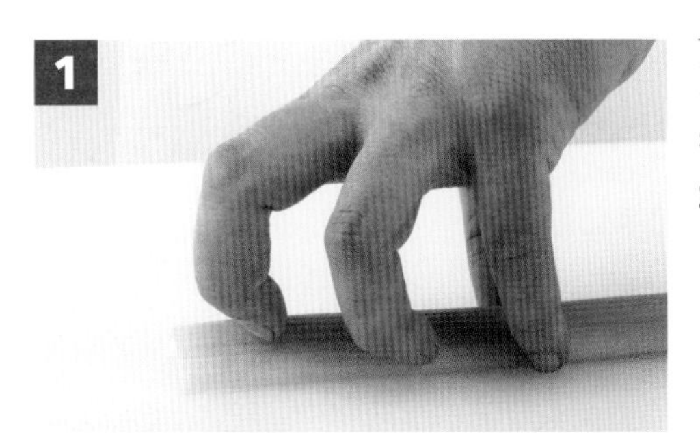

1. Lay the stalk on the cutting board, hollow side down. Steady the stalk with your guide hand in the claw position.

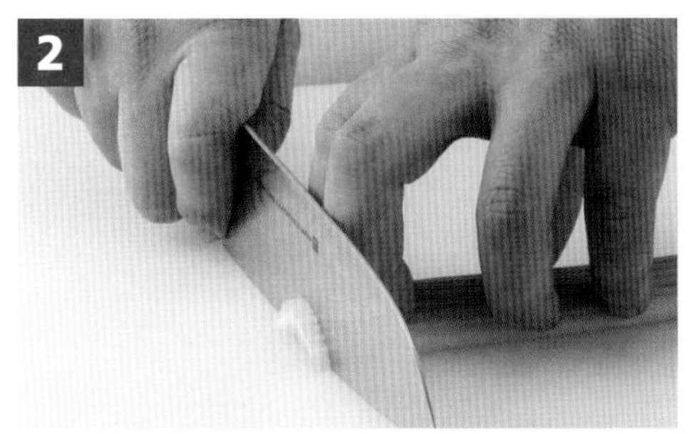

2. Place the knife blade flush against your guide fingers and cut straight down to create your first paysanne.

3. Keeping the blade against your guide fingers, move them back slightly and cut off another paysanne.

4. Repeat step 3 until the entire stalk is cut into paysannes.

Citrus Fruits

In this section, we'll show you how to peel citrus fruit and cut its individual segments into beautiful little crescents of flesh without any tough membrane attached. For instructions on creating decorative citrus curls and crowns, see pages 384 and 386.

Peeling Citrus Fruits and Other Large Fruits

In addition to citrus fruits, this is a great way to peel any large fruit, such as mangos, melons and pineapples, and even eggplants split along the equator and winter squash. We'll demonstrate the technique with an orange.

RECOMMENDED KNIFE

Chef's knife, fillet knife or paring knife

1 Place the orange on the cutting board with the top facing your knife hand. Steady it with your guide hand in the claw position. Cut off a slice that's just thick enough to uncover the flesh completely, leaving none of the white pith behind.

If you cut off the right amount of flesh, the orange will look like this:

If you leave too much pith behind, the orange will look like this:

Rotate the orange 180 degrees and cut off a slice from the bottom of the orange, again leaving none of the white pith behind.

Place the orange on one of its cut sides and secure it with your guide hand in the claw position. Following the natural curve of the orange, cut off a strip of peel. You'll be cutting in an arc, at first moving at an angle outward and then, as you cross the orange's equator, angling back in. The idea is to remove the peel and the white pith while taking as little flesh as possible.

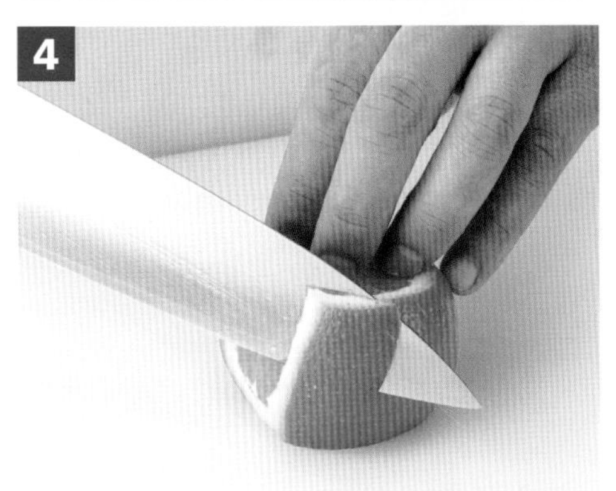

Rotate the exposed portion of the orange toward you just enough to allow you to make your next cut. Line up the knife at the edge of the newly exposed flesh and cut off another strip of peel.

Cut off remaining bits of pith and peel

Continue rotating and cutting until the entire orange is peeled. Check the orange for small bits of peel or pith you may have missed and cut them off.

Preparing Melons

Melons can be peeled exactly like citrus fruit, after which you can use a chef's knife to cut them into sticks (see page 90), dice (see page 95), paysannes (see page 106) or lozenges (see page 107). Or you can use a melon baller to make balls.

Preparing Winter Squash

Winter squash, such as butternut, acorn and kabocha, can be cut in half, seeded and baked, or they can be peeled, seeded and cut into chunks for roasting or simmering. Peel squash as you would citrus fruit, then cut in half and scrape out the seeds with a heavy spoon. Use a chef's knife to cut squash into large chunks.

Cutting Citrus Suprêmes (Segments)

This technique may look a little dangerous, since it requires you to hold the fruit in your guide hand while you cut it. But in fact, you're not really cutting so much as moving the knife forward and letting gravity pull its weight into the middle of the fruit, where the central gathering of membranes will stop it from cutting all the way through to your hand. We'll use an orange to demonstrate the technique, but it will work on any citrus fruit.

RECOMMENDED KNIFE

Paring knife, chef's knife or fillet knife

1

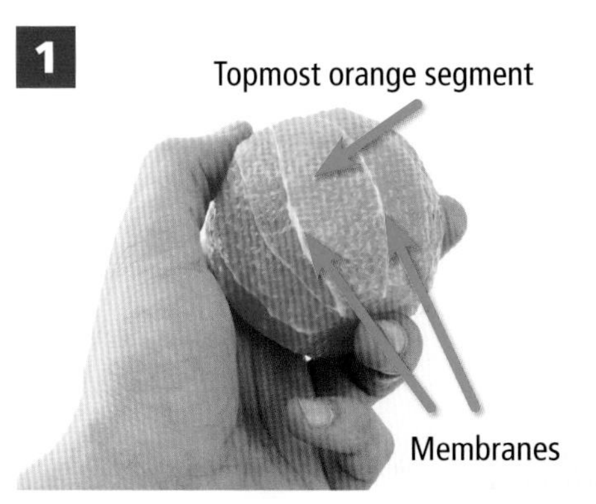

Hold a peeled orange (see page 159) in your guide hand with one of the ends pointing toward you. Look at the topmost orange segment and identify the membranes that surround it.

2

Place the knife blade on the topmost orange segment, just inside the membrane on the knife-hand side. Tilt the blade slightly to the side so that it is perfectly parallel with the angle of the membrane.

Make sure your blade stays parallel to the membrane as you cut. Otherwise, your segment will have unsightly strips of membrane attached to it.

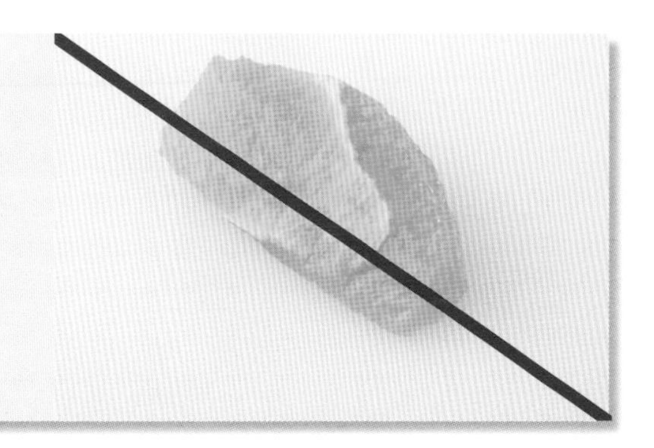

Push the knife straight into the orange, letting its weight cut through the flesh alongside the membrane. (Once again, the knife will stop when it reaches the center of the orange.)

Cut as close to the membrane as possible, so that all the flesh comes out with the segment. If you cut too far from the membrane, you'll leave bits of flesh attached to the skeleton and the segment won't be as pretty.

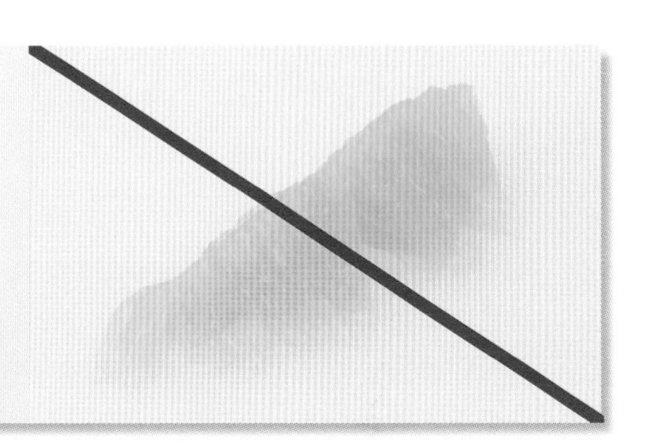

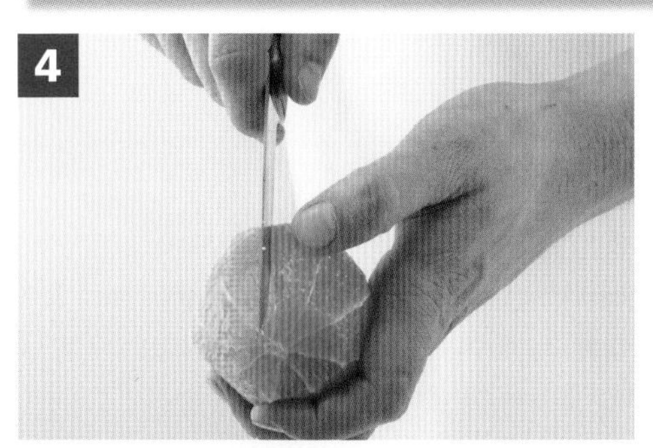

Remove the knife and place it back on top of the segment, this time just inside the membrane on the guide-hand side. Tilt the blade so that it is perfectly parallel with the angle of the membrane.

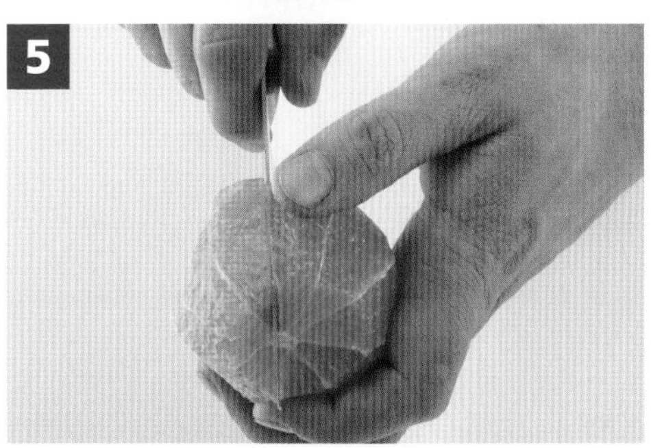

Push the knife straight into the orange, letting its weight cut through the flesh alongside the membrane.

If you are using a fillet knife, instead of cutting down both sides you can simply turn your wrist and push the segment out when you get to the bottom of the first slice.

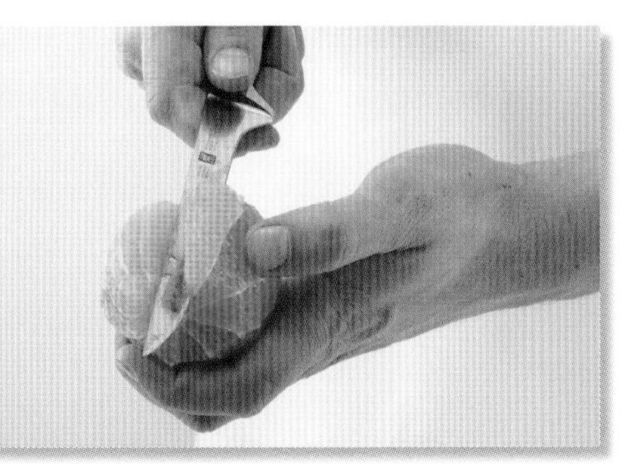

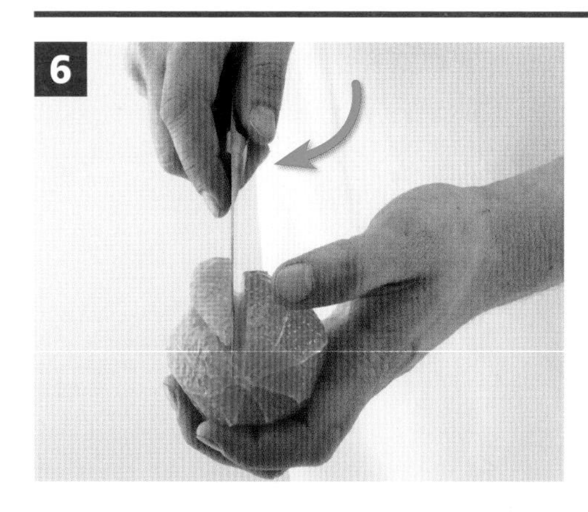

With a gentle flick of your wrist, tilt your knife slightly to lift the orange segment onto the blade and remove it.

When you encounter a seed, try to pull it out with the segment, then just cut it away with the tip of your knife. That segment will have a small chunk missing, but there's no way around it.

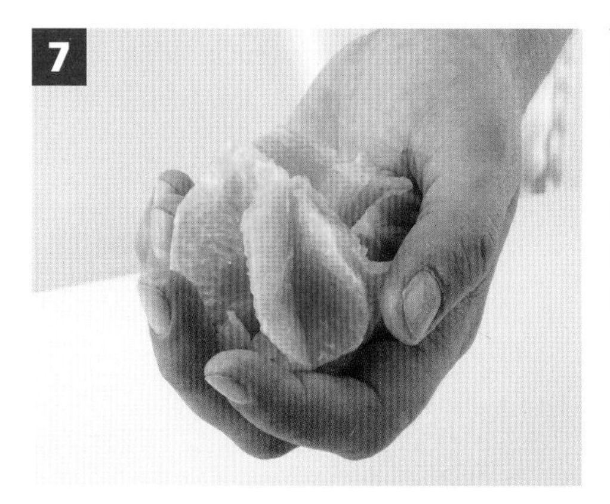

Rotate the orange in your guide hand until the next segment is straight up. Repeat steps 2 to 6. Continue rotating and cutting until all the segments are removed, leaving you with the empty skeleton of the membranes.

Don't discard the skeleton until you squeeze all the juice out of it. Each skeleton will yield only a small amount of juice, but if you're doing a number of oranges, you'll end up with a useable quantity.

Corn

Most people experience corn in one of two ways: on the cob or with the kernels already removed and either canned or frozen. Cutting kernels from the cob is, admittedly, a messy task. They tend to fly about the kitchen, leaving little streaks of their milky juice, which must then be wiped up. Still, if you're making any dish that requires corn, the difference between fresh and canned or frozen is as remarkable as the difference between home-grown and store-bought tomatoes. There's just no comparison.

Cutting Off the Kernels

To start, remove the husk and as much of the silk as you can by hand. After that, the technique is pretty much the same as the method for peeling a potato on the cutting board (see page 207).

RECOMMENDED KNIFE

Chef's knife or Santoku

1

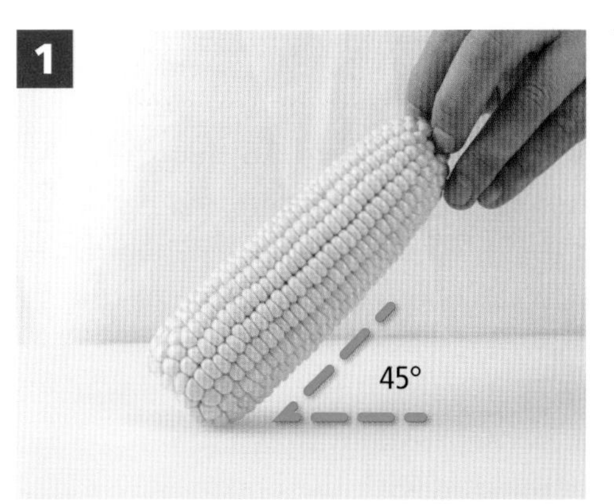

Lay an ear of corn on the cutting board. Using your guide hand, lift one end so that the ear is at a 45-degree angle to the cutting board.

2

Starting near the center of the ear, cut straight down along the cob to remove the kernels.

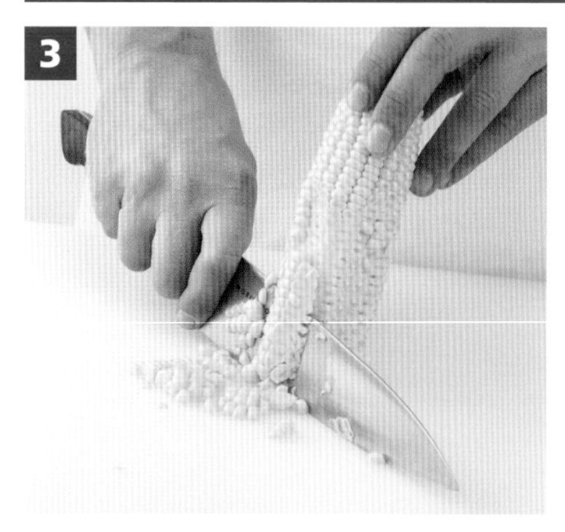

Rotate the cob with your guide hand and continue cutting strips straight down along the cob until the lower half of the cob is cleared of kernels.

Turn the ear over so that you are holding the cleared end in your guide hand at a 45-degree angle to the board. Cut straight down along the cob to remove the kernels from the other end, rotating the cob after each cut, until the entire cob is cleared of kernels.

Turn the knife upside down, so that the spine is toward the board. Still holding the cob at a 45-degree angle to the board, scrape down the cob with the spine of the knife. This will release some of the thick, milky juice that was left behind when you cut off the kernels. Add it to whatever dish you're making with the corn.

Garlic

Nothing enhances a dish like fresh garlic. Eat it in abundance, as garlic has many health benefits.

A head of garlic is made up of small cloves covered in layers of thin, papery husk. The cloves are joined at the root end of the head, which is covered in more of the papery husk. It can be difficult to get a clove out of its husk without damaging it; fortunately, garlic is often minced, so it doesn't matter if you crush the clove while peeling it, since smashing the clove is the first step in mincing anyway.

It is rarely necessary to take apart the entire head; most of the time, you'll just use a few cloves. To remove an individual clove, you can use your fingernail or any knife to cut through the husk between two cloves. Then just pull out one of the cloves and use the resulting cavity to give you purchase on other cloves.

Breaking Up a Garlic Head

Occasionally you may need an entire head of garlic or more. Fortunately, there's an easy way to break up the head into individual cloves.

Set the head of garlic on the cutting board, stem side up. Place your knife on top of the garlic head, with the blade parallel to the cutting board.

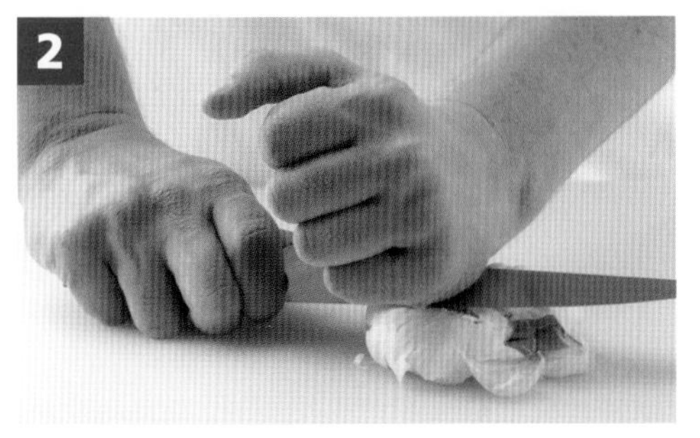

Form your guide hand into a fist and gently rap the knife, using just enough power to break the cloves apart from the head without crushing them.

When working with garlic, some chefs prefer to remove the germ — the light green bit that runs down the center of the clove — as it is often bitter. To do so, split the clove lengthwise, then use the tip of your knife to remove the germ.

Peeling the Cloves

There are many ways to peel a garlic clove, but since this is a knife skills book, we'll show you how to do it with a knife.

RECOMMENDED KNIFE

Chef's knife or Santoku

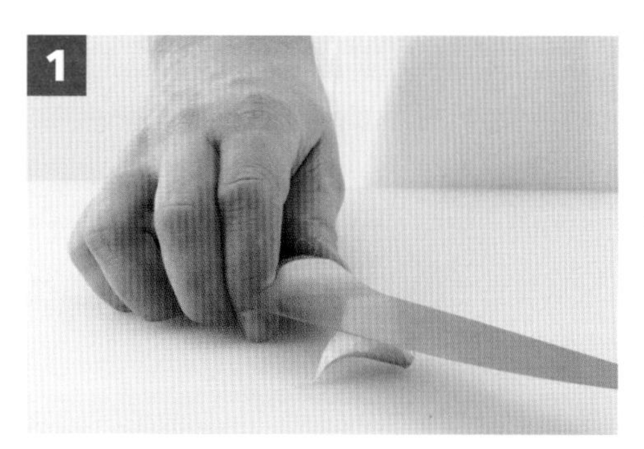

1. Lay an unpeeled clove of garlic on its side on the cutting board. Place your knife on top of the clove, with the blade parallel to the cutting board.

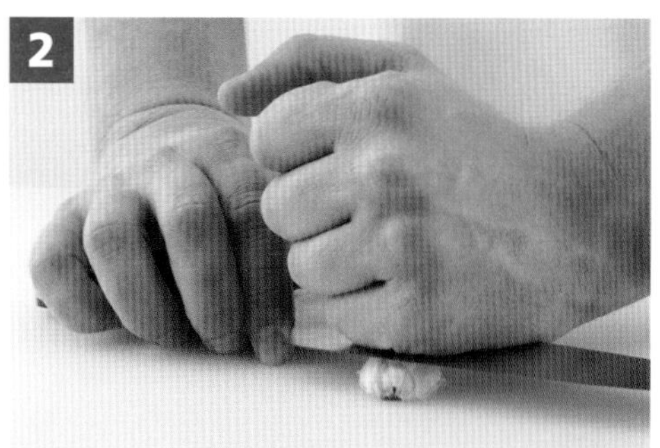

2. Form your guide hand into a fist and gently rap the knife, using just enough power to crack the husk without smashing the clove. (Of course, if you're going to mince the garlic, it doesn't matter if the clove is smashed.)

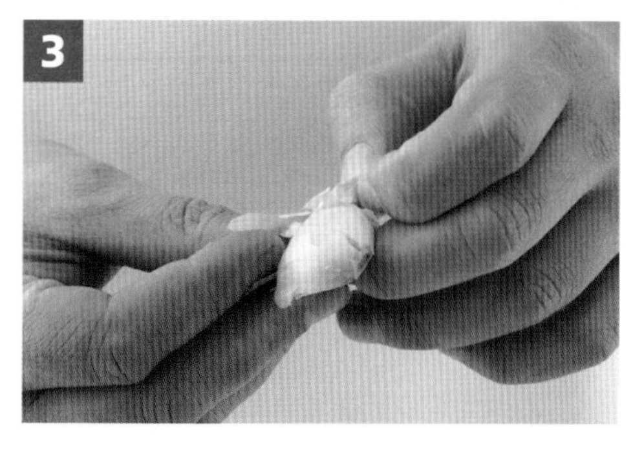

3. Set down your knife and peel off the husk.

Cut off flat root end

Lay the peeled clove on the cutting board, with the hard, flat root end facing your knife hand. Steady the clove with your guide hand. Cut off the root end and discard.

Mincing Garlic

For instructions on mincing garlic, see page 84.

Creaming Garlic

RECOMMENDED KNIFE

Chef's knife or Santoku

You can take minced garlic to another level of smoothness by creaming it. Creamed garlic is great in dishes where you want the taste of fresh garlic without having to bite into a chunk of it. The process of creaming garlic takes several minutes, but the more you do it, the faster you'll get.

In this technique, the knife is held nearly upside down, so you'll be using a different grip. As when you're dicing onions (page 189), the work should be done close enough to the edge of the cutting board that your knife handle is beyond the edge of the board, not directly above it.

Before you start, get some kosher salt ready to sprinkle on the garlic. The salt will help grind down the garlic, making your job much easier.

Mound the minced garlic on the board and sprinkle with kosher salt.

2

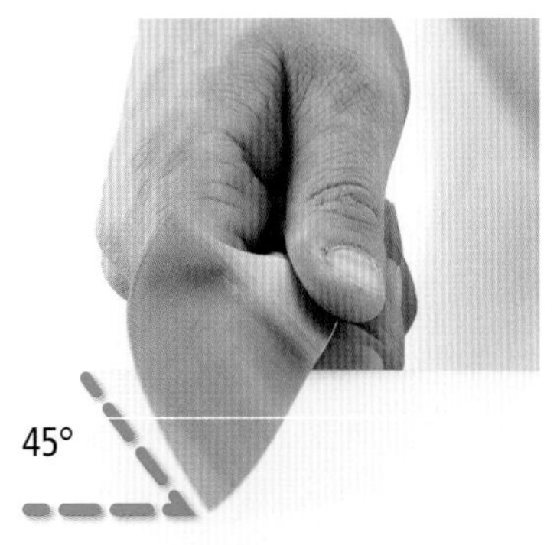

Holding the knife upside down, wrap all four fingers of your knife hand around the handle, extending your thumb so that it rests comfortably on the side of the blade. This thumb position ensures that the blade is held at about a 45-degree angle, with the edge pointing away from you.

3

Place the spine of the blade on the board, just in front of the pile of garlic. Place your guide fingers on the same side of the blade as your thumb, but closer to the tip.

4

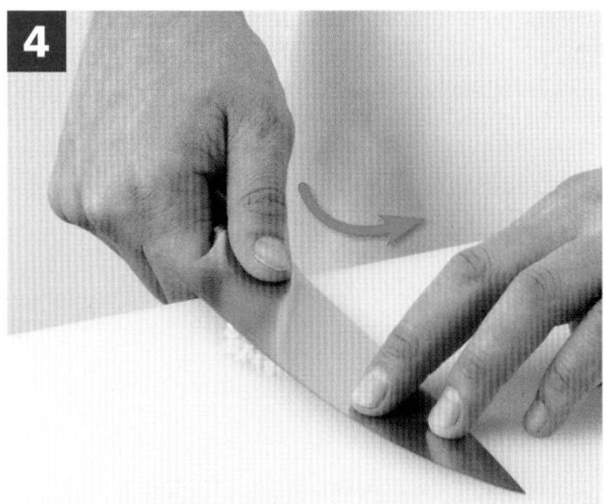

Imagine that the spine of the knife is hinged to the board. Twisting your knife hand from the elbow so that your palm rotates toward you, press down on the blade with the thumb of your knife hand and your two guide fingers. The idea is to crush the garlic with the edge of the blade.

5

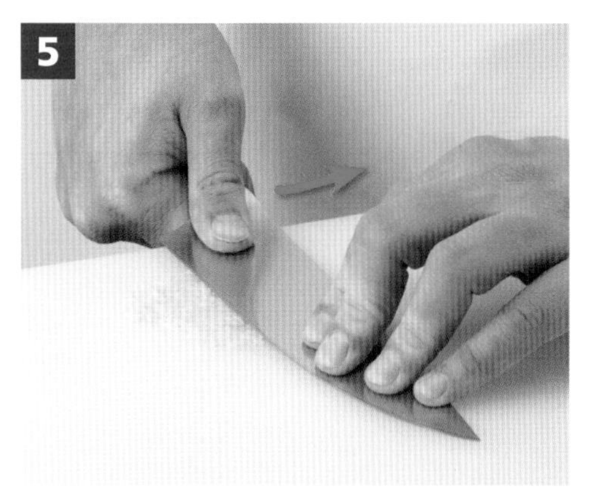

With the edge of the blade still crushing the garlic, and your thumb and guide fingers still applying pressure, pull the knife back toward you, smearing the garlic across the board. At this point, the spine may come up off the board a little bit.

Tilt the blade back up to a 45-degree angle and push the spine against the smeared garlic, gathering it up into a pile again.

Repeat steps 4 to 6 until the garlic is reduced to a paste. Remember that it's the edge of the blade, not the side, that's doing the bulk of the work.

Cutting Slices

Paper-thin slices of garlic add flavor and give a dish an interesting look.

RECOMMENDED KNIFE

Chef's knife or Santoku

Steady a peeled clove of garlic on one of its ends. Shave off a thin slice from the side of the clove to create a flat surface.

Lay the clove on this flat surface and steady it with your guide hand in the claw position.

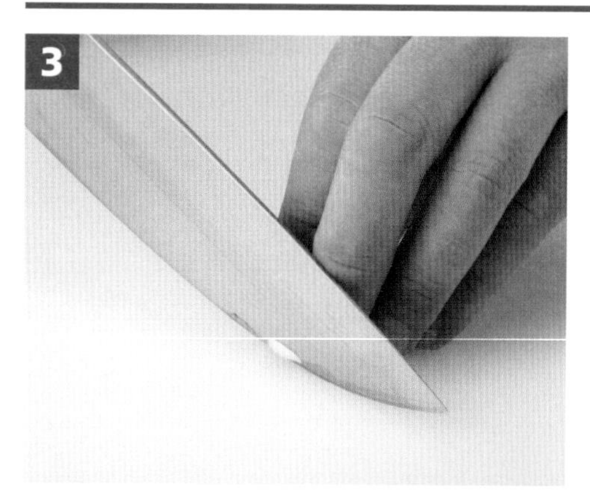

Place the knife blade flush against your guide fingers and cut off a paper-thin slice of garlic.

Keeping the blade against your guide fingers, move them back slightly and cut off another slice.

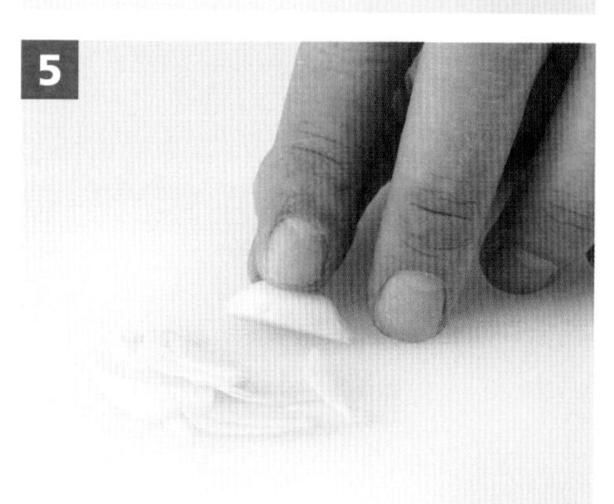

Repeat step 4 until the entire clove is cut into paper-thin slices. As you get close to the end, lay the cut side down on the board, so that the piece is easier to hold.

To get the smell of garlic off your hands, don't reach for soap, reach for steel. Many companies make soap-shaped bars of stainless steel, but you can save your money and just use a stainless steel spoon. While holding your hands under running water, rub the back of the spoon all over them. The smell will be gone — guaranteed!

We also recommend using a separate cutting board for strong-smelling produce such as onions and garlic.

Leeks

Leeks are delicious braised, grilled and in soups. The edible part of the leek is the white and light green area at the root end. The dark green leaves can be discarded or used as part of a bouquet garni.

Trimming and Cleaning Leeks

Because of the way leeks are grown, with dirt mounded around the bulb to keep it white, there's often dirt and grit in between the layers. So before you can cut a leek into sticks or dice, you'll need to learn the technique for trimming and cleaning it.

RECOMMENDED KNIFE

Chef's knife or Santoku

1. Lay a leek on the cutting board and steady it with your guide hand on the root end. Place the knife blade at the point where the leek starts to turn from pale green to a darker green. Cut into the leaves at a 45-degree angle to the leek, stopping when you reach the center, as if you're whittling a stick.

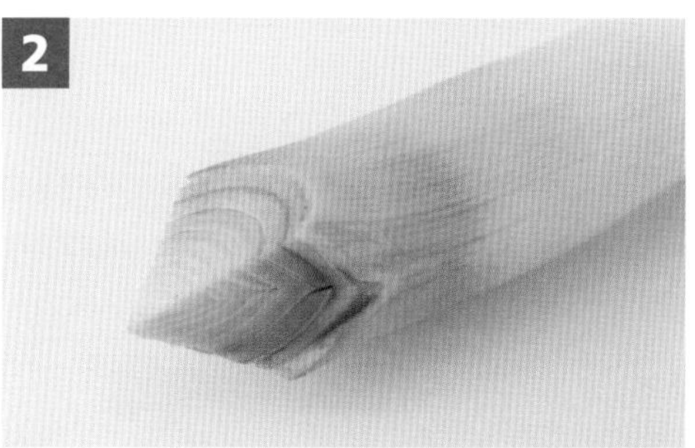

2. Rotate the leek and make another 45-degree cut into the center. Continue rotating and cutting until you have removed all the green leaves, leaving a point.

3. Lay the leek on the board, with the root end facing your knife hand. Steady the leek with your guide hand and, with the knife blade flush against your guide fingers, cut away the root.

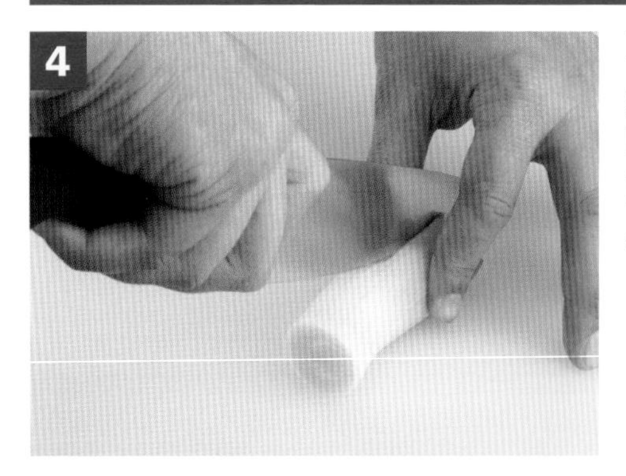

Hold one end of the leek steady with your guide hand. Carefully place the tip of the knife in the space between the end of the leek and your hand, so that your hand is arching over the blade.

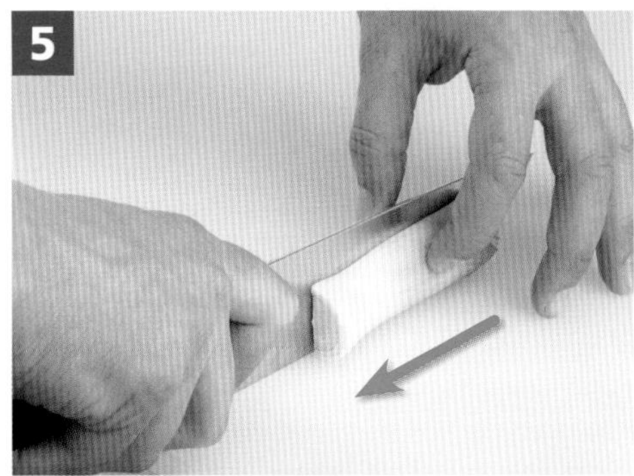

Cut the leek in half lengthwise, pulling the knife away from your guide hand.

Rinse the leek halves under cold running water, fanning the layers like a deck of cards to expose the interior layers to the water.

Cutting Juliennes and Brunoises

Because a leek is already in thin layers in its natural state, the process of cutting it into sticks and dice is a bit easier than with many other vegetables, which need to be cut into planks as the first step. The thinness of the layers does mean, though, that your only options for uniform sticks and dice are juliennes (see page 90) and brunoises (see page 95).

RECOMMENDED KNIFE

Chef's knife or Santoku

Cut a trimmed and cleaned leek half into 2-inch (5 cm) lengths.

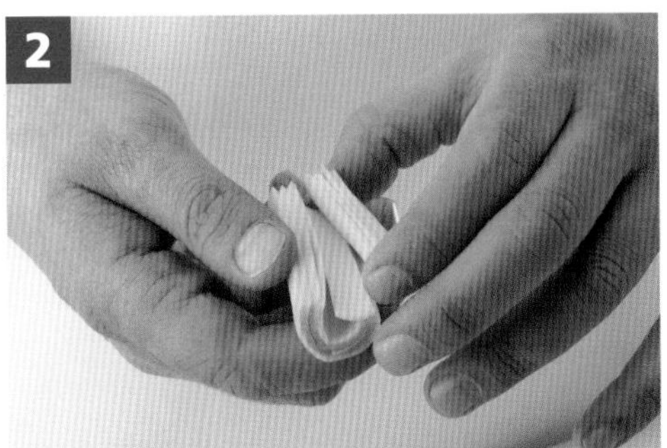

Pull the inner layers of the leek out of the 2-inch (5 cm) sections and set them aside to cut into juliennes separately. (Removing these inner layers makes it easier to flatten the leek, which makes it easier to cut it.)

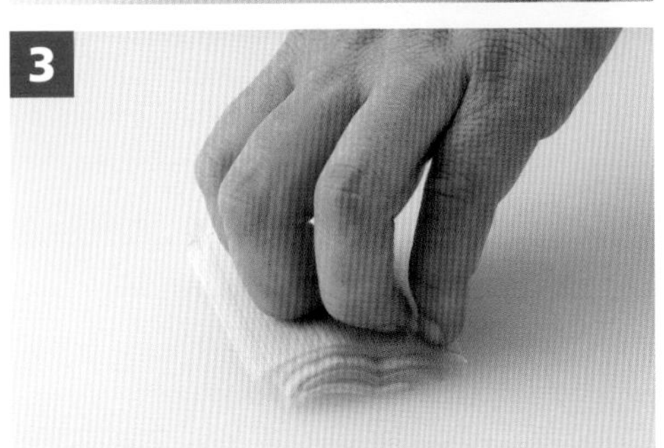

Lay the leek on the cutting board, cut side down, with the long edge facing your knife hand, and flatten the leaves.

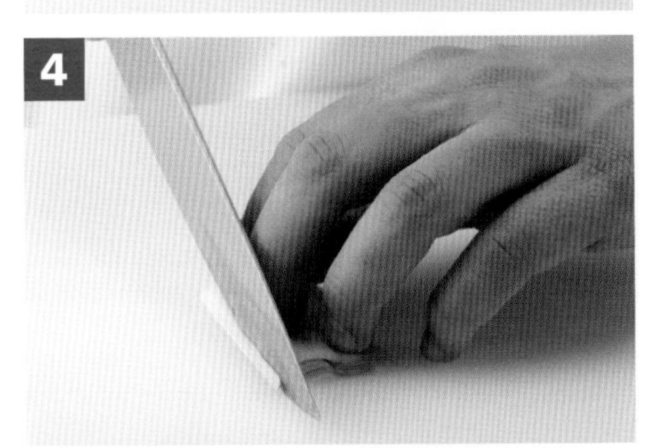

Steady the leek with your guide hand in the claw position. Place the blade flush against your guide fingers and line it up to cut off a $\frac{1}{8}$-inch (3 mm) strip.

Cut straight down through the leek along its length. Because you're cutting through several layers, the pieces will come out as juliennes.

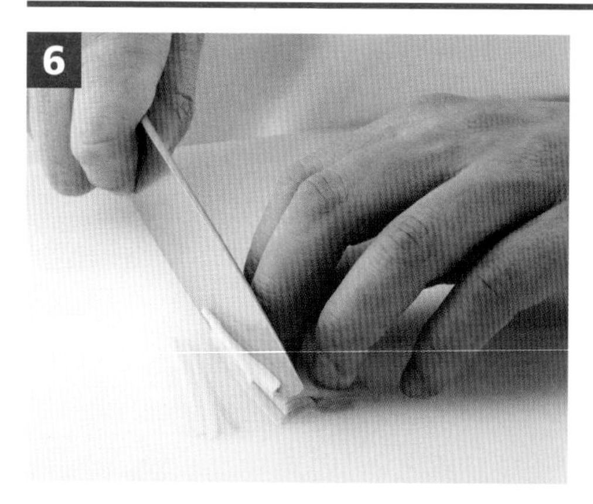

6 Move your guide fingers back $\frac{1}{8}$ inch (3 mm) and make another cut.

7 Repeat step 6 until the entire piece is cut into juliennes.

8 To make brunoise, simply gather the juliennes into a pile, rotate the pile 90 degrees and secure it with your guide hand in the claw position. Cut the juliennes into $\frac{1}{8}$-inch (3 mm) brunoises.

Cutting Paysannes

This will give you pieces of uneven size, but it's a quick and easy cut. Simply lay a leek half on the board, cut side down, and cut it into slices as you would for celery paysannes (see page 158).

Mangos

Mangos have an odd, spearhead-shaped seed in the center that can't really be cut out; instead, you have to cut around it. But if you've ever had fresh mango salsa with red onion, jalapeño, lime juice and cilantro, you know that it's worth every bit of trouble.

The fruit is the shape of a slightly flattened pear, with the seed right in the middle. To make things clear in our instructions, we'll call the narrow sides of the mango the edges and the wide sides the faces.

While the peel of a mango is technically edible, it tends to be tough and contains urushiol (a chemical that can cause contact dermatitis), so it's best to remove it. The technique is the same as for peeling citrus fruits (see page 159).

Cutting the Flesh off the Seed

The first step in getting rid of the seed is to cut off the two faces. Once that's done, you'll be left with a piece about $^3/_4$ inch (2 cm) wide, with the seed buried inside. The next step is to cut off the edges. Depending on the straightness of your cuts when removing the faces, your edge pieces may end up being different sizes. In fact, it is possible to end up with only one edge piece. That's okay. The goal is simply to remove as much of the flesh as possible. The number of pieces you get is more or less irrelevant.

Stand a peeled mango on its wider end on the cutting board, with an edge facing you. Place your guide hand on top of the mango and position your knife blade a little way out from the center.

Try to cut straight down through the flesh. If you encounter resistance, move the knife away from the center slightly and try again until you are able to cut straight down to remove one face of the mango.

Rotate the mango 180 degrees and repeat steps 1 and 2, cutting straight down to remove the other face.

Rotate the mango 90 degrees and cut down, following the shape of the seed, to remove the flesh from one edge.

Rotate the mango 180 degrees and repeat step 4 to remove the flesh from the other edge.

After the faces and edges are removed, there will still be a small amount of flesh attached to the seed. There isn't much point in trying to trim it off, as it will be small and oddly shaped, so we recommend nibbling it right off the seed (one of the perks of being the chef!).

Cutting Sticks and Dice

RECOMMENDED KNIFE

Chef's knife or Santoku

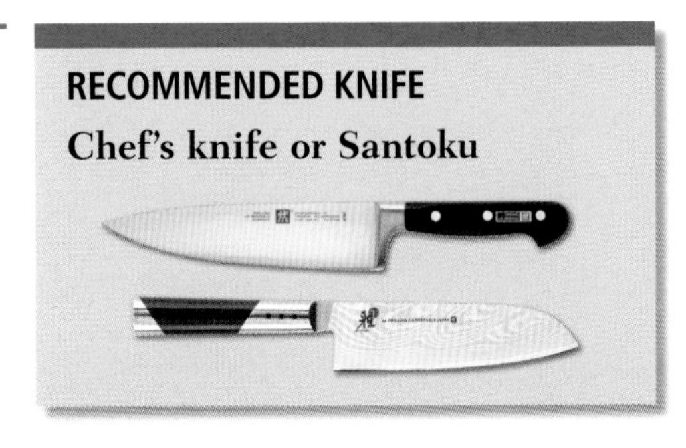

When we cut the faces and edges off the seed (see page 178), we cut as close to the center as we could, to remove as much flesh as possible. We weren't trying to end up with pieces of a specific thickness, yet that's what we need for even sticks and dice. So before we can cut our sticks or dice, we'll have to cut our mango pieces horizontally to a consistent thickness. If you want to end up with batonnets or small dice, cut ¼-inch (6 mm) horizontal slices. If you want juliennes or brunoises, cut ⅛-inch (3 mm) horizontal slices. (See pages 90 and 95 for an explanation of the different stick and dice sizes.) We'll use a face piece in our demo and cut it into batonnets and small dice.

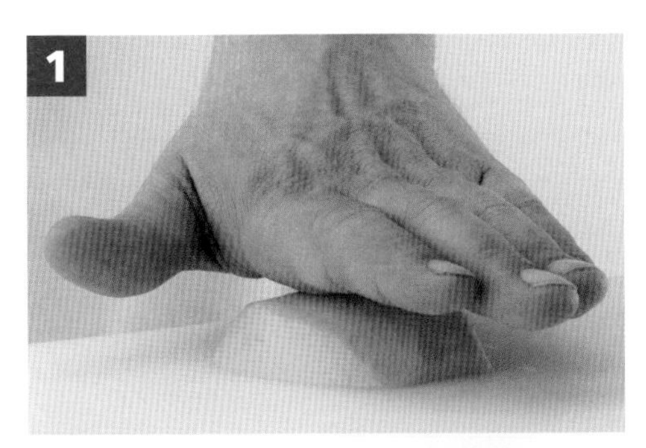

1. Lay a mango piece on the board, cut side down, with the tapered end facing your knife hand. The mango should be fairly close to the edge of the cutting board nearest you. Steady the mango with your guide hand.

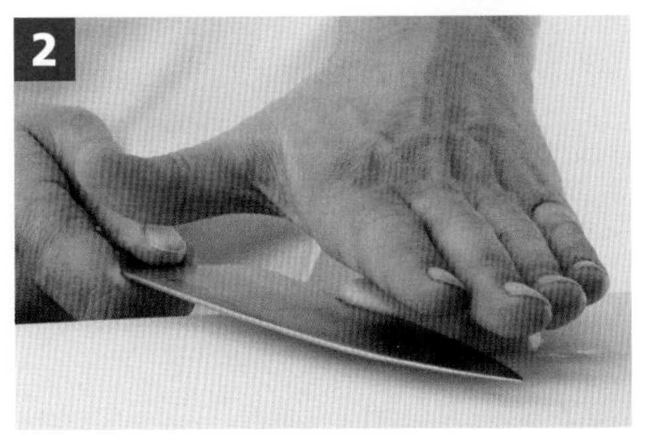

2. Hold the knife ¼ inch (6 mm) above the board, with the blade parallel to the board.

The mango piece should be close enough to the edge of the board that the knife handle is beyond the edge of the board, not directly above it. If you hold the handle directly above the board, you'll have a tendency to tilt the knife toward the tip, which will result in uneven slices.

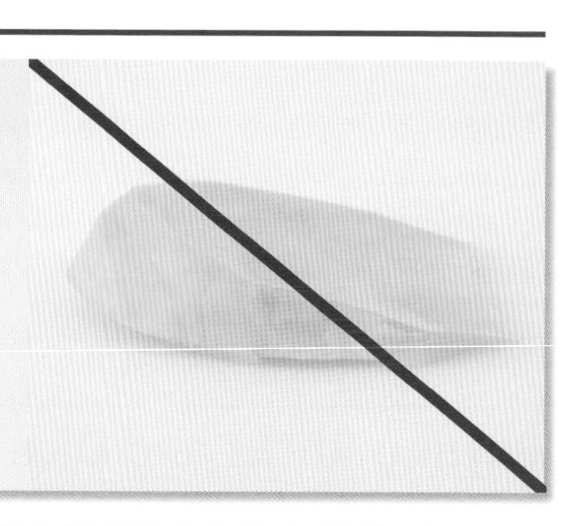

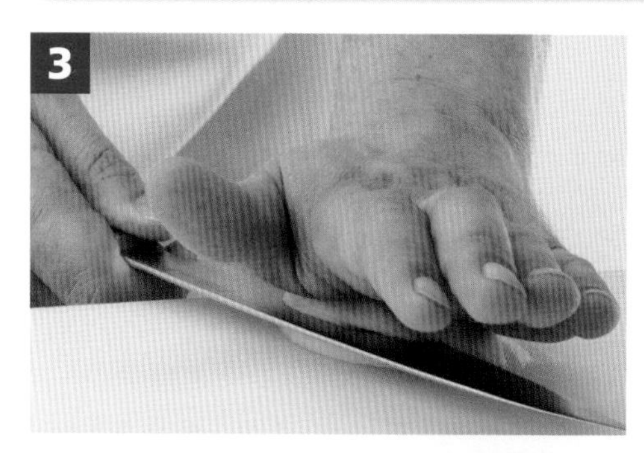

Cut straight through the mango horizontally. Leave the slices stacked as you cut them.

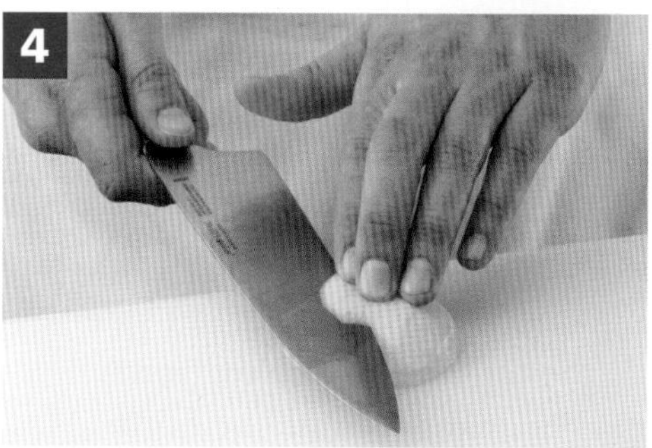

If the top slice is thicker than $\frac{1}{4}$ inch (6 mm), raise the knife that amount and cut another horizontal slice. Repeat until you have cut as many $\frac{1}{4}$-inch (6 mm) horizontal slices as the mango piece allows.

If you end up with a top slice that's the right width, cut it into sticks or dice too. If it's too thin, just give it a rough chop and enjoy a snack!

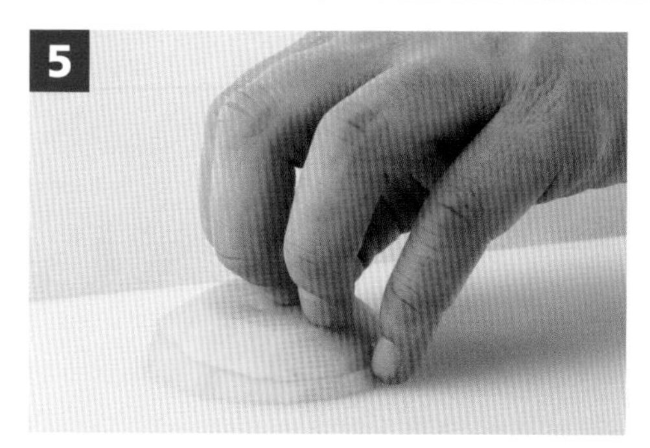

When you have completed your horizontal cuts, place your guide hand on top of the stack in the claw position.

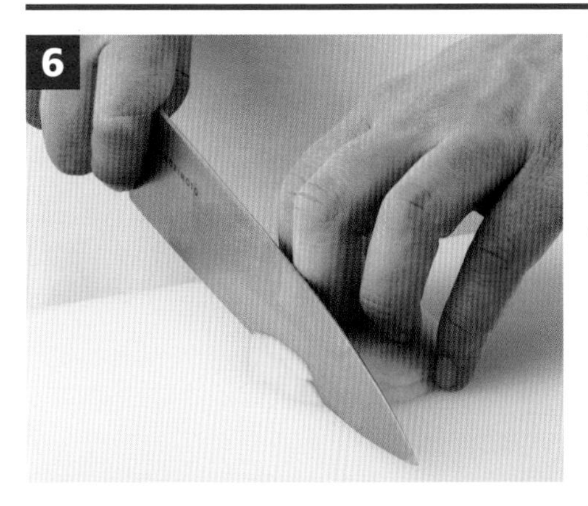

Place the knife blade flush against your guide fingers. Make sure the distance from the edge of the stack to your knife is $\frac{1}{4}$ inch (6 mm). Cut straight down to create your first set of batonnets.

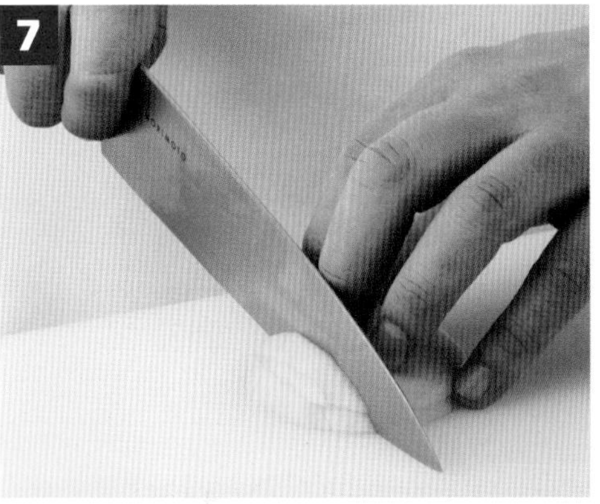

Keeping the blade against your guide fingers, move them back $\frac{1}{4}$ inch (6 mm) and cut off another set of batonnets.

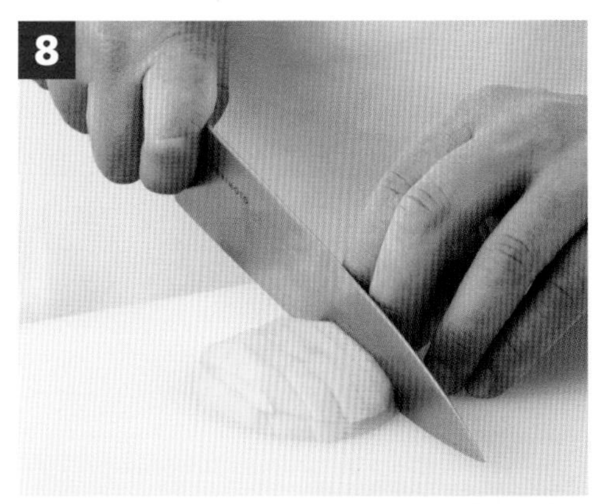

Repeat step 7 until the entire stack is cut into batonnets.

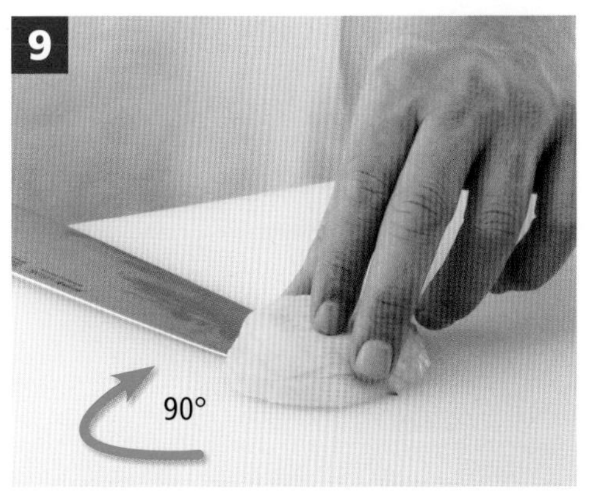

To make dice, slide your knife under the stack and use it to carefully rotate the sticks 90 degrees.

Steady the batonnets with your hand in the claw position. Place the blade flush against your guide fingers. Make sure the distance from the edge of the batonnets to your knife is $\frac{1}{4}$ inch (6 mm). Cut straight down to create your first set of dice.

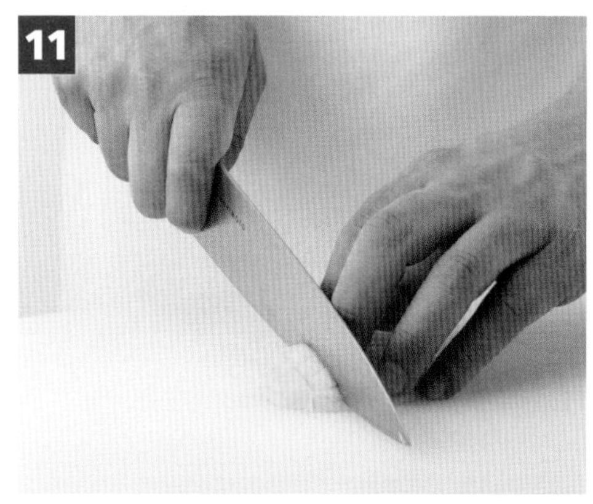

Keeping the blade against your guide fingers, move them back $\frac{1}{4}$ inch (6 mm) and cut off another set of dice.

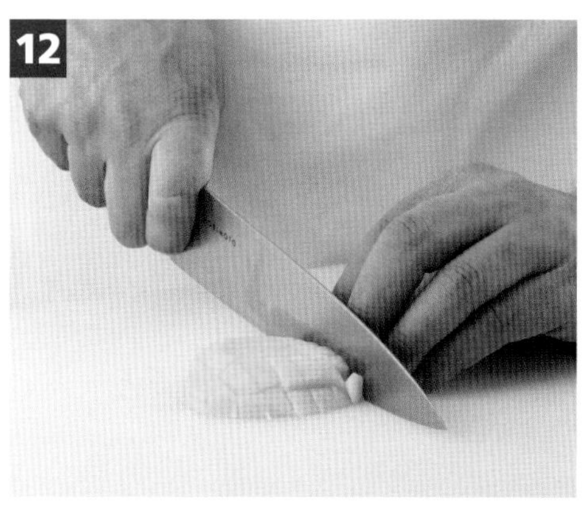

Repeat step 11 until the batonnets are completely cut into dice.

Alternatively, you can slice planks off the whole peeled mango, getting as close to the seed as possible, then proceed from there.

Mushrooms

The world is filled with thousands of varieties of mushrooms. Of course, only a small percentage of these are edible, and white button mushrooms are the ones most commonly eaten in North America. These, then, will be the mushrooms we use to demonstrate mushroom cutting techniques. But since the key to knowing how to take something apart is knowing how it's put together, once you're comfortable with these techniques, you need only look at other mushrooms to figure out how you should handle them.

One thing you need to ascertain before cutting a mushroom is whether the stem is edible. Shiitake stems, for example, are woody and tough, and should be removed before you cut up the cap. (Don't throw them out, though; they add wonderful flavor to stocks and sauces — just toss them in whole and make sure to remove them when you're done cooking.) If the stem is edible, as with a button mushroom, it can remain attached to the cap as you cut.

Mushroom pieces of different shapes and sizes have decidedly different mouth feels, so as you practice cutting and cooking mushrooms, be sure to observe how the various shapes affect the dishes in which you're using them. You can then adjust your cuts to match the dish, so that each one is prepared just the way you like it.

Finally, regardless of the type of mushroom you're using or the dish you're using it in, we recommend buying individual mushrooms rather than presorted containers. It's worth the effort of sorting through a bin of mushrooms to gather specimens of roughly the same size. This will allow you to cut pieces of an even size, which will ensure that they all cook at the same rate and will give your dish a more uniform, and therefore more elegant, appearance.

Peeling Mushrooms and Removing the Gills

Some mushrooms, such as portobello, cremini and black truffles, benefit in taste and appearance from peeling. Insert the tip of a paring knife under the edge of the mushroom and lift up the skin, pulling it toward the center to remove it.

Some recipes call for the removal of gills from gilled mushrooms. To do this, place the stemmed mushroom cap on the cutting board, gill side up. Place the tip of a chef's knife or paring knife in the center of the cap and scrape it toward the edge to shave off the gills. Rotate the cap and repeat until all the gills are removed.

Mushroom peels and gills can be added to stocks and sauces that will be strained. Truffle trimmings can be used to make truffle oils and butters.

Cutting Slices

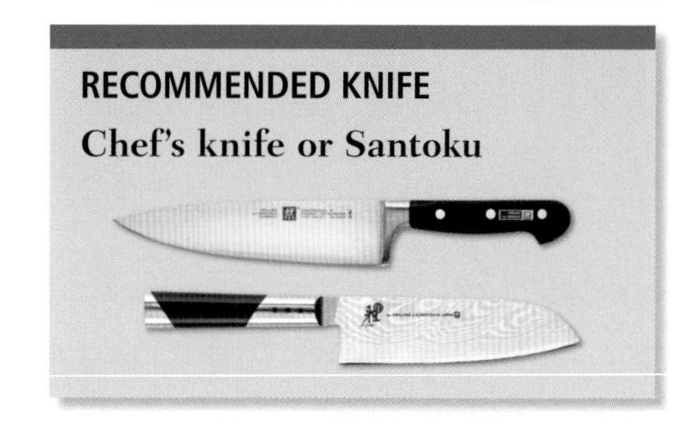
RECOMMENDED KNIFE
Chef's knife or Santoku

Mushrooms take well to the chopping technique (see page 81) because the knife passes through them easily, without sticking. If you're working with a very large mushroom, you may choose to cut it in half before cutting it into slices. In that case, you can place the mushroom halves cut side down. When you're working with a smaller mushroom, you'll lay it on its side, as we do in our demonstration.

Keep in mind that you want all of your slices to be the same width so they will cook at the same rate. What that width should be is determined by what you plan to do with the slices: for example, cut thin slices for quick preparations such as stir-fries and sautés; cut thick slices for soups and braises. As you cut, make sure to keep your knife perfectly perpendicular to the board and cut straight down so that each slice is a uniform thickness all the way around.

1. Lay a mushroom on the board, leaning on its cap with the stem facing you. Steady the cap with your guide hand in the claw position.

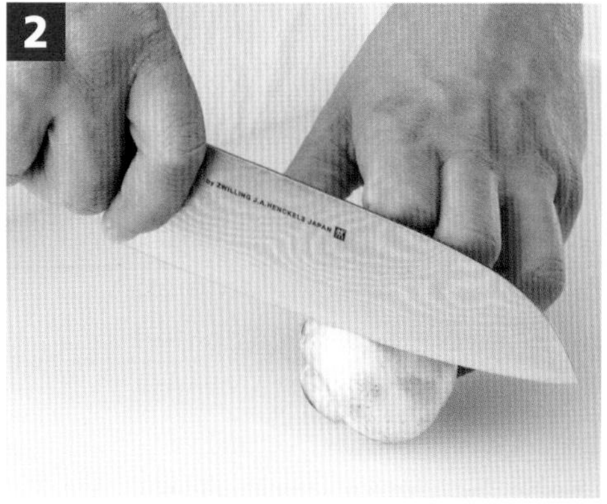

2. Place the knife blade flush against your guide fingers and cut straight down to create your first slice. (Depending on how thick you're cutting your slices, the first and last pieces may or may not have stem attached to the cap.)

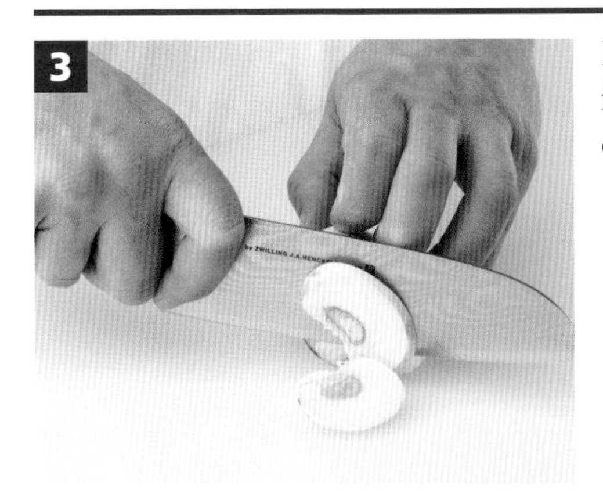

3

Keeping the blade against your guide fingers, move them back slightly and cut off another slice.

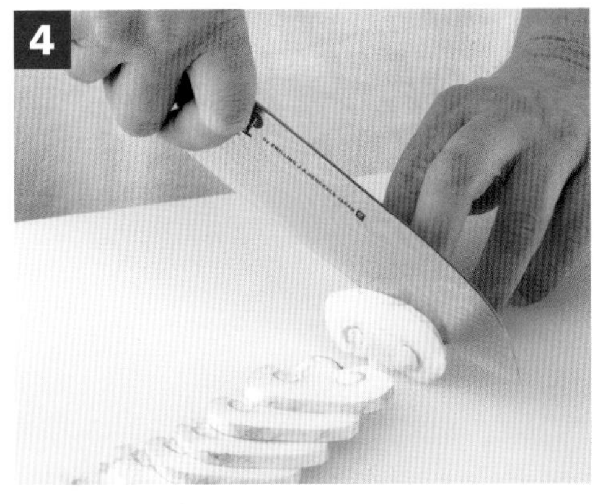

4

Repeat step 3 until the entire mushroom is cut into slices.

Quartering Mushrooms

Quartered mushrooms are often used in classic dishes like beef bourguignon and beef stroganoff. They also make a great addition to quick sautés.

RECOMMENDED KNIFE

Chef's knife or Santoku

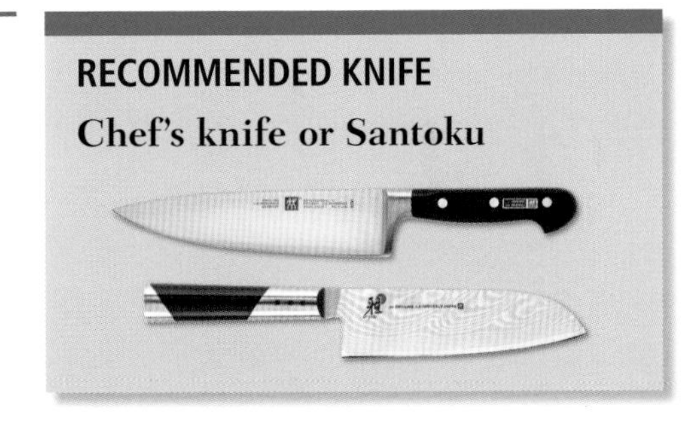

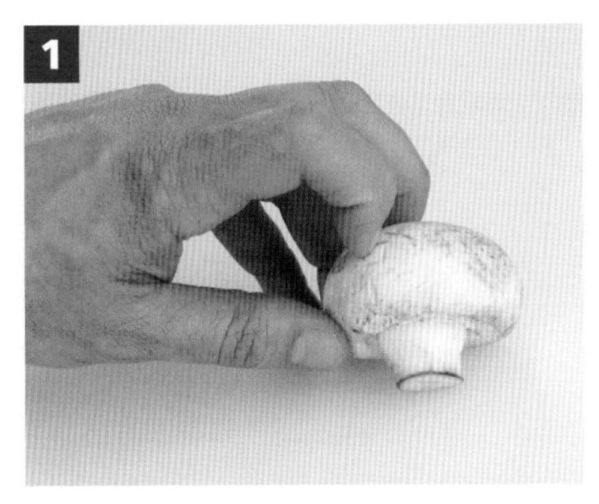

1

Lay a mushroom on the board, leaning on its cap with the stem facing you. Steady one side of the mushroom with your guide hand.

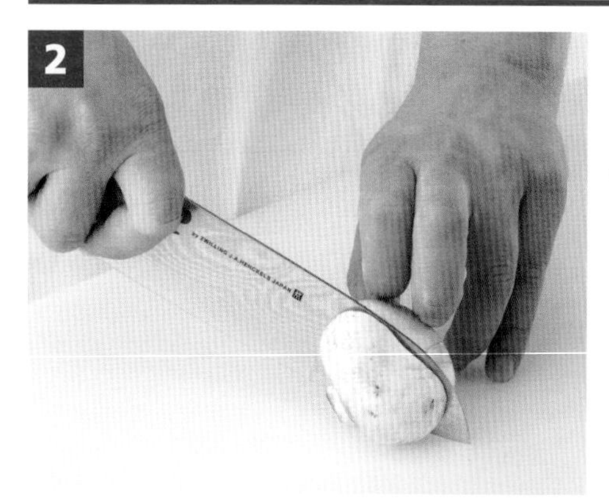

Place the knife blade flush against your guide fingers and cut straight down through the center of the mushroom. You should now have two identical mushroom halves.

Lay the two halves cut side down, cap to cap, with one stem facing you. Steady them with your guide hand.

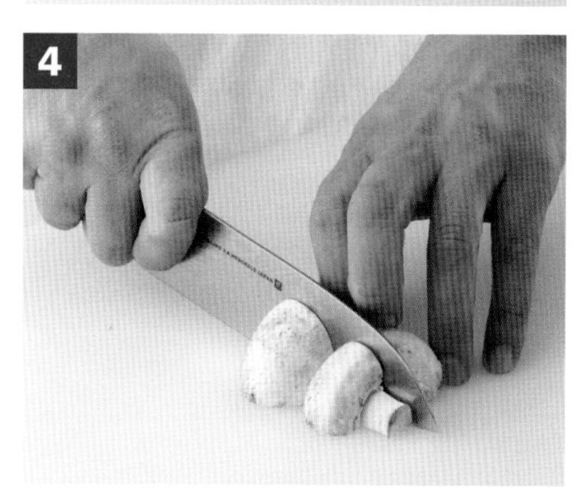

Place the blade flush against your guide fingers and cut straight down through the center of both halves. You should now have four identical mushroom quarters.

Cutting Dice

Diced mushrooms are a great addition to stuffing and are an essential ingredient in duxelles, a mixture of finely diced mushrooms, shallots and herbs used to flavor sauces and soups.

RECOMMENDED KNIFE

Chef's knife or Santoku

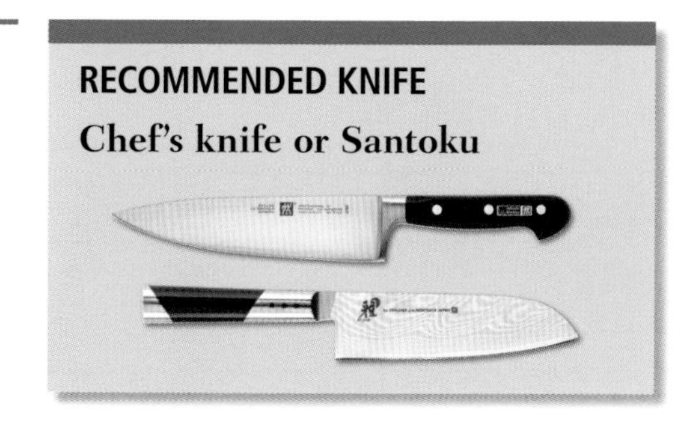

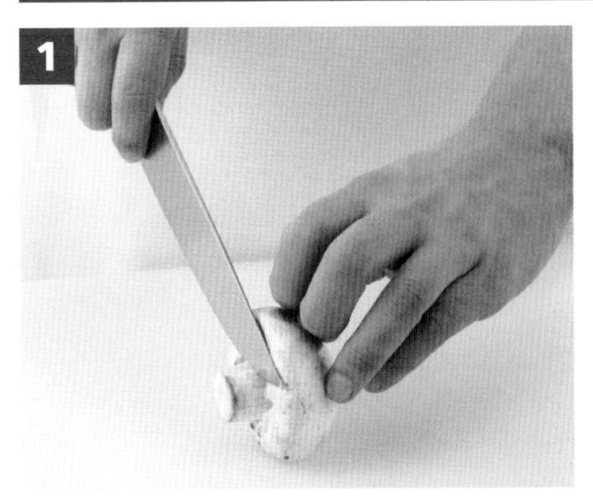

Cut off the stem and reserve it if it's edible.

Balance the mushroom cap on its side, with the top facing your guide hand, and steady it with your guide hand in the claw position.

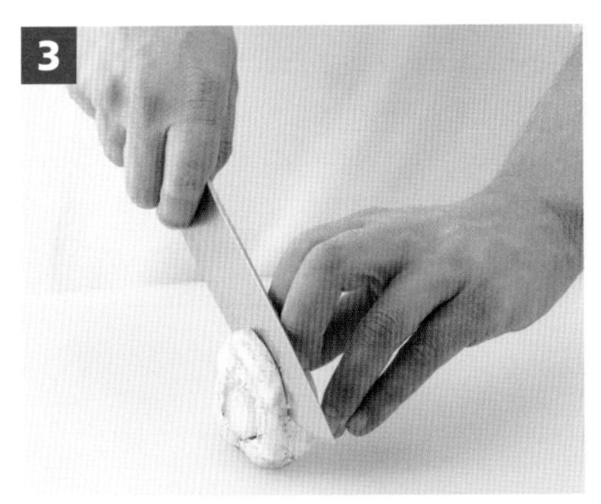

Place the knife blade flush against your guide fingers and line it up to cut off a $\frac{1}{8}$ inch (3 mm) slice. Cut straight down through the mushroom cap.

Keeping the blade against your guide fingers, move them back $\frac{1}{8}$ inch (3 mm) and cut off another slice.

Repeat step 4 until the entire mushroom cap is cut into slices. When you reach the end of the cap, lay it down and cut the last slice horizontally.

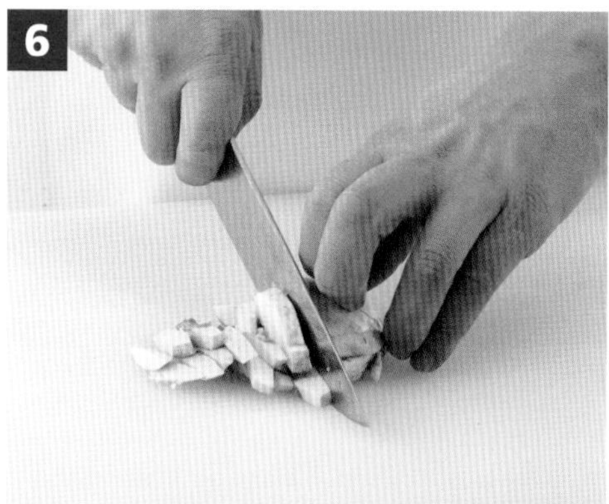

Stack the slices and steady the stack with your guide hand in the claw position. With the blade flush against your guide fingers, cut the stack into $\frac{1}{8}$-inch (3 mm) sticks.

Slide your knife under the stack and use it to carefully rotate the sticks 90 degrees. Steady the stack with your guide hand in the claw position. With the blade flush against your guide fingers, cut the stack into $\frac{1}{8}$-inch (3 mm) dice.

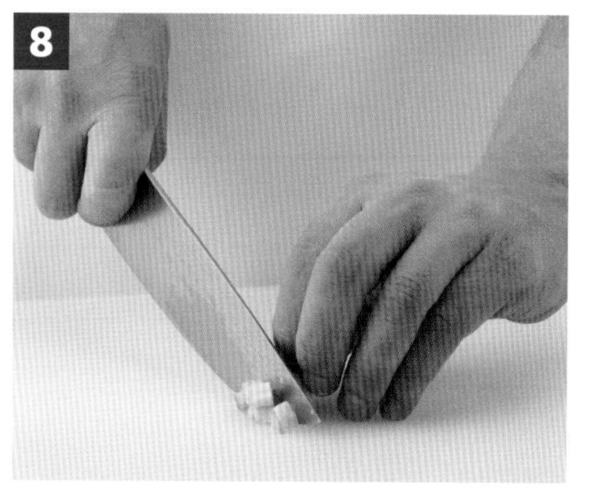

Repeat steps 3 to 6 with the reserved stem.

Onions

Because so many recipes call for onions, it's certainly worthwhile to learn the fastest way to cut one up.

An onion has a stem end and a root end. The stem end tends to be a bit pointy, as if there were a stem growing out of it (hence the name "stem end"). The root end has little hairs growing out of it.

Before cutting up onions, there is one important step you can take to lessen the waterworks: keep your knife very sharp. A sharp knife cuts cleanly through the individual onion cells. A dull knife smashes them, squirting the onion juices into the air, where they float around and irritate your eyes.

Cutting Dice

Diced onions are one of the most common ingredients in savory recipes and are an important part of mirepoix, a 2-1-1 mix of diced onion, carrot and celery that is the building block of many Western sauces and soups.

RECOMMENDED KNIFE

Chef's knife or Santoku

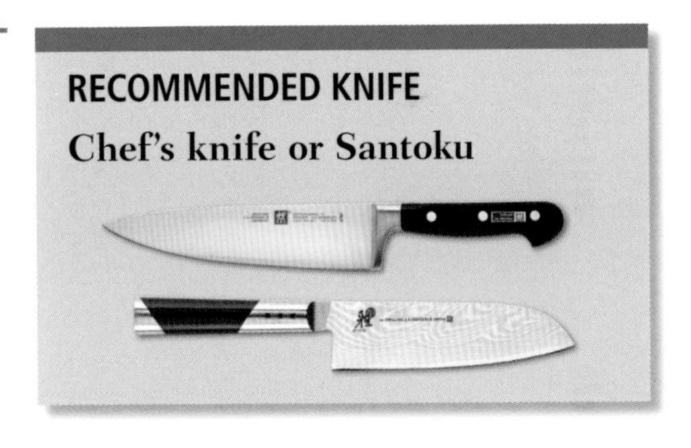

Lay an unpeeled onion on its side, with the stem end facing your knife hand. Steady the onion with your guide hand. Cut straight down to remove a thin slice from the stem end, leaving a small, flat circle of onion flesh where the stem used to be.

At this point, you can trim the roots, making sure to leave the base of the onion intact, or leave them on. It's a matter of preference.

Set the onion on this flat circle. Steady it with your guide hand and place the knife blade directly over the center. Cut straight down to create two equal halves.

Peel the onion halves, removing layers until the outermost layer is moist and firm.

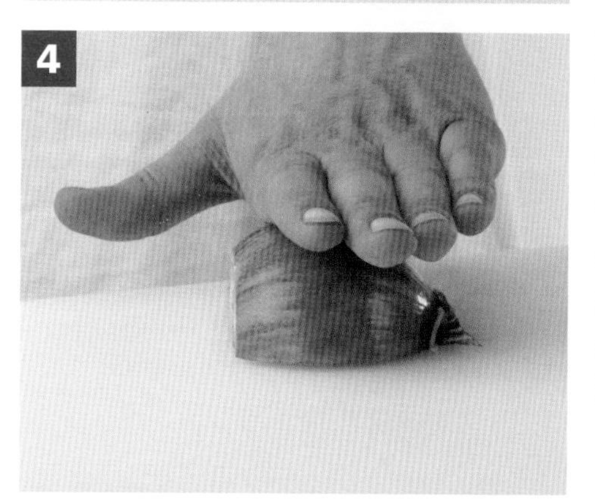

Set one onion half on the cutting board, cut side down, with the flat stem end facing your knife hand. Steady the onion with the palm of your guide hand, taking care to keep your fingers bent up and away from the blade (or just use the claw position, as shown in the photo for step 5).

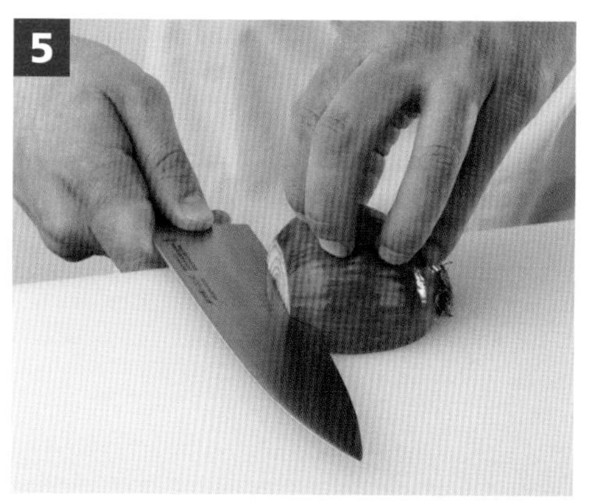

Hold the knife just above the board, with the blade parallel to the board.

The onion half should be close enough to the edge of the board that the knife handle is beyond the edge of the board, not directly above it. If you hold the handle directly above the board, you'll have a tendency to tilt the knife toward the tip, which will result in uneven slices. (Note: In the picture, the guide hand has been removed for clarity.)

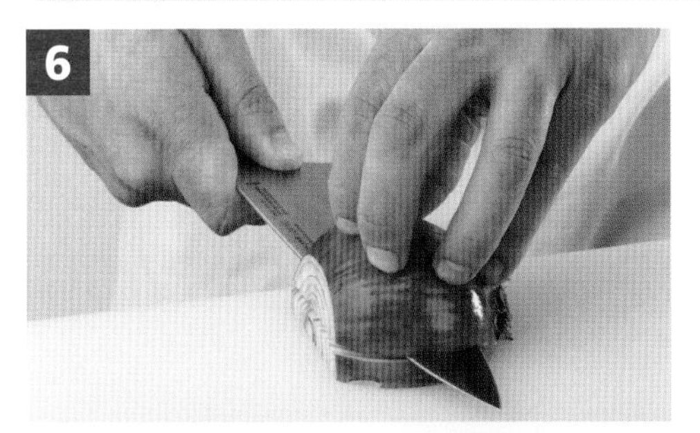

6 Cut back toward the root end horizontally at the desired height. The narrower the cut, the smaller the dice will be. Don't cut all the way through; just go back about 80% of the way. That way, the onion will hold together until you cut the dice.

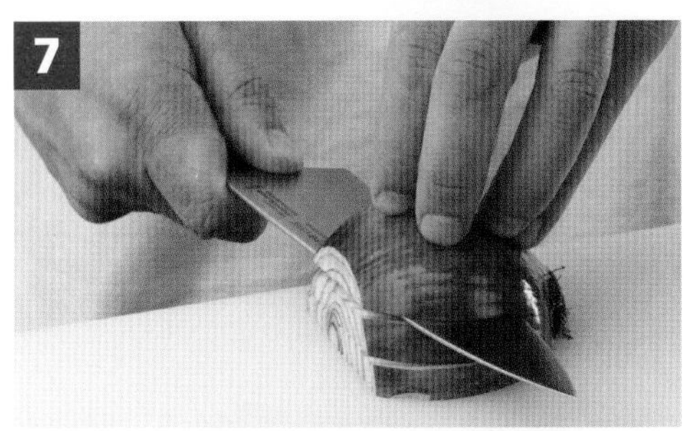

7 Raise your knife and make a second horizontal cut the same width as the first. (Depending on the size of the onion and the preferred size of your dice, you may not need to make this second cut, or you may make several cuts.)

8 When you have completed your horizontal cuts, rotate the onion 90 degrees so that the stem end is facing you. Place your guide hand on top of the onion in the claw position.

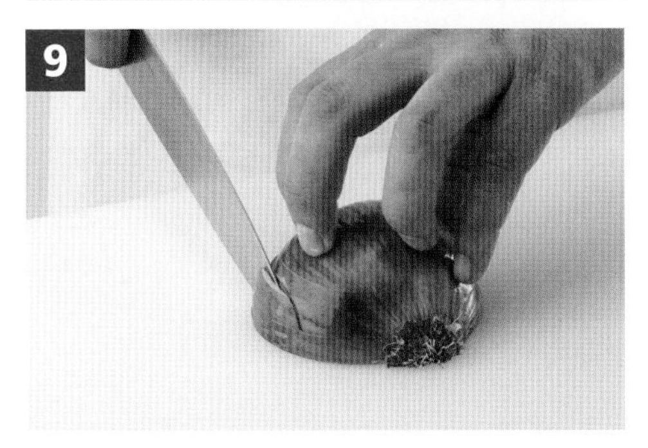

9 Place the blade near the edge of the onion so that your first cut will be the same width as your horizontal cuts. (If possible, the blade should be flush against your guide fingers, but this may be difficult with a larger onion because of its curve.) Cut straight down, once again allowing your knife to go about 80% of the way toward the root end.

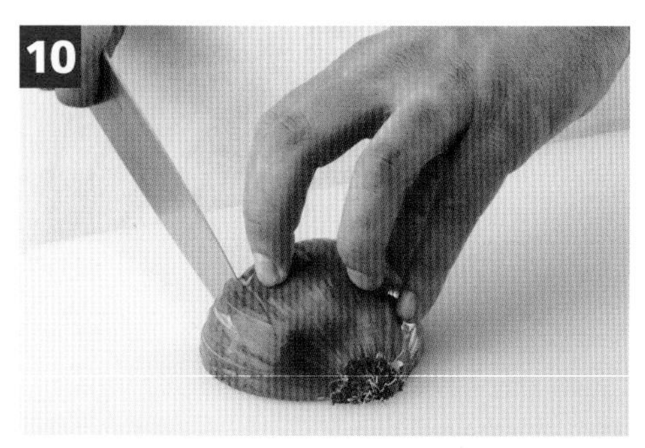

Move the blade back the appropriate amount and make another cut.

Repeat step 10 all the way across the top of the onion, keeping the blade flush against your guide fingers as soon as it is possible to do so.

If you prefer, you can make the vertical cuts first, followed by the horizontal cuts. It's a matter of personal preference.

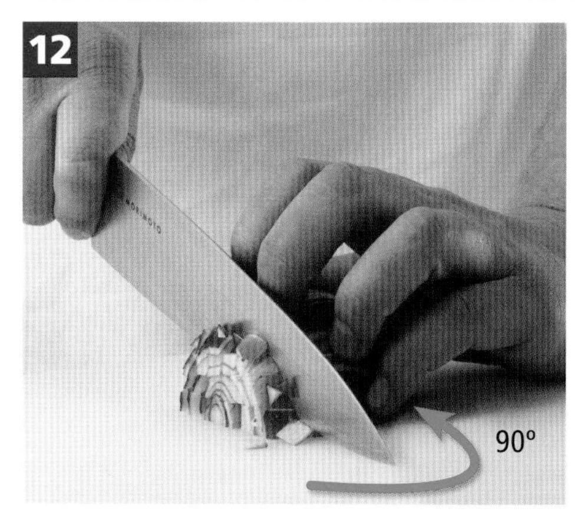

Rotate the onion back to its original position, with the stem end facing your knife hand. Steady the onion with your guide hand in the claw position. Place the blade flush against your guide fingers. Make sure the distance from the edge of the onion to your knife is the same as the width of your previous cuts. Cut straight down through the onion. The dice are now spilling from your knife.

Keeping the blade against your guide fingers, move them back the appropriate amount and cut off another set of dice.

Repeat step 13 until you approach the area of the root end that is uncut.

When it begins to become difficult to hold on to the root end due to its shrinking size, tip it forward onto the board and cut the usable flesh into dice.

Cutting Thin Slices

In France, this technique is called *émincer*. Some people call these slices juliennes. Regardless of what term you use, you'll end up with perfectly even onion slices that are all roughly the same length. These thin pieces are perfect for grilled onions or as the base for a delicious French onion soup. We'll cut 1/8-inch (3 mm) thick slices, but you can cut thicker slices if you prefer.

RECOMMENDED KNIFE

Chef's knife or Santoku

Lay an unpeeled onion on its side, with the stem end facing your knife hand. Steady the onion with your guide hand. Cut straight down to remove a thin slice from the stem end, leaving a small, flat circle of onion flesh where the stem used to be.

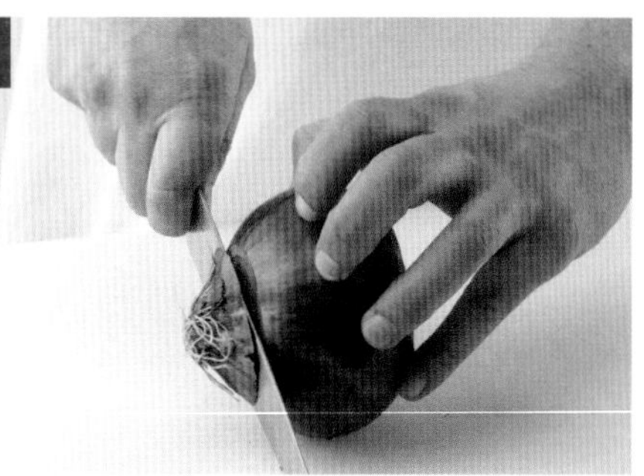

Rotate the onion 180 degrees and cut off the root end.

Be sure to cut off enough of the root end that the "wood" is completely gone.

Set the onion on one of the flat ends. Steady it with your guide hand and place the knife blade directly over the center. Cut straight down to create two equal halves.

4

Peel the onion halves, removing layers until the outermost layer is moist and firm.

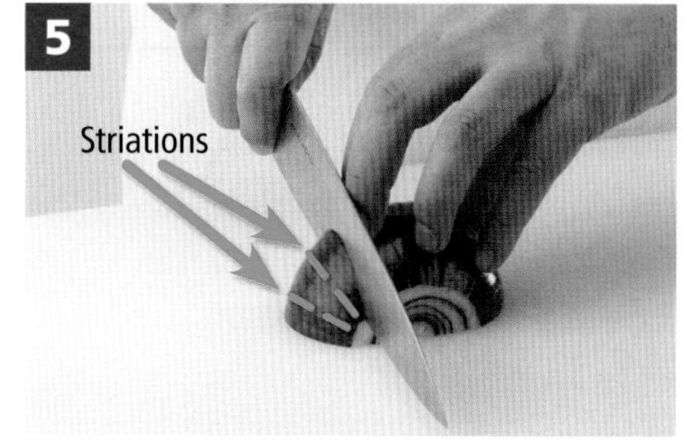

Set one onion half on the cutting board, cut side down, with the striations parallel to your knife.

6

Cut off about a quarter of the onion, in one piece.

7

Knock this piece over onto its side and rotate it 180 degrees, so that the lower end is facing your knife.

8

Steady the piece with your guide hand in the claw position. Place the blade against your guide fingers. Make sure the distance from the edge of the piece to your knife is ⅛ inch (3 mm). Cut straight down to create your first set of slices.

9

Keeping the blade against your guide fingers, move them back ⅛ inch (3 mm) and cut off another set of slices.

10

Repeat step 9 until the entire piece is cut into slices.

11 Return to the main piece of the onion and steady it with your guide hand in the claw position. Place the blade against your guide fingers. Make sure the distance from the edge of the onion to your knife is $\frac{1}{8}$ inch (3 mm). Cut straight down to create your first set of slices from this piece.

12 Keeping the blade against your guide fingers, move them back $\frac{1}{8}$ inch (3 mm) and cut off another set of slices.

13 Repeat step 12 until only about a quarter of the onion remains.

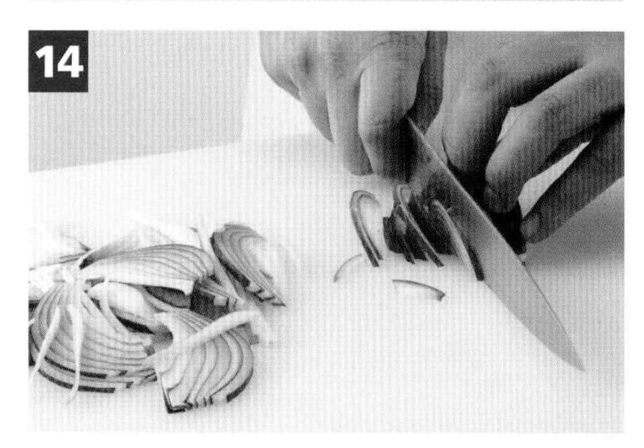

14 Knock that remaining piece over and repeat steps 8 to 10 to cut this piece into slices.

You can also cut an onion into slices using the fan method described for an avocado on page 137. Or, for quick but uneven slices, simply cut slices all the way across the onion.

FAQs about Onions *Émincés*

There are a couple of seemingly counterintuitive instructions in this technique, and we should explain why it is done the way it is. Remember, the goal is to make all of the slices as close to the same size as possible.

Why do we cut along the striations?

It might seem like it would make more sense to cut across the striations, so let's do that and see what happens. We'll set our onion half on the board with the striations perpendicular to the knife.

We'll make our cuts straight down all the way across, moving our guide fingers back ⅛ inch (3 mm) after each slice. The individual pieces fall nicely apart from each other and are all the same width.

However, notice that the closer the pieces are to the center of the onion, the shorter they are. There's a huge difference in the lengths of the various pieces.

Compare those pieces to the ones we cut doing the technique correctly.

Why do we treat the first and last quarters of the onion half differently, and what's with the knocking over?

If we were to start simply by cutting slices on the side of the onion, we'd end up with one big, oversized piece that would contrast starkly with the rest of our pieces.

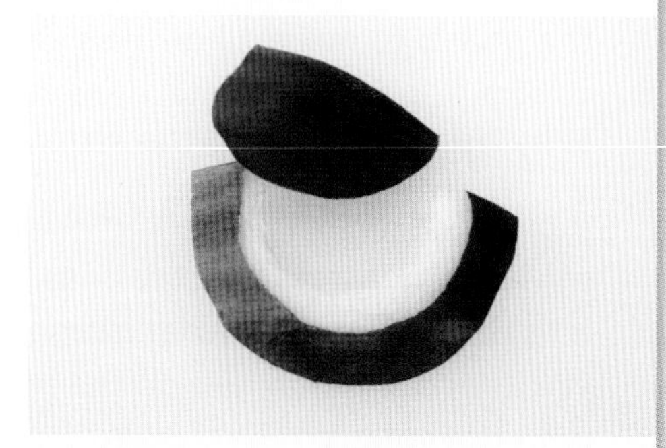

By cutting off that first quarter and knocking it down, we get nice, even pieces.

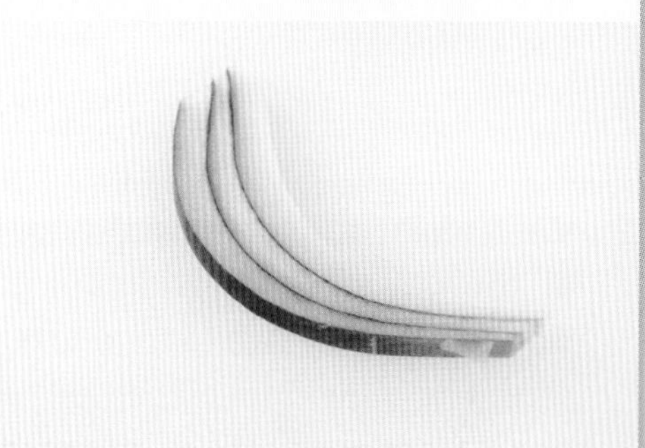

Why do we rotate the first quarter 180 degrees?

This is simply our personal preference. After we rotate the piece, the low end is closer to the blade, so that as we make our cuts, the knife moves "uphill." We find it a bit easier to grab the small piece with our guide hand that way.

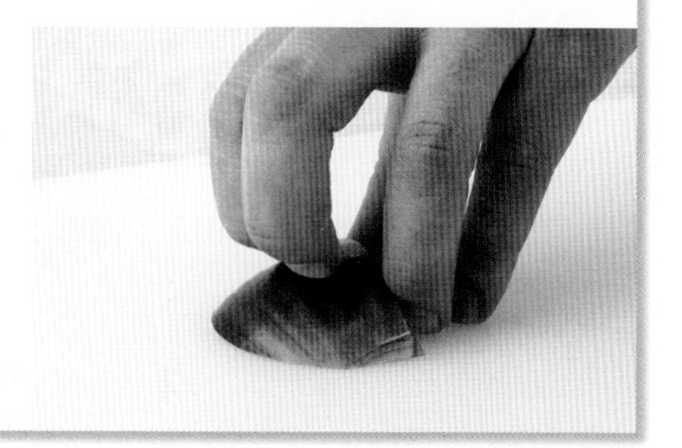

Cutting Rings

Onion rings are great raw on sandwiches or battered and fried for a side dish or a garnish for grilled steak. Onions cut this way can be left in slices, or the rings can be broken apart. For our demo, we'll make $\frac{1}{4}$-inch (6 mm) thick rings but you can cut them to any thickness you like. First, cut off the ends and peel the onion, but leave it whole.

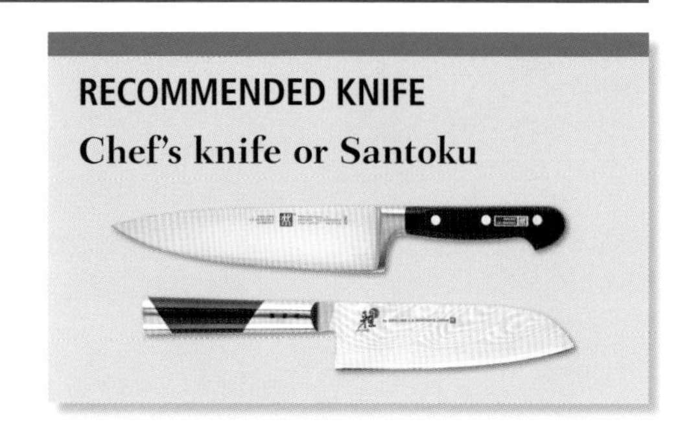

RECOMMENDED KNIFE

Chef's knife or Santoku

1. Place the onion on the cutting board, with the root end facing your guide hand. Steady the onion with your guide hand in the claw position.

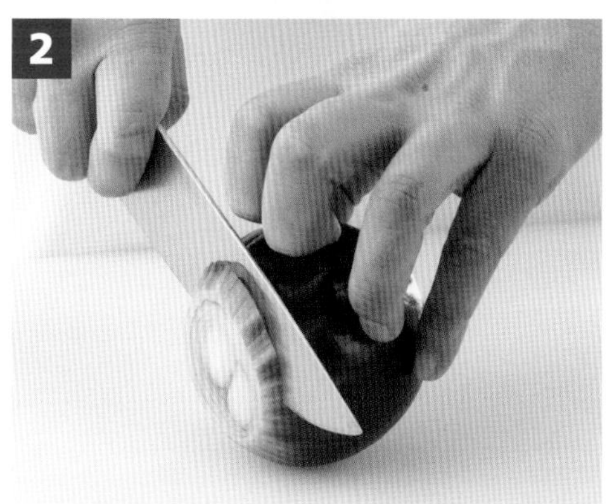

2. Place the knife blade flush against your guide fingers and line it up to cut off a $\frac{1}{4}$-inch (6 mm) slice. Cut straight down through the onion.

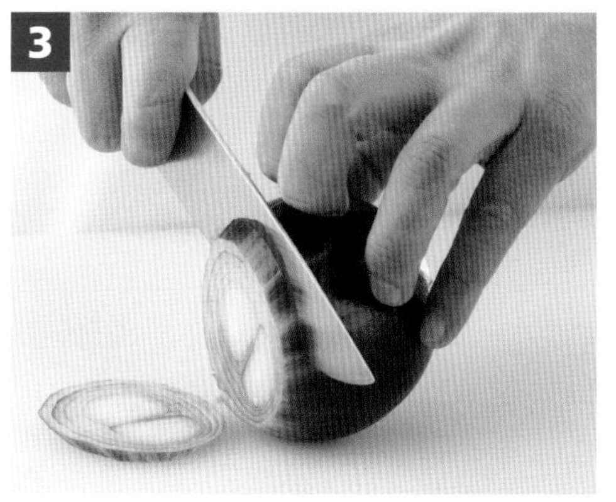

3. Keeping the blade against your guide fingers, move them back $\frac{1}{4}$ inch (6 mm) and cut off another slice.

4 Repeat step 3 until you have cut the entire onion into slices.

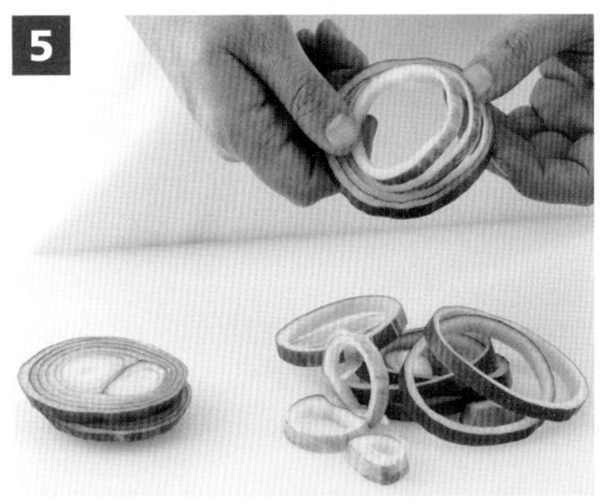

5 If desired, break the slices into rings.

In restaurants, when large amounts of onion rings are needed, cooks often use an electric meat slicer to save time.

Pineapples

Pineapple is delicious on its own and is a great addition to salads and salsas. Its sweet-tart flavor also makes it an excellent counterpoint to the saltiness of ham.

Peeling a Pineapple

The peel of a pineapple is inedible and must be removed. A challenge is presented by the eyes hiding underneath the peel — you must either cut deep enough to remove them along with the peel (which results in some wasted flesh) or, after peeling, spend a little more time cutting the eyes out in a spiral pattern (see the box on page 202).

RECOMMENDED KNIVES

Chef's knife or Santoku; paring knife

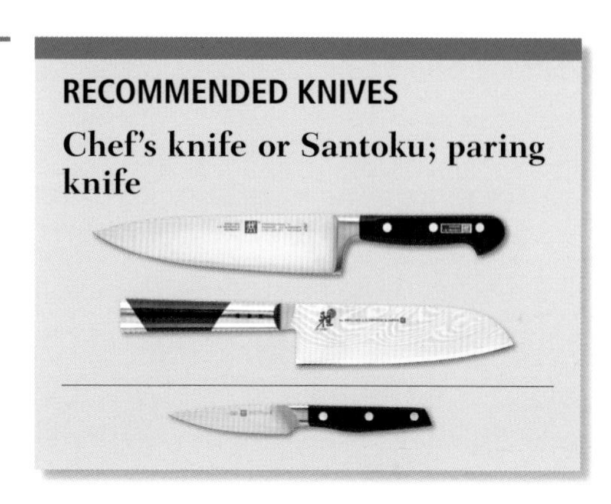

1

Lay the pineapple on the cutting board with the leafy end facing your knife hand. Place the blade of the chef's knife ½ to ¾ inch (12 mm to 2 cm) back from the leaves and cut straight down to remove the top.

2

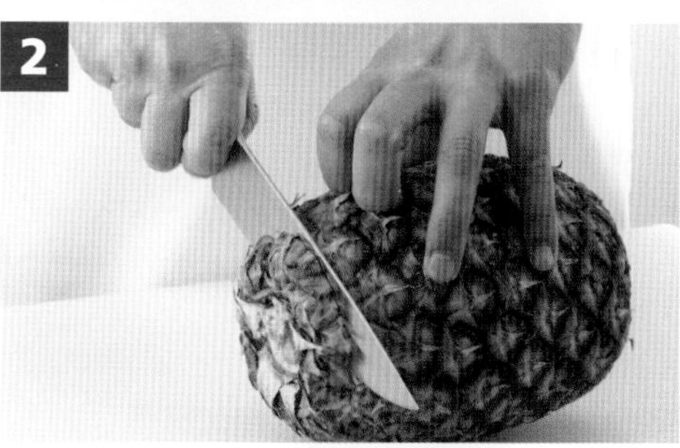

Turn the pineapple 180 degrees so that the base is facing your knife hand. Place the blade ½ to ¾ inch (12 mm to 2 cm) behind the stem and cut straight down to remove the base.

3

Stand the pineapple on its base and peel it as you would citrus fruits (see page 160, steps 3 to 5), following the slight curve of the pineapple and cutting deep enough to remove the eyes. Each slice will expose the eyes you'll need to remove in the next slice, telling you how deep to make your next cut.

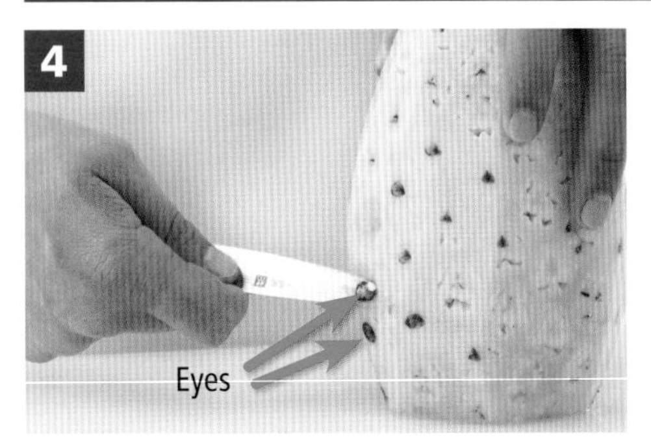

Once the pineapple is peeled, hold the paring knife in the shucking grip (see page 86) and steady the pineapple with your guide hand. With the point of the knife, cut out any remaining eyes, using a circular motion.

To remove the eyes with less waste, when you're peeling the pineapple, cut just deep enough to remove the skin. Then use the paring knife to cut a V-shaped channel through the pineapple flesh, following the diagonal lines of the eyes to create a spiral around the pineapple. Cut just deep enough to remove the eyes.

Coring a Pineapple

Pineapples have a thick core that is edible but not very tasty. It is best to remove it.

RECOMMENDED KNIFE

Chef's knife or Santoku

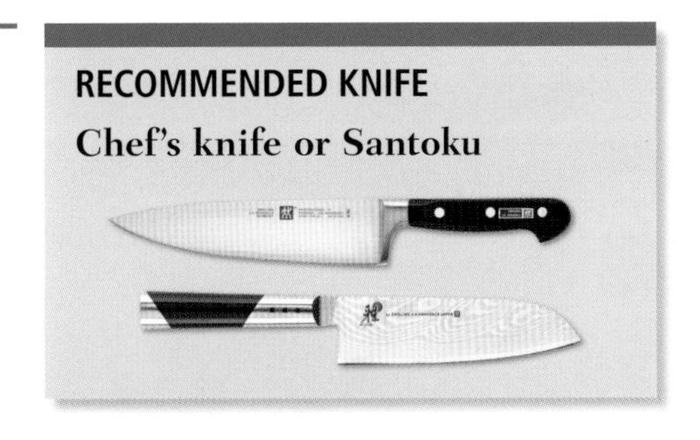

Stand a peeled pineapple on the cutting board and steady it with your guide hand. Place the knife blade on top of the pineapple at the center line and cut the pineapple in half.

2

Lay one of the halves on the board, cut side down. Steady it with your guide hand and cut in half. Repeat with the other pineapple half.

3

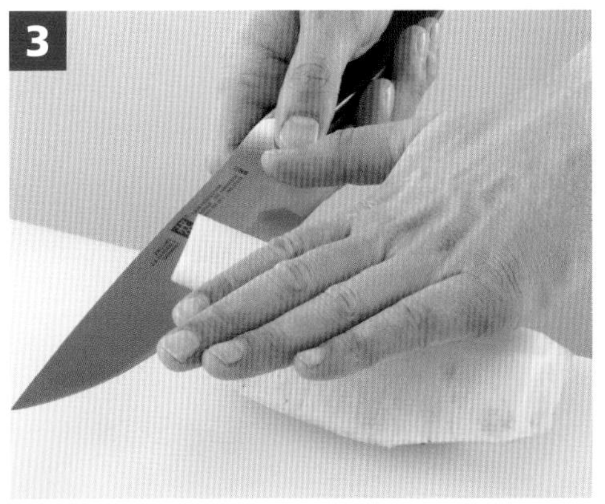

Place a pineapple quarter on the board, with the core facing up. The pineapple should be fairly close to the edge of the cutting board nearest you, and parallel to it. Place your guide hand flat across the pineapple quarter to steady it. Make sure to keep your fingers bent up and away from the blade.

4

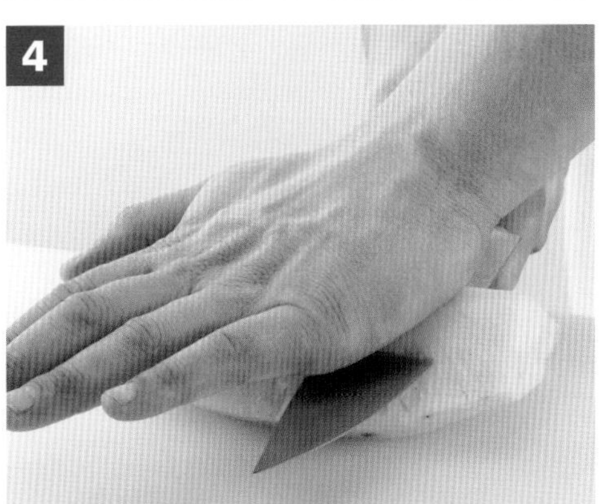

Hold the knife blade parallel to the board, just below the core on the knife-hand side. Slide the knife through the pineapple quarter to remove the core.

5

Repeat steps 3 and 4 with the remaining three pineapple quarters.

Dicing Pineapple

Pineapples can be cut into small, medium or large dice, depending on what you intend to do with them. If you're using the dice as a pizza topping, for example, you'll want to cut small dice. For a fruit salad, large dice would be prettier. Use peeled, cored pineapple quarters and cut them into dice following the basic technique detailed in chapter 3.

Cutting Rings

To cut pineapple rings, you'll used a peeled pineapple that hasn't yet been cored. You can choose to cut 1⁄4-inch (6 mm) rings or 1⁄2-inch (12 mm) rings. For our demo, we'll cut 1⁄4-inch (6 mm) rings.

RECOMMENDED KNIVES

Chef's knife or Santoku; paring knife

1

Lay a peeled pineapple on its side on the cutting board, with one end facing your knife hand. Steady the pineapple with your guide hand in the claw position.

2

Place the blade of the chef's knife flush against your guide fingers and line it up to cut off a 1⁄4-inch (6 mm) slice. Cut straight down through the pineapple.

Keeping the blade against your guide fingers, move them back $\frac{1}{4}$ inch (6 mm) and cut off another slice.

Repeat step 3 until you have cut the entire pineapple into slices.

Lay a slice flat on the board and place your guide hand on the edge of the slice to steady it. Holding the paring knife in the stabbing grip (see page 86), cut around the circumference of the core.

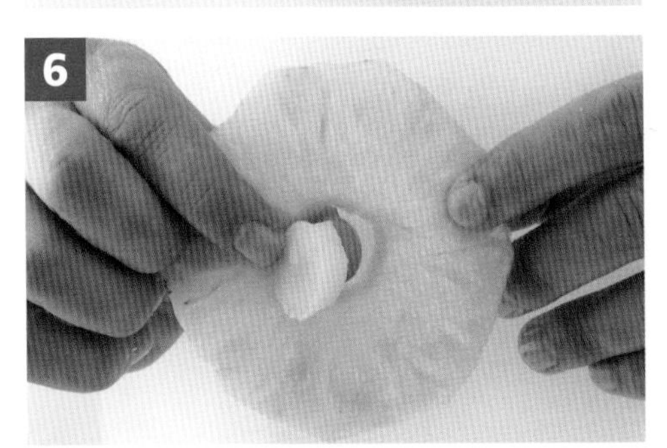

Pick up the slice with your guide hand and push out the core with your knife hand.

Repeat steps 5 and 6 until you have removed the core from all of the slices. With a little practice, you'll be able to core several slices at once by stacking them on top of each other.

Potatoes

Before you can cut a potato into sticks, dice, paysannes, lozenges or tournés (see chapter 3), you need to decide whether to peel it (most of the time, you'll want to, but in some cases you might decide not to, for a more rustic look). There are two ways to peel a potato, either holding it in your guide hand (the "old school" way) or resting it on the cutting board. Which method you use is simply a matter of preference.

With either method, after you've peeled the potato there may be some eyes left with bits of peel in them. Use the tip of your paring knife or peeler to gouge them out with a circular motion.

Peeling a Potato the "Old School" Way

If you don't mind holding the potato in your guide hand while you cut off the peel, this can be a very speedy method. If you're more comfortable with resting the potato on the cutting board, use the method on page 207.

RECOMMENDED KNIFE

Paring knife or peeler

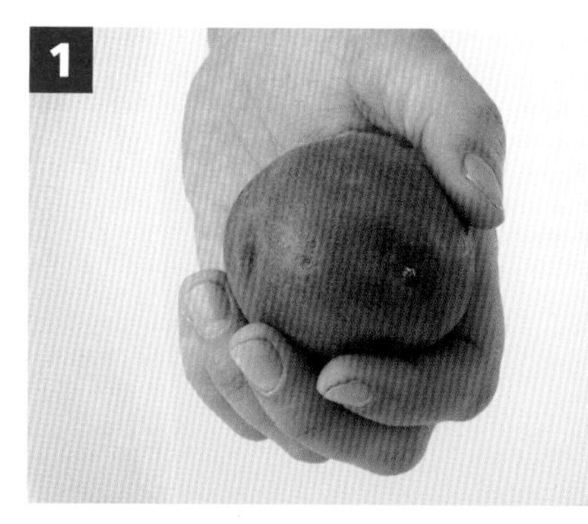

1 Hold your guide hand with the palm up and the fingers relaxed and slightly curled. Rest the potato on the index, middle and ring fingers of your guide hand and support it with your thumb.

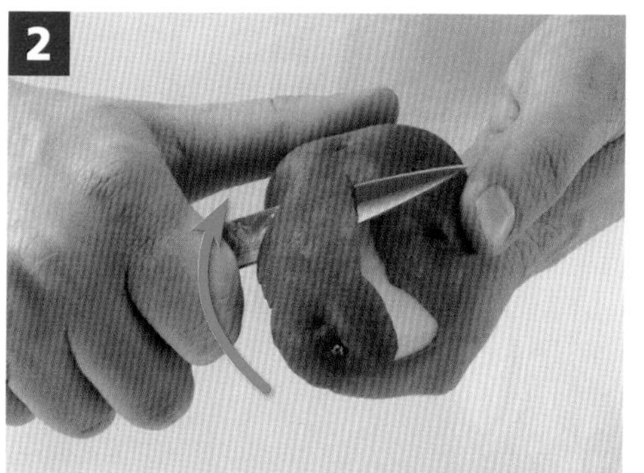

2 Holding the knife in the paring grip (see page 85), rest the thumb of your knife hand at the bottom of the potato, perpendicular to the thumb of your guide hand. Starting at the top of potato, drag the blade toward your thumb, just underneath the skin of the potato.

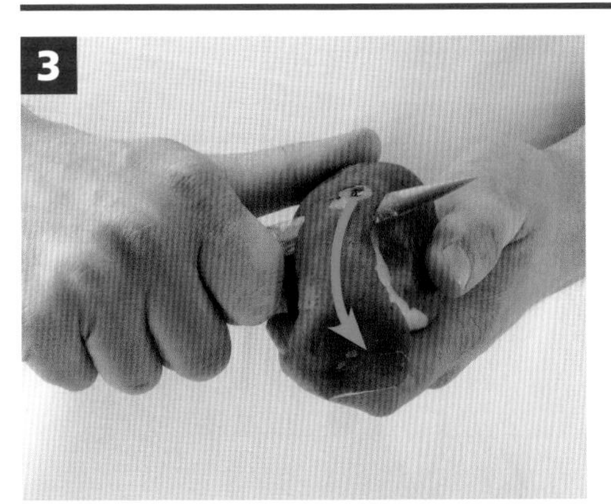

At the same time, use the thumb and index finger of your guide hand to rotate the potato away from the thumb on your knife hand. This will make it easier to follow the curve of the potato so that you take off as little of the flesh as possible.

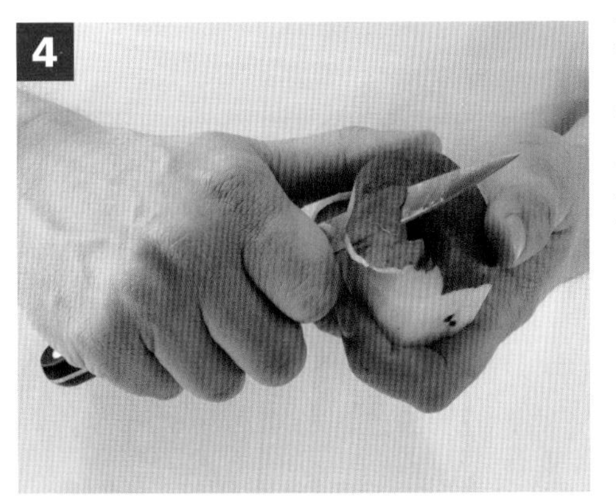

Turn the potato slightly to bring more of the peel into the path of the knife and repeat step 3. Continue until you've peeled the entire potato.

Peeling a Potato on the Cutting Board

If you like the convenience of a peeler and prefer to rest the potato on the cutting board while you peel it, this is the method for you. It works well with large potatoes.

RECOMMENDED TOOL

Peeler

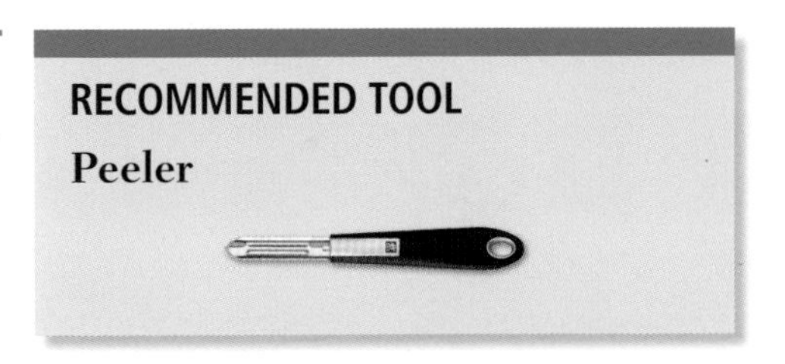

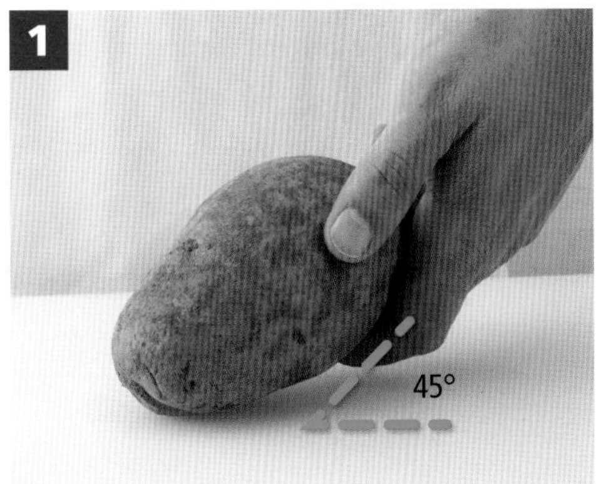

Hold one end of the potato with your guide hand. Tilt it away from your knife hand so that it's at a 45-degree angle to the cutting board.

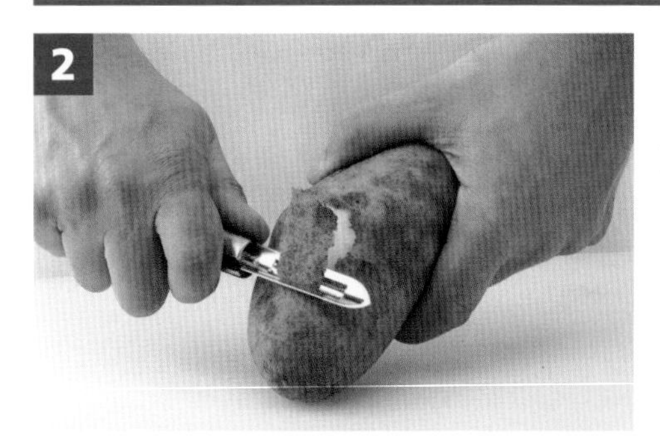

Holding the peeler in your knife hand, scrape it down along the surface of the potato from the center to the bottom to remove a strip of skin.

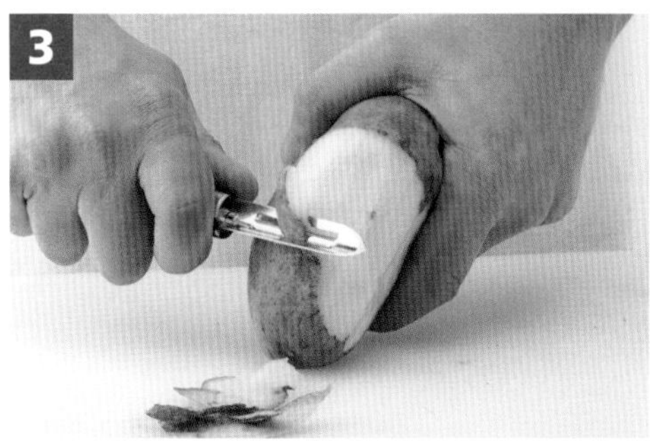

Rotate the potato so that the peel moves into the path of your knife hand and repeat step 2.

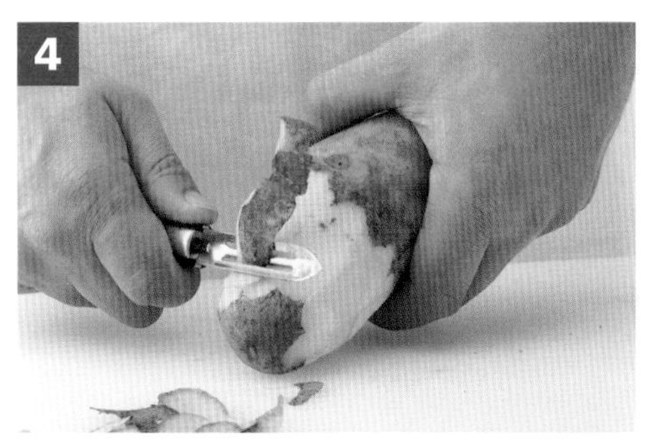

Continue rotating the potato and scraping down with the peeler until you've gone all the way around the potato.

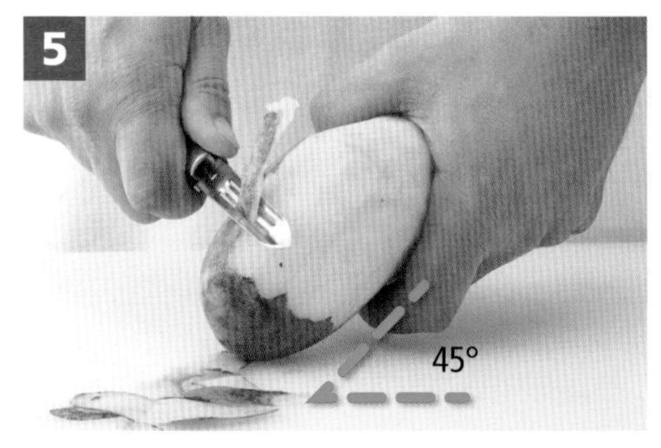

Flip the potato and hold it by the other end at a 45-degree angle to the cutting board. Repeat steps 2 to 4 until the entire potato is peeled, except for the two ends.

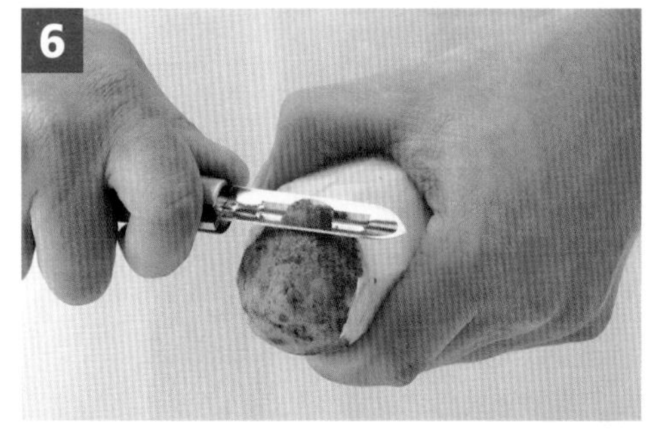

Hold the potato in your guide hand and scrape the skin from both ends.

Stone Fruits

This category of fruits, which includes peaches, plums, nectarines and apricots, is so called because the fruits contain a large stone in the center of the flesh, which should be removed before you cut the flesh into slices or dice.

Although the peel of stone fruits is edible, some recipes may call for you to remove it, especially in the case of peaches. To do so, use a paring knife to remove the stem with a circular motion and cut a small X through the skin on the bottom of the fruit. Drop the fruit into boiling water for 10 seconds — just long enough to loosen the skin without cooking the flesh. (This step is called blanching.) Remove the fruit from the boiling water and immediately immerse it in a bowl of ice water. (This step, called shocking, halts the cooking process.) Now you can easily peel the fruit by gripping the flaps created when you cut the X and pulling the skin away from the flesh.

Removing the Stone

Removing the stone involves cutting the fruit into its two hemispheres. Before you pick up your knife, examine the top of the fruit (and if there's still a stem attached, pull it off). You'll see a slightly elongated path across the top that divides the fruit into two obvious halves. You'll be using that path as the guide for your cuts.

This technique can be done on peeled or unpeeled fruit. We'll use an unpeeled nectarine to demonstrate it.

RECOMMENDED KNIFE

Chef's knife, Santoku, Kudamono or paring knife

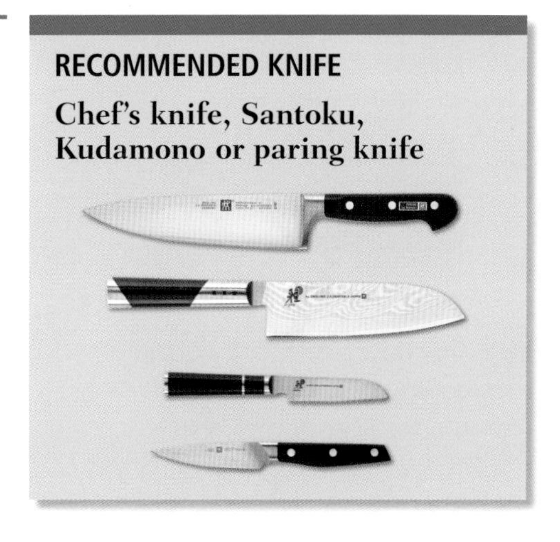

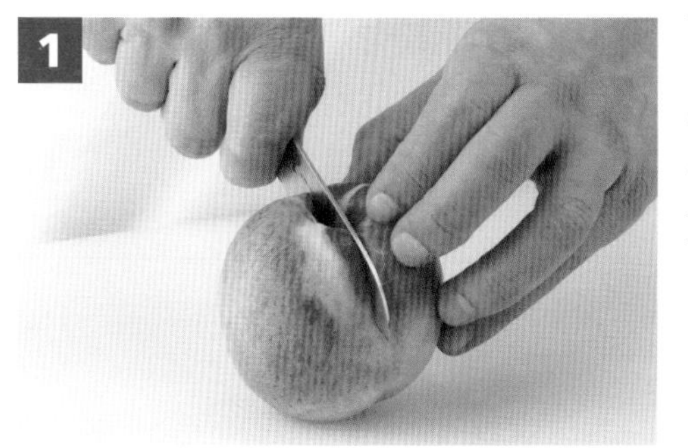

Hold the nectarine in your guide hand, stem side up. Place the knife blade directly in the center of the elongated path. Cut straight down to the stone.

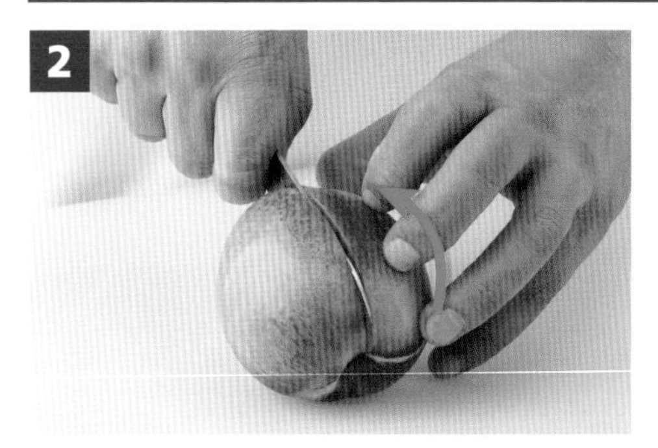

Maintaining constant contact between the blade and the stone, use your guide hand to rotate the nectarine into the blade, cutting through the flesh.

Continue rotating the nectarine into the knife until you have turned it 360 degrees and cut all the way around the stone.

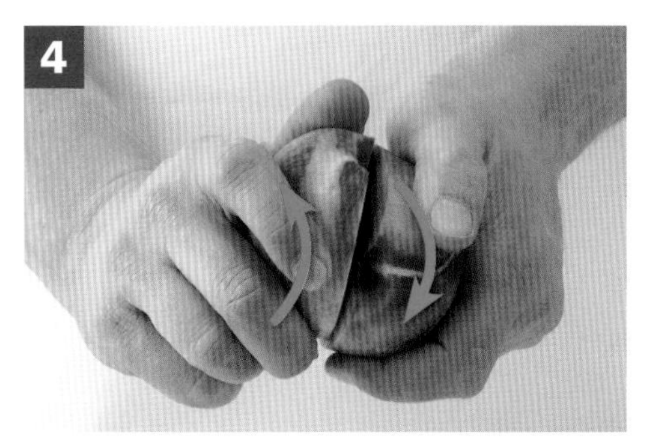

Set your knife down and grab one side of the nectarine in each hand. Twist the halves in opposite directions to loosen one of them from the seed.

Pull the two halves apart. Hold the half with the stone in your guide hand and pull out the stone with your knife hand.

Once the stone is removed, try using the fan method, explained using an avocado on page 137, to cut each nectarine half into even slices. You can then cut sticks or dice following the technique explained for apples on page 123.

Tomatoes

For our money, a ripe red tomato fresh from the garden is just about the best thing on the planet. Mass-produced varieties from factory farms rarely compare to those from local farmers or those we grow ourselves.

Cutting Slices

Tomato slices are a great accompaniment to most sandwiches, and a BLT would be just a BL without them.

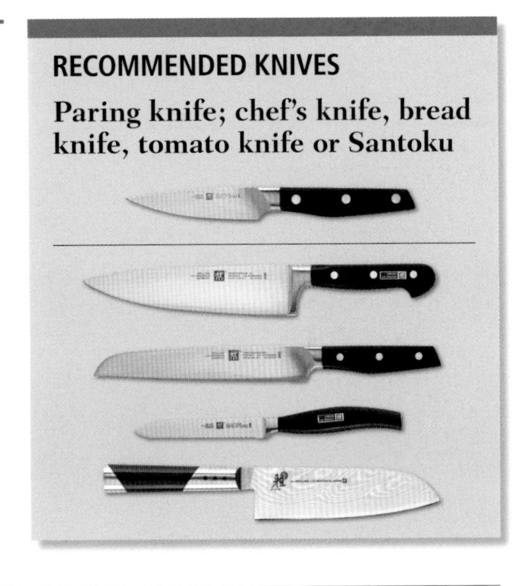

RECOMMENDED KNIVES

Paring knife; chef's knife, bread knife, tomato knife or Santoku

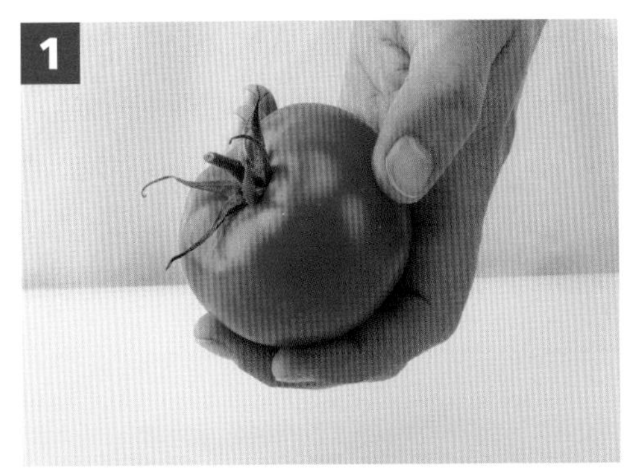

1. Hold the tomato in your guide hand, with the stem side facing away from your palm.

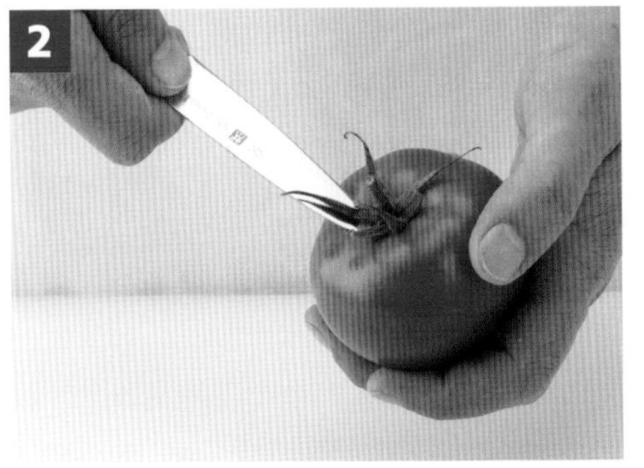

2. Hold the paring knife in the shucking grip (see page 86). Press the point into the tomato at the edge of the stem, holding the blade at a 45-degree angle to the stem. You're going to cut out the stem and a conical piece of tomato from directly below it.

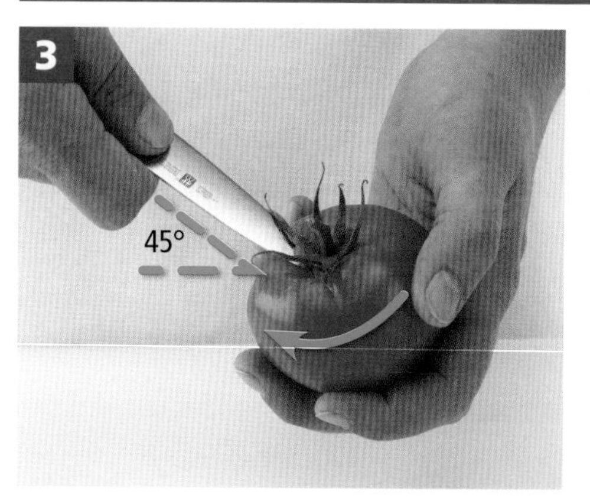

Using a sawing motion, cut down at a 45-degree angle as you rotate the tomato.

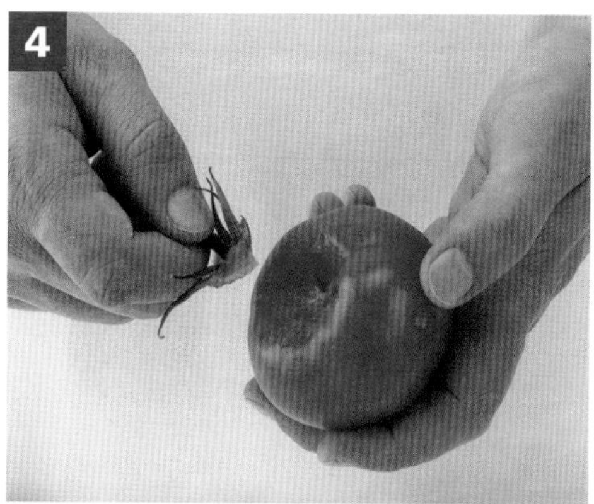

When you've gone completely around the stem, pull it out and discard it.

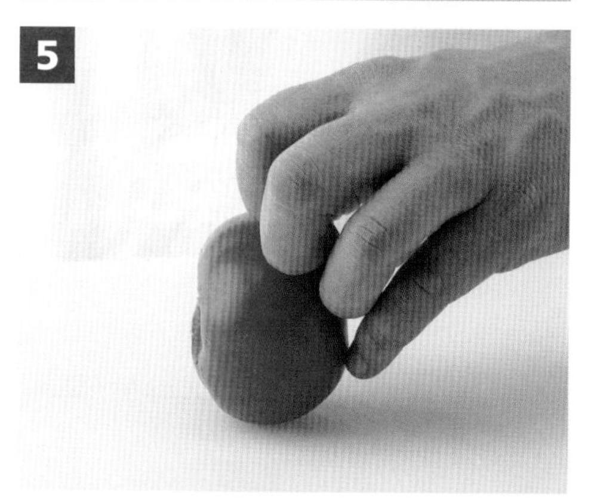

Lay the tomato on its side on the cutting board, with the top facing your knife hand, and steady it with your guide hand in the claw position.

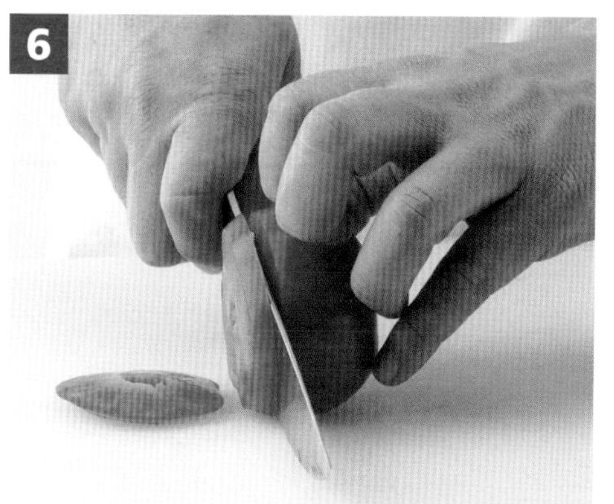

With the blade of the chef's knife flush against your guide fingers, cut the tomato into thick slices.

Cutting Concassé

RECOMMENDED KNIFE

Chef's knife or Santoku

Technically, "concassé" refers to a rough chop of any vegetable. Nonetheless, the term is almost always applied only to tomatoes. Because concassé, unlike other dice, is understood to be a rough cut, you don't have to worry about making all the pieces the same size.

Although a whole tomato can be used for concassé, the tomato is usually peeled and seeded first. To peel a tomato, use a paring knife to remove the stem with a circular motion and cut a small X through the skin on the bottom of the tomato. Drop the tomato into boiling water for 10 seconds — just long enough to loosen the skin without cooking the flesh. (This step is called blanching.) Remove the tomato from the boiling water and immediately immerse it in a bowl of ice water. (This step, called shocking, halts the cooking process.) Now you can easily peel the tomato by gripping the flaps created when you cut the X and pulling the skin away from the flesh.

To seed the tomato, cut it in half around its equator and squeeze gently to force the seeds out. Now it is ready to be chopped.

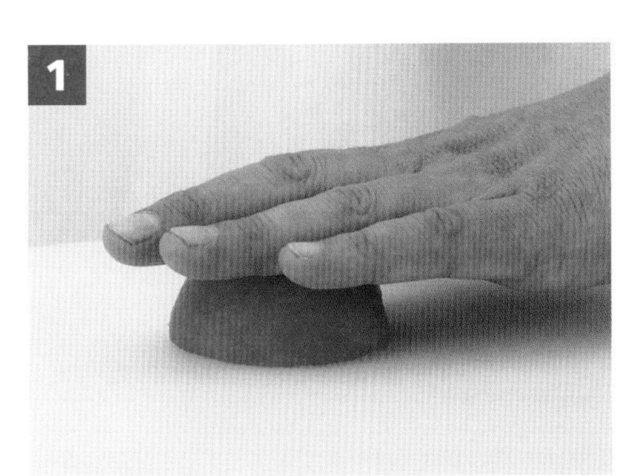

Place a tomato half on the cutting board, cut side down, and steady it with your guide hand.

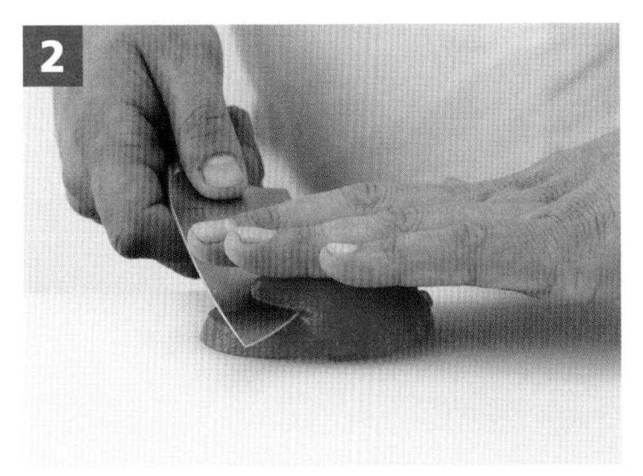

Holding your knife parallel to the cutting board, make a series of horizontal cuts through the tomato, cutting it into slices.

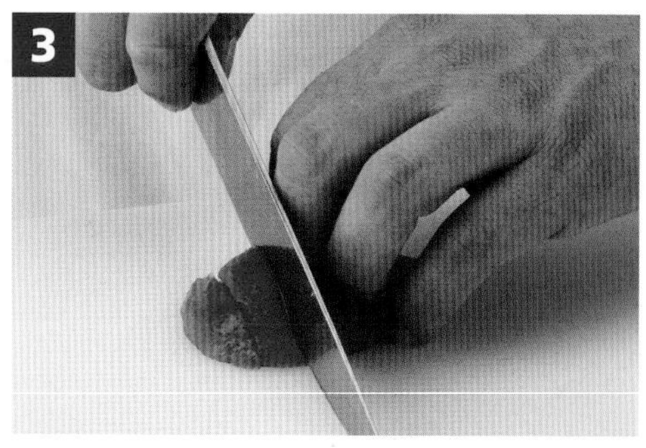

Place the blade flush against your guide fingers and make a series of vertical cuts through the stack of slices, making an effort to keep all the pieces stacked.

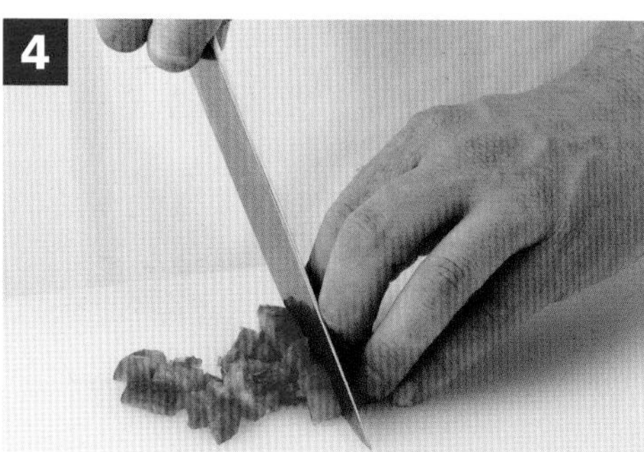

Rotate the stack 90 degrees and make another series of vertical slices through the stack until all the pieces are cut into rough dice.

Cutting Juliennes and Dice

While julienning tomatoes is a fairly uncommon practice, it's an attractive cut in dishes in which the tomato is used raw (so the pieces won't be broken down by cooking), such as salads. To do so, we'll first cut the tomato into quarters and remove the seeds. In doing so, we will have created tomato "leaves," the culinary term for deseeded tomato quarters — you'll understand why when you see their distinctive shape. The leaves are then cut into juliennes.

Cutting the juliennes into dice gives you much more precise cubes than those you get following the concassé technique (page 213).

RECOMMENDED KNIFE

Chef's knife or Santoku

Lay the tomato on the cutting board, with the stem end facing your knife hand. Steady it with your guide hand in the claw position.

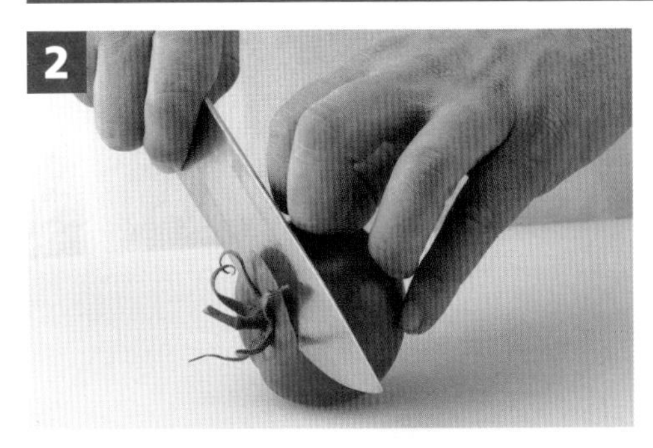

Cut off the top of the tomato, removing just enough to get the stem.

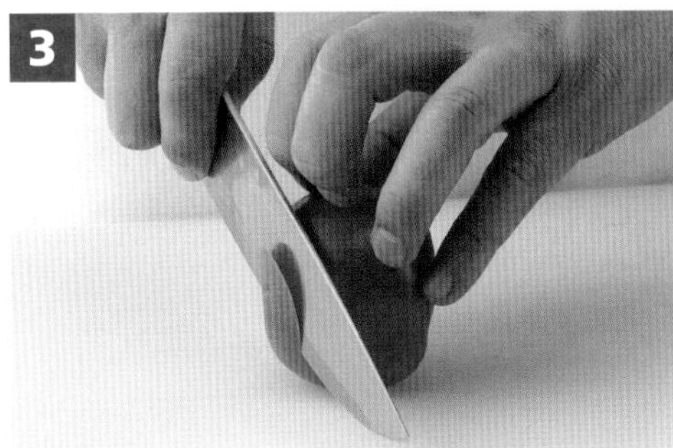

Rotate the tomato 180 degrees and cut off the bottom end.

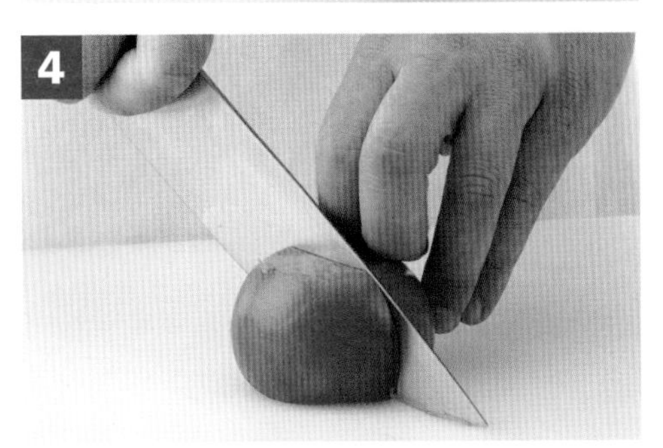

Stand the tomato on one of its cut ends and steady it with your guide hand. Place the knife blade on top of the tomato at the center line and cut the tomato in half.

With the tomato still standing, rotate it 90 degrees, place the knife blade on top of the tomato at the center line and cut the tomato into quarters.

Place a tomato quarter on the board, skin side down. Place the knife at one of the pointed ends, sliding it between the firm outer flesh and the pulpy inner flesh.

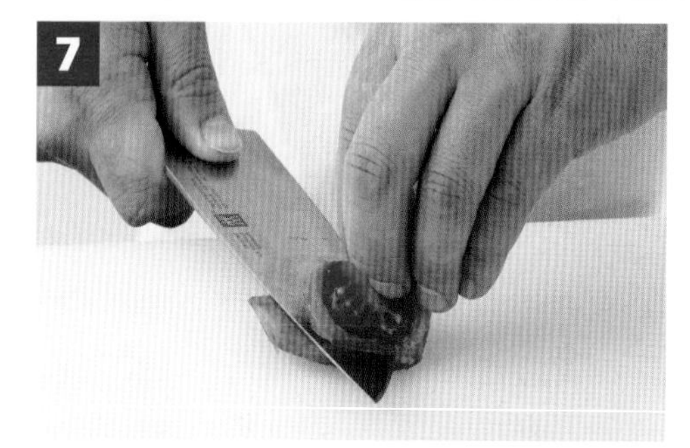

Slide the knife horizontally across the surface of the outer flesh to separate the pulp and seeds from the leaf.

Repeat steps 6 and 7 with the remaining three tomato quarters.

Stack the four tomato leaves skin side down, with a short side facing your knife hand. Steady the stack with your guide hand in the claw position.

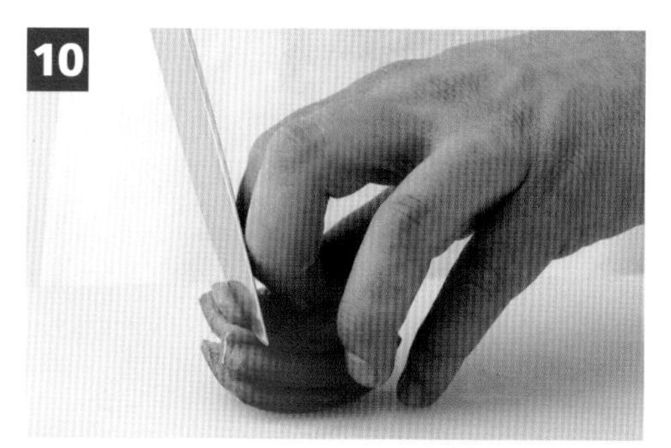

Place the blade flush against your guide fingers. Make sure the distance from the edge of the stack to your knife is $^1/_8$ inch (3 mm). Cut straight down to create your first set of juliennes.

Keeping the blade against your guide fingers, move them back $^1/_8$ inch (3 mm) and cut off another set of juliennes.

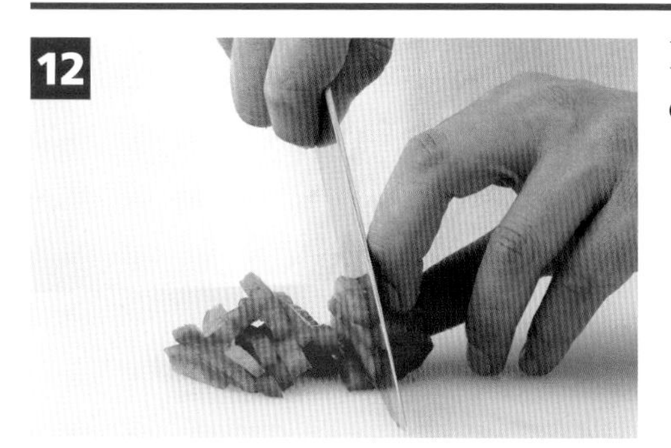

Repeat step 11 until the entire stack is cut into juliennes.

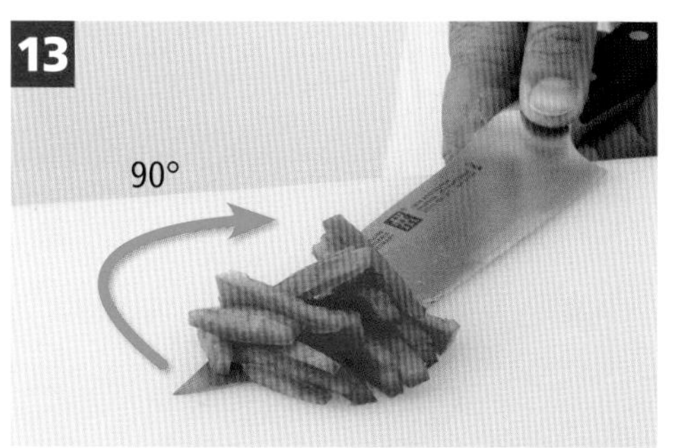

To make dice, slide your knife under the stack and use it to carefully rotate the juliennes 90 degrees.

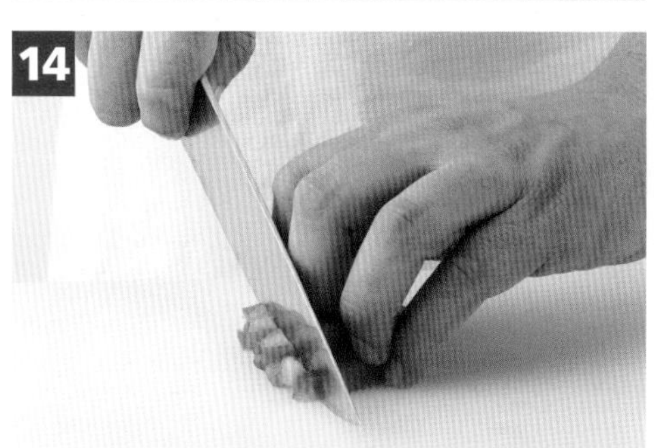

Steady the juliennes with your hand in the claw position. Place the blade flush against your guide fingers. Make sure the distance from the edge of the juliennes to your knife is $1/8$ inch (3 mm). Cut straight down to create your first set of dice.

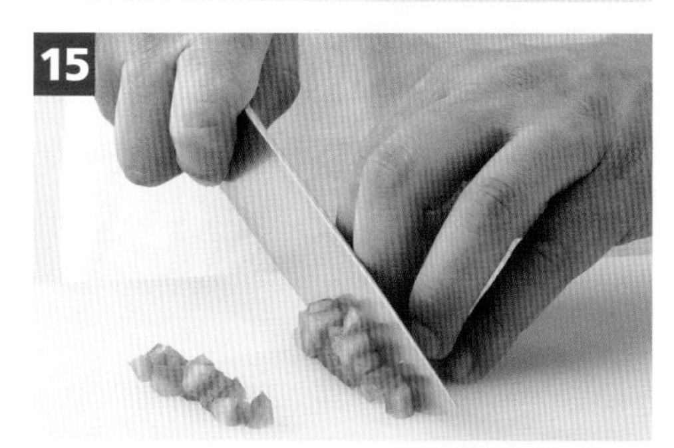

Keeping the blade against your guide fingers, move them back $1/8$ inch (3 mm) and cut off another set of dice.

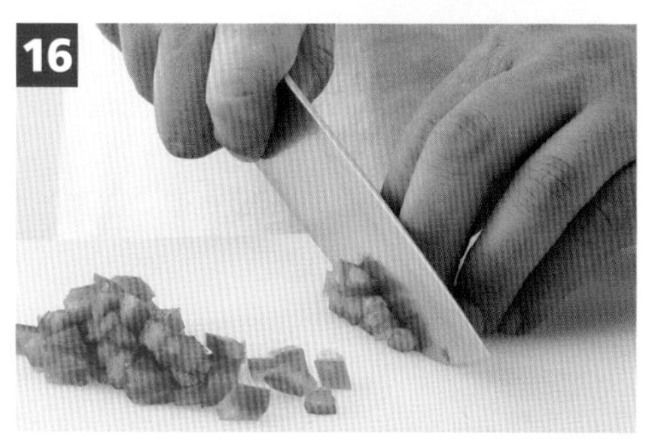

Repeat step 15 until the juliennes are completely cut into dice.

Chapter 5

Cutting Poultry

Avian anatomy is virtually identical across the species. The main differences are in size and relative position of the various pieces (for example, duck wings are set much higher on the back than chicken wings). Hence, while all of the techniques in this chapter are illustrated using chicken, they can be applied to turkey, duck, quail — essentially anything with wings.

Chicken Anatomy

Study the pictures below, preferably while holding a whole chicken. Let your hands explore the chicken, feeling where the legs and wings meet the body, noticing how the bones sit in the joints, and so on. Refer back to these illustrations frequently as you are practicing the techniques in this chapter. Knowledge of the chicken's anatomy will help you master the steps involved in taking it apart.

Breast view

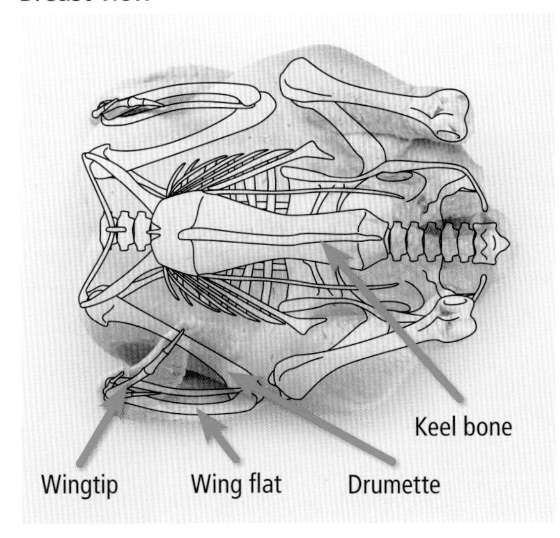

Back view

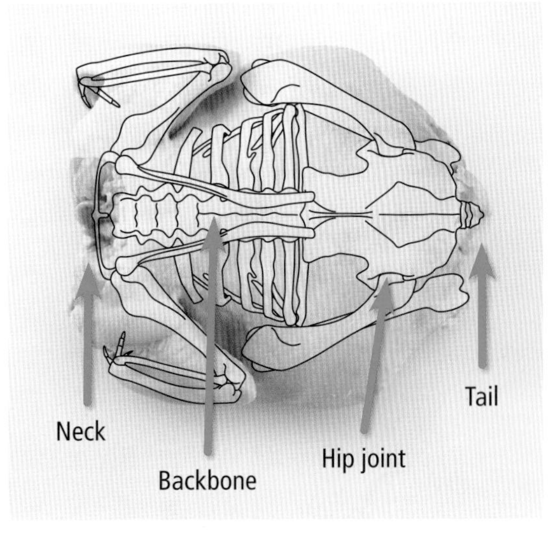

Side view

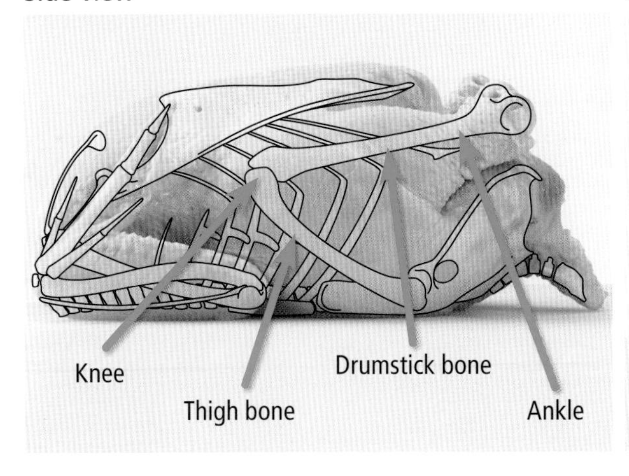

Tail view

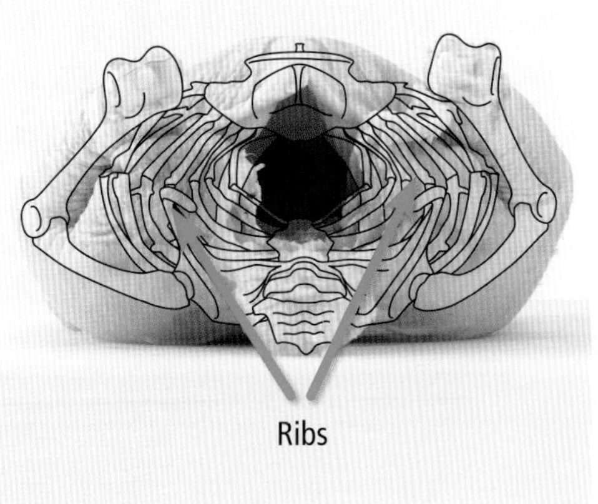

Cutting a Chicken into Eight Pieces

Whole chickens, as a rule, are cheaper by weight than packages of parts. Buying whole chickens and cutting them apart yourself can save you money. But if you've ever labored over a chicken, taking 30 minutes or more to get from whole chicken to eight good-looking (or not) pieces, you might think it's simply not worth the effort. And if it really took 30 minutes, we'd probably agree with you. But you can break down a chicken in just a few minutes, and once you learn how to do it, it's nearly effortless.

Removing the Legs

The joints of a chicken are fairly easy to locate. When you know where they are, separating the chicken into its component pieces becomes a simple task of splitting joints.

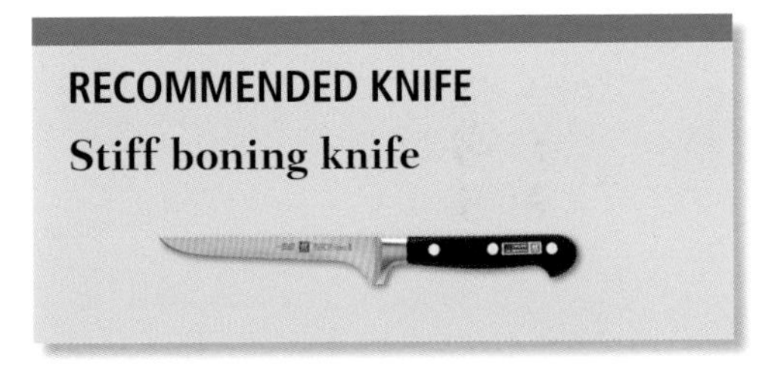
RECOMMENDED KNIFE

Stiff boning knife

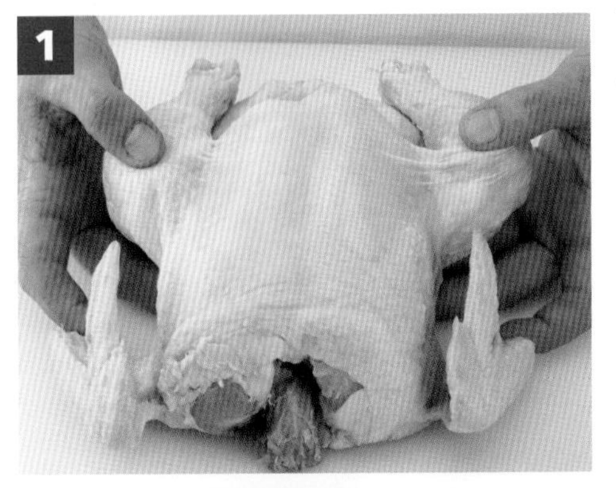

Place the chicken on the cutting board, breast side up, with the legs pointing toward you.

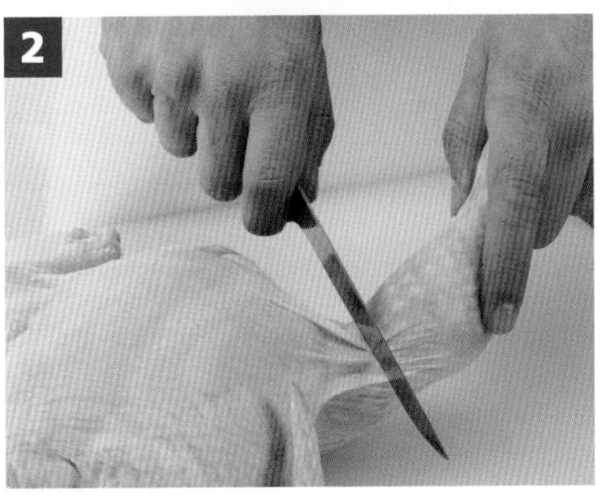

Pull one leg out from the body and cut through the skin, closer to the leg than to the breast. You'll notice that there's nothing but air beneath the skin; cutting it frees up the leg a bit, allowing you to see where the leg is connected to the body.

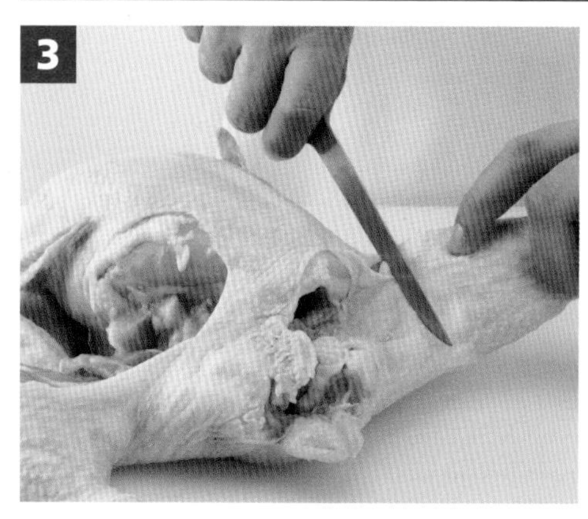

Turn the chicken 180 degrees, so the legs are facing away from you, and repeat step 2 with the other leg.

Set down the knife and place one hand under each leg, gripping the legs with your thumbs. Place the tips of your fingers at the joint where the legs are attached to the body.

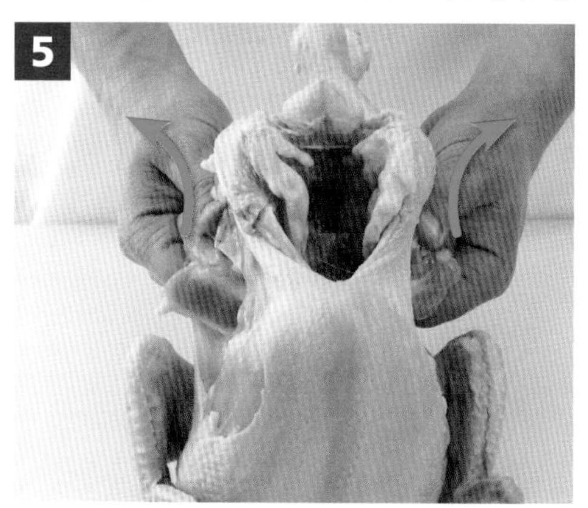

Rotate your forearms from the elbows, pulling back on the legs with your thumbs as you push up with your fingers, until you feel the leg joints pop out of the body.

Turn the chicken over and locate the oysters, the two little meaty circles on either side of the backbone. You want to include these when you remove the legs.

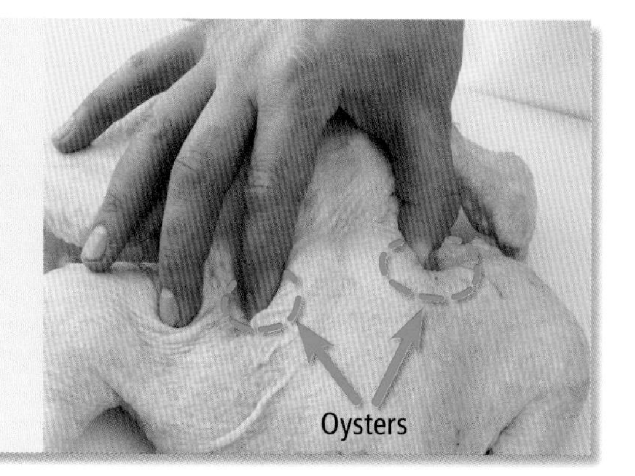

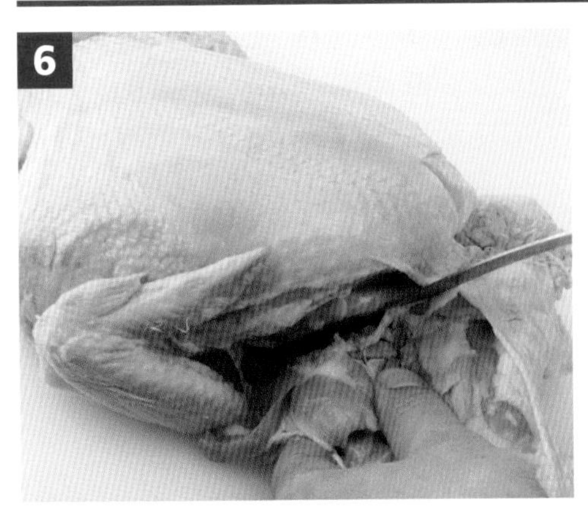

With your guide hand, grip the leg on the guide-hand side and pull it away from the body. Cut through the skin behind the oyster and follow it to the joint. Because you've disjointed the leg, you should be able to work the knife fairly easily between the leg bone and the socket.

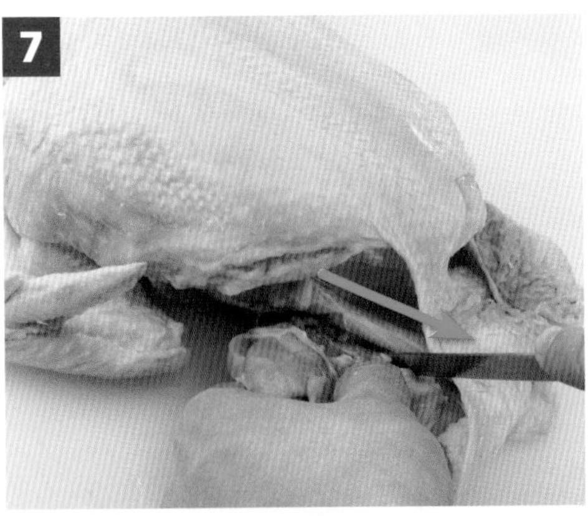

Once you've gotten past the joint, cut straight through the skin to remove the leg.

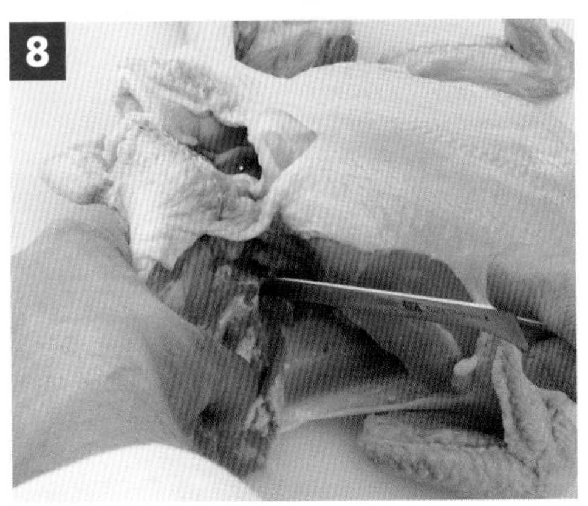

Rotate the chicken so that the other leg is facing your guide hand and repeat steps 6 and 7.

Separating the Drumstick and Thigh

Once again, familiarity with the chicken's anatomy (see page 220) will render this task effortless.

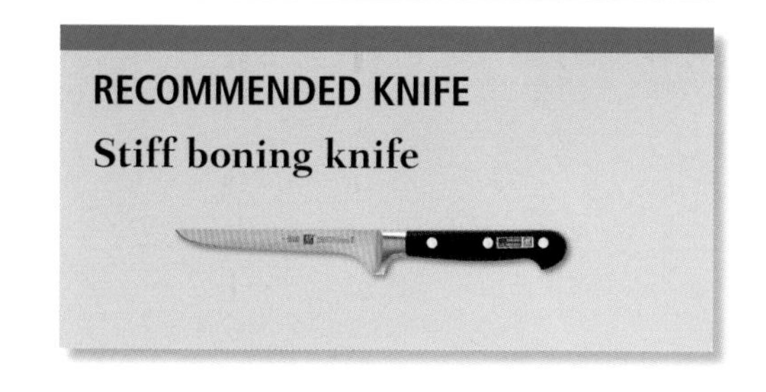
RECOMMENDED KNIFE

Stiff boning knife

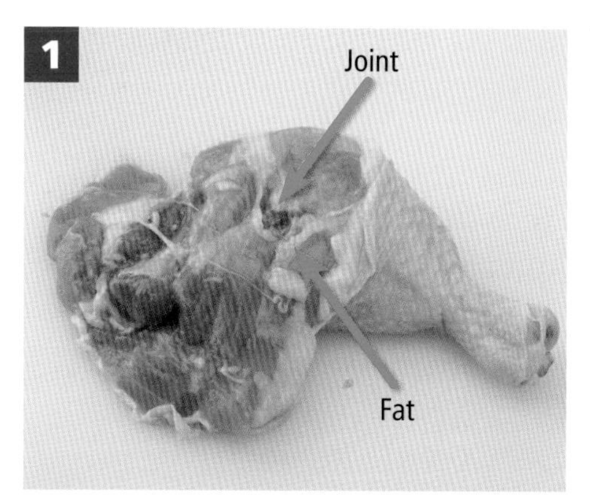

Lay the leg on the cutting board, skin side down. Pull the skin back to expose the joint connecting the drumstick and thigh; you'll see a thin white line of fat.

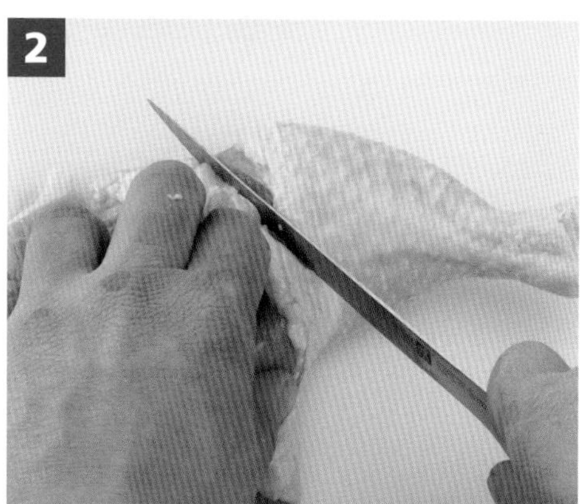

Place the knife blade just on the drumstick side of the line of fat and cut straight down. The knife will go right through with virtually no effort, separating the drumstick from the thigh. If it feels like you've hit solid bone, line up the blade and try again.

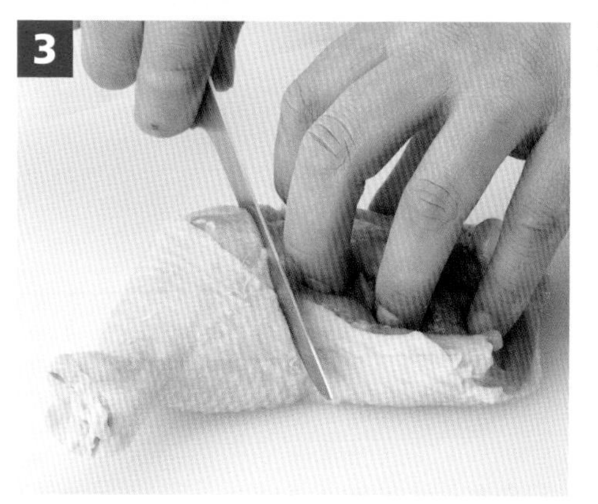

Repeat steps 1 and 2 with the other thigh.

Removing the Backbone

Unlike the previous steps, in which we only cut through skin and joints, here we'll be cutting through some of the ribs, so expect to hear a little bone crunching as the knife goes through.

RECOMMENDED CUTTING TOOL

Stiff boning knife or kitchen shears

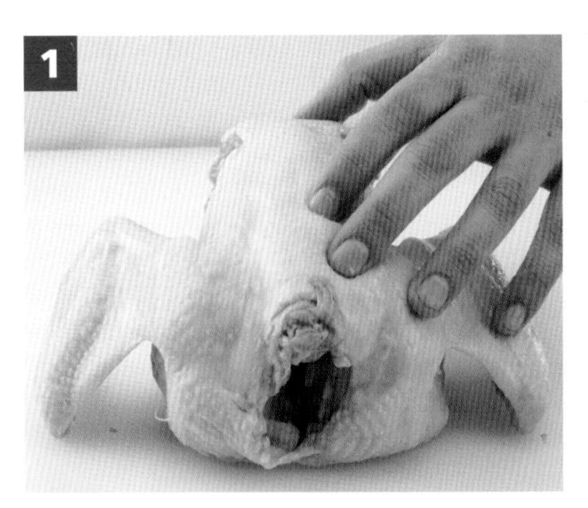

Set the chicken on the cutting board, breast side down, with its tail facing you.

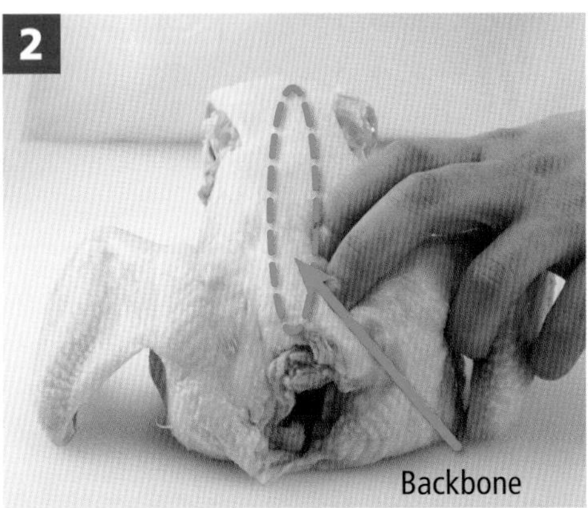

Grip the top of the chicken with your guide hand, just beside the backbone on the guide-hand side.

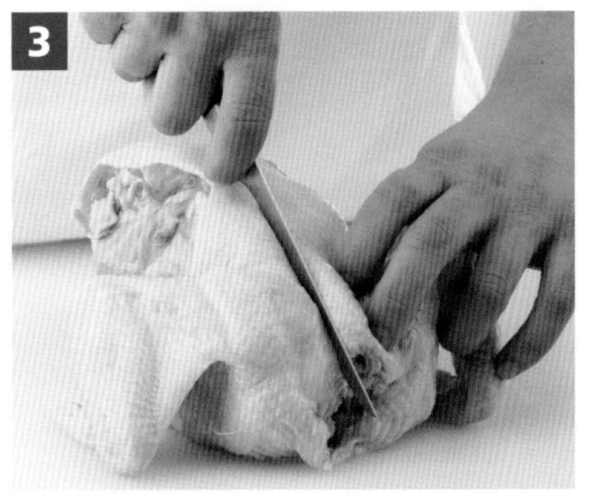

Place the knife blade on the side of the backbone opposite your guide hand.

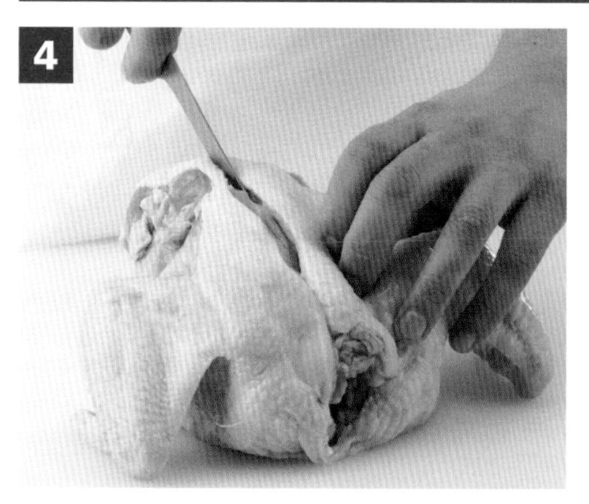

4 Cut down along the side of the backbone, using it as your guide. (You'll be cutting through rib bones as you do this, so expect it to take a bit of effort.)

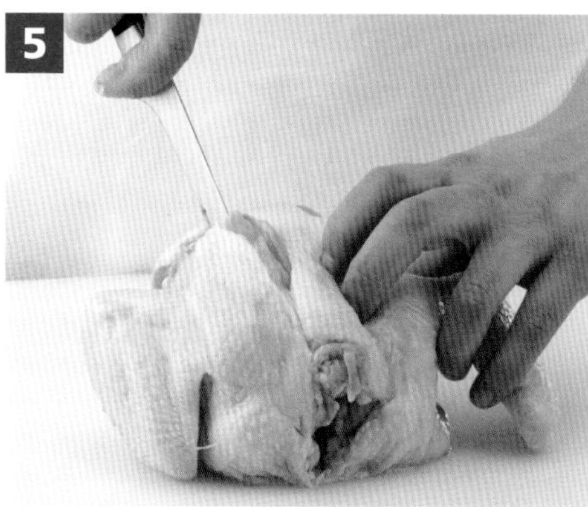

5 Once you're about two-thirds of the way down, adjust the angle of your knife to compensate for the flare of the hip.

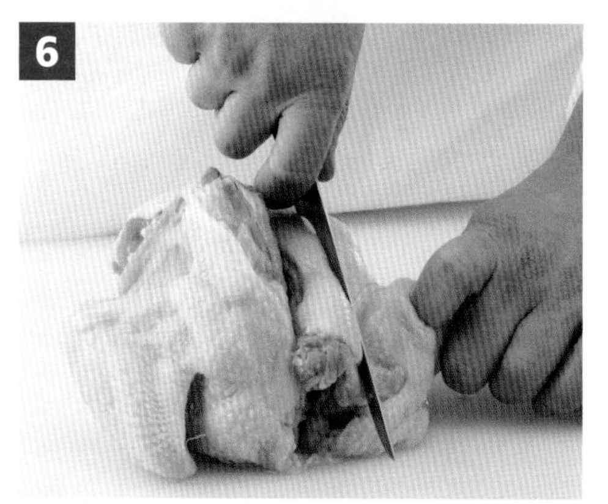

6 Return the knife to the top of the spine, placing the blade on the same side of the backbone as your guide hand. Grip the chicken by its wing.

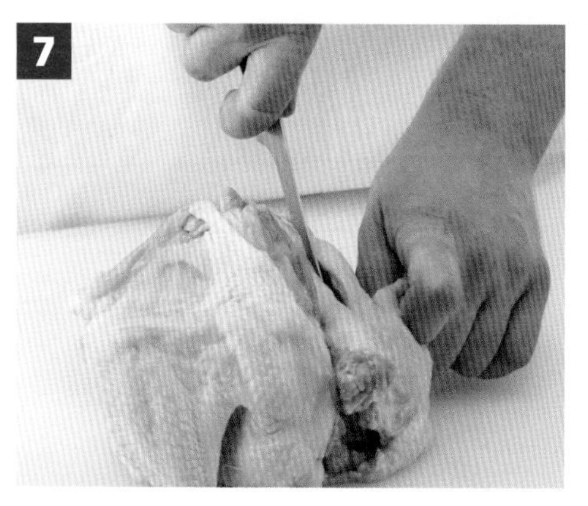

7 Repeat steps 4 and 5, and the backbone will come completely free. Use the backbone for stock.

Cutting the Breast in Half

The term "chicken breast" is a little misleading, because we typically use it to refer to just half of the breast. The whole breast is the entire front of the bird.

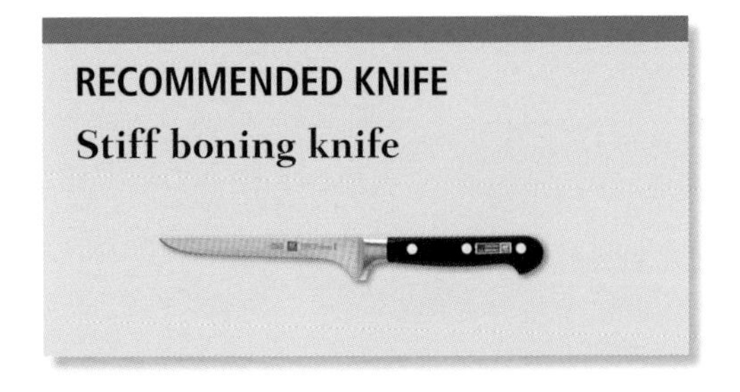

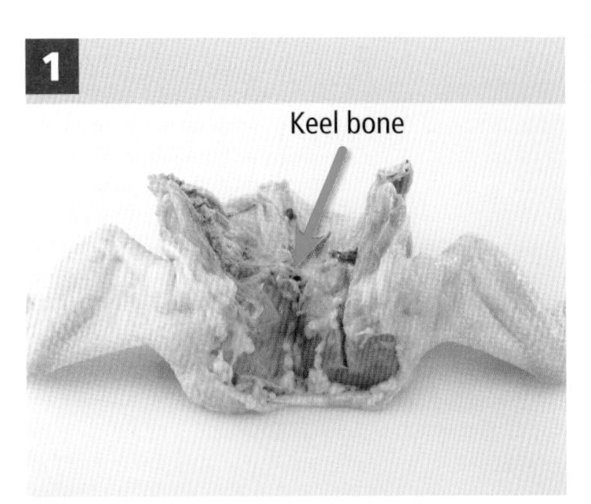

Place the breast on the cutting board, skin side down, with the wings pointing away from you.

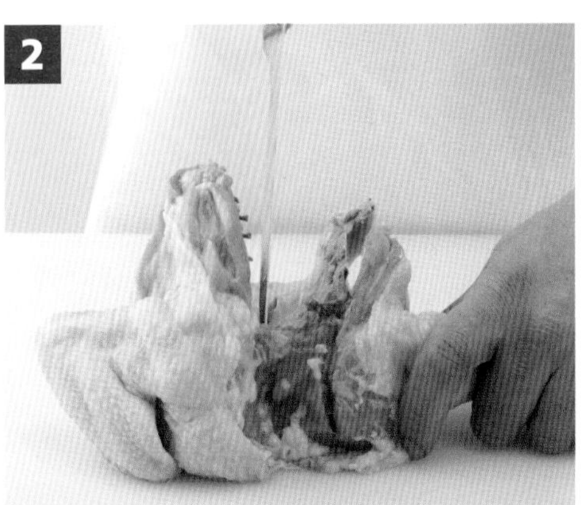

Hold the knife in the stabbing grip (see page 86), with the point in the center of the keel bone (the dark piece of bone between the two breast halves) and the blade facing you.

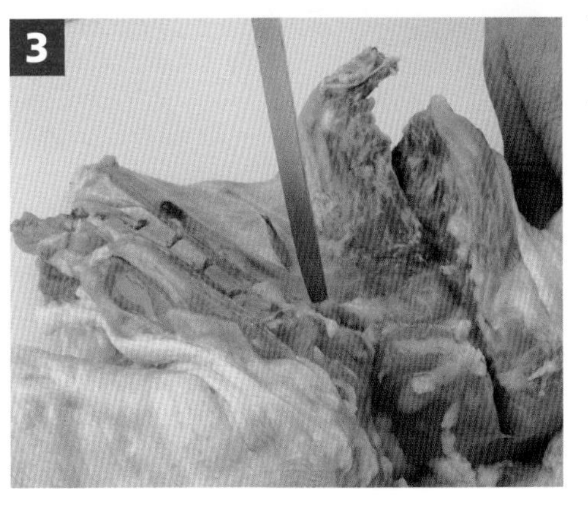

Make a slit about ½ inch (12 mm) long on the keel bone.

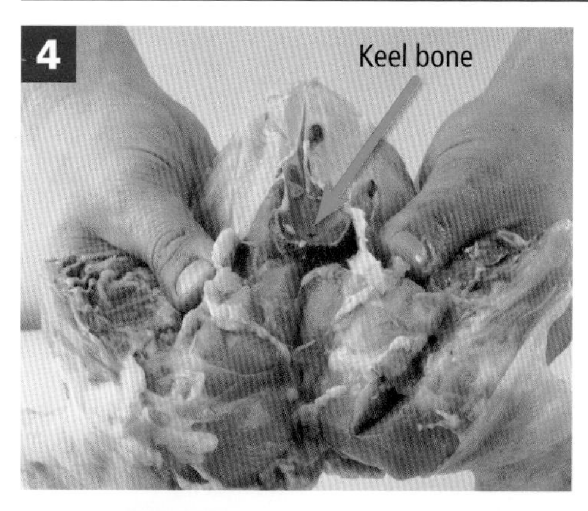

Pick up the breast in both hands and bend each half back until the keel bone pops up.

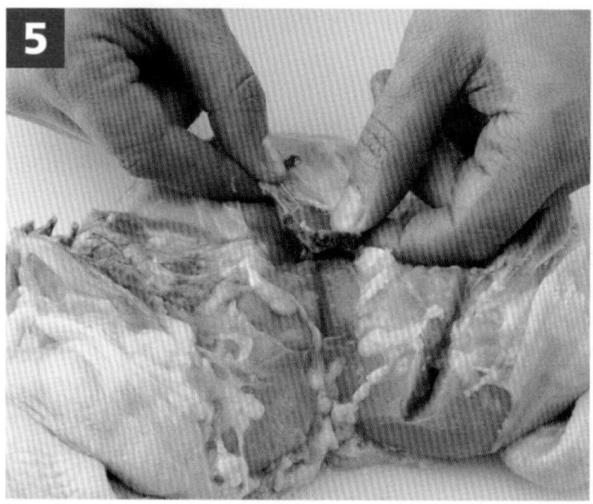

Return the breast to the board, skin side down. Grip the keel bone with your guide hand and run the index finger and thumb of your knife hand along each side of the bone to loosen it.

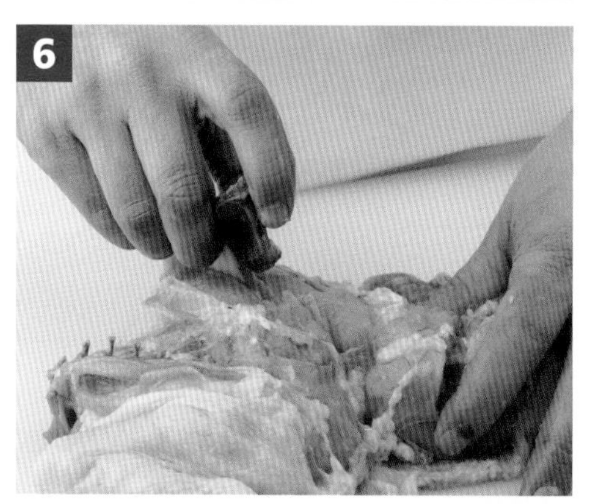

Pull out the keel bone with your knife hand.

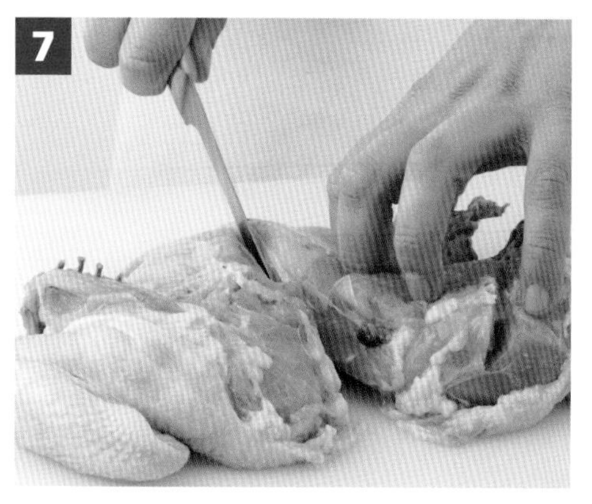

Cut between the breast halves to separate them.

Cutting the Breast into Quarters

Some recipes call for the breast to be split into quarters. To do so, lay each breast half on the cutting board, bone side down. Place the blade of the chef's knife in the center of the breast half and cut down and forward, cutting all the way through the flesh and bone.

Removing the Wings

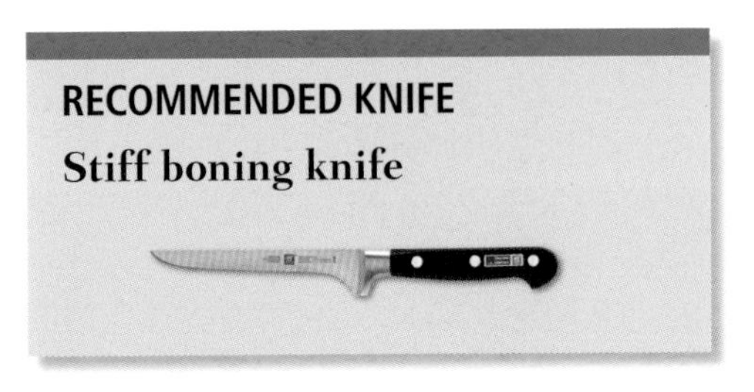

When you're removing the wings, you have a decision to make after you cut through the joint: how much breast meat, if any, to leave attached to the wing. The more breast meat left attached, the more substantial the wing — but keep in mind that you're also making the breast itself smaller. We've given instructions for removing the least amount of breast meat with the wing; if you want to leave some breast meat on, angle the blade toward the breast after you cut through the joint.

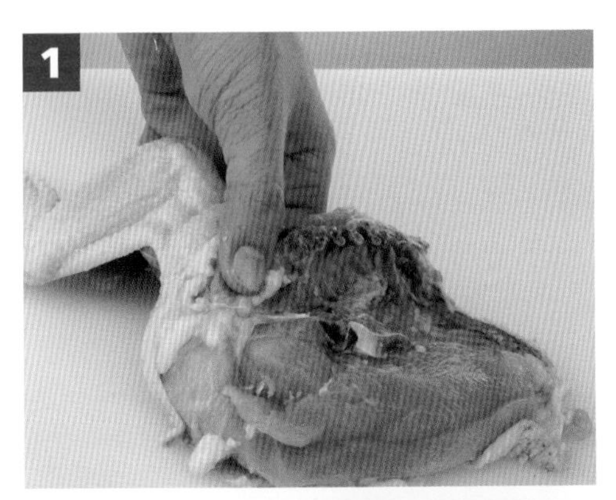

Set the chicken breast and wing section on the cutting board, breast side down, with the wings pointing toward you. Grip the wing with your guide hand and move it back and forth to get a feel for the joint that attaches it to the back. Place the knife blade directly on that joint.

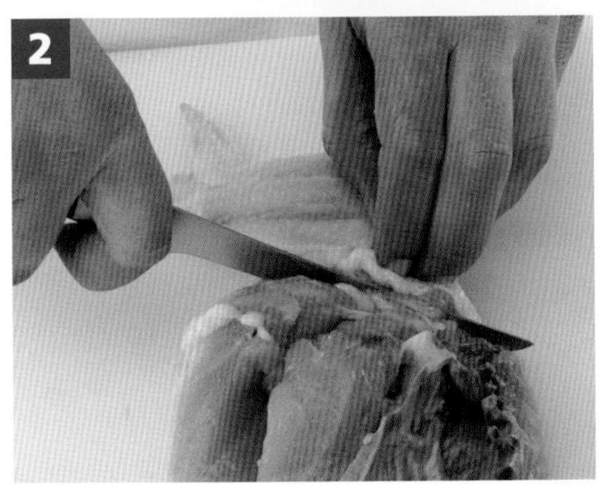

Pull out on the wing, twisting it a little to encourage the bone to come out of the socket, and cut straight through the joint.

3

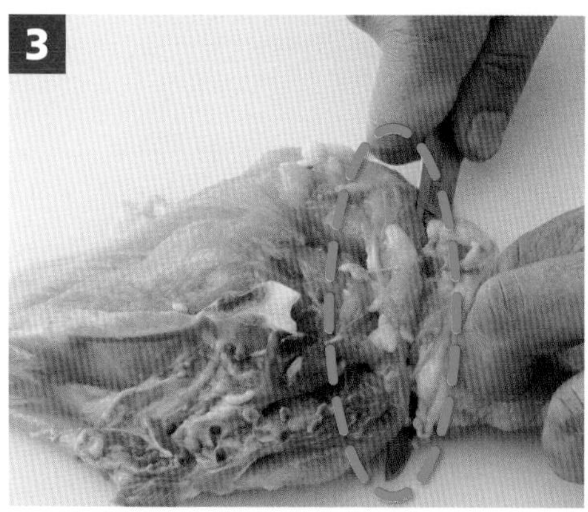

Blade angled away from breast

As soon as you have cut through the joint, angle the blade away from the breast and cut through the skin to release the wing from the breast.

4

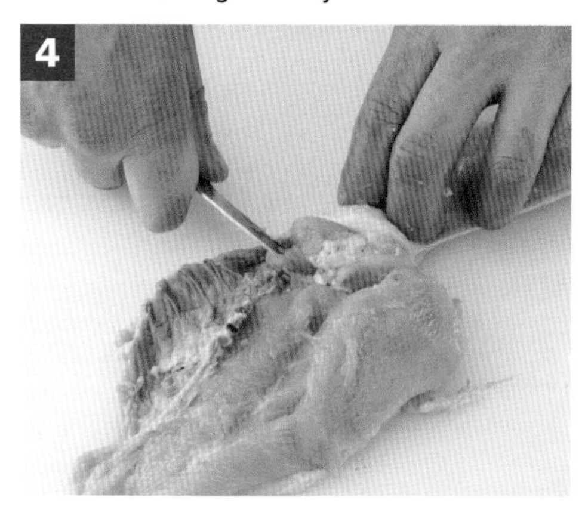

Repeat steps 1 to 3 with the other wing.

Parts of a Chicken Wing

Chicken wings are divided into three parts, not unlike the human arm. The end section of the wing, called the wingtip, is nearly always discarded or used for stock because it contains no meat, only skin and cartilage.

The section that attaches to the carcass has a single bone inside and is often called a drumette because, when prepared on its own, it resembles a miniature drumstick.

The middle section has two thin bones that surround a strip of tender meat. Unfortunately, there is no general agreement on the name of this section. Some people simply call it the two-boned section or the middle section. Others call it the winglet. We're going to go with wing flat, a term used by, among others, the U.S. Department of Agriculture and the Australian Chicken Meat Federation.

Removing the Wingtips (Optional)

Wingtips have no edible meat, only skin and bone and cartilage, so many chefs opt to get rid of them. If you choose to remove the wingtips, you can use them to make stock.

RECOMMENDED CUTTING TOOL

Stiff boning knife or kitchen shears

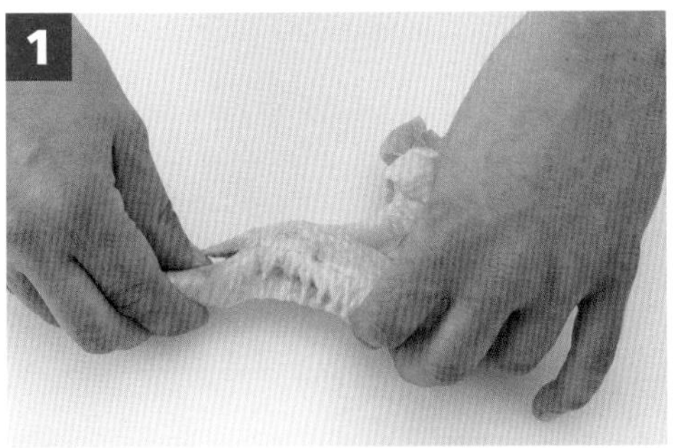

1. Pull a wingtip away from the rest of the wing to stretch out the wing. Grip the wing flat (the middle section with two bones) with your other hand. Bend the wingtip back and forth to get a feel for the joint between it and the wing flat.

2. With your guide hand, hold the wing so that the joint between the wingtip and the wing flat is on the cutting board.

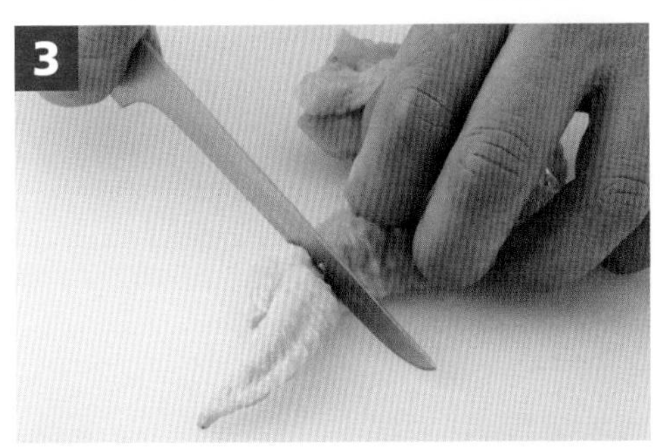

3. Place the knife blade directly on the joint and cut straight down to separate the wingtip.

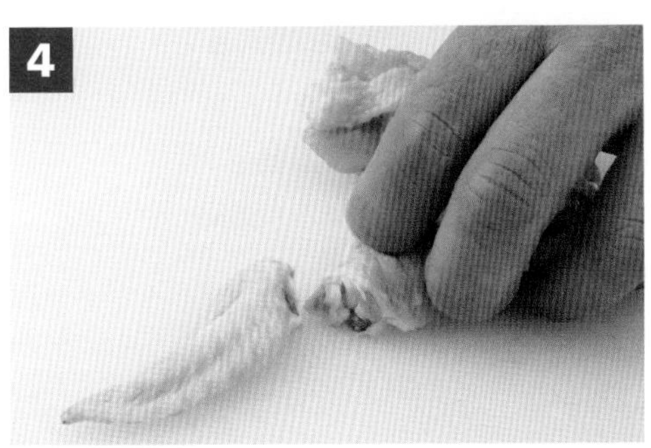

4. Repeat steps 1 to 3 to remove the wingtip from the other wing.

Cutting the Wing into Two Pieces

Most chefs go the extra step of separating the drumette (the single-bone section) from the wing flat. Simply grab a section in each hand and bend the joint the wrong way to snap it, then use a stiff boning knife or kitchen shears to cut through the snapped joint.

Making "Lollipops"

These cute little two-bite pieces, made with drumettes, are terrific for amuses bouches or passed hors d'oeuvres.

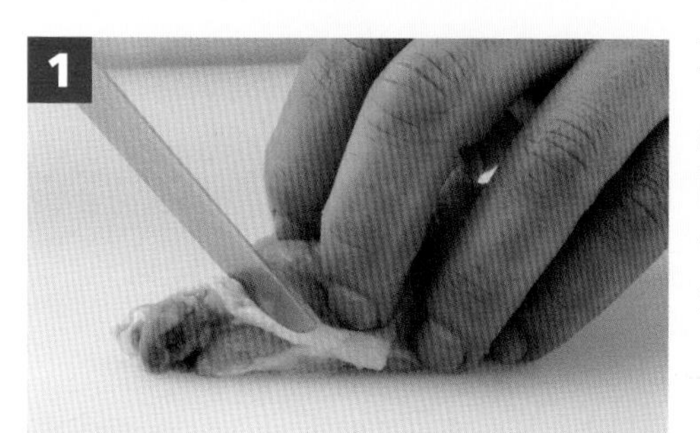

1. With your guide hand, hold the drumette by the meaty end. Use a stiff boning knife or paring knife to cut the tendons at the opposite end, freeing the muscle from the joint.

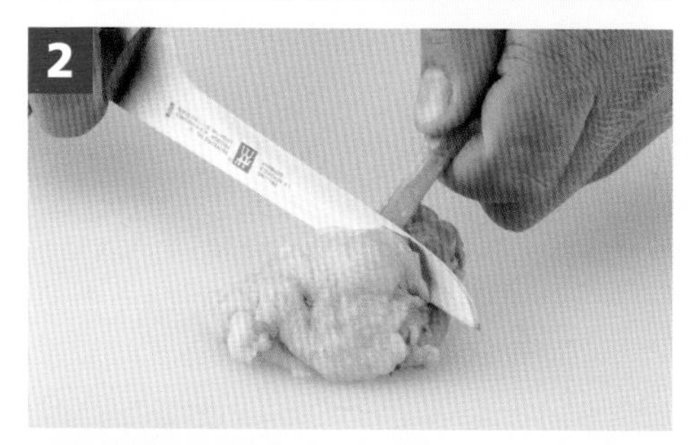

2. Hold the drumette by the other end and use the spine of the knife to scrape the meat down the bone — but rather than simply pushing it, flip it back over on itself, like turning a shirt sleeve inside out.

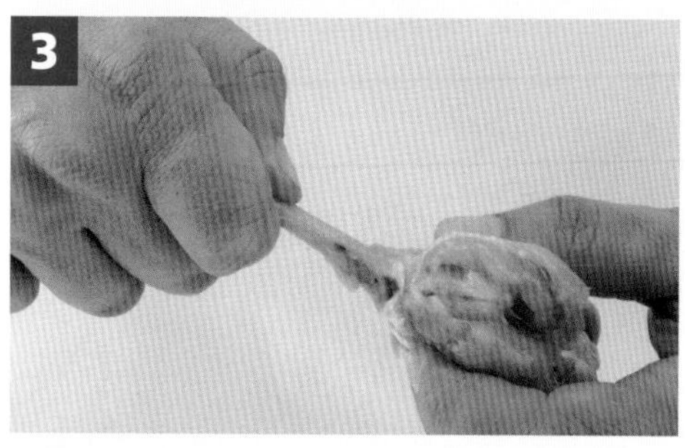

3. When the bottom "hem" of the meat is flipped inside out, set down the knife and use your knife hand to pull the meat toward the end until it's completely bunched up.

Fabricating an Airline Breast

An airline breast is a semi-boneless breast half, typically with skin on, with the drumette bone still attached but scraped free of all meat and tissue. Theories abound as to why these are called airline breasts. One is that airlines like to serve this cut because the little piece of wing attached makes the portion look more substantial. Another is that the wing section makes it look like the breast is going to take off.

The French call this cut a suprême, and in some parts of the United States, it is called a Statler breast, named after Boston's old Hotel Statler, where it was commonly served.

RECOMMENDED KNIFE

Chef's knife

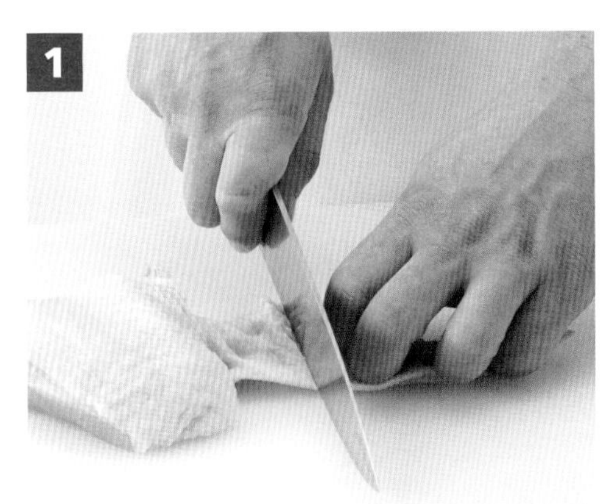

1 Place the breast with wing attached on the cutting board, skin side up, with the wing facing your guide hand. With your guide hand, pull on the wingtip to extend the wing as far as you can. Place the knife blade on the joint that attaches the drumette (the single-bone section) to the wing flat (the two-bone section). Cut straight through the joint to separate.

What you do with the wing flat is up to you. There's not much meat on the wing flat and none at all on the wingtip. You can separate the tip and cook the wing flat separately as a little snack, or you can save both pieces for stock.

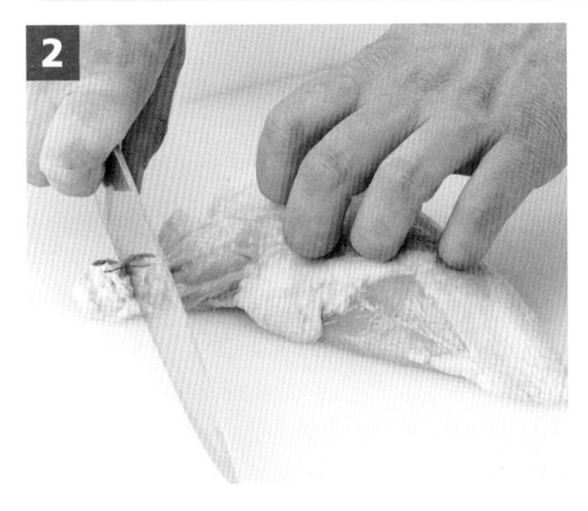

2 Rotate the breast so that the drumette is facing your knife hand. With your guide hand, hold the drumette where it attaches to the breast. Place the heel of the blade about 1/4 inch (6 mm) away from the end of the drumette. Lift the knife and bring it down with a hard chopping motion, using enough power to cut cleanly through the bone.

The chopping motion in step 2 sounds easy, but it's hard to perfect your aim. You might want to try it with celery or carrot sticks first. Practice cutting ¼-inch (6 mm) pieces, chopping with increasing force as you feel more comfortable with your aim. Remember, it takes a lot more power to chop cleanly through bone than it does vegetable matter. If you don't use enough power, you might crush the bone, causing it to splinter and ruining the look of the airline breast. Make sure to keep your guide hand away from where you're chopping, with your fingers in the claw position.

3

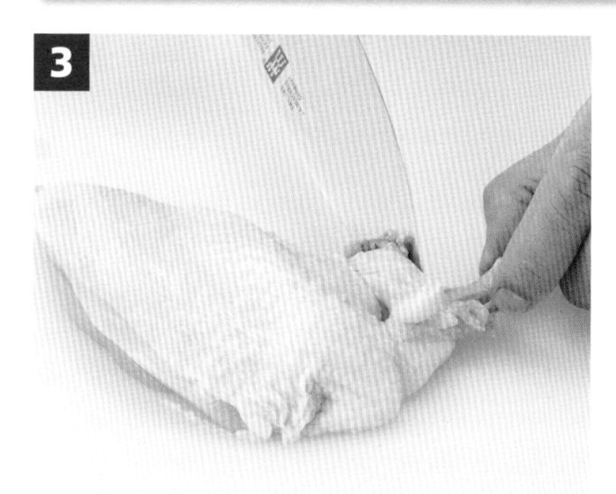

Using the spine of the knife, scrape the drumette meat down toward the breast. It will bunch up a bit toward the end.

4

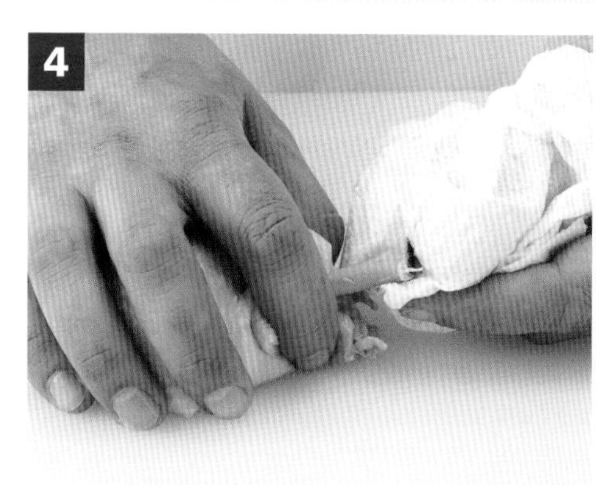

Using a dry paper towel or cloth, clean the now bare bone of any bits of meat or tissue.

Here's what your finished airline breast will look like:

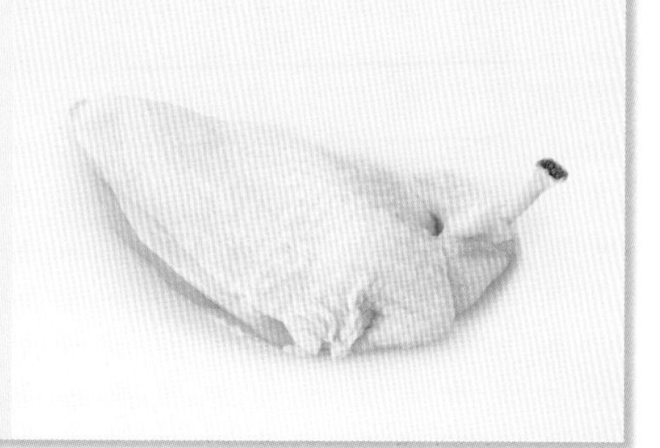

Boning a Breast Half

If you're a fan of boneless or boneless skinless chicken breasts, you know that any food purveyor will carry these cuts. But the more work that's been done to the bird, the more expensive the meat is. Thus, bone-in breasts are considerably less expensive than boneless, even taking into account the weight of the bone. If you want to save yourself some money but you still want a boneless breast, here's how to remove the bone from a bone-in breast half.

RECOMMENDED KNIFE

Stiff boning knife

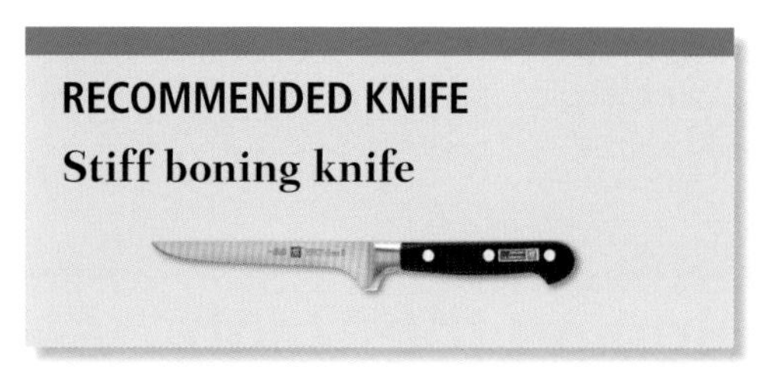

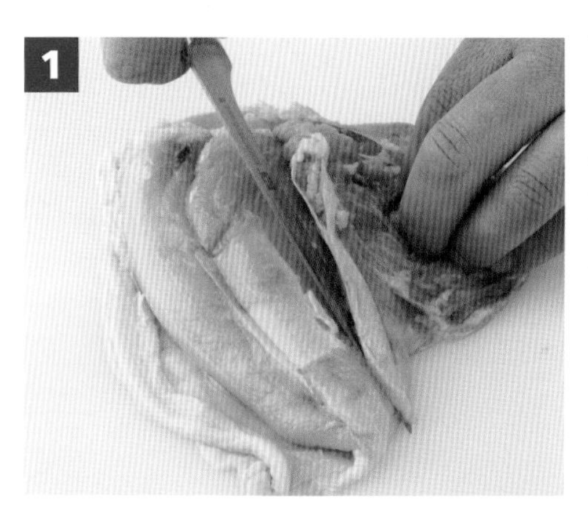

Lay the breast half on the cutting board, skin side down, with the ribs close to your knife hand. Slip the point of the knife directly underneath the ribs and grip the ribs with your guide hand.

Pull back on the ribs with your guide hand as you work the blade along the underside of the ribs, separating them more and more from the breast until the ribs are free from the meat.

To bone a whole breast, first follow the instructions for removing the keel bone in steps 1 to 6 on pages 227–228, then remove the ribs, starting with step 1 above.

Boning a Leg

There are two good reasons to bone out a leg. First, many recipes call for boneless dark meat, which is all from the leg. Second, a boned leg can be stuffed for a nice presentation.

Boning the Thigh

Thigh meat is dark and rich and works well in stews and other full-flavored preparations.

RECOMMENDED KNIFE

Stiff boning knife

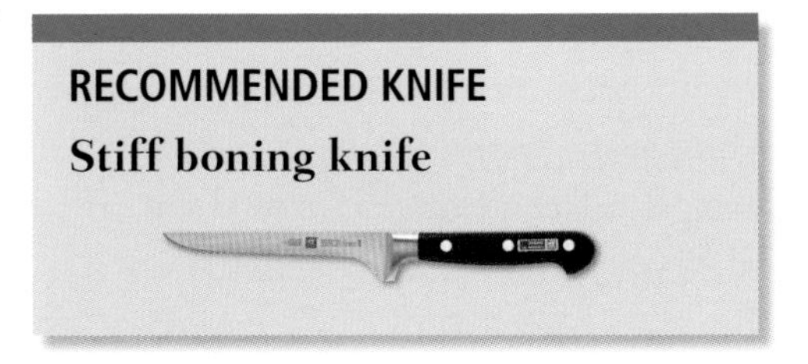

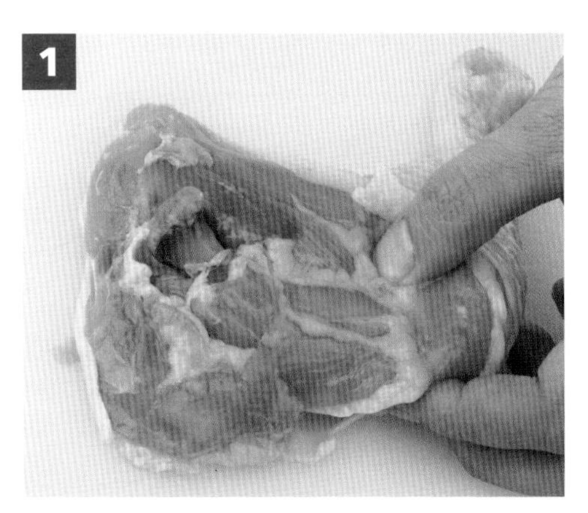

1 Lay the leg on the cutting board, skin side down, with the thigh end facing your knife hand. Hold the leg steady with your guide hand. Run the index finger of your knife hand along the thigh and drumstick bones to get a feel for where they are.

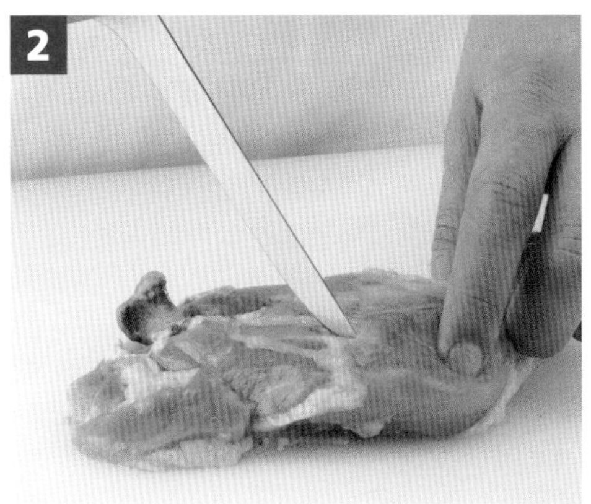

2 Use the tip of the knife to pierce the flesh just to the thigh side of the knee. Pierce it directly on top of the thigh bone, but then angle the blade so that it goes down the side of the bone closest to you. The idea is to cut along the bone, to remove as much of the flesh as possible.

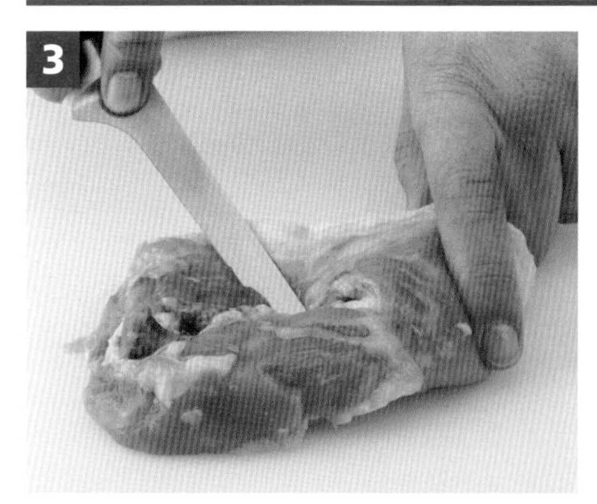

When the tip of the knife has gone halfway down through the flesh toward the board, angle the blade back in so that it cuts under the bone. When the tip hits the board, it should be directly under the place where it first went in.

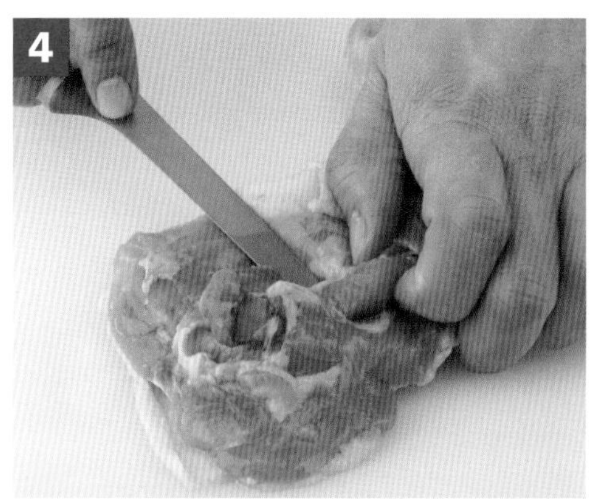

Grip the knee with your guide hand and saw up and down to cut along the thigh bone all the way to the other end.

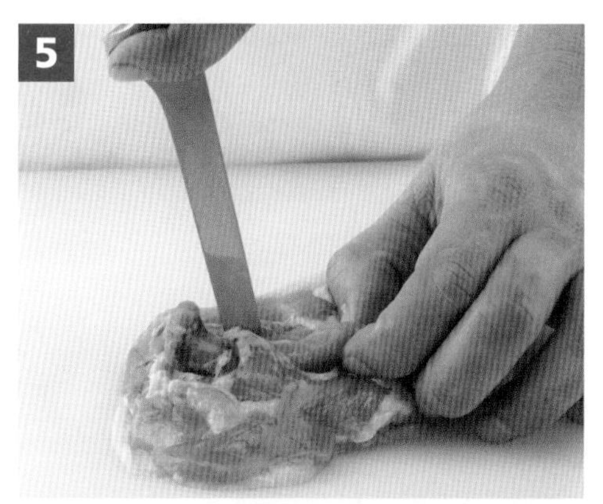

Place the knife tip back on top of the bone where you started (see picture 2). This time, angle the knife toward the other side of the thigh and repeat steps 2 to 4.

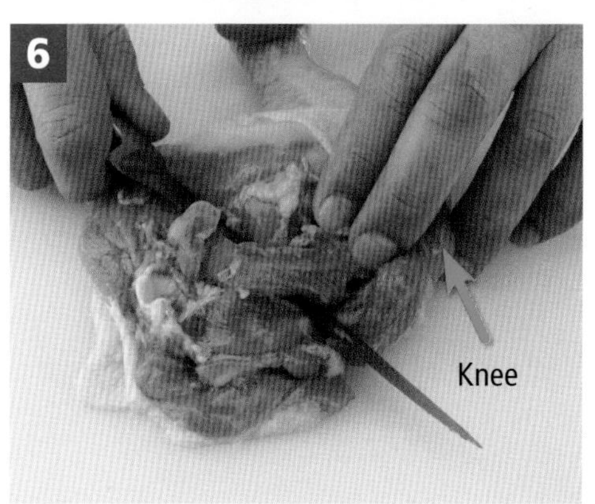

Use the thumb and index finger of your guide hand to pry apart the meat just below the knee and thrust the knife horizontally through the thigh, directly underneath the bone. Make sure the edge of the blade is facing away from the knee.

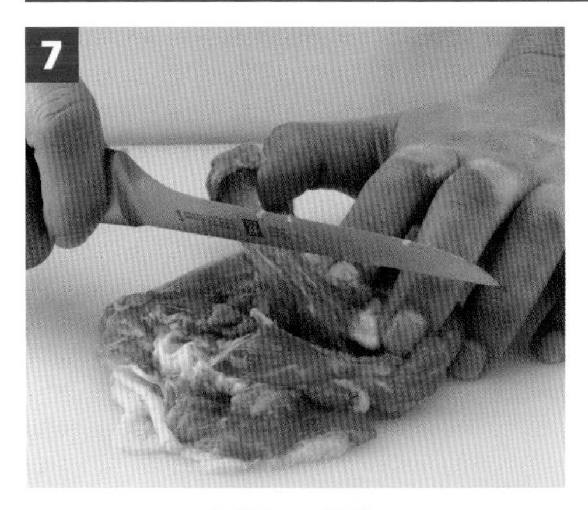

Saw back and forth, keeping the knife flush with the underside of the thigh bone, until the knife emerges from the other end of the thigh.

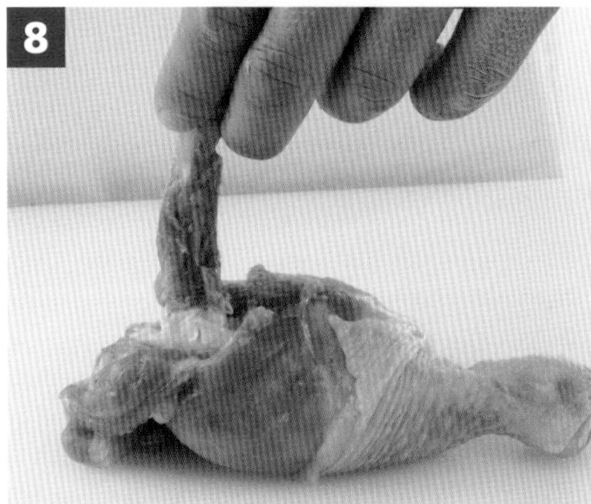

Pick up the exposed bone and hold it vertically, so that the drumstick is resting on its side on the board. Most of the thigh meat should be draping down toward the board.

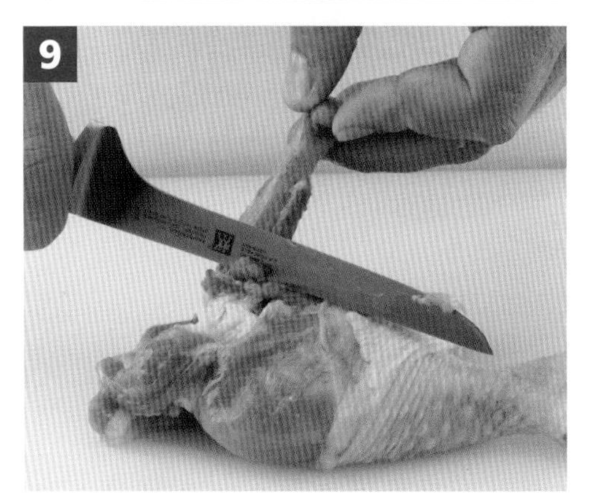

Use the spine of the knife to scrape all remaining meat down the bone toward the knee.

Boning the Knee

This is the hardest part, as the meat around the knee is held in place by quite a bit of connective tissue.

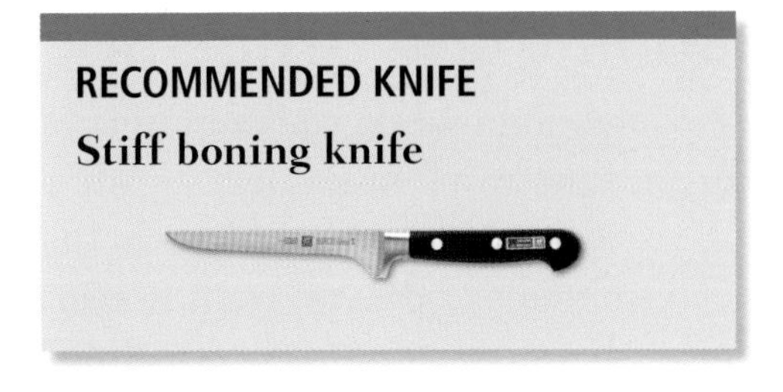

RECOMMENDED KNIFE

Stiff boning knife

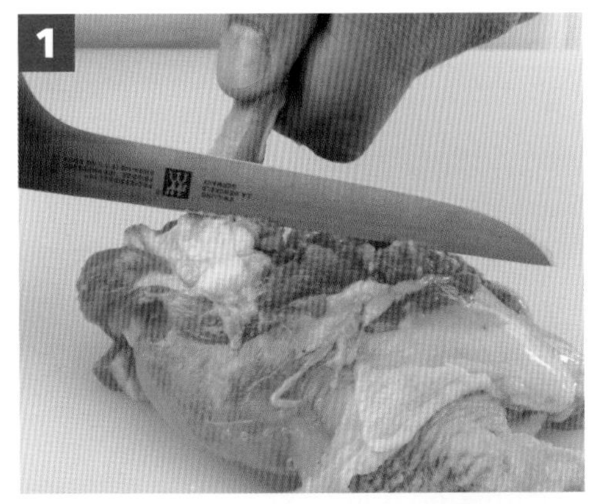

With the spine of the knife, scrape the flesh down the sides of the knee as best you can. You'll notice plenty of connective tissue.

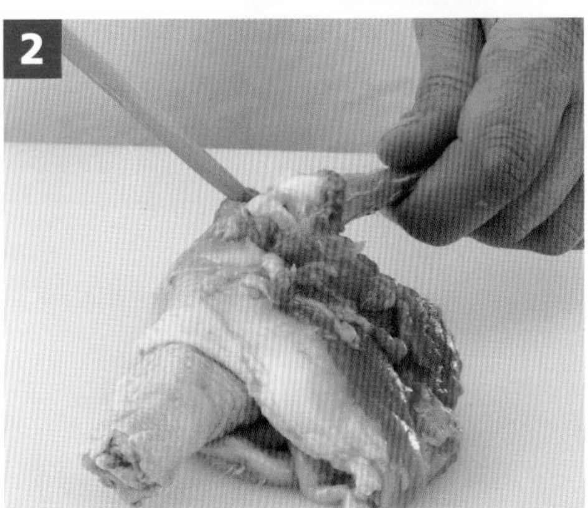

If it helps you to see, once you've gotten past the knee socket, you can cut through the cartilage holding it together and remove the thigh bone.

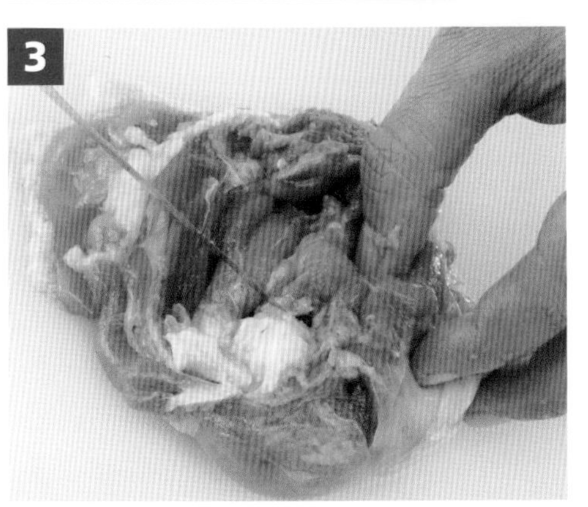

As you move past the knee, you'll notice more tendons. These may be severed with the knife to make further boning easier.

Boning the Drumstick

At some point while you're boning out the drumstick, you'll use a heavy knife to chop through the bone. Where you do that is determined by how you want to use the meat. If you're planning on stuffing the leg, you'll want to cut the bone from inside (see Option 1). If you're planning on cutting up the boneless meat for use in a stew, braise or stir-fry, you'll want to take off the very end of the leg bone to make it easier to separate the meat from the bone (see Option 2).

RECOMMENDED KNIVES

Stiff boning knife; cleaver or chef's knife

Option 1

1 After you've gotten past the knee joint, continue scraping the spine of the knife down the drumstick bone.

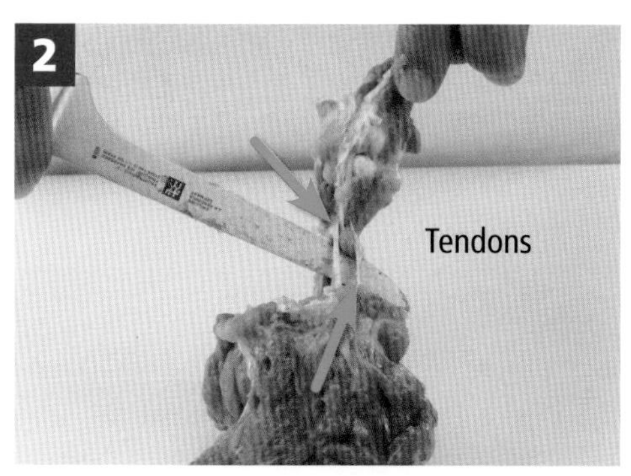

2 As you scrape, cut through all of the tendons holding the meat to the bones near the knee.

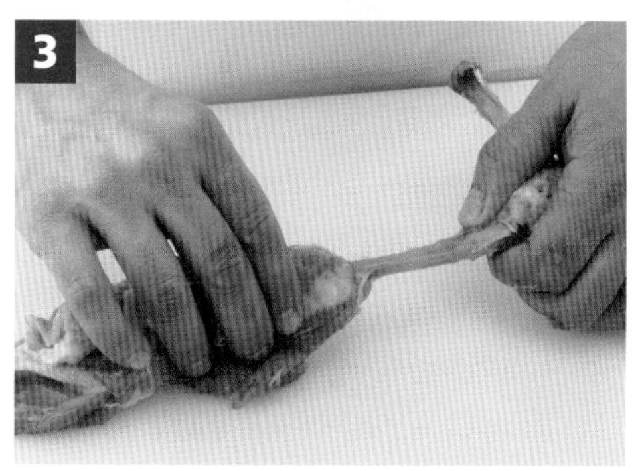

3 When you've scraped most of the way down the bone and are within about 1 inch (2.5 cm) of the end, stop. Pull the meat back toward the end, turning the leg inside out.

4

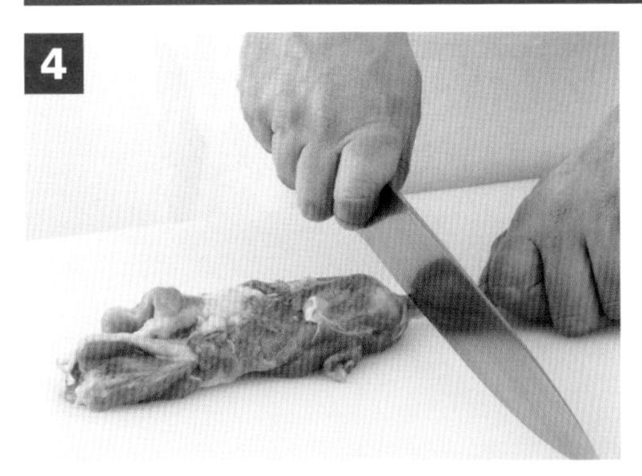

With your guide hand, anchor the drumstick bone while holding the meat out of the way of the bone. With as much force as you can muster, chop down with the cleaver or the heel of the chef's knife to sever the bone about 1 inch (2.5 cm) from the end.

5

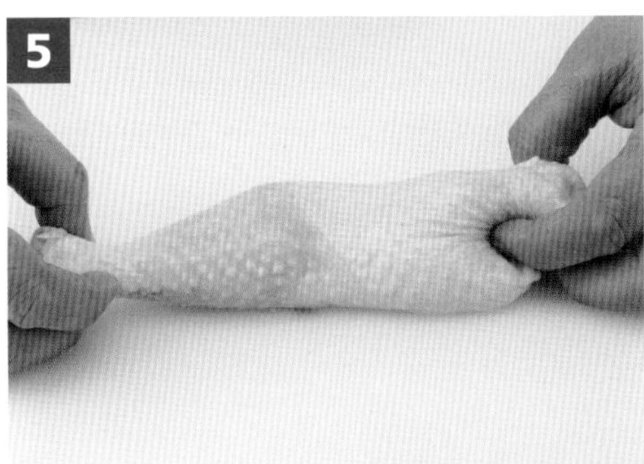

Pull the meat back over the stump of the leg bone and straighten it out.

The leg is now ready to be stuffed. The end of the drumstick bone will act as a plug for the stuffed leg.

Option 2

1

After you've gotten past the knee joint, stop scraping and grip the thigh with your guide hand, with the end of the bone (the ankle) facing your knife hand.

2

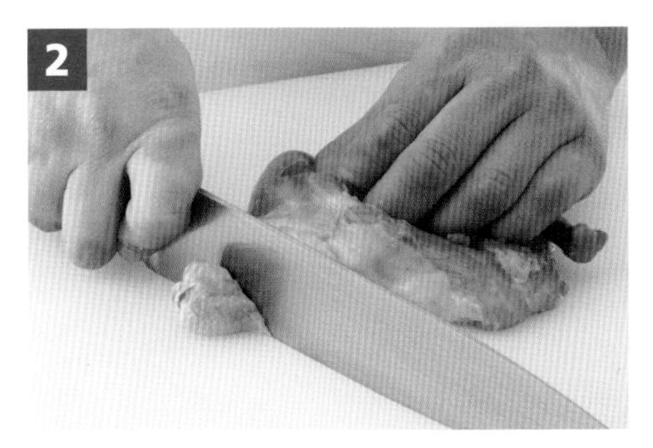

With as much force as you can muster, chop down with the cleaver or the heel of the chef's knife to remove the ankle.

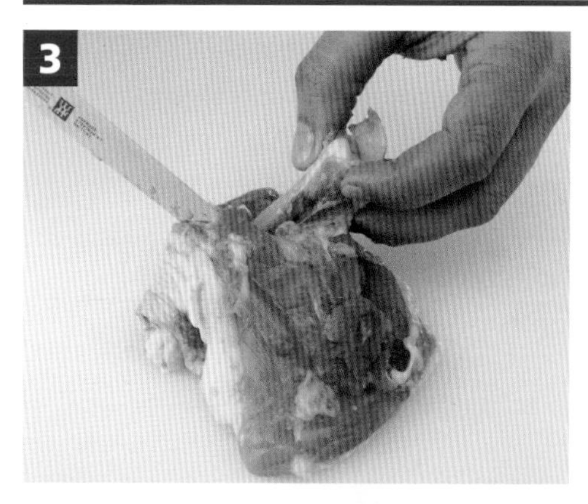

Grip the bone with your guide hand and use the spine of the boning knife to continue scraping the meat away from the knee.

Continue scraping down until the meat is completely free of the bone.

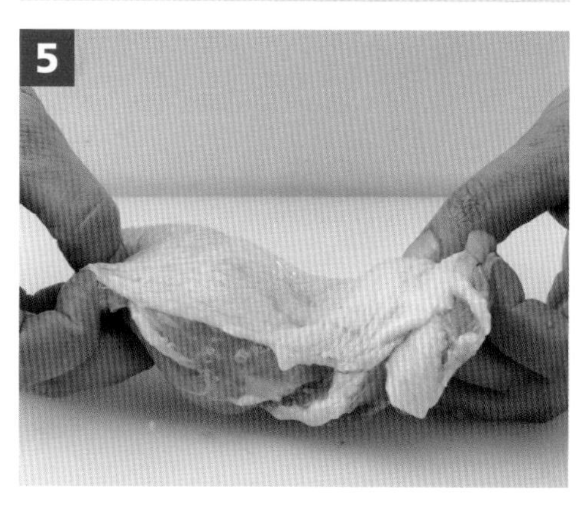

If you've turned the meat inside out, so that the skin side is now on the inside, use your fingers to turn it skin side out again.

The meat is now ready to be cut into bite-size pieces for your recipe.

Alternative Leg Boning Method

Here's another quick technique for boning out the leg. It's a good option only when you don't intend to stuff the leg, as the meat gets cut up a little more.

RECOMMENDED KNIVES

Stiff boning knife; cleaver or chef's knife

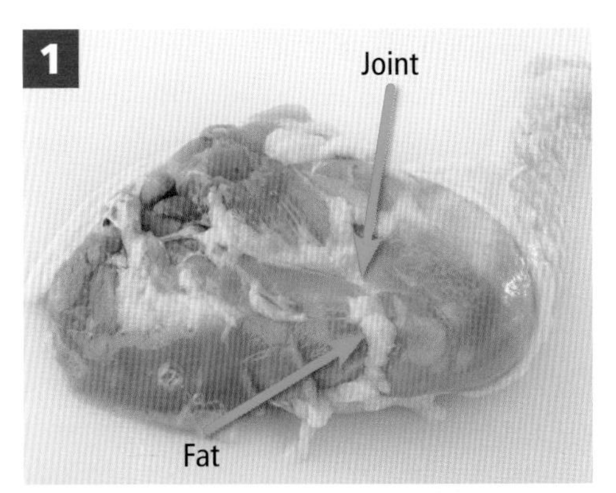

Lay the leg on the cutting board, skin side down. Pull the skin back to expose the joint connecting the drumstick and thigh; you'll see a thin white line of fat.

Place the knife blade on the drumstick side of the line of fat and cut straight down. The knife will go right through with virtually no effort, separating the drumstick from the thigh. If it feels like you've hit solid bone, line up the blade and try again.

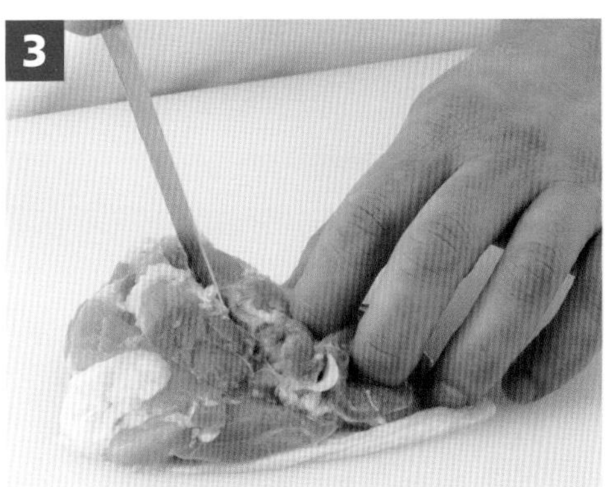

Starting on top of the thigh bone, cut along one side of the bone down the entire length of the thigh.

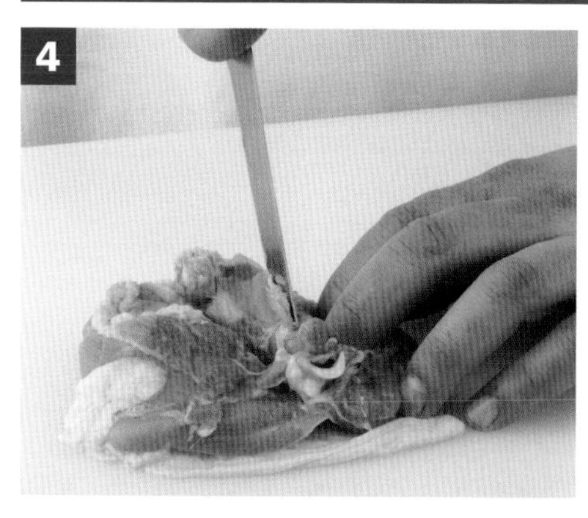

Repeat step 3 on the other side of the thigh bone.

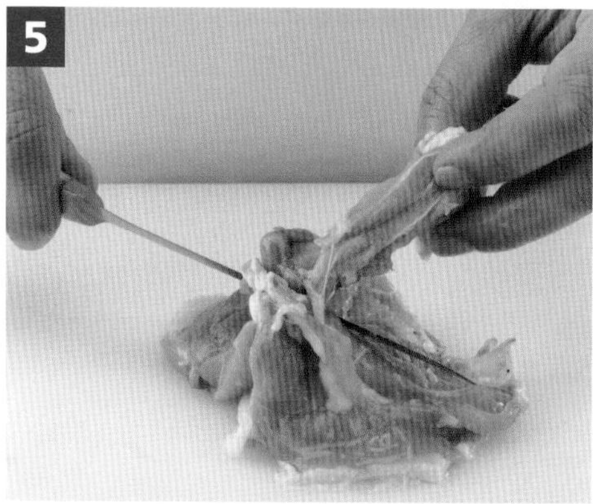

With the blade horizontal, poke the tip of the knife through the meat just under the bone at one end and cut along the underside of the bone to free it from the meat.

With the cleaver or the heel of the chef's knife, chop off the end of the drumstick bone (the ankle). This will also sever any tendons holding the flesh to the bone.

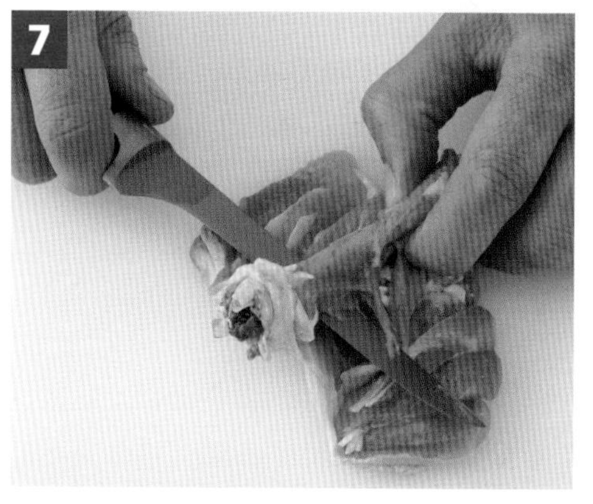

Remove the meat from the drumstick exactly as you did with the thigh in steps 3 to 5.

Boning a Whole Chicken

This is a great technique to learn if you want to make chicken ballotine or galantine, dishes in which a boned chicken is stuffed with forcemeat, vegetables, cheese and/or grains, then rolled up and trussed. Ballotine is roasted and served hot or cold, while galantine is poached and is typically served cold.

If you've never tried this before, we recommend getting two chickens and doing them one right after the other. The second one will go much faster than the first.

Boning Advice

Knowing how to remove the bones from chicken — whole and parts — is an excellent skill to have, but it takes practice and lots of patience. Don't be afraid of destroying the chicken or any of its parts. No matter what horror you inflict upon it, it will still be edible. The key is to just jump right in and not worry about mistakes.

Be sure to use your sense of touch as well as your sense of sight. Let your hands feel what's going on and tell you how to proceed.

Finally, remember that you're pulling muscle away from bone, not cutting through muscle or chopping through bone. Think of it as disassembling the chicken.

Preliminary Steps

Before we get to the actual work of boning the chicken, there are a couple of steps you can take to make the process go more quickly: disjointing the legs and removing the wing flat and wingtip.

RECOMMENDED KNIVES

Stiff boning knife; cleaver or chef's knife

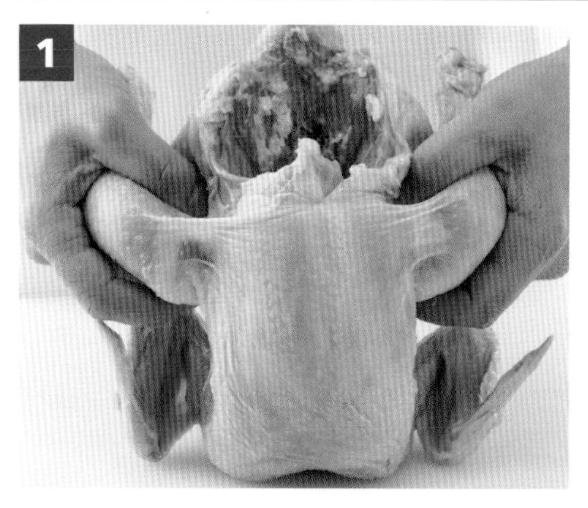

Pick up the chicken with one hand under each leg, gripping the legs with your thumbs. Place the tips of your fingers at the joint where the legs are attached to the body.

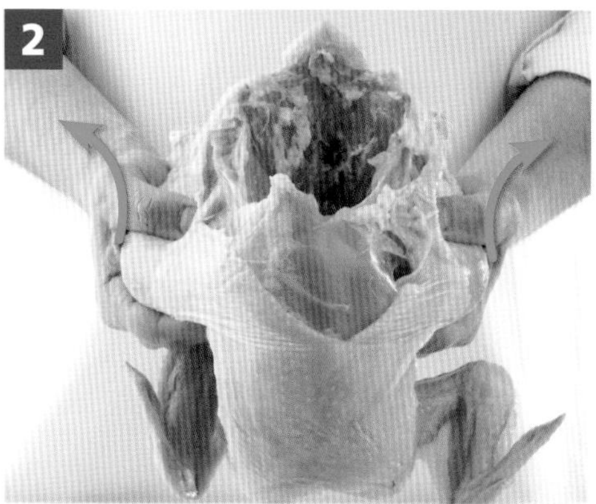

Rotate your forearms from the elbows, pulling back on the legs with your thumbs as you push up with your fingers, until you feel the leg joints pop out of the body.

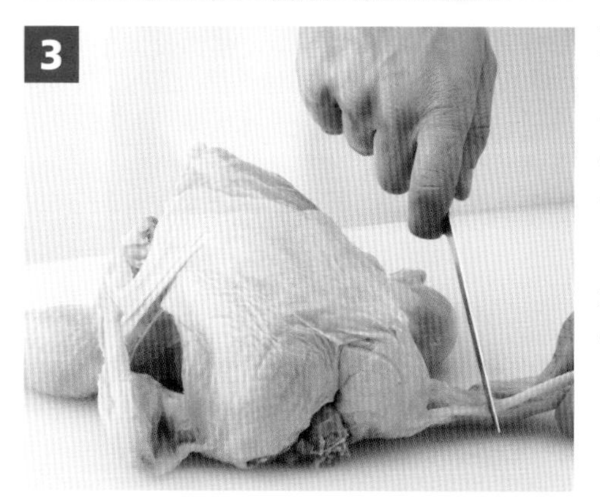

With your guide hand, grip a wingtip and stretch out the wing as far as you can. With the boning knife, cut through the joint that separates the drumette (the single-bone section) from the wing flat (the two-bone section). Repeat with the other wing.

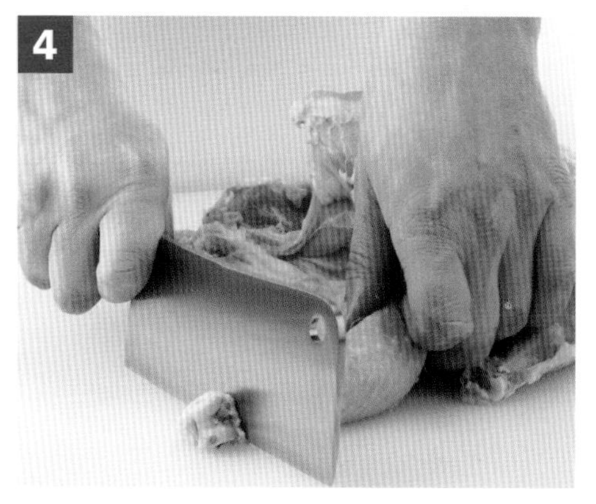

Steady the leg with your guide hand and use the cleaver or the heel of the chef's knife to cut through the joint at the end of the drumstick (the ankle). Repeat with the other leg.

Removing the Wishbone

The wishbone is located on the neck (wing) end of the chicken. Cutting it out first makes boning the chicken much easier.

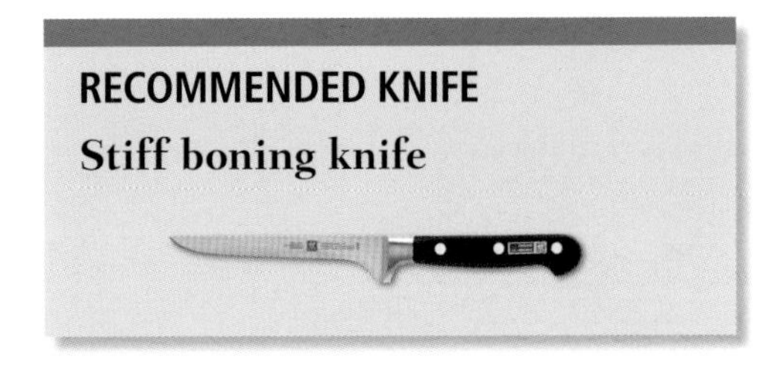

RECOMMENDED KNIFE

Stiff boning knife

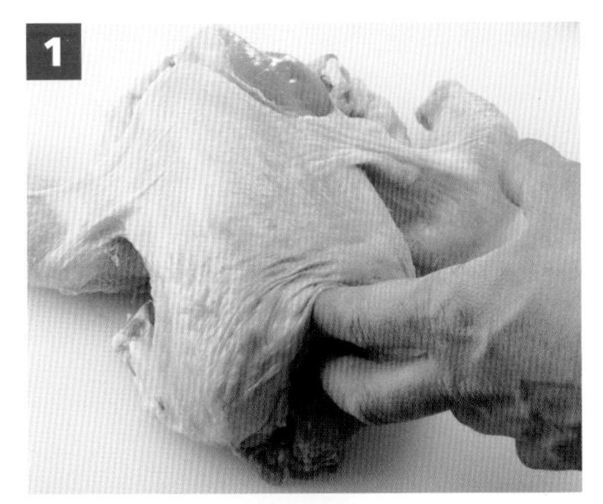

1 Place the chicken on the cutting board, breast side up, with the wings pointing toward you. Use your fingers to feel around the rim of the neck cavity until you locate the wishbone just underneath the flesh.

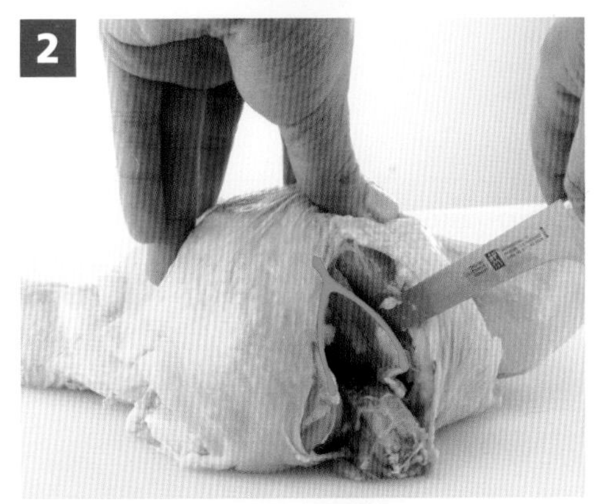

2 Rest the point of the knife on the flesh just off to one side of the wishbone. Puncture the flesh, keeping the knife blade against the bone, and cut straight down along the bone.

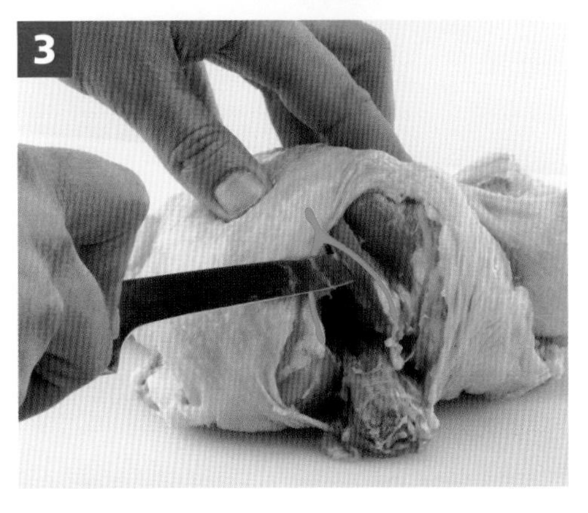

3 Puncture the flesh on the opposite side of the same part of the bone and cut straight down along the bone. This will more or less free up that side of the wishbone.

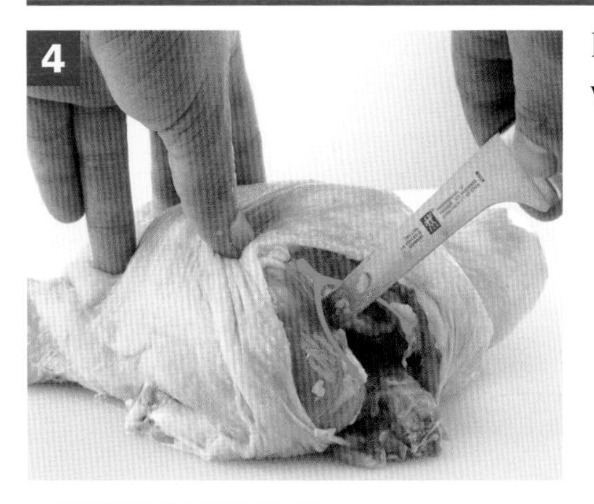

Repeat step 2 on the other side of the wishbone.

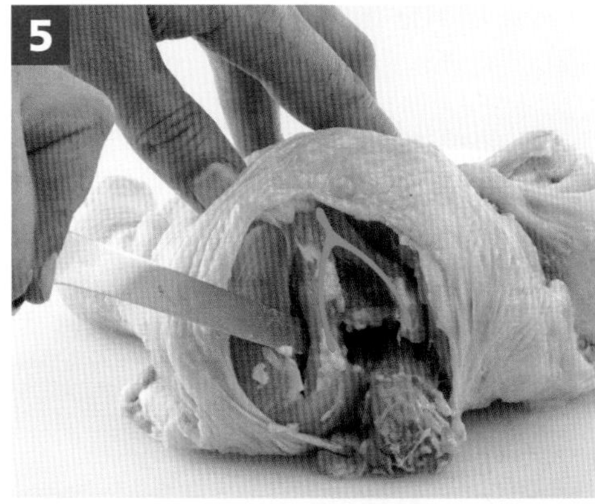

Repeat step 3 on the other side of the wishbone.

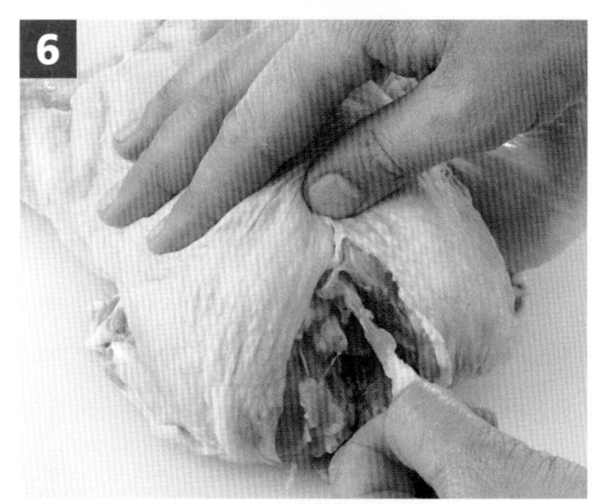

Set the knife down and use your fingers to strip any remaining flesh from the wishbone.

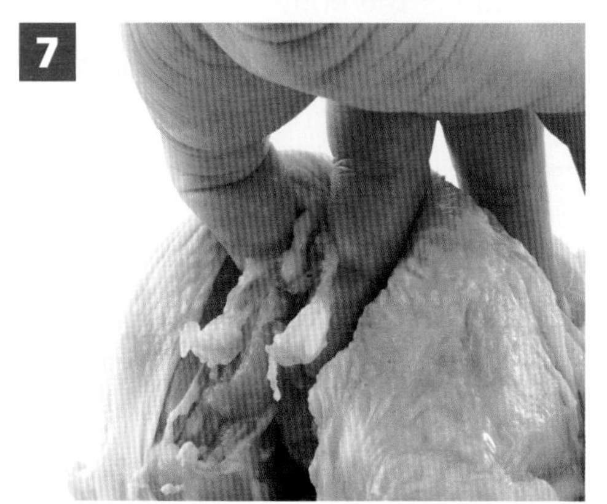

Place the thumb of your knife hand on one side of the wishbone and your index finger on the other. Slide them up until you feel the top of the wishbone. Grasp it at that junction and pull it free. Save the wishbone for stock.

Boning the Chicken

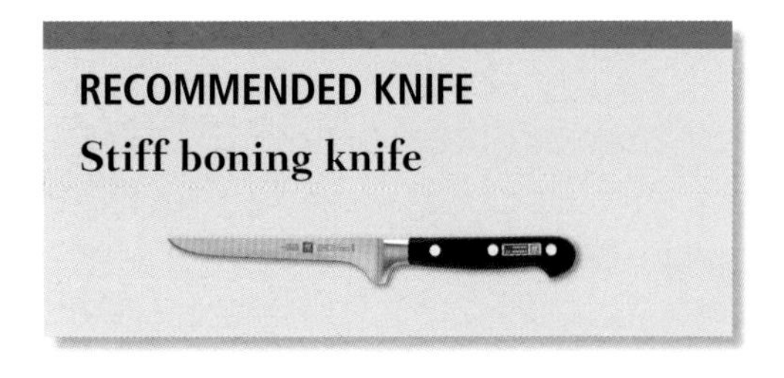
RECOMMENDED KNIFE

Stiff boning knife

This technique is different from glove boning (see page 259), in which the carcass is pretty much pulled right out of the skin, leaving the meat intact. Here, we'll start by making an incision along the backbone, allowing us to pull the meat away from it. Next, we'll separate the leg and wing bones on each side, then bone out the breast. Finally, we'll remove the leg and wing bones.

To start the boning process, we're going to cut through the skin along the backbone, then use the knife to scrape the flesh away from the bone. Remember, the breast is the meaty side and the back is the bony side.

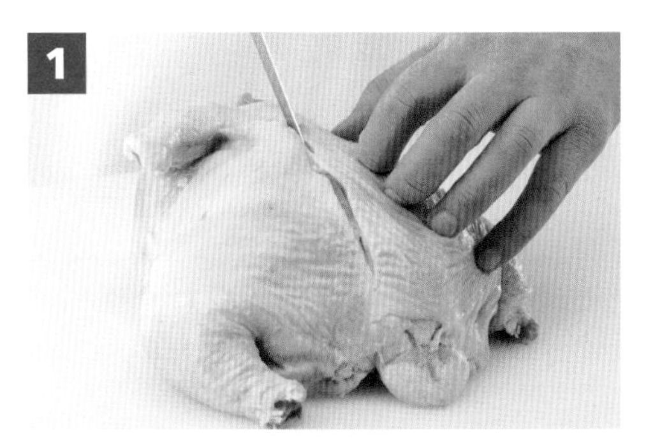

1 Lay the chicken on the cutting board, breast side down, with the legs pointed away from you. Cut through the skin down the center of the backbone. (Don't cut through the bone, just the skin.)

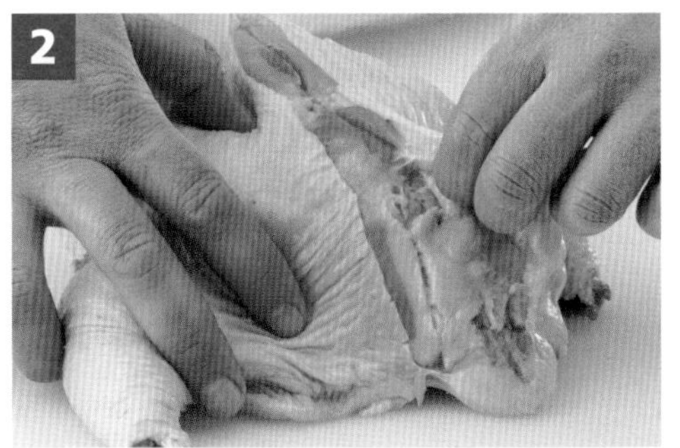

2 Working on the side closest to your guide hand and starting at the back of the bird, use your guide fingers to peel back the skin a bit.

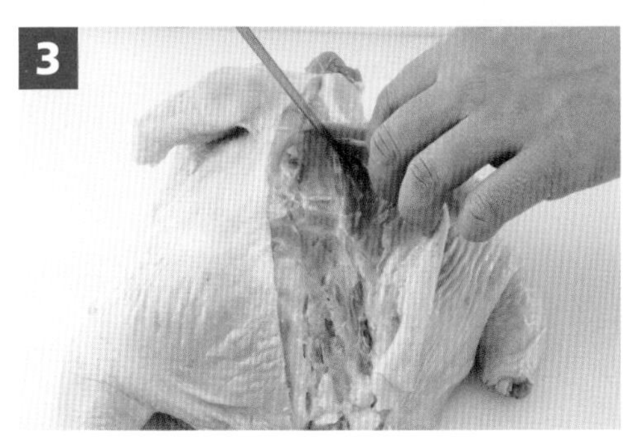

3 Slip the tip of the knife between the flesh and the backbone and cut toward you along the bone, feeling the scrape of the blade against the bone. Pull the skin and flesh away from the bone as the knife moves forward. Continue cutting until you reach the wing.

Next, we're going to cut through the joints connecting the wing and leg to the body, disjointing them but leaving them attached to the body by the skin.

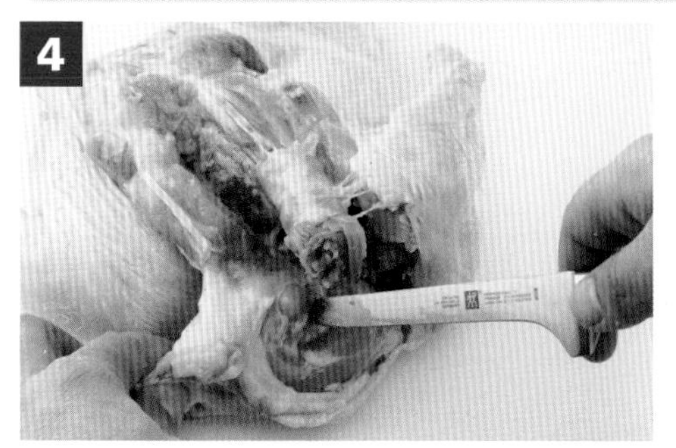

4 With your guide hand, wiggle the wing back and forth to loosen it in its socket. Use the tip of the boning knife to cut through the joint, without cutting the skin.

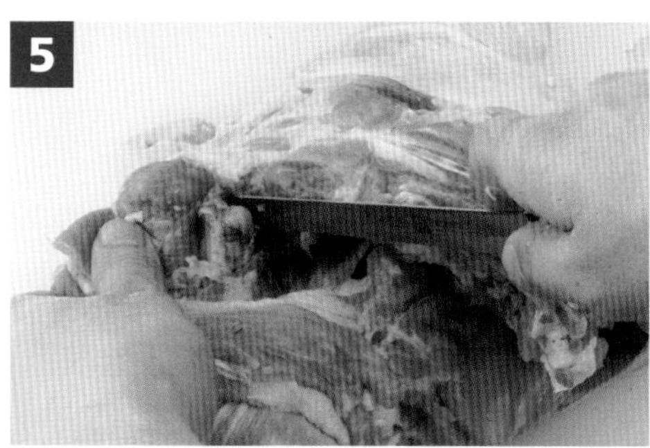

5 Grip the leg with your guide hand and pull it away from the body. Because you disjointed the leg in the preliminary steps, you should be able to work the knife fairly easily between the leg bone and the socket. Make sure you don't cut through the skin.

Now that the leg and wing are disjointed on one side, it's time to loosen the backbone and separate the leg and wing on the other side before moving on to the breast.

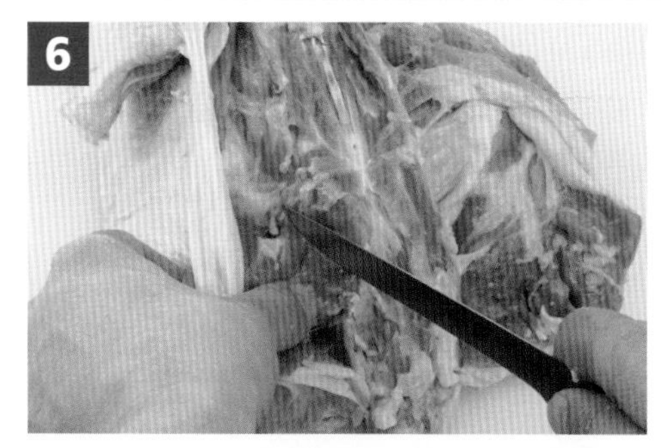

6 Rotate the chicken 180 degrees and repeat steps 2 and 3 on the other side, but this time cutting along the backbone from front to back.

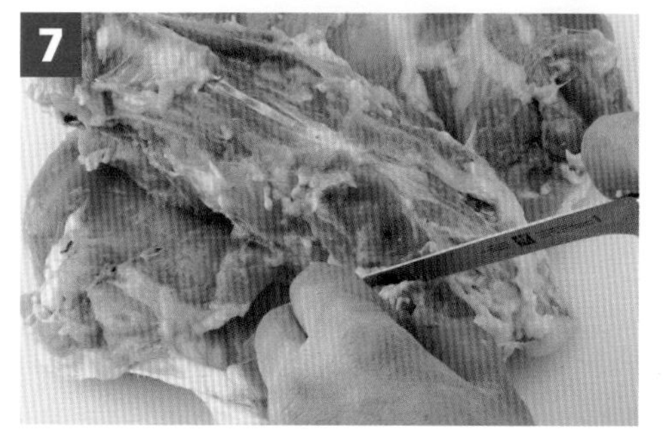

7 Repeat steps 4 and 5 to disjoint the wing and leg on the other side.

The next step is detaching the carcass from the breast.

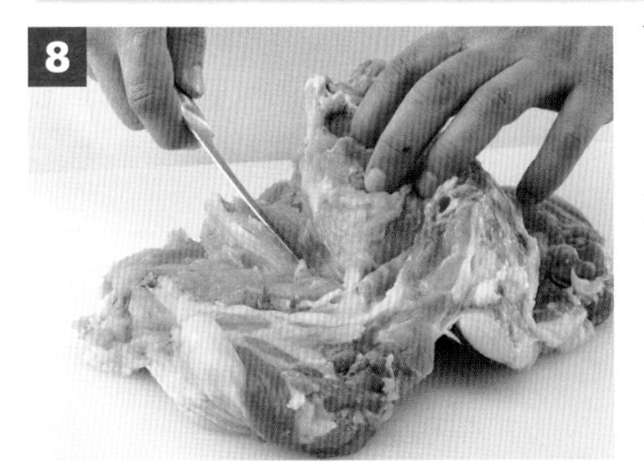

8

Use the tip of the boning knife to gently scrape the breast meat away from the ribs on one side, stopping when you get to the keel bone.

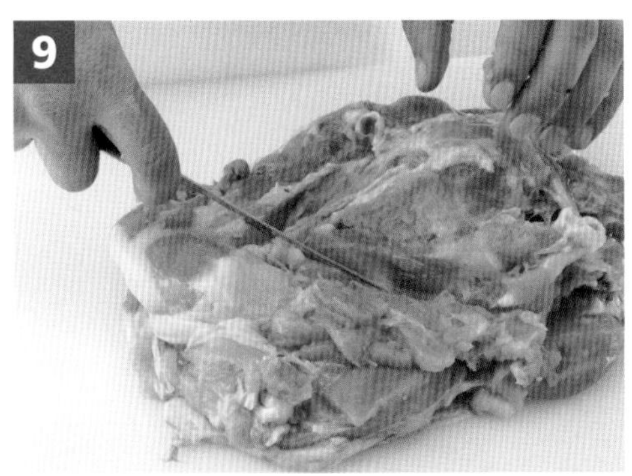

9

Repeat step 8 on the other side of the breast, again stopping at the keel bone.

At this point, the meat is just barely attached to the carcass at the keel bone, and if you lift the carcass, the meat will hang loosely.

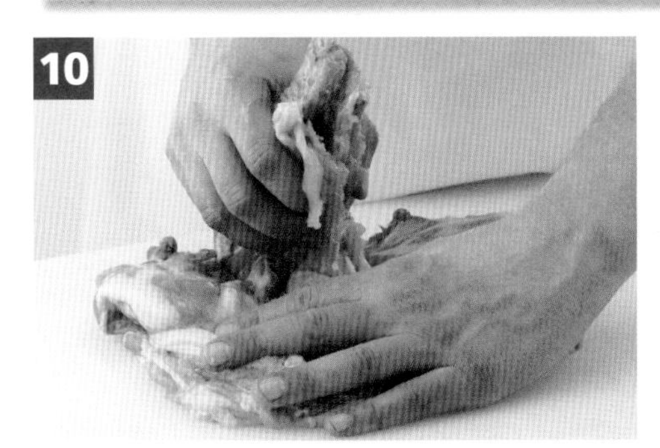

10

Grasp the carcass with your knife hand and hold down the breasts with your guide hand. Gently but firmly rock the carcass back toward the legs, pulling the keel bone out of the breast.

If the keel bone is stubborn and won't come out, use the boning knife to cut along the bottom of the bone, where it's attached to the meat, to free it completely.

Now that the carcass is removed, the only bones left to deal with are the ones in the legs and the wings.

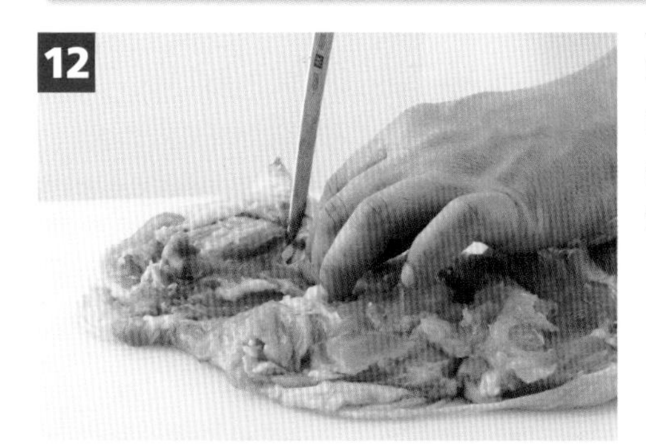

Using the tip of the knife, cut through the meat down the length of the drumstick and thigh bones on one of the legs.

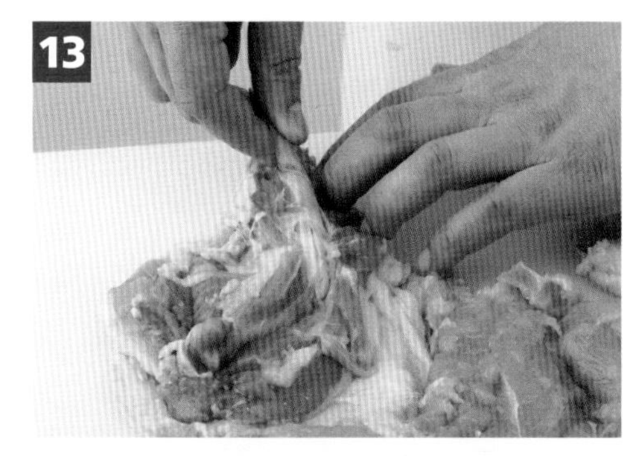

Use the thumb and index finger of your guide hand to push the meat down both sides of the bones.

Slip the tip of the knife underneath the drumstick bone and cut along it, freeing the bone from the meat.

Repeat step 14 with the thigh bone.

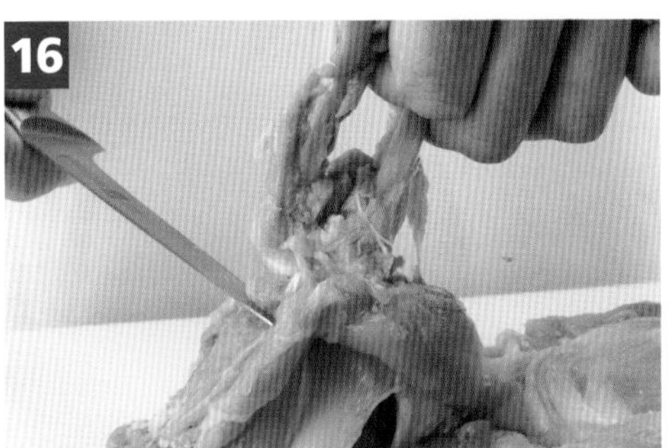

At this point, the bones will still be attached at the knee. Lift up the drumstick and thigh bones to see where the knee is attached by ligaments and tendons, and use some force to cut it out.

Repeat steps 12 to 16 with the other leg.

Using the tip of the knife, cut through the meat down the length of one drumette.

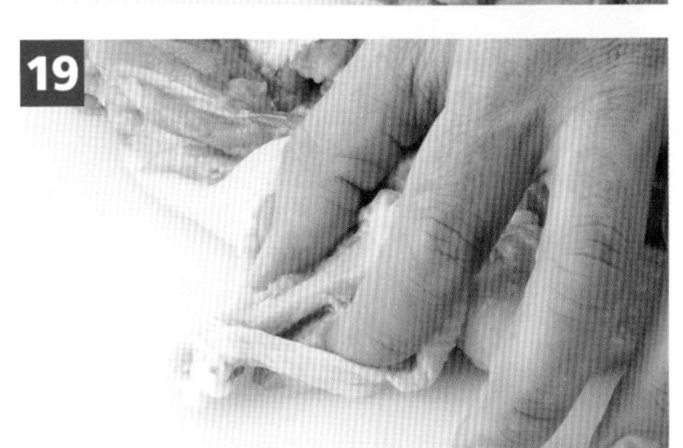

Use the thumb and index finger of your guide hand to push the meat down both sides of the bone.

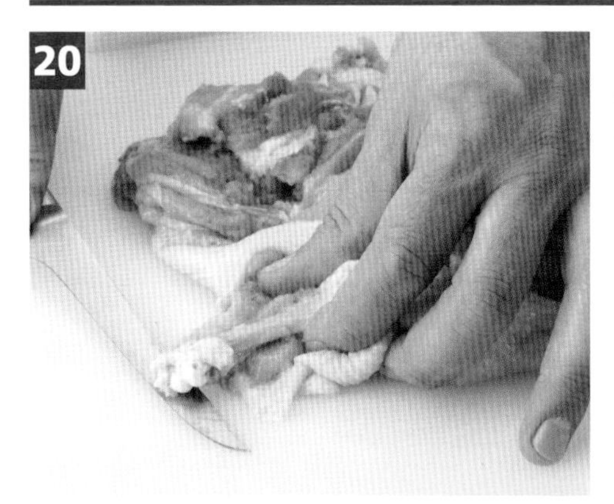

Slip the tip of the knife underneath the drumette bone and cut along it, freeing the bone from the meat.

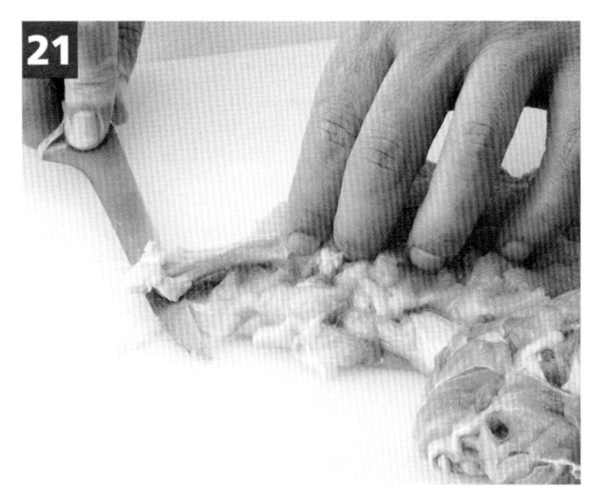

Rotate the chicken 180 degrees and repeat steps 18 to 20 with the other drumette.

Now that your chicken is boned, you can use the carcass and other bones and scraps to make stock.

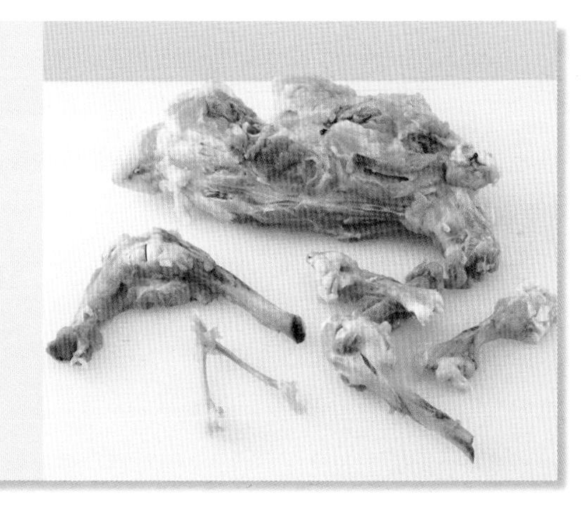

Spatchcocking

This is a relatively simple technique that gives a great outcome. According to the *Oxford English Dictionary*, the term "spatchcock" originated in 18th-century Ireland and is a shortened form of the phrase "dispatch the cock."

RECOMMENDED KNIFE

Chef's knife or cleaver

Spatchcocking involves removing the backbone and the breast bone of the chicken so that it can be opened up and laid flat. This substantially cuts down on the cooking time (you can roast a spatchcocked chicken in just over half an hour, as opposed to an hour for a trussed whole chicken), while at the same time giving the bird an interesting look.

Some people call this technique "butterflying," and indeed, a spatchcocked chicken does resemble a large butterfly.

A common preparation for a spatchcocked chicken is to roast or grill it while pressing it down with something heavy — such as bricks.

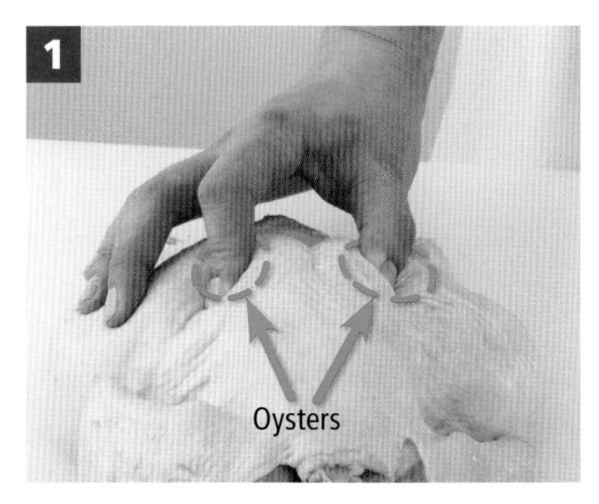

Set the chicken on the cutting board, breast side down, with its tail facing you. Locate the oysters, the two little meaty circles on either side of the backbone, just above where the thighs meet the body. When we cut the backbone out, we're going to leave the oysters attached to the body.

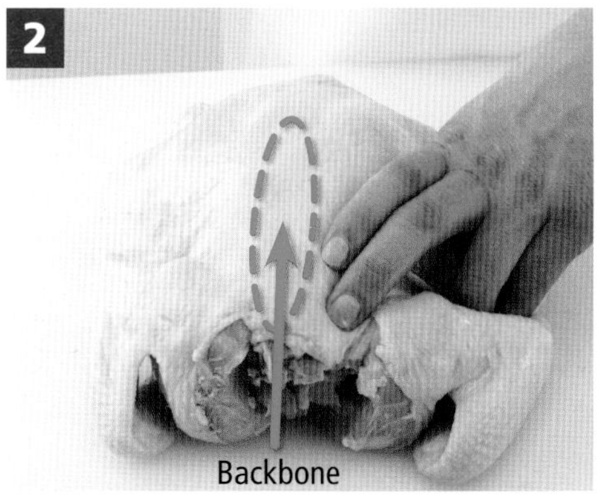

Grip the top of the chicken with your guide hand, just beside the backbone on your guide-hand side.

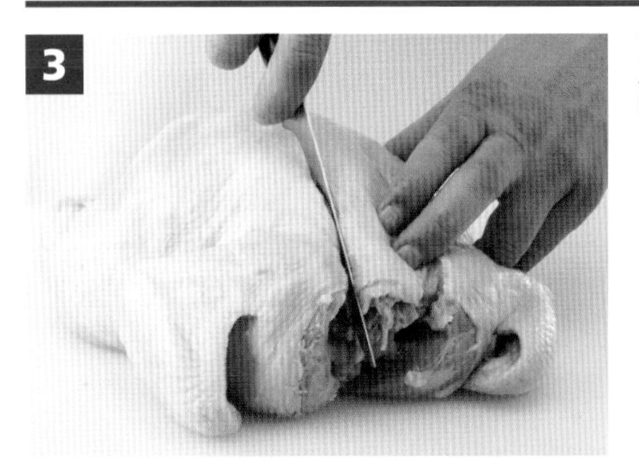

Place the knife blade on the side of the backbone opposite your guide hand.

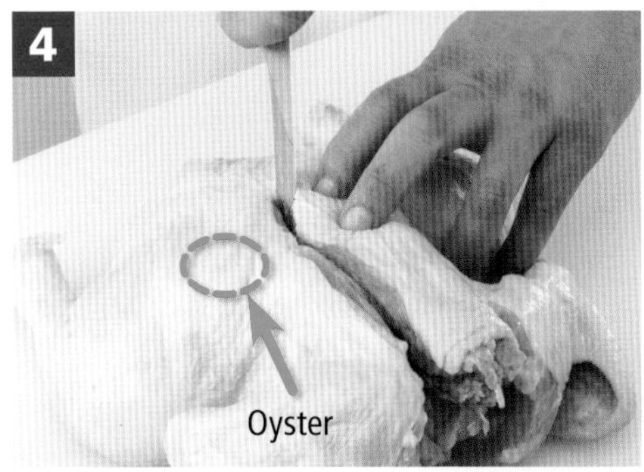

Cut down along the side of the backbone, using it as your guide. (You'll be cutting through rib bones as you do this, so expect it to take a bit of effort.) Watch out for the oyster. When you reach it, angle your blade in slightly toward the backbone and cut around the oyster, leaving it attached to the body.

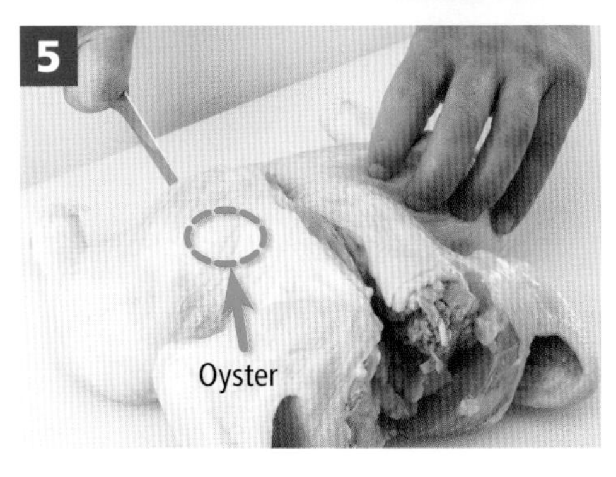

Once you've gotten around the oyster, continue cutting straight down until you cut through the bottom of the chicken.

Now that you've opened up the chicken along one side of the backbone, you can remove the backbone altogether in a couple of different ways.

Method 1

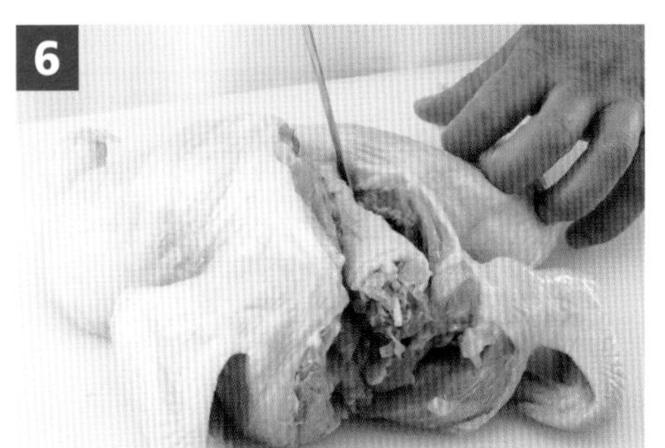

Start with the blade on top of the chicken on the guide-hand side of the backbone.

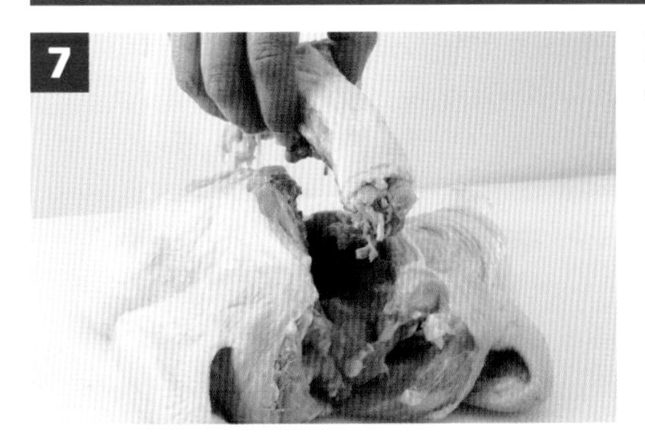

Repeat steps 4 and 5, and the backbone will come completely free.

Method 2

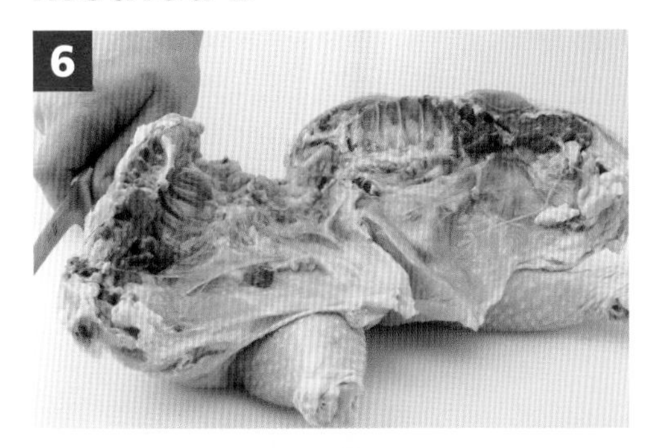

Open the chicken flat and lay it skin side down on the cutting board, with the backbone next to your knife hand.

Hold the chicken with your guide hand and cut down the other side of the backbone. Remember to cut around the oyster and leave it attached to the carcass.

Once the backbone is completely free, save it for stock. The next task is to remove the keel bone, the dark piece of bone between the two breast halves.

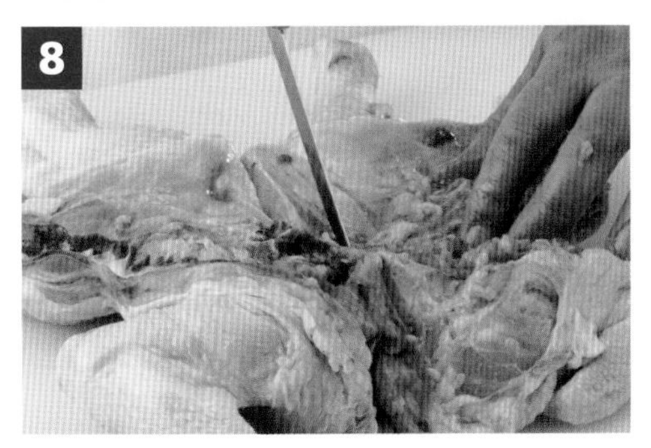

Steady the chicken with your guide hand and run the tip of the knife down the length of the keel bone to score it.

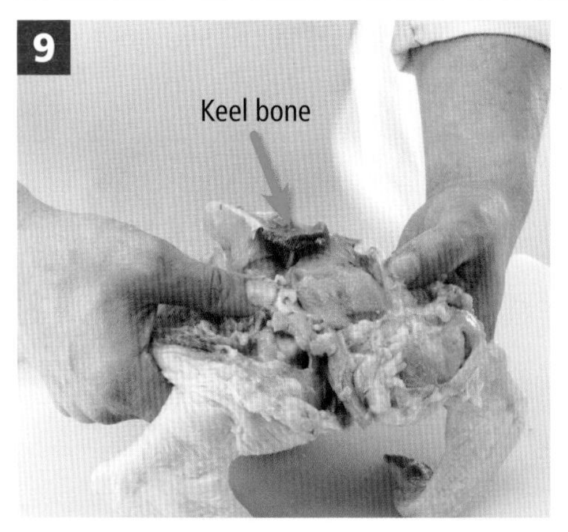

Hold the chicken in both hands, with the skin side down and the legs pointing toward you. Your thumbs should lie on either side of the keel bone, and the tips of your other fingers should meet directly below the keel bone. Bend the chicken back to release the keel bone. You may or may not hear a loud snap as it breaks free.

Grasp the keel bone firmly in one hand and strip it away from the breast meat. If it breaks, simply pull the pieces out with your fingers, or, if they're lodged in there, use the knife to cut them free.

Here are two views of your spatchcocked chicken:

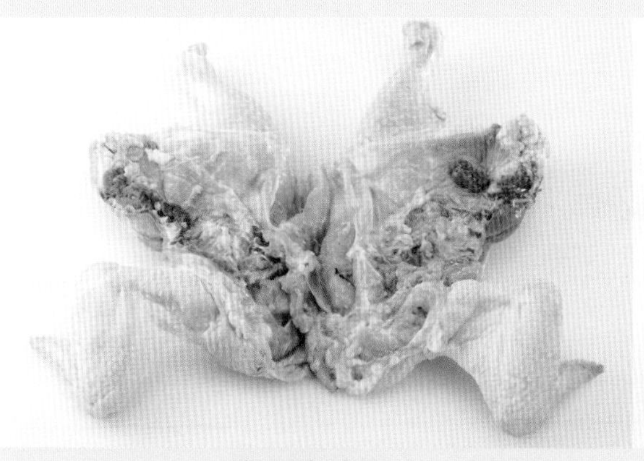

Skin side down

Skin side up

If you want to flatten it even more, set it skin side up on your cutting board, place a sheet of plastic wrap over it and pound it with the bottom of a cast-iron skillet or a meat mallet.

Glove Boning a Small Bird

This technique, also called tunnel boning, is not all that common, but it does have its uses, particularly with smaller birds, such as quail, pigeon and Cornish game hen. In our demo, we use a Cornish game hen.

RECOMMENDED KNIFE

Stiff boning knife or paring knife

Unlike the procedure for boning a whole chicken (page 245), in which a slit is made through the skin at the back, in glove boning the skin is left whole and the carcass is pulled out of the meat, like pulling a hand out of a glove, leaving the bones in the legs and wings.

Some chefs prefer to start at the neck end, where the wings are, while others prefer to start at the tail end, where the legs are. We'll give directions starting from the neck end, but the technique is basically the same either way: Scrape the meat away from the carcass and cut through the joints that connect the wings and legs.

While you're doing this, keep in mind that, unlike the skin on the breast, the skin along the back has no protective layer of muscle underneath. Therefore, be extra careful not to rip or poke through the skin.

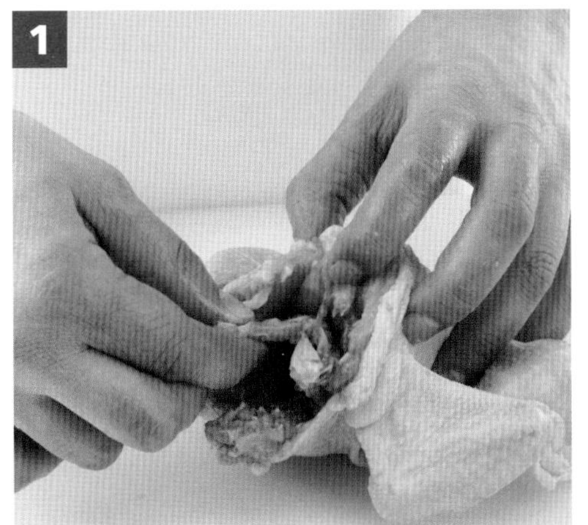

Remove the wishbone (see page 247).

Stand the game hen on its tail end on the cutting board, with the side of the hen facing you. Slip the point of the knife between the skin and the carcass at the back side of the neck cavity. Scrape the knife along the edge of the cavity, loosening the skin as you go, being careful not to tear it.

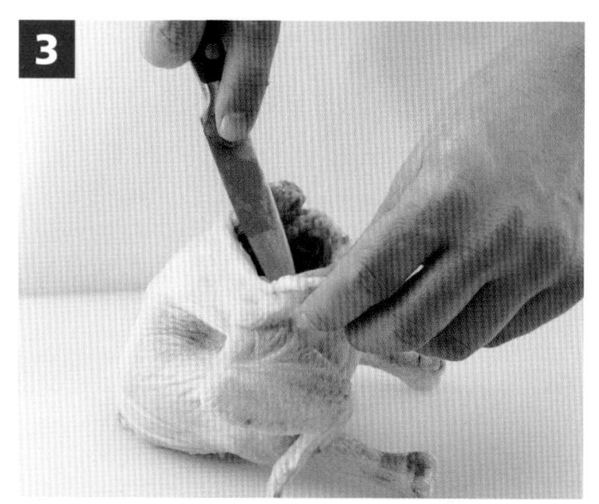

Turning your attention to the breast side of the cavity, slip the point of the knife between the carcass and the breast. Scrape down one side of the carcass until you get to the joint where the wing is attached.

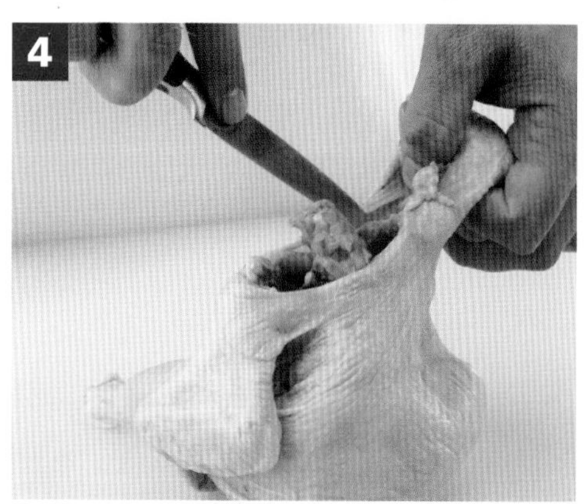

Scrape away any meat, sinew and connective tissue from the wing joint so you can see it clearly. Pull back on the wing with your guide hand while you slip the point of the knife between the wing bone and the carcass.

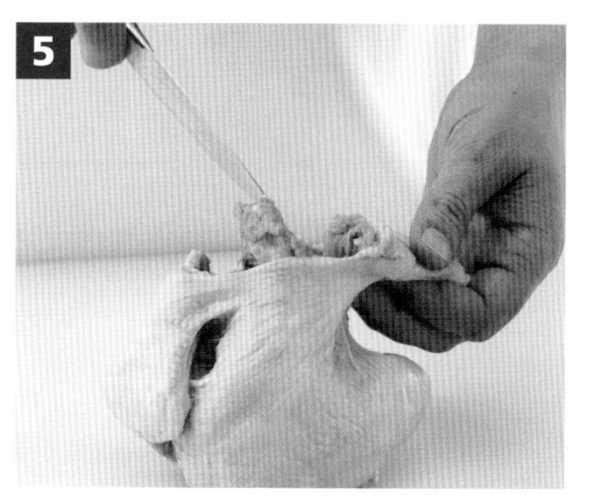

Cut through the joint, but not the meat or skin on the other side. The wing bone will now be detached, but the wing will still be attached.

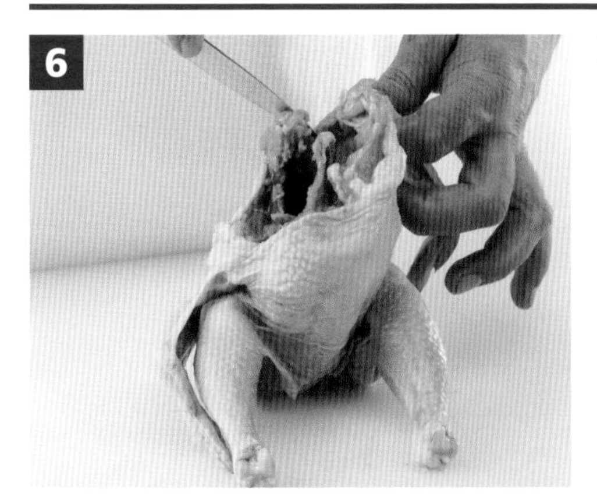

Repeat steps 3 to 5 with the other wing.

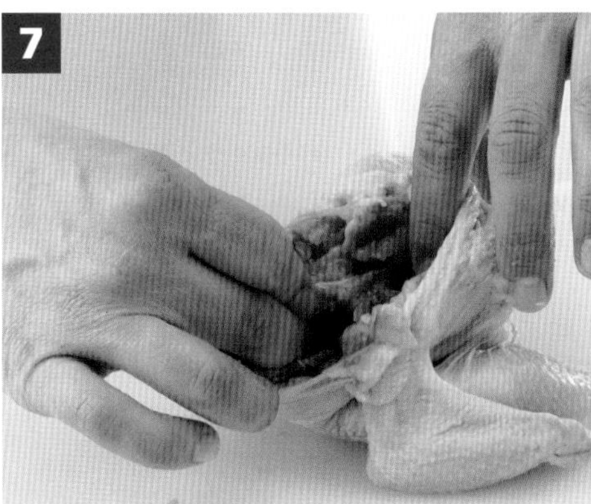

Use your fingers to separate the breast meat from the carcass. It should pull away without much resistance. If you encounter resistance around the keel bone, use the tip of your knife to detach the meat from the bone.

We've now peeled the top half of the breast meat away from the ribs. We'll separate the bottom half in step 12, after we've finished the back and legs.

Return your attention to the back, running the knife underneath the skin to scrape it away from the carcass and pushing the skin down as you go.

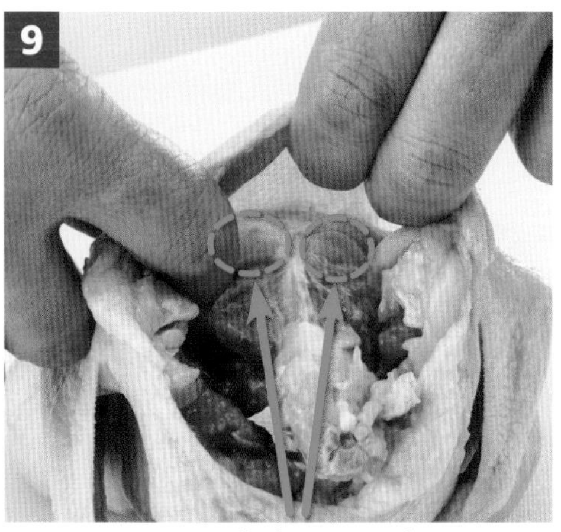

Oysters (before cutting)

When you reach the oysters (the two meaty circles of meat on either side of the backbone), dig them out with the point of the knife, leaving them attached to the skin.

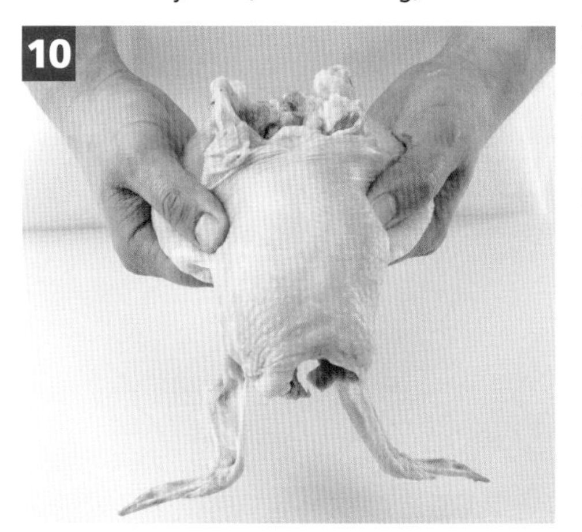

Lay the hen on its back and bend the legs back gently to dislocate the thigh bones from their sockets. Be careful not to tear the skin.

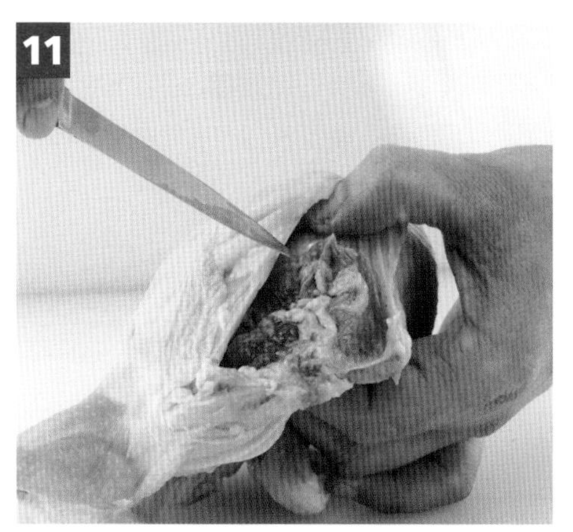

Use the point of the knife to cut through the sinew at the joint between each thigh and the carcass, leaving the legs attached by the skin.

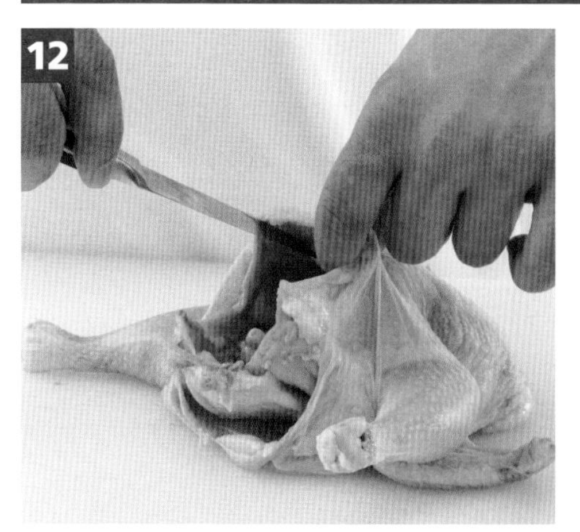

Starting at the bottom of the breast on the side farthest from you, slide your knife between the breast and the bone. Follow the bone around to the other side of the breast, separating the flesh from the bone.

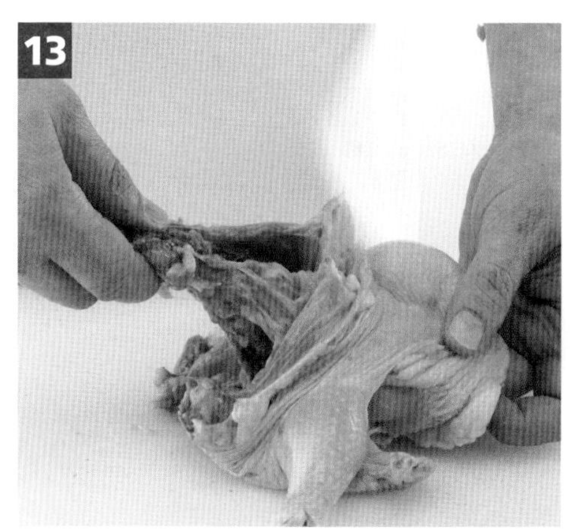

Grip the top of the breast with your guide hand. Reach in with your knife hand and carefully pull out the carcass.

Depending on what you intend to do with the hen, you can stuff it or cook it as is for a semi-boneless dish (there are still bones in the legs and wings, of course).

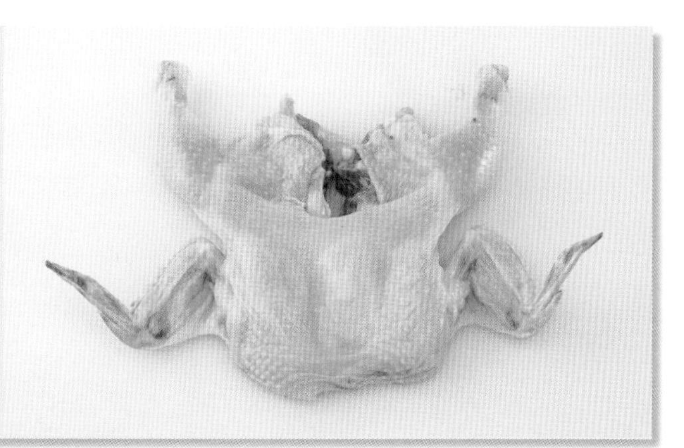

Chapter 6
Cutting Meat

Unlike with poultry, where it's common to start with a whole bird and break it down, it's fairly rare to start with a whole hooved animal. Butchers first break down animals into a few large pieces, called primal cuts. The pieces are then "fabricated" into individual cuts, which may in turn be further prepared for cooking. In this chapter, we'll explain some of the most common techniques for preparing beef, lamb, pork and veal from fabricated cuts. Some of these techniques may also be used on poultry or fish.

Cutting Bacon Lardons

Strictly speaking, lardons are long, thin strips of fat that are inserted into roasts to add moisture. Bacon lardons are thin strips of bacon that are cooked and used as a garnish. They are different from crumbled bacon in that they are cut before they're cooked, so they all end up the same size. Traditionally, they'd be cut from slab bacon into batonnet-sized strips, but since it's much easier to purchase precut bacon strips, we'll use those for our lardons.

RECOMMENDED KNIFE

Chef's knife or Santoku

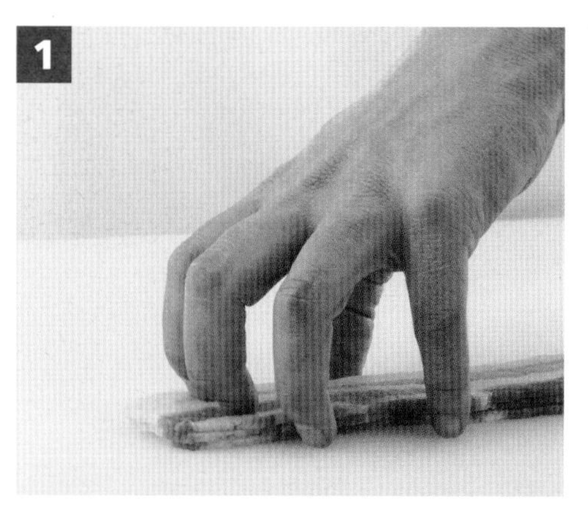

Lay several strips of bacon on top of one another on the cutting board. Place your guide hand on top in the claw position.

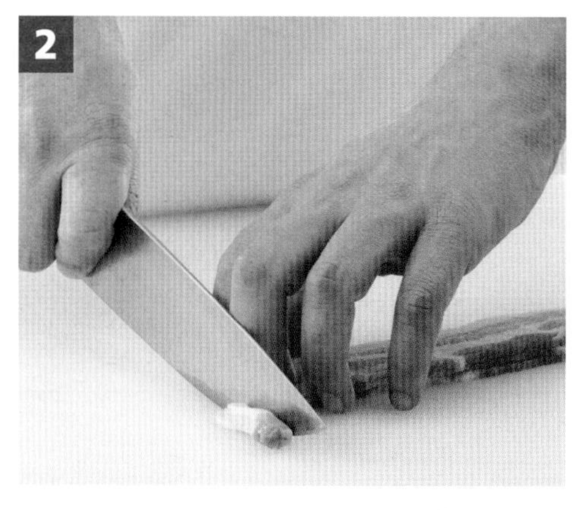

Place the knife blade flush against your guide fingers and line it up to cut off a ¼-inch (6 mm) slice. Cut straight down through the bacon.

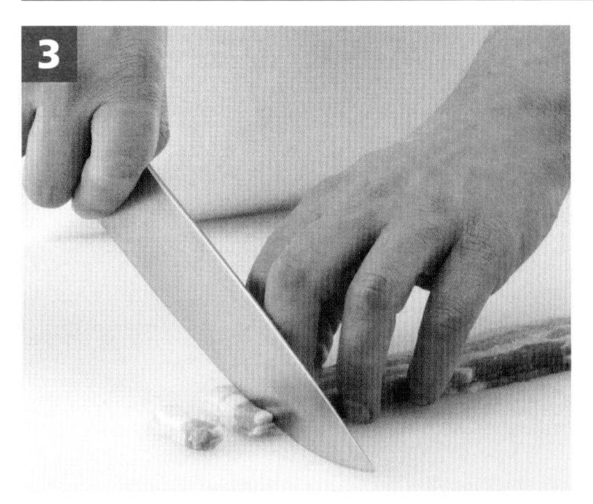

Keeping the blade against your guide fingers, move them back ¼ inch (6 mm) and cut off another slice.

Repeat step 3 until you have cut all the bacon into slices.

Don't be concerned that the individual lardons are sticking together. When they are cooked, the fat holding them together will melt and the lardons will cook individually.

Butterflying

To butterfly a piece of meat, you simply cut horizontally most of the way through it and use the uncut part as a "hinge" to open it into two thin pieces, thereby increasing its surface area. Any boneless meat, including poultry and fish, can be butterflied. It is a useful technique when you want a short cooking time or plan to cover the meat with a filling and roll it up.

Pieces of meat come in many shapes, sizes and thicknesses. When deciding which side to start cutting at and which to use as your hinge, remember that the meat will be half its original thickness when you're done, while the hinge will remain its original thickness. Thus, we recommend using the thinnest side as the hinge.

For our demo, we'll use a boneless pork chop cut from the loin.

Don't worry too much about making your butterflied meat an exact shape or thickness. Butterflied meat is very often pounded afterward, at which time you can control its shape and thickness.

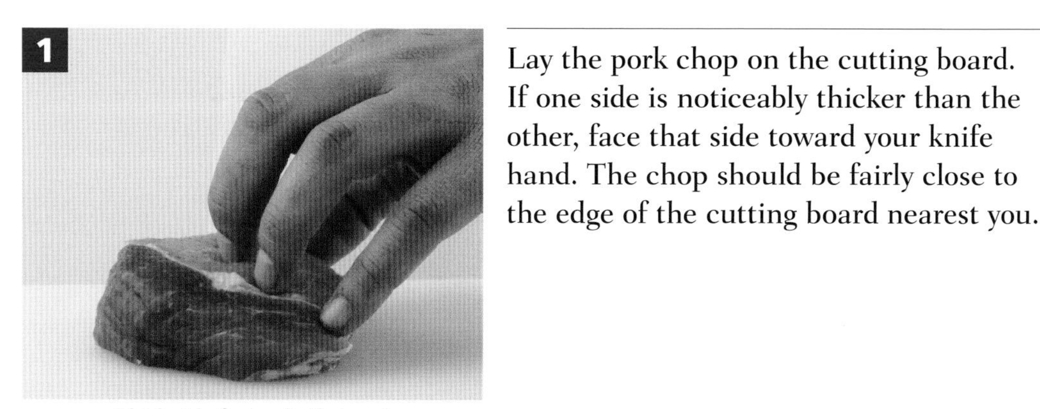

Thick side facing knife hand

Lay the pork chop on the cutting board. If one side is noticeably thicker than the other, face that side toward your knife hand. The chop should be fairly close to the edge of the cutting board nearest you.

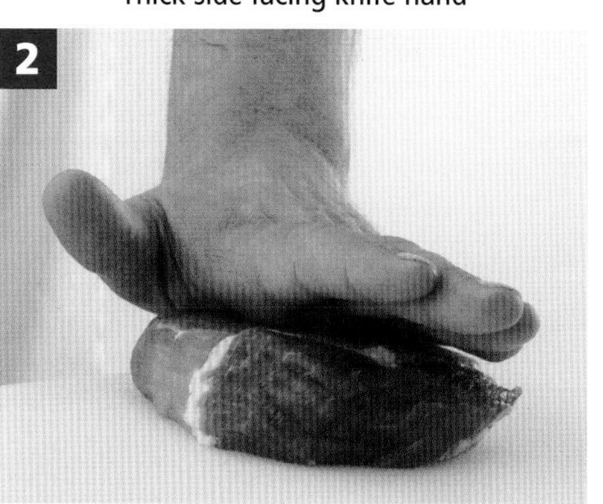

Steady the chop with the palm of your guide hand, taking care to keep your fingers bent up and away from the blade.

Hold the knife with the blade parallel to the board, halfway up the side of the chop.

The pork chop should be close enough to the edge of the board that the knife handle is beyond the edge of the board, not directly above it. If you hold the handle directly above the board, you'll have a tendency to tilt the knife toward the tip, which will result in an uneven cut. (Note: In the picture, the guide hand has been removed for clarity.)

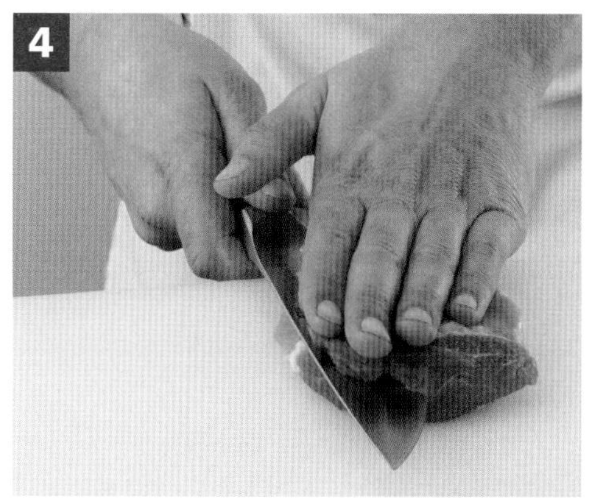

Cut horizontally through the chop until you get close to the other side; do not cut all the way through.

When trying to decide when to stop cutting, keep in mind that when you open it up, you want the hinge to have the same thickness as the cut parts. For example, if the piece of meat you're starting with is 1 inch (2.5 cm) thick, when it's butterflied, it will be ½ inch (12 mm) thick. Thus, you should cut through to within ½ inch (12 mm) of the other side.

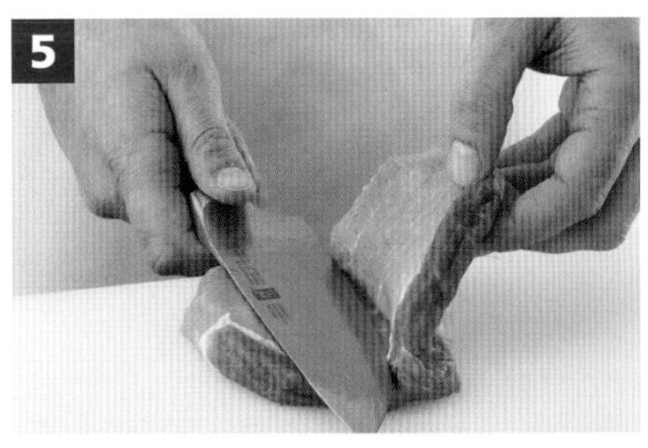

Open up the two "wings" of the butterfly as if you are opening a book.

If the whole piece of meat is relatively flat, you are ready to proceed with your recipe.

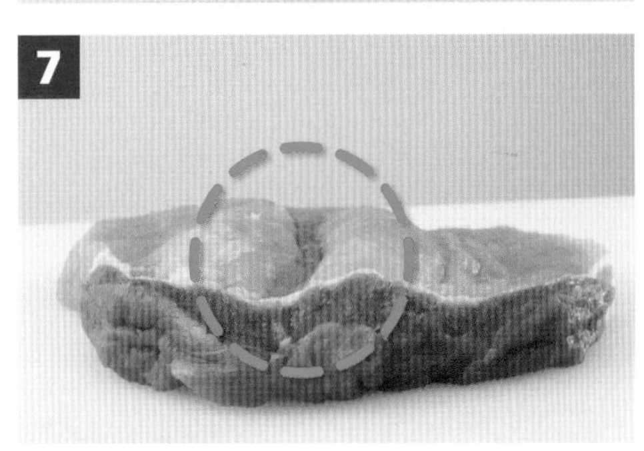

If you didn't cut far enough through the meat, the hinge will be too thick and will bulge along its length.

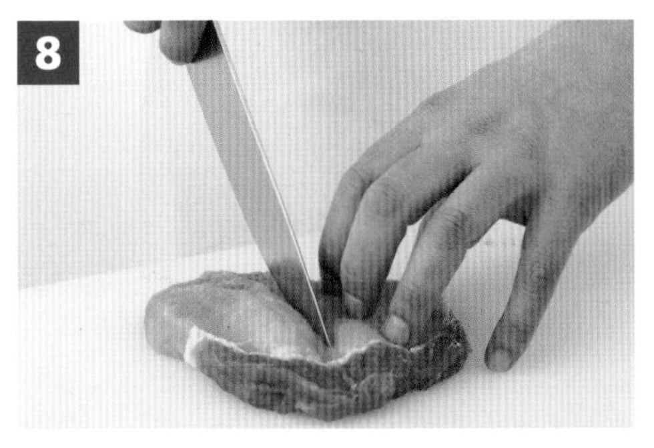

Run the blade down the length of the hinge very lightly, making a slight incision.

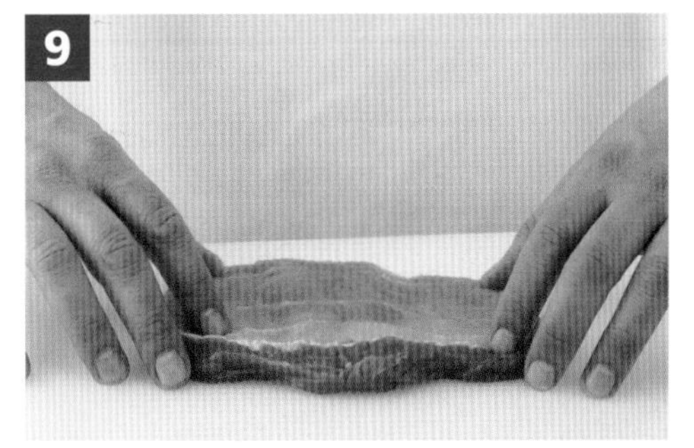

Set the knife down and use your hands to open the hinge a little more. If the whole piece is now relatively flat, you are ready to proceed with your recipe. If the piece is still too thick along the spine, repeat step 8 until the desired thickness is reached.

Cutting Pouches for Stuffing

Steaks, chops and poultry breasts — any relatively flat cut of meat — can be made a little more interesting if you create a small pocket and stuff it with something delicious. We'll demonstrate this easy technique with a boneless skinless chicken breast.

RECOMMENDED KNIFE

Paring knife or stiff boning knife

Before you get going, it's a good idea to get an understanding of exactly what you'll be doing with the blade. To do so, lay the knife on top of the breast, with the handle off the edge at the midline of the breast and the point about 3⁄4 inch (2 cm) from the other edge. Pivot the blade back and forth to get an idea of the outline of the pocket you'll be cutting.

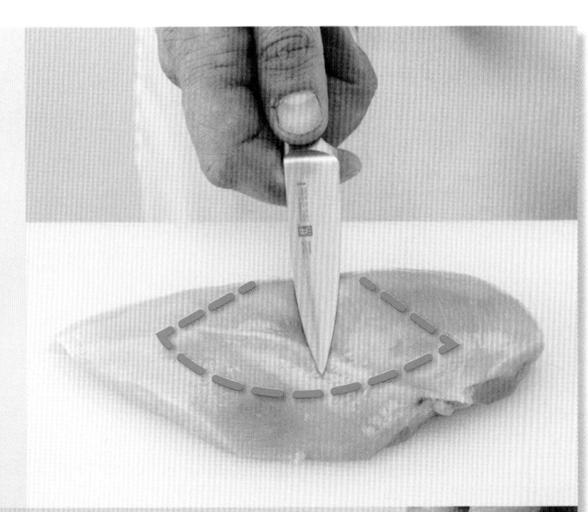

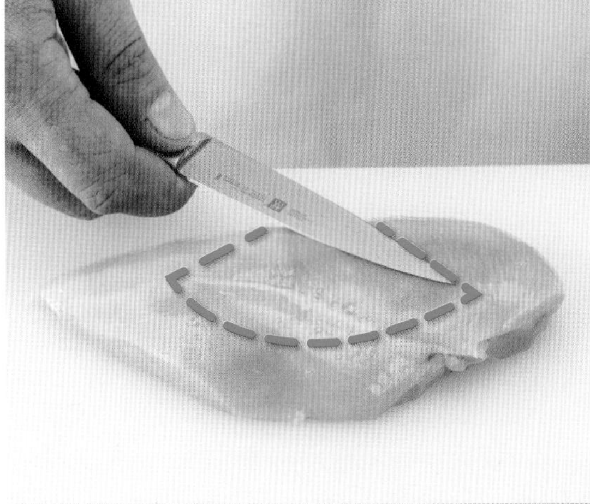

Cutting Pouches for Stuffing

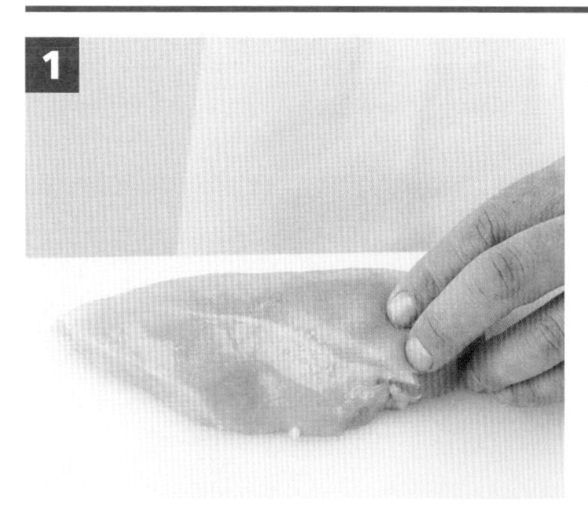

Place the chicken breast on the cutting board, with the thickest part facing you.

Steady the breast with your guide hand. Hold the knife blade parallel to the board and insert the point into the breast at the midline, and halfway between the top and the bottom.

Make sure the breast is the same thickness above and below the pocket to promote even cooking and a better final product.

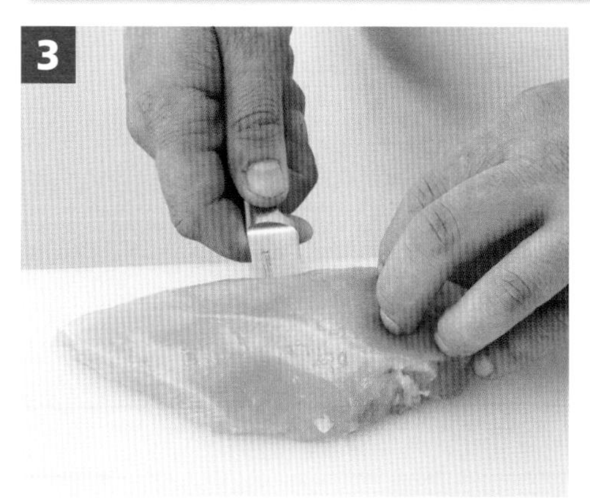

Push the blade about three-quarters of the way into the flesh. Be sure to keep the blade perfectly horizontal so as not to poke through the top or bottom.

Keep the entry hole as small as possible. As much as you can, avoid cutting through the edges of the hole as you pivot your knife around the inside of the meat. When it comes time to stuff the breast, you can use a piping bag.

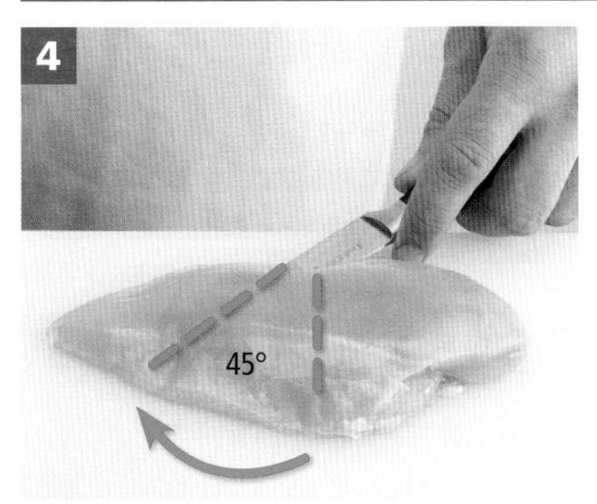

With the blade inside the breast, pivot the knife about 45 degrees from the entry hole to enlarge the pocket. As you cut, feel the motion of the knife under your guide hand and keep track of its location in the breast. (Note: In the picture, the guide hand has been removed for clarity.)

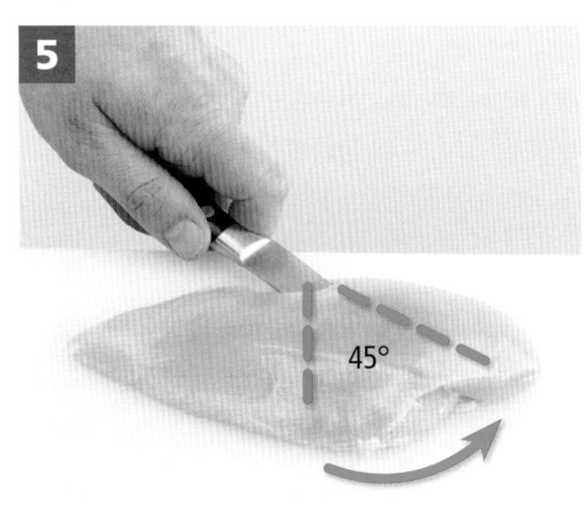

Remove the knife from the breast, flip it over so the blade is facing the other direction and reinsert it into the breast. Pivot the knife about 45 degrees from the entry hole. (Note: In the picture, the guide hand has been removed for clarity.)

You should now have a nice, even pocket, with an entry hole not much bigger than the height of the blade.

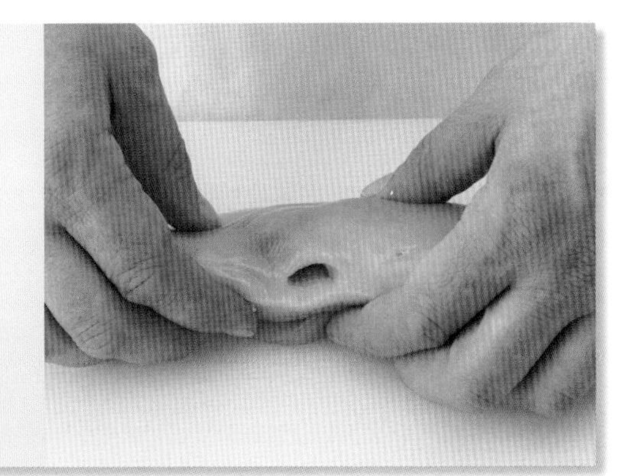

Trimming Tenderloins

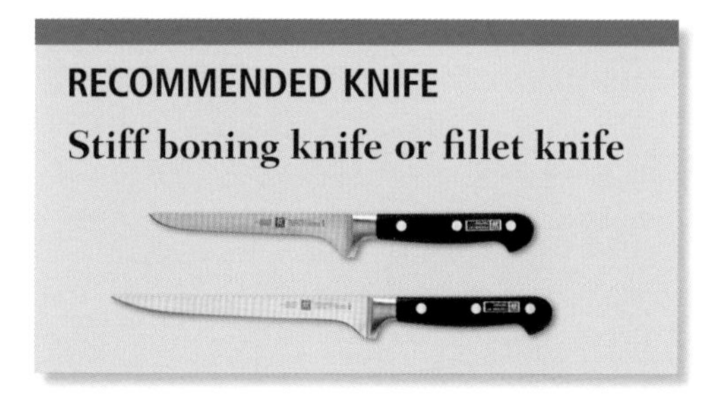
RECOMMENDED KNIFE
Stiff boning knife or fillet knife

The tenderloin is the most naturally tender portion of the cow or pig (or, for that matter, game animals such as bison, deer or elk). Owing to its placement on the back, it gets the least amount of use of any major muscle, which means it has very little of the tough connective tissue that makes other cuts of meat so chewy.

Whole beef tenderloins are in the 6- to 8-pound (3 to 4 kg) range and are much cheaper than trimmed tenderloins, even after accounting for waste, so it makes sense to trim off the fat and silverskin (inedible white connective tissue) yourself. Whole pork tenderloins are considerably smaller, usually in the 1-pound (500 g) range.

Tenderloins are much thicker at the butt end and taper gradually to the other end. The top side has most of the fat and silverskin, but the underside has a few big clumps of fat, which make it look somewhat wavy.

We'll demonstrate the technique with a beef tenderloin. It has considerably more fat and silverskin and therefore requires considerably more work than a pork tenderloin, which can be cleaned up in a couple of minutes.

Top side

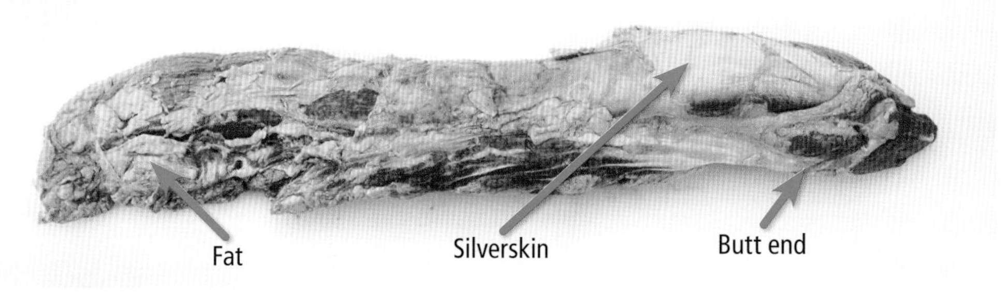

Underside

Place the tenderloin on the cutting board, top side up. Use your hands to pull away any loose pieces of fat that come off easily.

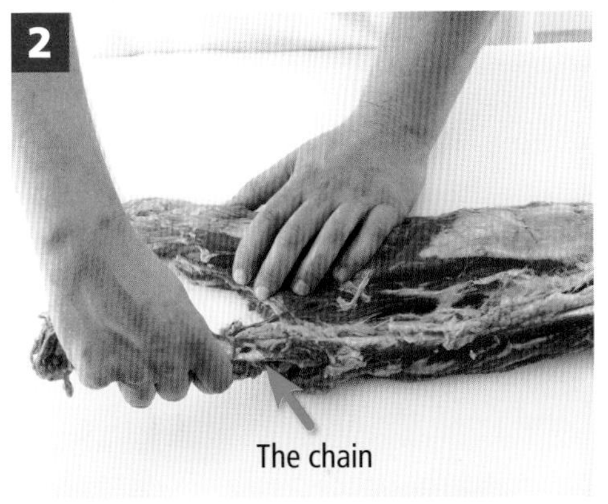

Locate the “chain,” the long, thin strip of meat, fat and gristle that runs along one side of the tenderloin. It’s attached to the tenderloin with strips of connective tissues and pulls away easily by hand.

Pull the chain free of the tenderloin. If any of it is particularly troublesome, cut through it with the knife. Use the chain for stock or clean it up and use it for stews, stir-fries or ground beef.

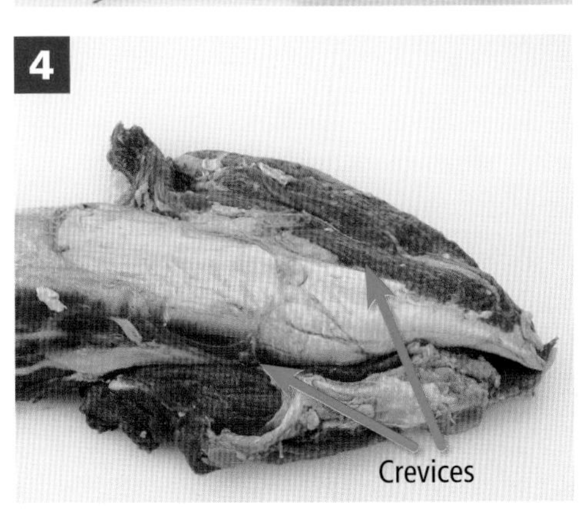

Turn your attention to the butt end and locate the two crevices that define the three distinct pieces of that end of the tenderloin.

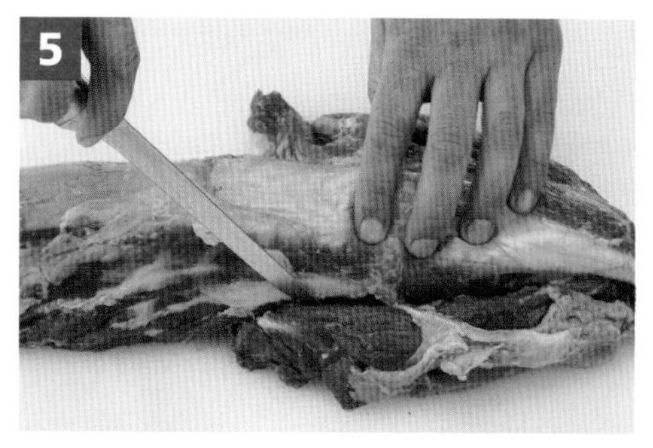

Use the knife to make shallow cuts down both sides of one crevice to remove any fat and silverskin.

Repeat step 5 with the other crevice.

Hold the knife with the blade parallel to the board and poke the tip just under the silverskin.

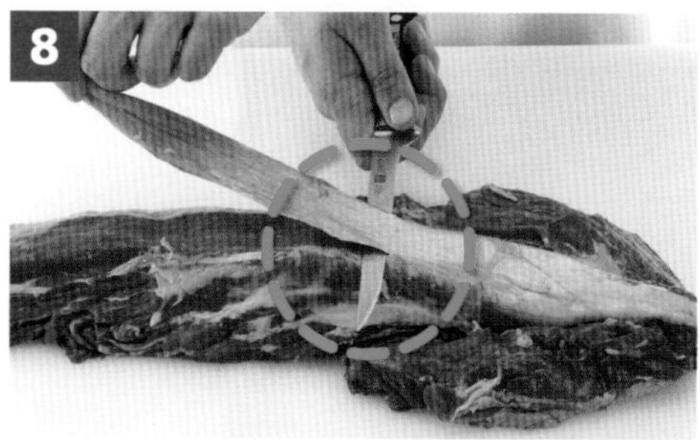

Blade tilted up slightly

Tilt the blade up slightly and cut along the underside of the silverskin. The idea is to limit the amount of meat you take off with the silverskin. You won't be able to get all the silverskin in one pass. Be patient and keep going back for more until it's all off.

Cut away big clumps of fat

Flip the tenderloin over and cut away any big clumps of fat. Repeat steps 7 and 8 to get rid of any silverskin.

Frenching Chops

This easy technique strips the excess meat, sinew and connective tissue off the bone of chops. It has two distinct advantages: it gives chops a cleaner look and it gives the diner a convenient handle with which to grab the chop.

Frenching can take place anywhere along the bone; it's up to you where to start. You can clean just the end of the bone, or you can take off everything except the main piece of meat, called the eye.

For our demo, we'll use a pork chop.

RECOMMENDED KNIFE

Paring knife or stiff boning knife

End of bone frenched

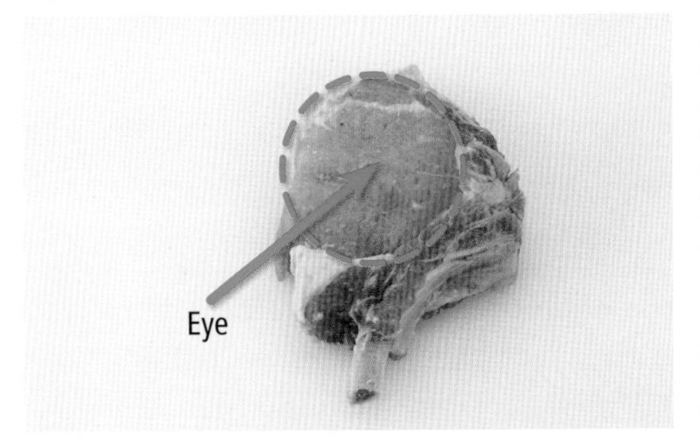

Entire bone frenched

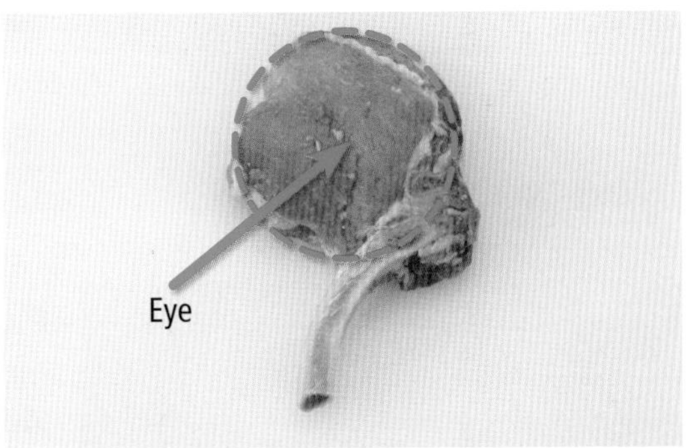

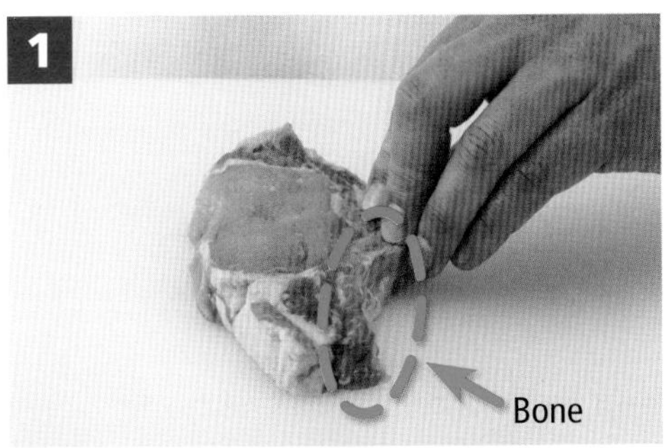

Lay the pork chop on the cutting board, with the side of the bone facing your guide hand. Steady it with your guide hand. Note that the bone is covered in a layer of meat, which you'll have to slice away.

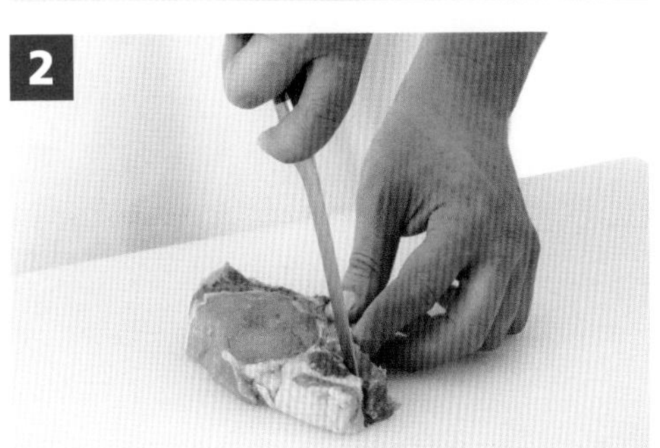

Using the tip of the knife, start cutting along the inside of the bone, getting as close to it as you can.

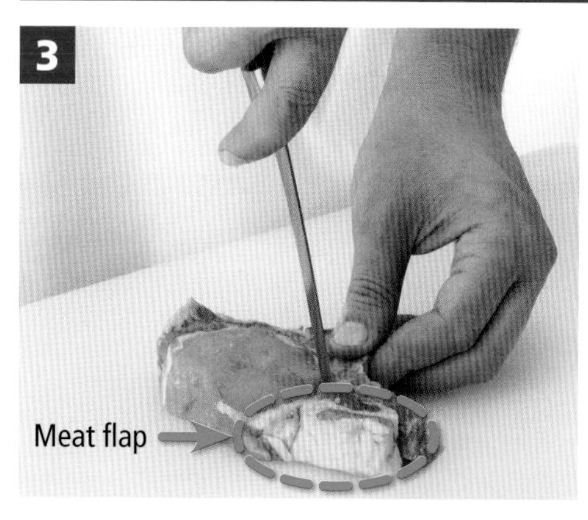

Continue cutting along the bone until you reach the eye. This will free up one side of the flap of meat and fat beneath the eye.

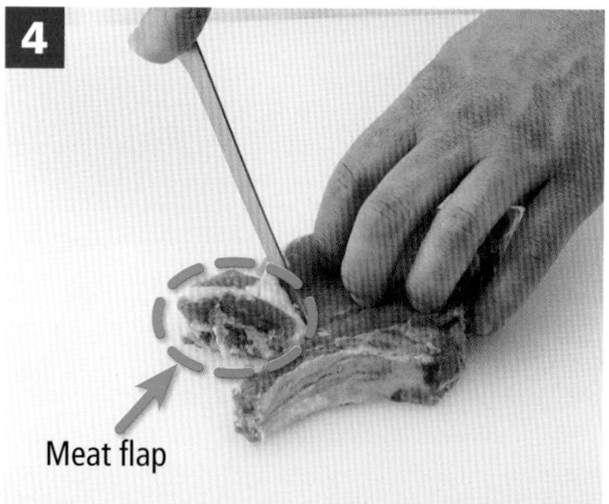

Rotate the pork chop 90 degrees so that the bone is facing away from you. Steady the eye with your guide hand. Cut along the line of fat just beneath the eye to remove the meat flap.

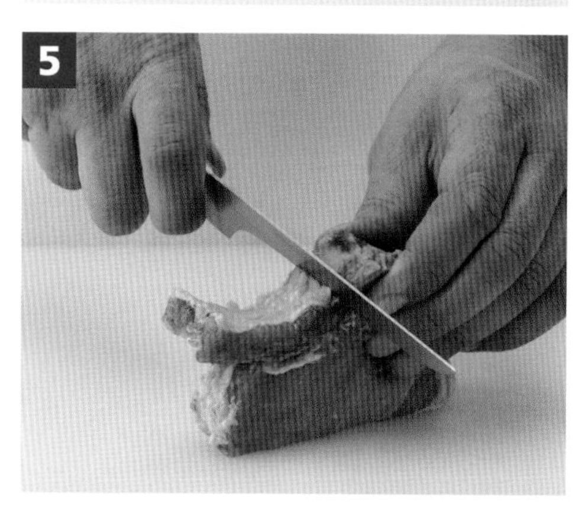

Flip the chop onto its side, with the bone in the air. Place the blade on the bone about 1 inch (2.5 cm) from the highest point of the chop and cut down to score the bone.

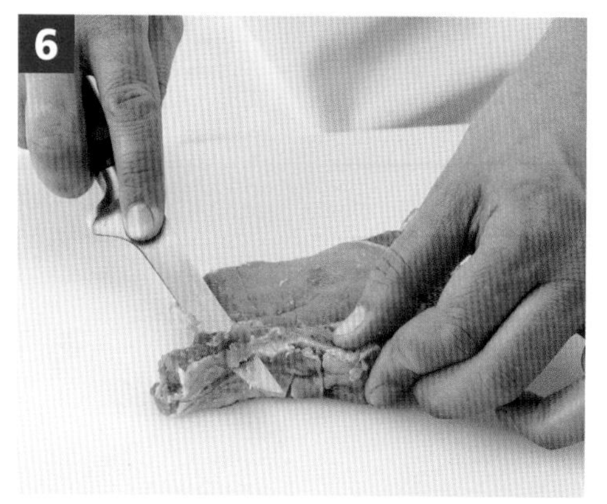

Lay the chop back down, with the bone facing away from you. Hold the blade parallel to the board and, starting at the score mark, cut away the meat, fat and sinew from the top of the bone.

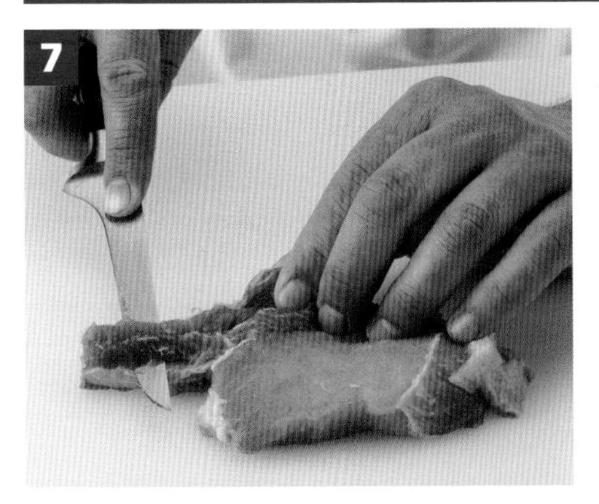

Flip the chop over and repeat step 6 on the other side of the bone.

Hold the knife perpendicular to the board and, starting at the score mark, cut away the meat, fat and sinew from the outside of the bone.

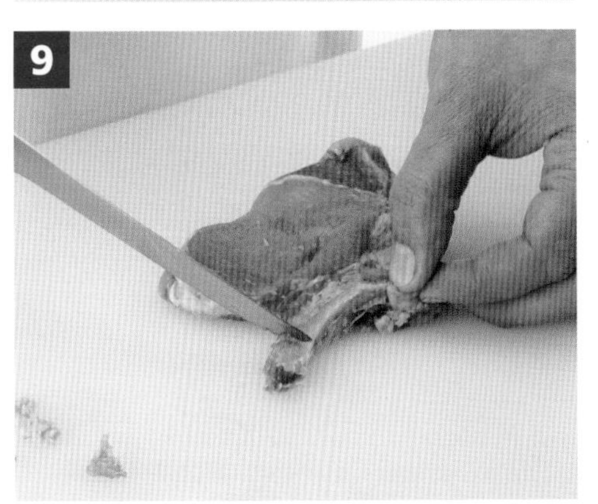

Use the tip of your knife to scrape off any remaining bits of tissue. (For an extra-clean bone, when you're done scraping, hold the chop by the eye and use a clean, dry towel to pull off any last stubborn bits of tissue.)

Before you cook the chop, wrap the frenched bone in foil to protect it from getting blackened or burned.

Frenching a Lamb Rack

RECOMMENDED KNIFE

Stiff boning knife

Few dishes are as elegant as a frenched lamb rack, where all of the meat, fat, tendons and connective tissue have been removed from the bones, leaving only the succulent eye of meat at the end. If you purchase whole lamb racks and french them yourself, you'll save money and have scraps left over for lamb sausages or patties or to make a sauce for your rack.

As with individual chops (see page 277), racks can be frenched to varying degrees depending on the chef's intended use. If you look at a whole rack from the side, you can see the main eye of meat. No matter what, the eye is left on, as it's the primary edible portion. Above the eye are thin layers of meat, interspersed with layers of fat. You may choose to remove all of this or leave some portion of it. Removing everything but the eye is by far the most attractive choice, though it provides the smallest portion. This is the style we'll be demonstrating.

This technique can also be used to create a frenched roast of pork, beef, veal or venison.

Part of bone frenched

Entire bone frenched

First, we'll cut through the meat, fat and membrane on top of the rack.

1

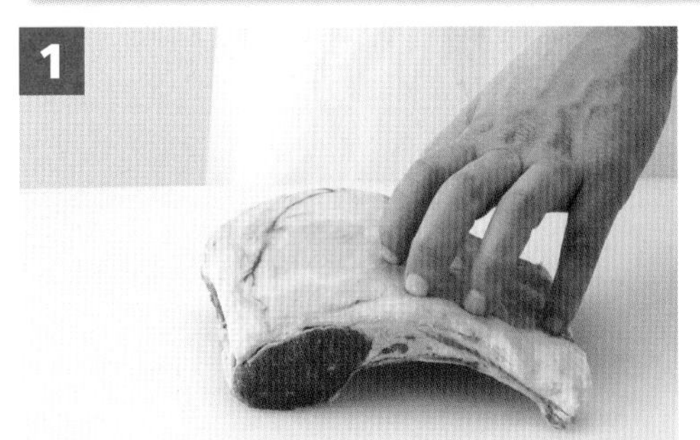

Place the rack on the cutting board, fat side up, with the bones facing your guide hand. Steady the rack with your guide hand.

2

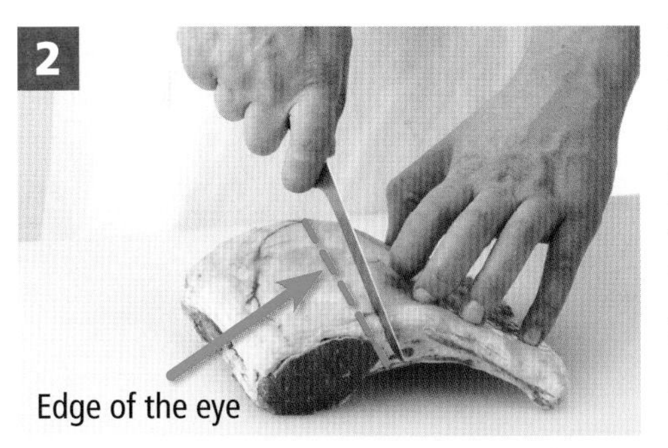

Locate the top edge of the eye on both sides of the rack. Starting at the side of the rack farthest from you, place the knife blade perpendicular to the bone at the edge of the eye. (If you want a smaller frenched handle, place the knife farther away from the eye.)

3

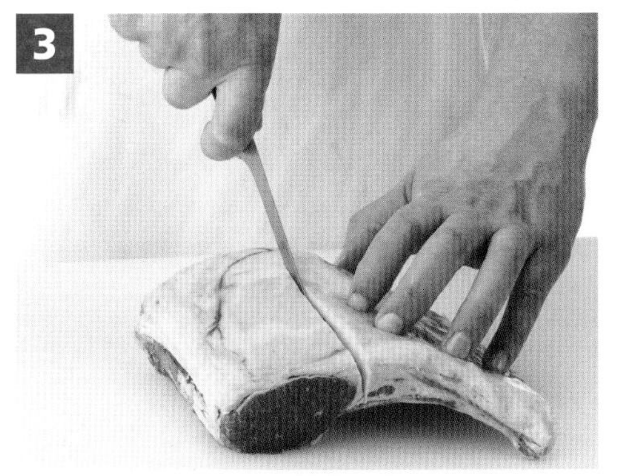

Make an incision across the rack, cutting down to the bone, until you reach the top edge of the eye closest to you. (Your impulse will be to cut a straight line across the bones; however, because the eye is smaller on one end of the rack than the other, you should cut evenly along the edge of the eye. This will result in a slightly angled cut.)

The top of the rack is covered with a thick layer of fat, interspersed with a bit of meat. If you like, you can pull this layer off very easily. If you choose not to remove it, skip to step 6.

4

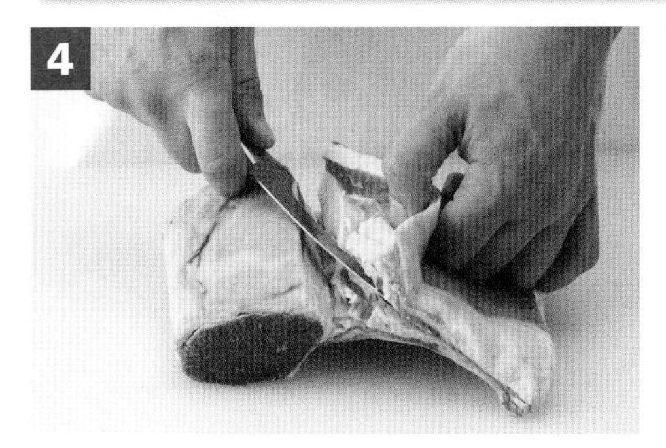

Peel up the corner of the fat cap at the side of the rack farthest from you. Slip the tip of the knife underneath the fat and scrape across the top of the bones to remove the fat.

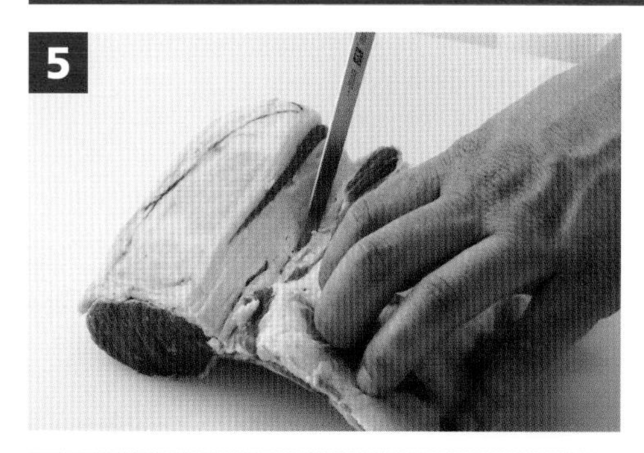

5

If your knife didn't cut through the membrane on top of the bones in step 4, cut through it across the bones now.

Next, we're going to cut through the membrane on the bottom of the rack.

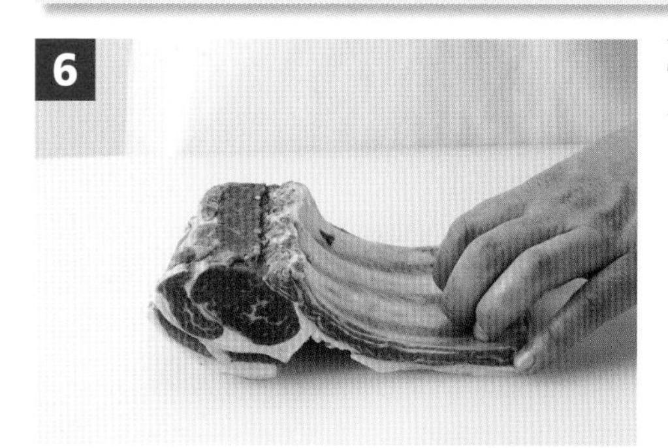

6

Turn the rack fat side down, with the bones still facing your guide hand. Steady the rack with your guide hand.

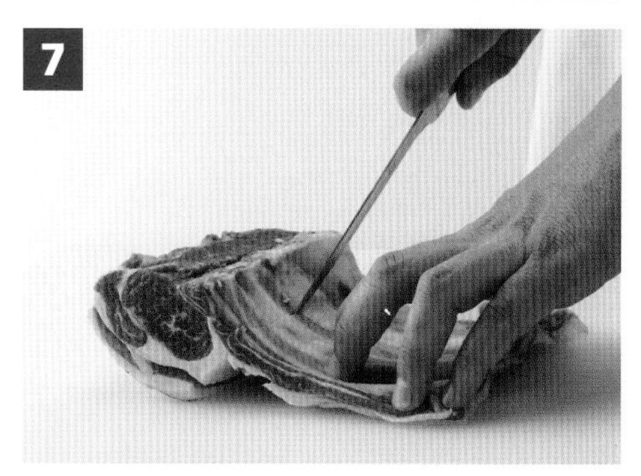

7

Starting at the side of the rack farthest from you, place the blade perpendicular to the bone at the top edge of the eye (or the same distance along the bone you chose on the top of the rack in step 2). Make an incision across the rack, cutting through the membrane to the bone, until you reach the top edge of the eye closest to you.

Now we're going to free the individual bones by slicing through the membranes along the length of each bone, then cutting through the meat at the point where the bones meet the eye. At that point, the meat can easily be pulled off the bones.

8

Rotate the rack 90 degrees so that the bones are facing you. Starting with the bone farthest from you, use the tip of your knife to cut through the membrane along each side of the bone, being careful not to cut through the meat between the bones.

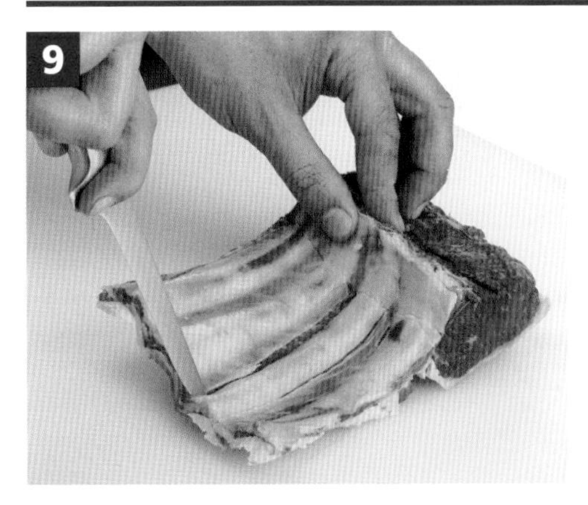

Repeat step 8 for all of the bones, ending with the one closest to you.

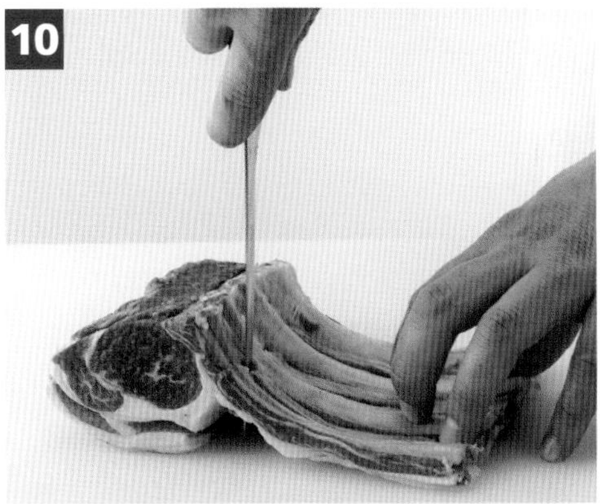

Use the tip of your knife to cut through the meat between the bones at the top edge of the eye.

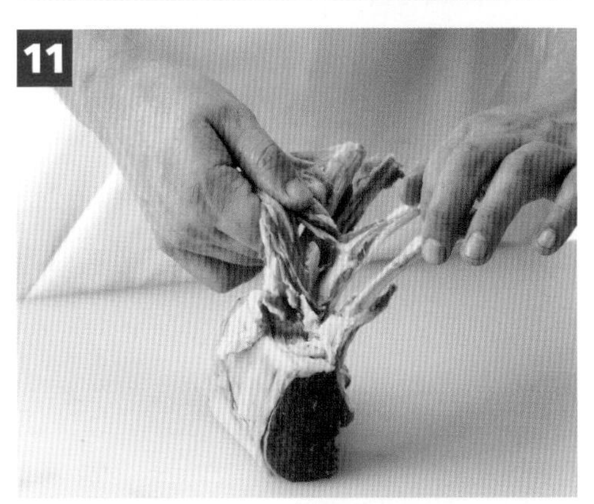

Stand the rack on end, with the bones in the air, and steady it with your guide hand. Pull out the meat from between the bones.

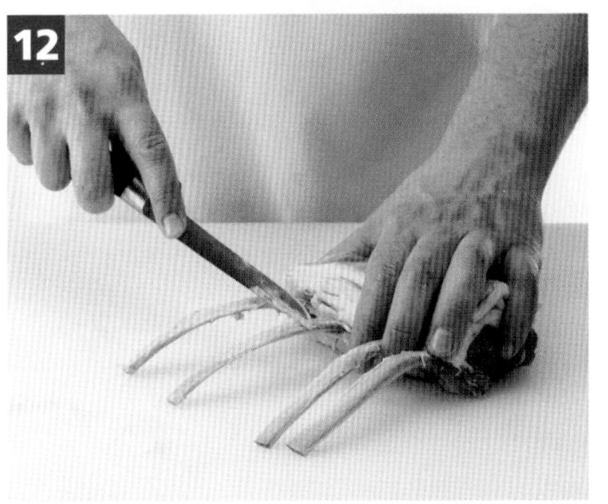

Scrape the bones with the spine of the knife to remove any remaining tissue.

Instead of scraping the remaining tissue off with the spine of the knife, as described in step 12, try this fast, easy and effective alternative: Loop a 6-inch (15 cm) piece of kitchen string around one of the bones, where it meets the eye. Cross the ends of the string a couple of times to keep it relatively tight around the bone. Pull the string down the length of the bone to strip off all the remaining tissue. (While you're doing this, hold the base of the bone with your guide hand to keep it from being pulled from the eye.) Repeat until all the bones are clean.

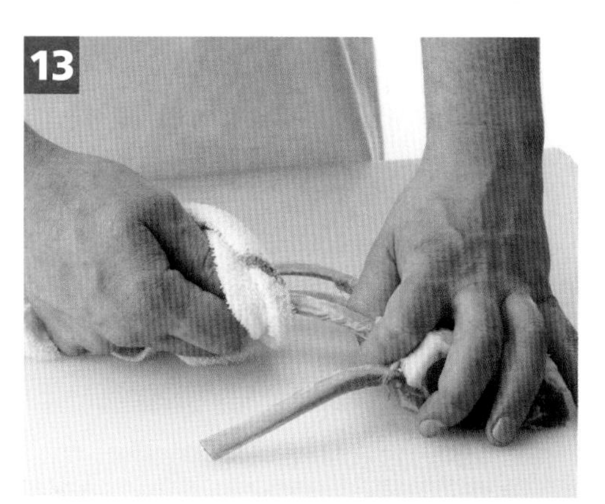

Wipe the bones with a clean, dry towel to remove any last stubborn bits of flesh.

If you french an eight-bone rack, you can turn it into a crown (circular) rack by lacing the two ends together.

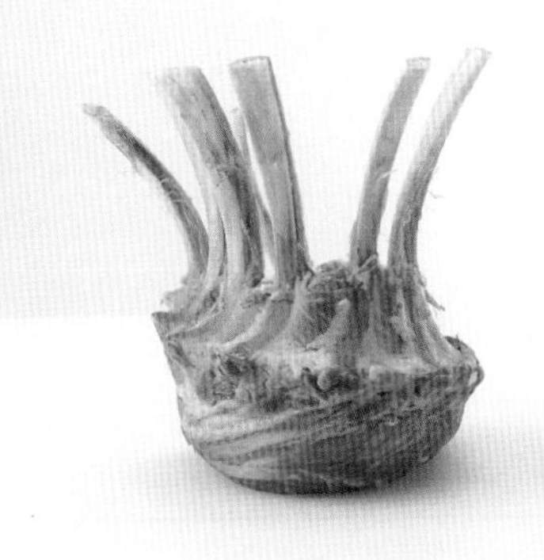

Boning Out a Leg of Lamb

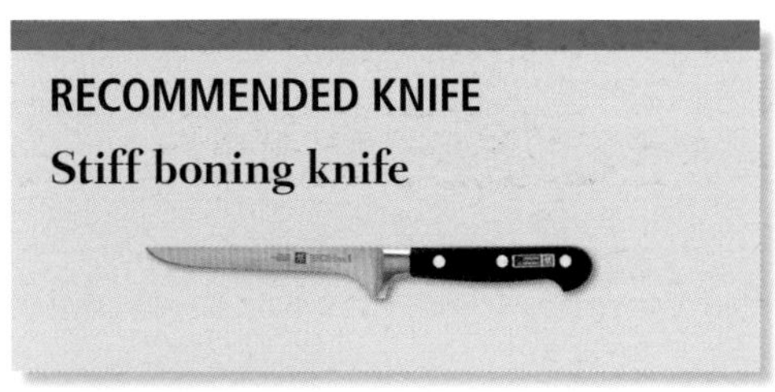

Full lamb legs have four bones: the aitchbone (part of the pelvic bone); the femur (thigh bone); the patella (kneecap); and the shank (shin bone). It is common, however, for butchers to remove the aitchbone when they split the hind leg.

The skeletal structure and musculature of calves and deer are virtually identical to those of lamb, so this technique can also be used on veal or venison.

Removing the Fell and Silverskin

The fell is the parchment-like membrane that covers much of the leg. The individual muscles are held together with connective tissue called silverskin. Because neither the fell nor silverskin are palatable, it's best to remove as much of them as you can.

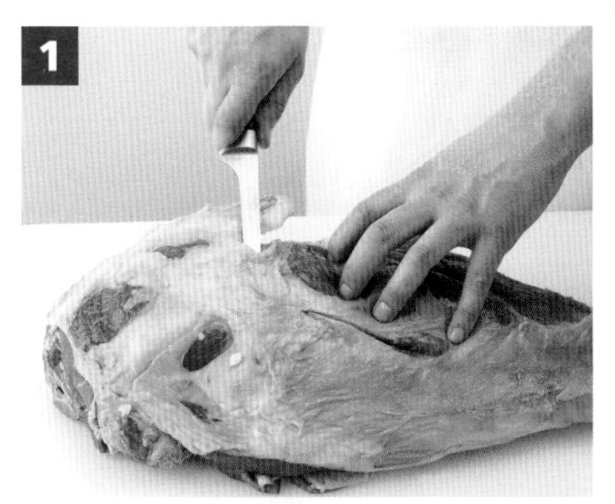

Lay the leg on the cutting board and steady it with your guide hand. Poke the tip of your knife through the fell and slide it just underneath the surface until the blade is about halfway in.

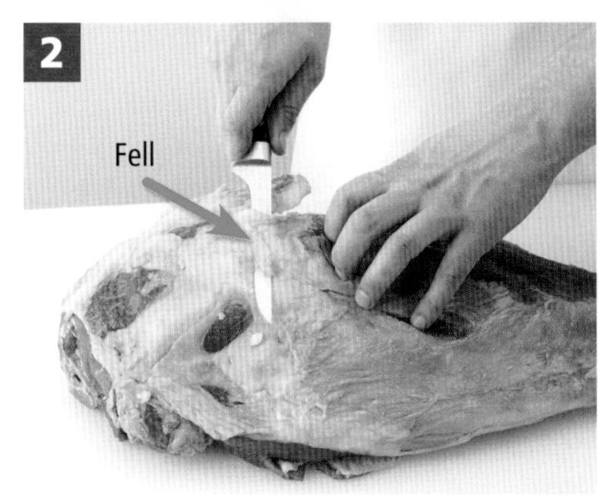

Poke the point of the blade back out through the fell, then slice away a piece of fell.

3

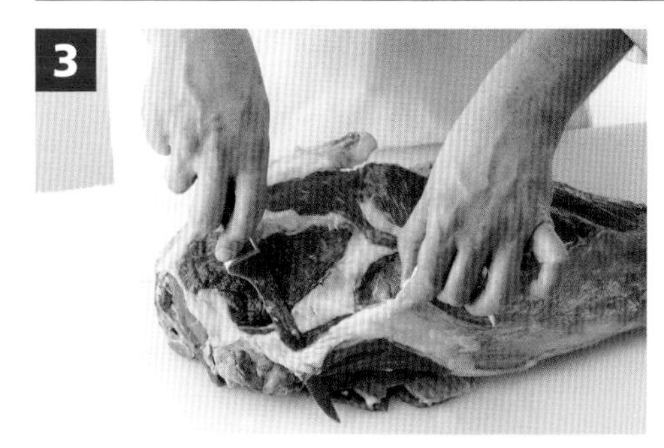

Repeat steps 1 and 2 until the fell is completely removed.

4

Once the fell is removed, the seams of silverskin that separate the individual muscles will be visible. Holding the blade parallel to the board, poke the point just under one seam of silverskin.

5

Tilt the blade up slightly and cut along the underside of the silverskin. As much as possible, try to avoid taking off any meat with the silverskin.

6

Repeat steps 4 and 5 until all the visible silverskin is removed.

7

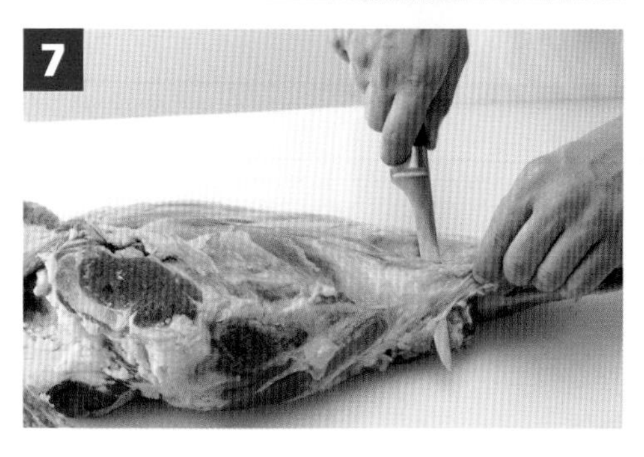

Flip the leg over and repeat steps 1 to 6 to remove the fell and visible silverskin from the other side.

Boning Out the Leg

This technique, also called "butterflying," is designed to separate the shank and remove all other bones, leaving the thigh meat intact. The boned thigh meat is most often stuffed, rolled up and tied, then roasted. The shank meat is tough and is usually removed from the bone and ground. Another option is to leave it on the bone and braise it, either whole or cross-cut into serving-size pieces.

1

Lay the leg on the cutting board with the shank facing you. Holding the knife in the stabbing grip (see page 86), insert the tip of the blade between the meat and the aitchbone on one side of the leg. Cut along the aitchbone all the way to the ball and socket joint between the aitchbone and the femur.

2

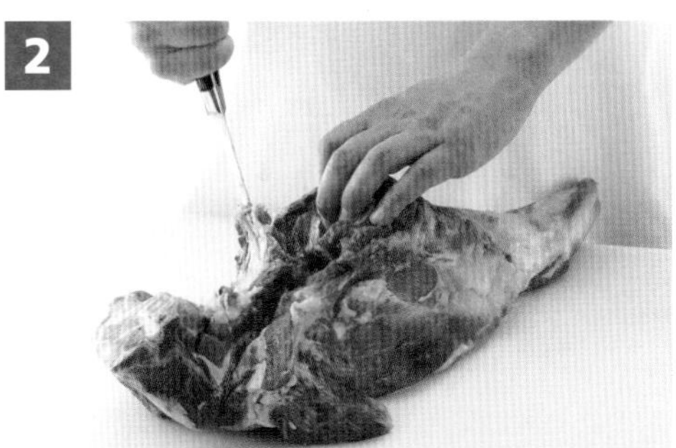

Remove the knife and reinsert it on the other side of the joint. Cut along the aitchbone until you reach the edge of the meat.

3

Insert the tip of your knife into the ball and socket joint to cut the femur away from the aitchbone. Save the aitchbone for lamb stock.

4

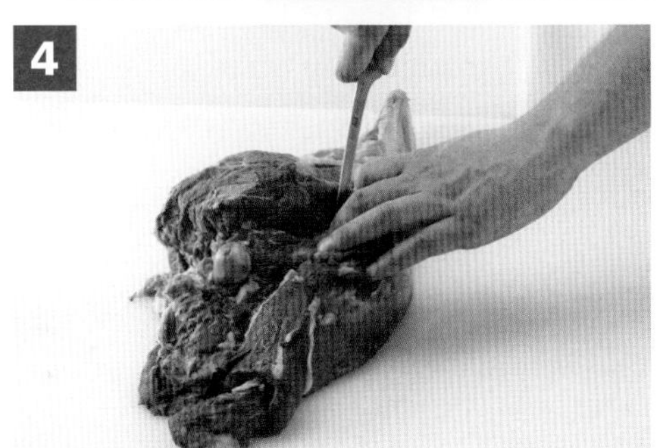

Holding the knife perpendicular to the board, run the blade down the top of the femur from the ball joint to the shank.

Insert the knife into the cut you just made and, starting on the guide-hand side of the leg, cut along the femur from end to end. (For better visibility, you can pull the meat away from the bone with your guide hand as you go.) Be careful not to cut all the way down to the board, just alongside the femur.

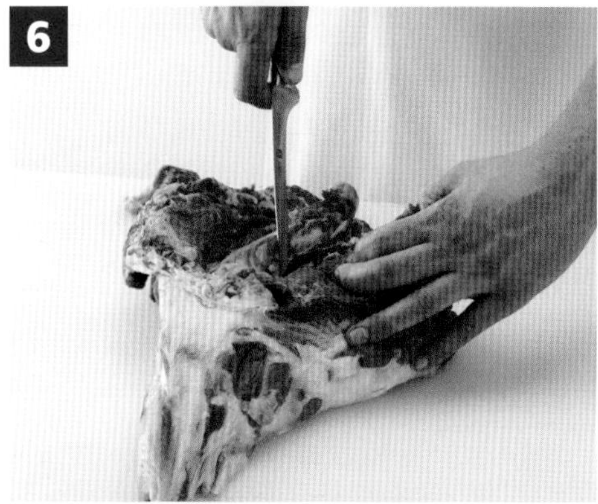

Rotate the leg 180 degrees, so the shank is facing away from you, and repeat step 5 on the other side of the femur.

Grip the femur with your guide hand and cut around the knee joint, below the patella.

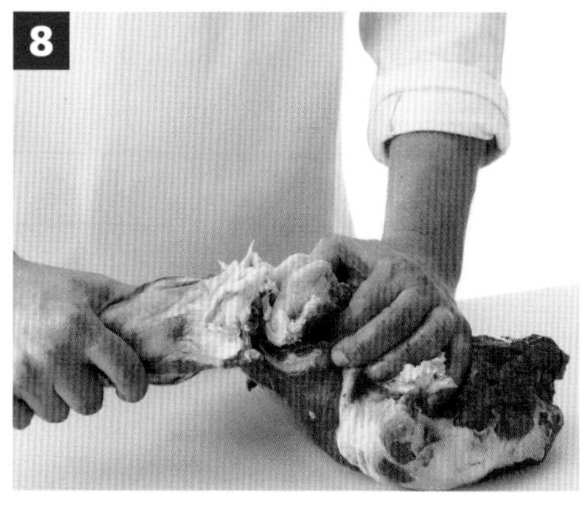

Twist the shank and bend it backward at the knee to break it free of the femur. If necessary, cut through any remaining tissue holding the two bones together.

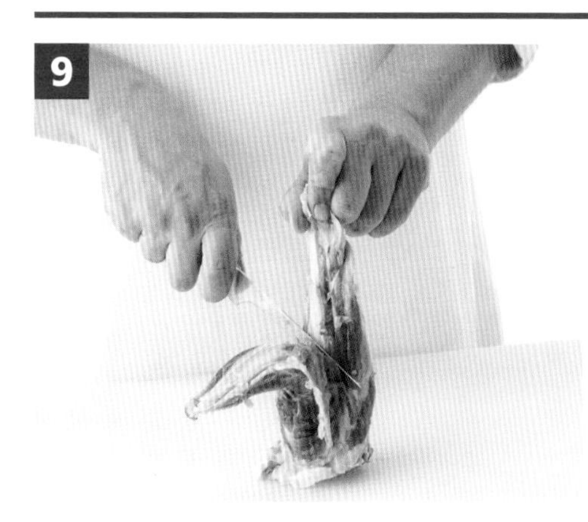

If you plan to grind the shank meat, hold the shank perpendicular to the board and cut straight down along the bone on all sides to remove the meat. Save the shank bone for stock.

If you want to braise the shank, do not remove the meat from the bone in step 9. Instead, leave the shank whole or use a bone saw to cut it crosswise into individual pieces.

Grip the knee end of the femur with your guide hand and pull up on the bone as you cut from the knee to the ball joint along the bottom of the bone. Lift the femur free of the meat and save it for stock.

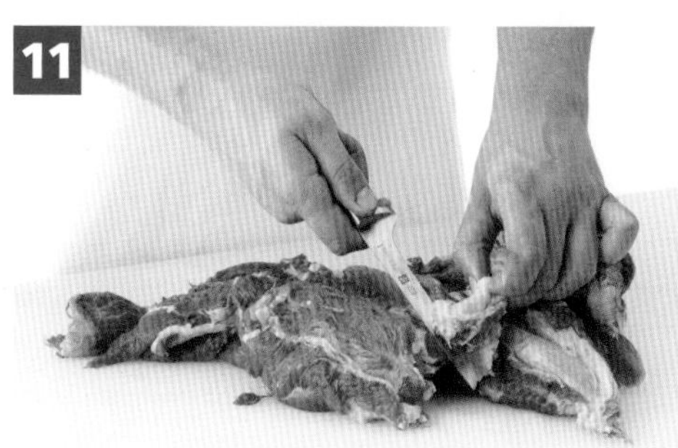

If the patella is still attached to the meat at the knee, trim it away and save it for stock.

Trim off any fat, sinew or connective tissue from inside the meat. The thigh meat is now ready to be stuffed, rolled and tied.

Chapter 7
Cutting Fish

Fish fillets and steaks are readily available to professionals and home cooks alike. Still, you'll never get a precut fillet or steak that's as fresh as the ones you cut yourself from a whole fish, because the closer a fish is to whole, the longer it stays fresh.

Fish Anatomy

Most fish can be divided into two categories: flatfish and roundfish. The vast majority of fish are roundfish, so called because their cross-sections are somewhat round. Salmon, trout and mackerel are all examples of roundfish. They have two fillets, which run the length of their bodies, one on each side of the backbone.

Flatfish, such as flounder, sole and fluke, start life looking like roundfish, but as they mature, their bodies gradually roll onto one side and one of their eyes migrates across the head so that both eyes are looking up. Their bottoms are light-colored and their tops are dark to protect them from predators. Flatfish have a total of four fillets, two on top and two on the bottom.

As with land animals, the more you know about fish anatomy, the easier it is to cut one up. Before you start practicing the techniques in this chapter, have a look at the pictures below to see where the various parts are located on a roundfish and a flatfish.

Roundfish

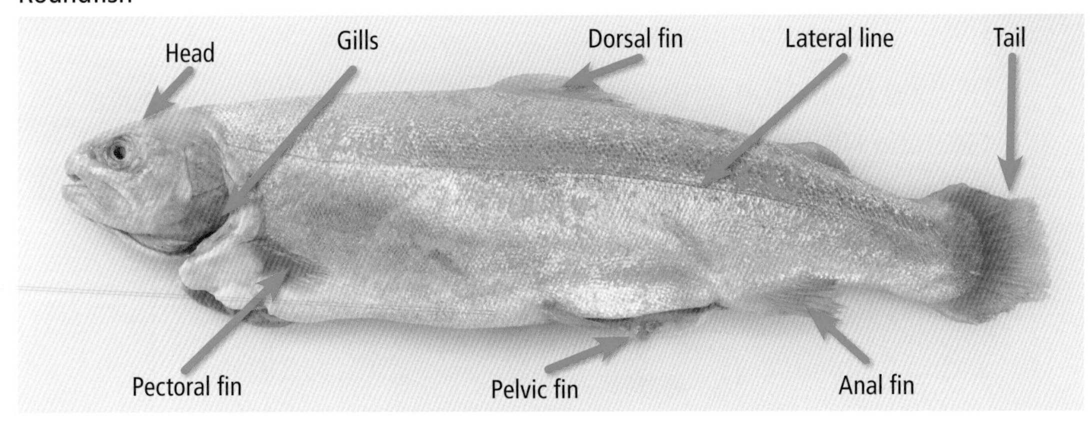

Flatfish

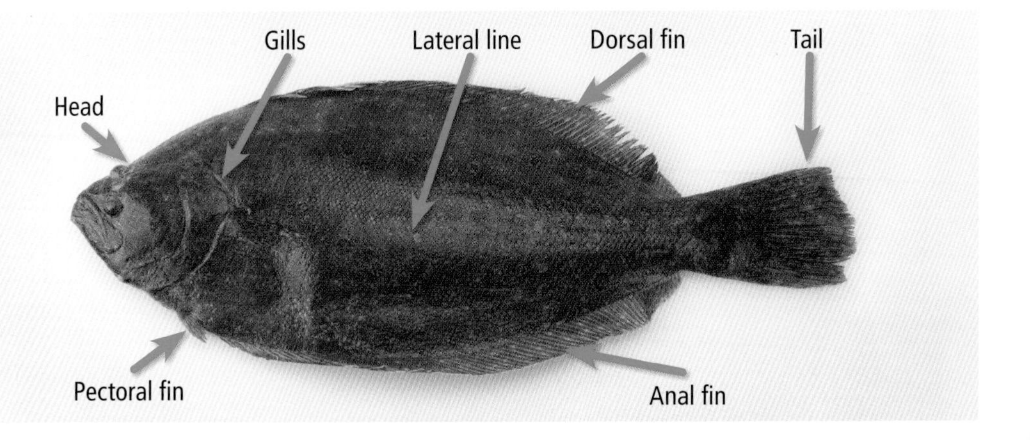

Scaling Fish

It's not uncommon to find fish at the market that need to be scaled. You can ask the market to do it for you, or you can do it yourself. If you're catching your own, of course, you'll have to do it yourself, but if you are catching your own, chances are you don't need to read about how to scale a fish.

RECOMMENDED KNIFE

Chef's knife or fillet knife

Scaling is not difficult, it's just messy. Scales tend to fly around the room and stick to surfaces, where they dry quickly and are hard to clean up. We suggest scaling fish inside a plastic bag, either in the sink or outside your home. (Since we have to illustrate the technique clearly, however, we won't be using a plastic bag in our photographs.)

1. Wrap a clean, dry towel around your guide hand and hold the fish by the tail.

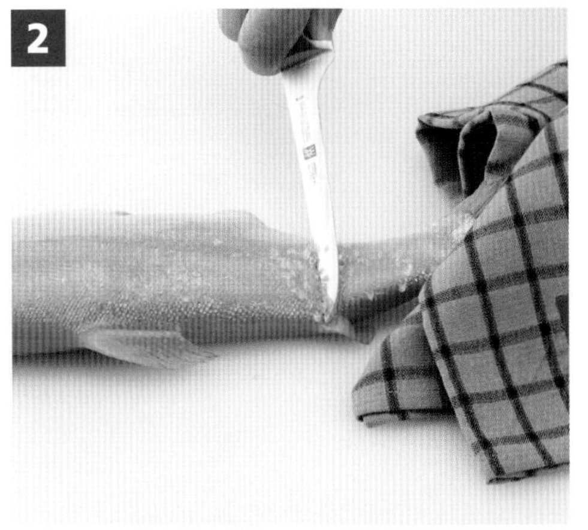

2. Beginning at the tail and working toward the head, scrape the spine of the knife down the side of the fish, detaching the scales.

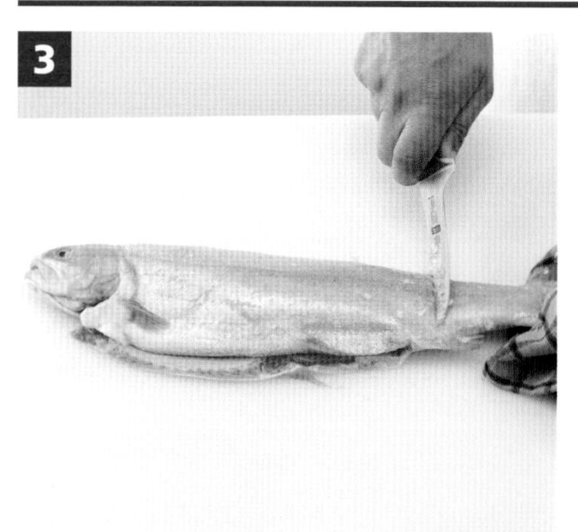

3

When one side is scaled, flip the fish and scale the other side.

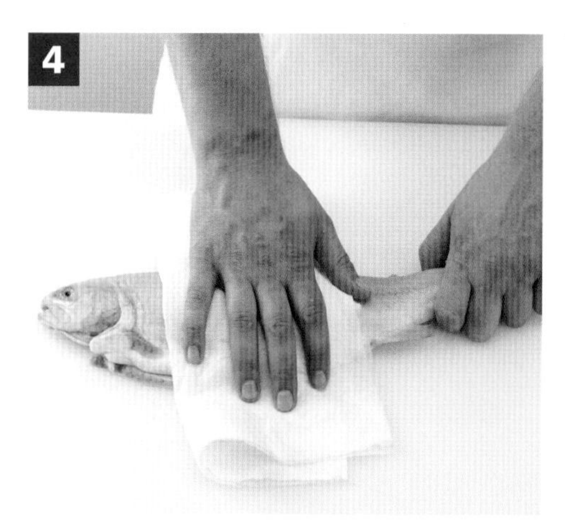

4

Rinse the fish under cold running water, then rub a paper towel over both sides to remove any loose scales adhering to the fish.

For a fish to be identified as kosher, it must have scales that are visible and easily removable by hand or knife without tearing the skin. Examples of fish that are not kosher include swordfish, catfish and shark. Debate rages over whether sturgeon is kosher.

Cleaning Roundfish

Most store-bought whole fish are already cleaned, meaning they've had their guts removed. This is not always the case, of course, especially if you're shopping at specialty markets or you caught the fish yourself. If you've never done this before, we won't blame you for a bit of squeamishness. Still, like anything else, the more you do it, the easier it gets.

RECOMMENDED KNIFE

Fillet knife

1

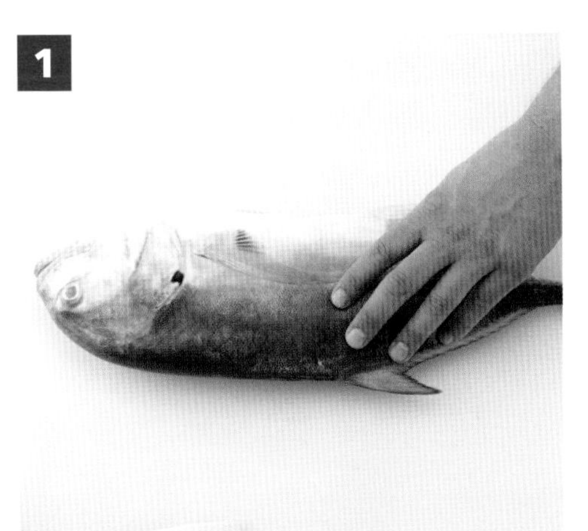

Lay the fish on the cutting board, with the head facing your knife hand and the belly facing you. Steady the fish with your guide hand.

2

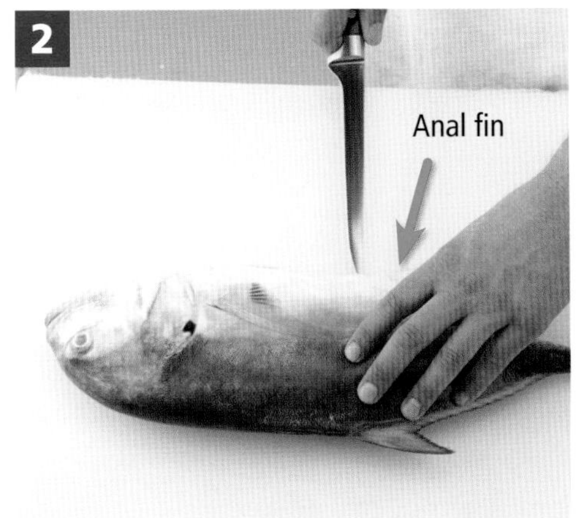

Locate the anal fin. With the edge of the knife blade facing the head, insert the tip of the blade into the belly just on the head side of the anal fin. Insert it about $\frac{1}{4}$ inch (6 mm) — just far enough to pierce the belly cavity but not so far that you puncture any organs.

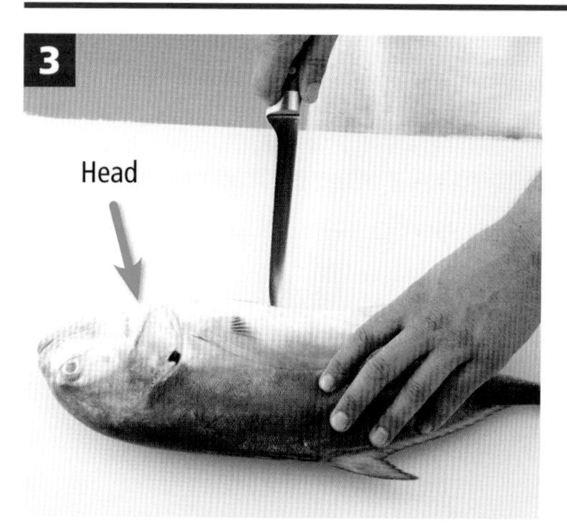

Slit the belly all the way up to the head.

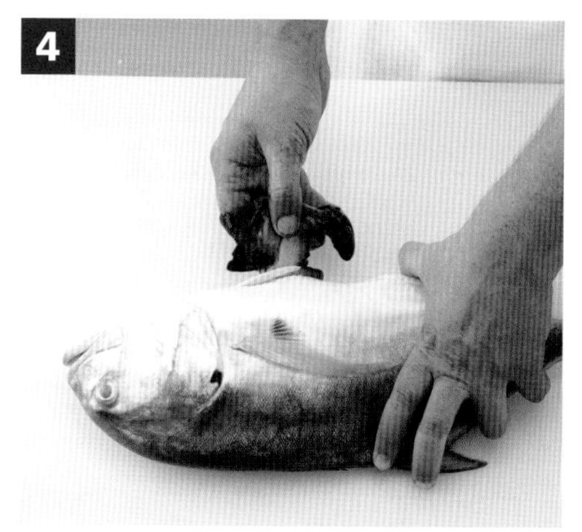

Use your hands to pull out the organs. Rinse the interior of the fish thoroughly under cold running water.

Sushi chefs recommend using salt water with a 3% salt ratio (roughly the composition of seawater) to rinse fish. They believe this helps saltwater fish maintain its fresh sea flavor.

Filleting Large Roundfish

Roundfish come in all shapes and sizes, and include salmon, grouper, snapper, cod, pompano, swordfish and tuna. We'll demonstrate this filleting technique using a large salmon.

RECOMMENDED TOOLS

Chef's knife or cleaver (optional); fillet knife; needle-nose pliers or tweezers

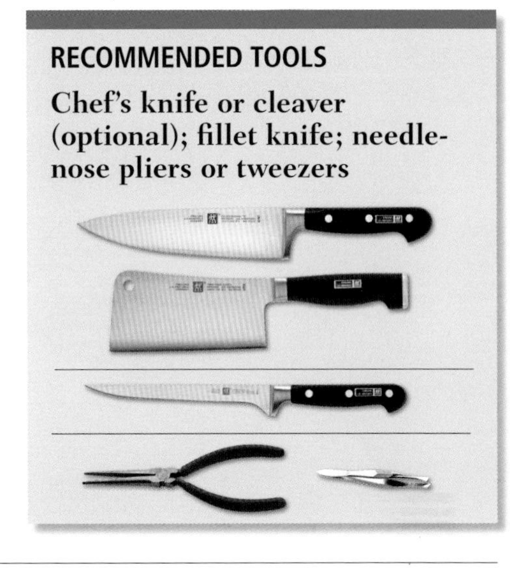

1

Lay the cleaned fish on the cutting board, with the head facing your knife hand and the back facing you. Steady the fish with your guide hand.

2

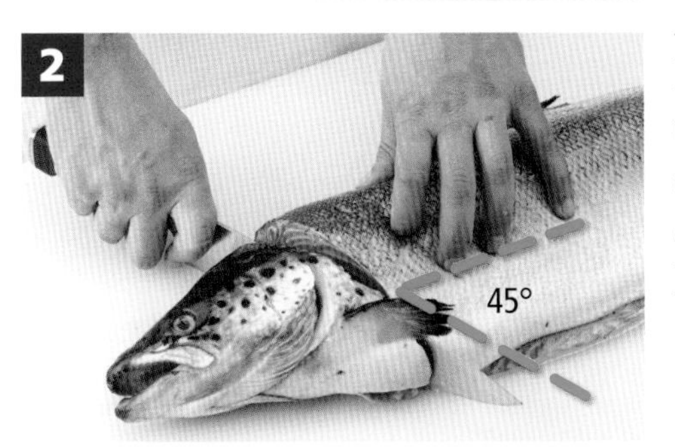

If you prefer to remove the head, place the chef's knife just behind the head, angling the tip 45 degrees toward the tail end. Cut straight down to remove the head, then skip to step 5.

3

If you choose to leave the head on, place the fillet knife just behind the head with the edge of the blade at an angle toward the head.

4

Cut toward the head at an angle until your blade hits the backbone. Do not cut through the backbone. Pull the knife out of the fish.

5

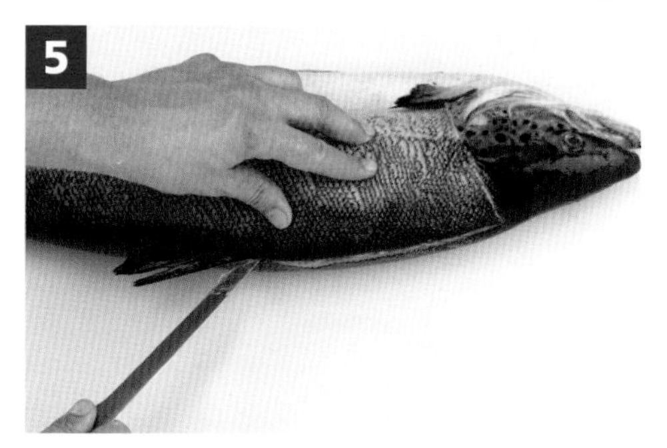

Holding the fillet knife parallel to the board, make a slit along the backbone down the entire length of the back.

6

When you near the tail, insert the tip of the knife under the fillet so that it emerges from the belly of the fish with the edge facing toward the tail.

7

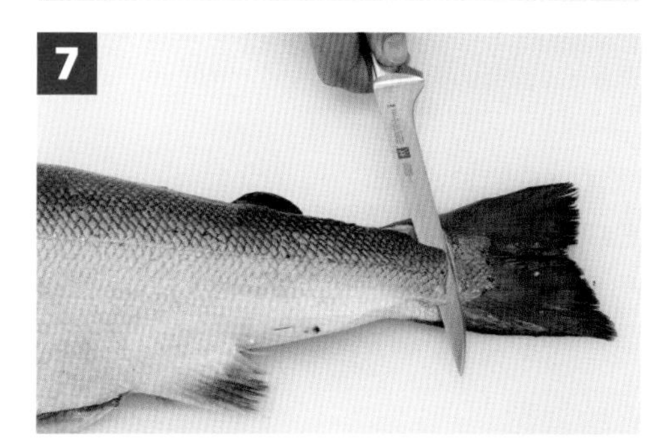

With the blade flush against the top side of the backbone, cut straight back to free the tail end of the fillet.

8

Return to the head end of the backbone and, working from the backbone down to the belly of the fish, use the tip of the blade to scrape the fillet away from the bones, pulling the fillet up with your guide hand as you go.

9

Gradually working your way back to the middle of the fish until the whole fillet is free of the bones. (You should be able to feel and hear your knife scrape across the bones.)

10

Flip the fish over so that the tail is facing your knife hand and repeat steps 3 to 9 (if you left the head on) or steps 5 to 9 (if you removed the head) to remove the fillet on the other side.

11

Run your guide-hand fingers across the fillets from tail to head to locate the pin bones. Use the pliers or tweezers to remove them.

If you're saving the bones and the head to make fish stock — a terrific idea — make sure to remove the gills and fins with kitchen shears, if your fishmonger hasn't done so already; they'll add a bitter taste to the stock.

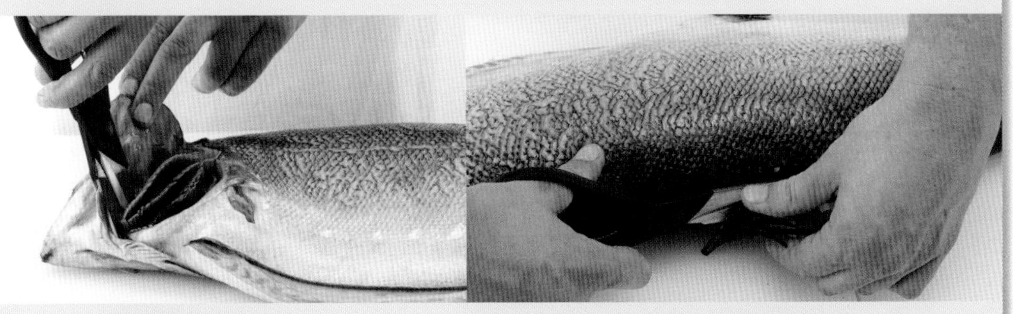

Removing the gills

Removing the fins

Filleting Small Roundfish

Whereas with the large roundfish, we cut the fillets right off the skeleton (page 297), with smaller roundfish, it's easier to remove the fillets from the backbone first and then remove the rib and pin bones (small, flexible intramuscular bones that aren't attached to the skeleton).

Removing the Fillets

This technique starts out just like the one for filleting large roundfish, but after step 4 it should go a bit more quickly, since you're not trying to scrape the fillets carefully off the bones this time.

RECOMMENDED KNIFE

Fillet knife

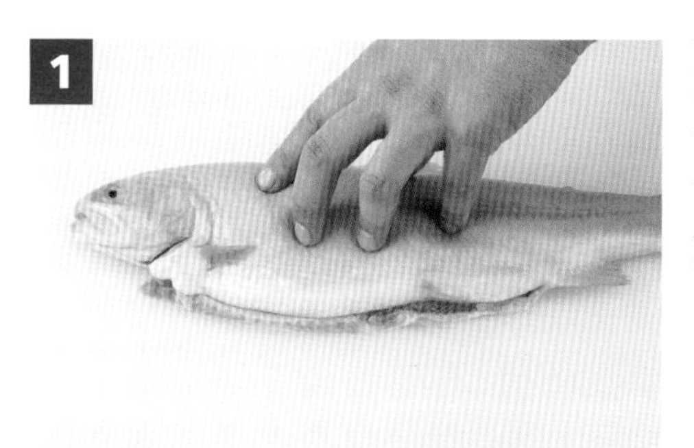

1. Lay the cleaned fish on the cutting board, with the head facing your knife hand and the back facing you. Steady the fish with your guide hand.

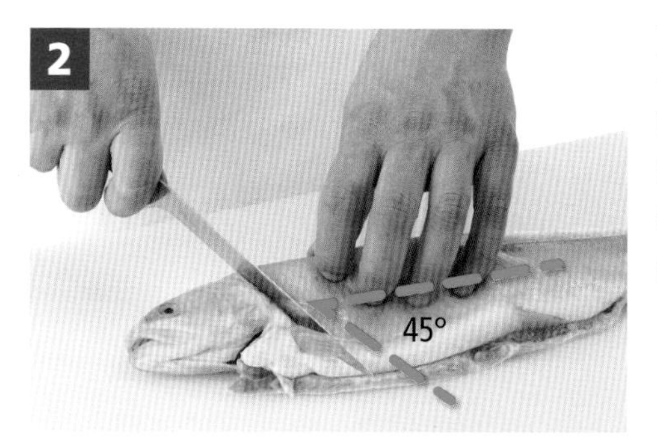

2. If you prefer to remove the head, place the knife just behind the head, angling the tip 45 degrees toward the tail end. Cut straight down to remove the head, then skip to step 5.

Depending on the size of your fish, you may want to use a chef's knife or a cleaver to remove the head in step 2.

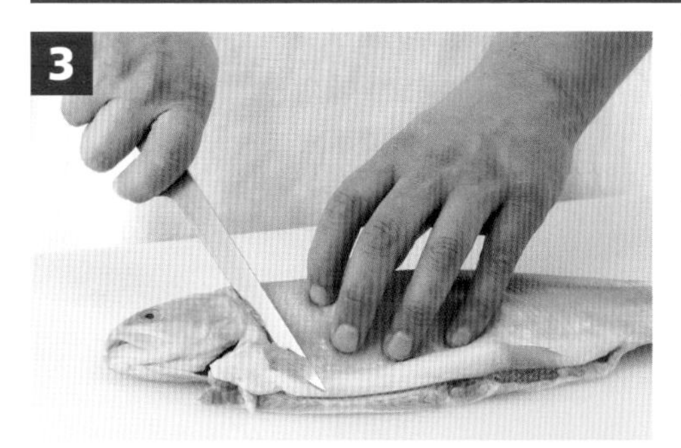

If you choose to leave the head on, place the fillet knife just behind the head with the edge of the blade at an angle toward the head.

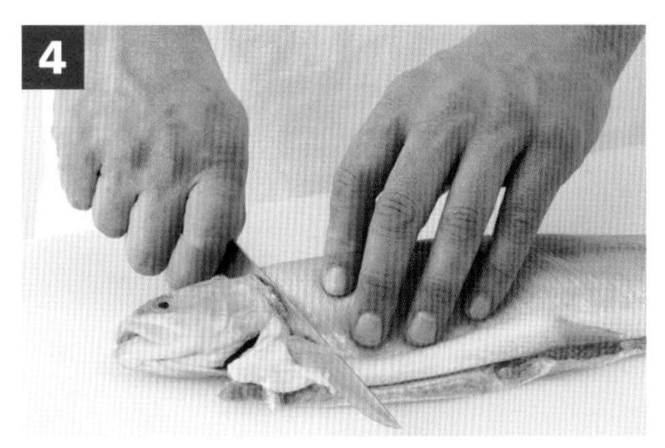

Cut toward the head at an angle until your blade hits the backbone. Do not cut through the backbone. Pull the knife out of the fish.

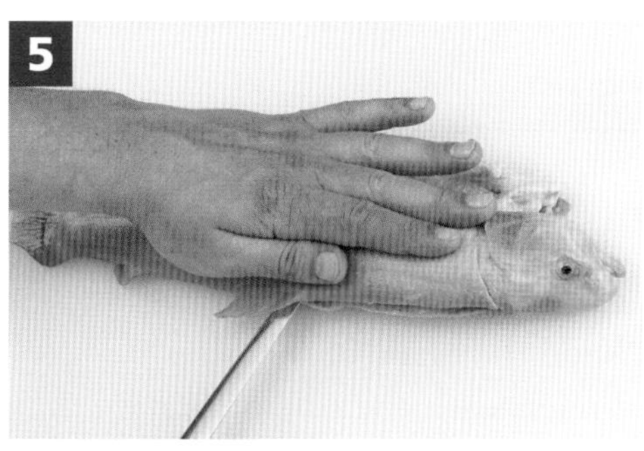

Holding the fillet knife parallel to the board, insert the tip just above the backbone. Cut toward the tail, keeping the blade flush against the top side of the backbone. If it helps, pull the fillet up with your guide hand as you go.

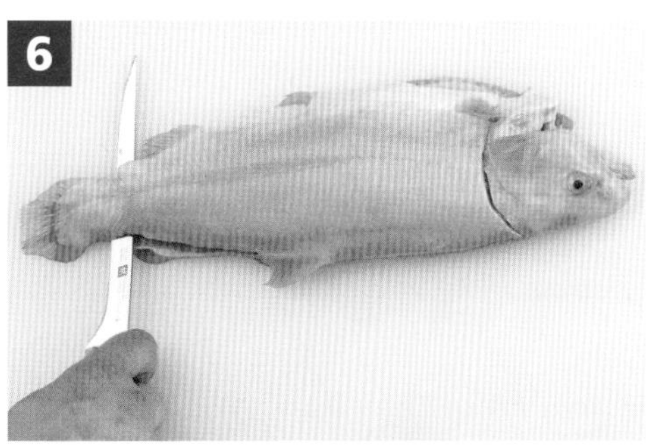

As you near the tail, push the tip of the knife all the way through the fish so that it emerges from the belly. Continue cutting back to the tail, separating the fillet completely where it joins the tail.

Flip the fish over so that the tail is facing your knife hand and repeat steps 3 to 6 (if you left the head on) or steps 5 and 6 (if you removed the head) to remove the fillet on the other side.

Removing the Rib and Pin Bones

Because we removed the fillets by cutting straight across the backbone instead of scraping the fillet free of the skeleton, the rib bones are still attached to the fillets. They won't make for pleasant eating, so here's how to remove them, as well as the pin bones.

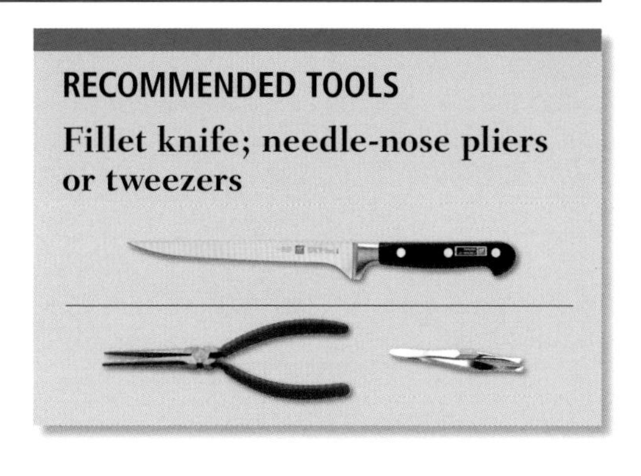

RECOMMENDED TOOLS

Fillet knife; needle-nose pliers or tweezers

1. Lay a fillet on the cutting board, skin side down, with the belly side facing your guide hand. Note how the rib bones lie across the top of the meat, connected by a thin, translucent sheet of tissue.

2. Starting at the end of the fillet farthest from you, slide the blade of the fillet knife just underneath the rib bones.

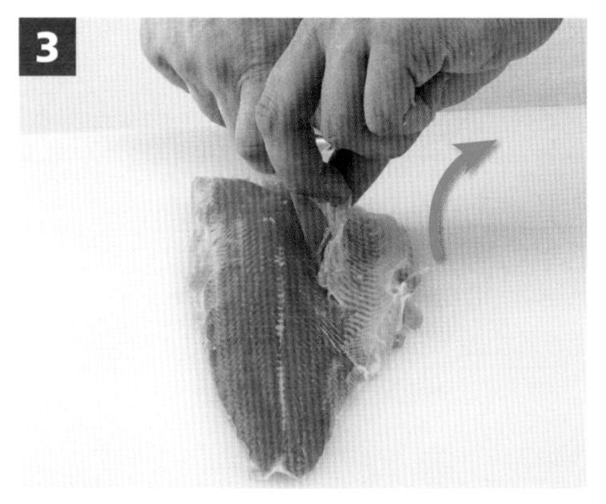

3. Twist your arm from the elbow to rotate the bones up. Grab the bones with your guide hand.

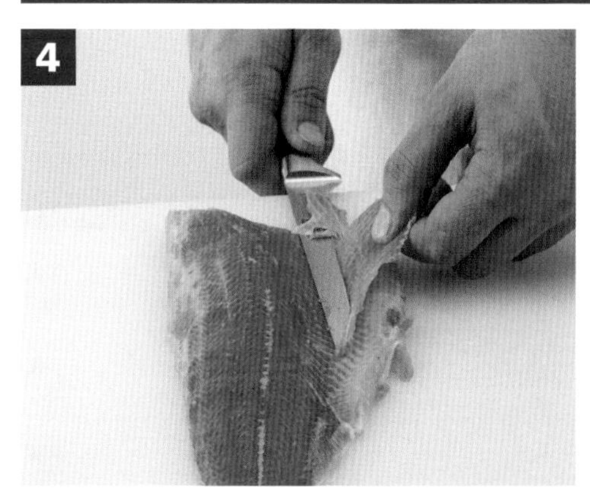

Keeping the knife nearly horizontal, make broad slicing strokes just underneath the rib bones, pulling them up with your guide hand as you go.

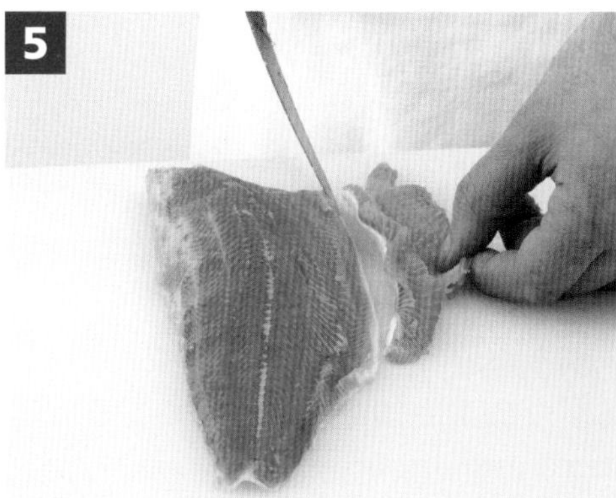

When you reach the bottom of the fillet, cut the bones completely away and discard.

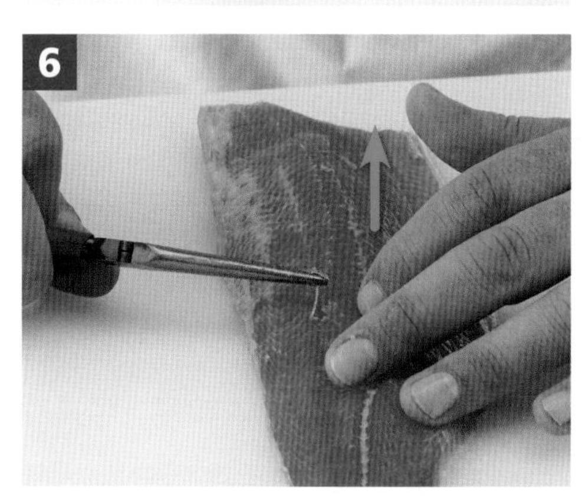

Run your guide-hand fingers across the fillet from tail to head to locate the pin bones. Use the pliers or tweezers to remove them.

Filleting Roundfish with a Deba

Japanese chefs use a Deba instead of a fillet knife when filleting fish. Whereas fillet knives are narrow and flexible, a Deba is wide and stiff, with a thick spine. A smaller version of the Deba, called a Kodeba (*ko* means "small" in Japanese), is used for smaller fish.

You can use the Deba just as you would a fillet knife to fillet small roundfish (page 300) or large roundfish (page 297). The Japanese call this method *daimyo oroshi* ("straight filleting") and consider it the quickest, but most wasteful, way to cut fish.

Here, we'll show you the *sanmai oroshi* ("three-piece filleting") method for filleting roundfish, which yields the least amount of waste, as you use the geometry of the single-beveled blade to get as close to the bones as possible. Start with a cleaned fish, with the head either on or off.

RECOMMENDED KNIFE

Deba (for a large fish) or Kodeba (for a small fish)

1

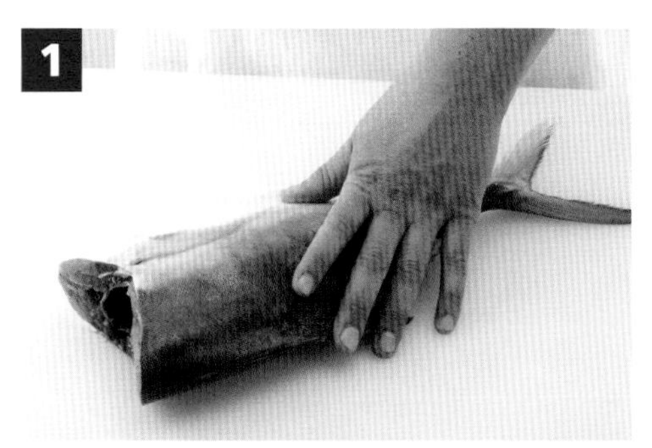

Lay the fish diagonally on the cutting board, with the tail closer to you and the belly facing you.

2

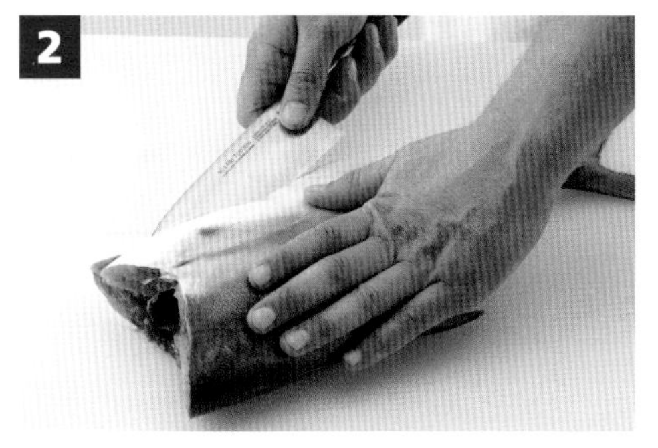

Steady the fish with the palm of your guide hand. Holding the knife blade parallel to the cutting board, place it on the belly at the head end of the fish, lining it up just above the pelvic and anal fins.

3

Using the entire length of the blade, cut along the belly to the tail. Use a fluid motion, without starts and stops, and keep the blade as close to the rib bones as possible, feeling the bones beneath your knife, as you cut up to the spine. This may require a few passes for a larger fish.

Use your guide hand to lift the fillet as you cut, so that you can better see the position of the knife.

4

Turn the fish so that the dorsal fin is facing you and the tail is pointing diagonally away from you.

5

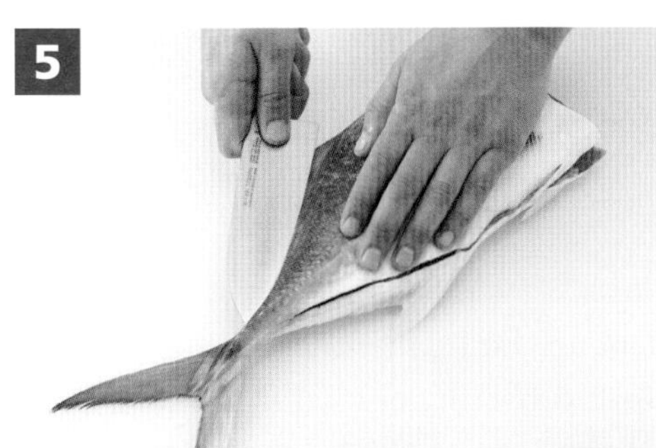

Steady the fish with the palm of your guide hand. Holding the knife blade parallel to the cutting board, place the edge just above the dorsal fin at the tail of the fish.

6

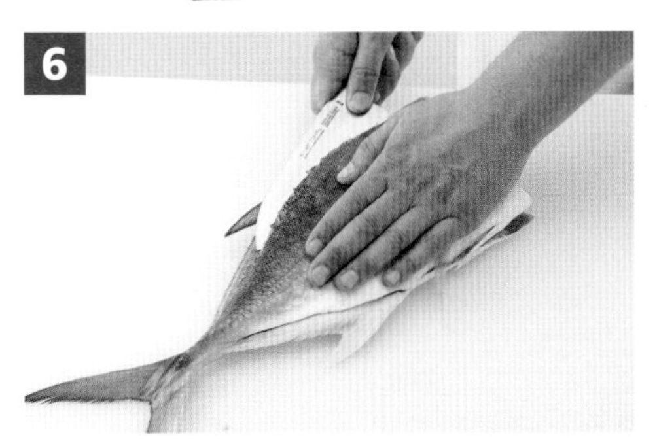

Using the entire length of the blade, cut along the back to the head end. Use a fluid motion, without starts and stops, and keep the blade as close to the rib bones as possible, feeling the bones beneath your knife, as you cut through to the spine. This may require a few passes.

At this point, both sides of the fillet are freed from the ribs, but the center of the fillet is still attached to the spine.

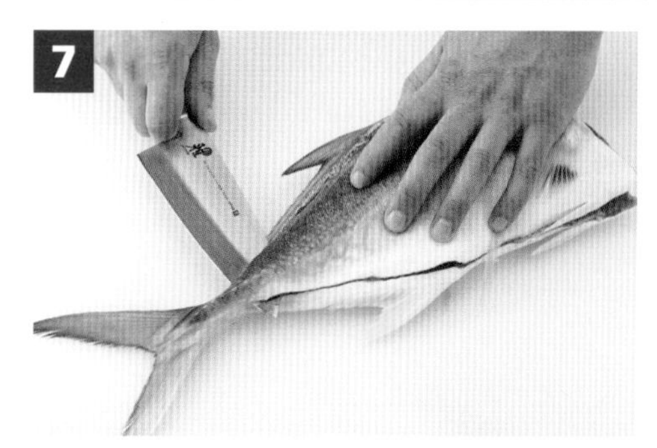

With the edge of the knife facing away from you, make an incision just above the tail, but do not cut through the tail.

Remove the knife and rotate your wrist so that the edge of the knife is facing you. Reinsert the knife in the incision at the tail until you feel the top of the spine underneath the blade.

Holding the knife parallel to the board, cut across the top of the spine.

As you get near the head end, cutting will become more difficult. Use your guide hand to lift the side of the fillet and use the tip of the knife to cut through the tough part.

11

Make a downward incision to detach the fillet from the tail.

12

Flip the fish over and position it diagonally, with the tail closer to you and the dorsal fin facing you. Repeat steps 2 and 3, but cutting along the back instead of the belly.

13

Turn the fish so that the belly is facing you and the tail is pointing diagonally away from you. Repeat steps 5 and 6, but cutting along the belly instead of the back.

14

Repeat steps 7 to 11 to detach the second fillet. You now have two fillets and a skeleton: the three pieces in the name of the method. Save the skeleton to make stock.

When stacking fillets to store them, prevent sticking by stacking flesh to flesh or skin to skin, not skin to flesh.

Cleaning Flatfish

Unlike roundfish, which are usually sold with their guts removed, flatfish often have to be cleaned. Don't let that dissuade you from purchasing and cooking flatfish, though. Once you've practiced this technique a couple of times, you'll be totally comfortable with it.

RECOMMENDED CUTTING TOOLS

Kitchen shears; chef's knife or Santoku

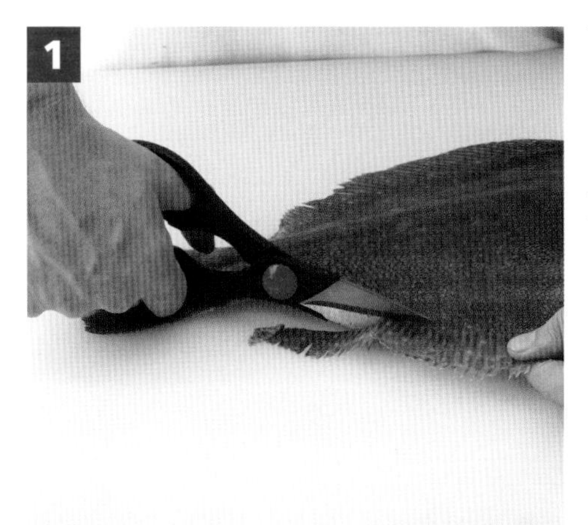

1 Lay the fish on the cutting board, with the head facing your guide hand. Grip the dorsal fin with your guide hand and pull it out to extend it. (Be careful — the sharp ends of the fin can puncture your skin.) Use the shears to cut off the fin.

2 Repeat step 1 with the anal and pectoral fins.

3

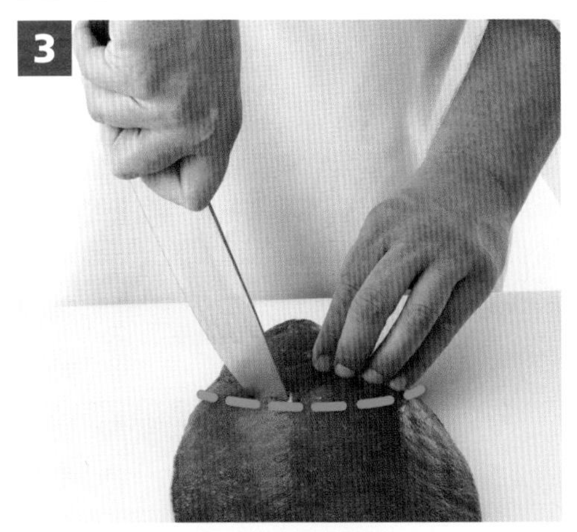

Turn the fish so that the head is facing you. Steady the head with your guide hand. Using the chef's knife, remove the head by cutting a curved line around it just behind the gills, keeping as close to the head as possible.

4

Hold the fish upside down above a garbage bowl and squeeze out the guts. Rinse the interior of the fish thoroughly under cold running water.

If you're saving the bones and the head to make fish stock — a terrific idea — make sure to remove the gills and fins with kitchen shears, if your fishmonger hasn't done so already; they'll add a bitter taste to the stock.

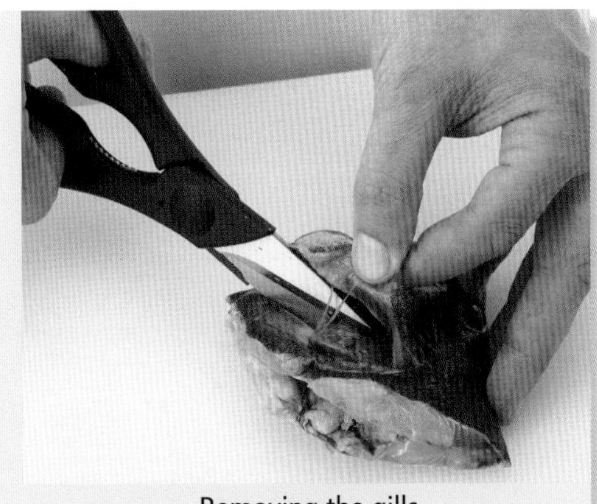

Removing the gills

Filleting Flatfish

Freshly cut fillets are always better than store-bought, because the closer a fish is to whole when you get it, the longer it will stay fresh. Once you cut into a fish, it begins to degrade quickly.

Instead of a fillet knife or chef's knife, you can use a Deba to fillet flatfish if you prefer. The Japanese call this method *gomai oroshi* ("five-piece filleting").

RECOMMENDED KNIFE

Fillet knife or chef's knife

1

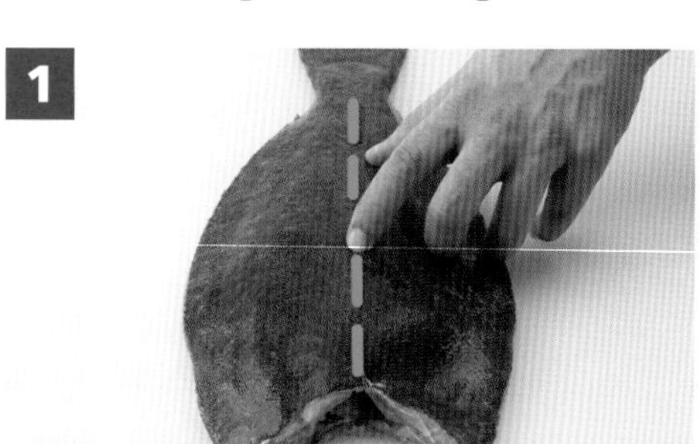

Lay the cleaned fish on the cutting board, dark side (top of the fish) up, with the tail facing you. Note the faint line running down the middle of the fish from head to tail. This is called the lateral line, and it runs directly above the backbone.

2

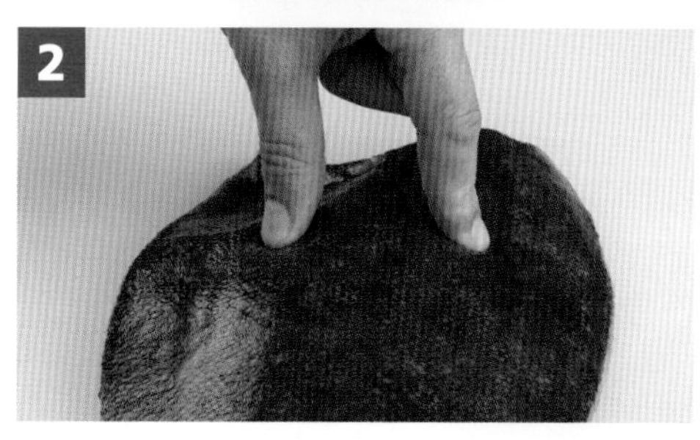

Place your guide-hand thumb at the top of the backbone and on one side of it, and place your index finger on the other side, forming an upside-down V with your hand. Push the skin away from the backbone so that it's taut.

3

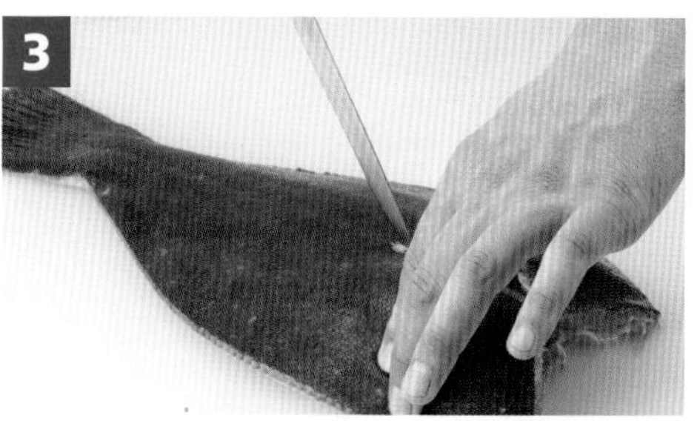

Place the knife blade beneath the V of your guide hand, directly on top of the backbone, and draw it toward you, cutting through the skin.

4

Move your guide hand toward the tail of the fish, tautening the skin farther down, and continue cutting. Repeat until you have cut down to the tail.

5

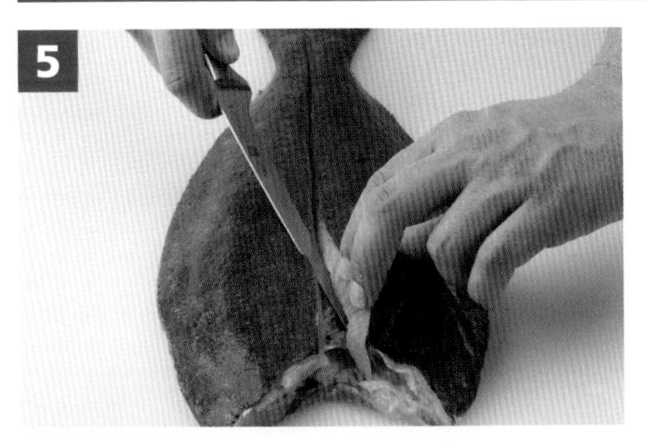

Returning to the top of the fish, insert the tip of the knife underneath the fillet on the same side as your guide hand and use your guide hand to pull the fillet gently away from the bone.

6

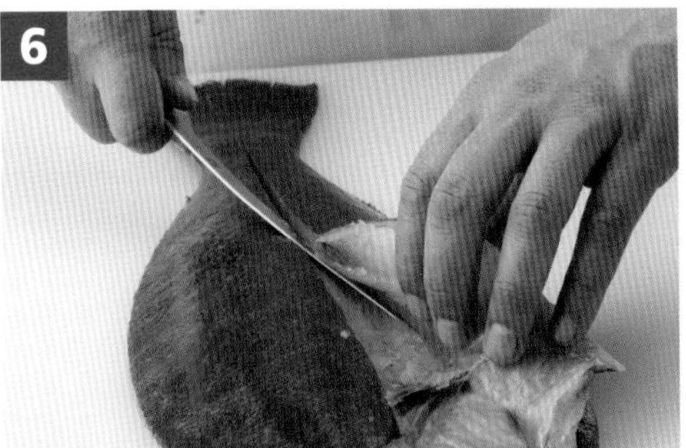

As you pull back on the fillet, use the tip of the knife to slice the flesh away from the bones below the fillet. Keep the blade angled so that you're cutting along — not through — the bones.

7

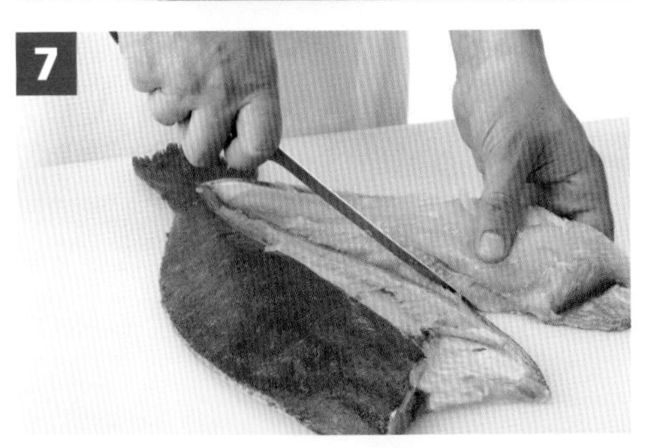

When you reach the bottom of the fillet, cut through the skin to remove the fillet.

8

Turn the fish so that the tail is facing away from you and repeat steps 5 to 7, this time working from the tail down.

9

Flip the fish over and repeat steps 2 to 8 to remove the fillets from the other side.

Removing the Skin from a Fillet

RECOMMENDED KNIFE

Chef's knife or fillet knife

Fish skin is edible — though not always palatable — and it sometimes pays in terms of flavor and presentation to leave it attached. Sometimes, though, we prefer skinless fillets. The technique for removing the skin is the same for both flatfish and roundfish fillets.

The skin should come off in one clean piece (if it doesn't, see the troubleshooting tips on page 314). Don't worry about patches of dark connective tissue that remain. When fillets are served skinless, the presentation side is the bone side, so the connective tissue won't be seen.

1

Lay the fillet on the cutting board, skin side down, with the thinner tail end facing your guide hand. Wrap a clean, dry towel around your guide hand (to keep the fillet from slipping out of your fingers), then grip the fillet at the tail end.

2

Knife angled away from guide hand

Place the knife blade as close as you can to the tail end and cut down through the flesh at a slight angle away from your guide hand, stopping when you get to the skin.

3

Rotate the knife until the blade is nearly parallel to the board, against the skin, with the edge pointed away from your guide hand. (You want the blade to be angled down slightly as you move forward, to keep it along the skin and prevent it from cutting through the flesh.)

4

Hold the skin taut with your guide hand and cut toward the head end of the fillet, using a sawing motion.

5

If the fillet is large (as with salmon), periodically move your guide hand up the skin so that it stays close to the knife.

6

Continue sawing until your knife comes out the head end of the fillet and the skin is freed completely.

Troubleshooting

There are still patches of skin here and there on the fillet.

Simply work the point of the knife underneath the skin and slice it away.

The skin breaks before you reach the end of the fillet, or you cut through the skin by mistake.

It's often easiest to turn the fillet around and start again from the head end. Because the head end is much wider than the tail end, though, we recommend starting at a corner and cutting toward the center of the fillet at a 45-degree angle.

Once your blade clears the other guide-hand corner, gradually straighten the angle of your knife until you are cutting straight toward the other end of the fillet.

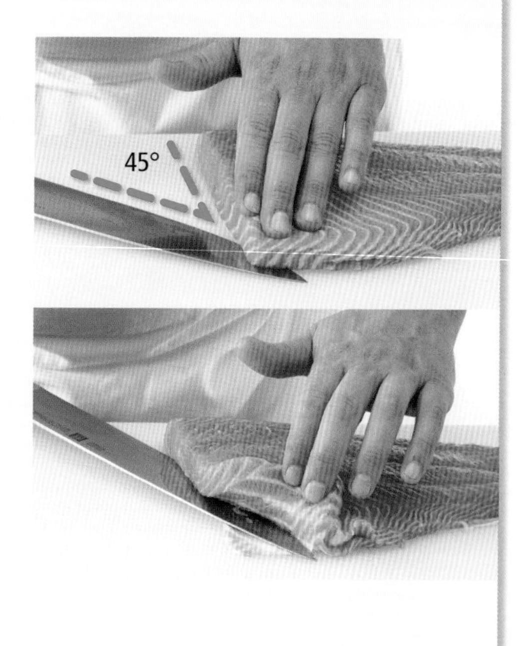

You purchased single-portion fillets with the skin on, and you want to remove it.

Starting at a corner of the fillet, work the knife between the flesh and the skin. Cut toward the center at an angle, then straighten the knife as directed in the troubleshooting tip just above.

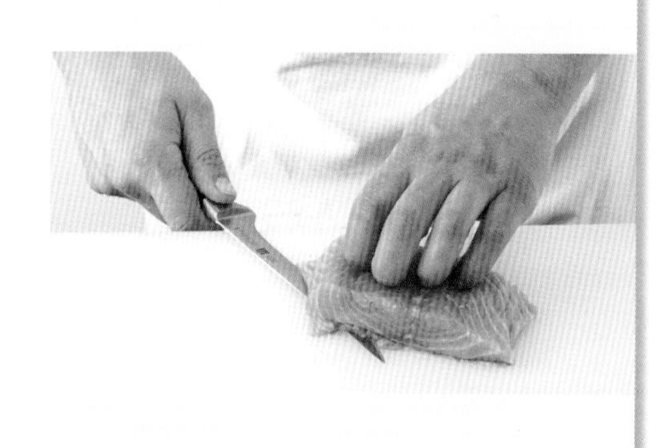

Cutting Steaks

RECOMMENDED KNIFE

Chef's knife or Santoku

Steaks are cross-sections of fish. They are most often cut from roundfish, but it's not uncommon to see steaks cut from halibut, one of the more popular flatfish.

You'll find that you cut steaks much less frequently than you cut fillets. For one thing, because steaks are cross-sections, it is only worthwhile to cut them from large fish, such as salmon or halibut. Also, people generally prefer fillets to steaks, because steaks have bones.

Cutting steaks is much easier than cutting fillets. We'll use a salmon to demonstrate the technique. Start with a cleaned fish, with the head on.

One-inch (2.5 cm) slices are standard, but you can cut the steaks to whatever thickness you like; the important thing is to make them all the same thickness.

Lay the fish on the cutting board, with the head facing your knife hand. Place the knife blade just behind the head, perfectly perpendicular to the fish. Steady the fish with your guide hand and cut straight through to remove the head.

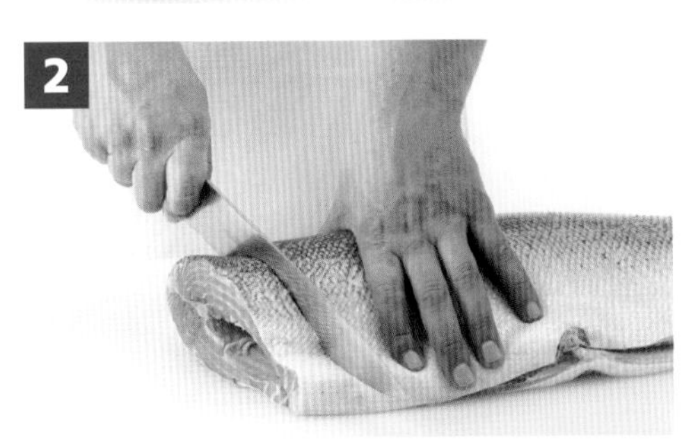

Grip the fish around its girth with your guide hand. Move the blade back 1 inch (2.5 cm) and cut straight down through the bones to remove the first steak.

Continue cutting toward the tail, moving the blade back 1 inch (2.5 cm) after every cut, until the entire fish is cut into steaks.

Slicing Sashimi

To maintain its structural integrity, sashimi (which is sliced raw fish, meant to be consumed that way) must be sliced with an extremely sharp knife, which is why the Japanese developed the Yanagiba.

RECOMMENDED KNIFE

Yanagiba or slicing knife

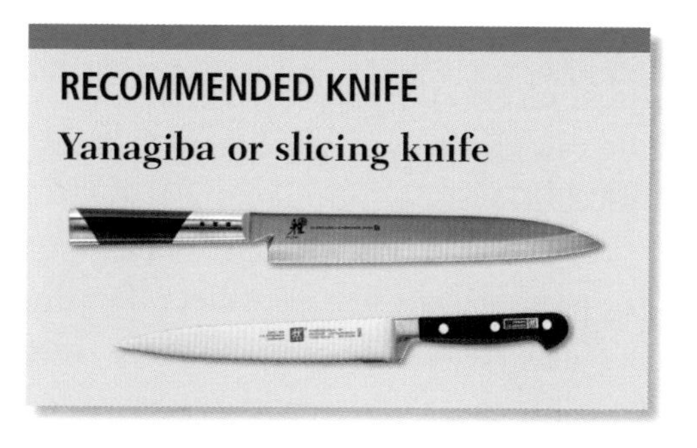

We will be demonstrating *hirazukuri*, the technique for cutting thick slices of fish, as that is the most common cut for fish like tuna and salmon. Other sashimi cuts include *usuzukuri*, for paper-thin slices, and *sogizukuri*, for thin slices.

We'll use a salmon fillet that has been skinned and sliced in half, first lengthwise, then crosswise, to create a narrow piece. Even though the fillet is skinless, we will still refer to the "skin side," meaning the side the skin used to be on. Similarly, although the fillet no longer has a head and a tail, we will still refer to the "head end" and the "tail end." (But if you purchased the fillets instead of cutting them yourself, don't worry about which end is which.)

Because you are cutting something soft and boneless in this technique, you can rest your index finger on top of the blade to control the pressure of the cut. For most other techniques, we recommend that you use the standard grip.

1

Lay the fillet close to the front edge of the cutting board, skin side up, with the tail end facing your guide hand. Steady the fillet with your guide hand in the claw position, with your guide fingers about 1⁄4 inch (6 mm) from the head end.

2

Hold the knife handle with your last three fingers and thumb and rest your index finger on the spine. Line up the heel just in front of the front edge of the fish and place the blade flush against your guide fingers.

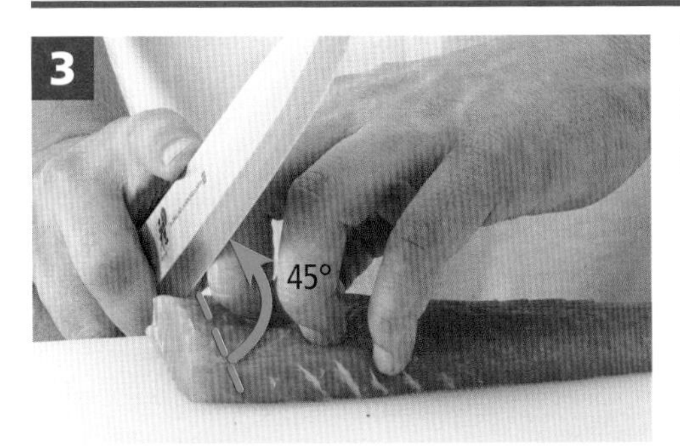

Tilt the handle down until the tip of the knife is in the air at a 45-degree angle to the board.

In one rapid motion, draw your elbow back while simultaneously bringing the tip down, using the entire length of the blade to make a clean slice.

Without lifting the blade from the board, move the slice aside with the tip of the knife.

Move your guide hand back $\frac{1}{4}$ inch (6 mm), line up the knife again and repeat steps 3 to 5.

Repeat steps 3 to 6 until the entire fillet is sliced.

Chapter 8
Cutting Shellfish

As with other fish, shellfish stay freshest longest when they're purchased as close to whole as possible. Some shellfish, like lobsters, clams, oysters and mussels, are just as commonly available live.

Deveining Shrimp

RECOMMENDED KNIFE

Chef's knife or paring knife

Although shrimp heads are edible, most Western preparations call for their removal. They are usually sold with the heads already removed; if you buy whole shrimp, just pull the heads off with your hands and save them for stock.

What we call the head also contains most of the shrimp's internal organs. One organ that is not limited to the head is the intestine, which runs the length of the shrimp, all the way down its back. Because the intestine carries waste material (primarily dirt or sand, but also bits of digested vegetable or animal matter), most cooks prefer to remove it before cooking the shrimp, as it can impart slightly off flavors or a gritty texture.

The removal of the intestine is called deveining. For our demo of this technique, we'll use peeled headless shrimp, though it works just as well with shrimp that still have the little tail section attached.

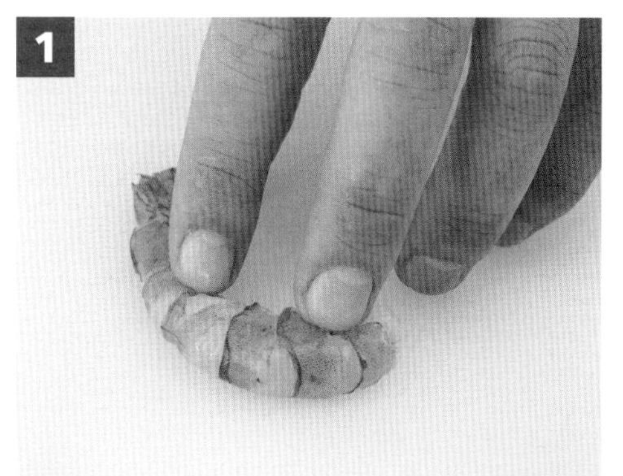

1 Lay the shrimp on the cutting board, with the back facing your knife hand and the tail facing you. Steady the shrimp with your guide hand in the claw position.

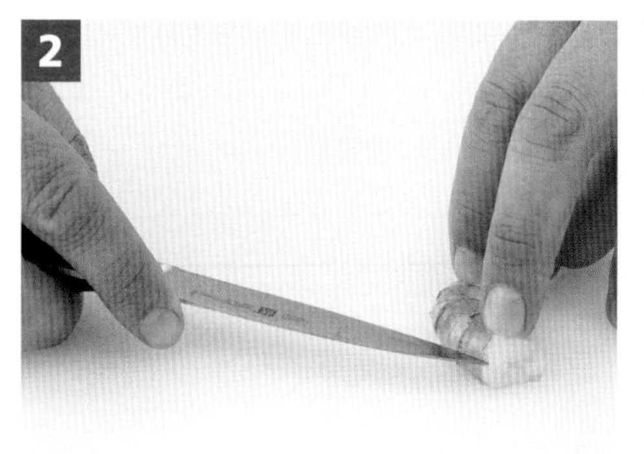

2 Holding the knife blade parallel to the board, place the point at the top center of the back.

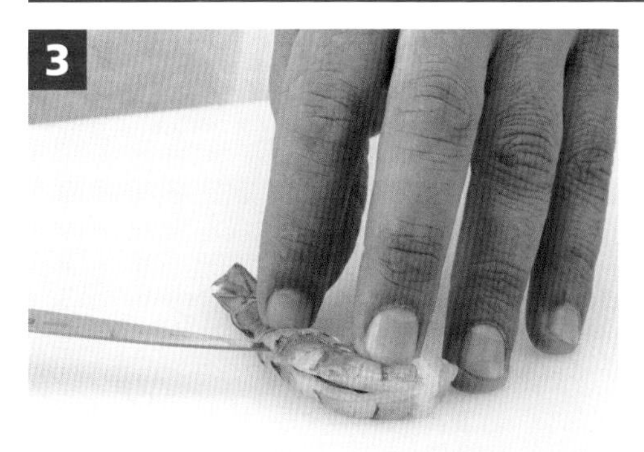

Follow the arc of the shrimp with the point of the blade, making an incision all the way to the tail, just deep enough to uncover the intestine.

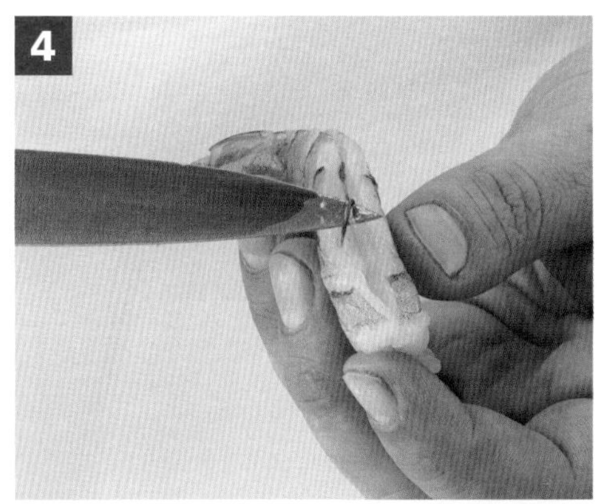

Work the point of the blade just underneath the intestine at the head side. Use the point to lift the intestine and pull it away.

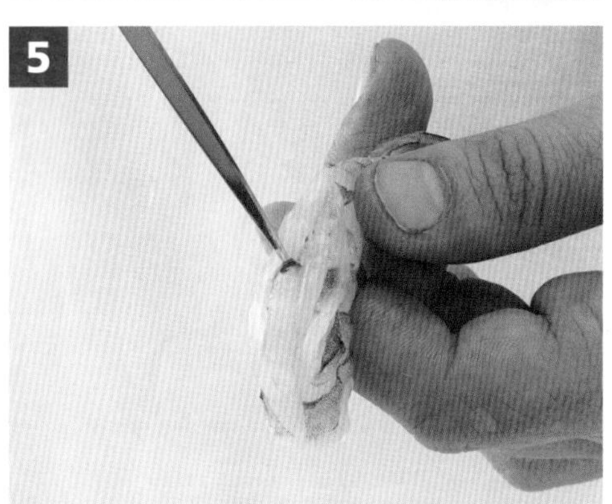

Use the point of the blade to scrape out any remaining pieces of intestine.

If you are doing a lot of shrimp at once, lining the shrimp up on the board will save time.

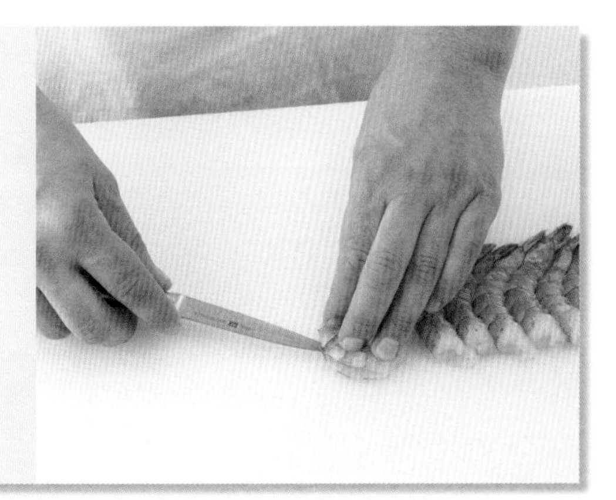

Butterflying Shrimp

Many recipes call for butterflied shrimp. The technique is pretty much like deveining shrimp (see page 320), only the cut is a lot deeper. We'll use a peeled headless shrimp.

RECOMMENDED KNIFE

Chef's knife or paring knife

1. Lay the shrimp on the cutting board, with the back facing your knife hand and the tail facing you. Holding the knife blade parallel to the board, place the point at the top center of the back.

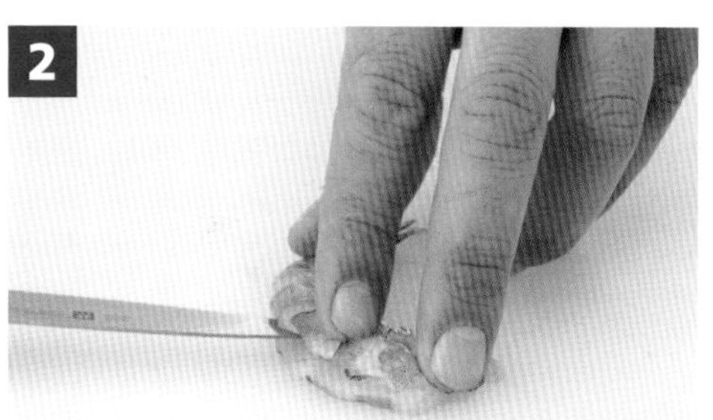

2. Follow the arc of the shrimp with the point of the blade, cutting nearly, but not quite, all the way through the shrimp from head to tail.

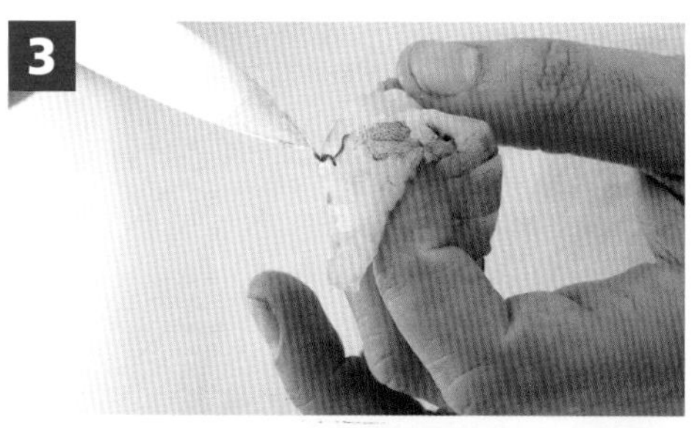

3. Work the point of the blade just underneath the intestine at the head side. Use the point to lift the intestine and pull it away, then scrape out any remaining pieces of intestine.

4. Open up the shrimp like a book.

Splitting a Lobster in Half

Grilled lobster, lobster à l'américaine, lobster Thermidor and many other dishes require the lobster to be split in half lengthwise. Unfortunately for the squeamish, this is best done while the lobster is still alive, to ensure freshness. Dead lobsters go bad very quickly, which is why they're only sold live, frozen or previously frozen.

RECOMMENDED KNIFE

Chef's knife

1

Place the lobster right side up on the cutting board, with the head facing your knife hand. With your guide hand, hold the lobster by the tail.

2

Hold the knife in the stabbing grip (see page 86). Place the point of the knife in the crevice that separates the head from the carapace, with the edge of the blade facing the head.

3

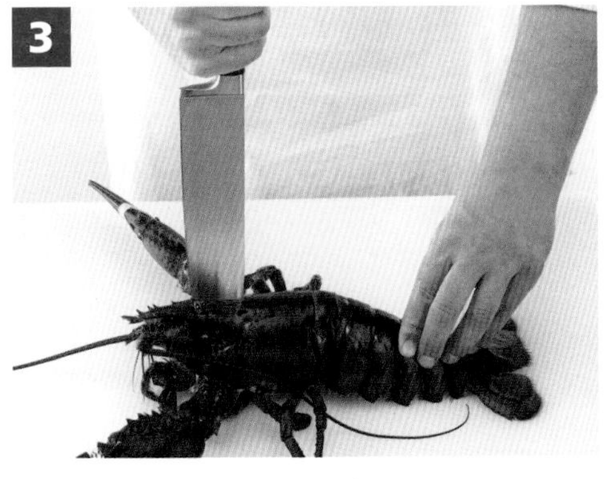

Press the knife straight down through the lobster until the point strikes the cutting board.

It may be difficult to get the point to pierce the shell. If you have trouble, adjust your grip on the knife so that your thumb and index finger are flush with the end of the handle and use the palm of your guide hand to press straight down on the top of the handle.

If you used your guide hand to help you pierce the shell, return it to the lobster's tail. With the knife still inside the lobster, change your grip to the basic grip (see page 70).

Keeping the point of the knife on the board, pull the handle down until the blade has sliced all the way through the head and come to rest on the board. (The amount of force this requires depends on the sharpness of your blade.)

Pull out the knife and turn the lobster so that the tail is facing your knife hand. Grip the head with your guide hand to steady the lobster. Insert the blade vertically into the cut you made in step 5, with the edge against the carapace.

7

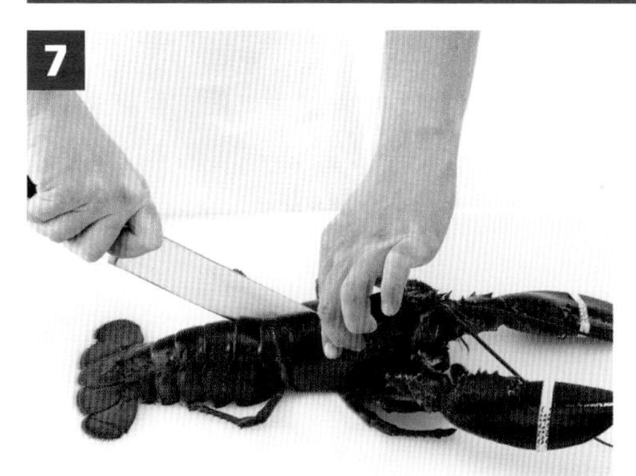

Holding the knife in the standard grip and keeping the point on the board, pull the handle down until the blade has sliced all the way down the back of the lobster and through the tail, splitting the lobster in half.

At this point, the lobster is dead, but you'll notice some reflex twitching in its organs.

8

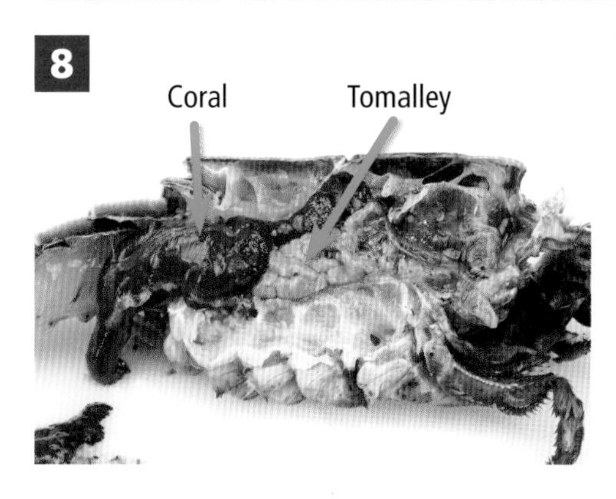

Remove the internal organs. Reserve the pea green tomalley and, if the lobster is female, any green coral.

Male vs. Female Lobsters

Female lobsters are preferred, as they often contain coral (lobster roe). To determine whether a lobster is male or female, simply flip it over and locate the top pair of swimmerets (the abdominal appendages). On a female, they are light and feathery; on a male, they are more rigid and substantial.

Removing the Meat from Cooked Lobster

To break down a cooked lobster, all you really need to know is what cutting tools to use and where to attack the shell.

RECOMMENDED CUTTING TOOLS

Kitchen shears; chef's knife

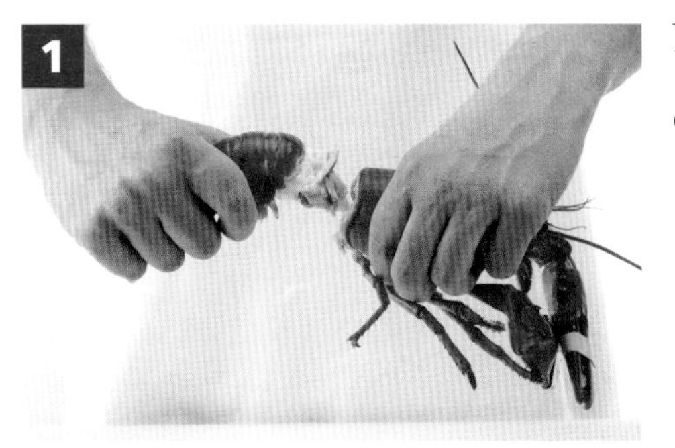

1. Use your hands to twist the tail section off the body.

2. Hold the tail in your guide hand, with the flipper sticking out between your thumb and index finger and the rest of the tail hanging down along your palm.

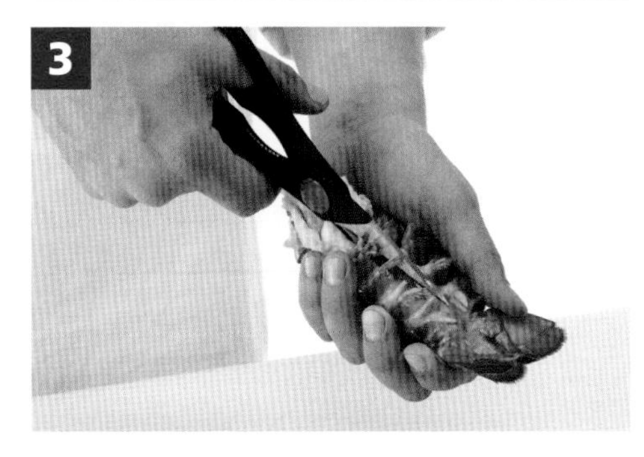

3. Use kitchen shears to snip apart the thin, flexible shell along the bottom of the lobster. Pull the meat out with your fingers.

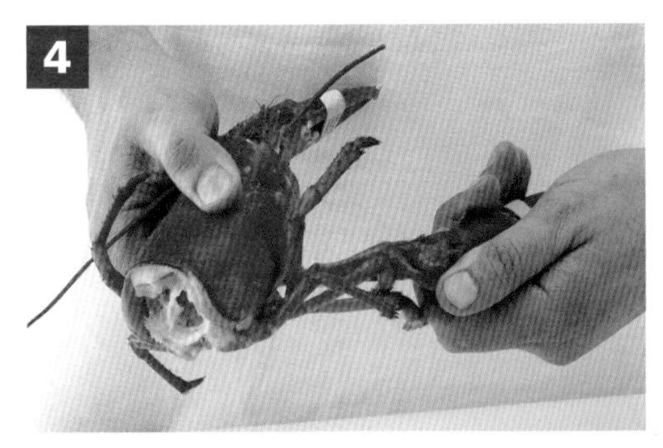

Use your hands to twist off the claws and legs. (The legs have very little meat and can be discarded, used for stock or eaten as a snack. To eat, hold the leg by one end and put most of it in your mouth. Close your front teeth on the shell and pull the leg out through your teeth, forcing the meat into your mouth.)

Place a claw on the cutting board, with the pincers facing your knife hand. Grip the other end with your guide hand.

Hold the chef's knife upside down, so that the edge is facing up. Line up the heel of the knife just behind the pincer hinge. Raise the knife into the air, then bring it down with considerable force onto the claw, cracking the shell without cutting into the meat.

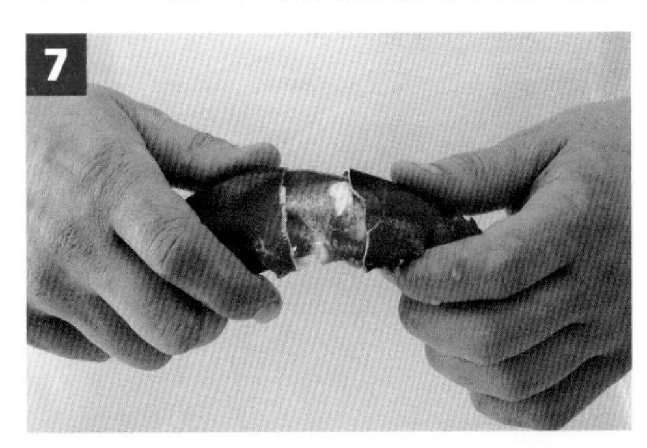

Pick the claw up and grip it with your knife hand on one side of the crack you made in step 6 and your guide hand on the other. Bend the claw backwards to sever the shell.

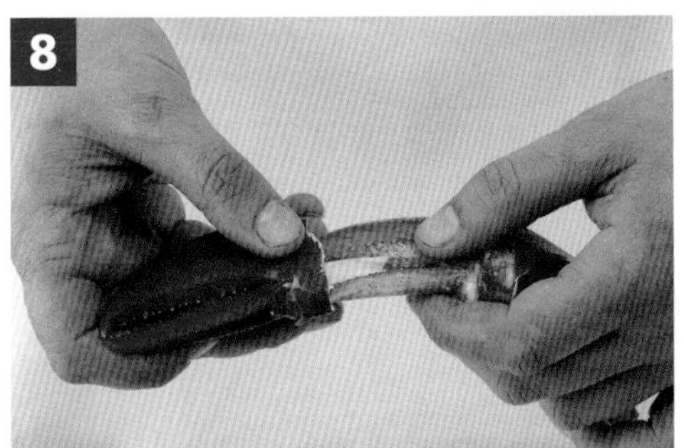

Use your fingers to pull the meat gently from the claw in one piece. Repeat steps 5 to 8 with the other claw.

Preparing Soft-Shell Crab

Soft-shell crabs are simply blue crabs that have outgrown their shell and molted (discarded the shell) so they can grow another. Because the newly forming shell is soft — hence the name — the crab can be eaten whole. Soft-shell crab season runs roughly from May to September. It's best to purchase soft-shell crabs live.

RECOMMENDED CUTTING TOOL

Kitchen shears

Hold the crab in your guide hand, with the front of the crab facing your knife hand. Use the shears to remove the face (the front part of the crab that contains the eyes). This will kill the crab.

Squeeze the innards out through the cut you just made.

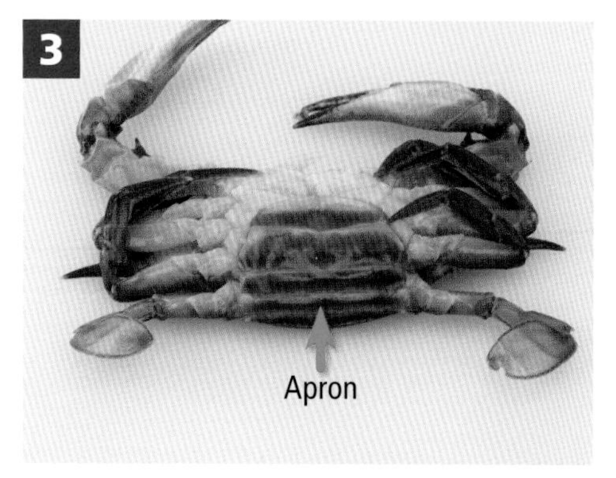

Place the crab on its back on the cutting board and locate the apron, a flap at the rear of the crab also known as the abdomen or tail flap.

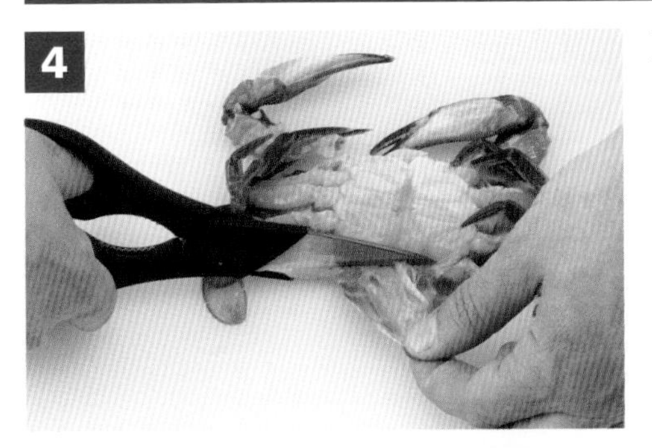

Peel back the apron and cut it off.

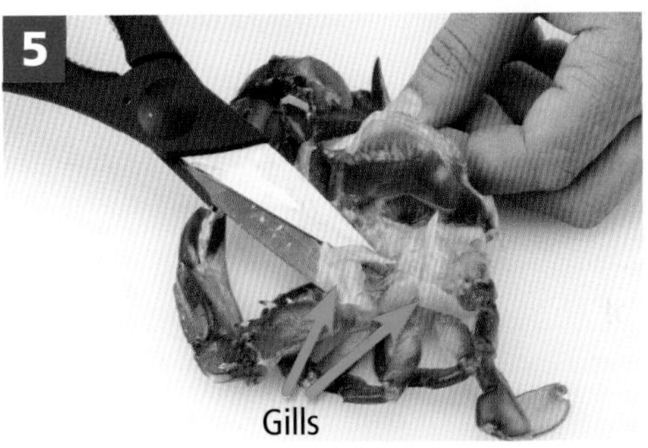

Flip the crab right side up and lift one side of the top shell. Use the shears or your fingers to cut or pull away the gills, a group of long gray tubes sometimes called "dead man's fingers."

Lift the other side of the top shell and remove the gills. The crab is now ready to be cooked.

Male vs. Female Crabs

Female crabs taste better than male crabs, so it's good to be able to tell the difference. At the rear of the underside of the crab, you'll see a sizeable flap that is variously called the apron, the abdomen or the tail flap. On a female crab, the apron stretches fairly far across the body and has a small, pointy protuberance at the top. The male apron looks much flatter and goes only a short way across the body, but its protuberance is much longer than the female's.

Male crab Female crab

Removing the Meat from Blue or Dungeness Crab

Blue crab and Dungeness crab are anatomically similar, but the blue crab makes its home off the coast of Maryland, whereas Dungeness crab comes from the waters just off Dungeness, Washington.

Crabmeat begins to spoil very soon after the crab dies. Hence, blue and Dungeness crabs are sold either live or cooked. If you purchase them live, you'll boil or steam them whole before taking them apart.

RECOMMENDED KNIVES

Paring knife; chef's knife

When it comes to removing the meat, there's no established set of steps followed by every chef, but we'll give you some guidelines that will allow you to get the easiest and fullest access to the cooked meat. We'll use Dungeness crab to demonstrate the technique, but it will work equally well with blue crab.

1. Place the crab on its back on the cutting board, with the apron (the flap at the rear of the crab) facing you. Insert the point of the paring knife underneath the tip of the apron and pry it up.

2. Use your fingers to pull the apron all the way off.

3. Flip the crab right side up, with the rear of the crab facing you. Insert the point of the chef's knife underneath the top shell and pry it up.

4. Use your fingers to pull the top shell all the way off. Note the membrane covers you've uncovered on both sides of the crab (we'll come back to them later).

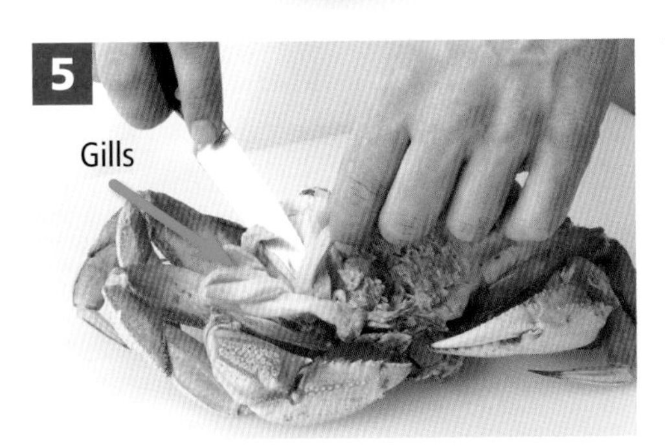

5. Use the point of the paring knife or your fingers to scrape or pull away the gills (also known as "dead man's fingers"), the six grayish tubes on either side of the body. Discard the gills, as they are not edible.

6. Use the point of the paring knife or your fingers to scrape or pull away the multicolored bits just behind the mouth of the crab. (These edible bits are the heart, fat and possibly, if it's a female crab, roe.)

7. Place the blade of the chef's knife along the center of the crab and cut it in half from front to back.

With your guide hand, hold one of the halves by the cut edge of the shell, with the side of the crab against the board. Cut straight down along the membrane cover to remove it. Pull out the large chunks of meat beneath the membrane cover. Repeat with the other half.

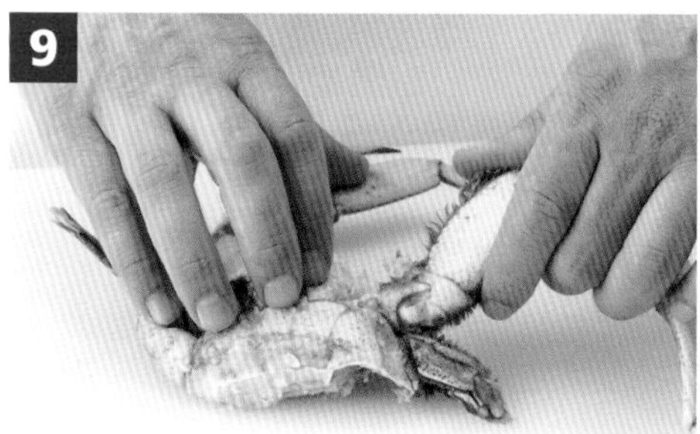

Twist off the claws and legs.

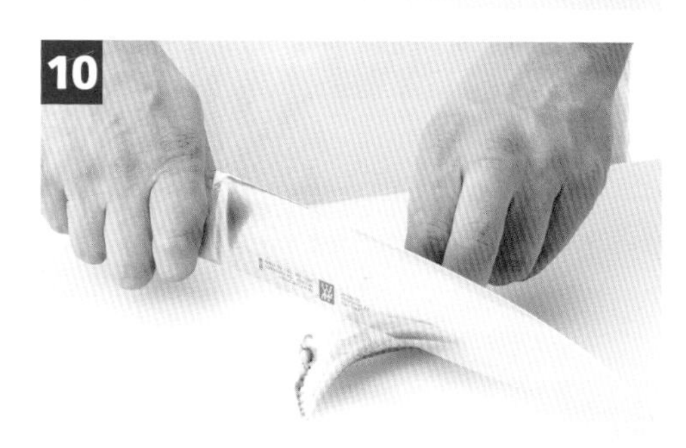

Lay a claw on the board. Hold the chef's knife upside down, so that the edge is facing up. Line up the heel of the knife just behind the pincer hinge. Raise the knife into the air, then bring it down with considerable force onto the claw, cracking the shell without cutting into the meat.

Use your hands to break off the pincers and pull the meat out of the claw. Repeat steps 10 and 11 with the other claw.

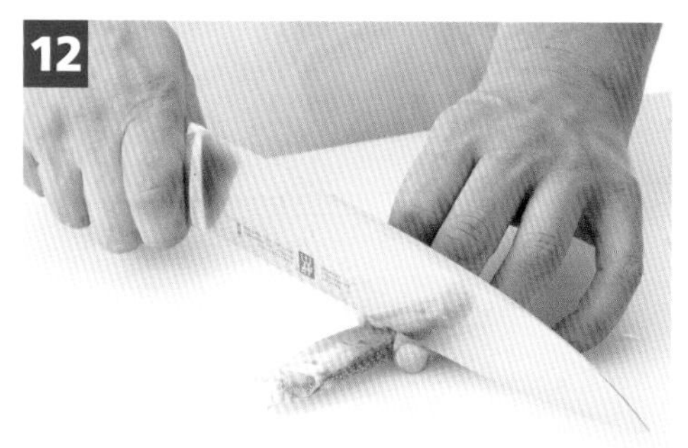

Lay a leg on the board and steady it with your guide hand. Cut one end off. Flip the knife over and scrape the spine along the leg, forcing the meat out the end. Repeat with the other legs.

Shelling King Crab Legs

King crab legs are always sold precooked, because the meat spoils very quickly after the crab dies. Here's how to remove the shell from the cooked meat.

RECOMMENDED CUTTING TOOL

Kitchen shears

1. Use your hands to break the legs apart at the joints.

2. Hold one leg section in your guide hand, with your palm up and thumb to the side of the leg section.

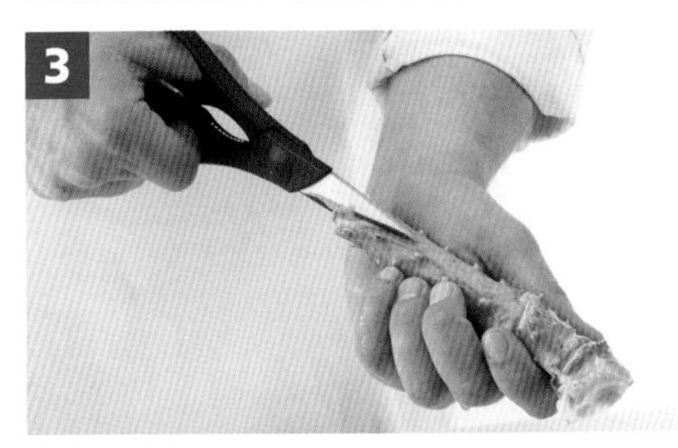

3. Use the shears to snip through the shell from bottom to top.

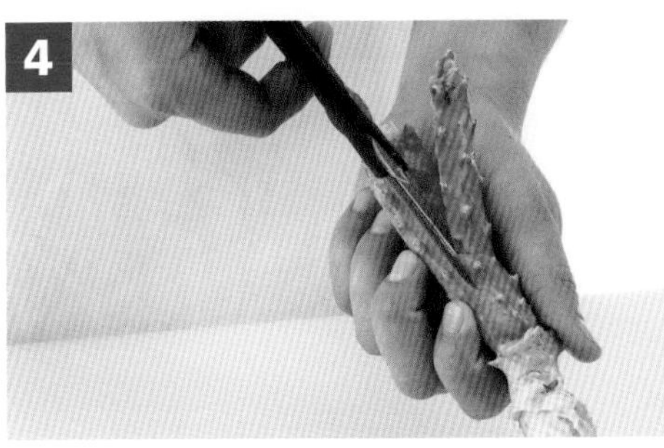

4. If you cannot open the shell after the initial cut, rotate the leg 90 to 180 degrees in your hand and make another pass with the shears to remove a wide piece of shell in one piece. Pull out the meat with your fingers or a fork.

Preparing Squid

The squid, like the octopus, is a cephalopod, which is Greek for "head-foot." This makes sense when you know squid anatomy: its head lies right on top of its "feet" — actually the arms and tentacles.

The top of the squid is a long, solid tube called the mantle, which holds all the internal organs. At the bottom of the mantle is the head, which contains the two eyes, and below that are the eight arms and two tentacles.

Depending on the size of the squid and what you plan to do with it, you may or may not need a knife to prepare it. The first step is to clean out the mantle and separate the arms and tentacles. A small mantle can be stuffed or cut crosswise into rings. Larger mantles can be laid out flat and cut into squares. Arms and tentacles can be prepared whole or cut into pieces.

Preparing Small Squid

Small squid are common in European cuisines. Look for squid with a mantle 4 to 6 inches (10 to 15 cm) long. This size is terrific for stuffing or cutting into rings.

RECOMMENDED KNIFE

Chef's knife or Santoku

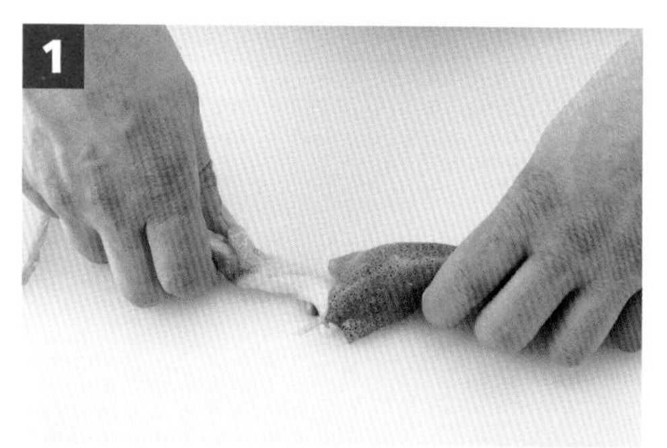

1 Lay the squid on the cutting board with the mantle facing your guide hand. Grip the mantle with your guide hand and the head with your knife hand. Gently pull the head away from the mantle so that all of the internal organs come out in one piece.

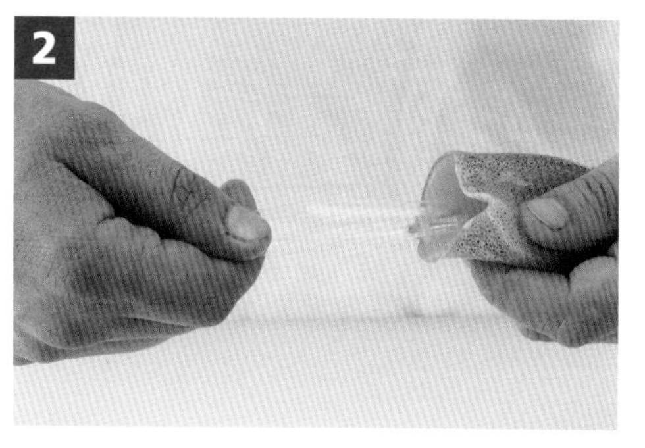

2 Reach inside the mantle and remove the quill, the long, thin, clear piece that looks like a shard of hard plastic.

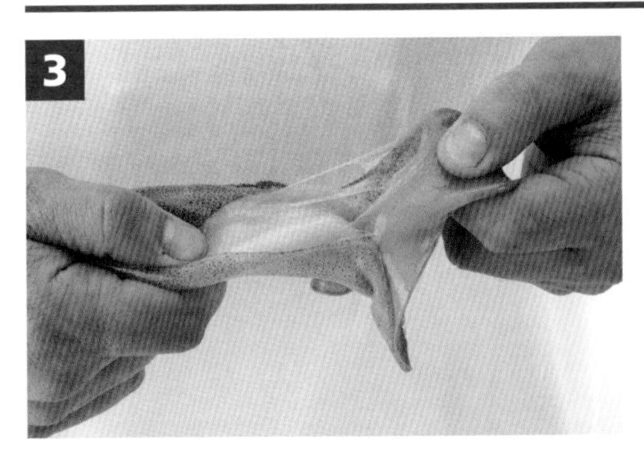
3

Pull off the fins on the side of the mantle, as well as the thin membrane that covers the mantle.

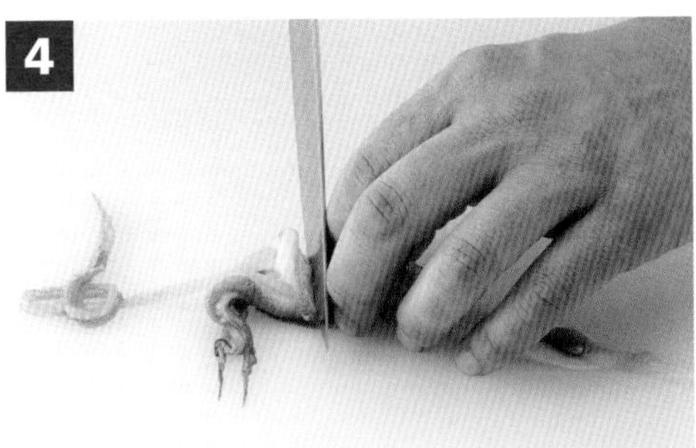
4

Gently pull or cut the arms and tentacles from the head. Discard the head and innards. If desired, cut the arms and tentacles into pieces.

5

If you want to stuff the mantle, leave it as is. To cut it into rings, lay it on the board, with one end facing your knife hand. Steady it with your guide hand in the claw position. Cut the mantle into $\frac{1}{4}$- to $\frac{1}{2}$-inch (6 to 12 mm) rings.

Preparing Large Squid

Some Asian markets carry squid with mantles that are 12 inches (30 cm) or longer. With these long mantles, it's not as easy to pull out all the organs in one piece. Also, because the mantle has such a large diameter, it's not as useful to cut it into rings. Mantles this large are usually scored and cut into rectangles that curl up into attractive little cylinders when sautéed. The arms and tentacles can be cut up and fried, braised or used in pastas.

RECOMMENDED KNIFE

Chef's knife

Preparing Squid

1

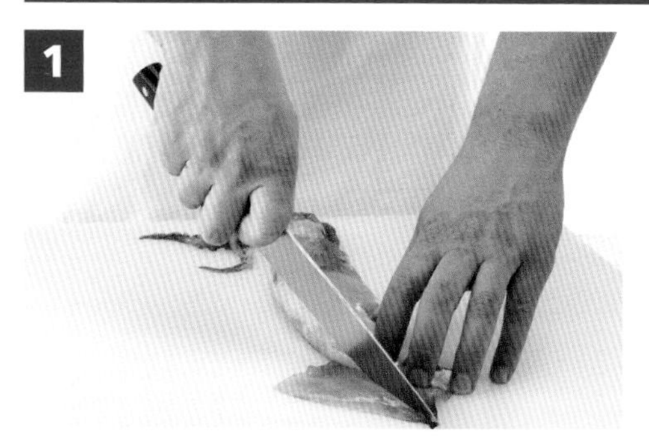

Lay the squid on the cutting board, with the mantle facing away from you. Place your guide hand on one side of the mantle and cut off one of the fins.

2

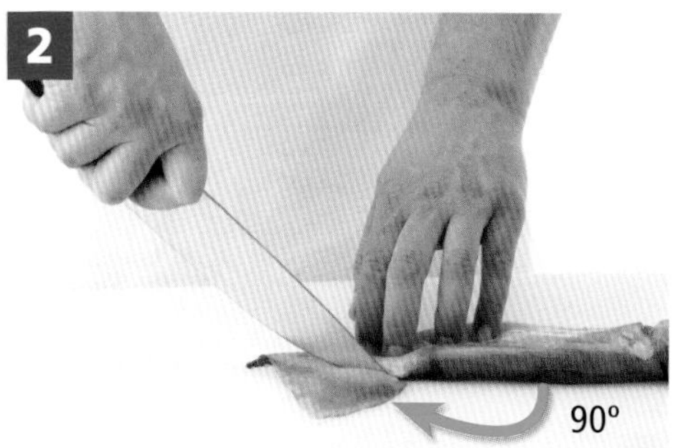

Turn the squid 90 degrees, so that the mantle is facing your knife hand, and cut off the other fin.

3

Return the squid to the starting position. Hold the knife with the blade parallel to the board and the edge facing the knife-hand side of the board. Lift the edge of the mantle and slip the knife inside, as far as it will go.

4

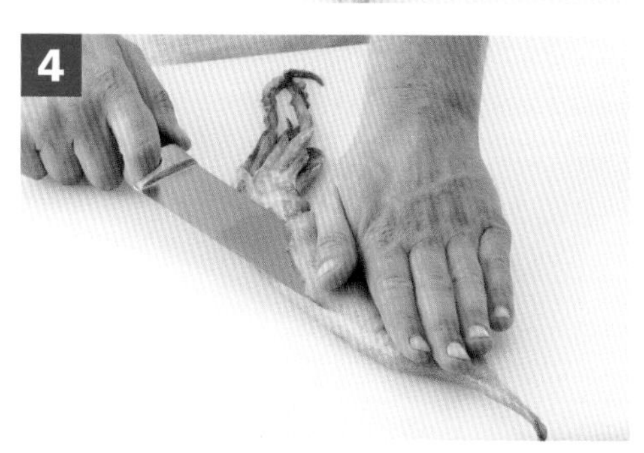

Rest your guide-hand palm on the mantle to stabilize it and move the knife out through the side of the mantle, cutting it all the way to the top (like using a letter opener).

5

Spread the mantle open. Grip the head of the squid and pull it away from the mantle to free the internal organs. Pull away any stray pieces attached to the inside of the mantle.

6

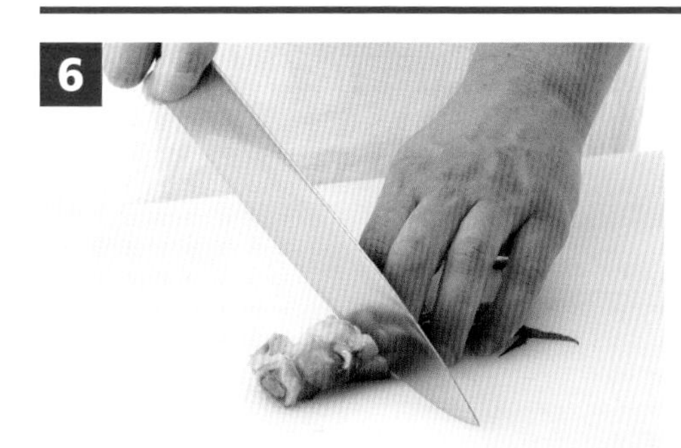

Gently pull or cut the arms and tentacles from the head. Discard the head and innards. Cut the arms and tentacles into pieces.

7

Score the inside of the mantle by drawing your chef's knife diagonally from one side to the other, cutting into the flesh but not all the way through. Space your cuts 1⁄4 to 1⁄2 inch (6 to 12 mm) apart.

8

Turn the mantle 90 degrees and make another series of parallel slits to create a crosshatch pattern.

9

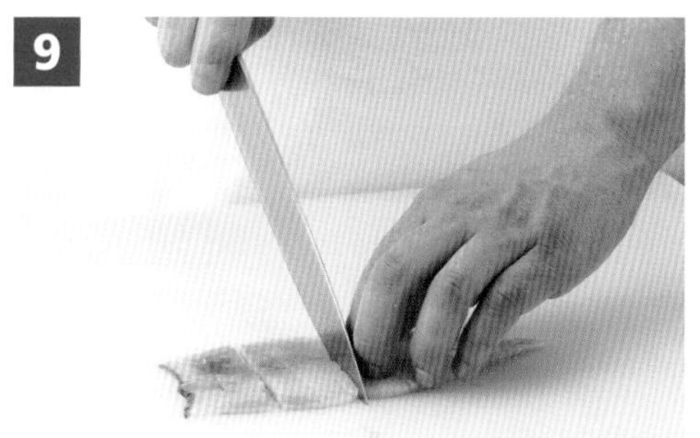

Cut the mantle into roughly 2- by 3-inch (5 by 7.5 cm) rectangles.

Shucking Oysters

The oyster is a bivalve, meaning that it has two shells: a top shell and a bottom shell. The shells are connected by a ligament at the narrow end, near the bulbous protuberances called the umbos. Typically, the bottom shell is slightly longer and has a deeper bowl than the top, so that's the side you want down when you open the oyster.

RECOMMENDED KNIFE

Oyster knife

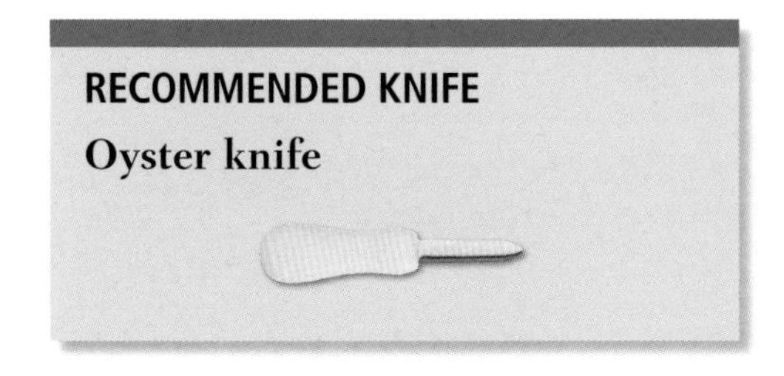

When shucking oysters, make sure to protect your guide hand with a wire mesh glove or a folded clean, dry towel. Oyster knives are not sharp, but it's not uncommon for them to slip, and you can do some serious damage to an unprotected hand.

Before you get started, examine all of your oysters to make sure they are tightly closed. Discard any that are open.

1. Grip the oyster by the rounded end with your protected guide hand. Make sure the longer bottom shell is facing down.

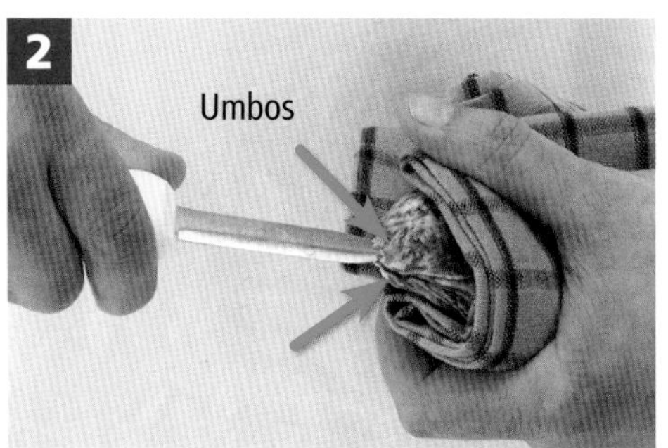

2. Locate the umbos at the narrow end. Hold the knife in the shucking grip (see page 86) and insert the point into the hinge between the top and bottom umbos.

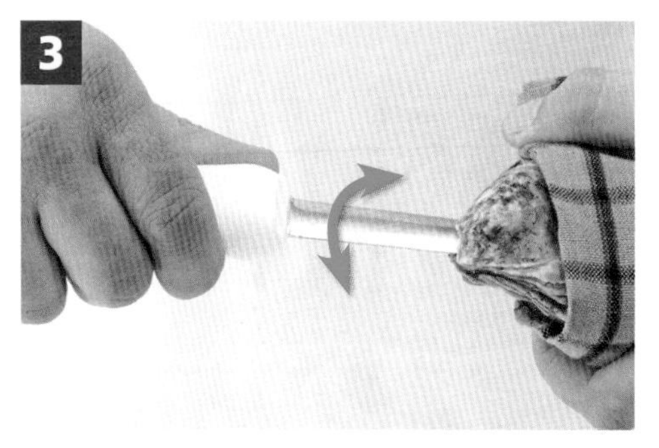

3. Moving your knife arm back and forth from the elbow, slowly work the knife point between the shells.

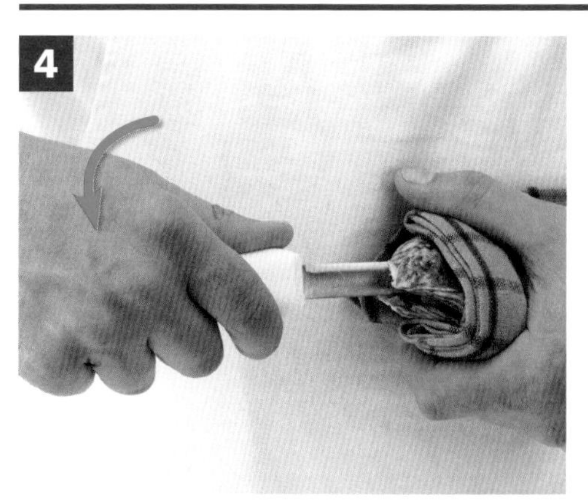

Once the shells part a bit, twist your wrist away from you to snap the hinge.

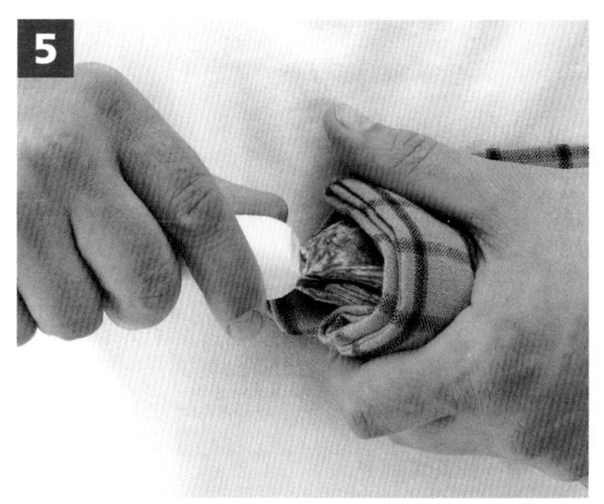

Rotate the knife handle down toward you. Scrape the point across the inside of the top shell to free the oyster from it.

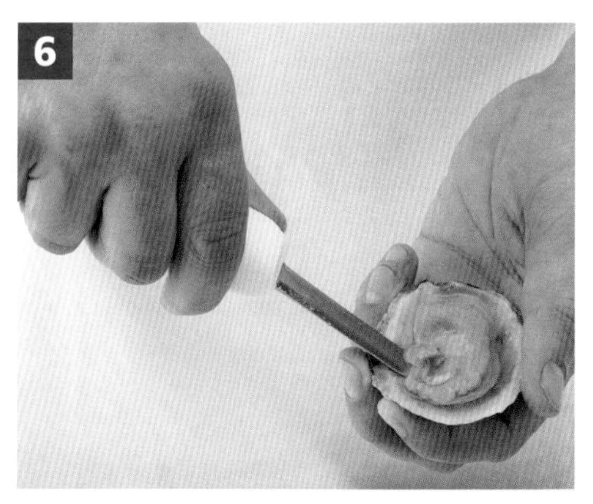

Use your hand to pull the top shell off. Carefully run the blade underneath the oyster to free it from the bottom shell.

If you prefer, you can place the oyster on the board instead of shucking in the air.

Shucking Clams

A clam knife is similar to an oyster knife, except that it is sharpened somewhat along one side of the blade. Besides the tool used, there are two other differences between shucking clams and shucking oysters. First, while you use the point of the oyster knife to open an oyster, you use the sharpened edge of the clam knife to open a clam. Second, whereas you open an oyster at the hinge, you open a clam on the side opposite the hinge.

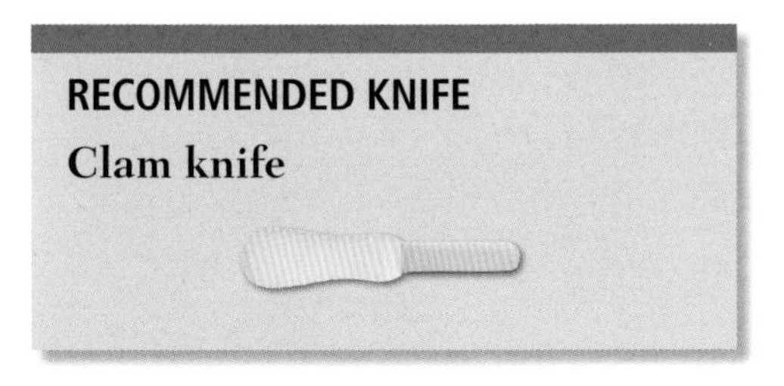

As with oysters, when shucking clams you should protect your guide hand with a wire mesh glove or a folded clean, dry towel in case the knife slips.

Before you get started, examine all of your clams to make sure they are tightly closed. Discard any that are open.

Grip the clam with your protected guide hand, with the hinge facing your hand.

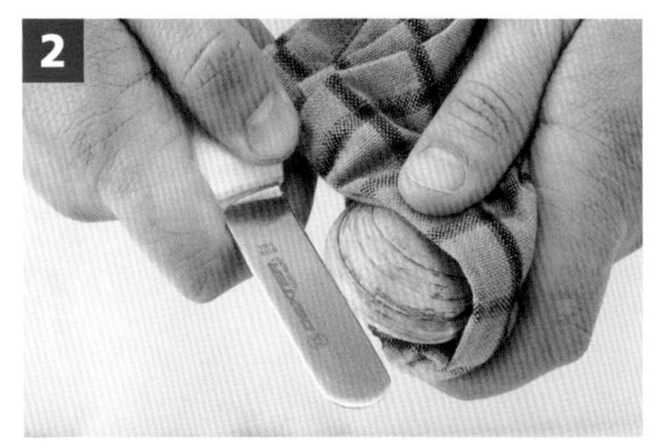

Hold the knife in the shucking grip (see page 86) and place the sharpened edge along the seam between the top and bottom shells.

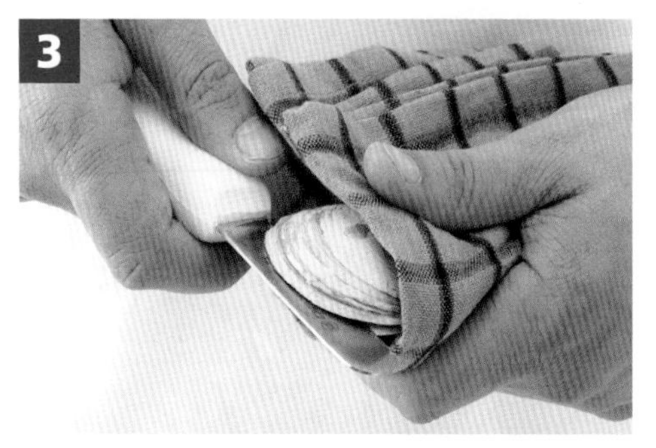

Using a slight sawing or waggling motion, slowly work the knife edge between the shells.

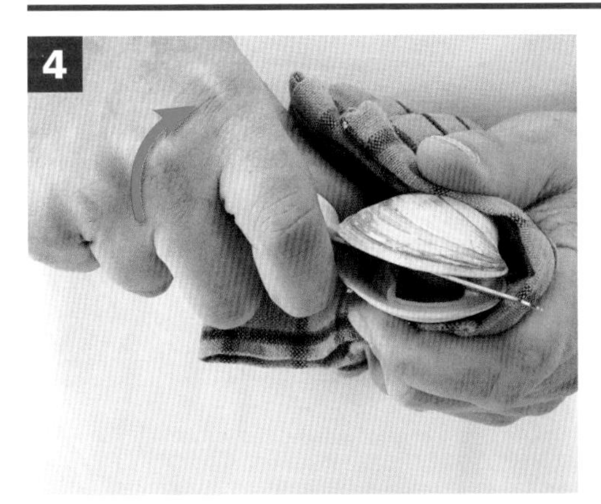

Once the shells part a bit, twist your wrist toward you to pry the shells apart.

Remove the knife, then insert the point between the shells and scrape it across the inside of the top shell to free the clam from it.

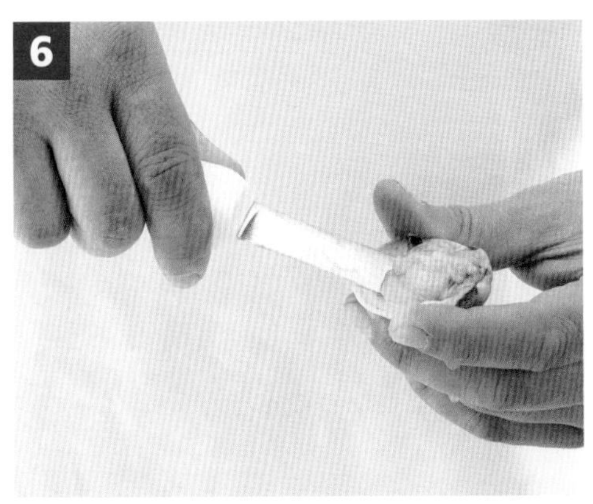

Use your hand to pull the top shell off. Carefully run the blade underneath the clam to free it from the bottom shell.

Chapter 9

Carving Cooked Meats

Knowing how to cook but not how to carve is kind of like knowing how to build a car but not how to drive it. But many people find carving large roasts or birds a bit daunting, probably because carving is so often done in the presence of assembled guests and no one wants to mangle dinner in front of an audience. Fortunately, carving well is simply a matter of knowing the anatomy of the animal you're carving. If you know where the bones are, you know how to avoid them.

One important note: all cooked meats need to rest after they are removed from the heat, to allow their juices to reabsorb into the flesh. Small pieces, such as steaks or chops, can rest for just a couple of minutes, but large roasts or birds should rest anywhere from 15 to 30 minutes before they are carved.

Carving a Turkey

How often do you really get to carve a turkey? Once a year? Twice, maybe, if you really love having people over for the holidays. Suffice it to say that this is one of the few techniques you are unlikely to develop muscle memory for, even if you're a pro. Having said that, remember that the skeletal structure and musculature of all edible birds are very similar. Thus, the techniques used to carve a turkey can be put to use carving a chicken, a duck or any other game bird.

But before you cook the turkey, let alone try to carve it, take a few moments to familiarize yourself with its anatomy by referring to the pictures on page 220 — after all, in terms of structure, a turkey is basically just an enormous chicken.

As you look at the pictures and become familiar with the different parts of the bird, feel around your turkey's legs and wings, breast and back. Note how the skin holds the legs tight to the carcass; once you cut through that skin, the leg is attached by a single joint. As when you're cutting up a chicken, you won't be cutting through bone to carve the turkey. Instead, you'll be cutting meat away from the bone and, on occasion, cutting through joints.

When the turkey is cooked and rested and ready for carving, start by cutting off the legs, then the wings. Then you can either remove the breast halves to carve on the cutting board or carve the breast meat right off the bird. You can carve the individual pieces immediately after you remove them from the bird, or you can break down the entire bird before carving the pieces.

Removing and Separating the Legs

A turkey leg conjures up images of Henry VIII, but for many people, it's their favorite part of the turkey.

RECOMMENDED TOOLS

Chef's knife or carving knife; carving fork

1

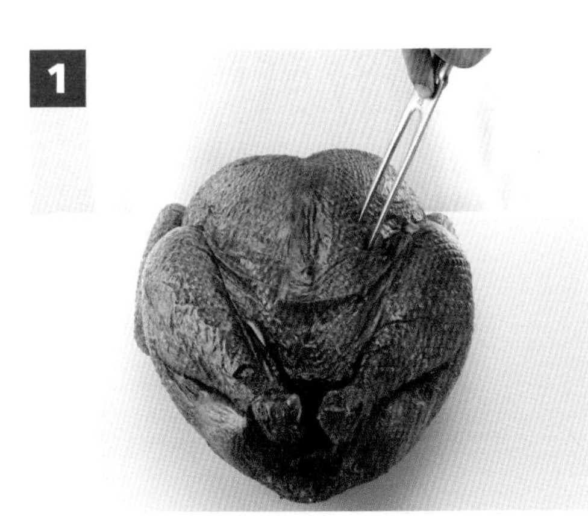

Place the turkey on the cutting board or a platter, breast side up, with the legs facing away from you. Steady it with the carving fork in your guide hand.

2

Cut through the skin that connects one leg to the carcass, cutting as close to the leg as possible.

3

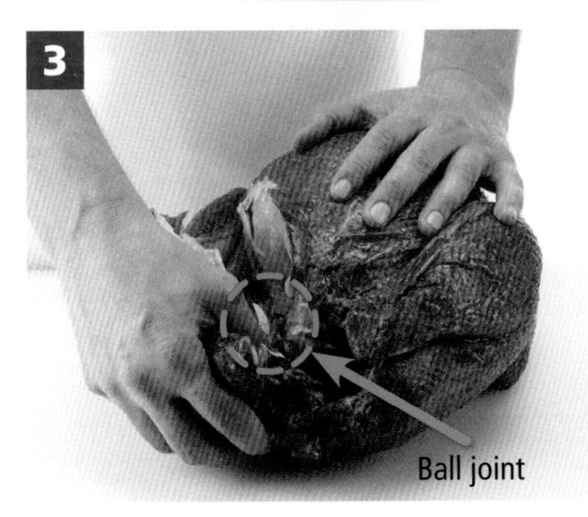

Set down the knife and pull the leg away from the bird until the ball joint that connects it to the carcass pops out of the socket. (If the turkey is too hot to handle, use a clean, dry towel to protect your hands.)

Cut straight through the joint with the knife. The leg will now pull easily away from the carcass.

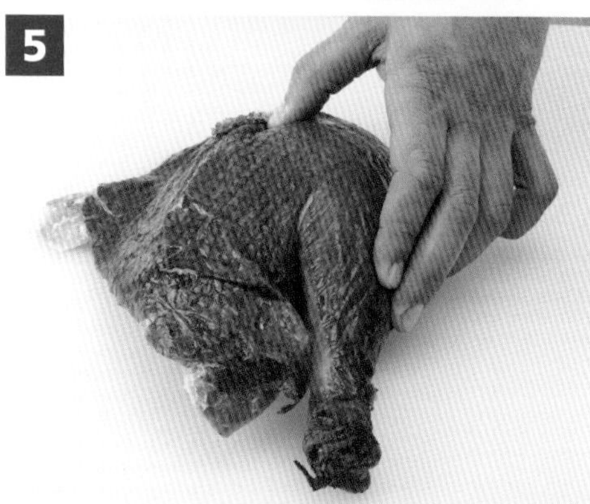

Lay the leg on the board, with the knee facing you, and feel for the joint connecting the drumstick bone and the thigh bone.

Place the knife blade directly on the joint and cut straight through to the board. (You shouldn't feel any resistance. If you do, the blade is on the bone, not the joint. Feel for the joint again and adjust the position of the blade accordingly.)

Repeat steps 2 to 6 with the other leg.

Carving the Drumsticks

Since there are only two drumsticks and many people gathered around the table, you'll need to carve the drumsticks up so that everyone gets a share.

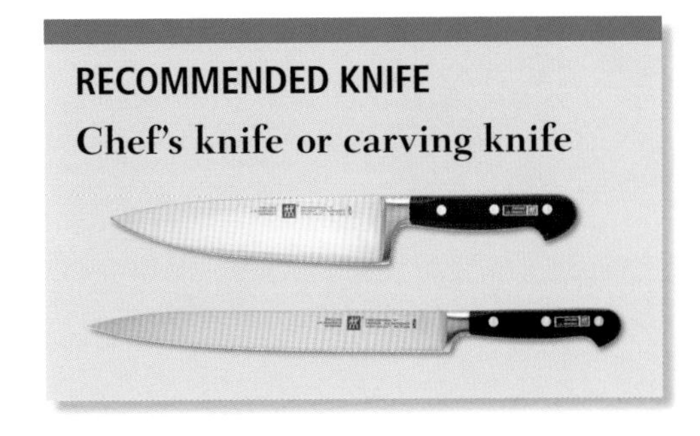

RECOMMENDED KNIFE

Chef's knife or carving knife

With your guide hand, hold a drumstick vertically by the end of the bone (the ankle) and let it rest on the cutting board.

2

Cut straight down along the bone, removing the meat in one piece.

3

Rotate the drumstick and continue cutting straight down along the bone until all the meat is removed from the bone.

4

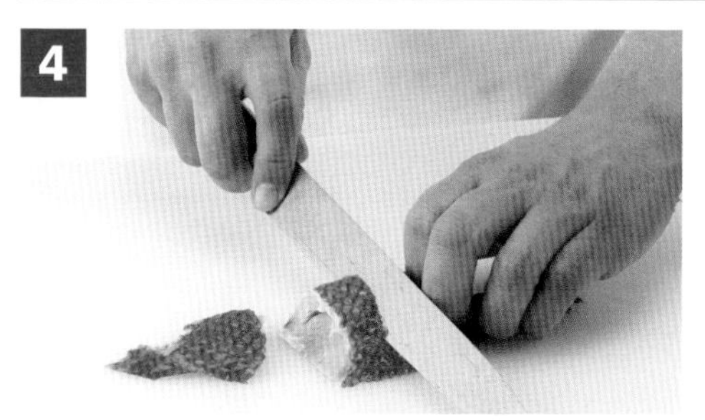

Bias-cut the drumstick meat into serving-size pieces (see page 360).

5

Repeat steps 1 to 4 with the other drumstick.

Carving the Thighs

Many people would argue that the thighs are the tastiest part of any bird, and especially turkey. Because they are fattier, they're juicier and more flavorful.

RECOMMENDED TOOLS

Chef's knife, carving knife or stiff boning knife; carving fork

1

Lay a thigh on the cutting board, skin side down, and steady it with the carving fork in your guide hand. Cut along both sides of the bone, from one end to the other.

2

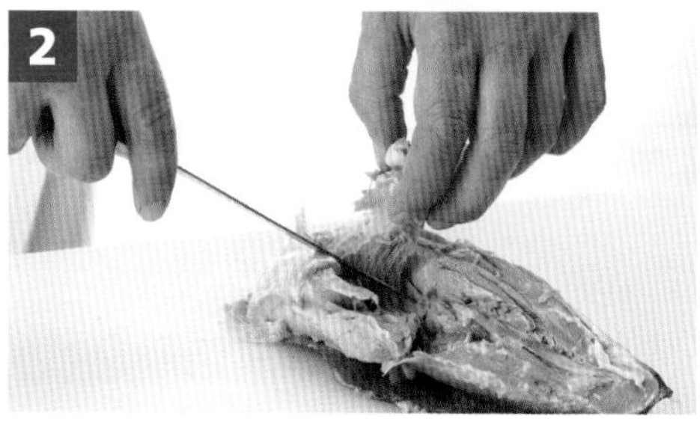

Hold the knife blade parallel to the board and slip it underneath the bone. Cut along the length of the bone to free it from the meat. Pull the bone away from the meat.

Flip the thigh so that it's skin side up and bias-cut it into serving-size slices (see page 360).

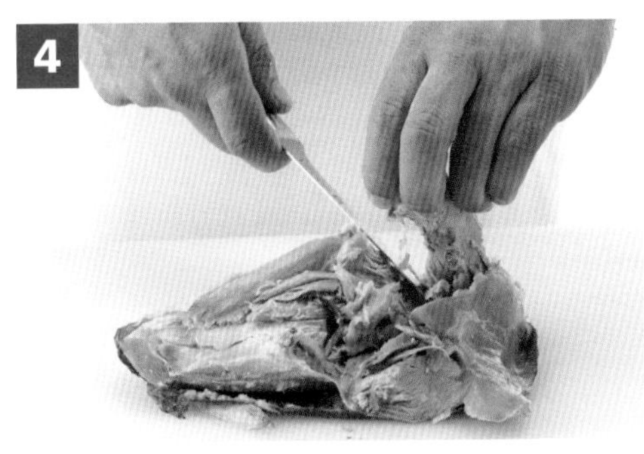

Repeat steps 1 to 3 with the other thigh.

Removing the Wings

The parts of a turkey wing are the same as the parts of a chicken wing: the wingtip (the end section), the wing flat (the middle, two-bone section) and the drumette (the single-bone section that attaches to the body).

RECOMMENDED KNIFE

Chef's knife, carving knife or stiff boning knife

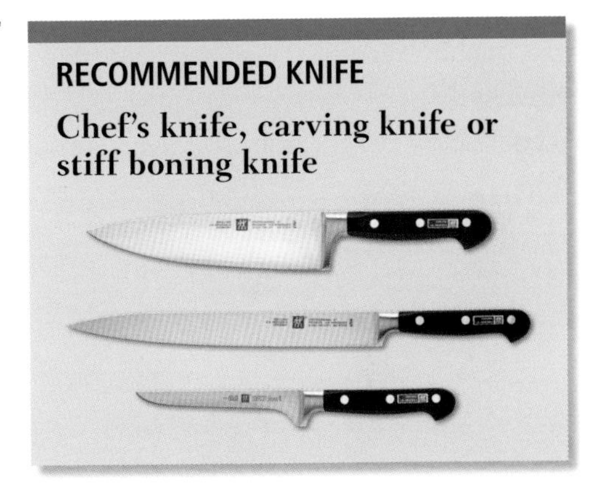

Grip a wing with your guide hand and pull it gently away from the carcass so you can see where it is attached.

2

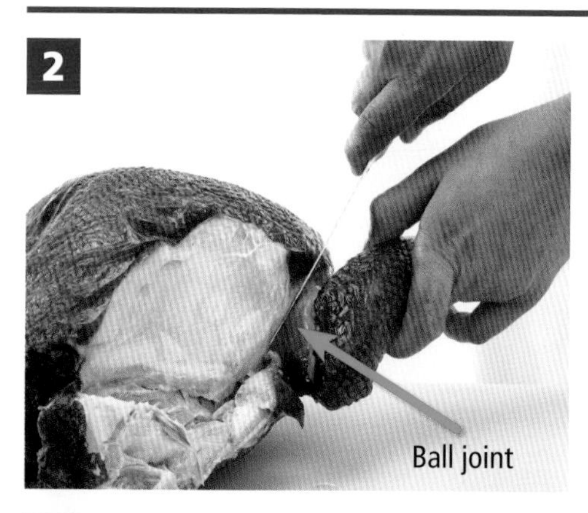

Work the tip of the knife between the ball joint of the wing and the socket.

3

Cut all the way through the joint, through any meat and skin, and remove the wing from the carcass.

4

Rotate the turkey so that the other wing is facing your guide hand. Repeat steps 1 to 3 to remove it.

The wings are commonly treated as snacks for the cooks and their helpers. They can be eaten whole or taken apart. To do the latter, first, cut off the wingtips at the joint and save them for stock. If you want to serve the wing pieces as finger food, separate the wing flats from the drumettes by cutting them at the joint. If you want to add just the meat to your platter, use your fingers to pull the meat off the bones.

Carving Slices of Breast Meat from the Bird

If you decide to carve slices of breast meat directly off the bird, here's how to go about it. If you'd rather remove the breast halves from the carcass first and carve them on the cutting board, see page 352.

RECOMMENDED TOOLS

Chef's knife; carving fork

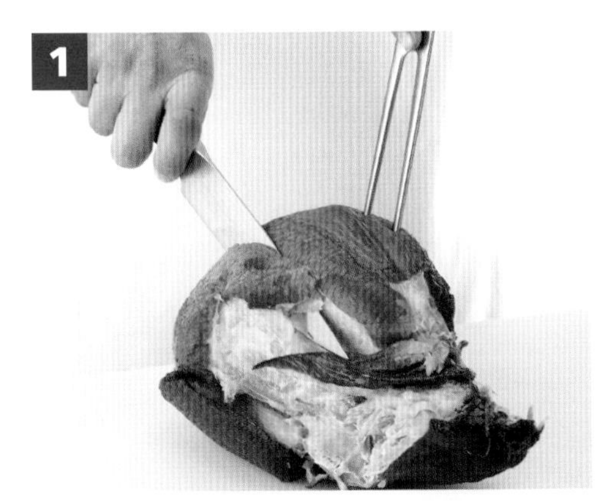

1. Steady the side of the breast you're not carving with the carving fork in your guide hand.

2. Holding the knife blade in line with the angle of the rib cage, cut thin slices off the breast until the meat is entirely removed from one side.

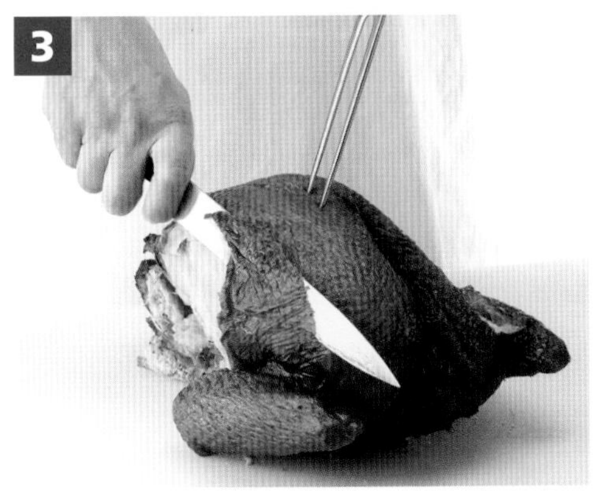

3. Steady the carcass with the carving fork and repeat step 2 on the other side of the breast.

Removing the Breast Halves to Carve on the Board

If you decide to remove the breast halves from the carcass and carve them on the cutting board, here's the technique. If you'd rather carve slices directly off the bird, see page 351.

RECOMMENDED TOOLS

Stiff boning knife or carving knife; carving fork

1

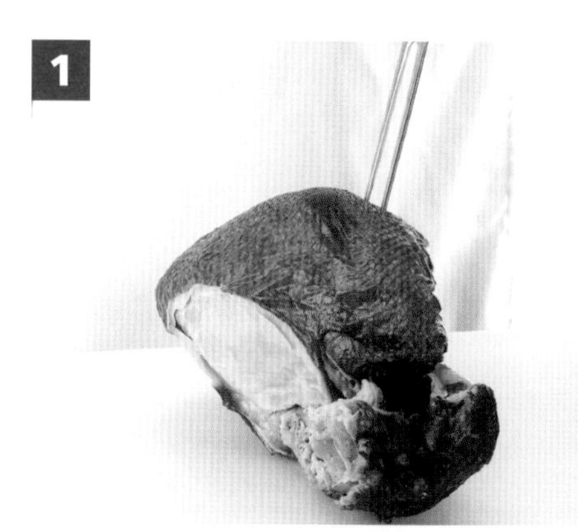

Steady the side of the breast you're not carving with the carving fork in your guide hand.

2

Make a long, thin cut along the breastbone, in the center of the breast.

3

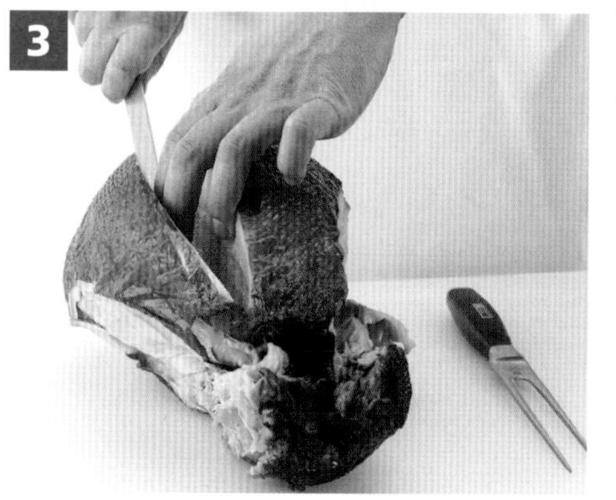

Using the tip of the knife, cut down along one side of the rib cage, then lay down the carving fork and use your guide hand to push or pull the breast gently away from the ribs as you go.

Let the knife blade ride the rib cage straight down to the socket where the wing was attached.

5

Cut along the bottom of the breast to remove that half completely.

6

Lay the breast half on the cutting board, skin side up, and bias-cut it into serving-size slices (see page 360).

Steady the carcass with the carving fork and repeat steps 2 to 6 with the other side of the breast.

Carving a Ham

While canned hams are easy enough to carve for anyone with a sharp knife, bone-in hams are a bit more challenging (giving rise, no doubt, to the popularity of the spiral ham, which comes presliced). The leg bone is pretty much in the center of the ham, which means you have to cut around it.

RECOMMENDED KNIFE

Carving knife

Whole cooked bone-in hams come in all shapes and sizes. When deciding where to start carving, look at the face of the ham (the largest end) and choose a spot that is narrower than your knife is long. Examine the ham to find a flat surface to rest it on. If you need to, cut a thin slice off one side.

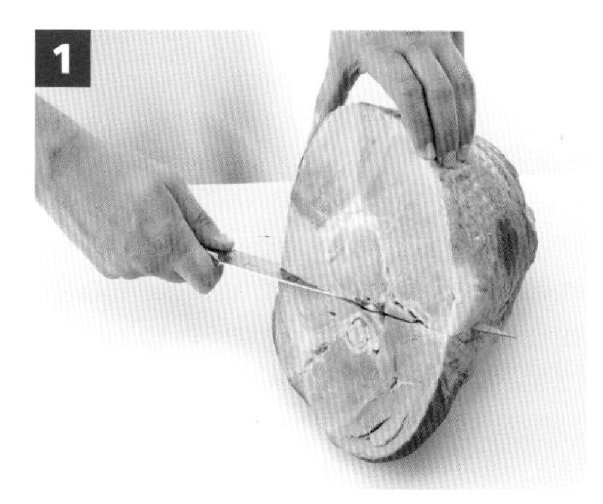

1 Lay the rested ham on the cutting board, flat surface down (see above), with the face facing your knife hand. Steady it with your guide hand. Holding the knife parallel to the board, place the blade just above the bone and begin cutting straight back.

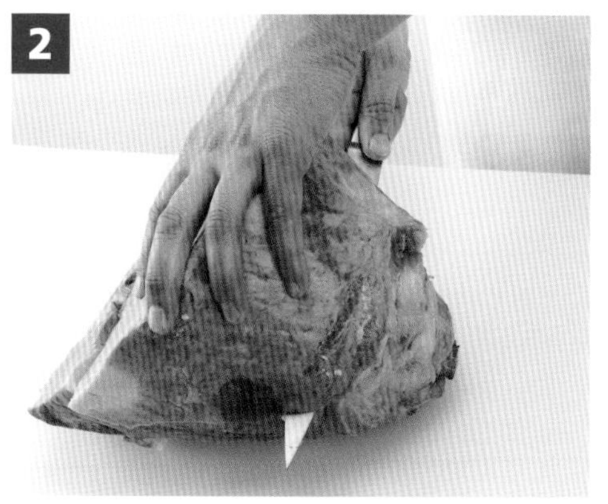

2 Continue cutting all the way back and remove the top piece.

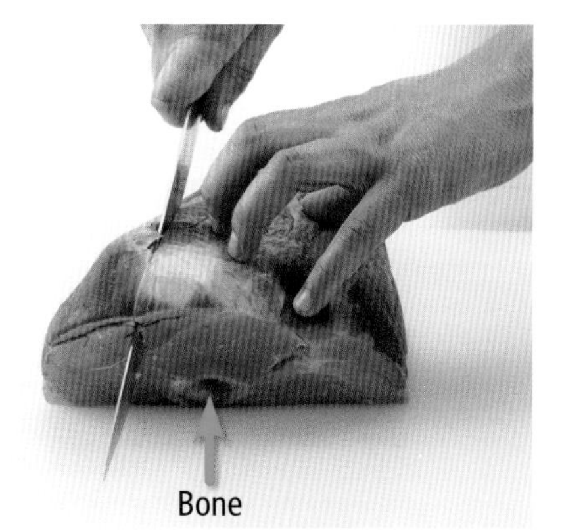

Lay the ham on the newly cut surface and steady it with your guide hand. Holding the knife perpendicular to the board, cut down along one side of the bone to remove another large piece.

4

Cut down along the other side of the bone to remove a third piece.

5

Tip the remaining ham onto its side and cut down along the bone to free the final piece.

The four large hunks of ham may now be cut into individual slices of the desired thickness.

Carving a Rib Roast

For beef rib roasts, we recommend that, after the roast has rested, you remove the bones before you carve the meat. This is an easy step, especially when you know what the bones look like: they are slightly curved and have a small bump just inside the meat.

RECOMMENDED TOOLS

Carving knife; carving fork

1

Place the rested roast on the cutting board, bone side down, with the ribs facing your guide hand. Fold a clean, dry towel and use it to grab the ribs with your guide hand and raise them to about a 45-degree angle.

2

Place the knife on top of the roast, with the blade flush against the bones and the edge just touching the meat.

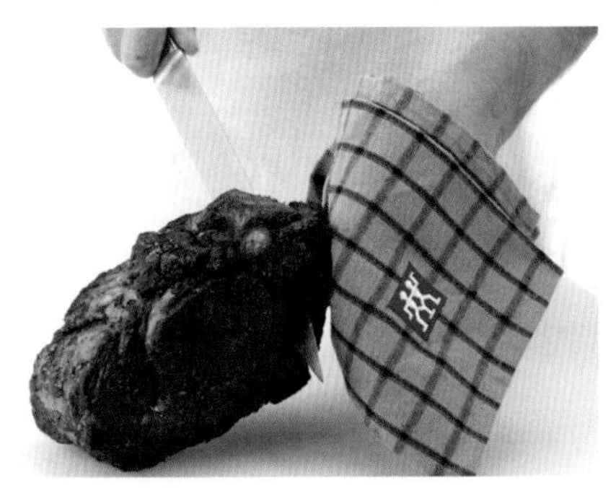

Cut back and forth through the meat, letting the knife ride just on top of the bones, following their curve.

4

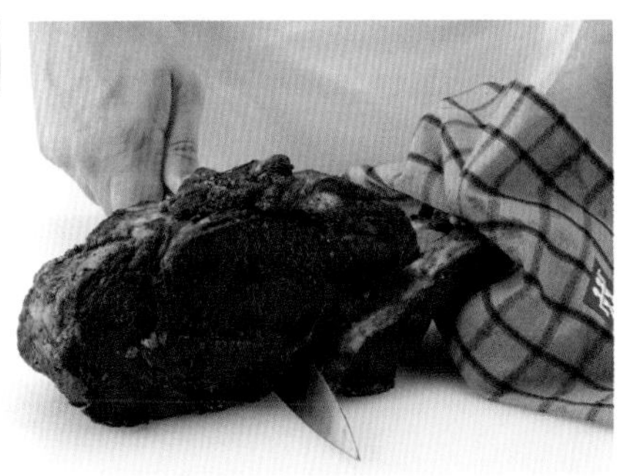

Continue cutting to the end of the ribs, so that the roast is completely free and the ribs come off in one piece.

There's not a lot of meat between the ribs, but they can be sliced apart for a snack or used to enhance a brown stock.

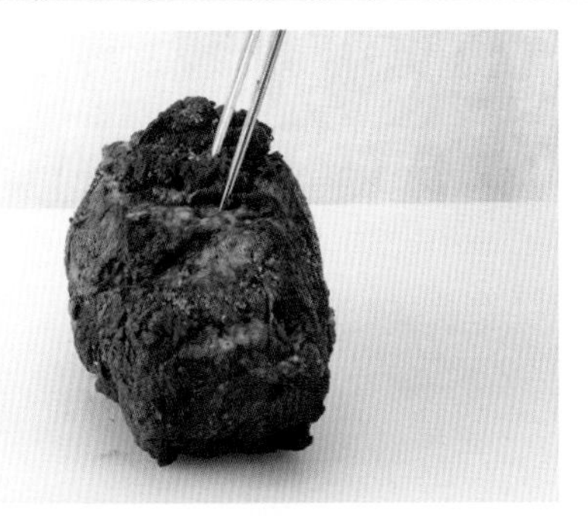

Place the roast on the board, bone side down (as if the ribs were still attached and facing you), and steady it with a carving fork held in your guide hand.

6

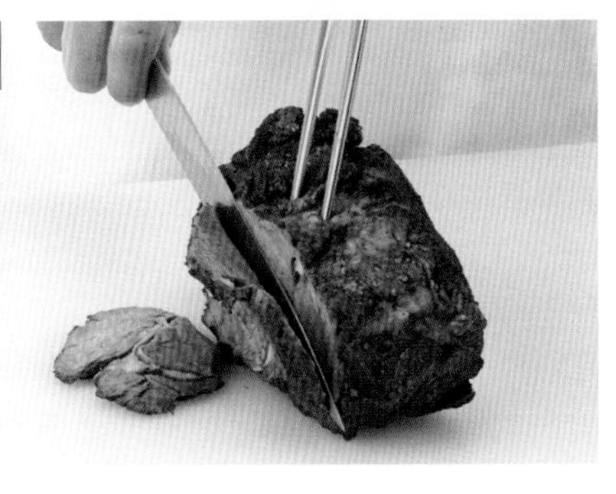

Cutting across the grain (in the same direction the bones used to lie), cut the roast into slices of the desired thickness.

Carve only as much of the roast as you need to give each guest one serving. If you carve the entire roast, the leftovers will dry out more quickly.

Carving a Leg of Lamb

A whole roast leg of lamb is a beautiful and festive sight. Carving a boneless leg is a no-brainer; all you needed is a sharp knife and a long-tined carving fork. Hence, we'll explain how to carve a bone-in leg.

If the leg of lamb you plan to purchase still has the aitchbone attached, ask your butcher to remove it (or do so yourself before roasting the leg, following the instructions on page 287, steps 1 to 3).

RECOMMENDED KNIFE

Carving knife

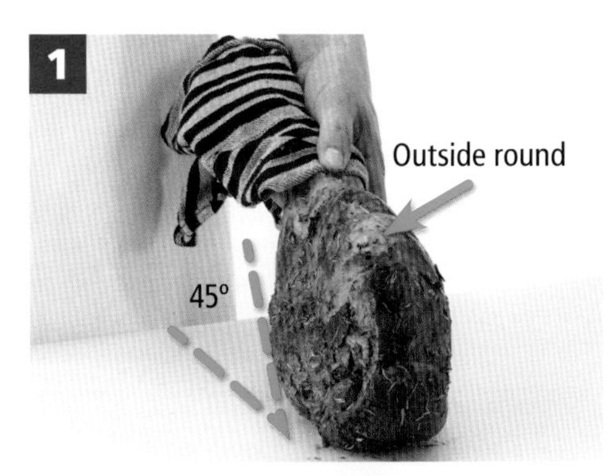

Lay the rested leg on the cutting board, with the shank (shin) end facing you and the rounded side (the outside round) facing up. Fold a clean, dry towel and use it to grab the end of the shank bone with your guide hand. Lift the shank to about a 45-degree angle.

Position the knife parallel to the femur (thigh bone) and cut off thin slices of meat from the outside in until you reach the bone.

Rotate the leg 180 degrees and repeat step 2, maintaining the 45-degree angle.

4

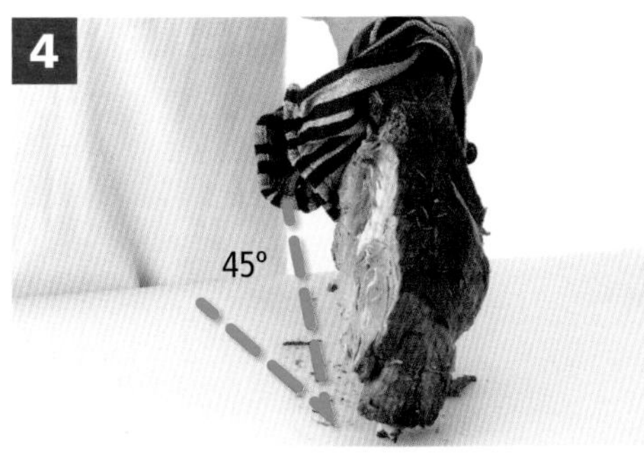

Turn the leg so that the shank is facing away from you and lift the femur to about a 45-degree angle.

5

Position the knife parallel to the shank bone and cut off thin slices of meat from the outside in until you reach the bone.

6

Rotate the leg 180 degrees and repeat step 5, maintaining the 45-degree angle.

7

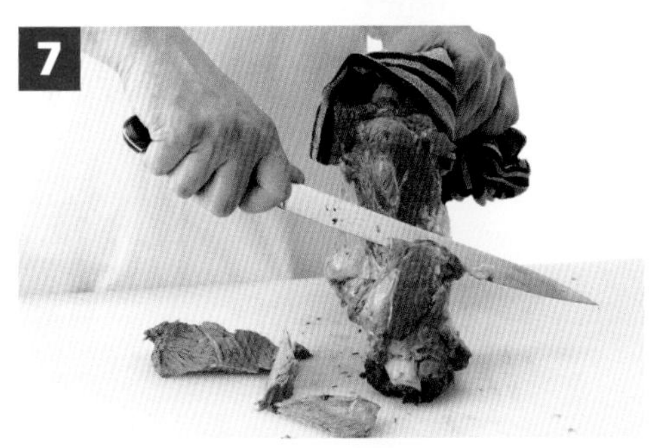

Rotate the leg 90 degrees and run the knife down the length of the femur and shank to remove any meat attached to the side.

8

Rotate the leg 180 degrees and run the knife down the length of the femur and shank to remove any meat from the other side.

Bias-Cutting

Cutting cooked meat on an angle, or on the bias, gives it an attractive look, with softer angles. In addition, each slice has more cooked surface area, which tends to be more flavorful thanks to the browning that occurs during the cooking process. For our demo, we'll use a boneless skinless chicken breast that has rested for a couple of minutes.

RECOMMENDED KNIFE

Chef's knife or carving knife

1

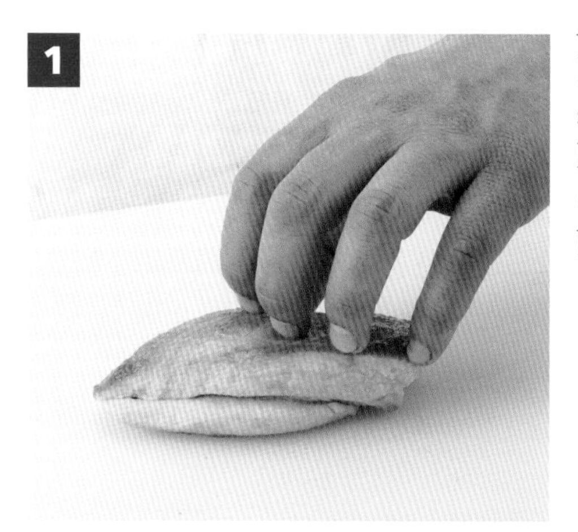

Lay the breast on the cutting board, skin side up, and steady it with your guide hand in the claw position, 1 to 2 inches (2.5 to 5 cm) away from the edge of the breast.

2

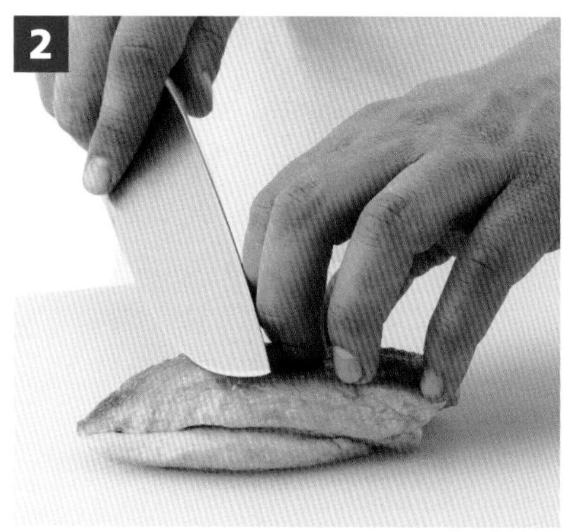

Place the knife blade on top of the breast, halfway between the edge and your guide fingers. Tilt the spine about 45 degrees toward your guide fingers.

Slice down through the meat at this angle to make your first bias cut.

Keeping the blade at a 45-degree angle, cut the entire breast into slices.

Bias-cut slices of meat are typically fanned out when they're plated, for an even nicer look.

Chapter 10

Creative Garnishes

Decorative garnishes are an art form unto themselves, and entire books have been written about them. In this chapter, we'll show you just a few of the cool things you can do to make your plates and platters more attractive.

Tomato Roses

For the best results, look for tomatoes that are as close as possible to a perfect sphere. Size doesn't really matter: cherry tomatoes work just as well as beefsteaks. For our demo, we'll use a medium-size vine-ripened tomato.

RECOMMENDED KNIFE

Paring knife

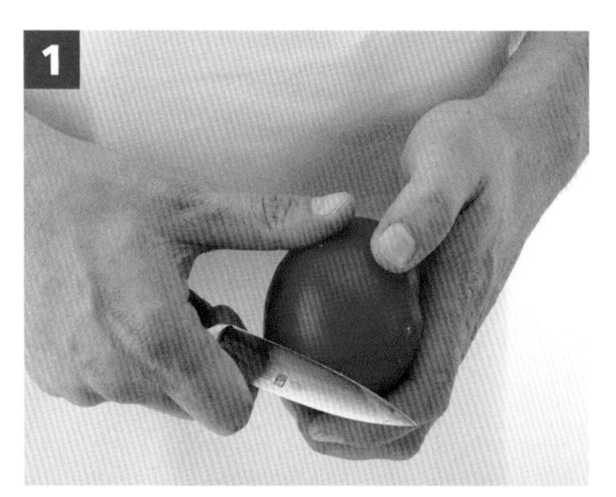

Hold the tomato in your guide hand, with the bottom facing you. Hold the knife in the paring grip (see page 85), with the edge of the blade about 1/4 inch (6 mm) from the bottom of the tomato.

Brace the tomato with your knife-hand thumb and pull the blade toward you through the bottom of the tomato, just underneath the skin.

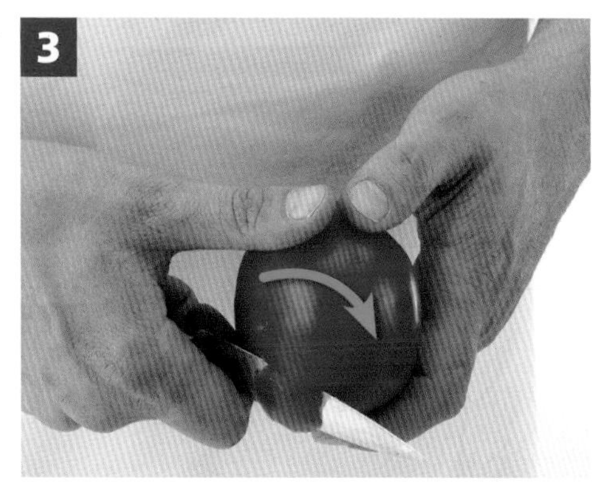

When you're close to cutting all the way through the bottom of the tomato and removing that strip of skin, rotate the tomato 90 degrees away from you.

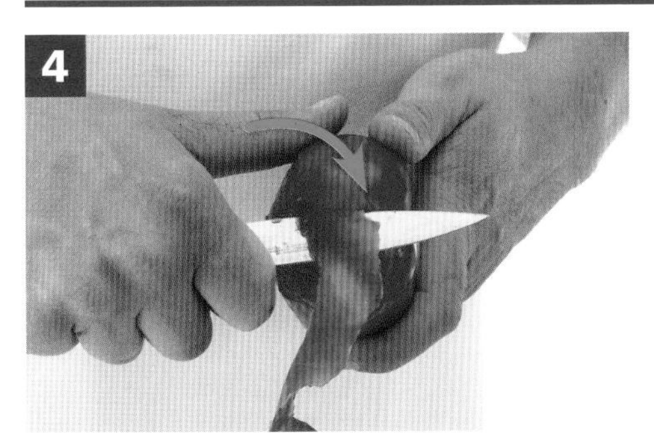

4 Continue removing the skin in one long, unbroken strip by running the blade just underneath the skin while simultaneously rotating the tomato up and into the blade. Reserve the tomato for another use.

5 Lay the strip of skin on the cutting board, skin side down, with the large circle from the bottom of the tomato facing away from you.

6 Roll the skin loosely all the way up to the large circle.

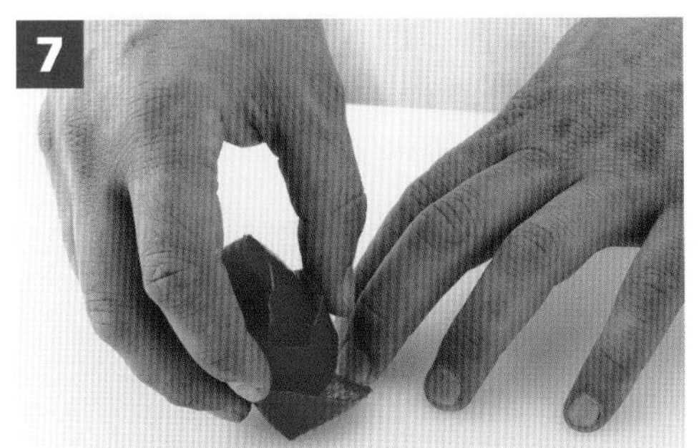

7 Set the rolled-up length upside down on the large circle.

Tomato roses — which look remarkably like the real thing — can stand on their own as a formal plate decoration or as part of a larger display on serving platters or buffet tables.

Radish Flowers

Of the many ways to make radishes look like flower buds, this technique is perhaps the easiest. It can be done on a cutting board or holding the radish in your guide hand. We'll demonstrate holding the radish, but try it both ways to see which is easiest for you.

One thing to bear in mind is that radishes come in many sizes. In our demo, we'll make two rows of cuts around the radish. If your radishes are small, you may want to go around only once; if they're larger, you can go around three or more times.

RECOMMENDED KNIFE

Paring knife

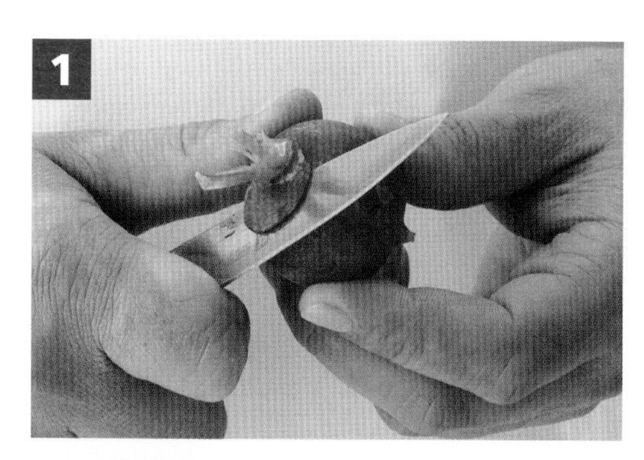

Hold the radish in your guide hand, as if you were going to pare it. Holding the knife in the paring grip (see page 85), cut off the top and bottom of the radish.

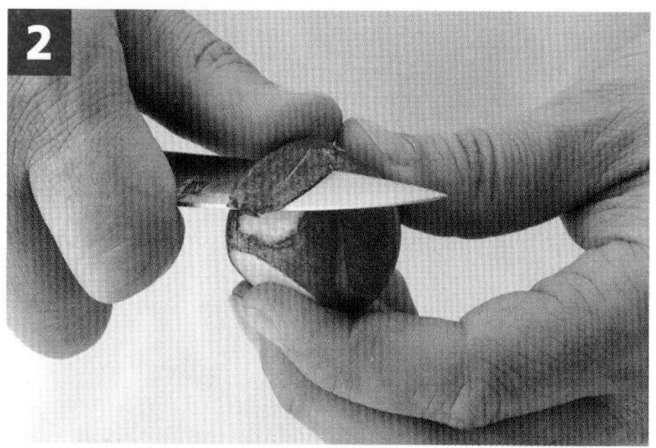

Place the knife blade near the top of the radish, with the edge facing the bottom. Cut straight down, without cutting all the way through at the bottom, to create a flap that looks like a curved flower petal.

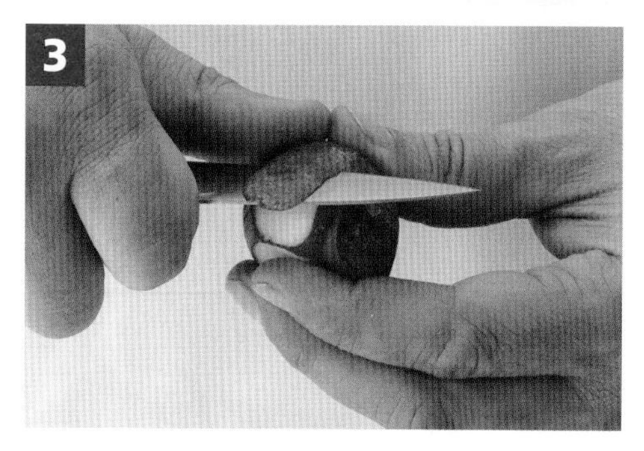

Rotate the radish and make a second cut the same size and shape next to the first, so that the bottom of petal 2 is touching or almost touching petal 1.

4

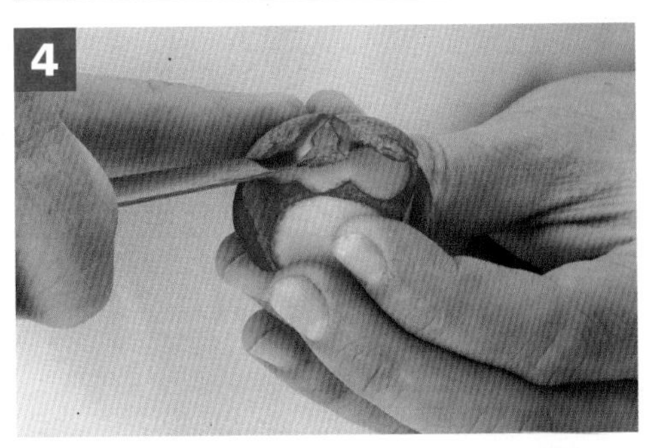

Continue making cuts like this all the way around the radish, so that it is ringed with petals.

5

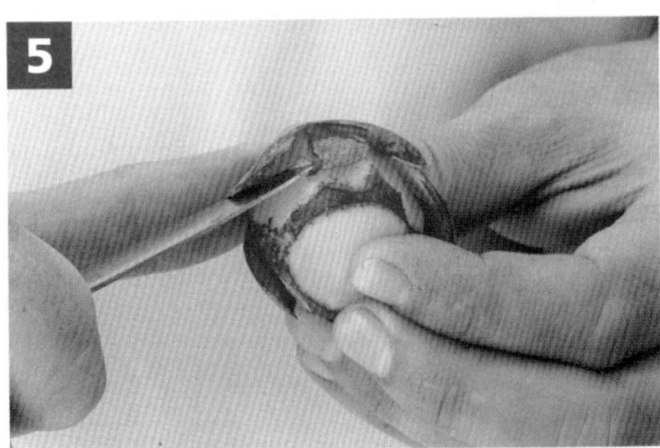

Using the tip of your knife, cut a petal between petals 1 and 2, directly behind and above them.

6

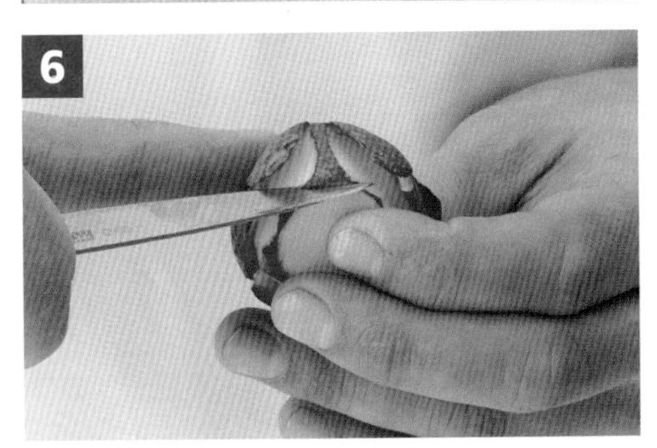

Rotate the radish and cut a petal between petals 2 and 3, directly behind and above them.

7

Continue cutting petals until every pair of bottom petals has a corresponding top petal. Soak radish flowers in salted ice water for 2 hours. (Soaking them causes the petals to open.)

Radish flowers are somewhat impressionistic — they don't exactly *look like* flowers so much as they *suggest* flowers. Use them alongside other flower garnishes on buffets or platters.

Carrot Flowers

This easy technique looks best when you use thin carrots. Larger, thicker "horse carrots" work just as well, but look rougher and less elegant.

RECOMMENDED KNIFE

Paring knife

1 Hold a peeled carrot in your guide hand, with the tapered root end jutting out from between your thumb and index finger and resting on the cutting board.

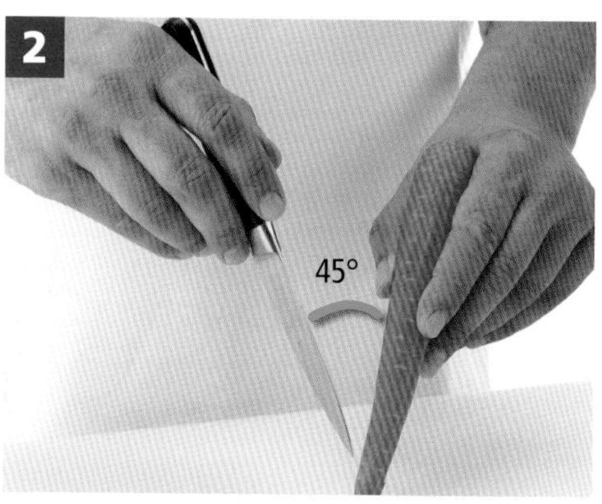

2 Hold the knife as you would a pen, gripping it by the handle, with the tip pointed down at about a 45-degree angle away from you.

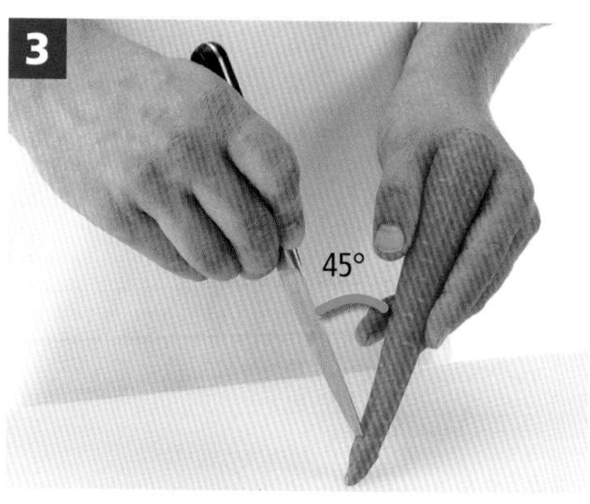

3 Starting $\frac{3}{4}$ to $1\frac{1}{2}$ inches (2 to 4 cm) up from the bottom of the carrot, and maintaining the angle of the knife, stick the point of the knife into the center of the carrot.

Withdraw the blade, rotating the carrot toward your knife hand as you do.

Push the point into the center again, at the same angle.

Repeat steps 4 and 5 all the way around the carrot until the blade meets the original cut, creating a point on the carrot while keeping the section you're cutting off in one cup-like piece. (When we say "creating a point," we don't mean a pencil point. It's more like a pencil with the tip broken off.)

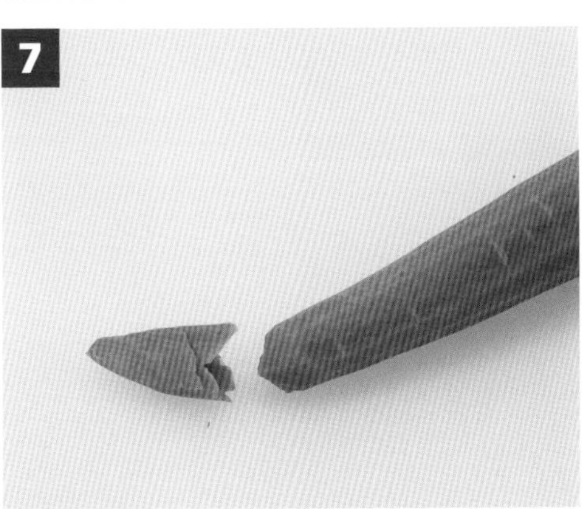

Set down your knife and twist the lower piece off the carrot. It should come off with just a little effort; if it's still solidly attached, run the point of your knife around the interior of the cut one more time. (This first piece is typically a throwaway piece.)

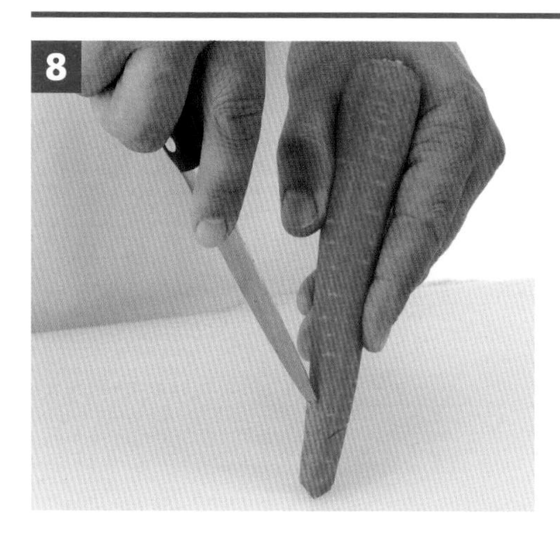

Moving your knife up $^3/_4$ to $1^1/_2$ inches (2 to 4 cm) each time, repeat steps 3 to 7 all the way up the carrot, producing ever-larger "flowers."

Carrot flowers are small, so use them on smaller platters. Because they're fairly rough-looking, it's best to include them in a display with other flower garnishes.

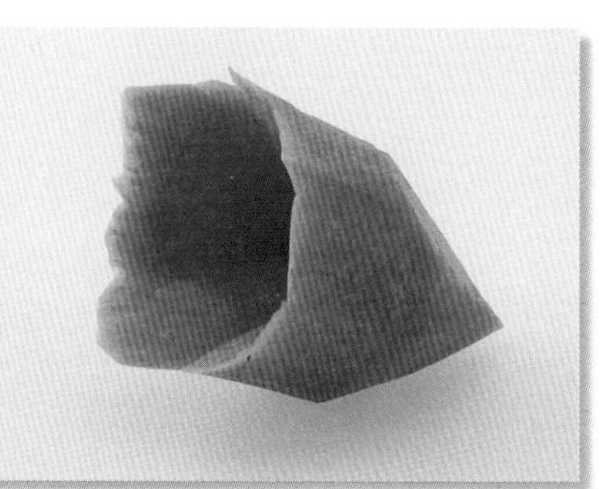

Fluted Mushroom Caps

Carving pinwheel patterns into the top of a mushroom is called either fluting or turning. It takes a lot of practice to get comfortable with the technique, and a lot more to get good at it, because the motion is unfamiliar and delicate.

RECOMMENDED KNIFE

Paring knife or tourné knife

Fluting is most commonly done with white button mushrooms, which must be clean and very fresh. If they're the least bit mushy, they become hard to work with, as the blade won't penetrate the flesh smoothly.

Some people prefer to remove the stems; remember, though, that the whole point is to make the mushrooms more attractive. If it helps to shorten the stem or remove it, go ahead. For our demo, we'll leave the stem in.

1

Hold the mushroom with the thumb and first two fingers of your guide hand, with the cap facing you.

2

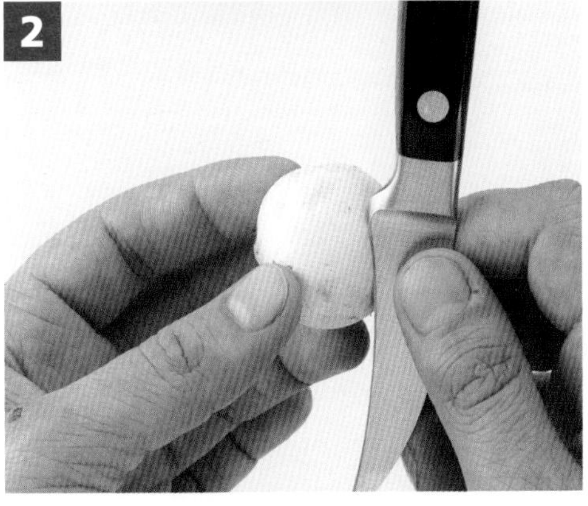

Hold the knife in the fluting grip (see page 87), with the edge facing your guide hand. Rest the heel of the blade just below and just to the knife-hand side of the center of the mushroom cap, angling the blade slightly down into the mushroom.

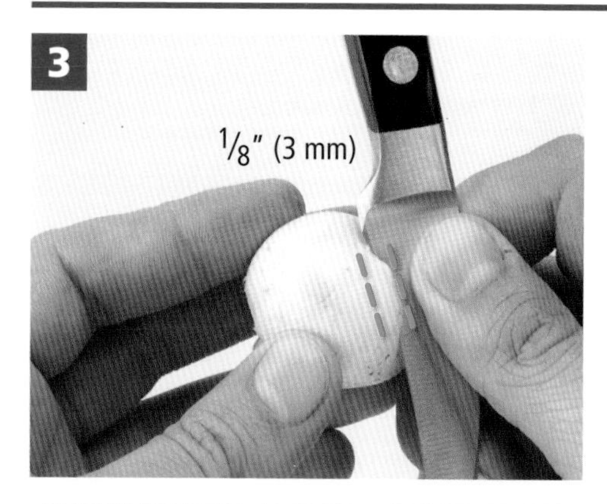

With a slight up and down flick of your knife-hand wrist, slice into the mushroom cap so that edge of the blade is buried about 1/8 inch (3 mm) below the surface. Note that the knife handle is pointed directly away from you.

Here comes the hard part. We're going to break it up into two steps (4 and 5), but as you practice, you'll be able to combine them into one fluid movement.

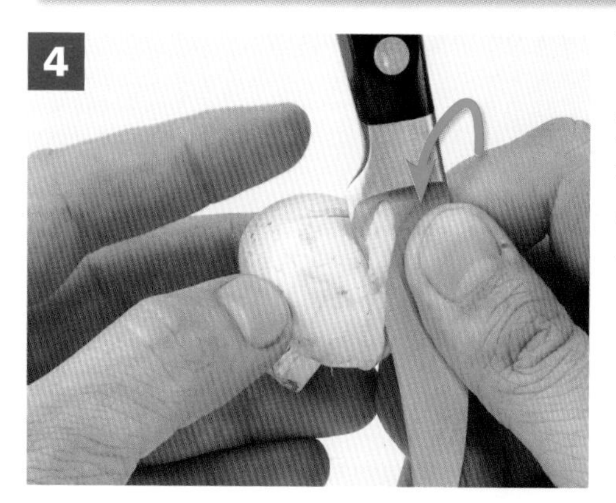

Slowly rotate your knife hand toward you from the wrist (like turning off the ignition in a car), while simultaneously exerting a small amount of pressure toward your guide hand.

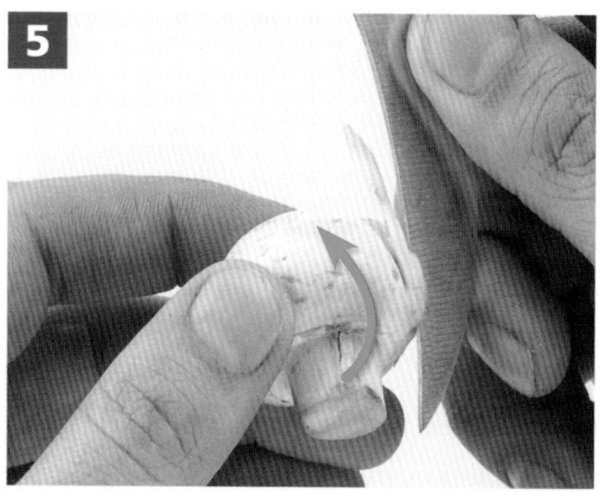

At the same time, rotate the mushroom so that it rolls down the blade as the blade travels from the top of the cap to the side to the bottom in a gentle curve.

Keep an eye on the little flap of mushroom cap that was covering the edge of your blade after step 3. As the edge of the blade moves along the mushroom, the slight sideways pressure you're exerting moves the blade under the skin in a way similar to a plow digging up the earth.

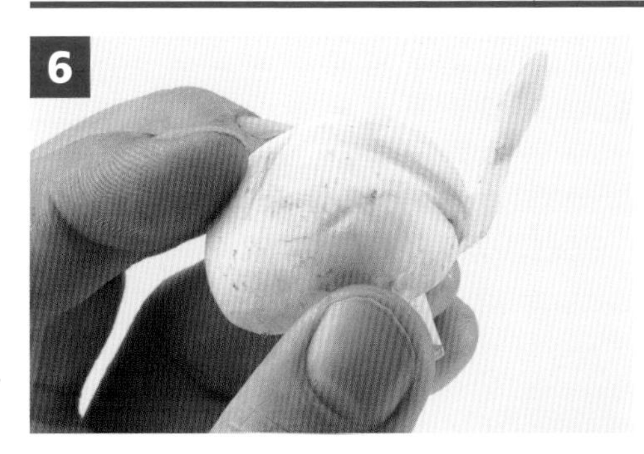

When you reach the underside of the cap, stop. The flute you've just cut will likely still be attached at the bottom. You'll remove it later.

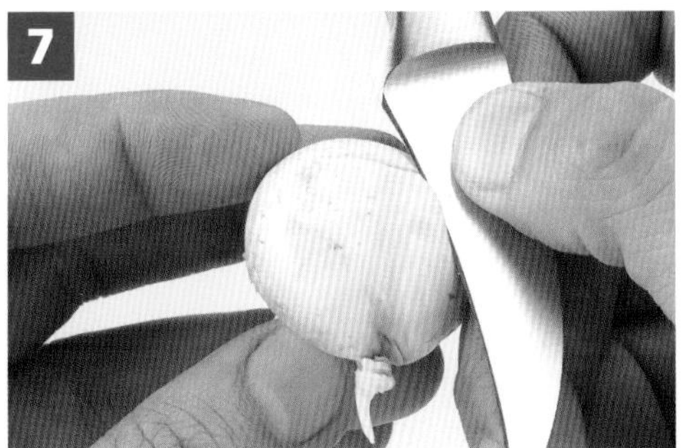

Returning to the top of the mushroom cap, position the blade just to the side of your first cut and insert the blade as you did in step 3.

Repeat steps 4 to 7 until you have gone all the way around the mushroom.

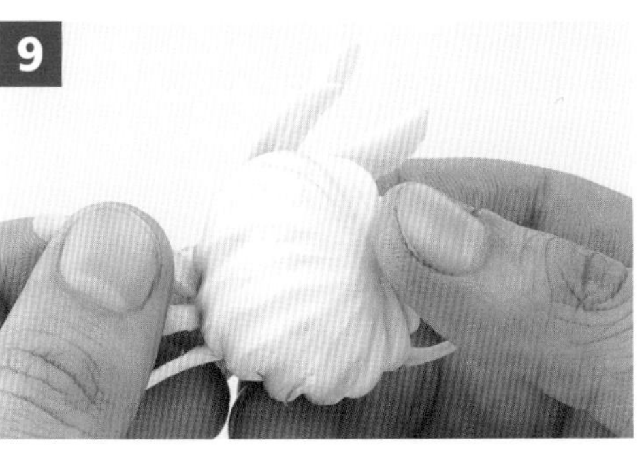

Use your hands to pull the flutes away from the mushroom.

Fluted mushrooms are typically sautéed or stewed and served on a formal dinner plate alongside hearty dishes such as filet mignon or salmon fillets.

Bell Pepper Threads

These brightly colored, shiny threads of pepper look terrific on any number of dishes, particularly steaks, chicken breasts or fish fillets. If stored in cold water in the refrigerator, they'll stay fresh for several days.

For the best results, choose large, meaty peppers with a good shape. Before you start this technique, you'll need to core the pepper, as explained on page 145. If the resulting long rectangle of pepper does not lie flat, cut it in half.

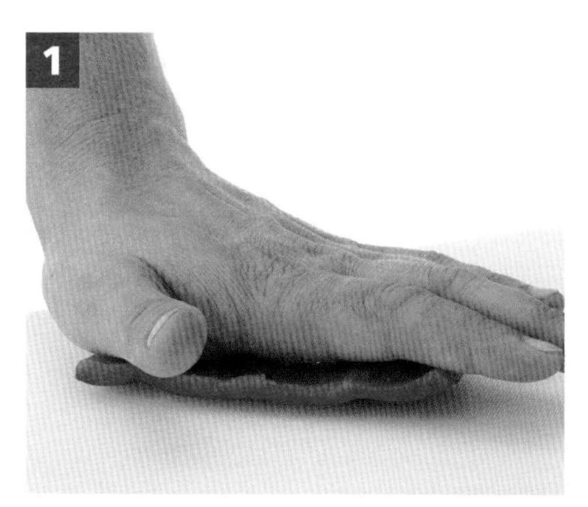

Lay the pepper flat on the cutting board, skin side down. Place the palm of your guide hand on top of the pepper, with your fingers splayed up and out of the way.

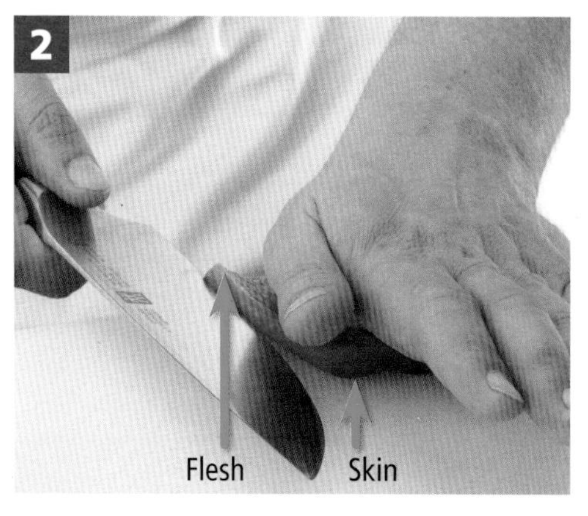

Hold the knife blade parallel to the board, with the edge facing the pepper and the handle beyond the edge of the board. Place the edge on the side of the flesh, getting as close to the skin as possible.

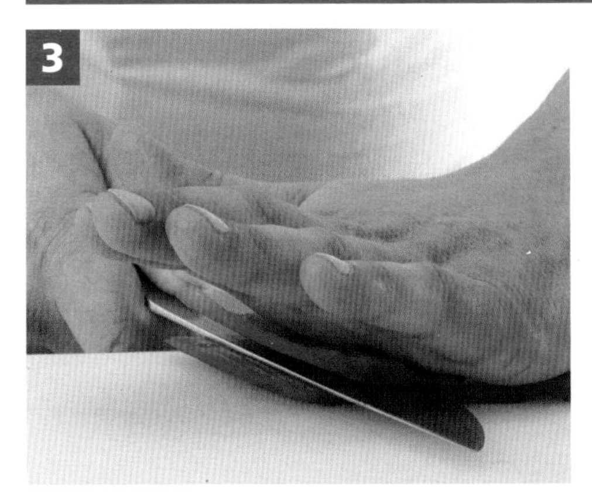

Slicing carefully back and forth and keeping the blade perfectly parallel, cut sideways between the skin and the flesh to remove the flesh from the skin. Save the flesh for another use, such as a salad or stir-fry.

Chances are you won't get all the flesh off in one even layer the first time you try this, and that's fine; just keep practicing. Go back over it as needed to shave away as much flesh as possible. After you remove the first piece, however, note the difference in color and texture between the flesh and the skin.

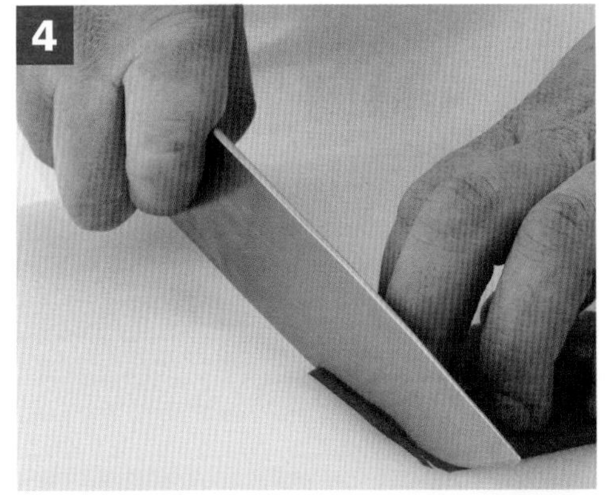

Secure the skin (still flesh side up) with your guide hand in the claw position. Place the knife blade flush against your guide fingers and cut off the thinnest possible slice of skin.

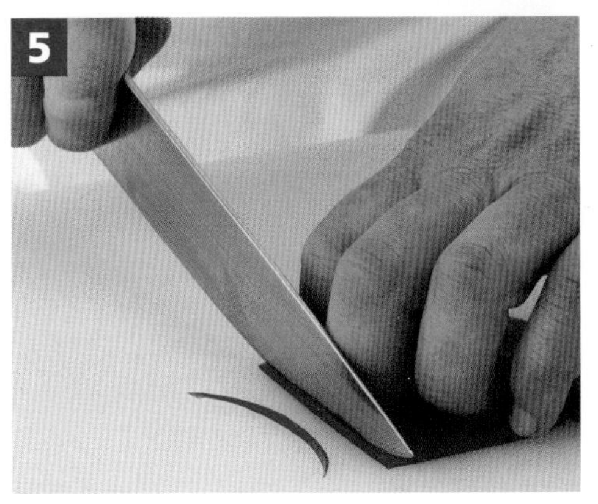

Keeping the blade against your guide fingers, move them back slightly and cut off another filament-thin slice.

Repeat step 5 until the entire skin is cut into slices.

To make curls, let the slices soak in ice water for a while.

To make confetti, rotate the slices 90 degrees and cut them into small pieces. (If the slices have curled slightly, lay them on their sides first, to make them easier to manage.)

Vegetable Ribbons

If you have eaten at a sushi bar, you may have seen the chef expertly cut a long ribbon from a daikon radish, cucumber or other soft, cylindrical vegetable. The technique, called *katsuramuki*, takes a sushi chef years to master, so expect to practice this one a lot before you get good results. A Usuba is the typical knife of choice, but you can also use a Nakiri or a Kamagata.

RECOMMENDED KNIFE
Usuba

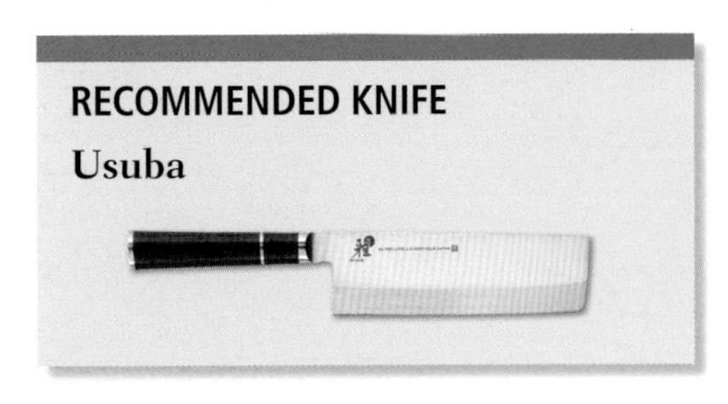

Before you start this technique, peel the vegetable and cut it into 3- to 4-inch (7.5 to 10 cm) lengths. For our demo, we'll use a piece of daikon radish.

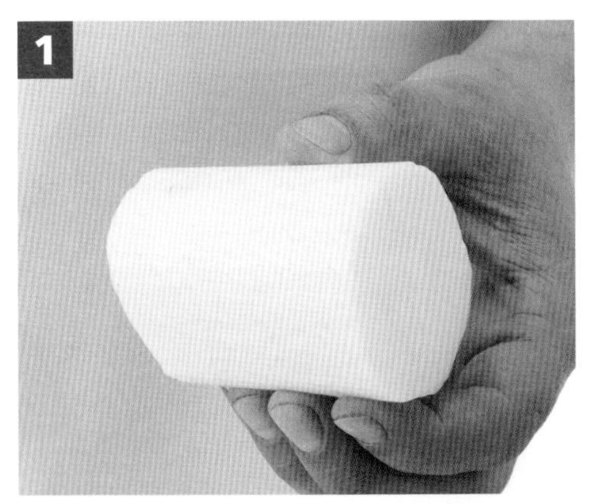

Hold the radish piece in your guide hand, with your thumb in the middle of the piece, parallel to the cut ends. Angle the top of the piece away from you.

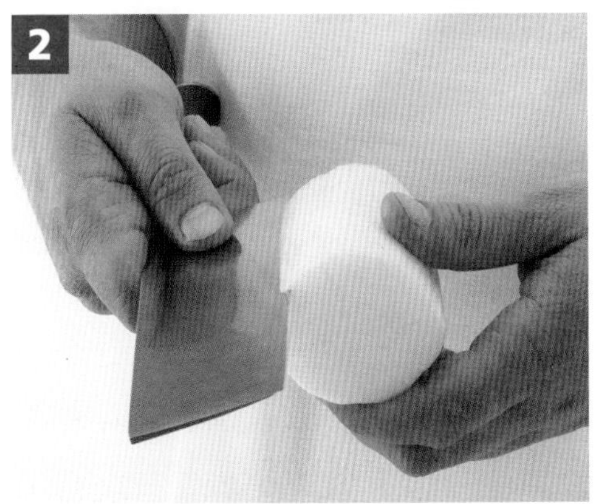

Holding the knife in the basic grip described on page 70, place the blade flat against the top of the radish piece and make a shallow incision into the radish.

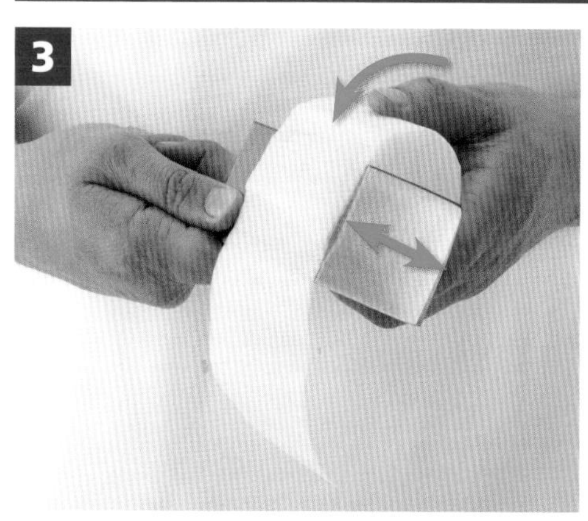

Keeping the blade parallel to and flush against the radish, use your guide-hand thumb to slowly rotate the radish into the blade while simultaneously shimmying the knife back and forth in tiny movements.

Repeat step 3 until the radish is reduced to a small cylinder and you have cut a long ribbon.

Vegetable ribbons can be used in place of seaweed to wrap sushi, or they can be cut into more workable lengths, stacked and julienned for use as garnish for sashimi.

Cucumber Fans

These pretty garnishes can be any size you like, and you can give them slightly different looks by varying the folds you make or by scoring the peel lengthwise before you start.

1

Lay the cucumber on the cutting board and use the chef's knife to cut off just enough of the ends that the remainder of the cucumber is roughly the same width all the way along its length.

2

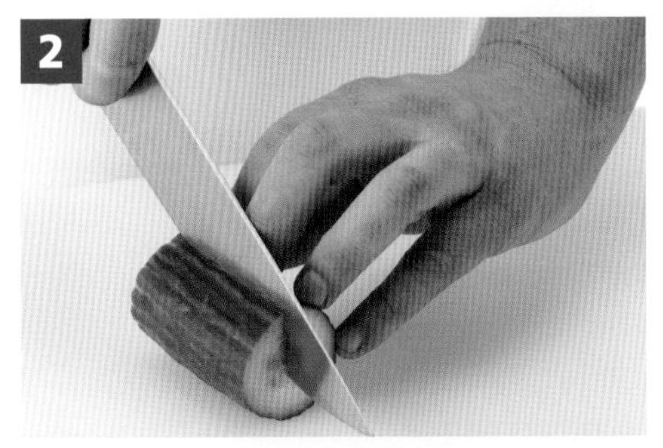

Cut the cucumber in half crosswise, then cut each piece in half lengthwise.

3

Lay one piece on the board, cut side down, with one end facing your knife hand, and steady it with your guide hand in the claw position.

Place the paring knife flush against your guide fingers about ⅛ inch (3 mm) from the end of the cucumber, aligning the point so that when you cut a slice, the cut will only reach about 80% of the way to the far side of the cucumber. Cut straight down to the board.

You want the pieces you cut to remain attached at the back of the cucumber like the teeth of a comb.

Move your guide fingers about ⅛ inch (3 mm) back and make another cut as described in step 4.

Repeat step 5 until you've made six cuts. On the seventh cut, cut all the way through the far side of the cucumber to remove the piece you're working on from the main piece.

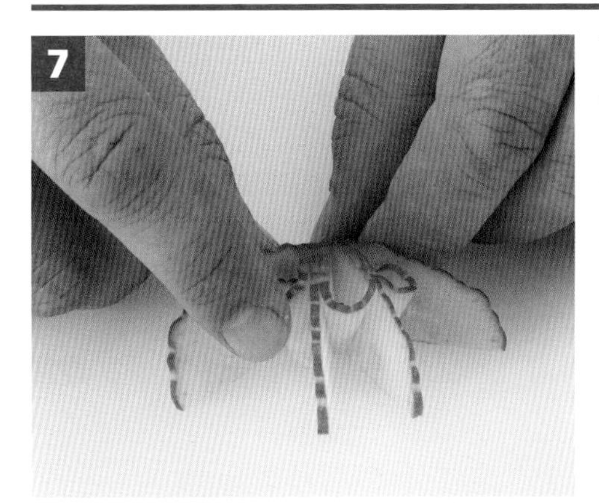

You now have a piece with seven "teeth" connected along the back. Bend the second, fourth and sixth teeth back on themselves to form curls.

Here's what your finished cucumber fan will look like:

For a different look, fold in all of the teeth except for the two outer ones.

You can make these fans any width you like; just make sure to cut an odd number of teeth.

To make longer fans, after you cut the cucumber into quarters in step 2, cut each quarter into 3- to 5-inch (7.5 to 12.5 cm) long pieces. Cut the teeth lengthwise instead of crosswise.

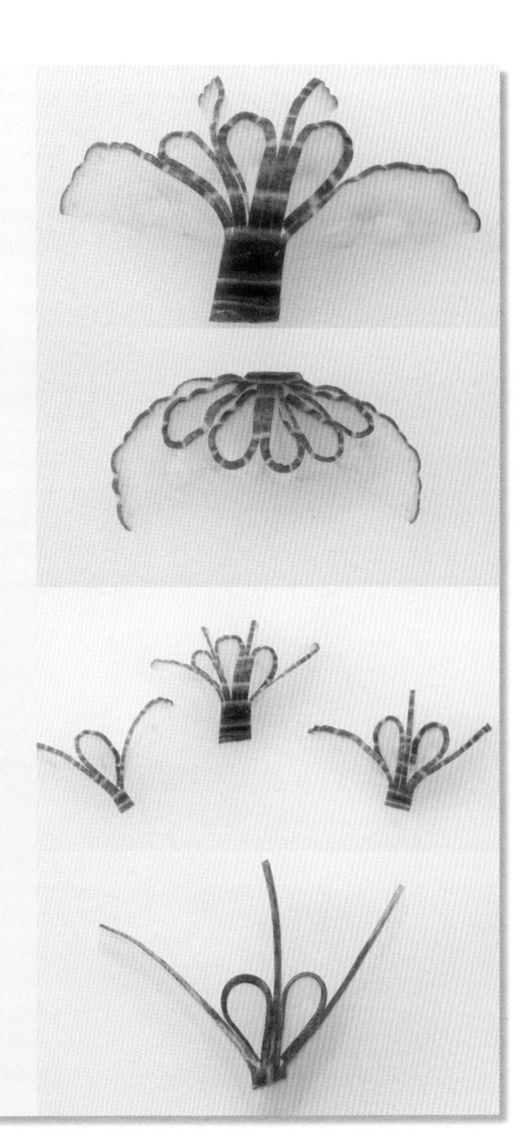

Strawberry Fans

This technique can be done on a variety of fruits, including peaches, avocados and mango face pieces, and makes for a very nice presentation.

RECOMMENDED KNIFE

Chef's knife or Santoku

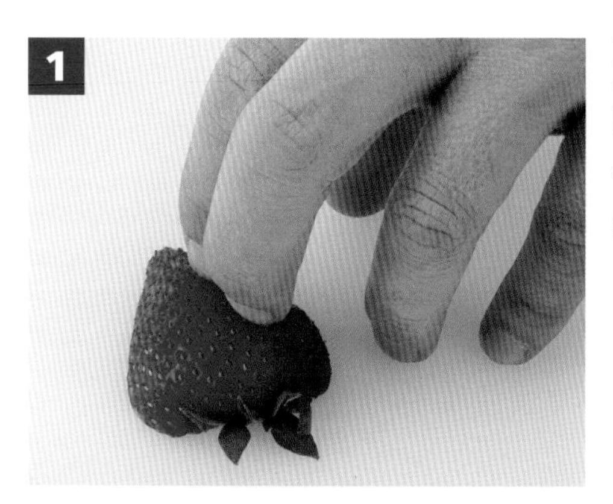

Lay a halved strawberry on the cutting board, cut side down, with the narrow end facing you. Steady it with your guide fingers.

Place the knife blade flush against your guide fingers on top of the strawberry. Make sure the point stops short of the top of the strawberry. When you cut down, you want to leave a small strip at the top uncut. This strip will hold all the slices together, like teeth on a comb.

Tilt the spine about 30 degrees away from your guide hand. Cut down through the strawberry at that angle, allowing the knife to pass safely beneath your guide fingers.

Reposition your guide fingers just past the cut. Repeat steps 2 and 3.

Repeat steps 2 to 4 until you have cut slices across the entire strawberry.

Spread the slices out in a fan by placing the palm of your guide hand on the strawberry and pressing down lightly in the direction of your knife hand, being careful not to break the slices off the strip that holds them together.

Strawberry fans look great atop a stack of pancakes or as a decorative garnish for fruit platters.

Citrus Curls

Citrus curls can be cut from any citrus fruit — choose one that matches the flavor profile of the dish you're garnishing. We'll use a lime for our demo.

RECOMMENDED KNIFE

Chef's knife or Santoku

1 Lay a lime on the cutting board, with one end facing your knife hand. Steady it with your guide hand. Cut the lime in half crosswise.

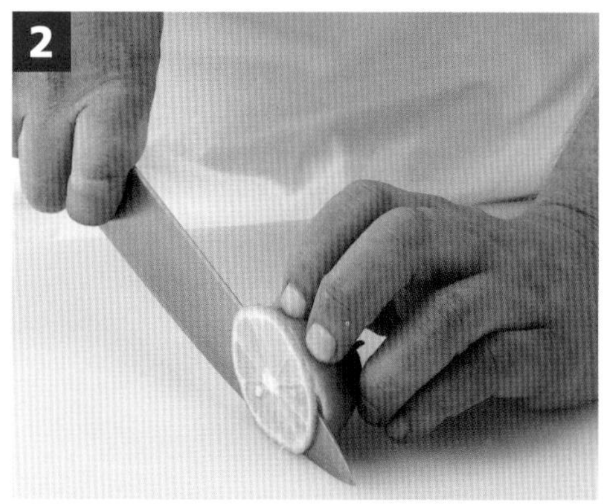

2 Hold one of the halves with the cut surface facing your knife hand. Steady it with your guide hand in the claw position. Place the knife blade flush against your guide fingers and cut off a ⅛-inch (3 mm) slice.

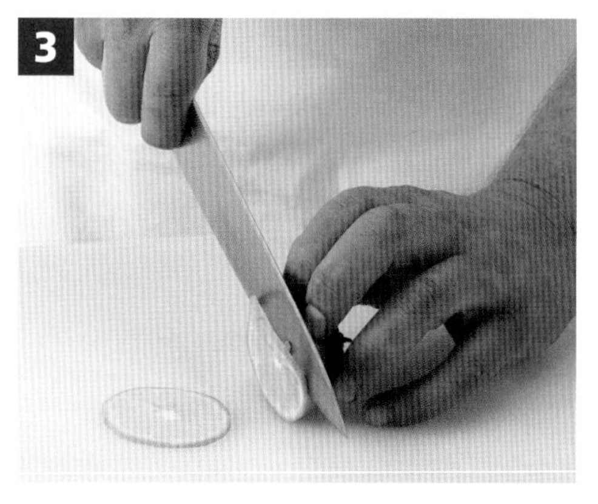

3 Move your guide fingers back ⅛ inch (3 mm) and cut off another slice. Continue until you have cut the entire lime into slices. Use your fingers to remove any seeds attached to your slices.

Lay the lime slices flat on the board. Starting just inside the peel on one side, cut straight through each slice all the way across and through the other side of the peel.

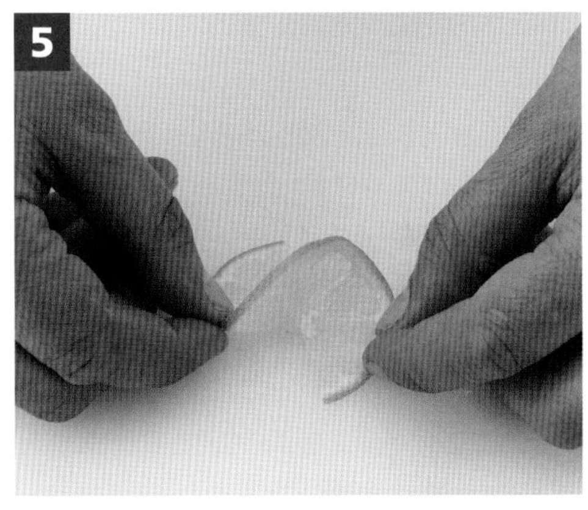

Pick up each slice and twist the two halves in opposite directions so that the slice forms a rough S.

Citrus curls are typically used as plate decorations. Lemon curls work well with fish entrées; other citrus curls look terrific as garnishes for tropical-style dishes.

Citrus Crowns

We'll use a lemon to demonstrate this technique, but it will work with any citrus fruit. Use the fruit that best matches the flavor profile of the dish you're garnishing. Each fruit yields two crowns. To sum up the technique in a nutshell, you're going to cut a zigzag pattern into the center of the fruit, all the way around its equator.

RECOMMENDED KNIFE

Paring knife

1

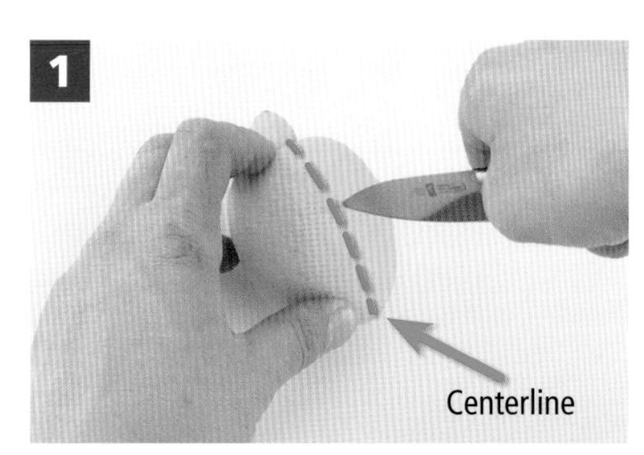

Hold the lemon in your guide hand. Place the point of the knife in the center of the lemon, with the edge facing the bottom of the lemon and the spine and edge aligned along the lengthwise centerline of the lemon.

2

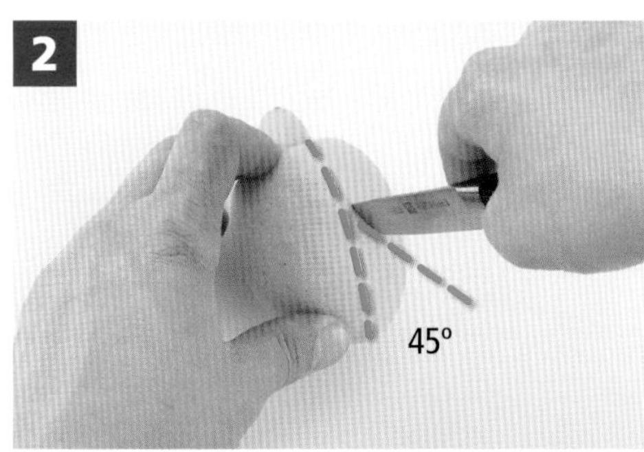

Rotate the edge of the knife 45 degrees from the centerline and push the tip into the center of the fruit.

3

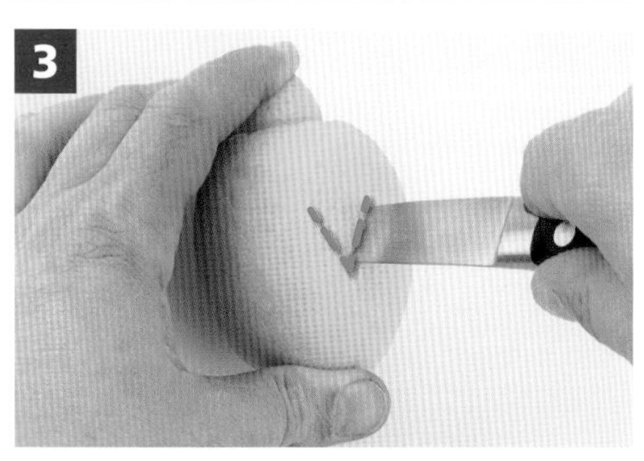

Pull the knife straight out and place the point at the bottom of the cut you just made. Rotate the edge 90 degrees toward the top of the lemon and push the tip into the center of the fruit. (You have now cut a V shape into the lemon.)

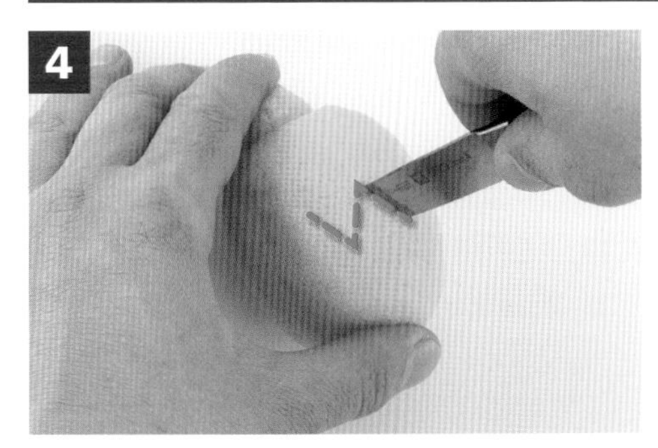

4 Pull the knife straight out and place the point at the top of the cut you just made. Rotate the edge 90 degrees toward the bottom of the lemon and push the tip into the center of the fruit.

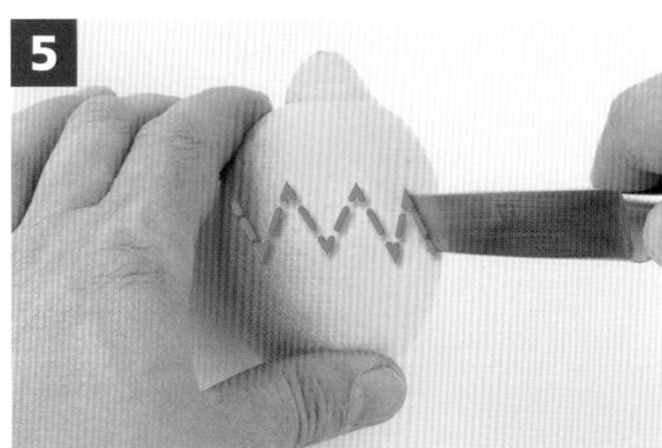

5 Repeat steps 3 and 4 all the way around the fruit, until the top of your last cut connects with the top of your first cut.

6 Pull the two halves of the lemon apart. If a few stray fibers are holding the halves together, just twist the halves in opposite directions as you pull.

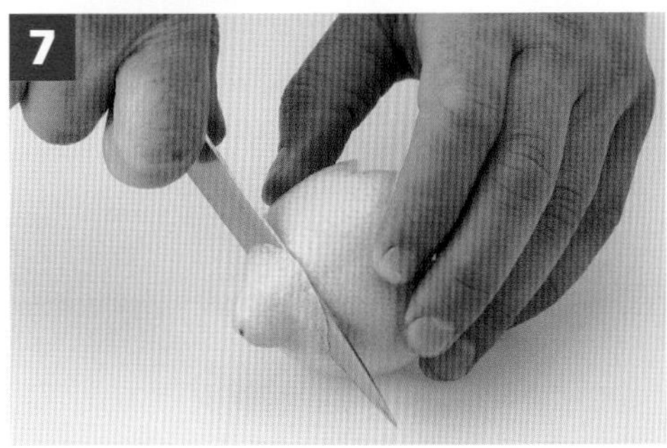

7 If desired, cut a flat surface on which the crown can rest. Depending on where you cut the surface, the face of the crown can be pointing at any angle.

Citrus crowns are typically used as plate decorations. Lemon crowns work well with fish entrées; other citrus crowns look terrific as garnishes for tropical-style dishes.

Apple Swans

This is definitely an old-school garnish, but it's beautiful and, despite appearances, easy to create. Choose the freshest, crispest, most perfect-looking apples you can find, preferably those with a uniform color, such as Red Delicious, Granny Smith or Golden Delicious. You'll also need two whole peppercorns or cloves (for eyes) and a toothpick for each swan you make.

RECOMMENDED KNIFE

Utility knife or paring knife

To prevent your apple pieces from turning brown when they're exposed to the air, place them in a bowl of acidulated water as you cut them. Use a mixture of 1 part lemon juice to 4 parts water.

1 Pull out and discard the stem, then place the apple on the cutting board, with the stem end up, and steady it with your guide hand in the claw position. Cut off a $\frac{1}{2}$-inch (12 mm) thick slice from one side and place it in the acidulated water. (It will be used later to create the neck and head.)

Next, you're going to cut a series of concentric wedges from the top of the apple. These wedges will ultimately represent the tail feathers on the finished swan.

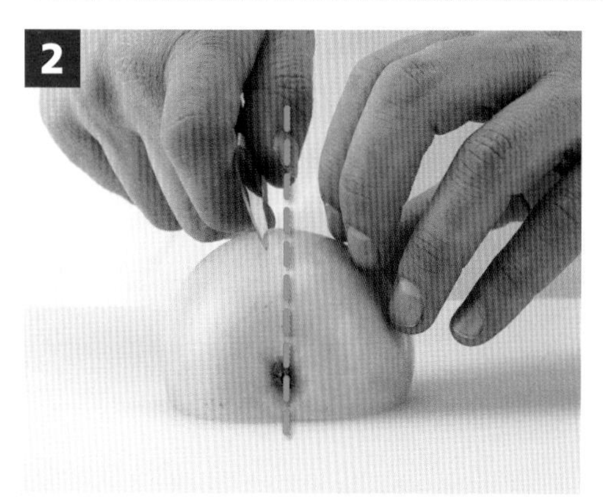

2 Place the apple on the cut side, with the stem end facing you, and steady it with your guide hand. Place the knife blade on top of the apple, exactly in the center. Tilt the spine about 20 degrees away from your guide hand and slide the blade about $\frac{1}{8}$ inch (3 mm) in that direction.

Keeping the knife at that angle, cut down into the apple, stopping when you reach the vertical centerline.

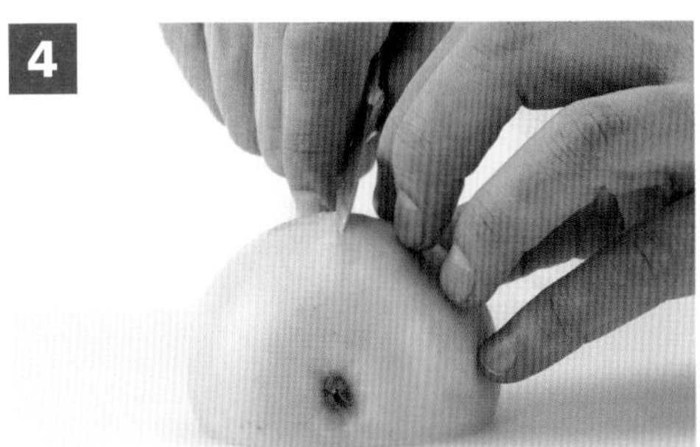

Remove the knife and place it on top of the apple, exactly in the center. Tilt the spine about 20 degrees toward your guide hand and slide the blade about $\frac{1}{8}$ inch (3 mm) in that direction.

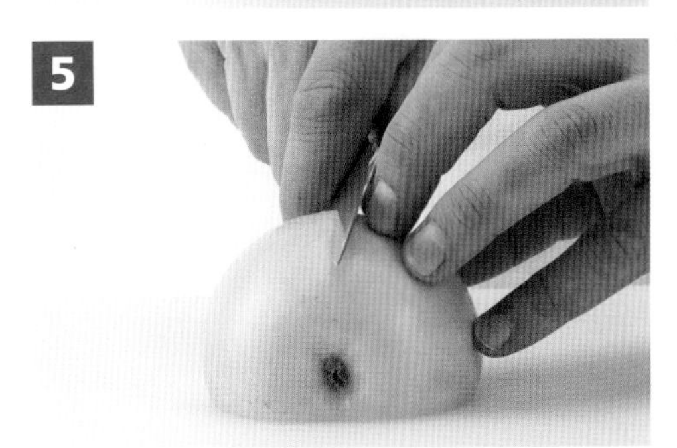

Keeping the knife at that angle, cut down into the apple, stopping when you reach the vertical centerline. Remove the wedge to the acidulated water.

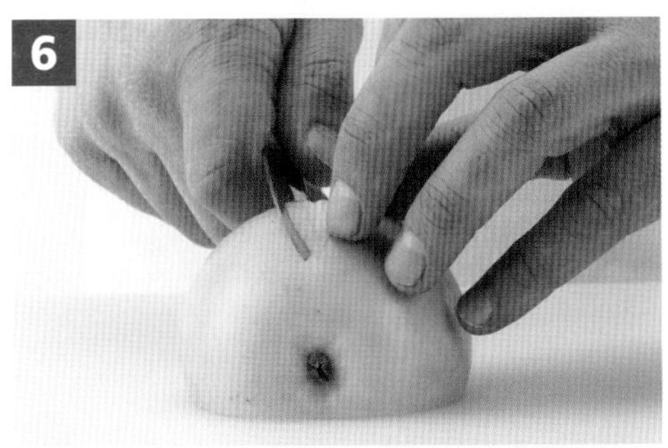

Lay the blade along the first cut. Keeping the blade at the same angle, move it about $\frac{1}{4}$ inch (6 mm) down the apple. Cut down into the apple underneath the first cut, stopping when you reach the vertical centerline.

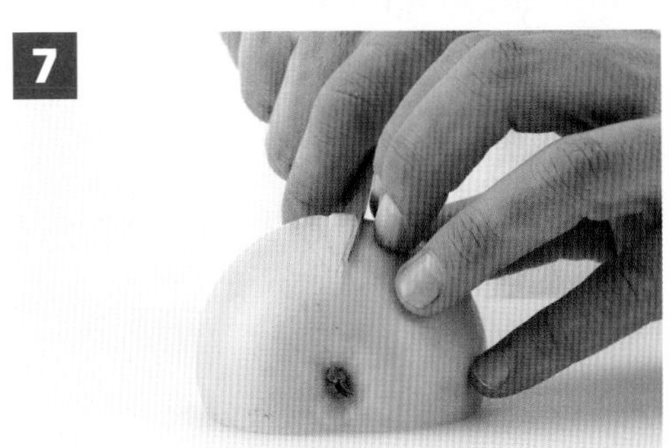

Make a complementary cut on the other side of center to create a second wedge that holds the first wedge. Remove the wedge to the acidulated water.

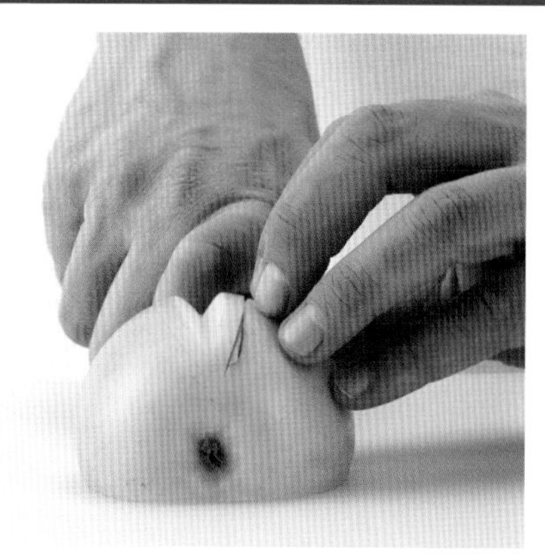

Repeat Steps 6 and 7 to create a third wedge underneath the second one. Remove the wedge to the acidulated water.

Depending on the size of the apple and how thin your wedges are, you can cut as many wedges from the top of the apple as you like — though unless you have an unusually large specimen, you'll probably be limited to about five.

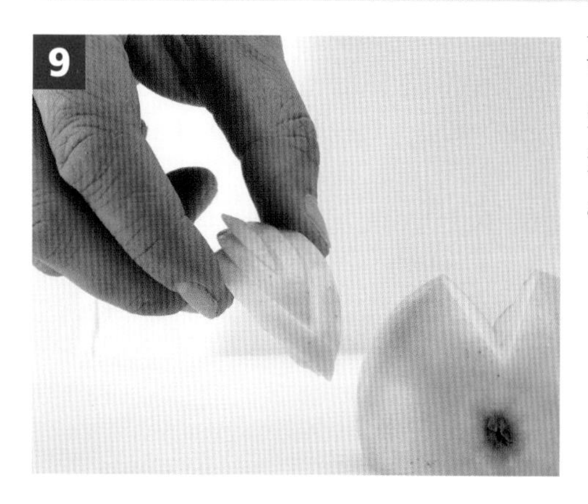

When you have completed all the wedges for your tail feathers, nest them one inside the other, then return them to the acidulated water.

The next step is to cut concentric wedges from each side that will represent the wings of the swan.

Move the blade down the knife-hand side of the apple until it's about ⅛ inch (3 mm) above the horizontal centerline. Cut another series of concentric wedges as described in steps 2 to 8, but using the horizontal centerline, rather than the vertical, as your guide. Nest the wedges and place them in the acidulated water.

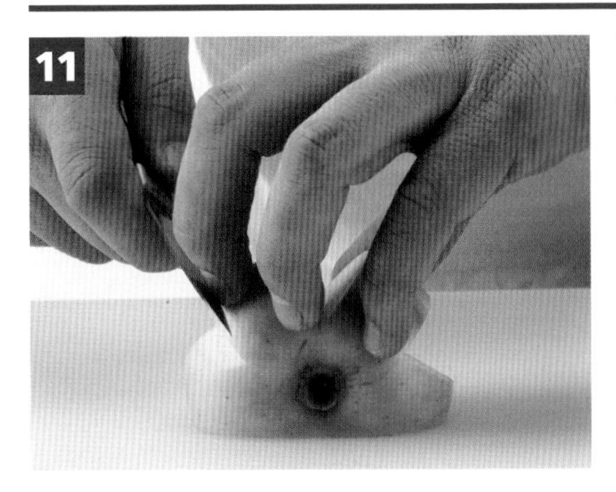

Rotate the apple 180 degrees and repeat step 10 on the other side.

Now you'll cut out the piece that will represent the head and neck.

Remove the slice you cut in step 1 from the acidulated water and lay it on the board, skin side up. Cut a ½-inch (12 mm) wide piece from the center of the slice. Eat the rest of the slice.

Place the piece you just cut flat on the board. Hold one end steady with your guide hand. Starting about ½ inch (12 mm) from the other end, cut a V-shaped notch into the straight edge. The point of the V should stop about ¼ inch (6 mm) from the curved edge. (The piece above the notch will be the swan's head.)

Starting at the point of the V, cut a curved arc down to the bottom of the piece, leaving a strip of ¼ inch (6 mm) of the flesh attached to the skin (this will be the swan's neck). Place the head piece in the acidulated water and eat the scrap pieces.

Finally, you're ready to assemble the swan.

Return the wing and tail feather wedges to their original notches and fan them out backwards (away from the stem end of the apple).

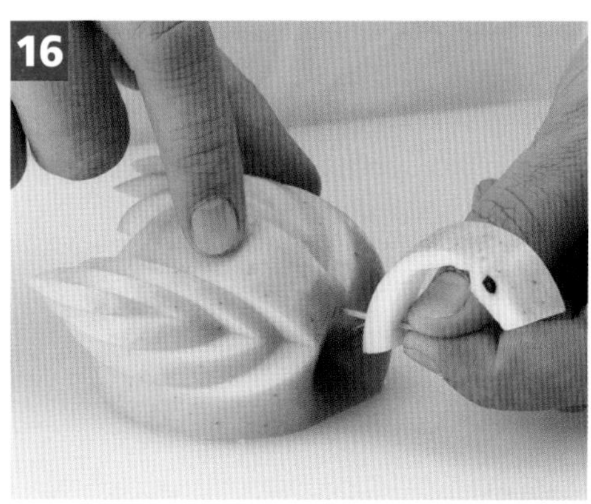

Push a toothpick into the neck section of the head piece, then use it to attach the neck to the top of the apple at the stem end. Push a peppercorn or clove into each side of the head to make the eyes.

Place apple swans in between dishes on your buffet table to add beauty and decorative flair to the display.

Acknowledgments

When we started writing this book, we didn't truly understand what a huge project we were undertaking. We are extremely grateful to everyone involved in helping us get from idea to finished book. Most importantly, we'd like to thank our publisher, Bob Dees, for believing in the book from the beginning, and our agent, Lisa Ekus, for introducing us to him. Our editor, Sue Sumeraj, a woman of infinite patience (which she needed to work with us), made everything we wrote better. And Joseph Gisini, our designer, made the words and pictures look incredible on the page. We spent a few weeks in a photo studio outside Chicago with photographer Al MacDonald and his unerring eye, and we borrowed the hands of Mark Steuer for all the photographs. Mark, a chef himself, also served as tiebreaker for our many Council of Trent–like disputes. Finally, thank you to proofreader Sheila Wawanash, proofreader and indexer Gillian Watts and all of the typesetters who assisted Joseph in laying out this book.

From Jeffrey

When I decided to write a book, Jim DeWan was my first and only choice for a co-author and, as you have seen, he was also the best choice.

My company, ZWILLING J.A. HENCKELS, was very generous in allowing me to write this book and in providing their help. I would like to thank U.S. CEO Guido Weishaupt for his belief in the book. Kerstin Schuetz, Bettina Thomas and Birgit Medeke were instrumental in getting the project off the ground. Mr. Hesse's insight into the manufacturing process was key.

I want to thank my parents, Sharon and Stuart, for sending me to culinary school, and my brother, Steven, for his unbending support. Thank you to all of the chefs who have shared their knowledge and skills with me. My unending gratitude to Mindy Segal for her friendship, understanding and cookies. Most of all, I'd like to thank Jill Sloane for her patience, encouragement and speed with a Band-Aid.

From Jim

Everything I know about anything I've learned from someone else. It would take pages to acknowledge everyone, but a few mighty chefs who have been instrumental in my education include the faculty of the Cooking and Hospitality Institute of Chicago (now Le Cordon Bleu College of Culinary Arts in Chicago), particularly chefs Tim Bucci, Germaine Peladeau and Mike Salzinski. Then there's the great Larry Smith, whose immense talents are matched only by his ability to impart them to others. I'm honored and humbled to be part of the Kendall College community, and I'm indebted both to my students, from whom I am constantly learning, and to my colleagues, especially chefs Michel Coatrieux, Mike Artlip, Chris Koetke and Renee Zonka.

I wouldn't be writing this book if it weren't for the generous invitation of Jeffrey Elliot. Thanks, Jeffrey.

And I wouldn't be writing at all if it weren't for the encouragement of Charles M. Madigan. Thanks, Charlie.

Finally, and most importantly, nothing would be possible without my lovely wife, Elaine Campbell Moore, and our totally excellent children, Violet and Seamus.

Library and Archives Canada Cataloguing in Publication

Elliot, Jeffrey
ZWILLING J.A. HENCKELS complete book of knife skills : the essential guide to use, techniques & care / Jeffrey Elliot & James P. DeWan.

Includes index.
ISBN 978-0-7788-0256-3

1. Knives. I. DeWan, James P II. Title.

TX657.K54E55 2010 641.5'89 C2010-901733-1

Index